4/2017

Measuring Wellbeing

Measuring Wellbeing

A HISTORY OF ITALIAN LIVING STANDARDS

GIOVANNI VECCHI

OXFORD
UNIVERSITY PRESS

Oxford University Press is a department of the University of Oxford. It furthers
the University's objective of excellence in research, scholarship, and education
by publishing worldwide. Oxford is a registered trade mark of Oxford University
Press in the UK and certain other countries.

Published in the United States of America by Oxford University Press
198 Madison Avenue, New York, NY 10016, United States of America.

Library of Congress Cataloging-in-Publication Data
Names: Vecchi, Giovanni, 1968- author.
Title: Measuring wellbeing : a history of Italian living standards / Giovanni
    Vecchi.
Description: New York, NY : Oxford University Press, [2017] | Includes
    bibliographical references and index.
Identifiers: LCCN 2016017264| ISBN 9780199944590 (hardcover) |
    ISBN 9780199944606 (updf) | ISBN 9780190218843 (epub)
Subjects: | MESH: Socioeconomic Factors--history | Health Status | Public
    Health | History, Modern 1601- | Italy
Classification: LCC RA418.3.I8 | NLM WA 11 GI8 | DDC 362.10945--dc23 LC record available at
https://lccn.loc.gov/2016017264

9 8 7 6 5 4 3 2 1
Printed by Sheridan Books, Inc., United States of America

Contents

3. Health   88

4. Child Labor   143

5. Education   175

6. Migration   215

7. Income   255

8. Inequality   293

9. Poverty   333

10. Wealth 373

11. Vulnerability 415

Acknowledgments

I take great pleasure in thanking the many people and institutions that helped me during the three-year-long research that led to presentation in the pages of this book.

I wish to start with Brian A'Hearn and Nicola Amendola, who are dear friends of mine as well as esteemed colleagues, untiring in coping with our infinite conversations to fine-tune my thoughts. Their help throughout the chapters of this book is greatly appreciated.

My special thanks also go to Alessandro Gambini for having read and commented on every single line of the manuscript. Although the authors take full responsibility for any remaining errors in these pages, many of the ones put right are thanks to Alessandro's work. I am similarly indebted to Alberto Iozzi, who patiently and expertly assessed all the chapters arriving on his desk. Finally, I would like to thank Jennifer Parkinson: she untiringly glossed both style and contents of each chapter without losing heart in the face of the imperfections of the first draft. My thanks also go to the two anonymous referees.

The research could not have been carried out without the financial support of Abbvie. I particularly wish to thank Fabrizio Greco and Roberto Girardello: their invaluable management of the project was enhanced by their extraordinary intellectual capacities enabling us to overcome the obstacles that arose from time to time. I would also like to thank Luca Paolazzi, director of the Centro Studi Confindustria that generously hosted the project.

I wish to thank Giovanni Alfredo Barbieri, Silvia Bruzzone, Aurea Micali, and Nicoletta Pannuzi, of the Italian National Institute of Statistics (Istat), who helped me in research, along with the staff of the Istat library for their assistance in the project: I cannot thank them enough.

I am indebted to the following people, colleagues in academia or otherwise: Andrea Brandolini, Leandro Conte, Giovanni Conti, Giovanni Federico, Stefano

Fenoaltea, Enrico Giovannini, Frank Heins, Alessandro Nuvolari, and Serafino Zucchelli. My debt to Nicola Rossi and Gianni Toniolo goes back a long way.

I wish to thank Giacomo Gabbuti for his excellent assistance in the research. Giacomo arrived with the project already well under way: had I known him before, the book would certainly have been better than the version going to press. I am also indebted to Francesco Olivanti for his good advice in reviewing the entire manuscript.

I would like to round off by thanking my family, Betta, Effe, and Emmegi, and also Mum and Dad, Liuccia and Filippo: any other word here is superfluous. I wish to dedicate this book to Martina, a young friend of mine whom I have never had the good fortune to meet.

Contributing Authors

Brian A'Hearn Brian A'Hearn is fellow and tutor in economics at Pembroke College, University of Oxford. He is an economic historian of modern Europe, particularly Italy, who has taught in Germany, the United States, and the United Kingdom.

Nicola Amendola is assistant professor at the University of Rome Tor Vergata. His main areas of research are monetary theory, measurement of poverty and inequality, and economic history.

Vincenzo Atella is professor of economics at the University of Rome Tor Vergata and Adjunct Affiliate del CHP/PCOR (Center for Health Policy) at Stanford University. His research activities are focused on consumption analysis, micro-simulation modeling, and health economics.

Alessandro Brunetti is researcher at the Consumer Price Statistics Unit of the Italian National Institute of Statistics (Istat). His main activity concerns the analysis of inflation. Currently, he has been working on the development of an Istat microsimulation model for Italian households.

Luigi Cannari is senior manager in the Bank of Italy's Directorate General for Economics, Statistics and Research. He has written extensively on income and wealth distribution and on various aspects of local economies.

Stefano Chianese is a Researcher at the University of Rome Tor Vergata, after a PhD in "History of Women and Gender Identity in the Modern and Contemporary Age" at the University of Naples L'Orientale. His research interest focuses on the history of migration, education, and the urban bourgeoisie.

Francesco Cinnirella is economist at the Ifo Institute for Economic Research at the University of Munich. His main areas of research are growth, development, and economic history. His research has been published in leading international journals.

Giovanni D'Alessio is a manager statistician at the Research Department of the Bank of Italy. He has extensively written on income and wealth distribution of Italian households and on various methodological issues related to sampling estimates and to the measurement of economic wellbeing.

Emanuele Felice is professor of economics at the University of Chieti-Pescara. His main areas of research are Italy's long-run economic growth, regional development, and economic history. He has published several books and essays in international journals, and is a leading columnist for Italian newspapers.

Silvia Francisci is senior researcher at the Italian National Institute of Health. Her research interests are on statistical methods applied to public health issues and patterns of cancer care and cost evaluation.

Giacomo Gabbuti is reading for an MPhil in economic and social history at the University of Oxford. His research interests covers European and Italian economic history, focusing on the interwar period, wellbeing and poverty, inequality and polarization, and the origin of the welfare state.

Matteo Gomellini is an economist at the Bank of Italy. He works in the Structural Economic Analysis Directorate—Economic History and Historical Archives Division. His research is focused on the economic history of Italian migration, international trade, demography, and urban development.

Lucia Latino holds a PhD in International Economics from the University of Rome Tor Vergata. Her research interests are vulnerability to poverty and food security measurement. Lucia is currently consulting for the World Food Programme.

Cormac Ó Gráda is Professor Emeritus of Economics at University College Dublin. He has published papers on topics ranging from the European Little Ice Age to the origins of the Industrial Revolution. His best-known books are on Irish economic history, the history of Irish Jewry, and the global history of famine.

Mariacristina Rossi is an associate professor of economics at the University of Turin and CCA affiliate at Collegio Carlo Alberto. Her research interests cover household decisions over the life cycle, precautionary savings, portfolio decision, and poverty analysis. Mariacristina has also worked as a consultant for the World Bank, ILO, and UNICEF.

Fernando Salsano has a PhD in social and economic history of modern and contemporary Europe at the University of Roma Tor Vergata. He is author of books and articles about the history of economic policies, urban history, and social history. He also teaches economic history at the University of Roma Tre.

Marina Sorrentino is a researcher at the Italian national statistical office, where she works on short-term statistics on labor input. She has worked on historical data and is a consultant for EU projects on labor statistics and for the World Bank on poverty and the labor market.

Gianni Toniolo—LUISS School of European Political Economy (Rome), and Duke University (emeritus)—is a CEPR Research Fellow and a member of the European Academy. His main research areas are the European economy in the nineteenth and twentieth centuries and financial history.

Giovanni Vecchi is a professor of economics at the University of Rome Tor Vergata. His main areas of research interest are the theory, measurement, and history of welfare, as well as economic history. He is the founding president of the Italian Association for Economic History, and a consultant to the World Bank on issues related to poverty and inequality measurement.

Measuring Wellbeing

Introduction

Economic History and the Elephant

In the course of my academic career, my interest has focused on measuring the wellbeing of the Italians during the last century and a half or so. Measuring wellbeing in a historical context is no easy task, either conceptually (how can we define the "wellbeing" of a society?) or empirically (where can we find data for hundreds of years of history?). Nor is it easy to build a narrative of this history, because the available material is fragmentary, with gaps and flaws. It is no accident that the Italian literature has traditionally ignored the subject of wellbeing altogether. This book is an attempt to bridge this gap.

Each chapter gives a piece of the overall story, reconstructing one of the many aspects making up the wellbeing of the Italians and studying its development over time. This brings up the concern addressed in the cautionary tale of the blind men and the elephant. In this parable, probably familiar to some readers, a prince arrives in a village of blind people on the back of an elephant—an animal unknown to the inhabitants. Six villagers, all blind of course, approached the animal to investigate. The first, touching the elephant's trunk, exclaimed that the animal was like a snake. The second, feeling its leg, claimed instead that it was like a tree. A third, finding an ear, judged the animal to be like a fan. Still another, grasping the tail, proclaimed the elephant to be like a rope. And so on. Each villager offered a good description of the part they had touched, but all six together could not provide a proper picture of the whole animal.

In the same vein, each chapter of this book measures the aspect of wellbeing assigned to it, much like each villager described the part of the elephant he was examining. What prevents this book from failing in the way that the villagers did is the coordinated approach taken to writing the various chapters. The chapters were not written by blind men and then assembled by a third party (sighted or not). If that were the case, then this introduction would have the task of solving the mystery of the elephant. Instead, all the chapters—each and every one of them—were coordinated before and during their drafting so as to relate their specific topic to the overall picture of the wellbeing of the Italians. The readers will be able "to see the elephant" right from the start, in chapter 1.

New Data, and a New Approach

The Kingdom of Italy—born on March 17, 1861—was a poor, overpopulated country, among the least educated in Europe. Most of its citizens lived short, difficult lives, with little or no prospect of giving their children a better future. Thus it had been for centuries in the Italian Peninsula. Since the the 1600s had buried the glories of the Renaissance, the inhabitants of the Italian Peninsula had scraped just to get by their circumstances slowly declining. The poet Giacomo Leopardi (1798–1837) described this state of affairs in verse in his famous poem "To Italy," written in 1818: "Ay, weep, Italia! thou hast cause to weep! . . . / Fallen! —ruined! —lost! who writes or speaks of thee, / But, calling unto mind thine ancient fame, / Exclaims, "Once she was mighty! Is this she?" / Where is thy vaunted strength, thy high resolve?"[1].

Starting from the 1850s, in the space of one and a half centuries, the Italians have amazed everyone by turning Italy into what many see as a little corner of paradise, defeating hunger, poverty, and early death to achieve a remarkable level of wellbeing. Italy is seen as the home of *la dolce vita* ("the sweet life"). How did such a transformation come about? In times of change, some people successfully take advantage of the moment, while others experience a painful worsening of their standard of living. Who were the winners and who were the losers in the course of Italian history?

The question of the distribution of income occupies a central position in this book, since the idea behind my research was to take a bottom-up approach, starting with basic data on the lives of individuals and households. The "macro" picture (the history) is built up from the "micro" data (the stories), taking great care not to leave anyone out. The most innovative, and also effective, tool for my task was the study of *household budgets*. Family accounts—records detailing incomes and expenditures through a year—are a source familiar to economists today, but conventional wisdom holds that in a historical context their number and quality are insufficient for analysis following modern best practice. In the case of Italy, fortunately, this is not the case. In this book I demonstrate that household budgets are a relatively abundant resource in Italy and that it is at last possible to lift the veil that has obscured the history of the country's income distribution. Traditional Italian histories have concentrated on per capita gross domestic product (GDP), that is, on the income of the "average Italian". In the presence of these household budgets, we no longer need to deal with such

---

[1] English translation from Longfellow (1877), *Poems of Places*.

abstractions; we are finally able to tell the history of *all* the Italians, of the disparities in their incomes, their deprivation and their wealth, all the way from 1861 to the present.

The Challenge of Defining Wellbeing

But let us proceed in an orderly manner. To document the extraordinary development of the wellbeing of the Italians, the first question to address is the *definition* of wellbeing. Although there is a mountain of literature on the subject, no *single* definition has emerged that has satisfied the whole academic community. In economics, which is my discipline, pragmatism has prevailed: the complexity of wellbeing has been reduced to simple monetary measures such as income, consumption expenditure, or wealth. Knowing full well that "money" does not always or necessarily imply wellbeing, economists have accumulated enough empirical evidence to conclude that the two variables are closely correlated: when GDP rises, the living standards of the population usually improve. This has led to the practice of using GDP as a measure of collective wellbeing. In this book, while not denying the importance of GDP, I have instead adopted a *multidimensional* approach to wellbeing. I have gone "beyond GDP"—an expression much in vogue today—and shown that if we restrict ourselves to this variable, we will only obtain a partial and potentially misleading picture of the historical development of living standards of the Italians.

Yesterday's Achievements and Today's Problems

In giving shape to a history involving many aspects of wellbeing, one difficulty concerns the choice of aspects to examine: which ones to include and why? I addressed this problem by focusing on a small number of core variables, fully aware that my choice would not satisfy all my colleagues, let alone all readers. To be on the safe side, I started from the most essential of basic needs: health. I hope most people will agree that health is a fundamental component of wellbeing. When we study poor economies, whether referring to sub-Saharan Africa today or the Europe of the past, the first step is to understand the whether and how a population manages to provide itself with an adequate diet, a precondition for achieving good conditions of health and the start-up of economic development. This is why the first three chapters of the book are dedicated to the themes of nutrition, physical stature, and health.

The analysis of the *nutrition* of the Italians (chapter 1) required many calculations, such as estimates of the calories available to the population on average, as well as a hint of methodological boldness to formulate hypotheses on the scale of undernutrition, that is, estimates of the percentage of the population whose intake fell below a minimum energy threshold (e.g., 2,100 calories per person per day). The chapter teaches us lessons of a general nature that are sometimes unexpected. One concerns the *reversibility of history*. With respect to progress, which is often perceived as unstoppable if not inevitable, the results of the first chapter show that the Italians experienced unexpected shocks of a considerable scale. After World War II, for example, the average Italian had the same daily calorie intake (a little under 1,900 per person/day) as that of his great-grandparents in the late nineteenth century. Nobody would have expected a return of hunger in postwar Republican Italy, but hunger did return, as did poverty, and on a large scale.

The second chapter deals with the Italians' average height. I imagine not everyone knows that even today there is a significant difference between the height of the poor and that of the rich—the latter being taller, on average. This difference is not due to any genetic differences between the two groups of people, but rather to the influence of the environment on the development of the human body. In a difficult, hostile environment, the human body responds through a series of defense mechanisms including a slowdown or cessation of growth, resulting in short adult stature. Hence, the average height of a community may increase but also decrease, depending on the circumstances. Economic historians have exploited this biological regularity in order to explore the living conditions in periods for which we have information on heights but no other better data. Chapter 2 ("Height") offers the reader a discussion of the limitations of this approach, but shows the usefulness of looking at the development of the living conditions of the Italians through the lens of their heights. The height indicators used are based on the measurement of over thirty million men born between 1840 and 1980, taken on the occasion of their medical examination to assess fitness for military service. This dataset yields an amazing picture enabling us, for example, to get an idea of what happened at the time of the country's political and administrative unification. We find that, on the whole, Italy—fragmented and poor as it was—had already reversed its centuries-old decline *before* the time of its unification. The north of the country showed a significant economic advantage compared to the south even then. The height data also show that the impact of the country's unification on the people's living conditions was, all told, quite modest. The few benefits recorded by our data were of greater advantage to the south than to the north. The newborn central government after unification thus deserves no rebuke, at least not from southern Italians.

The chapter dedicated to the *health* of the Italians (chapter 3) is the product of a mammoth statistical effort aimed at building a series of basic indicators (life expectancy at birth, the child mortality rate, etc.) capable of portraying the profound changes taking place over time. Health is perhaps the brightest page of Italian history. Premature death—something that in 1861 prevented one child in every four from living to see their first birthday—decreased rapidly, even in periods where per capita GDP was growing at very modest rates. At the same time, life expectancy at birth (around 30 years at the time of unification) is now just under 80 years or more (79.8 for males and 84.6 for females), putting Italy among the countries with the longest-living people in the world. Progress has been *inclusive*, that is, it has involved all the country's regions, albeit at different rates. If all this (and much more) brings out pages of history to be proud of, the chapter suggests looking ahead, to ponder the sustainability of the results achieved, in the spirit of what historian E. H. Carr (1892–1982) taught. In a famous lecture series at Cambridge in 1961 Carr claimed that "Records of the past begin to be kept for the benefit of future generations." Modern Italy is a radically different place from what it used to be: do we have reason to assume that the progress recorded on the health front in the past can be maintained or improved in the future? The chapter suggests that yesterday's achievements sometimes sow the seeds for the problems of today and those of tomorrow.

Education is the Gloomiest Chapter in Italian Social History

The next set of chapters deal with another fundamental aspect of wellbeing: *education*. I shall comment here on just one of the three chapters dedicated to this theme, focusing on the spread of literacy among the Italians and the formation of the country's current human capital (chapter 5). The other two chapters— on child labor (chapter 4) and migration (chapter 6)—look at the wellbeing of the youngest members of the population (child labor effectively means a lack of education) and those who seek their fortunes elsewhere (emigration flows are associated with human capital losses and gains).

Chapter 5 presents the results of an in-depth analysis of sources printed and handwritten, published and archival. Although the results cannot easily be summarized here, they confirm what a foreign observer, historian Bolton King (1860–1937), wrote in 1901: "Education is the gloomiest chapter in Italian social history, a chapter of painful advance, of national indifference to a primary need, of a present backwardness, that gives Italy (next to Portugal) the sad primacy of illiteracy in Western Europe."[2] This disaster was attributed to the failure of Italian institutions, to a lack of will rather than a lack of means: "There have been thirty-three Education Ministers since 1860, each eager to distinguish himself by upsetting his predecessor's work. Money has been stinted, and State and communes, lavish in all else, have economized in the most fruitful

---

[2] From Bolton King and Thomas Okey (1901), *Italy Today*, p. 233.

of national investments."[3] Our data, in graphs, tables, and regressions, support
this conclusion, document its features, and identify its phases. The significance
of all this for today's Italy is soon revealed: if, as we can reasonably assume, the
wellbeing of future generations is largely in the hands of their education (Italy
does not possess other natural resources), failure to nurture talents, develop
cognitive abilities, and invest in skills is not an option. Italy dare not miss the
skill-biased, knowledge-intensive train that has set off in these years and which
all countries are committed to catch.

Italy's Great Divergence and Decline

The book goes on to deal with monetary measures of wellbeing. In chapter 7,
dedicated to the *income* of the Italians, I reconstruct the trend in per capita GDP,
producing separate long-term estimates for the various regions of the country.
What emerges is the history of a country that has taken a great leap forward in a
short space of time: for a hundred years the Italian economy struggled to achieve
a take off, but then accomplished this quite abruptly in the 1950s. What also
emerges from the new estimates is a picture of the "great Italian divergence,"
that is, the incapacity of the south to achieve the levels of wellbeing recorded in
the north. It is an important and politically delicate issue, which I have tried to
document it with meticulousness: the statistics show that the south has always
gone forward, without stopping, but at a slower pace than that of the north;
these different paces necessarily mean a widening of the north–south divide.
Was it reasonable to expect a convergence? Perhaps not, if we bear in mind the
role played by certain primary actors: institutions, social capital, corruption,
and crime. However, despite the secular persistence of its geographic divide, the
Italian economic history does not justify any nostalgia for the past. Nearly unin-
terrupted progress means that all the Italians—both northern and southern—
enjoy better living conditions today than even imaginable a few generations ago.
It is an achievement that few other countries can boast.

A lack of integration means a lack of wellbeing. This is an important point
in view of the fact that since the 1980s the country has embarked on a phase of
relative decline: not only has the pace of GDP growth in Italy slowed down more
markedly than the Organisation for Economic Cooperation and Development
(OECD) country average, but in recent years there even seems to be a regression
(i.e., per capita GDP growth rates have turned negative)—a situation not to be
found in any other OECD country. Over the decade from 2001 to 2010, Italy
had the the worst average growth rate *in the world*. Starting from this datum,
the chapter suggests that the country is indeed undergoing a process of relative

[3] Ibid.

decline. This diagnosis is not shared by all scholars, but the analysis of per capita GDP together with the other indicators examined in this book seems to leave little room for doubt: Italy is in decline.

From Rags to Riches, and Back Again

The most difficult and, in some respects innovative part of the book is found in the chapters dealing with inequality (chapter 8), poverty (chapter 9), wealth (chapter 10), and vulnerability (that is, the likelihood of those who are not poor today to become poor in the near future, chapter 11) . The analysis conducted in the first two of these chapters is based on a collection of almost 20,000 Italian household budgets assembled over twenty years of research. This is the only dataset of its kind in the world today, and the subject of great interest among the academic community. It forms the basis for a broader research project called the Historical Household Budgets (HHB) Project (http://hhbproject.com). The sources are meticulously described in chapter 13 ("Household Budgets").

Household budget surveys are a modern invention. In Italy, as in any other country in the world, the first surveys of household income and expenditure carried out on a national scale and based on a probabilistic sampling design started only after World War II. Since the 1960s the Italian National Institute of Statistics (Istat) has interviewed over one million households, assessing their consumption expenditures, while the Bank of Italy has regularly interviewed another 150,000 households, recording their income and wealth. Linking these modern data with the collection of older household budgets has made it possible to estimate the inequality of incomes and the (absolute) poverty of the Italians from 1861 to the present day. No country in the world can probably boast estimates of both inequality and absolute poverty trends covering such a long time-frame.

What can be learned from this wealth of household accounting data? The Italian "economic miracle" saw the country's GDP grow at unprecedented rates between 1950 and 1963. In chapter 8 ("Inequality"), a new "miracle" is brought to the reader's attention, one the country experienced in the 1970s: Italy's modern economic development combined growth with greater equity in income distribution. Every three years the country recorded a one percentage-point reduction in income inequality (as measured by the popular Gini index). This makes the country's economic history a very interesting case study for the national and international scientific community. While in the United Kingdom and United States, countries for which we have the best historical reconstructions of income distribution, modernization came at the cost of greater inequality (at least in the early stages of the process), this was not the case for Italy.

With regard to the analysis of *poverty*, chapter 9 conveys two fundamental messages: one positive, the other negative. The good news is that, regardless of current levels, the trend in the incidence of absolute poverty in Italy has been downward throughout Italy's postunification history. It is still too early to understand whether the great rise in poverty rates recorded in the Great Recession (underway since 2007) contradicts what has been said above, but the historic trend has virtuous features. The bad news concerns the territorial distribution of poverty. Despite the generalized decrease in poverty rates, the gap between north and south has widened over time, accelerating considerably in the last few decades. The chapter explains that the state's lack of interest in poverty has not changed throughout the country's history: even today Italy has not established an *official* absolute poverty line. The absence of a poverty line—one with enough consensus and clarity to be approved by the Italian Parliament—is a formidable obstacle to tackling the poverty issue. How can we fight a phenomenon if we do not know the scale of the problem? It is like asking a medical doctor to operate on a patient without a diagnosis. The chapter leaves the reader with hope that the country can finally manage to turn over a new leaf. It's never too late.

With respect to the theme of *wealth* (chapter 10), I present first-generation estimates of an annual time series of Italian household wealth. The chapter illustrates the history of households' private wealth, revealing when the Italians were able to put aside money in the form of savings and when they had to draw them down to face the hardships of life. Estimates show that wealth needed a long period of incubation for accumulation to begin, but once the process had begun, the saving accumulation mechanism proceeded at a rapid pace. Perhaps no other variable in the country's history shows such a rapid increase as per capita wealth. Indeed, the Italians have become so rich that some have voiced their concern. Italy, like France, the United Kingdom, and the United States, could fall prey to the "central contradiction of capitalism". Too much wealth may have destabilizing effects, triggering forces that lacerate the socioeconomic fabric and jeopardize democracy. The question posed is thus the following one: Can too much wealth really be a pitfall for the wellbeing of the Italians? Our answer is a comforting "no, it can't". The chapter suggests that the imbalance in the ratio between income and wealth is an alarm bell: the problem does not lie so much with excessive wealth, as with the country's reduced capacity to generate income. This in turn reflects the country's persisting difficulties in adapting to the great forces affecting the world's economy over the last few decades: the technological paradigm (now driven by new information and communication technologies), the acceleration in globalization (integration of world markets), and the process of European integration (culminating in the introduction of the single currency, the euro). Some call this incapacity to adapt an "economic decline."

Economic History and the Elephant—Reprise

In conclusion, and to be consistent with my opening remarks, I ask myself whether the chapters that make up this book can really convey the story I meant to tell.

When it is time to take stock, there is the problem of reducing the complexity of the results. How to go about this? In some spheres the Italians achieved a miracle—in the case of health, for example—but in others the results have been disappointing if not a outright failure with regard to education, for instance. In some moments of their history, the Italians progressed in leaps and bounds; in others they slowed down; in still others they regressed. The trend in GDP over the years, for example, has sometimes made scholars sound the trumpet in celebration; but the impasse of the last twenty-five years, aggravated by inequality, poverty, and vulnerability, has led some to sound the death knell and talk of decline. How can we find a synthesis of such divergent positions? What evaluation can we make, in the end, for the great deal of evidence collected in the pages of this book?

In chapter 12 ("Human Development") I explore the possibility of providing an *objective* answer, that is, an answer that emerges unambiguously from the data. Technically, the problem has a simple solution, which involves constructing a composite index—a combination of two or more elementary indicators to create a single one. The most famous example of a composite index is the Human Development Index (HDI) used by the United Nations and in vogue for over a quarter of a century. The HDI combines GDP, a couple of education indicators (literacy and school enrollment rates), and life expectancy at birth. The result is a number that reduces a great many dimensions of life to a single number. This is the very situation confronted in this book, which documents various aspects of the wellbeing of the Italians. I have explored the use of composite indexes in historical settings, but concluded that it is a dead-end. An index like the HDI necessarily provides an incomplete, and worse yet a *subjective* picture of the development of the living conditions of the Italians. There are periods, such as the interwar years, where the same index can indicate either progress or decline in Italy, depending on how the index is defined. This happens because a composite index reflects the value judgments of its creator. If the person who uses it is a historian, then the HDI will largely reflect the historian's judgment of history. There is nothing wrong with this, since judgment is inevitable and the judgments of the court of history are never unappealable, but we must be conscious of this fact. The attempt to deal with complexity by constructing an aggregate measure of social welfare is, at the end of the day, destined to fail: what we get is, at most, a conclusion based on the value system associated with the researcher—the least objective thing we can imagine.

The task accomplished in this book, measuring the many dimensions of the wellbeing of Italians and tracking their evolution over time, has been difficult and complex, but fascinating: the elephant has been recognized and subjected to a great number of empirical measurements. Economic historians are now better placed, hopefully, to take the next steps and address the mother of all questions: what factors explain the history of the wellbeing of Italians? Dealing with causation in economic history is a daunting task, but is the logical, inescapable, top-priority issue in my research agenda, from the day the manuscript of this book was sent to the printer.

1

Nutrition

WITH MARINA SORRENTINO

1 The Never-Ending Dispute between Optimists and Pessimists

In the mid-1800s, getting a proper meal was a daily problem fraught with difficulties for most Italians. Accounts of the times all agree that most of the population had an insufficient availability of calories and an imbalanced diet:

> Badly baked, damp and rancid corn bread, and soup containing the lowest quality ingredients when they were not downright harmful; rice or pasta of inferior quality, old and rotten pulses, unwashed greens, a little oil or rancid lard or even fat for condiment, this is the fare which was prepared for those who worked in the fields of the tenant farmer—a meagre meal for a man barely scraping a living on the land ... that he enriched through his sweat. And the meal was sometimes so revolting that the poor peasant was forced to leave it and to spend his own scant earnings in order to eat. (authors' translation from Cardani and Massara 1868, 28)

This bleak picture pervades the historiography of the times: dozens of descriptions like this can be found (Sorcinelli 1995). Economists and social scientists in general, but also hygienists and physiologists, who analyzed the deprived, poor, and very poor, almost inevitably came to the same dramatic conclusions.[1] A few large-scale official investigations conducted from the mid-1800s found similar results. These studies are notable for gathering detailed information on the eating habits of the kingdom's inhabitants, but—much like the studies of private scholars—they focused on the hardships and privations of less-affluent sections of the population. There was a need to further assess food scarcity and

---

[1] See Niceforo (1901, 1937); Giglioli (1903); and Bottazzi, Niceforo, and Quagliariello (1933).

to understand the scale of the phenomenon in order to arouse public reaction and to call for political intervention.

All these sources of information led to creating a pessimistic view, which gained consensus over time. In this view, during the first fifty years of postunification Italy, improvements in the population's nutrition were not as significant as other economic developments—especially per-capita gross domestic product (GDP) (Zamagni 1998).

The pessimistic view does not, however, appear consistent with evidence that emerges if, instead of focusing only on the poorest section of the population, we consider the whole population—the poor, less poor, rich, and very rich. One way to approach this task is to analyze estimates published by the Italian National Institute of Statistics (Istat) showing that, as far back as 1861, the average calorie intake was 2,520 calories per person per day (Istat 2011)—a figure greatly exceeding the one most scholars use as the threshold of undernutrition. Unlike the older sources, the reconstruction made by Istat concerned the whole population: estimates of food availability were the product of calculations based on figures deriving not from episodic observations of local contexts but from the processing of national statistics on agricultural production as well as from balance of trade figures (the food we consume is not just domestically produced, but also imported from abroad, while some domestically produced food is exported). The different origin of the data clears up why the empirical evidence produced by Istat can lead to formulating the rosiest hypotheses: this is because the calories available *per inhabitant* (a category that includes everyone—rich and poor alike) are by definition more abundant than the calories *per nonaffluent inhabitant* (as with figures noted in nineteenth-century sources). The second body of estimates—based on official statistics—thus corroborates a more optimistic hypothesis, according to which the population's availability of foodstuffs increased significantly in the decades after Italian unification and that, right from the beginning of the new Kingdom of Italy, the food supply was already sufficient to meet the population's average energy requirements.[2]

The above dilemma is something Italy shares with other countries. The optimists' view (that the population's standard of living improved during the industrialization process) and the pessimists' one (that living conditions improved only marginally, when they did not actually worsen) have been debated for almost a century in the United Kingdom's case (Cinnirella 2008). Similar debates can be found concerning the United States (Lindert and Williamson 1985) and other countries all over the world (Steckel 2008). However, while for most countries the debate between optimists and pessimists does not seem to lead to one side winning over the other, in Italy's case the dispute is more apparent than

---

[2] Federico (2003), Fenoaltea (2002), and Vecchi and Coppola (2003; 2006) come to conclusions in line with the optimists' view.

substantial since it may be reconciled by jointly examining the data on calories available to the population and their *distribution*. The idea is straightforward: if calorie distribution among individuals of the population is markedly unequal (that is, only a few individuals possess a large portion of the total calories available), then it is possible to observe a society characterized by an adequate average availability of calories and, at the same time, a significant percentage of the population in conditions of undernutrition. To the extent that the above situation is supported by empirical evidence, we would then have an explanation capable of resolving the apparent contradiction between a relatively abundant average calorie availability found in Italy since its unification (see Istat and more recent historiographic data) and the co-presence of broad sections of an undernourished population (sources of the times).

The general questions that we focus on in this chapter can thus be put as follows: *In what way did the economic growth process enable the spreading of improvements in the diet of the Italian population? How long did it take?* Answering such questions is a complex operation at the methodological level and a laborious one with regard to data gathering. We shall begin by constructing a time series of the calories available to the Italian population in each of the 150 years examined (sections 2 and 3). To see whether the available calories were sufficient to meet the population's needs, we shall also estimate the country's calorie requirements (section 4), that is, we shall calculate the calories needed by the average Italian to lead a healthy life. Once we have determined the calories available and the average requirements, we shall reconstruct the trend in the population's calorie distribution—an operation that is necessary in order to estimate the percentage of undernourished population (section 5). Finally, since an adequate availability of calories is a necessary condition, but not a sufficient one, to evaluate a population's diet, we shall reconstruct the evolution of the Italians' diet by examining its content in terms of macronutrients: carbohydrates, fats, and proteins (section 6).

2 Calories and Wellbeing

A country's system of national accounts (SNA) can provide very detailed information on the quantity of foodstuffs available for the population's consumption. In Italy's case, as far back as 1958, the national statistics institute (Istat) managed to calculate the daily availability of calories per inhabitant by tracing its evolution, year after year, starting from 1861.[3] However, the published

---

[3] Updates of the first reconstruction, published by Istat (1958), are contained in the subsequent three editions of the *Sommario di Statistiche Storiche* (Istat 1968; 1976; 1986).

statistical series were never accompanied by a suitable description of the methods and sources used, without which it is difficult today to evaluate the quality of the relative data. Nor has the time series of available calories been reviewed or updated for the years after 1985, not even on the occasion of the special edition of the *Sommario di statistiche storiche* (Summary of Historical Statistics), which was published during celebrations of the 150th anniversary of Italian unification (Istat 2011). The calculation of the daily calories available to the Italians is thus—de facto—no longer part of the statistics of national interest.

In the light of these considerations, our analysis begins with a reconstruction of the time series of daily calories available to the Italians over the last 150 years. By connecting among them the most recent series available for each subperiod (described in the Appendix), we obtain the result shown in Figure 1.1, where we see that average calorie availability per inhabitant in Italy has

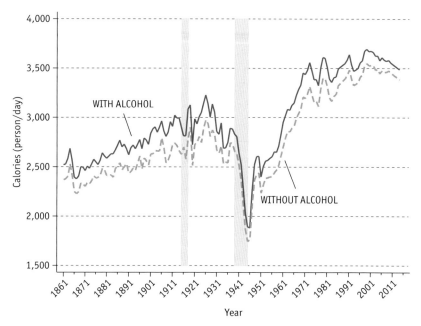

Figure 1.1 PER-CAPITA DAILY CALORIE AVAILABILITY, 1861–2014. The graph shows the trend in per capita daily calorie availability (vertical axis) over time (horizontal axis). The term "calories" is taken to mean "kilocalories" (Box 1). The unbroken blue line includes calories deriving from the consumption of alcoholic beverages, while the broken line shows calorie availability without alcohol consumption (alcohol does not provide the body with nutritional substances, unlike the proteins, carbohydrates and fats contained in other foods). The shading indicates the years of the two world wars.

been historically high. Immediately after the country's unification, the figure exceeded 2,500 calories per day—a value that is higher than the ones commonly used today to mark the threshold of undernutrition in developing countries (say, between 2,000 and 2,300 calories a day). A first conclusion is thus that calorie availability during the first fifty years of united Italy were such that, on average, the population did not have to endure periods of energy deficiency. Naturally, this does not rule out that parts of the population were undernourished, as we shall see by examining the unequal distribution of calories among Italians (section 5).

The years 1861–1913 saw a continuous upward trend in calorie availability. Now, when average calorie availability per inhabitant rises, it is reasonable to assume that the less affluent segments of the population enjoy greater benefits compared to those of the richer segments. This phenomenon—already observed by Balestrieri (1925)—can be illustrated by means of the following reasoning. If we assume that the rich are well nourished and always have the amount of calories satisfying their needs (otherwise, how could we call them "rich"?), every change in the *average* value of calorie availability will particularly reflect changes in the calorie availability of the poorest sections of the population. If this is true, then the average calorie availability per inhabitant, shown in Figure 1.1, contains some useful information not only with regard to development of the average diet but also—and above all—on how conditions of the less privileged changed. In this light, average calorie availability almost becomes an indicator of the spreading of wellbeing among the poorest sections of the population. If we adopt this interpretation, then Figure 1.1 tells a story that does not leave any doubt: over the first fifty years of unified Italy, the greatest benefits went to the "poor." Going back to the debate between optimists and pessimists with which we began this chapter, the increasing part of the curve in the years 1861–1913 is consistent with the "optimist" view, according to which the first decades of postunification Italy saw the whole population, but particularly the poorest segment, improve its conditions substantially.

In the period between the two world wars, there was not only a break in the continuous improvement in living conditions of the poorest sections of the population, but even an actual inversion in the trend. This change faithfully reflects the shift from the 1920s (which were years of strong economic growth that saw an increase in calorie availability) to the difficult 1930s. Starting from 1927, that is, two years after Mussolini's announcement of the "Battle for Grain", and in the year of the stabilization of the Italian lira at the ambitious "Quota 90" against the British pound, there began a decreasing phase in average calorie availability, which, even if it did not affect solely the poorest people in the population, certainly did not spare them.

Box 1 A Population's Calories: User Instructions

Calories. The term "calorie" has no univocal meaning. For physicists, a calorie indicates the quantity of energy needed to increase the temperature of one gram of water from 14.5 to 15.5 degrees Celsius. For nutritionists, a calorie is the quantity of energy needed to raise the temperature of not just one gram but a kilogram of distilled water by one degree. Thus, a "food calorie" is the equivalent of a thousand calories used by physicists. For our intents and purposes, we shall use food calories (abbreviated as "cal" or "kcal") since this is the unit of measurement for the energy contained in foods: when food is ingested, the cells come into contact with oxygen and release a certain amount of energy that the body can use. As we know, different foods contain and release different amounts of energy: fats and alcohol have the highest values (9 and 7 kcal per gram, respectively), followed by proteins and carbohydrates (4 kcal per gram). Eating a plate of pasta containing 100 grams of carbohydrates means providing the body with 400 kcal (besides the ones deriving from the proteins contained in the pasta), while a portion of cheese or cold cuts containing 100 grams of fats can provide 900 kcal (besides those deriving from the proteins and few

Figure 1.B1 Annibale Carracci, *The Beaneater* (1584–1585).

carbohydrates contained in these foods). In our daily life we normally use the word *calories* when we refer to quantities actually expressed as *kilocalories*: we say a dish contains 400 calories when we should really say 400 kilocalories. We shall adopt the same simplification in the rest of this chapter and talk in terms of calories meaning kilocalories.

Assimilated calories. To evaluate whether a person, and thus even a population, is undernourished, we must assess the assimilated calories, that is to say, the actual amount of energy provided to the body and absorbed by it throughout the day. Measuring the assimilated calories requires laboratory analysis as well as information on how the foods are treated and whether they are cooked before being consumed. This leads us to conclude that it is not even imaginable to reconstruct a time series of assimilated calories of the Italian population over the last 150 years.

Ingested calories. Equally impractical is measuring the average calories ingested by a population. This would call for: *(a)* an estimate of the quantity of food *purchased* by households (for Italy, this would only be possible from the late 1960s, with the advent of sample surveys on household consumption), and *(b)* an evaluation of the food wasted inside the household and along the distribution chain from producer to retailer. Prudent calculations show that today this wastage amounts to at least 26 percent of total food availability in the United States, 25 percent in Japan, and 10 percent in the United Kingdom (Bleich et al. 2007).

Available calories. In order to study the evolution of the diet of the Italian population over the decades, the only practical approach is to estimate the calories actually *available* after wastage. However, the estimation procedure is laborious. We start by estimating the national production of each foodstuff (how many thousands of tons have been produced by domestic agriculture for each type of foodstuff). To this domestic production must be added an evaluation of how stocks change (the difference between stocks at the start and at the end of the year for each type of foodstuff). From this amount we must deduct the quantity of foodstuffs exported (evidently what is sold abroad is not available for domestic consumption), and add the quantity of foodstuffs imported (the food purchased from abroad contributes positively to domestic availability). The last stage consists in deducting the quantity of foodstuffs destined for uses other than consumption as actual food, such as for sowing or for animal feeds, as well as foodstuffs lost or deteriorated in the distribution process. There are thus so many stages to be considered when estimating each one of the items listed above that it is no wonder that some authors lament the inaccuracy or limited reliability of final estimates (Somogyi 1973).

The Italian population experienced immense suffering during World War II. Average calorie availability fell to 1,884 calories—a figure that overestimates what was actually available to the civilian population if we consider that the army had a higher than average proportion of the available food. The peak level of calorie availability reached in 1926, with 2,975 daily calories per capita, including alcohol consumption, would be regained only in 1967. After the war, calorie consumption increased rapidly towards current levels, which, as we shall see, may be considered excessive.

2.1 THE CALORIES OF ITALIANS COMPARED TO THOSE OF THE REST OF THE WORLD

The first data enabling researchers to place Italy within an international context and to compare the Italians' diet with those of other peoples in the world date back to the late 1930s. In the five years from 1934 to 1938 the country was pursuing economic recovery, a task made difficult by the international situation (the aftermath of the Great Depression) and by constraints of the autarchic policy of the Fascist regime. Mussolini had wanted a strong currency and had managed to achieve it, but in order to defend the new parity of the Italian lira, he was forced to keep interest rates high—indeed, extremely high (Italian rates were the highest in Europe in the five-year period considered). The inexorably negative side effects weighed heavily on production levels and, obviously, on employment rates (Toniolo 1980; chapter 6, "Migration", this volume). A large proportion of the wage increases gained during the 1920s were thus eroded in the latter half of the 1930s (Zamagni 1993, 396). In view of the above situation, which countries at the time had more calories available for their populations than Italy? And how did Italy's relative position change in the decades following World War II? By working on the figures provided by the first World Food Survey—published by the Food and Agriculture Organization (FAO) of the United Nations in 1946, less than three months after its foundation—we obtain new, accurate, and eloquent quantitative answers.

In the late 1930s the average calorie availability of Italians was probably sufficient to shelter them from situations of mass undernutrition and malnutrition. However, it is also clear that the gap separating Italy from its neighboring countries and the best-nourished ones was broad. If we ranked countries on the basis of their calorie availability and grouped them into homogeneous classes, Italy would not be in the same class as countries from Central and Northern Europe, but rather in the one including countries like Spain, Portugal, and Greece, and even countries of the Soviet bloc, most of Eastern Europe, and many North African and Middle Eastern ones as well. The *extent* of this gap between Italy and the other countries can be grasped by looking at Figure 1.2 (upper panel). The graph shows a curve that statisticians call the "cumulative distribution

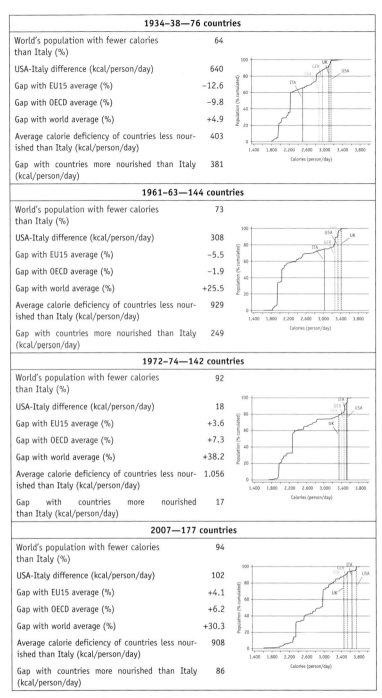

1934–38—76 countries	
World's population with fewer calories than Italy (%)	64
USA-Italy difference (kcal/person/day)	640
Gap with EU15 average (%)	−12.6
Gap with OECD average (%)	−9.8
Gap with world average (%)	+4.9
Average calorie deficiency of countries less nourished than Italy (kcal/person/day)	403
Gap with countries more nourished than Italy (kcal/person/day)	381

1961–63—144 countries	
World's population with fewer calories than Italy (%)	73
USA-Italy difference (kcal/person/day)	308
Gap with EU15 average (%)	−5.5
Gap with OECD average (%)	−1.9
Gap with world average (%)	+25.5
Average calorie deficiency of countries less nourished than Italy (kcal/person/day)	929
Gap with countries more nourished than Italy (kcal/person/day)	249

1972–74—142 countries	
World's population with fewer calories than Italy (%)	92
USA-Italy difference (kcal/person/day)	18
Gap with EU15 average (%)	+3.6
Gap with OECD average (%)	+7.3
Gap with world average (%)	+38.2
Average calorie deficiency of countries less nourished than Italy (kcal/person/day)	1.056
Gap with countries more nourished than Italy (kcal/person/day)	17

2007—177 countries	
World's population with fewer calories than Italy (%)	94
USA-Italy difference (kcal/person/day)	102
Gap with EU15 average (%)	+4.1
Gap with OECD average (%)	+6.2
Gap with world average (%)	+30.3
Average calorie deficiency of countries less nourished than Italy (kcal/person/day)	908
Gap with countries more nourished than Italy (kcal/person/day)	86

Figure 1.2 WHO EATS MORE THAN ITALIANS? CALORIE DISTRIBUTION IN THE WORLD, 1930S–2000S. The graphs show Italy's progress along the foodstuff availability scale constructed at a global level taking into account the different sizes of the countries in terms of population. The vertical axis of each curve measures the percentage of the population which has a number of available calories *lower* than the values given on the horizontal axis. For example, in the years 1934–38, the curve shows that over 60 percent of the world's population had a lower number of available calories than Italians, that is lower than about 2,500.

function", a very useful analytical tool that can be illustrated in nontechnical terms. The horizontal axis shows the average daily available calories per inhabitant. If we take any value along this axis, such as 2,510 calories (the one relative to Italy, shown as a blue line), the value that the curve gives on the vertical axis, 64 percent, tells us that 64 percent of the world's population had a *lower* calorie availability than Italy (the remaining 36 percent thus had a *greater* calorie availability). The overall finding that emerges from the curve for the years 1934–38 is Italy's backwardness compared to the countries highlighted (France, Germany, the United Kingdom, and the United States). Behind the French we find 82 percent of the world's population; behind the British, 90 percent; and behind the Americans, 93 percent.

To the left of this graph is a panel of useful indicators that can help us to more deeply analyze the Italian situation with regard to the rest of the world. The first indicator (line 1) shows the percentage of the world's population that had *fewer* calories than the Italians (64 percent). The second indicator (line 2) gives the number of daily calories separating Italy from the United States, the leading country of the times (640 kcal/person/day). The third (line 3) shows the gap—this time expressed as a percentage and not in calories—between Italy and the group of countries making up the so-called EU15, the first fifteen member states of the European Union: the calories available to Italians were 12.6 percent *fewer* than the EU15 average. The fourth indicator (line 4) shows the gap between Italy and the group of countries of the Organization for Economic Cooperation and Development (OECD), a broader and more heterogeneous group compared to the EU15: the calories available in Italy were 9.8 percent fewer than the ones available in the OECD countries. The fifth indicator (line 5) compares the calories available in Italy with the world average (calculated based on the seventy countries covered in the first World Food Survey): the former exceeded the latter by 4.9 percent. The last two indicators measure the calories separating Italy from the group of less nourished countries (on average, 403 kcal/person/day, line 6), and from the most nourished ones (on average, 381 kcal/person/day, line 7).

If we analyze Figure 1.2 from the top down (from 1934–38, the first data available, to 2007 and the most recent data), we can see the progress made by Italy compared to the rest of the world. At the start (1934–38), the country was definitely backward compared to the other countries of reference. In the 1950s Italy managed to significantly reduce its gap with the other countries, but not to eliminate it (in the 1961–63 survey, there was still a slight calorie deficit compared not only to the EU15 and OECD countries but also to the other European ones considered in the figure). In the 1960s Italy first caught up with and then overtook the other European countries, coming close behind the United States. This leading position was maintained in the following decades, as shown in the 2007 graph.

3 Income and Satiation

The increase in the number of calories available to Italians over the 150 years since the country's unification is also spectacular considering the increase in average per-capita income during the period. Figure 1.3 compares Italy's calorie availability with that of many other countries, also taking into account the level achieved by every country in terms of GDP per capita. The graph shows that as per-capita income rises, the per-capita availability of calories also rises, but at a decreasing rate (this is the interpretation of the curve crossing the "cloud" of countries). The result, largely expected by economists, is in line with the common view of many and with the experience of other countries (Deaton 1997): as a society (or even an individual) progresses in terms of income,

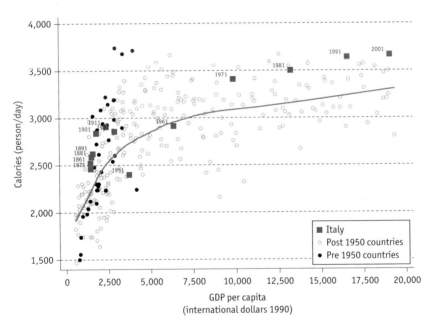

Figure 1.3 THE RELATIONSHIP BETWEEN AVAILABLE CALORIES AND PER-CAPITA GDP IN AROUND 60 COUNTRIES OF THE WORLD. In the graph, each small circle stands for a country whose average daily per capita calorie availability is represented on the vertical axis, and whose GDP per capita, expressed in 1990 dollars appropriately corrected to allow for purchasing power differences among countries, is indicated on the horizontal axis. The small dark circles show 19th century data of more uncertain reliability, while the small light circles indicate countries observed since 1961. The small blue squares identify Italy. The curve passing through the cloud of circles is an estimate of the relationship explaining how—on average for all the countries considered—calorie availability varies with changing income. The graph shows that, with rare exceptions, Italy has a number of per capita available calories that is always higher than the international average.

expenditure on food rises, but at a decreasing rate—larger and larger shares of the additional income are used not for calories, a basic good, but for other things (Box 2).

Figure 1.3 reveals that, except for 1951, Italy is always above—and often well above—the international average. Nineteenth-century Italy is no exception, despite the fact that it could not enjoy the advantages brought by modern technology in lowering the unit cost of a calorie over time. Moreover, having made up for the great drop in available calories in the years 1927–46, Italy progressively moves away from the international average, indicating an excess availability of calories. The increase in available calories after the end of World War II is a continuous trend that led the country to the top of the ranking of countries in

---

Box 2 **Mr. Engel and Expenditure on Food**

It is worth clarifying at the start that the "Mr. Engel" we are talking about here is Ernst Engel (1821–1896), a German statistician, and not Friedrich Engels (1820–1895), the German philosopher and politician who cowrote

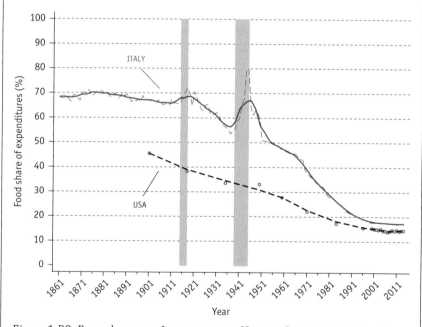

Figure 1.B2 Engel's law in Italy and the United States. By taking the proportion of household expenditure on food as an indicator of wellbeing (the lower the proportion, the greater the average wellbeing of the country), the graph shows the decades-long US advantage over Italy.

the Communist Party Manifesto along with Karl Marx (Kindleberger 1997). In 1857, Engel made an observation that has become famous over the years—so much so that it is still found in economics textbooks today. Engel observed that "the poorer a family, the greater the *proportion* of its total expenditure that must be devoted to the provision of food" (Engel 1857, 28–29; Stigler 1954, 98). At the time, this was an empirical finding that emerged examining just 132 household budgets. Since then, though, Engel's observation has been confirmed in the consumption behaviors of households of every period and country. Household budgets seem to tell the same story: expenditure on food on the part of rich households is, on average, greater than that of poor households (the diet of the "rich" is more abundant and of better quality than that of the "poor"), but if we equate total expenditure to 100, then the proportion of expenditure allocated to food is greater in poor households than in rich ones (food takes up a greater percentage of total resources the poorer the individual). The universal nature of this result led Engel to use the term "law" (Chai and Moneta 2010), from which today we have the expression "Engel's law" (Houthakker 1957; Lewbel 2008). The innovative aspect of this "law" is that it attributes to the proportion of expenditure allocated to food the role of indicator of wellbeing: the greater the proportion of expenditure, the lower the wellbeing. Engel also suggested, albeit in passing, that what was found for households could be applied to countries: "The proportion of the outgo used for food, other things being equal, is the best measure of the material standard of living of a population" (Engel 1857, 28–29; Zimmerman 1932). In Figure 1.B2, we have reconstructed the pattern of the proportion of expenditure on foodstuffs in Italy over the 150 years since the country's unification. If the long-term trend is clearly decreasing and in line with what Engel's law predicts, on closer examination we see periods that do not really fit in with this observation. This can be seen, for example, in the first fifty years of postunification, a time in which the proportion of expenditure on food does not show any decreasing trend despite the fact that per-capita GDP was rising (in real terms) by 60 percent (chapter 7, "Income"). Compared with the United States, the gap between the two curves shows *(a)* the scale of the initial U.S. advantage (from the late nineteenth century to the eve of World War II, the gap widened); and *(b)* Italy's gradual convergence, which started in the aftermath of World War II, but ended only in the last two decades (Deaton 1975).

terms of number of per-capita available calories. Italians are today second only to Americans: they can dispose of about 30 percent more than the calories available to the Japanese and have higher levels compared to the Germans, French, Spanish, British, and Swedes. The consequences of this are easy to imagine: the average Italian is getting fatter.[4]

4 The Energy a Population Needs

To understand whether a person is adequately nourished, we must take into consideration not only how much food is available but also the amount the person's body actually needs in order to carry on with daily activities (Fogel 1984). The human body uses up energy and thus needs calories to perform vital functions (breathing, blood circulation, digestion, maintaining body temperature) as well as to sustain everyday physical activity, including work. In some situations, energy needs rise. In the case of women, for example, pregnancy and lactation require supplementary calories; for people who are sick, greater energy needs arise during convalescence. In general, energy needs vary from one individual to the next, depending on age (children have lower energy needs than adults), gender, physical build (body weight), and lifestyle, as well as climate, the environment, and state of health. Not all of these factors have the same importance, but each one affects total energy needs, and understanding their significance is a first step in evaluating the conditions of absolute poverty in a country (Ravallion 1994).

According to the definition of international organizations—the FAO, the World Health Organization (WHO), and the United Nations (UN)—"energy requirement" consists of:

> the amount of food energy needed to balance energy expenditure in order to maintain body size, body composition and a level of necessary and desirable physical activity consistent with long-term good health. This includes the energy needed for the optimal growth and development of children, for the deposition of tissues during pregnancy, and for the secretion of milk during lactation consistent with the good health of mother and child. (FAO/WHO/UN 2004)

---

[4] This is confirmed by Istat data showing that, today, one man out of every two is overweight, while the ratio for women (and children) is 1 in 3 (www.istat.it, 2010). The United States has a greater incidence of overweight and obese adults (in 1999–2004, almost one adult aged 20–74 years out of every three was obese [Rhum 2007, 2010]), while the figure is similar for children (Ogden et al. 2010).

This is the definition of "calorie requirement" adopted in this chapter.

In Italy's case, studies on average calorie requirements are rare, and estimates of how energy requirements have changed over time are totally nonexistent (Ferro-Luzzi 2005). The calculation is a complex operation because it must take many factors into account, and these factors often act in opposite directions and with irregular intensities over time. An example can clarify this. Over the years, the demographic structure of a country changes if—as was the case with Italy during the period examined—the proportion of children out of the total population decreases and the average calorie requirement of the population rises. What changes is also workforce composition: while it is initially involved, above all, in agriculture, over time it gradually shifts toward industry, and later to services, where most of the population is employed today. These changes, along with mechanization, which reduces physical demands in individual activities, lead to a decrease in average calorie requirements. In Italy's case, we can say that demographic changes have boosted energy requirements (the birth rate has decreased over time), while changes in production methods have driven them down (agriculture has given way to services). The problem is that of estimating the net effect of these and other phenomena affecting energy requirements and of calculating how it has changed over time. In the remainder of this section we shall present the first estimates of the average calorie requirements of Italians for the entire 150-year history of postunification Italy.

To illustrate the procedure for estimating the calorie requirement of the Italian population since 1861, we shall begin by considering the demographic structure of the population. With other things being equal, the calorie requirement of a population depends on its composition in terms of gender and age. Figure 1.4 shows the so-called demographic pyramids at the end of the first year of the new Kingdom of Italy (1861, upper panel) and for the most recent year (2014, lower panel). The demographic pyramid describes the distribution of a population by age and gender: from the graph, for example, we can see that in 1861 the number of girls aged 0–4 years was a little under 7 percent (a percentage similar to boys of the same age), while in 2014 it was slightly over 2 percent (still similar to the percentage of boys in that year).

The transformation of the demographic pyramid—from a "triangle" in 1861, a typical shape seen in developing economies of any period, to a "kite" in 2014, a typical shape of mature economies (Rowland 2003)—reveals that in the 150 years since unification, population structure by age has changed radically. In 1861 the Italian population was a "young" one characterized by a high birth rate, as shown by the wide base of the triangle, which indicates the strong presence of young and very young individuals. It was also a population with

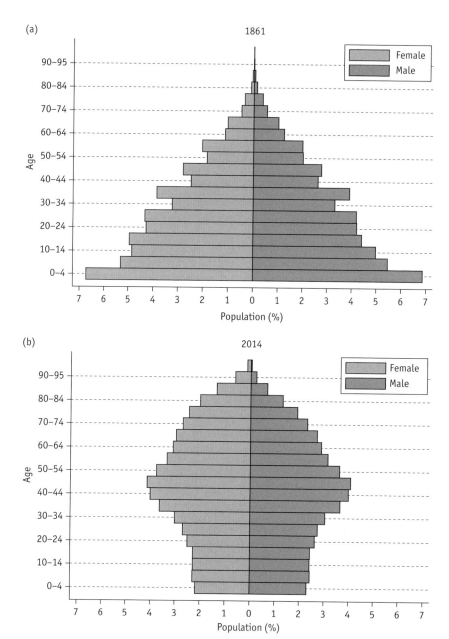

Figure 1.4 THE DEMOGRAPHIC STRUCTURE OF THE ITALIAN POPULATION, 1861 AND 2014. The demographic pyramids illustrated in the two graphs describe the distribution of the population by age and gender. The gray colour bars show the percentage of females of a certain age group out of the total population. The blue colour bars refer to the male population.

a low life expectancy at birth: the apex of the triangle suggests the presence of few elderly people. The 2014 pyramid describes a fundamentally different situation: a mature population with low birth rates (the base of the pyramid is narrow) and a high life expectancy (the top of the pyramid has become more like a rectangle).

Each age group has a different calorie requirement, with infants who need less than adults, who in turn need more than the elderly. This implies that, with other things being equal, changes that are observed over time in the demographic structure of a country bring about changes in the average calorie requirement. The method we have used allows for the demographic transition illustrated in Figure 1.4, recalculating the average calories required by the population as its demographic structure by age and gender changes over time.

Apart from demographic changes, energy requirement crucially depends on the development of a second parameter that we shall refer to as "lifestyle," which describes the everyday physical activity individuals are involved in. For example, let's consider the activity connected to the kind of work performed: the body needs greater calories per unit of time when digging a field with a spade than when working in front of a computer. Since, over the postunification years, most of the population has set aside the spade for a computer keyboard, it is reasonable to try to allow for these changes when calculating calorie requirements. The phenomenon is of a significant scale in the Italian context: in Italy in 1861, 59 percent of employed persons worked in agriculture, compared with under 4 percent in 2014.[5] Lifestyle changes also due to transformations in nonwork activities that today are significantly less physically demanding than in the past: think of the effect of electrical appliances in household chores (the washing machine and dishwasher, first and foremost, but also food processors and the like), or the means of transportation available today compared to 150 years ago.

To work these changes in with the lifestyle of the population when calculating average energy requirement, we can use appropriate coefficients that nutritionists have devised by measuring the energy consumption associated with various everyday activities. Thanks to these calculations we can see, for example, the calorie requirement of someone who is about to cut down an oak tree is about ten times greater than the one for someone who is about to play the flute. By using these coefficients (FAO/WHO/UN 2004) and the data on the population's

---

[5] Along with changes in workforce composition we must also consider the effects of changes in the length of the working day (Brandolini and Vecchi 2013) as well as the intensity of work as a result of mechanisation and technological innovations that have revolutionized production methods over the 150 years examined.

employment structure (how many loggers and how many flautists there are), as well as demographic data, we have reconstructed the average energy requirement of the Italian population, with the results illustrated in Figure 1.5.

On the basis of the estimates shown in Figure 1.5, in 1861 the average inhabitant of the new Kingdom of Italy needed just under 2,300 calories a day. With respect to Massimo Livi Bacci's intelligent conjectures, our estimate is a little higher, but not by much.[6] The energy requirement of Italians has tended to decrease over the decades: if about 2,300 calories per person were required in 1861, today a little under 2,000 are enough. The FAO estimates, obtained by means of a procedure that is independent from ours, point to an average requirement of 1,960 calories for the three-year period 2004–2006 (FAO 2009).

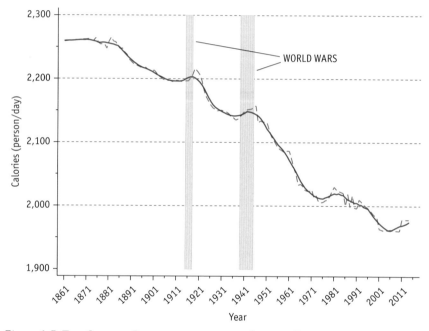

Figure 1.5 THE CALORIE REQUIREMENT OF THE ITALIAN POPULATION, 1861–2014. The graph shows that the average daily calorie requirement per person (vertical axis) has decreased over time (horizontal axis), as a consequence of changes in the population's demographic structure and lifestyle. The unbroken line is obtained by smoothing out the annual fluctuations present in the broken line. The shaded areas correspond to the two world wars.

---

[6] As Livi Bacci (1993, 55–56) noted: "Apart from inequalities in income distribution, we may conclude that a population which could have counted on a normal consumption of 2,000 calories per capita would, in the past centuries, have been a sufficiently nourished population, at least from the energy standpoint."

If we compare average energy requirement (Figure 1.5) with the average calorie availability calculated in section 2 (Figure 1.1), we end up discovering that *available* calories have always exceeded energy requirement by so much that if they had actually been *assimilated* calories, they would have produced an increase in the average Italian's body weight by an absurd amount (equal to 11 kilograms per year in 1861, for example, when the gap between calories available and those required is of about 263 calories a day, or equal to about 80 kilograms per year in 2011, when the calorie surplus is 1,699 calories per person per day). It is evident, from this, that the availability of calories, as calculated on the basis of national accounts, is a starting point for studying a population's diet and certainly not a point of arrival. The series of calorie availability is a useful analytical tool because it lends itself to corrections and integrations enabling an approximation of the series of ingested calories. Once this result is obtained, it will be possible to estimate for how many people in the Italian population the calories ingested were insufficient to meet their energy requirement, calculated for each one of the 150 years of postunification Italy.

5 Well-fed, on Average. What about Those under Average?

To estimate the percentage of undernourished people in the population, we need to deal with the problem of calculating the calories *ingested*, on average, by Italians during the period under consideration, starting from the data on the calories available. In the light of the discussion in Box 2 to shift from available calories to ingested ones we cannot but put forward a hypothesis on the scale of the waste. Specifically, we have assumed that the quantity of food wasted in Italy in more recent times lies between 15 and 30 percent—an interval that includes levels similar to those estimated for the United Kingdom and the United States today—and that the quantity wasted decreases as we go back in time, up to a threshold of between 2.5 and 5 percent (these are the values applied to the period before World War II). Reducing the series of calorie availability (Figure 1.1) by means of these percentages, we obtain an approximation of the calories ingested that we can, at this stage, compare with the energy requirement (Figure 1.5).

Since what we wish to calculate here is the percentage of the population that cannot afford a sufficient level of nutrition from a calorie standpoint, it is essential to know the calories consumed by each individual (or household) of the population. In Italy's case, we are unable to estimate this distribution: we lack data not only for the nineteenth century but also for the recent times. We know average calorie availability, but we do not know how calorie availability is distributed around the average. To get around this lack of figures, we constructed a dataset composed of over 5,000 observations of countries all over the world, on the basis of which we econometrically estimated the relation between calorie dispersion and GDP per capita. We thus obtained a model for estimating the evolution of the variability of calories available in Italy on the basis of the dynamics of GDP per capita throughout the postunification years (see chapter 7, "Income"). By virtue of these estimates, we reconstructed the calorie distribution for each one of the years under consideration, and calculated the proportion of the population that is undernourished. That is simply the count, year by year, of the number of people who have a calorie consumption lower than the calorie requirement estimated in section 4.

Figure 1.6 illustrates the aforesaid procedure. The graph calls for a certain interpretative effort because it considers three dimensions (as many as there are axes), unlike standard graphs that have only two dimensions, generally represented by a vertical axis and a horizontal axis. In Figure 1.6, two axes establish the floor of the graph: one axis measures time (from 1861 to 2011), while the other measures calories. On this floor there is a first curve showing the evolution in average per-capita ingested calories over time (broken line). The second curve on the floor of the graph shows the evolution in average calorie requirement over time (blue line). The graph also contains some bell-shaped curves that we must imagine as "jutting out" of the surface of the page and standing up along a third dimension—the one represented by the vertical axis with which we measure the number of people who consume a certain amount of calories. Each one of these curves gives a representation of how the ingested calories are distributed within the population. The curve plotted in relation to 1861, for example,

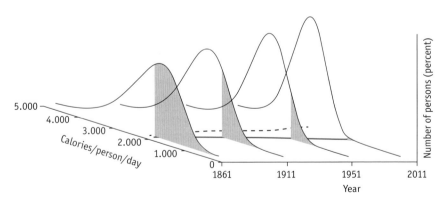

Figure 1.6 THE ESTIMATE OF UNDERNUTRITION IN ITALY. The graph shows the trend of the ingested calorie distribution (bell-shaped curves) over time. Each curve refers to a specific year and is centred around the estimate of average ingested calories for that year (broken line); the gray area shows the proportion of the population that does not meet the average calorie requirement (blue line).

represents the distribution of calories ingested by the Italian population in that particular year: the shape of the distribution shows that relatively few people had extreme consumptions (the curve is low at both ends), while most of the population has consumptions distributed around the mean value. The gray area under the 1861 distribution measures the percentage of the population with food consumptions lower than the average calorie requirement of 1861, that is, in technical terms, the incidence of undernutrition (Svedberg 2000). The other distributions in the graph are interpreted in a similar way: the 1911 curve, for example, shows a lower gray area than the 1861 one, which means that the percentage of undernourished people decreased between 1861 and 1911.[7]

In Figure 1.7 we focus on the fraction of undernourished population and build up the gray areas of Figure 1.6 in sequence: the result shows the development of the incidence of undernutrition in the course of Italy's postunification history.

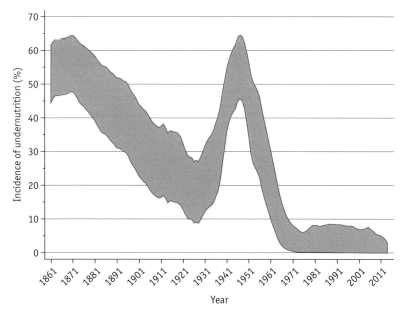

Figure 1.7 UNDERNUTRITION IN ITALY, 1861–2014. The graph shows how the percentage of undernourished people in the population (vertical axis) varies over time (horizontal axis). For each year, the percentage of undernourished people falls within the blue band: it is not possible to establish whether this value lies at the center or near one of the margins of the band, thereby preventing an analysis of short term changes of the phenomenon. The evolution over the 150 years is well shown by the curve.

[7] Two factors came into play here: the average available calories *increased* ("growth effect") while the dispersion of calories around the mean *decreased* ("distribution effect") (Datt and Ravallion 1992).

Box 3 **The Poorest of the Poor: The Food Budgets of the Common Folk of Naples**

The macroeconomic sources used in estimating the extent of undernutrition in Figure 1.7 do not allow us to grasp the variability of diets at the household and individual levels. We can get around this limitation if we have sample surveys on household consumption: in Italy's case, though, the first surveys date back to the late 1960s and so do not enable us to analyze the long period of time we are interested in. An alternative source consists of household budgets containing detailed information on household food expenditure, dealt with fully in chapter 14. There is a third source, which we shall refer to as *food budgets*, that analyzes the diet of households (single ones, but more often of groups of households) and individuals. Using food budgets for historical-economic analysis is nothing new. There are estimates of the population's calorie availability based on collections of household food budgets for France, the United Kingdom, and the United States (Fogel 1990; Oddy 1990). For what concerns Italy, the first useful studies in this regard date back to the latter half of the nineteenth century and were carried out by nutritionists, hygienists, physiologists, and physicians in general. Of the ones available to us, we chose the one conducted in Naples by the physiologist Luigi Manfredi (1861–1952), who considered eight individuals "chosen from the most numerous class of the *popolo minuto*—the common folk: small-scale workers performing a rather light and not always steady job (cobbler, carpenter, mason); or people without a steady job and often without any job altogether, almost stray beings, who spend their whole day in the streets living from hand to mouth and taking their chances (*lazzarone*, pedlar, beggar etc.)" (Manfredi 1893, 50). It is a small sample that not only focuses on the less privileged section of the population but also includes individuals in conditions of extreme poverty, those who normally escape sample surveys because they have no fixed abode—the poorest of the poor.

Table 1.B1 shows some analyses carried out on Manfredi's data. We have the age, height, body weight, and lifestyle of each individual. The second and third parameters enable us to work out the body mass index (BMI), a biometric indicator that tells us the adequacy of a person's body weight with respect to his/her height. It is easy to calculate a person's BMI by dividing mass (measured in kilograms) by height (expressed in meters) squared: for example, 82 kilograms divided by 1.7 x 1.7 meters gives 28.37. Today, BMI values ranging between 18.5 and 24.5 are considered within the norm; values lower than 18.5 indicate thinness (which becomes serious for values lower than 16); and values between 24.5 and 30 indicate a person is overweight (while values above 30 indicate obesity).

Judging from the BMI, *none* of the individuals analyzed by Manfredi can be classified as "undernourished". This is surprising since we are looking at the poorest segment of the population. However, this is in line with Manfredi's opinion, who noted that, once we allow for individual diversity, "from a quantitative point of view, (the diet) of the common folk of Naples [. . .] well suits the body's physiological needs" (Manfredi 1893). Therefore, although the sample examined is not representative of the Neapolitan people or even of Italy's population as a whole, the food budgets analyzed suggest a less gloomy picture than the one we may have expected. When calorie intake (column 7 in the table) is compared with each individual's actual requirement, only half of the individuals concerned show a significant calorie deficiency, even if it is, presumably, a temporary condition since the BMI does not in any way indicate persistent problems of nutrition such as those that lead to excessive slimness.

Table 1.B1 The diet of the poorest of the poor (Naples, ca. 1890)

Name	Occupation	Age (years)	Height (m)	Weight (kg)	Body mass index	Calories intake (cal/day)	Calories requirement (cal/day)	Energetic balance (%)
Felice C.	Cobbler	34	1.66	55.0	20.0	1997	1929	+4
Nicola M.	Errand boy	18	1.55	47.5	19.8	2423	2463	−2
Carmela M.	Beggar	70	1.36	38.1	20.6	1794	1607	+12
Vincenzo A.	Carpenter	40	1.62	62.3	23.7	2855	2119	+35
Maria n.	Servant	40	1.40	48.3	24.6	1848	2023	−9
n. n.	Mason	29	1.65	55.2	20.3	2156	3047	−29
Luigi S.	Lazzarone	25	1.62	50.2	19.1	1982	2244	−12
Antonietta G.	Pedlar	30	1.46	52.9	24.8	1727	2232	−23

Owing to the—sometimes discretional—decisions underlying the estimation method, we are unable to provide a traditional time series that can summarize the incidence of undernutrition in a single number for each year. What we can estimate, for each year, is a "plausibility interval," that is to say, a band of values within which the "real" one is plausibly found: the percentage of undernourished people in a certain year. Figures 1.6 and 1.7 are thus connected to one another with a dual bond: for each one of the 150 years considered, the proportion of undernourished people represented in Figure 1.6 by the gray area has margins of uncertainty measured by the breadth of the blue bands of Figure 1.7.

The scope of the results summarized in Figure 1.7 is considerable: for the first time, they provide a quantitative assessment of the evolution of the Italian diet over many decades and, more specifically, of the adequacy of the ingested calories. We can identify five stages of this development: let's go through them.

Firstly, it is without doubt that, at the time of unification, there was widespread dietary hardship. The estimates show that in the decade following the birth of the Kingdom of Italy, one person in two (but, perhaps, even two in three) did not ingest enough calories to lead a healthy life. Let's recall this again: the threshold used in estimating undernutrition is *not* a threshold below which there is starvation, but rather a threshold below which the body does not have sufficient energy in order to work and carry on daily activities, the ones connected to the context in which the individual lives, without running the risk of energy deficiency and thus, in the long run, suffering negative consequences for one's health. If at least half the inhabitants of the Kingdom did not have sufficient calories, it is possible to conclude that hunger was commonplace in the country and that a non-negligible section of the population—not less than 10 percent, and perhaps even 30 percent—was chronically and severely undernourished (these values are obtained if we establish the threshold of undernutrition as 2,000 calories per person per day). The result is in line with the estimates by Vecchi and Coppola (2003), according to which, in 1881, over a third of Italian households were undernourished.

Throughout the Liberal period and right up to the early 1920s, the diet of Italians improved significantly and steadily. In these decades, the proportion of undernourished people dropped continuously. The estimates suggest that in 1922 one Italian out of every five could have been in this condition. Dietary hardships were thus still significant in absolute terms, but the improvement with respect to the previous decades was a clear and quantitatively significant one.

In a third stage, the combination of autarchic economic and foreign exchange policies implemented by the Fascist regime, along with the Great Depression and the outbreak of World War II, set Italy back by almost a century with regard to food consumption. According to our estimates, the two-year period 1926–27 was a turning point that saw undernutrition incidence rates soar: in 1938, once again, about one Italian in three was undernourished. At the end of World War II, percentages of undernutrition were around 50 to 60 percent. The magnitude of this estimate is consistent with the descriptions of a great many studies and surveys. As Pierluigi Ciocca (2007, 227) put it: "Italy was on its knees; one Italian in four was jobless, millions in poverty, not few, especially in urban areas, were starving. The country had to accept, indeed beg for, food and sanitary aid from the victors."[8]

In the decades following World War II, undernutrition at last began to decrease and at a rapid rate. The new economic policy, focusing on a clear opening-up to international relations, along with an increase in per-capita income, contributed to the availability of calories the population needed in order to live, work, and enjoy the spreading progress. Productivity per hectare increased for many crops, as did the capacity to import foodstuffs from countries that had comparative advantages in production techniques. Within two decades, approximately from 1950 to 1970, hunger in Italy gave way to abundance.

What about today? The data show that undernutrition is *not* extinct. This finding is not new to experts in the field, but may be surprising to the reader. The survey *Income and Living Conditions*, carried out annually by Istat, collects information on households' "economic hardship." For 2010, 5.5 percent of Italian households declared they had difficulties in affording their food expenditures (Istat 2011, 5). This finding is not perfectly comparable with our estimates, but the substance of the message is certainly in line with our conclusion: undernutrition is still alive in Italy.[9]

6 Carbohydrates, Proteins, and Fats

Calories are important in evaluating the adequacy of a diet, but not enough to measure its consequences for an individual's wellbeing. A person may have an adequate number of calories per day, but inadequate nutrients. Although malnutrition is often a consequence of undernutrition, the two concepts are rather different; their relation is not automatic, and that is why we shall deal with both here. *Malnutrition* is a situation of any diet imbalanced in terms of the availability of macronutrients (carbohydrates, fats, and proteins) and/or

---

[8] We can mention another finding, taken from an enquiry into poverty in Italy (*Inchiesta sulla miseria in Italia e sui mezzi per combatterla*), conducted in 1951–52. According to the enquiry report, a percentage of Italian households ranging between 44 and 62 percent had an unsatisfactory "food standard" (measured on the basis of meat, sugar, and wine consumption), an estimate that is exceptionally in agreement with that in Figure 7. See also Heltosky (2004).

[9] Campiglio and Rovati (2009) found that undernutrition concerned about 5 percent of Italian households, a finding in line with the estimates in Figure 7.

micronutrients (minerals and vitamins). In this section we shall focus on the availability of macronutrients and not deal with micronutrients: measurement of the latter's availability is too sensitive to the way food is preserved and prepared—aspects on which information is lacking—to attempt any long-term quantitative evaluation.

Figure 1.8 shows the composition of the Italians' diet according to the number of average grams available per person, per day, and per category of macronutrients. To begin with, we consider the data for carbohydrates. Carbohydrates (sugars and starches that are particularly abundant in cereals—bread, pasta, and rice—but also in many tubers, like potatoes) not only provide energy to all the body's cells but also have a plastic function, that is to say, they contribute to building essential structures of the body and have a regulatory function for embryonic development, for infection and immune processes, as well as for the hormonal system. Figure 1.8 shows that the quantity of carbohydrates available to the Italian population has remained remarkably stable throughout Italy's postunification years. In 2011 we see the same per-capita availability as in 1861 (about 445 grams). However, while in 1861 the calories deriving from carbohydrates accounted for 70 percent of the total generated by available macronutrients, the increase in the availability of other macronutrients today has reduced this proportion to just under 50 percent. If we consider that, for a balanced diet, the contribution of carbohydrates must be maintained between 45 and 65 percent

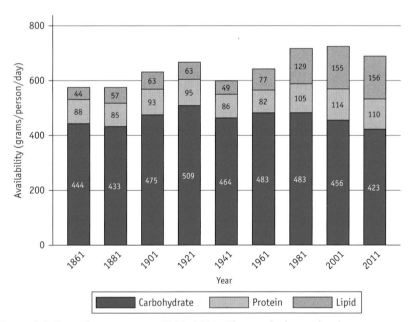

Figure 1.8 DIET COMPOSITION, 1861–2011. The graph shows the change in availability of the main macronutrients (how many grams per person per day, vertical axis) over time (horizontal axis).

of total calorie intake (Institute of Medicine of the National Academies 2005), we may conclude that, with regard to this macronutrient, the diet of the average Italian has always been quite well-balanced.

Proteins are the second category of macronutrients in Figure 1.8. Proteins are necessary for building the organs and tissues of the body: they are thus particularly important at the individual's developmental stage, but also later so that cells can regenerate; they are also essential for immune and hormonal system functioning, and can be used as a source of energy in the case of carbohydrate deficiency. Thus a diet that is lacking in proteins (mainly found in meat, fish, eggs, milk and dairy products, and pulses) has negative consequences for adults and particularly serious ones for children. Throughout the century and a half considered, the average availability of proteins has always been higher than the amount considered sufficient by nutritionists. The most recent studies by the FAO suggest that the average daily protein requirement is 0.66 grams/kg/day: this means that an adult weighing 65 kilograms (kg) needs 42.9 grams (g) of proteins per day (a chicken breast of 100 grams, for example, contains 22.2 grams of protein). On the basis of these standards, as far back as 1861 the average availability of proteins was more than double the amount today deemed necessary for a proper diet. The WHO recommendation is that proteins should account for 8 to 12 percent of total calorie intake: in Italian history, the average availability has always been within this range or even higher. Figure 1.8 does not show how protein sources have varied over time. What nutritionists call "complete proteins" or "whole proteins," that is to say, the ones containing all the varieties of amino acids that the body has to obtain from food because it is not able to produce them by itself, all come from animal sources. They accounted for 15 percent of total proteins in 1861, but reached 55 percent in 2011. This is an important finding that shows the improvement in *quality* of the Italian population's diet—something that is not easy to grasp through other statistics.

We now have to examine lipids, that is, fats. Contrary to what many people believe, fats are fundamental for the body: they are an energy reserve and thus a defense against periods of food deficiency—fundamental for babies and children, but also for pregnant women and for the sick. Fats also have a plastic function since they are components of the cell structure and help the body to absorb certain vitamins—particularly vitamins A, D, E, and K, as well as other nutrients contained in food. Finally, some kinds of fats cannot be produced by our body and thus must be obtained through our food. Figure 1.8 shows that the availability of fats was three-and-a-half times higher in 2011 than in 1861. In percentage terms, the proportion of the total calories generated by the available macronutrients deriving from fats rose from 16 percent in 1861 to 39 percent in 2011. For most of the considered period, the proportion of fats in the average diet has been in line with the recommendations made by nutritionists, who suggest that fats should account for 15 to 35 percent of total calories. In the last few decades, however, the average availability of fats has been excessive and shows the widespread phenomenon of diets too rich in this macronutrient.

7 The Defeat of Hunger

In the aftermath of unification, hunger was the norm for most Italians. Those who denounced the existence of a "dietary issue" were right. Our assessments indicate that in 1861, and in all likelihood during the following decade, at least one Italian in two (but perhaps even two out of every three) did not have a proper diet. Although we cannot precisely measure the statistic precision associated to the estimates of the percentage of undernourished people in the population, it has been possible to trace the evolution of undernutrition over the years since Italy's unification. From this reconstruction we have learned that those who stressed progress in the population's diet were right: undernutrition decreased steadily without interruption from 1861 to the mid-1920s.

It is not easy to establish the causal connections between the phenomena we have described. Did a better diet enable economic growth, or did the increase in per-capita income enable an improvement in the way Italians ate? What we can observe is that we do not *always* find an association between increased per-capita income and a decrease in undernutrition and malnutrition. We see many developing countries today that, although boasting an increase in per-capita income, have still not managed to eradicate undernutrition and malnutrition (see, e.g., Behrman and Deolalikar [1987], on India; and Alderman and Garcia [1994], on Pakistan).

In the mid-1920s, Italy's virtuous progress not only stopped, but began to show a trend reversal. The autarchic policies and revaluation of the Italian lira implemented by the Fascist regime are clearly correlated to a reduction in the average calories available to Italians, which meant an increase in the share of people inadequately nourished. With the Great Depression and World War II, available calories decreased dramatically; the country's population suffered a setback, returning to a nineteenth-century diet. After the war, the new Italian Republic had to start all over again. In 1947, one citizen out of every two, but perhaps two out of every three, did not meet his/her daily food energy requirement.

Between 1950 and 1970, the decades in which the Italians experienced the so-called economic miracle, there was a great decrease in the number of undernourished people in the population. However, the latest figures show that the process of deliverance from undernutrition has not been accomplished: in the last thirty years a notable percentage of the Italian population has not had an adequate diet. A huge problem for the few, but a small one for the many.

Appendix—Sources and Methods

Figure 1.1 Calorie availability (person/day), 1861–2014 Sources are as follows. For the period 1861–1911: Federico (2003) and Barberi (1961); for 1912–1960: Istat (1958; 1968; 1976; 1986); for 1961–2011: Faostat (2012), the version available in February 2015; for 2012–2014: estimates obtained by linear extrapolation.

Figure 1.2 Who eats more than the Italians? Calorie distribution in the world, 1930s–2000s Our analyses used FAO data (1946; 1952; 1963; 2012). The EU15 group consists of: Austria, Belgium, Denmark, Finland, France, Germany, Greece, Ireland, Italy, Luxembourg, the Netherlands, Portugal, Spain, Sweden, and the United Kingdom. The OECD countries are the following 34: Australia, Austria, Belgium, Canada, Chile, the Czech Republic, Denmark, Estonia, Finland, France, Germany, Greece, Hungary, Iceland, Ireland, Israel, Italy, Japan, Luxembourg, Mexico, the Netherlands, New Zealand, Norway, Poland, Portugal, Slovakia, Slovenia, South Korea, Spain, Sweden, Switzerland, Turkey, the United Kingdom, and the United States.

Figure 1.3 The relationship between available calories and per-capita GDP in around 60 countries of the world For the period 1861–1960 the available calories were taken from the following sources. Belgium: Bekaert (1991); France: Toutain (1971); Germany: Hoffmann (1965), Lemnitzer (1977); Japan: Kaneda (1968), Shay (1994); the Netherlands: Horlings and Smits (1998); Spain: Simpson (1989); Sweden: Jureen (1956); the United Kingdom: Oddy (1976), Fogel (1997); the United States: Bennet and Peirce (1961), Komlos (1987); Union of Soviet Socialist Republics (USSR): Wheatcroft (1999). For all countries, the data since 1961 have been taken from the FAO database (2012). Data on per-capita GDP are from Maddison (2010). The curve in the graph has been plotted non-parametrically by means of the procedure described in Cleveland (1979), with bandwidth set to 5.

Figure 1.B2 Engel's law in Italy and in the United States Italy: the proportion of expenditure on food was calculated on the basis of the series at current prices in Istat (1958; 1968; 1986; 2012), and includes beverages and tobacco. The United States: for the years 1901–1967: U.S. Department of Labor and U.S. Bureau of Labor Statistics (2006); for 2000–2013: our calculations from the U.S. Consumer Expenditure Survey (2014); for 2014: estimates obtained by linear extrapolation.

Figure 1.4 The demographic structure of the Italian population, 1861 and 2014 Calculations based on Istat data.

Figure 1.5 The calorie requirement of the Italian population, 1861–2014 To work out the average Italian's calorie requirement for each year, we calculated the average calorie requirement of a twenty-year-old man by means of the Schofield equation, used by FAO (2008): $ER = PAL \times (692.2 + 15.057 \times kg)$, where ER is the energy requirement, PAL the physical activity level, and kg the weight in kilograms. It has been assumed that the average PAL varies as a function of the distribution of employed persons among economic sectors of activity and of the degree of mechanization (from a maximum of 2.06 in 1861 to 1.65 for recent years). Body weight was calculated as the desirable weight for a twenty-year-old man on the basis of data available on the average heights of men of this age (chapter 2, "Height") and of a Body Mass Index (BMI) of 20 (Bekaert 1991). The relationships between the requirement of a twenty-year-old man and those of men of other age groups, and between those of a man and woman of the same age, were calculated on the basis of the recommended levels of energy and nutrient intake for the Italian population, established by the Italian Society of Human Nutrition (1986–87). These coefficients, applied to the energy requirement calculated as described above for a twenty-year-old man, along with the composition of the Italian population as regards age and gender, enable calculation of the calorie requirement of the average Italian for each of the considered years. To allow for pregnancy or lactation for women, an additional 210 kilocalories (kcal) per day, multiplied by the birth rate, were added to the population's average energy requirement. This meant adding to the average requirement a number of per-capita daily calories varying from about 8 for the first thirty years of postunification Italy to about 2 for the last twenty years. To allow for child labor, estimates of the number of working children were considered (chapter 4, "Child Labor") as well as an additional energy requirement of 360 kcal per day for every working boy and 330 kcal per day for every working girl. These values correspond to the extra consumption of a child aged 10–14 years who shifts from an average to a high level of activity. The increase in the average energy requirement of the Italian population, taking into account child labor, was thus estimated as 29 kcal per day per person in 1861, and it gradually decreased to zero in the 1980s. For 2012–2014 estimates are obtained by linear extrapolation.

Figure 1.6 The distribution of calories in Italy To work out the percentage of undernourished people for each year, we compared the distribution of calories ingested by Italians in that year with the average calorie requirement for the same period. For the latter, we used the estimates presented in section 4 whose calculations are described for Figure 1.5. To estimate the distribution of calories ingested by Italians in any given year, we had to *(a)* estimate the average ingested calories, *(b)* estimate the standard deviation of the ingested calories, and *(c)* assume a specific functional form for the distribution. The mean value of ingested calories is obtained by correcting the estimates of available calories (see the note to Figure 1.1) to allow for wastage, assuming that it has grown throughout the considered period and that in Italy today its level is similar to that estimated for other countries with comparable consumption levels (Bleich et al. 2007). The standard deviation of per-capita ingested calories in Italy for the period 1861–2001 was calculated after estimating, through ordinary least squares (OLS), a regression between the standard deviation of per-capita available calories (dependent variable) and average per-capita GDP (independent variable) on a sample of over 5,000 observations on countries all over the world (in the period 1961–2001, the former variable is available in the Food Balance Sheets, FAO (2012), while the latter one in Maddison (2010), as purchasing power parity adjusted to per-capita GDP, expressed in 1990 USD). Thus the standard deviation of per-capita ingested calories in Italy over the considered 150 years was estimated by means of the just described regression parameters and the actual per-capita GDP values for Italy given by Maddison. With regard to calorie distribution, three different functional forms were experimented with: the log-normal distribution, the beta distribution, and the type 2 generalized beta distribution (Jenkins 2009). Of these, we chose the beta distribution on the basis of the argument put forward by Bekaert (1991). The sensitivity analysis of the described procedure is represented by the bandwidth in Figure 1.7.

Figure 1.7 Undernutrition in Italy, 1861–2014 The sources are the same ones used for Figure 1.6, with figures for 2012–2014 obtained through linear extrapolation. The bandwidth captures the uncertainty associated with the point estimates of undernutrition, due not only to the sampling errors but also to the many assumptions necessary to reconstruct the information needed to carry out the exercise (how many of the available calories are lost in food wastage, which parametric form to use for density function, and so on). The percentage of undernourished people for each year lies plausibly within the bandwidth shown in the figure. It is worth noting that the band estimated for each year does not coincide with the confidence interval of the estimates, and therefore the "real" value of the percentage of undernourished people does not necessarily lie at the center of the plausibility interval.

Figure 1.8 Diet composition, 1861–2011 The data for the period prior to World War I were reconstructed starting from the series of the quantities of available foodstuffs. We wish to thank Giovanni Federico for providing these series. For the subsequent periods we used information on the composition of available foodstuffs published in the Sommari by Istat (1911–1960) and in the FAO Food Balance Sheets (since 1961).

2

Height

WITH BRIAN A'HEARN

1 Wellbeing and Centimeters

As we all know, medical doctors are the ones who deal with people's health. As early as the first weeks after conception, even before the individual is morphologically complete, the doctor starts a process of checkups and measurements that begin during pregnancy and then continue throughout a person's life. The thing most parents remember at the end of their first prenatal appointment with their doctor is a small number, typically expressed in millimeters, which represents the "height" of their little creature, assessed through an ultrasound scan. Once born, the baby's state of health is assessed by means of less sophisticated diagnostic tools: in effect, a yardstick and some weighing scales. As long as the baby grows up in line with standards established in growth charts, then parents can be reassured by the pediatrician that their child is in a good state of health.

For babies, children, and young teenagers, considering height as a good indicator of *physical wellbeing* is an established fact. Less well known, perhaps, is the fact that a child's height may be a useful indicator of their *economic wellbeing*. A child that grows up in a difficult context—such as with a diet poor in calories or lacking certain nutrients (proteins, vitamins, and minerals), or in a risky epidemiological environment—will show clear signs of these stresses with regard to appearance (lower height than his or her peers, thinness), a high propensity to illness, and problems in cognitive development.

An eloquent "natural experiment" was conducted by the anthropologist Barry Bogin. Bogin compared the average height of a group of Maya children born to poor families in the village of San Pedro, Guatemala, with a second group of Maya children in Los Angeles, California, born to refugee families who had fled the civil war in their native Guatemala. While the children of the first group grew up in rural areas of Guatemala, where poverty is endemic, food scarce, water contaminated, and health care practically nonexistent, those of the second group grew up in California, where they experienced conditions of poverty compared to the living standards of their American peers but without the serious hardships of the first group. Bogin found that the conditions of relative affluence enjoyed by the Californian Guatemalan children meant that they were as much as 11.5 centimeters taller, on average, than their native Guatemalan counterparts. The quality of the environment that children grow up in makes for huge differences with regard to their height.[1]

The relationship between children's height and their socioeconomic conditions was established further back in time than is normally supposed. In *A History of the Study of Human Growth*, James Tanner (1981) offered a fascinating reconstruction of the progress of auxology, the science that studies all aspects of human physical growth. Tanner recalled the work of physiologist Luigi Pagliani, a little-known figure of pride for Italy, who had been ahead of his times with a series of anthropometric studies published in the latter half of the nineteenth century. It is worth mentioning one of them, a study carried out in the summer of 1872 on around eight hundred boys and girls from Turin. The study aimed to "mathematically evaluate the energy of the influence of the hygienic conditions of the environment in which man lives on his growth activity" (Pagliani 1878, 230). Pagliani distinguished the children depending on their family's standard of living, dividing them up between the "affluent class" and the "poor class," and recording their weight and height. By comparing the average heights of the two groups at various ages, he obtained the results that we have summarized in Figure 2.1. The graph shows how the affluent children were systematically taller than the poor children. The bonus in terms of height deriving from good economic conditions was considerable: at the age of sixteen, an "affluent" boy measured an average 163.8 centimeters (cm) compared to the 151.2 cm of a "poor" boy. This height difference, 12.6 cm, showed the existence of a significant biological gap.[2]

Surprisingly, height differences reflecting social classes still exist today, albeit to a much lesser extent. They are found not only in developing countries but also in mature and affluent economies. A study carried out by Gabriel Lasker and Nicholas Mascie-Taylor (1989) in the United Kingdom, for example, shows that a father's occupation has a clear effect on his children's height. In the mid-1970s the sixteen-year-old sons of freelance professionals were almost 5 cm taller, on average, than the sons of unskilled workers (the difference was 4.1 cm for daughters). This finding has a general validity: the higher the social class of the parents, the greater the average height of their offspring.

---

[1] The Mayan children were between 5 and 12 years of age. See Bogin (1999) and Bogin et al. (2002).

[2] The data on the girls are less complete, but they show comparable differences between the two groups of children. At the age of 15, the affluent girls were an average 9.3 cm taller than their poorer peers.

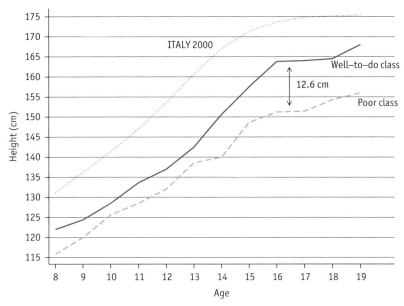

Figure 2.1 CHILDREN'S HEIGHT AS A MEASURE OF SOCIAL DIFFERENCES, TURIN CA. 1875. The graph shows that average height (vertical axis) varies with age (horizontal axis) for two groups of children in the latter half of the nineteenth century: the affluent (blue unbroken line) and the poor (blue broken line). The curve labeled as "Italy 2000" shows the average height of Italian children in the year 2000.

1.1 FROM CHILD TO ADULT, THROUGH THE ENVIRONMENT

If children's height yields useful information on their level of financial wellbeing, it is reasonable to ask whether this also holds for adults' height. In other words, is it possible to analyze the height of adults and draw conclusions on their financial wellbeing? Many readers would probably shake their head: the final height reached in adulthood is influenced by many factors and not just financial ones—first and foremost is the genetic factor, which is hereditary. Tall parents, tall children; short parents, short children: these are the equations that most people have in mind. Yet, the height people reach in adulthood is a formidable tool for assessing a population's economic conditions. How is this possible?

The answer lies in the fact that height "has a long memory" and, in particular, does not "forget" what occurred during childhood. If the individual did not have serious problems during development (such as nutritional deprivation or protracted illnesses), then the height reached in adulthood reflects the *potential height*, the one programmed in the individual's DNA. On the other hand, if the environmental conditions inflicted severe deprivations on the individual, the recovery mechanisms of the human body may not be enough to enable the individual to reach his or her potential (or maximum) height envisaged by his or her hereditary genetic code.

While it is true that genetics or, if we prefer, hereditary factors play a key role in determining an individual's height, it is also true that the environment the individual grows up in interacts with his or her genetic makeup. The conclusion is a general one and is worth stressing with the words of John Thoday, a world-famous British geneticist: "[K]nowledge of the genetic endowment is of little use without knowledge of the environmental circumstances also. Every character is both genetic and environmental in origin. Let us be quite clear about this. Genotype determines the potentialities of an organism. Environment determines which or how much of those potentialities shall be realized during development" (Thoday 1965, 94).

Once it was established that the environment, and thus economic conditions, influence height, it is self-evident that economists and economic historians started to take interest in issues linked to individuals' height, adults included.

1.2 HEIGHT AND ECONOMIC HISTORY

The interest of biologists and anthropologists in people's heights and in the impact that socioeconomic factors have on them dates back to the early nineteenth century. In the social sciences, economic historians were perhaps the first, in the 1970s, to grasp the potential of anthropometric data.[3] The fact that an individual's eventual height is sensitive to conditions of life during pregnancy and in the postnatal phase, say in the first three to five years of life, has pointed to the need to have anthropometric data surveyed during military service medicals in order to reconstruct the economic conditions prevailing in the years when soldiers themselves were children. For many countries, including Italy, military recruitment was based on compulsory conscription, which made a great deal of data available on heights of the whole male population aged 18 to 20 years.

The literature produced on the basis of this insight is huge, as demonstrated by the reviews made by Richard Steckel (1995; 2009), along with efforts made by many countries to reconstruct the secular trend in the population's average height. With the first edition of the *Sommario di Statistiche Storiche* ("Summary of Historical Statistics"), published by Istat in 1958, Italy could boast the completion of the historical series of the mean height of national service military recruits starting from those born in 1861. This result shows the old traditions of excellence, as we shall see further on.

Starting from these premises, this chapter has four aims. The first is to run through the 150 years of Italy's postunification history, documenting the

---

[3] See Le Roy Ladurie, Bernageau, and Pasquet (1969) and Fogel, Engerman, and Trussel (1982).

Box 1 It's (Not All) in Our DNA

Figure 2B.1 A MOTHER (MARIO INGROSSO, 1965)
Epigenetics suggests that parents' lifestyle can affect the health of their children (and grandchildren). Even if the actual DNA remains unchanged, the environment a person lives in can trigger or deactivate certain genes, with effects that are transmitted to successive generations.

It is common currency that our physical traits, and even aspects of our character, are determined by genetic inheritance—programmed by our DNA. But DNA is better understood as common hardware that is operated by different software in different contexts. All cell types—liver cells, muscle cells, nerve cells, etc.—contain the double-helix of 20,000 or so genes that make up our DNA. But not all genes are activated or fully expressed in every cell. Particular genes can be turned on or off when chemicals bind to the relevant location on the DNA helix in a process called methylation. The intensity of gene expression, too, can be regulated by chemical modification of the proteins (called histones) around which the double helix is coiled. The study of these mechanisms is known as epigenetics.

While an individual's DNA is fixed from the point of conception, epigenetic change is possible throughout a lifetime. Epigenetic reprogramming can be the source of abnormal cell behaviors that manifest as disease later in life—type 2 diabetes, for example, or some cancers. It was long believed that only DNA was heritable, while traits acquired during a lifetime were not. Experimental results have more recently demonstrated that epigenetic traits, too, are transmissible.

Among human populations, historical studies have uncovered similar links across generations. One influential study links mortality risk among individuals born in the early twentieth century to nutritional conditions prevailing during the adolescence of their mid-nineteenth-century grandparents in the isolated rural parish of Överkalix, in northern Sweden (Kaati, Bygren et al. 2007).

Epigenetics offers the hope of effective disease therapies based on identifying and stripping away the relevant epigenetic markers. At the same time, it delivers the chastening message that our behavior—overeating or smoking, for example—can have adverse effects not only on our own health, but on that of our as yet unborn children. Of particular relevance to the history of Italian heights, epigenetic analysis suggests that today's health outcomes, including mean stature, may reflect historic living conditions of previous generations as much as the current environment.

development of the average height of the Italians at both the national level and with regard to smaller territorial units such as regions and provinces. The second aim consists of dealing with a little-explored theme in the literature that is of great interest: What impact did the country's political and administrative unification have on the conditions of life in the population? Was it worth unifying the country in terms of the population's wellbeing? The third aim is to compare Italy's historical experience within the broader international context: How does our view of the height of the Italians change when we proceed to an international comparison? Finally, we shall try to move into the most difficult of terrains, the search for the "why": What factors underlie the growth in the height of Italians over the centuries?

2 Height and Economic Wellbeing: User Instructions

Before taking advantage of the unusual abundance of anthropometric data available for Italy, it is worth looking more closely at some conceptual questions relating to the extent to which height can be used as a sort of per-capita income indicator. Is the link between height and living conditions sufficiently close to enable us to use height to study the development of living conditions over time and their territorial differences?

This is no easy question. The difficulty stems not only from the complexity of the subject (at the intersection between social and natural sciences) but also because scientists cannot—for practical and ethical reasons—perform experiments on human beings. That is why we are devoting this section to the analysis of some fundamental teachings emerging from such a vast, deep scientific literature: the summary that we will provide is a sort of "quick user's guide" for the benefit of the reader who, even if interested in using height as an economic indicator, may not have specific knowledge of anthropometric matters and the like.

2.1 ALFRED AND HARRY

According to the *Guinness World Records*, the tallest man in history was the American Robert Pershing Wadlow (1918–1940), at 272 cm; among the living, the record goes to the Turkish basketball player Sultan Kösen, born in 1982, at 251 cm tall. Among the women, Zeng Jinlian (1964–1982) held the world record height of 248 cm. At the other end of the scale there are adults who do not reach one meter in height. At the present time, the shortest person in the world is only 54.6 cm tall. In between these two extremes lies the rest of the human species, with an average height estimated at around 175 cm for men and 163 cm for women. In general, the variability of height within a population, even if ethnically a cohesive one, is considerable and reflects how Mother Nature distributes genotypes.

At the individual level, the genetic makeup inherited from parents is the key factor explaining height.[4] With regard to this factor, it must be stressed that a person's height is not a hereditary trait. What is hereditary is potential height, that is, the maximum height an individual can reach. Whether or not an individual reaches this potential height depends on environmental conditions, especially those prevailing during childhood. The story of Alfred and Harry, British twins who came into the limelight in the 1950s, will allow us to clarify the point. Our story starts in 1953, when the British TV network BBC aired the program *Twin Sister, Twin Brother*, within which an appeal went out to the nation inviting viewers who had an identical twin to step forward "in the interests of science."[5]

---

[4] According to Karri Silventoinen (2003), in contemporary societies about 80 percent of individual height differences is due to genetic differences.

[5] As we know, the term "twins" refers to individuals born in the same delivery. Twins are called *monozygotic* (or, more commonly, *identical*) when they are born from the same cell fertilized by a single spermatozoon. In some rare cases, and for reasons still not completely clear, the cell may split into two during the early stages of development. The individuals born from this separation are called *dizygotic* or *fraternal* twins since they have the same genetic makeup. Being the sole case of genetic identity in humankind, researchers use monozygotic twins in order to study how the environment affects human development. The case of dizygotic twins is different. These are individuals who, although born during the same delivery, are the fruit of the fertilization of two different eggs by two different spermatozoa, and the twins thus do not completely share their genetic makeup.

Over 2,500 couples of twins answered the call, 44 of whom were homozygote twins separated during their first year of life and raised in separate homes by different people for the rest of their lives. The opportunity offered by the TV program was grasped by James Shields, who was working at the psychiatric institute of a London hospital at the time: the chance to observe a group of individuals with the same genetic makeup, but who had been separated at birth, was an extraordinary opportunity to measure the influence of the environment on the human body without spoiling a comparative analysis according to the genetic factor—homozygote twins have the same genes and thus genetics cannot be responsible for any differences found between the twins (body weight and height).

From the study by Shields (1962), we shall deal with the case of Alfred and Harry, homozygote twins separated from each other three weeks after birth. Harry stayed inside his own family, growing up surrounded by care and affection. Alfred, on the other hand, had a worse fate since he was entrusted to a psychotic and cruel maternal aunt, who used to keep the child under lock and key, in the dark, for long periods, without even giving him the chance to get a glass of water. Figure 2.2 shows Alfred (left) and Harry (right) as adults. Their anthropometric differences are evident; and their height difference in particular, 8.3 cm, is great. The natural experiment of the twins shows just how large and dramatic the effects of environmental deprivation in childhood can be on

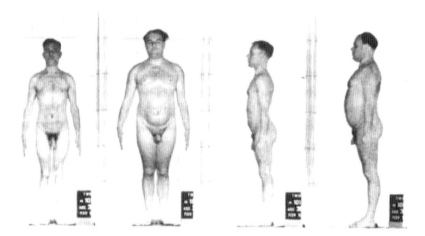

Figure 2.2 ALFRED AND HARRY, MONOZYGOTIC TWINS SEPARATED AT BIRTH. The figure shows the different height reached in adulthood by two monozygotic twins separated at birth. The one in the first photograph on the left grew up in difficult conditions and is 8.3 cm shorter than the second, who grew up in a normal family. Adult height is thus significantly affected by childhood deprivations.

an adult body: the genetic potential of Alfred, the "more unfortunate" twin, was not reached because of environmental obstacles.

The above case firstly teaches us that the genes we inherit from our parents establish a ceiling on our adult height, while the environment (that is, the material living conditions we grow up in) affects the extent to which we manage to achieve our potential maximum height. However, genes are far more important than environmental factors in determining our overall height, which leads us to conclude that for *individual people*, height *cannot* be taken as a measure of economic wellbeing.

2.2 AN INDIVIDUAL'S BIOLOGY AND A POPULATION'S HEIGHT

The fact that genetics is largely responsible for our individual height has not discouraged economists, who are not concerned with specific cases, of individual people, but rather with populations or groups characterized by a large number of individuals. The difference between the study of an individual's height and the mean height of an entire population is fundamental, which justifies economists' interest in the historical background of peoples' stature.

To start with, we note that an individual's height depends on his or her *net* nutrition. This term means the balance that remains when we take away unassimilated nutrients (for example, owing to illnesses such as diarrhea) and the energy necessary for basic metabolic functioning and for all daily activities, including work, from the value of all the food ingested (*gross nutrition*).[6] For children and teenagers, net nutrition is a source not only of energy but also of the "building blocks" the body needs in order to develop one's stature. Therefore, it is not just the amount of calories that is important, but also the quality of our diet. The importance of milk, rich in proteins and calcium, is a familiar example; iodine is another, since a deficiency in this micronutrient leads to goiter, cretinism, and stunting (that is, a slow-down in the speed of growth), which were all sadly widespread phenomena in nineteenth-century Italy. When there is an extraordinary event such as an illness, the body needs additional energy in order to deal with it, and so the individual's (gross) nutrition does not improve while net nutrition worsens. Inadequate nutrition and the illness interact, thereby increasing the negative impact on the body: an inadequate diet increases the likelihood

[6] The term "basal metabolism" indicates the energy consumption needed to maintain minimum vital functions (such as breathing and maintaining blood circulation and body temperature), without moving, digesting, etc. The energy needs of the basal metabolism account for 45–70 percent of total daily energy consumption (Oxley and Meredith 2013).

of getting ill, which in turn tends to reduced appetite and prevents the body from absorbing nutrients.

When net nutrition becomes insufficient, the body's first reaction is to slow down the growth process, with consequences that can be slight and transient, but also severe and permanent. The human body has its own defense mechanisms enabling it, within certain limits, to recover and offset the damage caused: if nutrition is insufficient for short periods and not extreme, the individual still manages to completely make up for it, delaying the growth process or slowing it down, with the result that no trace will remain in his or her height as an adult. However, when the deprivations are severe and long-lasting, the consequences may be great and permanent: the individual's final height will be below its potential.

The considerations made so far with reference to a single individual also hold when we deal with a community of individuals (a social class, a province, a population): in this case, *mean net nutrition* can condition the community's *average height*. When we calculate a population's average height, we sum the heights of all its individuals and, in so doing, do away with all the individual variability due to genetic factors.[7] When mean net nutrition in the community improves, the community's average height increases and thus approaches its potential average height. Vice versa, when net nutrition worsens, the population's actual average height decreases and individuals' growth stops short of its potential average height. Since net nutrition is determined by the community's economic and material conditions, the conclusion is that variations in a population's average height effectively measure the variations in its material living conditions. This holds true as much for populations consisting of millions of individuals as for less numerous communities (regions, provinces, districts, etc.) and, in particular, for groups of individuals with well-defined socioeconomic characteristics.[8]

[7] The dispersion of individual heights around the group mean is of interest in itself, as this inequality of heights results in part from an inequality of living conditions. Because it also responds to the average level of living standards and the age at which individuals are measured, height inequality is problematic as a measure of economic inequality. See A'Hearn, Peracchi, and Vecchi (2009) for a discussion of the distribution of heights.

[8] There is widespread evidence supporting this result, even in today's world. In France the average height of males who complete high school is systematically higher than the one of individuals who have no academic qualifications, with a bonus associated to social status, ranging from 2.8 and 4.9 cm, depending on the individuals' age (Singh-Manoux et al. 2010). A comparative study of ten European countries shows that the height differences among individuals with different education levels are not only systemic, but are true as much for men as for women. In Italy's case, the less educated men (having a primary education certificate at most) turned out to be 2.5 cm shorter, on average, than their peers who had completed high school (1.3 cm in women's case) (Cavelaars et al. 2000).

Box 2 **Growing Smaller**

A population's height may increase, but it can also decrease (Tobias 1985). In effect, history abounds with cases showing considerable and lasting decreases in average height of a population. The most studied cases concern the United States and United Kingdom (Komlos 1998; Steckel 2008): in both countries, during their industrialization, despite the fact that per-capita income was on the rise, the average height of the population decreased considerably. In the United States, the decrease in height in the years 1830–1890 was by as much as 4 cm; in Britain's case the decline in heights over the years was even more marked: -8.5 cm between the latter half of the eighteenth century and the first half of the nineteenth century (Cinnirella 2008). In both these cases, the decrease in height was due, at least in part, to the urbanization accompanying the industrialization process in the two countries. The towns and cities of the times were characterized by high mortality rates, endemic diseases, overcrowding and thus rapid contagion of disease, and poor or nonexistent health facilities (no sewerage system, no access to clean drinking water), as well as relatively high prices of fresh and nutrient-rich foods such as meat and dairy produce.

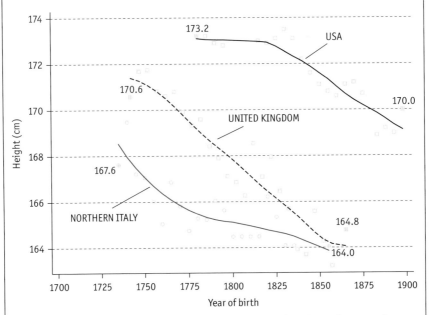

Figure 2.B2 SHRINKING POPULATIONS. Some examples of populations whose height has decreased in time due to the deterioration of the economic and epidemiological environment.

> Italy's history offers similar scenarios. The demographic growth in the north of the country had negative effects also on the height of Lombard soldiers between the mid-eighteenth century and mid-nineteenth century, where it decreased by about 3 cm (from 167 to 164 cm) — see A'Hearn (2003).

3 Military Anthropometric Data: From Abundance to Extinction

A few months after the birth of the Kingdom of Italy in 1861, the Ministry of War created the Directorate General of Levies, Low Level Ranks and New Recruits, a department charged with introducing military service in all the country's regions and coordinating recruitment operations. Lieutenant General Federico Torre (1815–1892) was appointed as its head, and he started the tradition of reporting the results achieved by his department to the Cabinet of His Excellency the Minister of War, by means of a report containing hundreds of statistical tables that he published on a regular basis from 1864 (the Torre Reports). All the young men of the new Kingdom were eligible for conscription, and all conscripts had to undergo a thorough medical examination in which the person's state of health and height were recorded.[9]

Overall, the Torre Reports contain data on the heights of over nineteen million individuals aged around twenty years, with an extremely detailed geographic resolution: the figures are available for each province in the Kingdom and often, but not always, for each of the over two hundred districts the country was divided into. What makes the material of these reports even more valuable is that they contain information dating back to the preunification period, seeing as the height of the first conscripts, measured in 1861, gives us information on the living conditions prevailing twenty years earlier. This is no small detail: on the contrary, it is a fundamental point. One of the most important questions in historiography concerns the effects of Italy's unification on the population's living standards: "Was it worth it?" (Rossi, Toniolo, and Vecchi 2011, xix). How did the unification process affect the wellbeing of the Italians? The availability of data on the conscripts' heights for the twenty years before and twenty years after unification allows us, for the first time (as we shall see in section 7) to

---

[9] If well below 156 cm in height, the young man was deemed ineligible to serve in the King's army and was rejected (*riformato*) However, if the military doctor considered his insufficient stature to be a temporary phenomenon and open to improvement, the man was declared "subject to review" (*rivedibile*) and invited to come back for the medical the following year. The reasons for exemption from, or deferment of, military service were not only based on height but also considered other biometric parameters (such as chest circumference), the presence of evident physical defects (limb impairments or blindness), and diseases such as pellagra, malaria, and syphilis (Ilari 1989).

assess the impact of the country's political and administrative unification on the wellbeing of the populations of the preunification Italian states.

General Torre left office in 1891, but the reports carried on without significant interruptions until 1930 (that is, including those born in 1910). In the interwar period the task passed to the National Institute of Statistics (Istat), which has since diligently updated the height series through the *Sommario di Statistiche Storiche* ("Summary of Historical Statistics"), on data supplied by the Ministry of Defense.

This abundance of Italian anthropometric data ended with the new millennium. Legislative Decree no. 215 of 8 May 2001 (Amato government) provided

---

Box 3 Of Size and Sex

The tale told by military anthropometric data is only half the story: it does not include women—that is, at least half the population (Sen 1990). In Italy, as elsewhere, there are no statistics that can describe the evolution

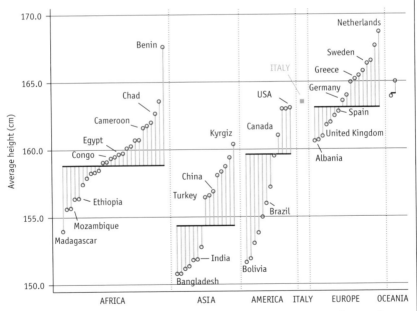

Figure 2.B3 AVERAGE FEMALE HEIGHTS AROUND THE WORLD. The graph shows average female height (horizontal segments, vertical axis) in the five continents (horizontal axis). Within each continent, the graph shows the dispersion of national heights around a mean value. There is almost an 18 cm difference between Bangladeshi women (150.8 cm, on average) and Dutch women (168.7 cm). Italian women (163.5 cm) rank slightly above the European average (163.1 cm).

of average women's height over this long period. There is, at most, sparse information on particular occupational categories and the most abundant, perhaps, concerns prison inmates, thanks to the data kept in penitentiary records offices (Nicholas and Oxley 1993, 1996; Baten and Murray 2000). The fact that almost the entire historiographical literature rests on the trend of just male heights instead of the average heights of both men and women is no small detail: the distribution of resources inside households has not always, and everywhere, been equal between the two genders (Sen and Sengupta 1983).

More recent data collection efforts are redressing this gender imbalance. For example, European Community Household Panel data show that the stature of Italian women grew by 3.2 cm between the early 1950s and the late 1970s (as against 2.7 cm for the men) (Garcia and Quintana-Domeque 2007). Meanwhile, the World Bank's Demographic and Health Surveys offer hundreds of thousands of height measurements of women and children in developing countries. In Figure 2.B3 we have tried to provide an overall picture by processing the data of 75 countries, corresponding to 70 percent of the world's population. The graph shows the estimates of the mean heights of women aged 25–50 years, measured since 2000. As we can see, the differences are great: starting with Asia (154.4 cm, on average), which has the shortest women in the world, to then go to Africa (158.4 cm), the Americas (159.6 cm), Europe (163.1 cm), and, finally, Australia and New Zealand (164.1 cm). Differences between countries are even more marked.

There is an overall lesson to be learned from these international comparisons: height is not determined only by economic conditions. African countries are among the world's poorest and suffer from some of the most dire diseases. Yet their women are, on average, almost as tall as those in the Americas and 4 cm above female stature in Asian countries that are mostly better off. Powerful selection effects of infant mortality could explain some of this, but genetic differences seem likely to be part of the explanation as well (Deaton 2006).

---

for the gradual replacement of conscripted servicemen with volunteers, and then law no. 226 of 23 August 2004 (Berlusconi government) envisaged the abolishment of compulsory military service—as of January 1, 2005. These two measures marked the end of an era, not just historically speaking, but also with regard to statistics: the generation born in 1980 was the last for which we have height data collected, processed, and published by Istat.

4 From Dwarves to Vikings: The Growth of a Population

As Luigi Pagliani wrote in the latter half of the nineteenth century: "There is no doubt that, with good nutrition and a suitable job, with hygiene and education, we see—day-by-day—the change in individuals previously destined to remain relatively dwarfish into individuals of more normal conditions" (1876, 159). In this section we shall show how right Pagliani was: he had grasped what was not easy to understand at the time, and had envisaged what we can easily observe today. That is to say, over the 150 years since Italy's unification, the average height of the Italians has reached, and perhaps even surpassed, the stature of the Vikings. The writer Ahmad Ibn Fadlan (877–960) had described these people: "They are the filthiest of all Allah's creatures, [...] but I have never seen more perfect physiques than theirs—they are like palm trees, are fair and reddish" (Montgomery 2000, 5). Recent studies have estimated that the average height of the Vikings was between 168 and 176 cm (Steckel 2004)—just what an average young adult Italian measures today.

Figure 2.3 shows the times and ways in which the Italians have reached the stature of the Vikings. In the graph, we follow the conventional practice of attributing average height to the birth year instead of to the year of

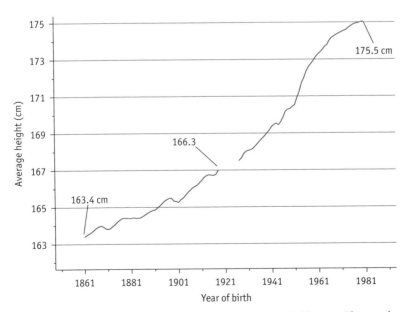

Figure 2.3 THE AVERAGE HEIGHT OF CONSCRIPTS AGED 20 YEARS. The graph shows the trend over time of average height, expressed in centimeters, of military service conscripts aged 20 years. The figure of 163.4 cm of 1861 represents the average height of those born in 1861 and measured in 1881.

measurement: gestation and early childhood is the overall period in which ill health can affect height irremediably (Eveleth and Tanner 1990).

Figure 2.3 highlights four important facts. The first concerns Italy's *backwardness* at the time of unification. The 163.4 cm height of the average Italian born in the aftermath of unification (and measured twenty years later) suggests that the country's economic conditions at the time of unification were such to severely stunt children's growth. Using the terminology introduced in section 2, we can say that the children's growth process found an environment in Italy that did not enable them to achieve their potential stature (the latter is, obviously, at least the same as the one actually reached by those born in 1980). Another sign of backwardness lies in the height fluctuations found up to the years of World War II. These would suggest that, although improving, living conditions were still low and made children vulnerable to dietary deficiencies and to illness.

A second comment concerns the trend in average height over the long period considered. The average stature of the Italian population has grown over 150 years, not without some halt, but never experiencing any falls. As we saw in Box 2, the fact that the average height of a population does not decrease is not such an obvious finding: many countries have experienced periods in their history in which the population got shorter.

A third remark with regard to Figure 2.3 concerns the magnitude of the increase in average height which, thanks to improvements in living conditions, has grown by 11.6 cm over a period of one hundred and twenty years. To judge this result, we can compare Italy's performance with that of other countries, and it turns out that the increase in the average height of the Italians is in line with the historical experience of European countries. Timothy Hatton and Bernice Bray (2010) have worked out that, between 1871 and 1980, the average height in twelve European countries increased at a rate of 1.08 cm a decade: during the same period, Italy recorded an increase of 1.07 cm a decade. Italy's gains are better that those of Ireland (+ 0.80 cm), France (+ 0.91 cm), and the United Kingdom (+ 0.93), but not as good as those of the Netherlands (+ 1.41 cm), Germany (+ 1.25 cm), and Spain (+ 1.19 cm). Hence, if the increase in average height was spectacular in absolute terms, it was not so extraordinary in relative terms: the Italians managed not to lag too much behind the leading European countries, but they ranked low in European height distribution, even lower than the Greeks and Spanish.

The final comment with regard to Figure 2.3 is the rate at which height has increased over time. Progress has not been uniform. The increases were more sluggish in the first fifty to sixty years (+ 6 millimeters [mm] per decade), accelerated during the interwar period (+ 12 mm per decade), and have increased further since World War II (+ 15 mm per decade). With regard to the most recent period, the height gains were resounding in the first two decades after the war (+ 25 mm per decade between 1950 and 1963), as with other Southern European countries, but mediocre thereafter up to 1980 (+ 8 mm per decade between 1964 and 1980). While Italy experienced the so-called economic miracle, young

Italian men experienced a nonmiraculous growth in height that was, however, unprecedented—as much in their remote as in their recent past.[10] On the whole, we can conclude that the Italians grew "very much," but not more than people in other Western European countries; this growth, in particular, occurred in the first twenty years after World War II.

We have still not said anything about the territorial distribution of these centimeters gained over the hundred and twenty years taken into consideration. What is the variability behind the average national figure? To go back to what Pagliani wrote, from the country's unification, did all the dwarves manage to turn into Vikings?

5 All Tall in the End?

The wealth of data in the Torre Reports and later Istat publications allows us to trace the path of mean heights not just for Italy, as a whole, but also for its 20 regions and, for the early part of this period, also for the 69 provinces in which the country had been divided at the start. In this section we present a series of actual maps of Italian statures. The maps were constructed on the basis of these data and we shall examine their trends over time. In so doing, we shall shed some light on the process spreading the benefits of economic development: if, as we have argued, height is correlated to living conditions, it is crucial to see to what extent the Italians managed to become "all tall." Is this not what we would expect to see after 150 years of a unified Italy?

Figure 2.4 plots mean heights for five macro-areas, all of which follow the same basic trajectory as the national series (section 4). No part of the country experienced declining heights over more than a transient period, and this is true of the underlying eighteen regional-mean height series as well.[11] It did not have to be so. Industrializing areas undergoing rapid urbanization might have suffered from a worsening disease-ridden environment or from a deterioration in the quality of diet, for example. Equally possible, other regions might have stagnated economically and experienced declining real wages and standards of living. The height evidence indicates that this was not the case: living conditions improved everywhere. This *universality* of the Italian growth process is not found in France (Chamla 1964), Spain (Martínez Carrión and Puche-Gil 2009), the United Kingdom, or the United States (Fogel, Engermann, and Trussel 1982).

[10] In 1953 the Istat data show an anomalous leap, probably owing to a change in survey and data-processing procedures. If we take this into account, the increase in height recorded in the first twenty years after World War II is + 19 mm per decade.

[11] The decreases in mean heights around 1900 relate to conscripts called up at ages as young as 17.8 years during World War I. To some extent, the declines may be real, reflecting wartime deprivation in the adolescent years preceding conscription. To a greater extent, they reflect shortcomings of our age-adjustment procedure, particularly in regions of the mainland South.

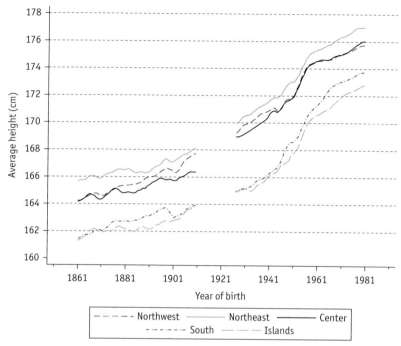

Figure 2.4 FIVE PATHS TO MODERN STATURES. The graph shows the trend over time (horizontal axis) of the average height of conscripts aged 20 years (vertical axis), for the five Italian macro-areas.

A less encouraging, but equally unmistakable, message in Figure 2.4 is the 125-year persistence of significant geographic disparities in height. One might expect statures to converge toward a common value as the benefits of economic development and medical advances reduced differences in living conditions. The south and the Islands (Sicily and Sardinia), in particular, might have been expected to enjoy more rapid growth and to catch up with the north and center of the country. It is clear that this did not happen to any significant degree; the north–south gap was 3.2 cm among those born in 1861 and 2.8 cm for the most recent data available, for those born in 1980.

The maps in Figure 2.5 allow us to better visualize the geographic variation in heights and to understand it at a finer level of disaggregation. In these maps, a darker color corresponds to a taller mean stature. The first two describe the situation in 1861 and 1910. There are large, contiguous swaths of territory in which similar heights predominate, and we do not see provinces more than one category apart bordering each other. The patterns, evidently, do not correspond to urban versus rural provinces, interior versus coastal provinces, or similar contrasts. Instead, we see a more nuanced version of the familiar north–south divide. The primary nuance is the leading position of the northeastern provinces (along with parts of the center) in 1861, followed by the rapid catching-up of provinces in the industrializing northwest. The latter feature of the data suggests that industrialization, Italian-style, was not dangerous to health.

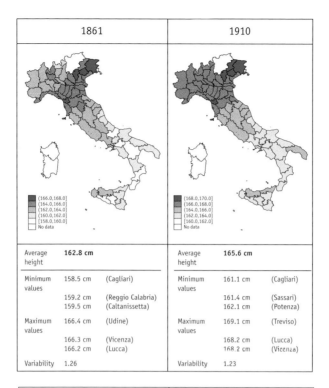

1861		1910	
	[166.0,168.0] [164.0,166.0] [162.0,164.0] [160.0,162.0] [158.0,160.0] No data		[168.0,170.0] [166.0,168.0] [164.0,166.0] [162.0,164.0] [160.0,162.0] No data

Average height	**162.8 cm**		Average height	**165.6 cm**	
Minimum values	158.5 cm	(Cagliari)	Minimum values	161.1 cm	(Cagliari)
	159.2 cm	(Reggio Calabria)		161.4 cm	(Sassari)
	159.5 cm	(Caltanissetta)		162.1 cm	(Potenza)
Maximum values	166.4 cm	(Udine)	Maximum values	169.1 cm	(Treviso)
	166.3 cm	(Vicenza)		168.2 cm	(Lucca)
	166.2 cm	(Lucca)		168.2 cm	(Vicenza)
Variability	1.26		Variability	1.23	

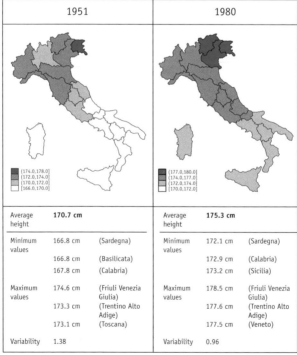

1951		1980	
	[174.0,178.0] [172.0,174.0] [170.0,172.0] [166.0,170.0]		[177.0,180.0] [174.0,177.0] [172.0,174.0] [170.0,172.0]

Average height	**170.7 cm**		Average height	**175.3 cm**	
Minimum values	166.8 cm	(Sardegna)	Minimum values	172.1 cm	(Sardegna)
	166.8 cm	(Basilicata)		172.9 cm	(Calabria)
	167.8 cm	(Calabria)		173.2 cm	(Sicilia)
Maximum values	174.6 cm	(Friuli Venezia Giulia)	Maximum values	178.5 cm	(Friuli Venezia Giulia)
	173.3 cm	(Trentino Alto Adige)		177.6 cm	(Trentino Alto Adige)
	173.1 cm	(Toscana)		177.5 cm	(Veneto)
Variability	1.38		Variability	0.96	

Figure 2.5 THE GROWTH OF THE ITALIANS (AVERAGE HEIGHT OF CONSCRIPTS PER PROVINCE). The maps show the average height of conscripts aged 20 years, born in 1861, 1910, 1951, and 1980. The lighter shade corresponds to a low stature while a darker shade to a high stature. The variability index (coefficient of variation) measures the dispersion of heights: a higher value indicates a greater variability.

The second set of maps present regional-level data for the birth years 1951 and 1980. The same patterns seen a century earlier are repeated: the regions of the northeast remain the tallest, and there is a clear north–south gap. One difference in the postwar decades is some degree of convergence, which we can see in the need for only three shades to cover all regions except Sardinia in 1980, and in the decrease in the index of variability from 1.38 to 0.96.

Regional convergence and divergence are so fundamental to understanding the history of wellbeing and its distribution that it is worth investing in some relevant conceptual tools. We can assess the issue from two perspectives. We can ask, firstly, whether the dispersion of regional mean heights tends to rise or fall. In the former case, we are dealing with a *divergence*, while in the latter, a *convergence*. On the other hand, we can ask ourselves whether or not mean heights grow faster in the regions with shorter heights, so that they catch up with those with taller statures. These are different ways of asking almost the same question.

Figures 2.6 and 2.7 illustrate these two convergence concepts. Figure 2.6 plots the dispersion of the eighteen regional mean heights, and namely their standard deviation. It is worth avoiding any possible misunderstanding by saying that the variation observed in the graph could be explained, even in part, by hypothetical genetic differences between regional populations. In Figure 2.6, genetic differences are ruled out in that, even if they existed, they would be a constant factor (the

Figure 2.6 THE FALL, RISE, AND FALL OF REGIONAL DISPARITIES IN HEIGHTS. The figure shows the trend over time (horizontal axis) of the dispersion of the 18 regional mean heights measured by the standard deviation (vertical axis).

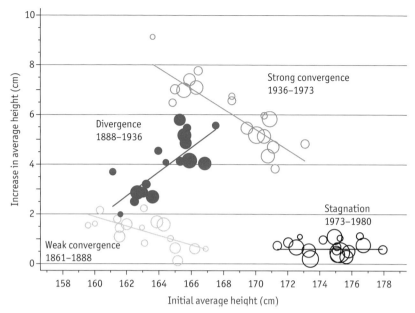

Figure 2.7 Catch-up and Fall-Back in Four Periods. The graph shows the relation between the increase in height experienced in different time periods (vertical axis) and the height at the start of the period (horizontal axis). Each circle in the graph stands for a region; the area of each circle is in proportion to the population of that particular region. A negative relation, shown by a downward sloping "best-fit" curve between the circles, indicates a convergence: the lowest regions are the ones that grew the fastest. An upward sloping curve, as in the period 1888–1936, indicates a divergence instead.

genetic makeup of a region does not change over a few decades) and a constant factor cannot, evidently, be held responsible for a phenomenon that varies over time. The curve in Figure 2.6 must, instead, reflect a variation in living conditions.[12]

Figure 2.7 illustrates the catch-up convergence by plotting the change of mean height against its starting level. In the graph, each small circle stands for a region (the area of the circle reflects the region's population), along with its initial stature (horizontal axis) and increase in average height (vertical axis) over the various periods.

For each subperiod, the gradient of the curve indicates whether there is a convergence or not. If a catch-up convergence is occurring, mean heights grow faster where heights are originally lower, and the points representing the regions should cluster along a negatively sloped line. The more negative the

---

[12] If genetic differences existed, migration flows, if sufficiently intense, could make a contribution to convergence. They would not be expected to produce divergence, however. And the likely motivation for significant migration flows is precisely differences in living conditions.

slope (e.g., the period 1936–1973), the greater the convergence. A positive slope (e.g., 1888–1936), instead, indicates a divergence of average regional heights.

Both Figure 2.6 and Figure 2.7 concur in identifying the early decades of unification as a period of gentle convergence in regional mean heights. Figure 2.6 shows that the variability decreased, while the circles in the lower-left part of Figure 2.7 show that regions of shorter stature enjoyed faster growth in mean stature from 1861 to 1888. Both measures indicate that this convergence was slow. This trend was rather abruptly reversed in the 1890s, coinciding with the acceleration of an industrialization process that focused in the northwest. Now it was the taller, northern regions that enjoyed the most rapid improvement in living conditions, and the variability of regional means widened.[13] This trend continued, or at least was not reversed, throughout the Fascist years, the Great Depression, and World War II. The Fascist period is thus characterized by growing divergence, but this was a legacy of the past. The period beginning just after World War II and continuing until the late 1960s was a phase of rapid convergence, in which it was again the poorer, shorter regions in which stature rose most rapidly and regional variability fell to levels last seen eight decades before. This phase coincided, of course, with Italy's economic miracle. Variability having returned to the levels of a hundred years earlier, catch-up convergence stopped, leaving in place the considerable disparities highlighted in the more updated map of Italian heights (Figure 2.5).

6 Why Did the Heights of Italians Increase?

The increase in the heights of Italians that we have documented in Figure 2.1 is an eloquent testimonial to the improvement in their physical wellbeing. There is simply no way to increase average stature without better health among ordinary families. But just what kind of story should we be telling based on the improvement in mean heights? Was it the triumph of economic growth in Italy, putting more resources at the disposal of households? Or the march of science worldwide, creating new medical treatments and public health measures? Or something else, such as changes in childrearing practices and child labor, or perhaps technical progress in the preservation and transportation of protein-rich foods like milk and meat?

The answers to these questions are not obvious since height is the product of many different factors. The body responds to several types of disease, the quality of housing, the distribution of resources within the household, the nutritional content of the diet, the climate, psychological stress, energy consumption

---

[13] The inverse U-shaped curve, evident after about 1890, recalls the "Williamson curve" discussed in chapter 6 (Williamson 1965).

in work, and mothers' health. To properly deal with so much complexity, we need suitable analytical tools and spaces going beyond the task we have taken on in this chapter. However, as we shall see in this section, something useful can still be learned from a simple explorative analysis in which we consider two key variables: per-capita gross domestic product (GDP) (from chapter 7, "Income") and child mortality (from chapter 3, "Health").

We have divided our analysis into two parts. In the first, we aim to exploit the time horizon of national data, which is exceptionally long (section 6.1): What can we learn from the cycles and trends observed in the 150 years of data we have at our disposal? In the second part, instead, we try to take advantage of the fact of having—albeit only for some benchmark years—historical experiences of each Italian region (section 6.2). In this case, the challenge consists of taking advantage of the great variety of regional behaviors and of establishing any regularity. Readers who do not feel inclined to follow the analysis—perhaps more technical than usual—of these two sections will find a summary discussion in section 6.3.

6.1 TIME

At the national level, we have annual series on mean height (for all but a few years), per-capita income, and infant mortality. In Figure 2.8, height is plotted against income (left panel) and infant mortality (right panel). It is clear that height is closely correlated with both variables. Consider the left panel. It looks as though height is quite responsive to per-capita income until 1950 (during which time incomes grew slowly), but is less sensitive thereafter (when income grew rapidly). At times, height increases autonomously, as from 1910 to 1920. The opposite is, perhaps, the case for mortality. Until 1900, infant mortality falls fairly dramatically, but heights rise slowly, while thereafter a given improvement in child health seems to "buy" a greater increase in height. Here, too, there are instances of height rising autonomously, as between 1930 and 1940.

An interesting aspect of Figure 2.8 that is more subtle, but worth highlighting, concerns the frequency of short-run fluctuations in both mortality and income, in the face of which heights remain unchanged. For example, if we look at the right-hand graph, we see many zigzag movements: these are sharp variations in child mortality (shown by the horizontally moving gray line) to which no variation in average height is attributed (it should move vertically but does not vary, though). The most visible examples in the graph concern the mortality peak associated with the Spanish flu epidemic in 1918 or the economic collapse associated with defeat in World War II. These trends suggest that it was *chronic* poverty, malnutrition, and disease that generated short statures, rather than *episodic* events (Dehejia and Lleras-Muney 2004). Italian history thus suggests that small negative shocks of an economic nature, or caused by a temporary

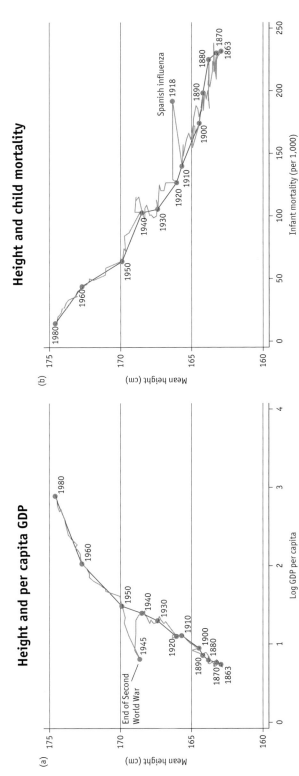

Figure 2.8 HEIGHT, HEALTH, AND INCOME OVER TIME. The graph on the left shows the strong *positive* correlation between the average height of the Italians (vertical axis) and per capita GDP (horizontal axis) over time. The graph on the right, instead, shows the close *negative* correlation between average height and child mortality. On the whole, the "average adult male height" indicator is again confirmed as a useful indicator of a population's economic wellbeing.

worsening of the epidemiological environment, can be completely absorbed and not leave any trace in the statistics of a people's average height. On the other hand, prolonged, chronic deprivations are the factors that leave a permanent mark in the evolution of a population's mean height.

Both per-capita GDP and child mortality can "explain" height statistically. But which of the two variables has the more powerful effect? And can we be sure that either of them is associated in a causal way with mean height? Is it not possible that some factor we have not considered is the real cause of rising stature, something like a gradual shift toward drinking more milk in childhood, or scientific advances in the prevention and treatment of (postinfancy) diseases? Figure 2.9 graphically presents an attempt to answer these questions by means of regression analysis. Mean height is explained as the sum of a time-trend, a child mortality effect, and a per-capita income effect. The strength of each effect is estimated from the data as detailed in the Appendix.[14] The three lines in Figure 2.9 show predictions of what height would have been had there been (i) only a secular trend; (ii) the time trend and the improvement in infant mortality only; and (iii) the joint effect of time, mortality, and the growth in income.

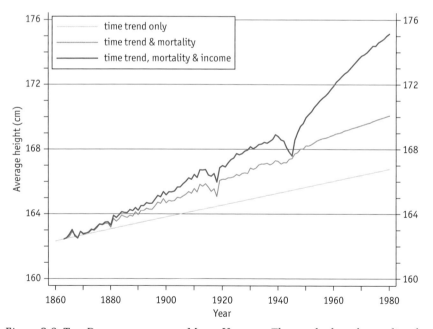

Figure 2.9 THE DETERMINANTS OF MEAN HEIGHT. The graph plots the predicted values from a regression of mean height on a time trend, child mortality, and the logarithm of per capita GDP. All three contributed to the rise in stature over the long run.

[14] Federico (2003) undertakes a similar exercise for the period 1854–1913, reaching conclusions not dissimilar to the ones described here.

The deterministic time-trend captures the steady accumulation of positive influences that we do not observe, such as improvements in diet or postinfancy medical care (Fogel and Costa 1997). Cumulatively, these factors are estimated to have contributed about 5.5 cm to mean height between 1861 and 1980. Our measures of health and wealth jointly explain a little more than 8 cm of improvement. The separate contributions of each were of similar magnitude, with fast-declining mortality the dominant influence in the early decades and rapidly rising incomes more important later, especially after World War II.[15]

6.2 PLACE

We have a particular interest in the determinants of *regional* mean heights: we want to understand whether persistent differences in regional mean heights imply enduring differences in wellbeing among the inhabitants of the various regions of the country. Regional data give us a further opportunity to investigate the effects of income and child mortality on mean height. As Figure 2.10 shows, the

Height and GDP   Height and child mortality

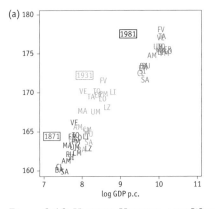
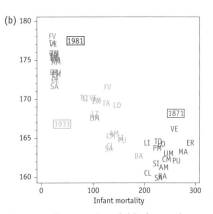

Figure 2.10 HEIGHT, HEALTH, AND WEALTH ACROSS SPACE. Panel (a) shows the relation between average regional heights (vertical axis) and regional per capita GDP (horizontal axis). Panel (b) is constructed in a similar manner and summarizes the relation between average regional heights (vertical axis) and child mortality (horizontal axis). In this case, except for 1871, which we shall talk about in the main text, the relation is a negative one: height is greater in those regions where child mortality is lower. Mean income, mortality and height are solidly correlated indicators in both time and space.

---

[15] The decreases in the predicted mean height series in the late 1910s and 1940s are not observed in the actual height series. They are due to a brief spike in mortality (part of which is associated with the Spanish influenza epidemic) and a brief postwar economic collapse, respectively.

same patterns seen at the national level are seen in the regions. The left panel plots regional mean height against regional per-capita GDP for three particular years: 1871, 1931, and 1981. Each point represents one region in one year and is labeled with an abbreviation of the region's name (e.g., "VE" for Veneto). There is a clear, positive relationship between income and stature in each year; the rich regions have always been tall since the time of the country's unification.[16] The right-hand panel depicts regional height and child mortality rates. Here, the picture is slightly more complex. In 1931, the expected relationship between height and health is evident: regions with a lower child mortality have taller statures. By 1981, this relationship almost disappeared, but the explanation is straightforward: child mortality rates are bunched near their lower bound of zero, while height differences remain. The intriguing case of 1871 is discussed below. A regression analysis similar to that of section 6.1 yields similar conclusions: both per-capita GDP and child mortality have strong and separately identifiable associations with regional heights. Indeed, in the regional analysis these effects are even stronger and there is no role for an autonomous trend. A doubling of regional income is predicted to raise height by 2.1 cm, while a 10-percentage-point fall in child mortality is expected to increase stature by 3.4 cm. These results suggest that regional height disparities are likely indicative of disparities in wellbeing.

But this interpretation may be premature because it ignores the possibility of genetic (or persistent epigenetic) differences between regional populations. These could potentially affect maximum achievable height or the body's responses to environmental conditions. Although there is no direct evidence for this, we do know that Sardinians differ from other Italians in genes associated with blood type, for example (Piazza et al. 1988). It would be a strange coincidence that the poorer regions with higher child mortality were precisely those with genetically determined smaller statures. But it is possible. Perhaps more relevant is the possibility that there were persistent differences between regions in factors that affect heights that were not included in our analysis. For example, protein-rich foods might consistently have been cheaper in some regions than in others, raising heights without affecting or being determined by either income or child mortality. Or, perhaps, the incidence of endemic diseases that affected children only after infancy, or that caused only morbidity rather than mortality, differed across regions.

The way to address this concern is to discard information on the regional *levels* of variables and to consider only their variation around their mean, or their changes over time. The question changes from "Were statures tall in times and places that were rich and healthy?" to "Did statures increase by more in times

---

[16] This is just as true for the other years for which estimates of regional GDP exist: 1891, 1911, 1938, and decennially from 1951, 1961 and 1971. These have been omitted from the graph for the sake of legibility.

and places where incomes grew more and mortality fell more?" The answer is clearly "yes." Estimated in this way, the effects of regional income and mortality are qualitative as before, albeit smaller in magnitude. A doubling of per-capita GDP is associated with an increase in height of between 0.75 and 1.5 cm, while a decrease of 10 percentage points in child mortality corresponds to a rise in stature of between 1.1 and 2.4 cm.[17]

The same regression analysis allows us to decompose persistent regional height differences into a component attributable to our observed explanatory factors and a component that is unexplained. The results are depicted in Figure 2.11. The bars in Figure 2.11 show the enduring difference between a region's mean height and the national average. Sardinian heights, for example, were almost 4 cm below the Italian average between 1861 and 1911 (leftmost bar), while those in Veneto (third from the right) were more than 2 cm above.[18]

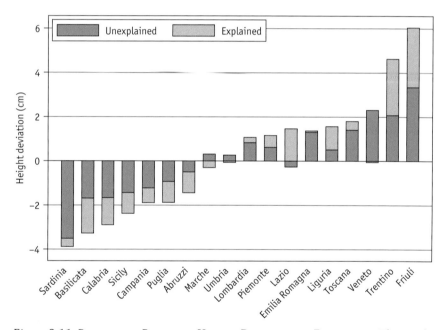

Figure 2.11 Persistent Regional Height Differences Explained. The graph shows that the difference between the average regional heights and the national average (the height of each bar) is only partly explained by the effects of average income and of the epidemiological environment of the regions. The tall stature recorded in Veneto, for example, seems to be due to other factors, while the one in Lazio is almost completely explained by income and child mortality.

---

[17] The range of the reported effects derives from estimates of two models: a model of the level of heights with regional fixed effects, and a model of changes in height.

[18] More specifically, estimates refer to averages over the years 1871, 1891, 1911, 1931, 1938, 1951, 1961, 1971, and 1981, for which we have estimates of regional GDP. The exceptions are Friuli–Venezia Giulia and Trentino–Alto Adige, for which the relevant years are those from 1931 onward.

The dark portion of each bar indicates the share that is *not* attributed to regional income and mortality with any confidence (the regional "fixed effect"), while the light portion is the share that is explained. In Basilicata, for example, there was an average deficit of 3.3 cm with respect to national mean height, and this discrepancy is predicted in roughly equal measure by observable deficits in health and wealth, and by an enduring unexplained Basilicata-specific effect. Trentino Alto Adige had an average 4.6 cm advantage, attributable in similar degree to income and mortality and to a region-specific effect. Sardinia and Veneto are extreme cases in which an unexplained regional effect "explains" most of the lasting deviation from the national average.

How do we interpret unexplained but enduring regional effects? They do not imply a failure of height as a measure of welfare. If anything, the opposite is true; if height were perfectly explained by child mortality and per-capita GDP, it would have no added value as an indicator. We cannot rule out genetic differences, even if—as noted earlier—it would be a surprising coincidence that they aligned so well with measures of welfare. However, the obvious path for further research is in the direction of region-specific factors affecting health and quality of life, such as child-rearing practices, diet, postinfancy health care, or inequality.

Let us now go back to the curious lack of a relation between child mortality and adult stature in the early years of postunification Italy (year 1871 in Figure 2.10). Of course, this may simply result from measurement error (i.e., poor-quality data). But it may also indicate a balance between the offsetting effects of *scarring* and *selection*. The scarring effect is the reduction in adult height that we expect to result from the deleterious living conditions that also cause high child mortality.[19] But child mortality can also generate a selection effect that works in the opposite direction. Among adults, mortality risks are higher for shorter individuals, and there is reason to think that this may be true in infancy as well: child mortality would be greater for the frailest children, having less growth potential, that is, the ones who achieve shorter statures in adulthood. If so, then as child mortality rises, more and more individuals who would have grown up to have a small stature (for some combination of genetic and environmental reasons) are missing from the population of adults when heights are measured. The mean height of the adult population is thus higher than it would have been had all the children survived. Where health conditions are truly dire and child mortality reaches tragic proportions, it is possible that this selection effect more than offsets the usual scarring effect, leaving a taller population of survivors (Bozzoli, Deaton, and Quintana-Domeque 2009). If the

---

[19] More generally, "scarring" is a *negative* and *permanent* effect on an individual's long-term health. For example, (respiratory) tuberculosis contracted in infancy may, without any effective treatment, not only reduce life expectancy but also prevent full body development (Elo and Preston 1992).

selection effect did predominate in the 1870s, we have another confirmation of just how poor living conditions were in the early years of postunification Italy. Mean stature, low as it was, might be too *optimistic* an indicator.

6.3 HEALTH, WEALTH, OR SOMETHING ELSE?

The evidence consistently supports the role of both wealth and health in explaining mean height. The results of sections 6.1 and 6.2 show, in statistically rigorous fashion, that, over time and across regions, decreases in child mortality and increases in per-capita incomes raised statures. The finding of significant child mortality effects even after controlling for income and time is important. It means there was an important role for factors that did not depend on local resources or on the steady march of progress (captured by time trends in our regressions). What might these region- or time-specific factors be? One possibility is exogenous differences in the disease environment, such as in the severity of winter weather or a suitable habitat for disease vectors. Another could be the variation in public health initiatives not driven by GDP. Irregular bursts of progress in medical knowledge are another possibility. The eradication of malaria through the application of DDT to anopheles mosquito breeding areas (chapter 3, "Health") is an example in which all three factors intersect.

There is also evidence of persistent regional "fixed effects" on average height that do not work through income or child mortality. These differences could be of a genetic or epigenetic origin. Or they might reflect differences in postinfant childhood mortality, or perhaps differences in diet that did not depend on income levels, such as greater protein consumption due to persistent differences in relative prices or culinary traditions. Hence, although there is no doubt about the centrality of health and wealth in determining heights, much still remains to be explained.

What caused the increase in Italian statures? An improvement in good health could come about through the economic resources of households (a nutritious diet, good-quality housing, medicine, and medical treatment), the resources of society as a whole (infrastructure improvements, a public health system), or through advances in scientific knowledge (antibiotics, quinine, surgical procedures).

Why did it slow down? Largely because height probably has a genetic upper bound that we are approaching, reaching the limits of what income, medicine, and favorable health outcomes can contribute. Taller statures in other countries suggest we are probably not quite at that limit, though, so we have to consider the possibility that progress was slowed by adverse developments relating to the distribution of resources between and within households—factors such as diet or environmental conditions. While further research is certainly necessary to find a more satisfactory answer, it is still interesting to note the parallels and synchrony between the slowdown recorded in the biological indicator of "average height" and the one seen in the usual macroeconomic indicators.

Why did it not eliminate regional differences? We cannot deny the possibility of enduring genetic and epigenetic traits, and there may be persistent differences in diet, child-rearing, within-household distribution of resources, inequality, the geographically determined disease environment, and other unmeasured factors. But there also remain significant differences across regions in the resources available to households, which continue to correlate strongly with average heights. A lack of economic convergence hindered convergence in biological living conditions.

7 Where It Is Claimed That Italy's Unification Did Not Affect the Wellbeing of the Italians

The years between 1859 and 1870 saw the disappearance of as many as seven sovereign states from the European geopolitical map: the Kingdom of Sardinia (corresponding to today's regions of Piedmont and Liguria in northwest Italy, plus the island of Sardinia), the Kingdom of Lombardy-Venetia (in the northeast of the country and formerly a dependency of the Austrian Empire), the duchies of Parma and Modena, the Grand Duchy of Tuscany, the State of the Church (including today's Lazio, Umbria, and Marche regions, plus part of Emilia), and, finally, the Kingdom of the Two Sicilies (approximately comprising the southern mainland regions plus Sicily). In their place there was now the new Kingdom of Italy, which was formally proclaimed on March 17, 1861, but became firmly established in its boundaries only in September 1870, with the taking of Rome. What was the impact of this geopolitical upheaval on the living conditions of the populations involved? To date, only a few scholars have looked into the issue and, to our knowledge, none of them have provided an answer—if not a mere speculative one.

The new Kingdom's draft records reach back into the past to inform us on the pre-unification period, since the heights of conscripts reflect conditions around the time of their birth. The first draft called up consisted of young men born in 1839: these were the first to serve in the new army of King Victor Emanuel II, and it is their heights that we can use in order to reconstruct the trend in the Italian population's living conditions before, during, and after Italy's unification.[20] Did the country's unification have any positive effects on the population's living

---

[20] From the generation born in 1843 onward we have usable data on the distribution of heights on an annual basis for all Italian provinces. Data on conscripts from the provinces of Veneto are available from the generation of 1846, for Rome from 1850.

conditions? The answer we find in the data is a negative one, at least as regards the first twenty years after unification: the wellbeing of the Italians was not really affected by unification, for better or worse.

The form in which the data are reported in the early years complicates the calculation of average height, and this is another reason why the data we are presenting here have been largely unused to date.[21] The solution we have adopted consists of using an alternative measure to the mean that is equally simple and functional: the share of heights of 170 cm or more. We can imagine that when statures grow, the number of people who manage to reach or go above a certain threshold increases more and more: in this case, a threshold of 170 cm.[22]

As Figure 2.12 illustrates for two important regions (Lombardy, in the north, and Sicily) and for Italy as a whole, 170 cm was quite a tall stature in the 1840s: only about one in ten Sicilian men reached this height. Lombardy's

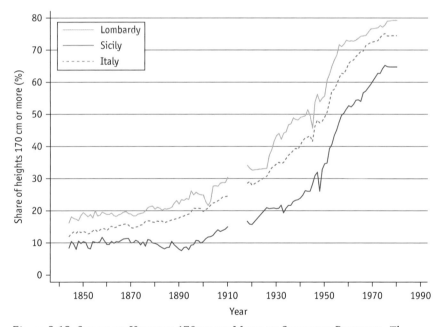

Figure 2.12 SHARE OF HEIGHTS 170CM OR MORE IN SELECTED REGIONS. The graph shows the increase over time (horizontal axis) of the share of individuals with a height above 170 cm (vertical axis) for Italy (broken line) and for the two most numerous regions representing the north (Lombardy, light blue line) and south (Sicily, dark blue line).

---

[21] One exception to this is Arcaleni (1998).

[22] The focus on what was in the early years the upper tail of the distribution has a drawback. It masks progress in average height that arises from reducing the share of individuals in the lower tail.

share of tall statures, though still a small minority of the total, was considerably greater. The difference between Lombardy and Sicily was typical of a more general north–south gap in initial conditions in the 1840s (Table S1, in the Appendix, gives the estimates in detail). The trajectories in Figure 2.12 show how the north–south gap widened from about 1880 and again in the 1920s and 1930s, with differences in the share of tall statures persisting to the very end of the period. Everywhere, though, the extraordinary became ordinary. Among the generation of 1980, a large majority of Italian conscripts—three-quarters—exceeded 170 cm in height. The distribution's upper tail had become its lower tail.

We can analyze the impact of the country's unification on local economic and health conditions by looking for changes in growth trends of the 170-plus share. Were tall statures becoming more common before 1861, and if so, at what pace? Did this growth accelerate or decelerate after unification?

The answer is found in Figure 2.13, in which we compare the growth trend of statures of the two decades prior to unification (1844–1861) and those after (1862–1879). Across the territories that would become Italy, progress was very slow prior to unification. The 170-plus share was increasing at a rate of about one-tenth of a percentage point per year. In other words, after a decade, only 1 percent more individuals would reach 170 cm or more in height. The most significant finding, though, is the fact that this rate of change did not alter perceptibly after unification in 1861, suggesting no acceleration in the rate of improvement of living conditions for ordinary households, but no disruption of that progress either. The other panels in Figure 2.13 show the effect of unification separately in the north and south, largely confirming the conclusion drawn for Italy as a whole.

If we delve into the underlying regional data, are there any signs of promising developments being stifled or reversed or, alternatively, accelerated? The answer is clearly negative: there are no systematic patterns of acceleration or deceleration. A particularly significant example concerns the future Industrial Triangle regions (Lombardy, Piedmont, and Liguria). Prior to unification, the share of tall statures was improving slowly in Piedmont and Lombardy, and rather more quickly in Liguria. In the two decades after 1861, growth speeded up a little in Piedmont, remained steady in Lombardy, and slowed considerably in Liguria. In the south and the Islands after 1861, there was a trend reversal from decline to increase in Campania and Abruzzi-Molise, but a mirror-image reversal (from growth to decline) in Basilicata and Sicily. Across the nation, growth accelerated in eight regions, decelerated in five, and changed not at all in two.[23] Growth

---

[23] Interestingly, one of the accelerating regions is Veneto, which did not become part of Italy until 1866. From 1861 to 1866, it was severed from Lombardy, with which it had previously formed the Kingdom of Lombardy-Venetia within the Habsburg Empire.

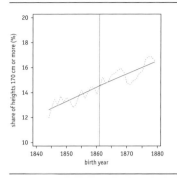

ITALY
Unity without any visible effects

The fact that Italy's political and administrative unification did not have any real impact on the living conditions of the populations of the pre-unification states is quite striking. The trend in average height in the pre-unification period (left of the line marking 1861) is perfectly aligned with the post-unification one (right of the 1861 line).

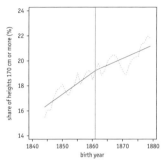

CENTRE-NORTH
Growth after unification, but at a slower pace

In the center and north of the country, the progress in average stature in the twenty years leading up to unification is sluggish: average height increased at the rate of 1.7% per decade. In the twenty-year period after unification, progress slows further to 1.1%. It is by no means a significant change in that it does not alter the conclusion arrived at in the text: unification had a negligible impact on the living conditions of central and northern populations

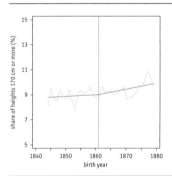

SOUTH
Unification was favorable to the south

In the south and islands (Sicily and Sardinia), stagnation gives way to imperceptible growth at 0.5 share points per decade. In the short-to-middle run, the view that the country's unification came about to the detriment of the south is without grounds. In fact, it was quite the opposite.

Figure 2.13 ITALY'S UNIFICATION HAD NO EFFECT ON THE STATURE OF THE ITALIANS. The figure compares the trends, separately for Italy (top panel) and the two macro-areas of the Center-north (middle panel) and south (lower panel), for statures (measured by the share of conscripts with a height above 170 cm, vertical axis) before and after Italy's unification (indicated with a line at 1861, horizontal axis).

rates remained modest and their changes—the "unification effects"—were small, whether positive or negative. In most cases, they cannot reliably be distinguished from random annual fluctuations in the data.

Provincial-level data confirm this highly varied picture. For the most part, rates of change are quite modest both before and after 1861. Trend growth in the share of tall statures accelerates in 40 provinces, decelerates in 28, and more often than not cannot be distinguished from a random variation. On the whole, it is difficult to discern a north–south, urban–rural, or other general pattern.

To the extent that heights are responsive to variation in the living conditions of ordinary households, the evidence considered here offers no support to grand interpretations of the economic impact of Italian unification on the wellbeing of the Italians. The lack of acceleration in the frequency of tall statures after 1861 suggests no generalized acceleration in the pace of economic development. This can hardly be surprising: the slow pace of per-capita GDP growth in the 1860s and 1870s (chapter 7, "Income"), if largely faster than what went before, would imply a truly dire situation in the 1840s and 1850s. Nor is there support for a redistribution effect from south to north. Higher taxes in the south to support infrastructure development in the north, where industry further benefited from access to wider new markets, should have slowed or reversed stature improvements in the south, and accelerated them in the regions that would become the Industrial Triangle. There is no evidence of such an impact. Indeed, quite the opposite.

Finally, the broad gaps in tall stature shares make it quite unlikely that per-capita incomes, child mortality rates, or other factors, such as the quality of the diet, were approximately the same in the north and south prior to unification. This supports the view that, at the time of unification, the southern regions were clearly backward with respect to the northern ones, while it discredits the "southerner" views according to which, in 1861, there was no great economic gap between north and south. Initial conditions differed, and unification failed, over its first two decades, to either diminish or broaden them.

8 Stature Gives Us Economic History Lessons

> Statements such as 'Height is an inherited characteristic' or 'Intelligence is the product of social forces' (or vice versa, of course) are intellectual rubbish, to be consigned to the trash-can of propaganda. . . . What is inherited is DNA. Everything else is developed. . . . Suppose, for example, we have two children, of different genotypes (i.e. arrays of genes). Under the environmental circumstances represented, let us say, by a contemporary well-off Swedish home, A grows to be 5 cm taller than B. Transplant the same two genotypes to a peasant environment in southern India, growing fitfully in the face of recurrent famines, chronic infections, physical labor and heat. Both children will probably end up smaller. (Tanner 1989, 119)

This is how James M. Tanner (1920–2010), a world-famous British pediatrician and scholar, summed up the point that inspired economists to use human stature, a biological indicator, as an indicator of economic wellbeing: the environment conditions the human growth process, and this makes it legitimate to study the evolution of stature over time in order to grasp the evolution of a population's living conditions. What lessons have we learned, then, from analyzing the heights of military service conscripts? Some things have been confirmed while some other results are new.

The confirmations include the *economic backwardness* of the country in the aftermath of unification. The anthropometric data highlight that in the mid-nineteenth century the living conditions of the Italians were difficult, perhaps dire, as much in absolute terms as in relative ones: the average height of the population was short compared to that of other countries, but even compared to the height reached by later generations of Italians. The genetic potential found a great constraint in the environmental conditions of the times. One and a half centuries later, Italy's growth trend has been in line with that of other countries that we consider to be rich and modern today. The statistics we have processed highlight how life—childhood in particular—has been transformed beyond all recognition since 1861. If the 13-year-old boys of Turin's working class in the 1870s (Figure 2.1) could meet the median 13-year-old of today's Center-North, it really would be a case of dwarves looking up to unrecognizable Vikings: the difference in mean stature would be 25 cm. What is more, the dwarves would be suffering from a range of chronic ailments including diarrhea, malaria, pellagra, and tuberculosis, mostly unknown to children of today (chapter 3, "Health"). Progress has not been uniform throughout the period, but concentrated more in the first twenty years after World War II.

A second confirmation concerns the benevolent process of Italian industrialization. The *modernization* and *urbanization* associated with the country's modern economic development did not have adverse consequences on the health of the Italians: on the contrary, heights increased at a greater pace in those very provinces in the so-called Industrial Triangle, where industrialization started up and went on with greater intensity (Fenoaltea 2003b). While it is true that the Italian population did not show bodily signs of the "dark satanic mills" found in the British industrialization process (Williamson 1981), it is also true that the progress recorded in Italian stature was characterized by broad and persisting disparities across the country: although people's height in the southern regions increased, it did not always keep up with the accelerated pace shown by the northern regions. This is why we even saw periods of divergence between the two parts of the country. Only after World War II do we find a clear and robust trend toward convergence: although we cannot, at the present state of knowledge, rule out a role for genetic differences in the lack of convergence in regional heights, it would be a strange coincidence that such differences should align so neatly with disparities in per-capita income (chapter 7, "Income") and the related variables. Not only this, but the fact that the variation in Italian regional statures remains broader than the one seen in such a large and diverse country as France (Pineau 1993) suggests that there is still room for significant improvement in the living conditions of the southern regions.

Let us now turn to the new results, to the lessons to be learned from our analysis in this chapter. The first result, a surprising one in some respects, concerns the period around the time of unification. The new data we have collected for the 1840s unequivocally show an advantage of the center-north: the northern Italians were not only significantly taller than the southern ones but also showed faster progress. The Italy of the unification period, although fragmented, was undoubtedly on the road to improvement with regard to the wellbeing of its population. Although revolutionary at political, administrative, and civil levels, unification does not seem to have affected the road to wellbeing of the populations of the pre-unification states: the growth rate was the same in the decades leading up to and after 1861. Some difference can be found if we consider the southern regions separately from the northern ones. In the novel *The Leopard* (*Il Gattopardo*) by Sicilian writer Giuseppe Tomasi di Lampedusa (1896–1957), the main character, Don Fabrizio, Prince of Salina, converses with the emissary of the Piedmontese government Aimone Chevalley. In the aftermath of Sicily's annexation to the new Kingdom of Italy, the Sicilian nobleman does not hide his skepticism on the effects this annexation would have on the lives of the Sicilians: "Sleep, my dear Chevalley, eternal sleep, that is what Sicilians want. And they will always resent anyone who tries to awaken them, even to bring them the most wonderful of gifts. And, between ourselves, I doubt very strongly whether this new Kingdom has very many gifts for us in its luggage" (Tomasi di Lampedusa 1896, 1957). The height data largely confirm Don Fabrizio's view: the southern population's living conditions—stationary in the twenty years leading up to 1861—improved only imperceptibly with annexation to the Kingdom of Italy. The north shows an opposite trend, however: although average heights were increasing in pre-1861 Italy, they slowed down, albeit imperceptibly, after unification.

A second lesson concerns the years between the two world wars. The more recent historiography describes these years as a period of contrast. The roaring 1920s (in which per-capita GDP increased by 3.1 percent a year) were followed by the troubled 1930s (+ 0.1 percent); the average incomes of the regions showed a rapid polarization process. While some indicators, such as child mortality or life expectancy, show improvements in line with international trends, others (such as widespread undernourishment, the incidence of absolute poverty, and enjoyment of civil rights and political freedoms) indicate a clear worsening of living conditions. The statistics on stature presented in this chapter temper the contradictory nature of these years by portraying them in rosier hues, on the whole. The average height of the Italians increased more rapidly between 1910 and 1950 than the overall hundred-year trend, despite the disastrous events occurring in this time period: two world wars and the worst economic crisis ever experienced by modern economies. Our econometric exercises suggest that the significant decline in child mortality counted for more than the disappointing growth in income, a pattern seen throughout Europe in the period (Hatton 2013). Still, in general, our models underpredict height improvement in much of this period, so there were clearly other factors at work, about which we can only speculate at this point. Was there a decline in illnesses during later childhood? Or a fall in malaria morbidity due to reclamation projects and later DDT spraying? Did diets improve, or did inequality perhaps decline? What of changes in the nature of children's labor and stress levels? Did the health of girls and young women prior to, and during, pregnancy improve particularly? And could the improvement in height mean that other aspects of child development, including cognitive abilities, were also favored (Heckman and Rubistein 2001)? We cannot say, but there is a clear suggestion that some positive, possibly synergistic, developments were under way.

The third lesson springs from an analysis of the time and space of the progress in statures recorded during the twentieth century. If this progress had been dominated by improvements in public hygiene and by innovations in medical science, and if these processes had been spread all over the country through state action, then we should have seen improvements in height that were *uniform* and approximately *synchronous* throughout the country. The results illustrated in this chapter show that this is not the case: the data revealed geographically localized improvements that were staggered over time and clearly dependent on local economic conditions. The convergence in the Italians' stature, as we saw, was the exception rather than the rule. This suggests that local economic conditions played a very important part in explaining local progress at a time when the most significant advances—the ones recorded by medical and scientific technology as well as those deriving from public infrastructure— were not (or should have been) due to local income. The *national* policymaking in the twentieth century seems not to have been able to cope with the biological inequalities or promote a real integration of the country. This political class was not up to the task.

The persistence of differences between the regions does not leave room for any complacency, all the more so if we add differences found among the social classes. Recent studies show that obtaining a secondary education diploma confers an advantage of + 1.75 cm with respect to those who only finished lower secondary school—and this bonus increases to + 2.19 cm for those who completed university education (Peracchi 2008; Cavelaars et al. 2000). These differences lie within a context of prematurely decelerating growth: the average height of the Italians born in the years 1966–1970 was the second-shortest in Europe, but its growth slowed dramatically over the 1970s, falling well below not only historically small-stature countries like Portugal or Spain but also taller nations such as Austria or the Netherlands (Hatton and Bray 2010). Recent history on statures suggests, therefore, that in terms of wellbeing, the Italians have not yet entered a golden age.

Appendix—Sources and Methods

Figure 2.1 Children's height as a measure of social differences, Turin ca. 1875 Our processing of data from Pagliani (1878) and Cacciari et al. (2002).

Figure 2.B1 *A Mother* (Mario Ingrosso, 1965) Picture by the neorealist photographer Mario Ingrosso: Frusci, Italy, 1965. Source: http://www.centrofotografia.org/img/images/thumb_2729.jpg

Figure 2.2 Alfred and Harry, monozygotic twins separated at birth Shields (1962), cit. in Tanner (1989, 121)

Figure 2.B2 Shrinking populations Northern Italy: A'Hearn (2003); United Kingdom: Cinnirella (2008); United States: Costa, Bleakley and Lleras-Muney (2013).

Figure 2.3 The average height of conscripts aged 20 years The data used are the ones provided in the Torre Reports (section 10), which are difficult to use for three main reasons: (*a*) *age* at the time of measurement is not constant over time—from 17.8 years for those born in 1900 (military draft of 1918) to 20.7 years for those born in 1873 (draft of 1984); (*b*) those measured of each cohort include the *rimandati* (those "subject to review"), that is, individuals deemed temporarily unsuitable for military service in previous drafts and who were then reexamined in medicals of later drafts; (*c*) statures for a fraction of the conscripts are missing because some of them did not turn up at the military medical (*non comparsi*—"not present").

The problem of those not turning up (the *non comparsi*) has negligible effects on the final estimates. The problem of age was dealt with in a recent work (A'Hearn, Peracchi, and Vecchi 2009) by employing a semiparametric method deriving from

a compromise—that of "letting the data speak for themselves," without imposing a parametric structure on the height distribution. The approach adopted in
this chapter is different—simpler, but less flexible. The conviction is that, faced
with old and "faulty" statistical material, as is the case with nineteenth-century
anthropometric data, it is worth including—formally and transparently—the
scholar's aprioristic knowledge, namely a set of constraints set by human growth
biology. Concretely, the method used proceeds by estimating the following equations by means of an ordinary least squares regression:

$$H_{it} = \alpha_i + \beta_{1i}A_t + \beta_{2i}A_t^2 + \theta_i R_{it} + \gamma_{1i}t + \gamma_{2i}t^2 + \gamma_{3i}t^3 + e_{it}$$
$$S_{it} = \delta_i + \phi_{1i}A_t + \phi_{2i}A_t^2 + \eta_i R_{it} + \lambda_{1i}t + \lambda_{2i}t^2 + \lambda_{3i}t^3 + v_{it}$$

$$(1)$$

where H_{it} and S_{it} stand for the mean and standard deviation of height in the
i-th province for those born in year t, A_t is the natural logarithm of mean age at
the time of measurement, R_{it} is the share of *rimandati* out of the total individuals measured, and t, t^2, and t^3 are the terms of a deterministic cubic trend. All
the parameters are specific to each province. The next step consists of imposing the following constraints on the parameters of the equation (1): $\beta_1 \geq 0$,
$\phi \leq 0$, $\eta \leq 0$ e $\theta = 0$. We also impose that the age effect decreases as age
increases up to becoming zero at age 22 years. All these constraints assure
that the values predicted by (1) satisfy some of the basic "laws" of human body
growth explained in the text. Once the restricted version of (1) was estimated,
we then calculated the mean and standard deviation of the height distribution
as follows:

$$H_{it} - \bar{H}_{it} = \phi_{1i}(A_t - \bar{A}) + \phi_{2i}(A_t^2 - \bar{A}^2)$$
$$\bar{S}_{it} = S_{it} - \phi_{1i}(A_t - \bar{A}) - \phi_{2i}(A_t^2 - \bar{A}^2) - \hat{\eta}(R_{it} - \bar{R})$$

$$(2)$$

To facilitate comparisons with other published series, the target age was fixed
at 20 years and the share of *rimandati* at 0.20 (instead of zero, in order to avoid
extrapolating the values in an interval outside the sample).

Once the provincial data were adjusted, through (2), for the age effect and
the presence of *rimandati*, it became necessary to aggregate provincial means
and variances to obtain the corresponding parameters at regional, macro-area
and national level. For the average height, aggregation is an immediate question
since it is enough to calculate the weighted averages of the provincial means.
As weightings we used the population aged 15–25 years present (census data
linearly interpolated for intermediate years). We used the following expression
in order to aggregate the standard deviations:

$$\mathrm{var}(H_t) = \sum w_{it}\left(\bar{H}_{it} - \bar{\bar{H}}_{it}\right)^2 + \sum w_{it}\bar{S}_{it}^2$$

$$(3)$$

where $\bar{H}_{it}$ derives from (2), $\bar{\bar{H}}_t$ is the mean of the provincial averages, and w_{it} is the weight (the number of individuals measured each year not counting the *rimandati*).

Figure 2.B3 Average female heights in the world The figure is the result of our estimates on data from the Demographic Health Surveys (DHS), available at: http://www.measuredhs.com. The databases used refer to February 2015.

Figure 2.4 Five paths to modern statures The graph plots average heights, aggregated and adjusted to age 20 and a 20 percent share of *rimandati* as described in the notes to Figure 2.3, for five macro-areas. These are defined as follows. *Northeast*: Veneto, Emilia-Romagna, Trentino–Alto Adige, Friuli–Venezia Giulia; *Northwest*: Piemonte (including Valle d'Aosta), Liguria, Lombardia; *Center*: Toscana, Marche, Umbria, Lazio; *South*: Abruzzi-Molise, Campania, Puglia, Basilicata, Calabria; *Islands*: Sicily and Sardinia.

Figure 2.5 The growth of the Italians, 1861–1910 (average height of conscripts per province) The maps for 1861 and 1910 display average heights of conscripts born in those years, adjusted as described in the notes for Figure 2.4, for the 69 provinces into which the Italian territory was divided at the time (Caserta and Napoli provinces being aggregated throughout, however, due to later changes in boundaries). The maps for the generations of 1951 and 1981 depict the official mean heights reported by Istat in the *Sommario di Statistiche Storiche* (with Valle d'Aosta suppressed and Abruzzo and Molise always aggregated). To allow the variability of mean heights to emerge fully in the maps, the categories denoted by each color change over time. For example, the darkest blue refers to heights of at least 164 cm in 1861, 166 cm in 1910, 174 cm in 1951, and 176 cm in 1981.

Figure 2.6 The fall, rise, and fall of regional disparities The graph plots the standard deviation of regional means for the years 1910 and earlier, adjusted as described in the notes for Figure 2.4. Post-1910, Valle d'Aosta is omitted and Abruzzo aggregated with Molise when these three regions are reported separately. Otherwise, no aggregations or omissions are made when new regions arise through territorial expansion or administrative organization (e.g., the creation of Friuli–Venezia Giulia from part of the old Veneto region and newly annexed territories). Calculating the dispersion of regional means using a consistent set of regions throughout yields a pattern very close to that in Figure 2.6.

Figure 2.7 Catch-up and fall-back in four periods The graph shows the initial level and subsequent growth of regional mean heights (adjusted as described in the notes to Figure 2.5 for the period before 1910, using official Istat figures thereafter) for several intervals of time: 1861–1888, 1888–1936, 1936–1973, 1973–1980. The markers each indicate a particular region, and are proportional in size to regional population (interpolated between census years). The best-fit lines are the predicted values from an ordinary least squares regression of the change in regional mean height on its initial level.

Figure 2.8 Height, health, and income over time We have used the logarithm of real per-capita GDP (taken from chapter 7, "Income") because, beyond some point, extra income is no longer able to buy much improved health, and better health does not buy much greater height. A preliminary examination of the data clearly revealed just such a nonlinearity in the height-income relationship. We do *not* transform child mortality (data taken from chapter 3, "Health") by taking its logarithm because the variable is trending down toward a lower bound of zero. The *logarithm* of mortality would change by the same amount as it decreased from 200 to 100 per thousand, and when it decreased from 2 to 1 per thousand, which we would not expect to have the same impact on stature. Nor do we transform heights, preferring to keep them in their natural units of measure, centimeters.

Figure 2.9 The determinants of mean height The graph is based on estimates of the following model.

Table 2.1 **Regression of national mean height on a time trend, income per capita, and infant mortality**

Variables	Mean height
trend	0.0371***
	(0.00940)
Log of GDP per capita	2.350***
	(0.200)
infant mortality	−0.0152***
	(0.00526)
Constant	164.2***
	(1.302)
Observations	103
R-squared	0.981

Standard errors in parentheses

*** p<0.01, ** p<0.05, * p<0.1

A model with differences in variables, instead of levels, produces similar results.

Table 2.2 **Regression of the change in mean height on the changes in income per capita and infant mortality**

Variables	Change in mean height
Change in log GDP per capita	2.345**
	(0.766)
Change in infant mortality	−0.0154
	(0.0145)
Constant	0.267
	(0.293)
Observations	12
R-squared	0.590

Standard errors in parentheses

*** p<0.01, ** p<0.05, * p<0.1

In this second regression, because it is *chronically* bad living conditions that affect adult height, we consider changes over approximately decade-long intervals. To further insure against the possibility of the chosen years being unusual ones (a business cycle trough, say, or an epidemic), we smoothed the variables by using a five-year moving average before differencing.

Table 2.3 **Regression of regional mean heights on a time trend, income per capita, and infant mortality, at ten-year intervals**

Variables	Regional mean height
Change in log GDP per capita	2.188***
	(0.200)
Smoothed infant mortality	−0.0244***
	(0.00509)
trend	0.0253**
	(0.0104)
Constant	150.7***
	(2.018)
Observations	155
Number of regnum	18
R-squared	0.967

Standard errors in parentheses

*** p<0.01, ** p<0.05, * p<0.1

Figure 2.10 Height, health, and wealth across space The sources were the same ones used in Figure 2.8. In order to smooth out the volatility of annual child mortality rates, a five-year moving average was calculated.

Figure 2.11 Persistent regional height differences explained, and section 6.2 The graph is based on estimates of the following model. The regional fixed effects are not reported.

Section 6.2 also deals with the following two models.

Table 2.4 **Fixed effects regression of regional mean heights on income per capita and infant mortality**

Variables	Regional mean height
Log of GDP per capita	3.232***
	(0.347)
Smoothed infant mortality	−0.0299***
	(0.00384)
Constant	144.5***
	(3.263)
Observations	155
R-squared	0.880

Standard errors in parentheses

*** p<0.01, ** p<0.05, * p<0.1

Table 2.5 **Regression of the change in regional mean height on the changes in income per capita and infant mortality**

Variables	Change in regional mean height
Change in log GDP per capita	1.281***
	(0.316)
Change in smoothed infant mortality	−0.0224***
	(0.00407)
Constant	0.537***
	(0.158)
Observations	137
R-squared	0.234

Standard errors in parentheses

*** p<0.01, ** p<0.05, * p<0.1

Figure 2.12 Share of heights 170 cm or more in selected regions The sources and adjustment method of the data follow the ones described in the notes to Figure 2.4.

Figure 2.13 Italy's unification had no effect on the stature of the Italians The source is the Torre Reports (see Figure 2.3 for details). Two linear trends are estimated separately prior to and after the year 1861.

3

Health

WITH VINCENZO ATELLA AND SILVIA FRANCISCI

1 The Right to Health

Health is a fundamental component of the physical and mental wellbeing of any individual and society. In 1946 the World Health Organization (WHO) stated the following with regard to the *right* to health: "the enjoyment of the highest attainable standard of health is one of the fundamental rights of every human being, without distinction of race, religion, political belief, economic or social condition" (WHO 1946). The following year the very same right was acknowledged by the Constitution of the Italian Republic, in article 32, which reads: "The Republic safeguards health as a fundamental right of the individual and as a collective interest, and guarantees free medical care to the indigent."

The affirmation of the right to health in the Italian Constitution is the endpoint of a process that began in the late nineteenth century, when the Crispi government created a Public Health Directorate inside the Interior Ministry. At the same time, however, this affirmation is a starting point: the Constitution has a normative nature in that it prescribes what citizens and institutions must and must not do; but, as with all prescriptions, these indications may be followed and respected or not (Onida 2007). In this chapter we thus aim to go through the process that led Italy to include health among its constitutionally guaranteed rights, by documenting to what *extent* and in what *ways* the affirmation of a principle has actually been achieved in the Italian population's everyday life over the 150 years of the country's postunification history. What do we learn by analyzing the country's history through the data at hand?

The attention devoted to measurement is a strength of this chapter. We shall, in fact, present the results of a laborious reconstruction of the trend of the most significant epidemiological indicators—from longevity to child mortality, from the general death rate to an analysis of its structure by cause, from the risk of getting ill to the probability of surviving a certain illness. Each indicator manages to grasp one of the many dimensions characterizing the population's state of health by describing what happened in specific historical periods over the century-and-a-half under consideration. However, no indicator, taken singly, can fully describe the progress recorded over the long period of time concerned. We shall thus bring together and substitute indicators that lose their capacity to account for development in the population's state of health with other indicators capable of grasping current trends.

We shall compare and contrast the process of improvement of the living conditions of the Italians, as shown by epidemiological indicators, with the one described by the gross domestic product (GDP)—the indicator that economists most commonly use in order to describe a country's wellbeing. As we shall see, this exercise is useful because it reveals how, with regard to wellbeing, GDP does not tell us the whole story, and not always the right one.

The second aspect at the heart of the chapter concerns the *universality* of the right to health, which must be guaranteed to *all* citizens. This aspect is stressed in the article following the aforementioned one of the WHO Constitution: "The extension to all peoples of the benefits of medical, psychological and related knowledge is essential to the fullest attainment of health" (WHO 1946). The concept is also found in the Italian Constitution, which reads that the state guarantees "free medical care to the indigent" (article 32). In the second part of this chapter we shall thus focus on *distributive equity*: over the course of economic development, have the benefits recorded with regard to health reached all parts of the country—the cities as much as the countryside, children as much as the elderly, women as much as men?

Italian historiography does not offer a comprehensive answer to this question. We know the existence of a territorial gradient, but we do not have an overall picture explaining the distributional aspects of Italy's postunification history. We shall try to fill in this gap in the second part of the chapter. The country's average progress must be read jointly with the equity of how it is distributed: only in this way can one appreciate just how much public action has been able to implement—*de facto* as well as *de jure*—the declaration of the principle stated in article 32 of the Constitution: health is a right belonging to all Italian citizens.

2 Long Live the Italians

Italy ranks among those countries in the world where people live the longest. The rankings compiled by international agencies do not always agree on how they rate Italy, but the conclusion is a robust one. In the latest data, issued in 2012 by the WHO's Global Health Observatory, Italy ranks fourth in the world, after Japan, Switzerland, and Australia, in a list of over two hundred countries.

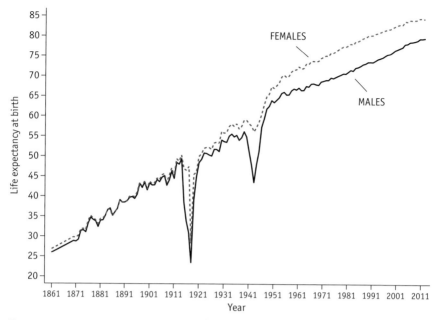

Figure 3.1 LIFE EXPECTANCY AT BIRTH, ITALY 1861–2012. The graph shows the trend in life expectancy at birth (vertical axis), over time (horizontal axis), separately for men and women.

The statistical indicator used for measuring longevity is called "life expectancy at birth" and measures the number of years that an individual can expect to live, on average, at the time of birth.[1] The Italian National Institute of Statistics (Istat) estimates that children born in 2011 in Italy can expect to live an average 82 years, and this expectancy goes up a couple of years or so if it is a baby girl (life expectancy for women is 84.8 years as against 79.3 years for men). The achievement of 82 years of average life is a considerable success if we consider that at the time of the Kingdom of Italy, in 1861, children's life expectancy at birth did not exceed 29 to 30 years. Longevity is probably the most eloquent achievement in the country's history.

Figure 3.1 shows that the process of lengthening average life expectancy has had an approximately linear trend, broken only in the war years.[2] Over the 150 years examined, the Italians have, on average, gained four months of life a

---

[1] Life expectancy at birth is commonly indicated with the expression "e0" (pronounced "e with zero"). It is possible to work out life expectancy at other ages. For example, life expectancy at 5 years of age ("e5") indicates the years that a person can expect to live starting from their fifth birthday. More generally, demographers indicate life expectancy at age x as "ex."

[2] The sharpness of the peak in mortality corresponding to World War I is due to other concomitant negative events: the earthquake in the Marsica area of the Abruzzo region (1915) and the so-called Spanish flu, the most devastating influenza pandemic (1918–1919) in modern history (Pinnelli and Mancini 1999).

year: every three years, newborn babies in the Kingdom had a life expectancy one year longer than the one of babies born just three years earlier.

Figure 3.1 highlights other aspects worth commenting. The first concerns the extraordinary *backwardness* of the country's average living conditions at the time of unification. The data estimated for 1861 show very modest progress even when compared to the remote past. For instance, if we consider the case of ancient Rome—which has been studied at length by historians and demographers alike—the estimates for life expectancy indicate values fluctuating around twenty-five years, and well express the idea of just how much living conditions in 1861 were more similar to those prevailing two thousand years earlier than the ones found today, "just" a hundred and fifty years later (Hopkins 1966).

If we compare Italy with other countries during the same period, the mid-nineteenth century, we will see that, on average, Italians lived ten years less than the French and sixteen to seventeen years less than the Swedes. In today's world, no country has a life expectancy as low as the one of mid-nineteenth-century Italy. According to WHO figures, the poorest countries of our planet today—all located in sub-Saharan Africa—have a life expectancy at birth of around forty years or above.

Italy's backwardness, measured through life expectancy, is much greater than the one emerging in comparisons—so dear to economists—based on per-capita GDP. The comparison with Sweden is very revealing. According to estimates by Maddison (2010), in 1861 Sweden was poorer than Italy (by about 5 percent in terms of per-capita GDP); but, as we saw earlier, it had a higher life expectancy—16–17 years higher than Italy. Hence, longevity and GDP do not tell the same story, and the overall lesson is the following: to get a more complete picture on the average progress achieved in a nation's wellbeing, per-capita GDP is not only insufficient but may also be misleading.

A second comment concerns *gender differences*. Figure 3.1 shows this clearly: up to World War I, being born a boy or a girl did not make much difference with regard to life expectancy.[3] Differences in life expectancy between men and women started to appear in the period between the two world wars, even if the gap widened considerably after World War II. On the eve of World War II, women had already gained three years of life more than men—a gap that broadened after the war to arrive at almost seven years more in the late 1970s. However, there has been an inverse trend since the latter half of the 1990s: the latest figures show that women live 5.5 years longer, on average, than men.[4]

---

[3] A tendency toward a much greater male mortality in some child and teenage age groups was already seen in the early years of postunification Italy (Mineo and Giammanco 1968).

[4] Currently, 60 percent of women's advantage is due to a lower mortality for heart disease and cancer, which together account for 70 percent of overall mortality (Istat-Iss 1999; Istat 2005; Egidi 2007). The phenomenon is common to most industrialized countries and is partly explained by the change in lifestyles, but especially by the fact that two pathologies—heart disease and cancer—are more commonly found in their gravest forms in men rather than in women (section 9).

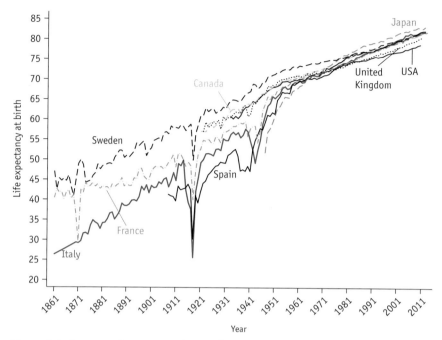

Figure 3.2 AVERAGE LIFESPAN IN ITALY COMPARED TO THE REST OF THE WORLD (SINCE 1861). The graph compares trends in life expectancy at birth (vertical axis) of Italy (blue line) and other countries. The process of convergence over the decades, broken only in the interwar years, accelerates visibly after.

To grasp the breadth of the *progress* achieved by Italy with regard to longevity over the postunification period, it is worth making some international comparisons. Figure 3.2 shows a history of chasing, catching up, and overtaking. We have decided to compare Italy with a small but significant group of countries including Japan (the country with the highest life expectancy today); the United States (the richest country in terms of per-capita GDP); France, Spain, and the United Kingdom (Italy's neighbors); Sweden (the country with the most generous healthcare system); and Canada (the United States' neighbor, but with a mostly public healthcare system, similar to those found in Western European countries).

The figure shows that during the first fifty years of postunification Italy, the country caught up with France (despite the fact that the latter had a 35 percent higher per-capita GDP than the Italian one). Italian life expectancy interrupted its increasing trend between the two world wars (interrupting its *relative* catching up with other countries, but continuing its increasing trend in *absolute* terms), but resumed its increasing trend in the aftermath of World War II. The late 1960s and early 1970s saw Italy overtaking the life expectancy of other countries that were leaders in this field, with the exception of Japan, Switzerland, and Australia, as we saw earlier.

Once again, the trend seen for life expectancy tells a different story than the one based on per-capita GDP: compared to the same countries considered in Figure 3.2, the success in terms of life expectancy does not correspond to a similar phenomenon when we look at per-capita GDP. Indeed, in 1870, Italy's per-capita GDP was higher than GDP in Japan and Spain, but lower than that of all the other countries considered. After a period of 150 years, Italian per-capita GDP remains lower than that of all the other countries (Italy is below all the others and has been caught up by Spain).

While life expectancy unequivocally tells a success story, two issues still remain. The first concerns the capacity of the "life expectancy at birth" indicator to adequately grasp the scale of the progress achieved in recent decades; marginal gains in terms of longevity are lower, and it becomes fundamental to turn our attention not only to the *quantity* (duration) of life, but also to the *quality* of life. The second issue to be examined concerns the causes of the spectacular increase in longevity: Which factors are responsible?

Measuring the *quality* of the years of life is a complex issue that calls for defining (before measuring) what can be considered a state of "good health."[5] Some *objective* measures have been proposed that identify good health as the absence of specific pathologies (for example, chronic diseases or cancer), whether they be declared by the individuals or clinically ascertained; *subjective* measures have also been put forward, based on individual perceptions of one's state of health. If we consider the "life expectancy in good health" indicator—constructed on the basis of life expectancy at birth, adjusted for the number of years lived with health problems—Italy confirms its position of wellbeing in international comparisons. WHO data relating to the last decade put Italy behind Japan, Switzerland, and Australia, but ahead of the other 194 countries of the world.[6]

On the whole, the progress made in life expectancy at birth (also in the modified versions that take into account aspects pertaining to the quality of life) leads us to conclude that the longevity of the Italians has increased in an extraordinary manner, both in absolute terms and as regards international standards. *Hic breve vivitur* ("life is short here") was written with reference to ancient Rome (Burn 1953), and the same could have been written in the aftermath of Italy's unification; *hic diu vivitur* ("you live long here") one can say today, not without some pride, a century and a half since unification.

---

[5] Economists and epidemiologists have long been dealing with measuring the quality of years of life without ever managing to establish any one preferable indicator (Torrance 1976; Jones 1977; Pliskin, Shepard, and Weinstein 1980).

[6] The index used by the WHO is called HALE (Health Adjusted Life Expectancy) and it does not only consider mortality, but also the multiplicity of conditions compromising part of an individual's wellbeing. Similar results can be obtained by looking at the DFLE (Disability Free Life Expectancy) index, similar to the HALE index, and where the adjustment is based on the prevalence of disability.

Behind the lengthening of lifespan, we find the dynamics of survival and its main determinants: improvements in public health services, progress in medicine (the introduction of prevention treatments and medical therapies), economic growth (responsible for improved nutrition), progress in terms of behavior (hygiene practices), and the role of better education and of environmental reclamation initiatives (Riley 2001). To unravel the relative importance of these factors, we must go beyond the analysis of mere life expectancy and broaden the picture by considering other indicators enabling us to distinguish what components—which pathologies, which categories of people—influence the dynamics involved. This is the task of the remaining part of this chapter.

3 We Don't Die Like We Used To

A picture that, in some respects, mirrors the one of life expectancy is provided by the trend in the general mortality of the population (Figure 3.3). The "raw

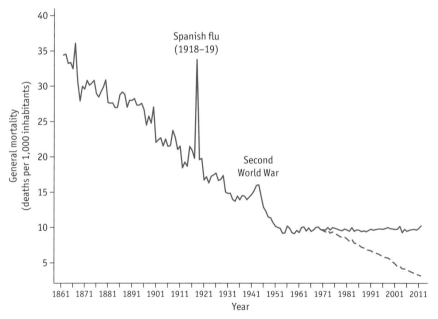

Figure 3.3 GENERAL MORTALITY, 1863–2012. The figure shows the trend in overall mortality for all causes (vertical axis) over time (horizontal axis). The unbroken line shows the *raw* death rate (deaths per 1,000 inhabitants) and the broken line shows the *standardized* death rate according to age (deaths per 1,000 inhabitants, the estimate adjusted to account for the population's age structure), available only as of 1970. The standardized death rate allows us to highlight improvements in the population's state of health even in more recent times, when the ageing of the Italian population tends to mask them.

general mortality rate" is defined as the total number of deaths recorded in the country in a certain year for every one thousand individuals. For example, a death rate of 20 means that, in that particular year, 20 people died out of every thousand inhabitants—which is to say, 2 percent of the population. It is considered that 45–50 deaths per thousand people represents a maximum figure that a society cannot sustain for very long, and is seen during exceptional times such as during a plague, famine, or the like (Rowland 2003); no country in the world today has a death rate above 30 per thousand (WHO 2010).

Figure 3.3 shows the trend in the overall mortality rate of the Italians over the last hundred and fifty years or so. The interesting aspects concern not only the lower number of deaths per thousand inhabitants (from 30 to fewer than 10), but also their lower *variability* over time (something that can be seen also in the life expectancy at birth curve). The peaks seen during the first hundred years since unification (notably the one immediately after World War I that reflects the outcome of the war and the Spanish flu epidemic) have become increasingly rare: mortality crises were frequent in the past, owing to serious famines and pandemics, but then became rarer, going on to disappear completely since World War II (Del Panta 1980)[7].

Around the mid 1950s, general mortality reached a plateau. Since then there have been no signs of improvement: mortality fluctuates within a narrow band between 9 and 10 deaths per thousand inhabitants—a figure found in most industrialized countries. The interpretation of the plateau shown in Figure 3.3 is not mundane and conceals a very interesting phenomenon. In particular, the fact that general mortality has reached a low point must not lead us to think that the progress made with respect to the death rate has come to a halt. To understand this point, we need to know the effects of population aging on the general death rate. With other factors being equal, the older a population is, the higher the associated death rate. In 2010 an "elderly" country like Italy (where 20 percent of the population is over 65 years old) had a death rate of 10 per thousand inhabitants; in the same year, Kuwait, a much "younger" country (only 2.7 percent of the population are aged over 65 years), had a death rate of 2 per

---

[7] The Spanish flu epidemic killed more people in one year than the bubonic plague did in a hundred years during the Middle Ages. Half a billion people are estimated to have been affected—just under a third of the whole world population of the times (Taubenberger and Morens 2006). The total deaths, some 40–50 million people, shows the extraordinary lethalness of Spanish flu: 2.5 percent of those who contracted the flu died, compared to the 0.1 percent of other flu epidemics (Taubenberger 2005). Sydenstricker and King (1931) showed how the victims tended to be concentrated in the less privileged classes of the population. The onset and characteristics of the Spanish flu epidemic in Italy were much like those in the rest of Europe, but with a much higher number of deaths: around 274,000 during the autumn phase. It is difficult, if not impossible, to establish the exact number of dead owing to the chaos created by the war and the change in Italy's frontiers (Tognotti 2002). Estimates of the deaths due to Spanish flu range from 300,000 to 600,000 (Maraffino 2010).

thousand inhabitants. The difference in general death rates between the two countries is not due to the fact that the Kuwaiti population enjoys better health, on average (in other words, that Kuwaitis show a better capacity to treat illness and lengthen their own life expectancy), but simply to the fact that Kuwait has a significantly younger population compared to Italy's.

The above example contains a general lesson: differences in demographic structure risk compromising comparisons based on raw overall death rates, both between populations and within the same population in different periods. Population aging alters the age structure of the population itself and creates a distorted view of the progress achieved with regard to mortality.

The solution to the problem consists of supplementing the raw death rate (the unbroken line in Figure 3.3) with a standardized death rate (the broken line), which can neutralize the effects of an aging population. While the raw death rate provides the *real* scale of the phenomenon (the number of deaths per thousand inhabitants), the age-standardized death rate is more suitable for comparisons in different time periods because they are conducted with *demographic structures being equal*: this adjustment allows us to appreciate the progress achieved by the Italians with regard to mortality even over the last fifty years. This very clearly emerges in Figure 3.3: the broken line can be interpreted as the trend in death rate that we would have observed if the population, instead of aging, had maintained a constant demographic structure, the same as the one observed in the 1970s. The conclusion is thus clear: although starting from extraordinarily backward initial conditions, Italy caught up with the more virtuous countries characterized by the lowest death rates in the world.

4 From the Greek Word *Nosos* (νόσος), "Illness"

Reconstructing the evolution of the nosological picture is a difficult, but fruitful, task. Understanding morbidity and mortality with respect to pathology is actually a fundamental analytical step in finding the *causal* connections behind the success of the longevity of the Italians, and also in grasping *who* has benefited from health progress within the Italian population and *when*.

Figure 3.4 shows how the picture of pathologies changes considerably over the 120 years examined (Pozzi 1990)[8]. In 1881, the first year for which we have

---

[8] From a methodological angle, reconstructing death statistics according to cause of death is no easy task. The ability to recognize an illness and to ascribe a death in the final stages of the illness has changed over time and probably unevenly so in Italy. We have used the International Classification of Diseases (ICD), considering the selection of large groups of causes proposed by Istat. The ICD has been updated over the years (and is currently in its 11th revised edition) to increase the details of the categories concerned, but this did not affect our analysis because we used an aggregate classification

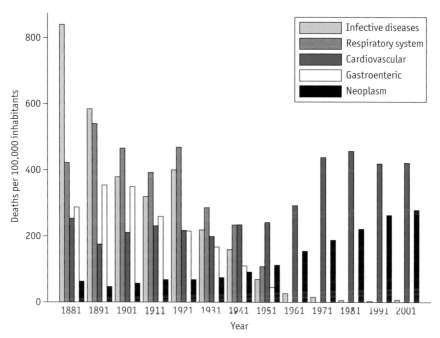

Figure 3.4 WHAT PEOPLE USED TO, AND STILL, DIE OF IN ITALY, 1881–2001. The graph shows the evolution of the main causes of death in the period 1881–2001. The above values have been adjusted with a 10-period moving average.

useful data, the main cause of death was *infective diseases*, a category includ-ing many pathologies existing today—measles, whooping cough, and scarlet fever, but also others that have completely, or almost, disappeared today in Italy: smallpox, diphtheria, malaria, and tuberculosis. In 1881 infective diseases accounted for about 30 percent of all deaths in Italy (Caselli 1991). These were followed, in order of importance, by illnesses of the *respiratory system* (bronchi-tis, pneumonia) and influenza, followed by *gastroenteric* disorders. Caselli (ibid.) estimated that both these categories of pathologies accounted for 25 percent of all deaths.

Figure 3.4 shows the main causes of death in the period 1881 through 2001. The trends over the decades emerge with clarity: we see the almost total disap-pearance of deaths caused by infective diseases; deaths caused by gastroenteritis (a pathology linked to environmental, socioeconomic, and climatic conditions) decrease as do those due to pneumonia, bronchitis, and influenza (all coming under the category of "respiratory system" pathologies in Figure 3.4). Alongside the decrease in these pathologies, what also clearly emerges is the gradual

for large groups of causes. However, we cannot rule out possible incongruities for 1968 when, in the shift from the 7th to the 8th edition, brain vascular damage (hemorrhages, ischemia, etc.) was placed in the category of circulatory system illnesses (it had previously been included among the central nervous system pathologies).

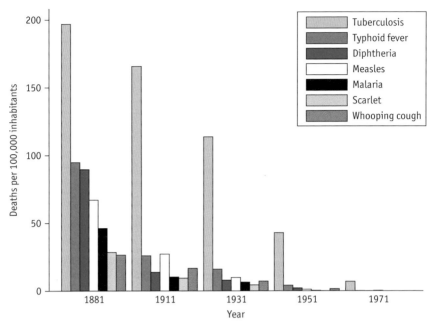

Figure 3.5 THE ERADICATION OF MORTALITY FOR INFECTIVE DISEASES. The higher the bar in the histogram, the greater the mortality associated with that pathology (different colors stand for different diseases). The figure shows that mortality has decreased over time for all pathologies: except for tuberculosis, this process of eradication of mortality was all but complete by 1951. Italy's "economic miracle" has no equivalent in health indicators.

increase in certain *chronic* diseases (the ones linked to the cardiovascular system and to cancer) that accompany the population aging process[9].

In Figure 3.5 we examine the development of infective diseases in greater detail. This is particularly interesting in that the drop in the death rate for these diseases has implications, as we shall see, that are very instructive on the development of the living conditions of the Italians. Figure 3.5 shows the trend in mortality associated with seven pathologies belonging to the category of infective diseases: tuberculosis, typhoid fever, diphtheria, measles, malaria, scarlet fever, and whooping cough. The picture that emerges shows rapid progress leading to the almost complete eradication of deaths owing to infective diseases at the national level.

It is worth noting that deaths due to infective diseases in Italy were down to almost zero during World War II and in its aftermath, and thus before the average income of the Italians "took off". There is thus no synchronicity between

---

[9] Other pathologies, not considered here for reasons of space, are also on the rise: diabetes, neurodegenerative diseases (such as Alzheimer's disease and Parkinson's disease), and asthmatic ailments.

the "economic miracle" in the post–World War II years and the eradication of mortality caused by infective diseases: the latter preceded the former. Not only this, but if we focus on the years 1881–1911, we will see that the trend in GDP seems to grasp little or nothing of the progress highlighted in Figure 3.5, and has probably little to do also with the underlying causes of the eradication of mortality for infective diseases. The latter result is due not only to the overall improvement in hygiene-health conditions, linked to income, but also to spreading knowledge in the medical field, vaccines, and pharmaceuticals—factors that are essentially not correlated to the country's economic growth.

Pharmacology, in particular, made a decisive contribution to improving the population's health conditions with a development accompanying that of the nosological picture examined in this section. The earliest contributions date back to the early 1900s, thanks to discoveries concerning vitamins, the antibacterial qualities of some sulfamides, and the therapeutic effects of insulin in diabetes treatment. Pharmacological therapy started taking on a leading role during World War II. The early 1950s saw important steps forward in the treatment and prevention of cardiovascular diseases, with the use of antihypertensive drugs (diuretics, calico-antagonists, beta blockers). The first therapy for metastasized cancer dates back to 1956. Later, in 1965, *official pharmacopeia* recognized sulfamides, antibiotics, antihistamines, cortisones, vitamins, hormones, oral antidiabetic agents, anti-inflammatory drugs, oral contraceptives, psychiatric drugs, and other specific vaccines and serums.[10] This changed pharmacological picture enabled the eradication of infective diseases—soon categorized as "diseases of the past"—and their replacement with diseases characterized by a multiplicity of risk factors, such as heart disease and cancer.

4.1 DEADLY TUBERCULOSIS

To explore the way the death rate for infective diseases decreased, shown in Figure 3.5, we shall consider the case of *tuberculosis* in more detail. In the mid-nineteenth century, tuberculosis accounted for more deaths than any other disease in Italy: about 220 out of every 100,000 people. It was an "obstinate and deadly" scourge, well known from time immemorial and feared like few others (Parola 1849). What made this pathology frightening was not just the painful suffering that it entailed, but also the relative ease of contagion. Tuberculosis

---

[10] Alongside the development of these pharmaceutical drugs, the pharmaceutical industry is working on complementary therapies in order to make chemotherapy less toxic and more tolerable: new adjuvant substances, antiemetic drugs, and anti-anemic drugs. Around the early 1990s, the appearance of new generation antipsychotic drugs enabled the treatment of even the most serious psychiatric patients in their own home, with positive effects for patients—who can now conduct a normal working and relational life—and for the hospital system.

is transmitted by inhaling a bacterium, and transmission through the air significantly increases the risk of contracting the infection. In nineteenth-century Italy, dwellings—overcrowded rooms—and working activities conducted in close and stuffy environments in the presence of people with this disease in the active phase made the less privileged classes of the population particularly exposed to it.[11]

In 1882 Robert Koch (1843–1910) discovered the pathogen (i.e., the infecting microorganism) of tuberculosis, *Mycobacterium tuberculosis*, showing for the first time the existence of a causal effect between a specific microorganism and a human disease. The news spread around the world with lightning speed: Koch announced the discovery of the bacterium during a presentation, made at seven o'clock in the evening on 24 March 1882, during the usual monthly meeting of the Berlin Physiology Society. In less than a month the news not only came out in the main scientific journals of the day, but also made the headlines of *The Times* of London and the *New York Times*. Koch had made and revealed a discovery of extraordinary interest for the whole world—something that had been unknown for thousands of years (Sakula 1982).

Once the cause of tuberculosis had been found, what was now needed was a treatment. A decade went by before Hoechst started up production of Tubercolidicin, or tuberculin, a glycerin extract of the tubercle bacilli, making it the new treatment for the disease. However, tuberculin did not turn out to be the hoped for remedy against tuberculosis, but it became an effective diagnostic tool for establishing its existence with certainty.[12]

In the following decades, the social nature of the disease became increasingly clear. It mainly affected the poor classes and spread with ease because of the overcrowding and terrible state of dwellings inside towns and cities, the unhealthy conditions in workshops and public places, the lack of hygiene education, and, in general, the insufficient nutrition of the lower classes.

Although effective treatments or vaccines were unavailable, measures aimed at enhancing prevention increased; that is to say, the degree of social control of the pathology increased. Actions aimed at combating the disease also increased, as much collectively as individually: practices of disinfection were started, dispensaries and sanatoriums were set up, the hypernutrition of the sick was encouraged (a robust organism is less vulnerable to bacteria), environmental reclamation operations were intensified by creating such things as drainage systems, and the fight against overcrowding in urban dwellings and the spreading of hygiene education was promoted.

---

[11] All this was naturally unknown to scientists of the mid-nineteenth century, who had only developed conjectures on the etiology of tuberculosis.

[12] It was observed that injecting tuberculin under the skin in healthy individuals did not produce any kind of reaction, but it caused an intense reaction in those already affected by the disease.

On the whole, all these measures led to a sharp decrease in deaths caused by tuberculosis, and this occurred well before the discovery of streptomycin, the first antibiotic—marketed in Italy in 1947—which would prove to be particularly effective against tuberculosis. The improvements recorded over the decades prior to World War I continued and were significant even during the 1920s and 1930s.[13] The process was a gradual one, though: the strong initial bond between poverty and the disease weakened as medical knowledge and the discovery of effective treatments began to eradicate the pathology in the whole population. Better nutrition of the population—documented in chapter 1 ("Nutrition")—was synergic, and it naturally made people's bodies more resistant to attack by the tuberculosis bacterium.

4.2 MALARIA AND PELLAGRA

As with tuberculosis, the fight against *malaria* lies within the sphere of social medicine, which became established in Italy between the late nineteenth and early twentieth centuries in order to combat diseases affecting specific sections of the population: the poor, lying at the fringes of society. Around 1881, malaria killed over 50 people out of every 100,000 inhabitants of the country.[14] However, this national figure must be interpreted with some caution because, although malaria was an acute and endemic problem in certain regions, it was almost nonexistent in others. In 1881, Basilicata, Calabria, Lazio, and Sardinia had mortality rates ranging from 150 to 200 deaths per 100,000 inhabitants as against the 4–12 deaths per 100,000 people in Liguria, Lombardy, and Marche. Where present, malaria was a factor that was "stable, permanent and strongly conditioning, both from an economic and demographic standpoint" (Rossi 1982, 233) and it hit the "poor" (rural workers) rather than the rich (the great absentee landowners and the "notables," variously classified as lawyers and miscellaneous professionals [Corti 1984]).

It was estimated that, in the 1880s, malaria accounted for more than 10 percent of the overall death rate, with peaks of up to 23 percent in regions like Sicily (Tognotti 1996). It is an interesting pathology for our purposes since malaria is associated with swamplands and is more generally linked to an unhealthy environment. It is, in other words, an illness revealing the degree of backwardness of a region.

---

[13] The Fascist regime's commitment in the fight against tuberculosis is documented in section 8.2. Preti (1982) offers a skeptical view. Tuberculosis was not definitively eradicated with the advent of antibiotics. The 1980s saw the emergence of tuberculosis strains that were "resistant to antibiotics"—something that has received WHO attention ever since.

[14] This imbalance was known to contemporaries and well documented. As early as 1880, the Ministry of the Interior had promoted an enquiry into the spreading of malaria in the country, showing that the situation in the southern regions was more serious even than the rice-growing areas of the north and of the Maremme, where there were also many hotbeds of infection (Torelli 1882).

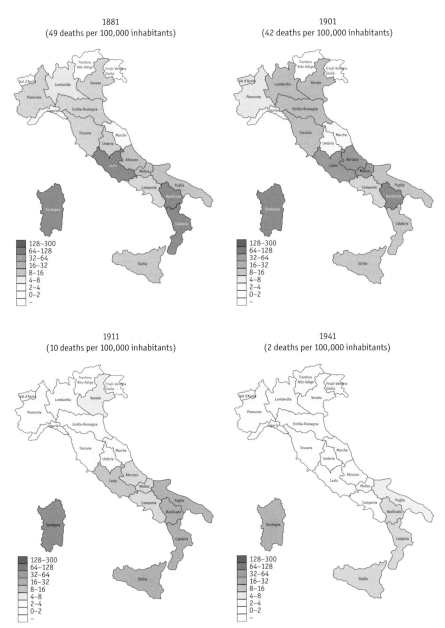

Figure 3.6 AN UNHEALTHY ENVIRONMENT AND MALARIA: MORTALITY IN ITALY'S REGIONS, 1881–1941. The maps show mortality for malaria (the number of deaths per 100,000 inhabitants) for some years between 1881 and 1941. A lighter shade indicates low mortality while a darker shade indicates high mortality.

In Figure 3.6 we have processed the data on malaria deaths, and these statistics enable us to grasp even regional differences. Malaria was combated both
through the reclamation of swamplands and through agricultural transformations, following the view that intensive cultivations are unfavorable to malaria.
The fight against malaria was also carried on through prevention and treatments
and through many legislative actions, starting from the one promoting the dissemination of quinine, which was made freely available to people working in
malaria-infested areas from 1901 onward. The data of 1911 already show significant progress: malaria now accounted for fewer than 10 deaths out of every
100,000 inhabitants.[15]

The decrease in malaria deaths confirms that the factors responsible for this
improvement were manifold—progress in medicine, in public hygiene, and in
economic policymaking—not all of which can be accounted for in the dynamics
of per-capita GDP. Figure 3.6 also shows regional differences; in the years 1881–
1941, in Lazio, the death rate plummeted tenfold, in Basilicata and Calabria
about sixfold, while in Sardinia progress was very modest indeed. In the latter
case, as we shall see further on (Figure 3.16), two other key factors were needed
to root out the disease: chemistry (namely, DDT); and the Americans.

To round off this section, we wish to tell the story of *pellagra* (a term that
originated in the Lombard dialect to indicate the "coarse skin" caused by the
disease [De Bernardi 1984a]). Pellagra deaths accounted for just 0.5 percent of
the overall death rate and so the disease was not quantitatively significant at
the national level. Interest for this disease is justified, however, for two reasons.
The first is the deficiency-related origin of the illness: pellagra is caused by the
non-absorption of B-group vitamins—a result of chronic malnutrition (typically, maize monophagism, that is, a diet essentially based on maize porridge or
polenta). The second reason is that it is a disease that only affected certain social
classes, the workers in rural areas of certain northern regions of the country
(Finzi 1982, 399). These two factors establish a strong connection between the
presence of this disease and the living conditions of the poorest of the poor in
the population, which suggests using pellagra as a marker in order to signal how
successful economic growth was in spreading its benefits to the neediest sections of the population.

By adopting this interpretation, Figure 3.7 leads us to judge the process of
economic growth in these regions positively: in Veneto, Lombardy, and Emilia-
Romagna—the three regions historically more affected by pellagra—the
death rate fell considerably from 1878. The situation was different in the various regions (for Umbria and Marche, not shown in the graph, as with Emilia-
Romagna, pellagra deaths even increased until the first decade of the twentieth

[15] Corti (1984) stressed the weakness of legislative measures taken by the Liberal state. See also
Tognotti (1996).

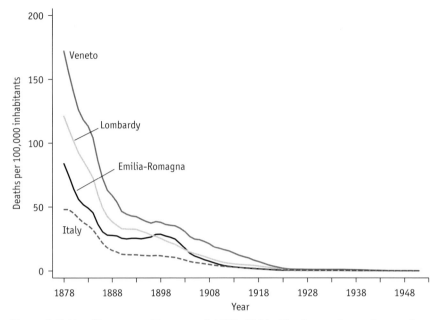

Figure 3.7 THE "PELLAGRA TRIANGLE," 1878–1951. The figure shows the trend in deaths per 100,000 people (vertical axis) over time (horizontal axis) caused by pellagra in the three Italian regions mostly affected by the disease: Veneto, Lombardy and Emilia-Romagna.

century). However, the overall picture shows not only a general improvement, but also a very fast process of eradication of the disease.

The result in Figure 3.7 is in line with the analyses carried out in chapter 2 ("Height"), particularly with regard to the estimates for the percentage of under-nourished people in the population (chapter 1). These estimates have led to the conclusion that the population's diet had improved significantly in the period concerned (1887–1951). The analysis concerning the "pellagra triangle" supports the thesis of a "benevolent industrialization" (Toniolo 2003; Vecchi 2003), according to which economic development successfully involved the periphery, that is to say, the poorest sections of the population; we should not forget, however, that to overcome these "deficiency diseases" like pellagra, besides the role played by the income effect (which allows people to have a better diet), there is also the knowledge gained in medicine (understanding the etiology of the disease means being able to act on the diet and to avoid death, even with income being equal).[16]

---

[16] Kazmierz Funk discovered vitamins in 1911, recognizing their vital role for the body and identifying the existence of "deficiency diseases".

What we have seen for tuberculosis, malaria, and pellagra also holds, mutatis mutandis, for all infective diseases: improvements in the living conditions of the Italians led to a fall in the death rate for these diseases—something that can hardly be attributed to the dynamics of per-capita GDP (the decrease is greater and earlier than what we would see if we adopted per-capita GDP and its dynamics as the summary indicator of wellbeing).[17]

5 Children Drive Away Death

At the time of Italy's unification, the chances of survival in the early years of life were not very great. The earliest data available for Italy date back to 1863 and show that, on average, one child out of every 10 did not survive the first month of life, while one in 4 did not live longer than the first year. Such a high likelihood of death is no longer found anywhere in the world today, not even in Angola, the Republic of Congo, or Chad—the three countries with the highest infant mortality in the world. The picture has radically improved over the last hundred and fifty years: today, only two children out of every thousand die in their first month of life, while infant mortality within the first year of life is lower than four in a thousand. Essentially, Italy has vanquished infant mortality and is among the world's most virtuous countries in this regard.

To understand how and when mortality by age structure changed, we have reconstructed the distribution of deaths by age in Figure 3.8, distinguishing between the male and female population, and with reference to four significant dates in Italian history. The first graph (top left) shows the situation in 1872, the first year that we have the necessary data available for our analysis. The figure shows that the highest percentage of deaths occurs during the first year of life (about 22 percent of the population died before their first birthday): in general, the broader the base of the graph, the more child deaths contribute to the population's overall death rate.

If we read the graphs in Figure 3.8 in a clockwise direction, we see that over the decades the base of the histogram narrows (owing to the drop in mortality among the younger age groups), and the upper part broadens (owing to the increase in deaths in the elderly). The finishing line of this process is shown in the graph concerning 2009 (bottom left): the distribution takes on a mushroom

---

[17] Public health spending increased significantly from the early 1900s: the increase is not visible in the series given in chapter 11 ("Vulnerability") because the focus is on the *composition* of social spending: by expressing health spending as a percentage of GDP, the increase in absolute terms of the series does stand out because it increases at the same pace as GDP. However, the increase in absolute terms is relevant in this section because it highlights the state's growing commitment in favor of public health.

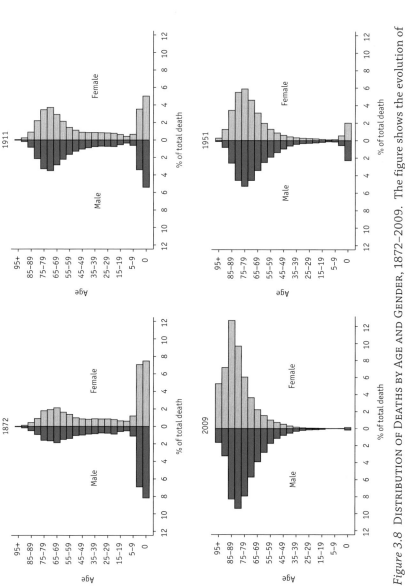

Figure 3.8 DISTRIBUTION OF DEATHS BY AGE AND GENDER, 1872–2009. The figure shows the evolution of the distribution of deaths by age and gender. Starting from the top-left graph, relating to 1872, the evolution of the structure of deaths by age and gender is seen by looking at the shape of the bars. If we compare the top-left graph (1872) with the bottom-right one (2009), we see that deaths are now rather infrequent in the younger sections of the population.

shape (Rowland 2003). The base of the distribution is narrow, almost disappearing, while the mushroom "stalk" is very thin, indicating that the likelihood of death in the middle-aged groups of life is very low. On the other hand, the breadth of the mushroom "cap" indicates that death now occurs most in the oldest sections of the population. The asymmetry of the cap reflects the fact that men die younger than women—something common to all industrialized countries.

On the whole, the evolution of the distribution of deaths by age illustrated in Figure 3.8 suggests that children were the first to benefit from improvements in health (see also Table S5 in the statistical appendix). The eradication of mortality for infective diseases and gastrointestinal pathologies documented in section 4 led to a marked decrease in mortality in the youngest section of the population, and this explains the extraordinary gains in life expectancy at birth that we saw in section 2: with other conditions being equal, a life saved in infancy enables adding many years to the average lifespan of the population.

The decrease in the death rate shown in Figure 3.8 has not been a linear process over time, nor has it concerned *all* children. To grasp these aspects, let's examine the historical series of the *infant mortality rate*—calculated on an annual basis, as the ratio between deaths in the first year of life and the total number of live births—which is an indicator that is sensitive to the population's hygiene and sanitary conditions. In 1863 the infant mortality rate in Italy was 232 (that is, out of every thousand babies born alive, 232 died during their first year of life), a lower figure than the one recorded in Germany in the same period, but almost 50 percent higher than the one found in France, and 100 percent higher than the one in England and Wales. Italy's economic backwardness in the aftermath of its unification was thus clearly reflected in the high infant mortality rate recorded in the mid-nineteenth century.

In the decades following unification, infant mortality decreased almost linearly in Italy (Pinnelli e Mancini 1991). Figure 3.9 shows that before the century was over, Italy caught up with France—a country that, in the mid-nineteenth century, had been characterized by a 30–35 percent higher per-capita GDP than the Italian one. Until around 1910, the infant mortality rate in Italy remained higher than the highest levels we see in the poorest countries today, such as in Sierra Leone, Liberia, and Angola, where we find values of around 150–160 deaths per thousand live births.

The process of convergence of Italy's infant mortality rate with that of the leading countries (Sweden, Britain, and the United States) was interrupted in the interwar period, unlike what occurred in France and Germany, for example, which continued to reduce their gap with the most virtuous countries. Convergence resumed after World War II: infant mortality decreased at an increasing annual rate from 1 percent in the period prior to 1942 to values equal to or above 5 percent afterward. This is an important and significant change of

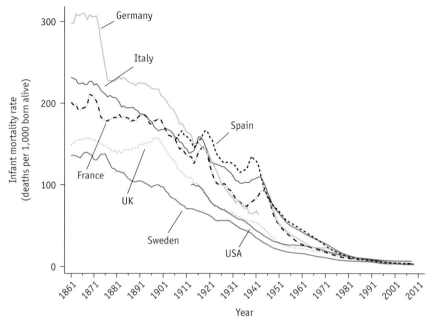

Figure 3.9 THE INFANT MORTALITY RATE: ITALY COMPARED TO THE REST OF THE WORLD. The graph shows the trend in infant mortality (vertical axis) over time (horizontal axis).

pace, but—it must be noted—not an extraordinary one: Spain (characterized by an over 40 percent lower per-capita GDP than the Italian one) experienced a similar decrease to the Italian one, while France and Germany had a faster pace compared to Italy (Berentsen 1987).[18]

On the whole, the data presented in this section document something of extraordinary historical importance: the vanquishing of mortality—at a general and infant level—such as had not been envisaged by any scholar: never, in any time or place. Indeed, in the mid-nineteenth century, when the demographic revolution started in Italy, the prevailing theory was the one of the Reverend Thomas Robert Malthus (1766–1834), according to whom improvements in death rates could only be temporary, of short duration: the view was that, on eradicating one disease, another would emerge (Fogel 1997). When the facts (the drop in mortality rate) started to disprove his theory, there was a real explosion in scientific studies, as much in medicine as in history, demography, economics, and the social fields, aimed at reconciling the theory with empirical evidence, as well as for understanding the *causes* of the age-old decrease in mortality (Fogel 1990).

---

[18] The analysis of the *neonatal mortality rate* (defined as the ratio of the number of deaths during the first month of life to the number of live births) leads to similar conclusions as the one of the infant mortality rate (Poston and Rogers 1985).

Among the causes of this age-old decrease, scholars have indicated the effects of public health system reforms, advances in medical science and technology, progress in personal and collective hygiene, improvements in economic conditions, and, above all, in nutrition (McKeown 1976; Harris 2004). Despite the many papers and books written to explain the fall in the death rate, no one universally accepted thesis has emerged (Schofield, Reher, and Bideau 1991). The case of Italy is no exception (Livi Bacci 1993; Del Panta 1997): thanks to the work of historical demographers, we have grasped many aspects of the mechanics of the progress made; as regards the causal explanations, however, we are still at the stage where scientific studies conclude with much use of verbal hedging.

6 Longevity Is Not the Same for Everyone

In the previous sections we examined the trend in a broad set of health indicators at the national level, but we have not yet talked about regional differences. Life expectancy at birth, for example, shows a wide and lasting regional variability.[19] We saw that in 1862, average life expectancy in Italy was 29 years (an average between men and women). The deviation around the national mean value in the same year was 12 years and 6 months: the inhabitants of Basilicata and Campania had the lowest life expectancy (23.6 and 24.2 years, respectively), while those of Liguria and Puglia had the highest (35.4 and 36.1 years, respectively). Longevity does not, therefore, appear to be evenly distributed throughout the country.

The evolution of regional differences in life expectancy is not an easy matter to summarize. Over the period considered, regional trends show an alternation of phases of rapid growth with phases of stagnation, giving rise to an interweaving of lines that is not always easy to unravel. Figure 3.10 provides an overall picture: from the unification of Italy, the inhabitants of the central-northern regions, on the whole, had a systematically greater life expectancy than those in the southern regions. The romantic image of the south as a relatively less wealthy land than the north, but healthier and more hospitable, requires a rethink in light of the data presented.

The north-south trend shown in Figure 3.10 obviously overlooks the complexity of the dynamics of individual regions (represented anonymously by the bundle of gray lines). There are southern regions in which people live longer than in northern ones (in 1862, for example, Sicily and Puglia had the edge on

---

[19] The data on life expectancy at birth presented in this section were provided by Lorenzo Del Panta, to whom goes our gratitude as well as the merit for the statistical reconstruction of the series. The Istat estimates of regional life expectancy start from 1980.

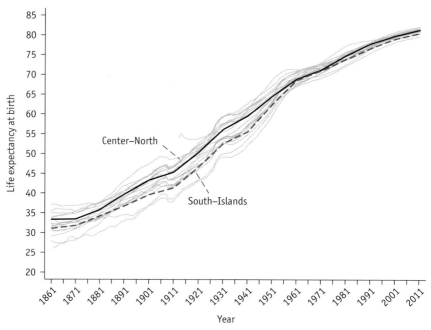

Figure 3.10 Northerners have Lived Longer Since Italian Unification. The figure shows the long-term trend in life expectancy at birth (vertical axis) over time (horizontal axis) for the set of central and northern regions (dark unbroken line) and the southern regions (broken blue line). The bundle of gray lines refers to each region. It took more than a century to close the gap between north and south. No sooner did integration seem to be achieved (around the 1960s) than the gap started to widen again, and has done so ever since.

many northern regions, including Piedmont); others in which people live not as long, but that show dynamics capable of rapidly making up the gaps; and northern regions that sometimes go against the trend with respect to generalized improvement (Lombardy, for example, had a life expectancy below the national average up until fairly recently).

To grasp the evolution of regional differences in various periods, in Figure 3.11 we have calculated the difference between the average life expectancy of the region with the highest longevity and that of the region with the lowest (broken line), for each one of the 150 years of Italy's postunification history. A value of 10 in the vertical axis of the graph, for example, means that in the region with the highest longevity, people live an average 10 years longer compared to the region with the lowest longevity. The trend of this indicator enables us to identify the features of the country's integration process: the lower the gap separating the most virtuous region from the less virtuous one, the greater the country's capacity to spread the benefits within its borders. On the other hand, a broad gap means a substantial failure of territorial integration.

The estimates in Figure 3.11 tell an unambiguous story: over the first hundred years of postunification, there was no integration; the gap between the regions grew wider instead of narrowing. The line describing the trend of the longevity gap during the eight or nine decades from the time of unification to the end of World War II not only remains broad (fluctuating within a band ranging from 10 to 15 years) but also shows a slight upward trend: for almost a hundred years of Italian history, the children born in the "less fortunate" region lived shorter lives than their peers in the "most fortunate" region. The luck of being born in the right region meant having about 12 extra years of life. In light of these data, we cannot evidently speak of a cohesive country: not with regard to the provision of basic health services, infrastructure, and practices normally responsible for the differences in mortality underlying the gaps observed in life expectancy.

Although the convergence in life expectancy between the various regions of the country required a considerable length of time to come about, there was convergence in the end: slow and discontinuous it may have been, but it was convergence nonetheless. The latest data show that the greatest longevity is in Marche (82.7 years) while the lowest is in Campania (80. 3 years): 2.4 years' difference are a significant gap, but still incomparably lower than the ones seen in the past.

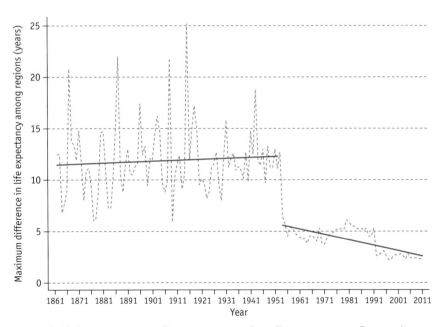

Figure 3.11 INTERREGIONAL DIFFERENCES IN LIFE EXPECTANCY AT BIRTH: A LASTING GAP. The figure measures how the difference in life expectancy at birth in the region with the highest longevity and in the region with the lowest longevity (vertical axis) varies over time (horizontal axis). The differences lasted for almost a century: the process of convergence only started up in earnest after World War II.

The jump that we see in Figure 3.11 starting from World War II deserves particular comment. This marks a reduction in the regional variability in life expectancy as well as the start of a process of interregional convergence. This result encapsulates two phenomena that acted in synergy: on the one hand, the different age structure between the northern and southern regions; on the other, the introduction of antibiotics and their dissemination throughout the country. To grasp the synergy between these two circumstances, we must start by observing that not all sections of the population get the same benefits from the introduction of antibiotics. The southern regions, characterized by a "young" demographic structure, had age groups more affected by diseases of bacterial origin and thus had the greatest benefits from the spreading use of antibiotics. On the other hand, in the northern regions that had a relatively more "elderly" population, there were more chronic and degenerative diseases of an inflammatory nature, as well as cancer, that benefited less from the progress made in medicine in those years (Mineo and Giammanco 1968). We can thus hypothesize that the spreading use of antibiotics, by acting rapidly and uniformly throughout the country and in combination with different demographic structures in the various regions, led to the sharp and considerable decrease in the variability of the average life expectancy shown in Figure 3.11. From this perspective, antibiotics promoted convergence between the regions by acting through two channels: they decreased the mortality of the southern regions more effectively than in the northern ones (antibiotics decreased infant and youth mortality in a mainly young southern population); and they acted as a compensating element for the backwardness of the health facilities of the southern regions.[20]

Which mechanisms are responsible for the lack of convergence between north and south of the country during the first hundred years of postunification and the convergence observed since World War II? Figure 3.12 highlights the factors in play, their strength and direction, through a statistical breakdown of the inequality in regional life expectancy. This exercise consists of dividing the Italian regions into two groups: the central and northern ones, on the one hand, and the southern ones (including Sicily and Sardinia), on the other, and then establishing the relative importance of two different sources of inequality to explain the trend in life expectancy at the national level. The first source of inequality is the difference in life expectancy *between* the center-north and south of the country; the second is the difference in life expectancy *within* each macro-area (the deviation from the mean life expectancy in the regions belonging to each macro-area changes over time).[21]

---

[20] The first national penicillin, marketed with the name of Supercillin (Prontocillin in the children's version), was manufactured in Milan in 1947 by the Società Prodotti Antibiotici.

[21] Similar exercises of breaking down inequality were carried out and commented on in chapter 2 ("Height") and chapter 8 ("Inequality").

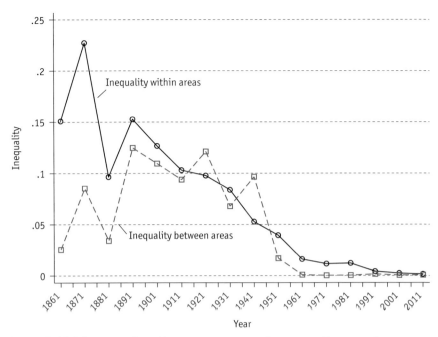

Figure 3.12 WHY DOES LIFE EXPECTANCY IN THE SOUTHERN REGIONS STRUGGLE TO ACHIEVE THAT OF THE NORTHERN REGIONS? The figure shows two curves representing inequality in life expectancy at birth of the regions within two macro-areas—the center-north and south (unbroken line, vertical axis)—and between the two macro-areas (broken line). The measure used is the mean logarithmic deviation (the value of which can be obtained, for each year, by summing the vertical axis values of the curves shown in the graph).

Figure 3.12 shows the role of the first component (the curve labeled "inequality between the areas") and the second ("inequality within the macro-areas"). Let's consider the period 1861–1891. In 1861 over 80 percent of the gap between the center-north and south of the country was caused by regional differences *inside* each macro-area, while the remaining 20 percent was caused by differences in the average lifespan between the two macro-areas. The figure thus depicts the country as a kaleidoscope, with the geographical macro-areas well-outlined and characterized. Over the three following decades, the inequality in life expectancy inside the two macro-areas was the most important component of total inequality, and its action was reinforced by a synergic trend of differences in average lifespan *between* the macro-areas. The overall effect is that during these first thirty years, the gap between the regions in terms of life expectancy decreased: this trend was the result of considerable immobility in inequalities inside the two macro-areas, but also of a significant widening of the average lifespan *between* north and south. In short, there was an "immediate" convergence in the years following unification, but there was also a parallel polarization process underway at the same time.

Starting in the 1890s, the regional differences *inside* the center-north and south of the country decreased and have continued to do so ever since: the center-north and south have become ever more homogeneous areas within themselves. In the decades 1891–1911, the equalizing action of the two sources of inequality was synergic and both were decreasing: the greatest intra-area homogeneity was accompanied by a corresponding decrease in the average gap *between* north and south of the country. Then something changed. In the interwar years the two forces acted in opposite directions, with similar intensity, and there were episodes of an *increase* in the average gap between north and south, of sufficient strength to more than compensate for the decrease in inequality inside the two areas. These movements were responsible for the lack of convergence observed at the national level in the period 1861–1941 shown in Figure 3.11.

After World War II the forces that had characterized the past trends changed rather sharply. Italy came out of the war with the territorial variability in life expectancy at the lowest levels in its history: between 1961 and 1991 the north–south dichotomy practically disappeared; the variability observed at the national level was all explained by the interregional differences inside the two macro-areas.

In the last two decades (1991–2011) there were again signs of a widening of the gap between north and south: despite the fact that at the national level the convergence of regional life expectancies continued, the gap between north and south *widened*. Figure 3.12 does not allow us to grasp the phenomenon described above because, in the section relating to the last two decades, the two curves are squeezed by the scale adopted. However, if we break down total inequality ("low" for the historical standards, but not negligible and considerably significant for health policymakers), we see that in the most recent decade, about 27 percent of the total is due to the north–south divide: in 1981 this value was less than 2 percent. This means that the two macro-areas, even if cohesive inside, tend to diverge from one another: Italy is more united, on the whole, and has continued to reduce inequality among its citizens' lifespan, but it seems unable to solve the polarization trends observed at the dawn of unification. The data show signs of reawakening of the gap in life expectancy between north and south.

7 Regions and Children's Health

As observed in section 5, the infant mortality rate is a useful indicator for analyzing a population's living conditions since it is closely correlated to the socioeconomic conditions of that community. Figure 3.13 shows the long-term series of infant mortality for each region. The numbers underlying the graph tell us that mortality in the first year of life decreased in all the Italian regions, both for males and females: from 250 deaths within the first year of life per thousand live births in 1861 to 47 in the 1960s, and then to 4 in recent years. This is in line

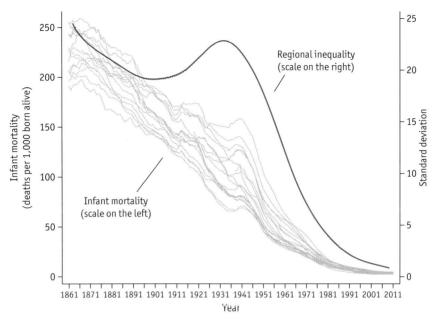

Figure 3.13 The process of Regional Convergence of Infant Mortality. The graph shows two phenomena. The bundle of gray lines indicates the decrease over the years (horizontal axis, calendar year) of the infant mortality rate (left vertical axis) for the regions: each line represents a region. The blue line, instead, shows the dispersion (measured by means of the standard deviation, right-side vertical axis) of the death rate among the various regions.

with what was found in section 5: Italy's decades-long trend is thus common to most other European countries (Corsini and Viazzo 1993).

What is more interesting to comment on in Figure 3.13 is the process of convergence of regional data. The risk of dying before celebrating one's first birthday varied considerably throughout the country: although the infant mortality rate decreased everywhere over time, the process of convergence of regional rates that we see in Figure 3.13 appears slow, characterized by a nonlinear trend over time and by very different regional dynamics.

The bundle of gray lines (each one representing the trend in the infant mortality rate for a given region) highlights a process of *divergence* among the regions—accentuated in the interwar period—which is followed by a phase of *convergence* in the years following World War II. To more rigorously delineate the trend in regional differences, Figure 3.13 also shows the trend in the standard deviation of the regional death rates (blue line, measured on the right-side vertical axis). The higher the standard deviation, the greater the interregional inequality in mortality rates. The trend in the standard deviation identifies three subperiods that overlap the traditional political periodization with extraordinary precision: we see a "slow" convergence during the Liberal period (the standard deviation falls), a divergence in the interwar period (the standard deviation rises), and a "rapid" convergence after World War II.

Although Figure 3.13 summarizes the trend in regional differences, it does not enable us to follow the individual regional trends: the curves are too many and interweave so that it is difficult to distinguish one region from another. That is why we have completed the descriptive picture with the maps of Figure 3.14, which refer to three symbolic dates: the beginning of the Kingdom of Italy (1863, the first year for which we have the necessary data), and the fiftieth and the hundredth anniversary dates of Italy's unification (Table S7, in the statistical appendix, gives the data in greater detail).

The first fact worth noting for the first years of postunification—and already grasped by Del Panta (1997)—concerns the high infant mortality rates in a broad area of central and northern Italy, particularly for the eastern regions: Lombardy and Veneto, first and foremost, but also Emilia-Romagna, Marche, and Umbria. Infant mortality was really high in these regions: 1 child out of every 4 died before its first birthday—a rate 20–40 percent higher than the one recorded in Campania or Puglia, where the ratio was 1 child in 5.

In the decades following unification, the geography of infant mortality changed rapidly, and in some respects even experienced an opposite trend. On the eve of World War I, Veneto and Emilia-Romagna had caught up and had managed to reduce infant mortality to levels lower than the national average. Lombardy, instead, failed to do so: although there was a drop in infant mortality, it did not match the one in other regions. The changes occurring in the southern regions are equally important: Sicily and Puglia, for example, had infant mortality rates equal to or lower than the national average at the time of the country's unification (Table S7 in the statistical appendix), but they then had such modest improvements over the first fifty years after unification that they slipped down the national infant mortality ranking.

The halt in convergence taking place in the interwar years was due to a very marked polarization process: between 1921 and 1941 all the *northern* regions experienced a rapid drop in infant mortality rates, below the national average (the only exception was Lombardy, which managed to catch up somewhat but not on a par with the other northern regions).

On the other hand, all the *southern* regions managed to improve their situation, and all show higher than average mortality rates (except for Sardinia). In the interwar years, Italy did not unify but actually accentuated the geographical divides within its borders: this is the story told by the infant mortality rates.

At the time of the hundredth anniversary of Italian unification, the country was thus clearly divided into two: the separating line was the border south of the Lazio and Abruzzo regions. Above the line, children survived to their first birthday more than was the case below the line. The differences are not even negligible: for every child that died in Tuscany, there were two who died in Campania. Although the overall variability index shows that the country was moving in the right direction, the southern regions lagged behind.

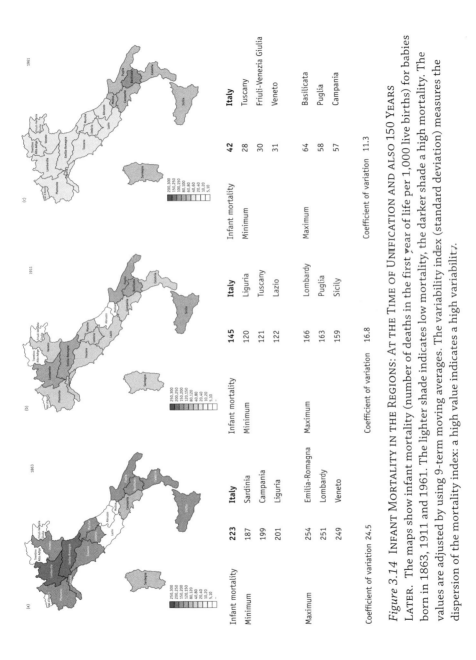

Infant mortality		Italy	**223**		Infant mortality		Italy	**145**		Infant mortality		Italy	**42**
Minimum		Sardinia	187		Minimum		Liguria	120		Minimum		Tuscany	28
		Campania	199				Tuscany	121				Friuli-Venezia Giulia	30
		Liguria	201				Lazio	122				Veneto	31
Maximum		Emilia-Romagna	254		Maximum		Lombardy	166		Maximum		Basilicata	64
		Lombardy	251				Puglia	163				Puglia	58
		Veneto	249				Sicily	159				Campania	57
Coefficient of variation 24.5					Coefficient of variation 16.8					Coefficient of variation 11.3			

Figure 3.14 INFANT MORTALITY IN THE REGIONS: AT THE TIME OF UNIFICATION AND ALSO 150 YEARS LATER. The maps show infant mortality (number of deaths in the first year of life per 1,000 live births) for babies born in 1863, 1911 and 1961. The lighter shade indicates low mortality, the darker shade a high mortality. The values are adjusted by using 9-term moving averages. The variability index (standard deviation) measures the dispersion of the mortality index: a high value indicates a high variability.

The data on infant mortality for the 150th anniversary of Italy's unification are still unavailable. The most recent year available is 2006, and it shows a formidable persistence of differences: the infant mortality rate is 2.9 per thousand in the north and 4.2 in the south. In Friuli–Venezia Giulia the rate is 2.3 (the lowest value after Valle d'Aosta and Molise, equal to 0.71 and 2.0, respectively), while it is 5.2 in Calabria. In short, what we wrote about the differences in life expectancy in the nineteenth century could be repeated here in commenting on the most recent data (2006) on infant mortality: the good fortune of being born in the right region means having a 250 percent better chance of surviving your first birthday and celebrating your first year of life with mom and dad.

If we now turn to the causes of death, we see that *infective diseases* (measles, typhoid fever, etc.), which are crucial for infant mortality purposes, affected southern regions more than those in the center and north of the country, especially at the time of unification, when mortality for infective diseases was at very high levels. Even in the years after World War II, when levels were by now low everywhere (thanks to antibiotics and sulfamides), there were still more deaths in the southern regions. Among the infective diseases, those of the *respiratory system* were, instead, more deadly in the central and northern regions, characterized by a harsher climate (Pozzi 1990). Death from respiratory tuberculosis was more common in the central and northern regions (with values above the national average) throughout the period examined.

Whatever the perspective, that of general infant mortality or one due to specific pathologies, what emerges is the selective nature of the progress signaled by health indicators. All the indicators show improvements in overall health, in the sense that they concerned all the country's regions. However, these improvements were not uniform throughout, either over time or geographically speaking: some regions clearly lagged behind. This happened as much with regard to illnesses requiring mere "public hygiene" treatments (most infective diseases and gastroenteric pathologies in the nineteenth century) as to other pathologies that required scientific and technological innovation for a solution (chronic and neurodegenerative diseases, which have seen a sharp increase since the mid-twentieth century).

Given the absence of obstacles and barriers, at least in principle, to the action of transferring and redistributing the benefits gained from certain medical and scientific discoveries, or to the dissemination of norms and principles of public or personal hygiene, or even to the distribution of pharmaceutical drugs and access to health centers, the conclusion to be drawn from past and present inequalities is that the country has struggled to redistribute the improvements in health conditions in the measure and times that were possible.[22]

---

[22] What is lacking, naturally, is the counterfactual: that is, we cannot document the health indicator trends that we could have observed if different health policies had been pursued.

8 The State and Health

The empirical evidence illustrated in the previous sections documents a story of a progress that is rarely linear and uniformly distributed, but is still such to place Italy among the leading countries in the world ranking of main health indicators. The measurement exercise allowed us to establish the essential features of the country's epidemiological transition. Having outlined the overall picture, what remains to be examined is the role of government and institutions in promoting and safeguarding their citizens' health.

Figure 3.15 shows the timeline for the main events discussed in this section. We have organized our historical reconstruction starting from the origins of the national health system (section 8.1), quickly running through the health policy during the Fascist period (section 8.2), to then deal with the more important reforms after World War II (section 8.3).

8.1 IT ALL STARTED WITH THE (POOR) MAYORS

Everybody knew it: the population's health at the time of Italy's unification was not in the best shape—not in absolute terms or when compared to other neighboring countries. The doctors knew, the country's parliament knew: Italy was in

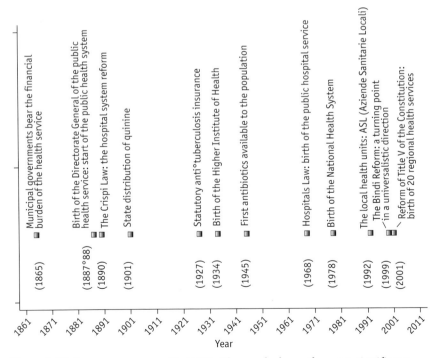

Figure 3.15 LEGISLATION AND HEALTH. The graph shows the most significant legislative measures and institutional innovations over time (horizontal axis).

a depressing situation of inferiority and the ruling class was well aware of the "public health" problem (Della Peruta 1980).

The first health administration act of the new Kingdom of Italy came out in 1865, by adopting the "Rattazzi Law", which had come into force in the former Kingdom of Sardinia in November 1859. This stated that the safeguarding of public health was entrusted to the Ministry of the Interior and to its peripheral representatives (governors, superintendents, and mayors). The effectiveness of these figures was, however, constrained by the limitedness and poor definition of responsibilities. The powers of mayors, in particular, were limited to generic tasks of hygiene monitoring in dwellings, public places, foods, and beverages. The law-implementing regulation (8 June 1865) added the imposition of the financial burden of the health service to municipal authorities, particularly for the free service addressed to the poor and carried out by district doctors.

The 1865 law had many shortcomings and ambiguities. Indeed, public action in the health field was confined to narrow limits established by the liberal thinking of governments of the historical center-right. A good example is what happened with the municipal regulations of public hygiene (issued in September 1870), which had envisaged compulsory anti-smallpox vaccinations for those aspiring to work in factories of the municipal territory: this provision was quickly withdrawn because, according to ministry authorities, it "naturally" went against individual freedom (Martino 1878).

The principle of limiting the state's role to the utmost was also applied to land reclamation initiatives in "unhealthy" areas. The first law on land reclamation, of 1862, entrusted the *private sector* with the task of draining and reclaiming lands, with the result that it favored the northern regions that had the largest swamplands and where there were many consortiums of landowners. The southern regions and Sardinia, instead, were characterized by marshlands of small pools and the almost total absence of landowner associations or consortiums (Corti 1984; Novello 2003).

Despite the delays and resistance, the new legislation favored the dissemination of the municipal doctor service (Table 3.1). In 1885, of the approximately 17,600 practicing physicians, almost 50 percent worked as municipal or district doctors (Detti 1994).

The most significant innovation in the health field was the creation of the Directorate General for Public Health in 1887, by the will of interior minister Francesco Crispi. The year after, as prime minister, Crispi promoted the birth of a real public health system, codified by law no. 5849 of 22 December 1888. In his *History of Italy*, Benedetto Croce places this law among the memorable feats of Italian "political and *moral* life" at the beginning of the new Kingdom (Croce 1928, cited in Cosmacini 2005, 345).

The law, drafted by Luigi Pagliani, created a detailed pyramid framework in the country: from the Directorate General at the top, down through various provincial councils to municipal doctors, transferring responsibility for health management from the technical-administrative apparatus to the "health technicians". The role of municipal doctor was thus enhanced by attributing

Table 3.1 **The municipal doctor service: an Italian glory**

Region	Spending per capita	1881 Municipalities with a doctor service for the poor (%)	Municipalities with a doctor service for all
Marche	1270	0	100
Umbria	1114	1	99
Roma	899	1	99
Lombardia	722	22	77
Emilia	657	72	27
Veneto	631	60	39
Toscana	592	27	72
ITALIA	492	41	50
Sardegna	471	30	39
Piemonte	392	56	19
Abruzzi	371	43	51
Liguria	291	35	46
Calabrie	290	48	45
Puglie	273	53	46
Basilicata	238	55	41
Sicilia	158	78	15
Campania	147	51	44

"The municipal doctors are those doctors who receive a salary from the municipal authorities for providing free treatment to the poor or to the whole population. This health system arrangement is one of the Italian glories right from the time when public health institutions were very imperfect everywhere" (Raseri 1882, 821; Cipolla 1985).

The data in the table on the right show that in the early 1880s about half the Italian municipalities had a municipal doctor service. For the times, the Italian figure (50% coverage of all municipalities in the country) was admirable compared to 20% in France, for example (Forti Messina 1982, 667). Regional variability was marked—a legacy of the pre-unification states. However, there were few rural doctor services, the institution of which was left to the discretion of local administrations, and they were not encouraged by the central authorities (Della Peruta 1985, 231). For a century, the municipal doctor service represented a crucial institution in the country's health system (Cosmacini 2005). This situation was reformed by the "hospital law" of 1968, which we shall deal with in section 8.3.

Source: Our processing of Raseri data (1882).

the qualification of health official. The municipal authorities had the task of providing health care to the poor registered in the municipal records, while hospital admissions continued to be handled by the *Opere Pie* ("Pious Organizations"). The "nonpoor" continued to be excluded from the public health service and were mainly catered to at home by free-practicing doctors (*medici libero-esercenti*), since fee-based hospital treatment was still not very widespread.

The main drawback of the law was that it did not extend compulsory free health care to the pharmaceutical field, with negative repercussions especially on rural populations. The 1888 reform also had some evident imbalances undermining its efficiency, such as the disproportionate burden of expenditure placed on municipal authorities compared to those of the state and of the provincial authorities, which all contributed to consolidating the regional imbalances between more and less developed areas.

The modernization task of the health legislation promoted by Crispi continued with *hospital reform*, which included hospital admissions for the chronically ill and home treatments. Hospital management had previously been almost exclusively in the hands of the *Opere Pie*. Hospitals mainly catered to the chronically ill or to the poor, whose admission and care were governed by regulations of the *Opere Pie* and of the municipal authorities. During the 1880s, in northern towns and cities, hospitals had started to admit the new working classes. Patients from rural areas were also on the rise, as a result of loosening bonds of family solidarity and the gradual reduction of resistance to hospital treatment, considered in rural culture as dishonorable, as a last resort after a long period of care with traditional healers (Lepre 1986).

Law no. 6972 of 17 July 1890 (the "Crispi Law," which we shall discuss in chapter 11, "Vulnerability") provided for the creation of charity institutes, supported not just by voluntary contributions and donations but also by programmed state funding and allocations, in order to provide care to the indigent "as much in sickness as in health".[23] The hospital reform of 1890 marked "a step forward along the road to the re-appropriation of the hospital organizations on the part of the medical community" as well as an easing of the path for "the advent of late-century technology" and for "building the clinical order" (Frascani 1986, 130, 133 e 203). Between 1885 and 1902, the number of patients treated by hospitals up and down the country rose by 50 percent.

---

[23] The possibility of introducing an "emergency rescue" service was granted even for the wealthy, in cases where the sick, the injured, or parturient women needed hospitals or charity institutes.

In the next two decades, contemporaries considered the new health legislation as the main cause of the drop in deaths from infective diseases. This period also coincides with years in which the main progress was made in bacteriology—something that public opinion increasingly appreciated also thanks to health education. Bacteriology decisively influenced preventive medicine policies to be implemented by acting on the environment, and it interacted in synergy with the Crispi-Pagliani Law, which established the key principles of city governance in the hygiene sphere. Public hygiene established the guidelines for building construction plans and for effective action on urban structures. The need to provide every home with potable water, to build healthy and comfortable buildings, to widen and straighten roads, and to move away harmful factories as well as any other source of unhealthiness, including organic waste, should have opened up the antiquated building structures of towns and cities to hygiene imperatives (Giovannini 1996; Pogliano 1984; De Luca 1991; Giuntini 1999a).

The health reformism tendencies starting in the early twentieth century have been described with masterly synthesis by Giorgio Cosmacini, who defined them in line with "the two directions of the Giolitti policy of social intervention: always grant with great caution and slowness, and when it is no longer possible to postpone without real danger, limit expenses to the utmost, and always and in every way public and state ones" (Cosmacini 2005, 347; Cherubini 1980). These directions underline the view at the turn of the century: improvements in public health would arrive without needing to involve the state, without needing active legislation and preventive action. They would come, and that was that. In chapter 11 ("Vulnerability") we shall examine and measure this aspect by looking at the evolution of social spending and highlighting the state's "light weight". In this context, the light weight, that is, the inertia of legislative action, is reflected in the relatively slow and uneven improvements made in the country with regard to health indicators.

8.2 FASCIST HEALTH POLICY

In the aftermath of World War I, public opinion once again focused on the need to face not just the sudden Spanish flu epidemic, but also the effects of "social illnesses" that struck certain sections of the population more heavily, and especially those that came about in the so-called triple endemic diseases: malaria (which had still not been eradicated despite the progress made at the start of the century), syphilis, and tuberculosis.

Box 1 **DDT, Rockefeller, Malaria, and Sardinia.**

Malaria has influenced the entire historical and economic life of Sardinia. As the historian Eugenia Tognotti wrote: "Fascism's grand land reclamation scheme had little effect. It was rather the 'State quinine' which led to a drastic drop in mortality rates, despite the resistance of a great many Sardinians who hated that extremely bitter medicine and considered it bad for their health. But what finally vanquished malaria was DDT, the insecticide destined to change the strategies in the fight against this anopheles mosquito transmitted infection. Selected by the Rockefeller Foundation after World War II for a grand technical-biological experiment to eradicate the indigenous insect, Sardinia was freed of the ages-old scourge between

Figure 3.1B Searching for Mosquito Larvae. Cixerri river, near Siliqua, in the province of Cagliari, 1948.

1947 and 1950, thanks to the extraordinary organizational and scientific capacity of the Americans, to the commitment of the ERLAAS (the regional agency for the fight against the anopheles mosquito in Sardinia), and to a mobilization that the island had never witnessed before in terms of people, equipment and intellectual and technical energy: from university hygienists to students of medicine and to municipal doctors, parish priests, teachers, health and political authorities, right down to the last worker" (2008, 36). On completion, in 1951, the "Sardinia Model" of de-malariazation using insecticides was applied to other malaria-infested areas: the Pontine area south of Rome, the Tiber delta, and Sicily.

Scholars all agree in denouncing the insufficiency of antimalaria legislation during the liberal period (Corti 1984). Fascist propaganda did not take long to criticize the guidelines that had inspired measures in the past, based on charity-type welfare initiatives (the distribution of quinine), and countered with a model hinging on the reclamation of unhealthy lands, not just by draining marshes but also by permanently transforming the reclaimed lands into intensive farmlands (Tognotti 1996).[24]

The most important provisions were issued between 1923 and 1934 through a series of legislative measures designed to arrive at a thorough land reclamation operation (*bonifica integrale*).[25] In the latter half of the 1930s, following the drop in financial resources, the land reclamation operation came to a sharp halt. What is more, the amount of quinine distributed for treatments fell drastically. Despite the legislative measures and the fact that research to combat malaria had made giant steps forward, during the twenty years of the Fascist period the scale of the malaria phenomenon and the north–south divide were still problems to be solved (we saw this in Figure 3.6).

To eradicate tuberculosis, the Fascist regime initially continued the policy decision of previous years by favoring the setting up of consortiums for combating the disease to make them compulsory in all provincial capitals (law no. 1276 of 23 June 1927). In this way, "urban and rural dispensaries" were set up for the

[24] Law no. 505 of 23 December 1900 instituted "state quinine"; law no. 460 of 2 November 1901 prescribed its free distribution to categories at risk as well as the obligation of the mechanical protection of homes; law no. 224 of 22 June 1902 granted easier conditions for the purchase of quinine; law no. 209 of 19 May 1904 established the obligation of preventive quinine treatment for workers in risk areas.

[25] The Consolidation Act on the reclamation of marshlands was approved with Royal Decree no. 3256 of 30 December 1923. Law no. 3134 of 24 December 1928, called the "Mussolini Law," granted financial resources to land reclamation and provided for integration regarding the supply of drinking water and the construction of rural buildings, hamlets, and roads.

tubercolizzati, that is, people with tuberculosis or prone to the disease, in order to provide preventive treatment (along the French model); "mountain sanatoria" with treatment functions for the *tuberculotici*, that is, people at an advanced stage of the disease but who were open to improvement or to being cured; and, finally, the "phthisis centers" (*tisicomi*) of the plains areas, for incurable patients in order to segregate the most serious cases.

Another area of legislative action during the Fascist period concerned hospitals, which were disrupted during World War I owing to the huge increase in hospitalized people (an effect of greater urbanization and of a change in the collective mentality) and the increasing costs of medical services. Decree Law no. 2841 of 30 December 1923 reestablished the obligation for municipal authorities to reimburse hospital fees for the poor who had their "rescue domicile" in the municipality. During the 1930s, the main innovation in the hospital sphere was the possibility of treating fee-paying patients, that is, the "nonpoor." This solution enabled hospitals to increase their revenues, to modernize their structures and equipment, and to compete with private clinics.

As Fascism developed into a totalitarian regime, health and welfare policies were aligned to the corporative structure of the economy. From the organizational standpoint, health policy moved in the direction of so-called corporative modernization (Preti 1984): the organization of public health came about through company and worker health insurance schemes funded by equal contributions made by workers and employers.[26]

This health insurance system envisaged health care in actuarial terms of risk, and the treatment or service provided was conditioned by the occurrence of the pathological event, thus excluding any kind of preventive treatment. The system was addressed to "the most numerous mass of citizens, not rich enough to afford to freely pay a doctor and not poor enough to be included in the list of the poor", the less-moneyed class, "the gray area of the countryside and of the towns—people who lived only if they worked, but who could not care for themselves if they got ill" (cit. in Cosmacini 1989, 223).

The Italy of the 1930s saw the spreading of a plethora of health care and insurance schemes based on a profession-focused organization of funds and their territorial distribution. If, at the start of the decade, the Sickness Funds—created through trade union initiatives—catered to just over 810,000 members, ten years later their numbers had risen to over thirteen million (Soresina 1987).

---

[26] The national institute for workers' accident compensation (INAIL) was created in 1933, the national social security institute (INPS) was set up in 1935, and the national agency for the social security and welfare of public sector workers (ENPAS) was created in 1942.

8.3 THE REPUBLIC AND THE NATIONAL
HEALTH SERVICE

The need to completely overhaul the health system emerged in the final years of World War II, when Allied military commanders set up an autonomous health administration—separate from other bodies of executive power—in the liberated areas in order to provide for the population's most pressing needs. Months later, the fathers of the Italian Constitution included the safeguarding of health among the fundamental rights of the individual (art. 32 of the Constitution). However, after the failure of the initial projects of reform, it was not possible to make any inroad toward the creation of a single, suitably organized health policy for the country. The insurance principle underlying the health insurance system was essentially confirmed.

Faced with a growing demand for health services, the funding system based on wage contributions soon proved to be insufficient, requiring the state to frequently top up health insurance funds. It took law no. 296 of 13 March 1958 to set up the Ministry of Health, but the ministry had insufficient staff and means to create centers of preventive medicine. Despite these difficulties, the theme of health reform started to be the subject of attention on the part of all political forces.

The first step toward a concrete renewal of health structures was the *hospital reform* implemented with law no. 132 of 12 February 1968, which established the definitive public status of hospitals. This law is one to remember because it marks the birth of the public hospital in its modern form, that is to say, organized through a basic unit (the so-called zonal hospital, in practice known as "the town hospital"), and also at provincial and regional levels. To grasp the scope of the innovation, it is worth recalling that the law made it compulsory to have three wards—medicine, surgery, and obstetrics—and two services—radiology and laboratory—in each zonal hospital. This was a significant step forward and a break with the past: it increased the pervasiveness of hospitals as well as their completeness and complexity with respect to previous structures.[27] It is this law that gave birth to the modern hospital and the profession of hospital doctor.

The years-long debate on the way to concretely implement article 32 of the Constitution only came about in 1978 with the creation of a National Health System (NHS, in Italian "SSN") of a universalistic nature (à la Beveridge) (Colucci 2010). This was the first structural reform of public health since the Crispi-Pagliani reform. Law no. 833 of 23 December 1978 defined the National Health System as "the complex of functions, structures, services and activities destined for the promotion, maintenance and recovery of the physical and mental health

---

[27] The law also marked the start of a hospital program giving the nascent regions the task of highlighting and planning their needs.

of the whole population, without any distinction of individual or social condition and according to methods which assure the equality of citizens before the service".

The birth of the NHS marked a new era going beyond a mere health insurance system. The reform of 1978 aimed to make a vast set of health services (general medical and nursing services, home and surgery care, specialist and hospital treatments, pharmaceutical and supplementary services), available free of charge to all citizens, abandoning the idea that only those registered with various health insurance organizations (à la Bismarck) had the right to health care.

Although organized at both national and regional levels, the NHS operated along decentralized management lines through local health units called *Unità Sanitarie Locali* (USL) based on the number of citizens, ranging from 50 to 200,000. The USL had the task of meeting the population's needs in various fields including health education; illness and accident prevention; the diagnosis and treatment of pathologies; the promotion of health; the safeguarding of a healthy environment; workplace safety; the overcoming of backwardness in health structures and of pathologies deriving from underdevelopment; and the protection of pregnant women, children, the elderly, and the mentally ill (Maccolini 1982).

The creation of the NHS involved a gradual and very conspicuous increase in costs, which was met by starting a corporatization of the various health units through Legislative Decree no. 502 of 30 December 1992, promoted by the then health minister Francesco De Lorenzo. The decree provided for turning the USL into the ASL (*Aziende Sanitarie Locali*), or local health firms having public health goals and not run by "management committees" linked to political parties, but by managers charged with the task of managing the units in line with budgetary criteria. The decree thus created—at least on paper—a division between health policy programming, entrusted to regional authorities, and health system management, entrusted to managers appointed by each regional government councilor responsible for health policy.[28]

There followed a new drive to recover the core idea of safeguarding health and the conscious need for proper sustainable health service management. Legislative Decree no. 229 of 19 June 1999 (the "Bindi Reform") restored the central role to the National Health Plan and to recovering the universalistic spirit of law 833/1978, clarifying the meaning of the ambiguous clause according to which the NHS had to only provide "essential" services. For decree 229/1999, the essential services to be assured are all those of proven effectiveness.

---

[28] A new way of paying for NHS services was also introduced and it replaced the previous method: the new system—invented in the United States and called Diagnosis Related Groups (DRG)—envisages a rigorous definition of treatment duration and of the reimbursement that the ASL must make to the service provider, for each type of treatment (Luzzi 2004).

In 2001, with the reform of Part 5 (*Titolo V*) of the Italian Constitution, the accent was placed on federalism (or devolution) and on the need to decentralize resources and decision making in NHS management, thereby introducing an element of "competition" between the powers of the state and of the regional authorities. The NHS thus ended its life to be replaced by twenty regional health services.

9 The Country's Health on Its 150th Birthday

Our brief look at certain illnesses in section 4 highlighted the fact that the main causes of death today for the Italians are heart disease and cancer. In this section we shall report the results of a more in-depth analysis on these two pathologies.

9.1 CARDIOVASCULAR DISEASES

An aging population is a key factor in the increasing impact of both heart disease and cancer on people's health. With regard to heart disease, however, the increase in new cases due to an aging population is largely compensated by the reduced risk of developing a cardiovascular pathology. The final outcome of this combination of factors for Italy is a *decrease* in the "population prevalence" of cardiovascular pathologies (that is, the whole set of people surviving a cardiovascular illness): from 1997 to 2007, the levels dropped from 227,000 cases to 191,000 for men, and from 41,000 cases to 35,000 for women (Giampaoli et al. 2001).

Even if cardiovascular pathologies are the primary cause of death in Italy and in the rest of Europe, the situation has changed in the last few years. While the number of deaths has risen dramatically in countries of central and eastern Europe, it has decreased constantly along with the relative incidence in countries of northern, southern, and western Europe (European Heart Network 2012). Heart diseases kill more than 4.3 million people in Europe every year and accounts for 48 percent of all deaths (54 percent for women and 43 percent for men). The main forms of cardiovascular pathologies are coronary cardiac diseases and strokes. Morbility in Europe is also very high: 23 percent of illnesses are due to cardiovascular pathologies, and this percentage drops to 17 percent in countries of the European Union that have a very low infant and adult mortality rate.

There are many risk factors that go to determine this overall European picture. The main ones include smoking, dietary problems, lack of proper physical activity, and alcohol consumption. Although the number of smokers has been falling in many European countries, this trend is slowing down, especially because of the increase in the number of women smokers who smoke as much as men, and adolescents who smoke more than their friends do. Dietary habits are converging: the diet in northern and western European countries is improving, while it is worsening in southern European countries, such as Italy, and in central and eastern Europe. Finally, the levels of physical activity tend to decrease owing to a sedentary lifestyle and a low propensity for sport activities: this is also reflected in the increase in child obesity.

In addition to inappropriate lifestyles, there are cardiovascular disease risk factors of a pathological or physiological kind such as diabetes, hypertension, and hypercholesterolemia. The 2012 Report of the European Heart Network calculated that 48 million adults in the European Union suffer from diabetes, and this number is rising. For Italy, the picture is generally improving: with reference to just the male population, Figure 3.16 shows the decrease in new cases (the incidence curves start falling from 1978) in *each* macro-area of the country and a corresponding drop in national mortality.

The analysis of heart disease incidence per macro-area enables us to see how the geographical distribution of the risk factors associated with cardiovascular pathologies and their trend over time have not been uniform processes. Although we see an improvement in the male population of the central and southern regions, initially characterized by a lower incidence than the national average, it

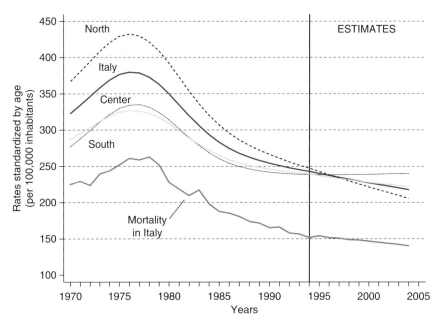

Figure 3.16 HEART DESEASE: INCIDENCE AND MORTALITY, MEN, 1970–2004. The graph shows two indicators for the male population aged 25–84 years. The curves in the upper part of the graph refer to the incidence of heart disease (number of new cases of heart disease per 100,000 people, vertical axis) over time (horizontal axis). The curve labeled as "Italy mortality" shows the trend in deaths for heart disease per 100,000 people.

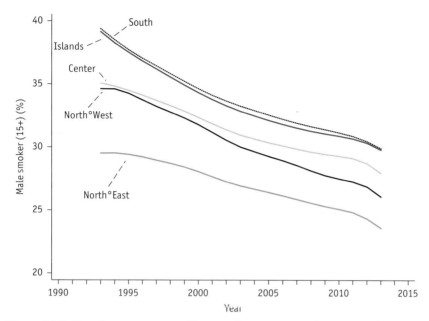

Figure 3.17 MEN SMOKERS IN THE VARIOUS PARTS OF THE COUNTRY. The figure shows the trends in percentage of male smokers above 15 years of age for the various macro-areas of Italy.

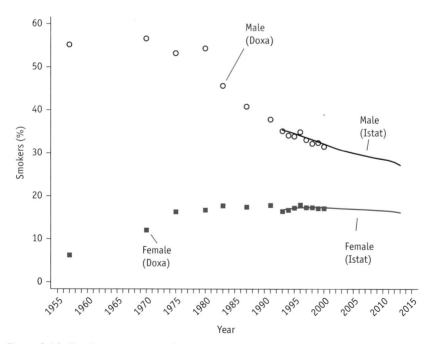

Figure 3.18 THE PREVALENCE OF SMOKING AMONG MEN AND WOMEN, 1957–2010. The figure shows the trend over time (horizontal axis) of the percentage of the smoking population (vertical axis) separately for men (black) and women (blue).

is a slower process compared to what we see in the northern regions. Around the mid-1990s, northern regions—along with central regions—bridged the gap and reached levels of incidence well below those found in the south. The trends are similar for women, but the incidence levels (not shown in the figure) are around half the ones of men; the national picture is, on the whole, homogeneous.

The statistics on the prevalence of smokers, illustrated in Figure 3.18, give a good example to illustrate the dynamics of the risk factors underlying Figure 3.17. The prevalence of smokers (males above 15 years of age) in the southern regions remained higher than that found in the central and southern regions between the early 1990s and 2008. This greater propensity to smoke is in line with the less

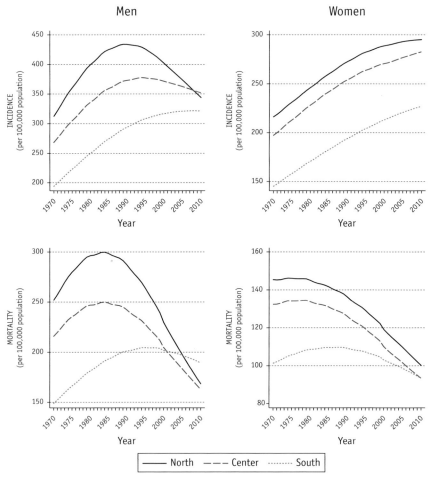

Figure 3.19 CANCER: RISK AND MORTALITY ACCORDING TO GENDER AND MACRO-AREA, 1970–2010. The upper part of the graph shows cancer incidence trends according to macro-area, that is, the risk of getting cancer. The lower part shows trends in mortality per 100,000 people.

advantageous picture of the incidence of heart disease in the south, where risk decreased less than in the central and northern regions, and has actually tended to remain stable in more recent years. Figure 3.19, instead, shows the differences in trends between men and women smokers from the mid-1950s to 2010. What is evident is an alarming process of convergence between men—traditionally more inclined to smoking, but who now show an inverse trend with decreasing consumption—and women, whose smoking habits are increasingly similar to men's and who are thus gradually losing their advantage in this respect.

9.2 CANCER

Death from cancer in Italy currently accounts for about 30 percent of total deaths: it is the leading cause of death in adulthood and the second in the elderly population (http://www.tumori.net). Both the levels and trends in cancer mortality in Italy are in line with European ones, and there is a declining trend in deaths for all kinds of cancer. It is estimated that about 250,000 deaths were avoided in 2014 compared to the peak in mortality recorded at the end of the 1980s (Malvezzi et al. 2014), with the sole exception of pancreas tumors, for which new cases and the number of deaths are on the rise everywhere.

Although cancer is a serious disease, it is possible to live with it for a long time and, in many cases, even to be cured. Over 50 percent of those affected survive longer than five years from the time of diagnosis, while 30 percent manage to live for longer than ten years. These figures eloquently show the progress made in Italy and in other economically advanced countries in the fight against cancer.

With regard to public health, we must consider the long-term impact of cancer and of its treatment on people's health. The long-term effects include organ damage and functional disabilities due to the pathology, to the treatment, or to both. There are also psychological implications such as the fear of a new outbreak of the disease; feelings of isolation, anxiety, and depression; and an altered perception of one's body and of one's social functions. These considerations must be at the center of attention of all public health workers dealing with cancer.

In Italy there are currently around 2.25 million people (4 percent of the population) who have been diagnosed with cancer in the more of less recent past (Dal Maso, De Angelis, and Guzzinati 2010). The same is true for Europe and the United States, where the first decade of the twenty-first century saw 3–4 percent of the population living their lives even after being diagnosed with cancer (Rowland 2013): this corresponds to 13.7 million individuals in the United States (Mariotto et al. 2011) and about 18 million individuals in Europe.

Over half of these are women (mostly elderly women) and the most frequent type is breast cancer (over half a million cases in Italy). Among men, although lung cancer is still the most frequent case, individuals diagnosed with prostate cancer live relatively longer than those diagnosed with other forms of cancer, and even account for most of the long-term survivors (almost 220,000 Italians).

To assess the state of health of a population suffering from cancer, we must enrich the picture of indicators used in the previous section of the chapter. We must, in particular, consider the *prevalence* of the pathology and its components: the *incidence*, which expresses the risk of getting cancer; the *survival*, which measures the effectiveness and appropriateness of cancer patient treatments; and the timeliness and accuracy of the cancer diagnosis.[29]

With regard to Italy, the cancer prevalence indicators show that the north of the country has around twice the number of people diagnosed with cancer (5 percent of the resident population) compared to the south (2–3 percent of the resident population). This is the result of the historical trends of all the aforesaid indicators, and particularly with regard to incidence. The risk of getting cancer in the south has been lower in the past—certainly owing to better nutrition (the so-called Mediterranean diet) and healthier lifestyles.

The historical series of indicators we have available starting from 1970—with projections for the set of tumors and for each macro-area until 2010, and for the more frequent locations at the national level, until 2015—enable us to accurately describe the evolution of the phenomenon (Baili et al. 2007; Rossi et al. 2013).[30] The trends in mortality and incidence are shown in Figure 3.19. The upper part of the figure (incidence) describes the *risk* of getting cancer according to macro-area and to gender. However, geographical differences with regard to risk are disappearing for all kinds of cancer: over the forty years examined, the data for the southern regions are coming closer to those of the central and northern ones, for both men and women. In some southern regions, the incidence of cancer is higher than the one observed in the center-north, as is the case with Campania (data not given in the figure), which, for some years now, has shown the highest incidence for all types of cancer in men (Grande et al. 2007), while the incidence for women is still highest in northern Italy.

---

[29] The terminology used in this section belongs to the sphere of epidemiology. *Prevalence* is a measure of the presence of the disease and is calculated as the proportion of people with cancer out of the total population, where onset of the pathology could have been at any time before. The term *incidence*, instead, measures the number of new cases out of the total of the population, within a certain time period, usually a calendar year. Measuring the number of new cases, the incidence provides a measure of risk (that is, the likelihood) of contracting the disease. Finally, the *survival rate* expresses the likelihood of an individual staying alive for a certain period of time once s/he has been diagnosed with cancer.

[30] Mortality according to cause is collected by the Italian statistics institute Istat for all types of cancer, while new cases are recorded in the resident population of specific areas covered by "cancer registers" (AIRTum databank). The information contained in these cancer registers enables epidemiologists to estimate the number of new cases (the incidence), the relative survival rate, and the percentage of those still alive who have been diagnosed with cancer at some time in their lives (prevalence), for the whole national territory.

The trends in mortality in the lower part of Figure 3.19 are in line with incidence and survival rate values. Male mortality is falling everywhere, albeit at a different pace in the macro-areas concerned. The southern regions' advantage, which was evident in the 1970s, has totally disappeared, giving rise to the opposite situation where risk of death from cancer is higher in the south than in the central and northern regions. On the other hand, the drop in female mortality is completely due to the increase in survival rate (Figure 3.20); the macro-areas of the country are tending to converge to common levels, to the main advantage of the central and northern regions. If we look at the trends in incidence and mortality according to location and type, at the national level we find that the most frequent forms of cancer are breast cancer for women, and prostate cancer for men, followed by colorectal cancer for both genders, while the risk of getting lung cancer is falling for men but rising for women. Mortality is decreasing for all the more frequent forms of cancer except for lung cancer in the female population.

As regards the *survival rate* of cancer sufferers, the trend throughout the country is far from uniform. The EUROCARE study shows that survival is generally on the rise for all forms of cancer, particularly with regard to prostate cancer, Hodgkin's lymphoma, and rectal cancer. The reasons for this improvement lie in the availability of more effective treatments, an early diagnosis, and the refinement of surgical techniques. With regard to prostate cancer, on the other hand, part of the increase in survival rates is due to the diagnosis of indolent tumors that are clinically not significant, but which are still detected in the prostate-specific antigen (PSA) test.

Significant differences still remain at the geographic level: the Eastern European countries included in the study (Bulgaria, the Czech Republic, Estonia, Latvia, Lithuania, Poland, and Slovakia) show lower levels, especially for those

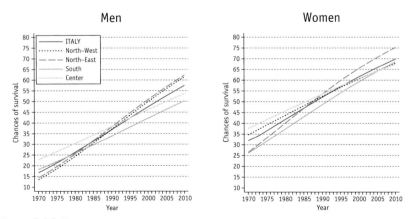

Figure 3.20 THE SURVIVAL RATE OF CANCER PATIENTS: GEOGRAPHICAL DIFFERENCES

forms of cancer that have a better prognosis, for which investments in early diagnosis, secondary prevention (organized screenings), and advanced therapies can improve expectations of greater survival and of healing in patients (De Angelis et al. 2013).

Also for Italy, the considerable improvement in survival shown in Figure 3.20 has not been uniform throughout the country. Over the forty years considered, the improvement is from 17 percent to 57 percent for men, and from 30 percent to 70 percent for women (Verdecchia et al. 2007). Improvement in the northern regions has been more marked than in the southern ones, for both men and women. The lack of convergence is particularly conspicuous with regard to men, for whom the persistence of regional differences is partly due to a different composition of cases per type of cancer. The south has more frequent cases of serious, often lethal, lung cancer, but bowel cancer is less frequent, with a better prognosis and greater probability of survival in the middle and long run. There has, instead, been greater convergence with regard to women: the north-eastern regions have seen a spectacular improvement, from a disadvantaged position compared to the national average in 1970 to a clear edge on all the other regions in 2010, with a survival rate that tripled over the forty years considered.

The overall success of all the indicators presented crucially stems from the combination of diagnostic accuracy and timeliness as well as the effectiveness and appropriateness of treatments throughout the country. Figure 3.20 suggests that certain regions have managed to adopt the most modern technologies more quickly than others, and to build the necessary structures to facilitate access to services, thereby reversing previous local trends: the male survival rate, in particular, shows how the modest initial *disadvantage* of the northern regions turned into a substantial advantage.

What conclusions can we draw from our analysis in this section? All the indicators considered (incidence, mortality, survival rate, and prevalence) point to the fact that Italy has made considerable progress over the last few decades. This is the result of a set of factors: firstly, *primary prevention*, which manages to reduce some forms of cancer connected to smoking, obesity, and lack of physical exercise. To this we must add *secondary prevention*, with the introduction of screenings for specific tumors (breast, prostate, and bowel cancer) and specific sections of the population (those more at risk).[31] We are witnessing a rise in the incidence of these types of cancer; although this may appear negative, we must bear in mind that the composition of cancer sufferers is changing, with an

---

[31] With regard to *prevention*, pharmacological research has taken on an important role: it is the case of the introduction of the vaccine against HPV (human papilloma virus) that prevents damage to the uterine cervix caused by four different types of the virus and opens the path to a possible prevention strategy for cervical cancer to be used alongside screening practices (http://www.epicentro. iss.it).

increase in the less serious and more curable cases (with less developed cancers at the time of diagnosis). The final factor underlying the progress made in this field relates to *treatments*, as demonstrated by the increase in survival rate for most forms of cancer all over the country.

The second conclusion that we feel we can stress here is that overall success is not evenly distributed: access to diagnostic and therapeutic tools increases with the level of education, and socioeconomic status affects the chance of having an early diagnosis and appropriate treatment (Quaglia et al. 2005; Caselli e Lipsi 2002; 2006). The trends in survival rate leave little doubt of the fact that, in Italy over the last few decades, the progress made in treating and curing cancers has proceeded at a different rate: southern Italy appears slower than the north.

The benefits of the southerners' "natural" advantage with regard to illnesses affecting wellbeing—given by their Mediterranean diet and relatively later taking to smoking—are weakening, and it is reasonable to foresee that the negative effects on health statistics on cancer, as things stand, will continue to be seen. A greater homogeneity in the geography of cancer is the result of a homologation in nutrition habits, increasingly more distant from the traditional Mediterranean diet, and of a convergence of the prevalence of smoking among southern women toward the level of those found in the central and northern regions.

10 As Long as There's Health (for Everyone)

Epidemiologists and economists have different souls, use different languages, and tend to associate with one another as little as possible; and when they do, their mutual suspicion hangs in the air. In this chapter we have tried to achieve a blend of these two disciplines in order to reconstruct the evolution of the Italian population's conditions of health throughout the postunification period.

In our concluding thoughts, it is worth starting by recalling the position from which Italy set off at the time of its unification. In 1873, Carlo Maggiorani, a Bolognese physician, reported the health conditions of the population to the senate of the new Kingdom: "pale looks, morbid flesh, frail machines and weak constitutions", the result of the "heap of ills" that afflicted the Kingdom's population (Della Peruta 1980, 200). Italy was, in short, hardly an enviable place to live in, as noted by visitors of the times. Charles Dickens came back dazed from his trip to mid-nineteenth-century Italy, charmed by the magnificence of its artistic heritage, but deeply disturbed and disgusted by the living conditions of the mass of the population (Dickens 1846).

Although Italian historiographical literature has produced hundreds of testimonies like Maggiorani's, it lacks three fundamental elements: (*a*) it does not offer a summary picture of long-term changes (capable of summarizing the many health indicators necessary to describe the population's living conditions over a century-and-a-half of its history); (*b*) it does not quantitatively measure the progress made; and (*c*) it overlooks the distribution aspects, that is, it does not offer the elements to assess whether the process of spreading the benefits achieved nationally was equitable. The chapter has tried to make good this gap.

The data examined show that the health of the Italians has reached extraordinarily high levels. The road has not been—as often happens—a linear or uniform one, but the degree of success has surprised everyone, Italians and the rest of the world. The analysis carried out in this chapter shows that, in some cases, it is worth toning down the enthusiasm because Italy took longer than other countries to achieve the same results (we saw this, for example, with regard to infant mortality). At the end of 150 years, though, Italy is now among the leading players.

Distribution analysis leads us to further play down the above success story: *all* the regions experienced the average improvements, all moved in the right direction, but not always, at not all of them, at the same pace. It is no use repeating the considerations made in this chapter, but it is useful to pay attention to the data of the last decades that show a country characterized by still-marked territorial differences. The reasons for concern emerge from the analysis of current trends. These are documented by the processed data and nurtured by the changes started up by the country with regard to its institutional and legislative framework.

The reasoning we feel we can share with the reader is the following. The paradigm within which the modern health system lies is very different from the one of the past. Seen through modern eyes, the health of the Italians since the nineteenth century has improved owing to a relatively simple recipe: once the importance of personal and public hygiene was grasped, along with the adoption of basic prevention and intervention measures that, on the whole, were not very onerous, the epidemiological transition got off to a start. The process that transformed the "pale looks" of the Italians thus got underway; it took over a century to make this come about, but, in the end, Italy finally made it: the citizens "have never had it so good" (Giorgio Amendola, quoted in Bertoldi 1993), and live a long life like few others in the world.

Over the twentieth century, the greatest progress was achieved thanks to improvements in medical technology and in pharmaceutical science, but also thanks to the health system's drive toward spreading health—even if not optimally—from the center to the periphery. As we note in many other chapters, even in the case of health indicators, the aftermath of World War II marks the beginning of an acceleration phase. It is not a homogeneous fifty-year period, though, and the date of 23 December 1978, which saw the birth of the National Health Service, is a decisive watershed, both with regard to institutional reform and to the results achieved by health indicators. After Christmas 1978, the health of the whole population—about 60 million Italians—enjoyed the protection established in the Constitution.

Italy proved able to defend its citizens' health, but not without a price. Health spending, as we can also see in chapter 11 ("Vulnerability"), began to grow considerably at an unprecedented rate. The data elaborated by the Organisation of Economic Cooperation and Development (OECD) stress that the Italian trend in health spending is in line with the main international players (Cergas 2009). Indeed, according to many indicators such as per-capita health expenditure or health spending as a percentage of GDP, Italy has spent less and obtained better results than France, Germany, and the Scandinavian countries, not to mention the United States. The Italian health system has, from this perspective, become a model admired and studied by the international community.

At the start of the new millennium, the celebrations for the 150th anniversary of Italy's unification took place within a context that appeared changed, but is rapidly evolving. The one word that, perhaps, best describes the new environment is "complexity." The modern public health system, on which the safeguarding of citizens' health depends, is a complex system: not only with regard to medical and pharmacological competence, and to technology, but also as regards organization: the complexity concerns the design of the whole national health organization. The pathologies of wellbeing require detailed actions, from primary prevention to the programming of screenings, from the implementation and rapid dissemination of effective treatments to investments in adequate resources and human capital. This is a complex picture that often poses questions—not easy to answer—about the sustainability of specific actions: we can mention the problem of lack of self-sufficiency (there are an estimated 800,000–900,000 so-called carers), or that of the incredible cost of some personalized chemotherapies.[32] The question posed with regard to public health is whether the country is equipping itself to find the answers to the population's health needs in a context that appears to be of growing complexity.

At the institutional level, as we saw when running through the legislative process over the hundred and fifty years of postunification, Italy is pointing toward further administrative decentralization of the health system. In the face of the federalist drive started up ten years ago, the country is experiencing a period of transition, with some of the objectives already achieved: twenty regional health systems. Already different from one another and autonomous in resource management, these regional systems have de facto replaced the national health system created in 1978—and are still the bone of political contention. Italy is thus preparing to take up the challenge of complexity with a new institutional

---

[32] Over the last two or three decades, a great boost to medicine and research has undoubtedly come from genetics, with the birth of *genomics*, a branch of molecular biology that deals with the study of the genome (the entirety of a living organism's hereditary information). The goal of *pharmacogenomics* is to personalize treatment and give each individual the most appropriate therapy, not just for the illness itself, but also for the patient, thereby minimizing any damage from side-effects.

arrangement of a federalist kind. At a hectic pace, when compared to the yard-stick of history, the country has created a group of "virtuous" regions (the central and northern ones), which are ahead—according to the criteria explored in this chapter—compared to other (southern) ones that are dealing with the complexity of managing citizens' health with some difficulty and delay. The decentralization appears to be accompanied by less equity: the gap in the health indicators considered is increasing along with the tones of political conflict and tension at the social level.

If Italy wishes to maintain what it has gained, it must grasp the need to act systemically, with reference to article 32 of the Constitution—the safeguarding of the health of *all* its citizens. Despite the complexity mantra, it is worth remembering that health system reform may not be enough if it is not accompanied by reforms in other spheres. The huge sums spent on health by each region (on average, about three-quarters of the regional budget is devoted to health spending) is an opportunity to catch up and redress the balance, but it may also be an opportunity for the ruling class to cultivate local clienteles and gain electoral consensus. If the new federalist arrangement does not envisage the necessary counterweights to avoid the latter possibility, then the scenario is that of a widening gap between the various regions. The mass migration toward the north of the country in search of a "better health service" is a painful thing to see, and it reflects the difficulties of actually implementing the Constitution the Italians gave themselves after World War II. To maintain the extraordinary and, in some respects, unexpected progress of the past, the country is looking ahead in an attempt to fully grasp the new nature of the complexity of the modern public health service.

Appendix—Sources and Methods

Figure 3.1 Life expectancy at birth, Italy 1861–2012 At national level, the sources are: for 1861–1871: values obtained by linearly projecting the trends in life expectancy at birth of the first three years, 1872–74, for which we have mortality data; 1872–2009: Human Mortality Database (HMD), University of California, Berkeley, and the Max Planck Institute for Demographic Research (http://www.mortality.org, retrieved December 2010); 2010–2011: Istat projections extracted by Health for All Italia (http://www.istat.it/sanita/Health, retrieved December 2010). At regional level, the sources are: for 1861–1991: Arturo Taraborrelli, *Una ricostruzione del regime demografico delle regioni italiane dal 1861 al 1991*, degree thesis, academic year 1999–2000, supervisor Prof. Lorenzo Del Panta, Faculty of Statistics, Bologna University; 1992–2011: Health for All Italia, the database of indicators on Italy's health system and state of health, Istat (http://www.istat.it/sanita/Health, retrieved December 2010). The life expectancy data for the two macro-areas of center-north and southern Italy were obtained as a weighted average of life expectancy values in the regions making up these macro-areas, using the corresponding resident population of each region as weights.

Figure 3.2 Average lifespan in Italy compared to the rest of the world (since 1861) Source: HMD (2010).

Figure 3.3 General mortality, 1863–2012 Sources: for 1887–1955: Causes of death 1887–1955. Istat, 1958; 1956–1957: *Annuario di statistiche sanitarie*, for years 1956–1957. Istat, 1959–1960; 1958–1975: *Annuario di statistiche demografiche*, for years 1958–1975. Istat, 1961–1978; 1977–1980: *Annuario di statistiche sanitarie*, for years 1977–1980. Istat, 1981–1984; 1980–2002: Mortality according to cause in Italy: 1980–2002. Online database, *Istituto superiore di sanità*; 2003–2007: Health for All Italia, Istat (http://www.istat.it/sanita/Health, retrieved December 2010).

Figure 3.4 What people used to, and still, die of in Italy, 1881 2011 The following groupings of large scale causes of death were taken into consideration: tuberculosis (all forms), typhoid fever, diphtheria, measles, whooping cough, scarlet fever, influenza, pneumonia (including pneumonia in newborns), bronchitis, gastroenteritis, complications in child birth and pregnancy, specific illnesses in infancy, smallpox, infectious and parasitic diseases (all forms), malaria, pellagra, malign tumors, diabetes, circulatory system pathologies. The sources used are: 1887–1955: Causes of death 1887–1955. Istat, 1958; 1956–1957, *Annuario di statistiche sanitarie*, years 1956–1957. Istat, 1959–1960; 1958–1975: *Annuario di statistiche demografiche*, years 1958–1975. Istat, 1961–1978; 1977–1980: *Annuario di statistiche sanitarie*, years 1977–1980. Istat, 1981–1984; 1980–2002: Mortality according to cause in Italy: 1980–2002. Online databank, *Istituto Superiore di Sanità*; 2003–2012: Health for All Italia, Istat (http://www.istat.it/sanita/Health, retrieved February 2015).

Figure 3.5 The vanquishing of mortality caused by infective diseases Sources: as in Figure 3.4.

Figure 3.6 An unhealthy environment and malaria: mortality in Italy's regions, 1881–1941 The averages are 9-term moving averages, centered on the target year of each map. Sources: as in Figure 3.4.

Figure 3.7 The "pellagra triangle," 1878–1951 Sources: as in Figure 3.4.

Figure 3.8 Distribution of deaths by age and gender, 1872–2006 Source: Human Mortality Database (2010).

Figure 3.9 The infant mortality rate: Italy compared to the rest of the world The sources are: for 1863–1972: "Tendenze evolutive della mortalità infantile in Italia," Istat, 1975; 1973–1980: *Annuario di statistiche demografiche*, years 1974–1981, Istat 1977–1985; 1982–1987: *Annuario statistico italiano*, Istat, ed. 1983–1989; 1988–1989: "Nascite e decessi," *Istat Annuari* nos. 1 and 2, ed. 1993; 1990–2007: Health for All Italia, Istat (http://www.istat.it/sanita/ Health, retrieved December 2010).

Figure 3.10 Northerners have lived longer since Italian unification Sources: as in Figure 3.1.

Figure 3.11 Interregional differences in life expectancy at birth: a lasting gap Sources: as in Figure 3.1.

Figure 3.12 Why does life expectancy in the southern regions struggle to reach that of the northern ones? Sources: as in Figure 3.1.

Figure 3.13 The process of regional convergence in infant mortality Sources: as in Figure 3.9.

Figure 3.14 Infant mortality in the regions: at the time of unification, 150 years later Sources: as in Figure 3.9.

Figure 3.16 Heart disease: incidence and mortality, men, 1970–2004 Source: The CUORE project for the epidemiology and prevention of cerebral and cardiovascular diseases (www.cuore.iss.it).

Figure 3.17 Men smokers in the various parts of the country Source: adjusted values taken from Health for All Italia, the database of indicators on Italy's health system and state of health, Istat, retrieved December 2010 (www.istat. it/sanita/Health).

Figure 3.18 The prevalence of smoking among men and women, 1957–2013 Source: Doxa (1966) and Health for All Italia, the database of indicators on Italy's health system and state of health, Istat, retrieved February 2015.

Figure 3.19 Cancer: risk and mortality according to gender and macro-area, 1970–2010 Source: Baili et al. (2007).

Figure 3.20 The survival rate of cancer patients: geographical differences Source: Verdecchia et al. (2007).

4

Child Labor

WITH FRANCESCO CINNIRELLA AND GIANNI TONIOLO

1 Children at Work

For many Italians today, the idea of child labor is something distant if not down-right alien. It brings to mind images of other ages in history, of a traditional, peas-ant economy where children became part of the production process almost as soon as they could stand upright. It also evokes images of the Industrial Revolution, where the first workshops made use of children for their malleability, so to speak, as much with regard to lower costs as to the discipline required in factory work.

Although there are still a great many children working in the world today—over 260 million according to the latest estimates of the International Labor Organization (ILO; ILO 2013)—they are mainly concentrated in Southeast Asia, sub-Saharan Africa, and Latin America. Political and economic news in Italy and other European countries thus devotes little attention to this theme. However, when mention is made, it is to stigmatize the multinational enterprises that use children in order to gain a competitive edge with respect to adult labor forces in Western countries. For most people in the West, it is enough to know that several international organizations are dealing with the plight of child labor—UNICEF, the ILO, and Save the Children, to name but a few—and they will finally manage to root out this phenomenon in due course as economic growth spreads throughout the world. In the Western world, child labor is thus seen as a distant problem in both time and space.

What about Italy? In fact, relatively little is known about child labor in Italy. Despite the country's membership in the Convention on Children's Rights and its cooperation with the ILO, Italy has conducted a relatively modest number of inquiries into child labor. The most significant data that we have to date on the history of child labor are the ones provided by the ILO (1996) and reported in Basu (1999). The data tell a little-known story in which Italy was characterized by exceptionally high levels of child labor, even in the post–World War II years. According to the ILO, in 1950 29.1 percent of Italian children aged 10–14 years were "economically active" compared to a European average of 6.5 percent. Over the following decades, still according to the ILO, the percentage of child workers in Italy rapidly fell to reach very low levels (0.38 percent), but this was still significantly higher than the European average (0.06 percent).

If the above data are correct, then the history of child labor in Italy is not only something much more recent than what is commonly supposed but also reveals a darker side of the country's economic development. If nearly one child in three went to work instead of school in 1950, what was the situation like in the early stages of Italian development? Was widespread use of child labor one of the ways in which a poor, peripheral Italy of the mid-nineteenth century managed to overcome the poverty trap and achieve levels of wellbeing among the highest in the world? If this is the case, then the process of Italian development reveals some iniquitous and even odious traits.

As regards the situation today, the latest studies all agree that child labor is by no means eradicated in Italy. The Italian National Institute of Statistics (Istat), in cooperation with the ILO, has carried out an investigation which found that, in 2000, about 144,000 children (of non-immigrant parents) aged 7–14 years did some form of work in Italy—accounting for 3.1 percent of the total population of that age group (Istat 2002). A more recent study carried out by the Associazione Bruno Trentin and Save the Children Italia found 260,000 children under 16 years of age in active employment, corresponding to 5.2 percent of the total population for that age group (Save the Children 2013). Even if the various methodologies underlying these studies prevent clear-cut comparisons over time, it is clear that child labor is still widespread today and perhaps is even on the rise.

This chapter aims to shed light on the evolution and trends of child labor over the 150 years of postunification economic development. The goal is to grasp the development of wellbeing in one of the most vulnerable sections of the population: children. To do so, we need to go beyond the limits of the existing literature, which may be rich in anecdotes, clichés, and stereotypes but poor in "facts" and evaluations based on statistics.

The first part of the chapter provides a statistical reconstruction of child employment for the period 1881–1961, based on ten-year population censuses, enabling us to overcome the limits and quality of data affecting the existing sample-based studies. For the first time, this reconstruction enables us to tell the story of children at work, with a narration extending over an extraordinarily long period of time and with a degree of detail that is not often equaled.[1] The

---

[1] The study by Toniolo and Vecchi (2007) is the first to systematically put together census data on child labor at the regional level for such a long period of time. Other studies are based on samples taken from industrial censuses (Goldin and Sokoloff 1982), household budgets (Horrell and Humphries 1995), parliamentary reports (Nardinelli 1990), or autobiographies (Humphries 2012). Moehling (1999) used census data for the United States, but only for the years 1880, 1900, and 1910.

second part of the chapter focuses on the factors underlying the decline of child labor over the twentieth century: What made the Italians send their children to school, thereby removing them from work in the fields, in the factories, and in the home? As we shall see, state laws were not enough; what was decisive in this regard was the degree of education of their parents, the supply of schooling, and the increase in household average income.

2 The Slow Progress of the Law

The task of sending children to school instead of to work essentially belongs to parents and the state. While parents may have mixed feelings in this regard, the state has developed an unambiguous position over the years: children have a *right* to their own childhood and an *obligation* to attend school.[2] Article 34 of the Italian Constitution guarantees that "first level education, provided for at least eight years, is compulsory and free of charge," and parents have the obligation to send their children to school.[3] In this section we provide the reader with some useful elements in order to assess the timespan and manner in which the Italian state arrived at this position.

2.1 EARLY LEGISLATION

The first attempts at drafting a series of laws to safeguard child labor in postunification Italy aimed to overcome the problem of child trading. This was especially widespread in the southern regions and consisted of the buying and selling of children, ceded by their families to operators called *conduttori* ("conductors"), who would transfer them abroad and start them off as beggars, peddlers, strolling musicians, and itinerant craft workers (Angelini 1996; Guerzoni 1868). In 1869, after the circulation of a report by the Italian Society of Charity in Paris, which denounced the sad conditions of Italian children in the French capital, the Italian government introduced a law bill in the Senate in order to prohibit child trading, considering it a crime punishable even with imprisonment. The bill sparked a long debate that prevented the approval of the law, despite the favorable opinion of broad sections of the progressive middle class. The main

---

[2] Articles 28 and 29 of the United Nations Convention on the Rights of the Child enshrine the right to education, to play (art. 31), and to be protected from all forms of exploitation and abuse (art. 34).

[3] "The child's parents or guardians who intend to provide for the child's education directly or privately must demonstrate they have the technical or financial means to do so and must notify the relevant authorities of this every year" (Consolidation act, legislative decree of 16 April 1994, part II, art. 111).

criticisms focused on the unacceptability of state interference in family life because it constituted a limitation on parental authority.[4]

The issue had already aroused interest in the years before unification and the proclamation of the Kingdom of Italy, and had prompted the promulgation of some legislative provisions on the part of the preunification states along with the setting up of inquiries on the phenomenon.[5] The need to take action at the legislative level became more and more pressing with the country's industrial development (see chapter 7, "Income"), something that made the problem of regulating the use of child labor in factories unavoidable in Italy as well. The first postunification governmental inquiry was ordered in 1869 by Bolognese minister Marco Minghetti (1818–1886), who set up a committee charged with studying the working conditions of women and children.

In 1876 the Ministry of Agriculture, Industry and Commerce (MAIC) presented a law bill that established the minimum age for factory workers. The bill also established a ceiling for working hours and prohibited certain kinds of jobs, such as the transport of minerals, which were considered harmful for child development. Industrialists and chambers of commerce immediately opposed the bill, opening a phase of tough confrontation between free-traders and supporters of state intervention; the former prevailed and the 1876 bill was never approved.

The debate had been opened up, though. In a report published in 1879, Alberto Errera (1841–1894) described the main provisions regarding child labor adopted "in the main civilized nations of Europe" in order to "influence public opinion in Italy thereby stimulating the national Parliament to vote a law on the work of women and of children." Twenty years after unification and the birth of the Kingdom of Italy, concluded Errera, Italy still did not have a law, but only law bills—as if to say the country did not belong to the club of "civilized" nations.[6]

2.2 A TORTUOUS LEGISLATIVE PROCESS

The first provision establishing a safeguard for child labor in factories was law no. 3657 of 11 February 1886, which put a minimum age of 9 years for

---

[4] The result of the debate was Law no. 1733 of 21 December 1873, which established the exclusion of minors under 18 years of age from certain itinerant occupations such as "acrobats, swindlers, charlatans, strolling musicians or singers, rope jumpers, soothsayers or dream explainers, animal displayers and the like." The "child trade" was not explicitly condemned, however.

[5] We should recall the studies made by Count Carlo Ilarione Petitti di Roreto (1790–1850), who was among the first to affirm the legitimacy of state intervention to safeguard the "health, religious, moral and intellectual education of the nascent generation" (Petitti di Roreto 1841, 123).

[6] In the United Kingdom, the first law on child labor was approved in 1833, in Prussia in 1839, and in France in 1841. In the United States, Massachusetts was the first state to regulate child labor with a law of 1837. By 1899, 44 states had passed laws on child labor (Ogburn 1912; Moheling 1999). Late adopters included Denmark (1873), Spain (1875), and Belgium (1886).

employability and 15 years as the minimum age for dangerous or unhealthy jobs. The greatest weaknesses of the law consisted of weak sanctions, with modest inspections envisaged, entrusted to a small group of ministerial inspectors, and its sole applicability to the industrial and mining sectors. All the other production sectors—small firms, the craft industry, home production, and agriculture—remained without any regulation in this sense. The exclusion of agriculture was not a mere detail: in the Italy of the times, the number of workers employed in farming was around, if not above, 70 percent (Broadberry, Giordano, and Zollino 2013). If the law thus represented a rather timid intervention at a practical level (concerning a minority of workers), its approval definitively established the affirmation of a fundamental principle: the legitimacy of state intervention in the employment field.[7]

Despite the approval of the 1886 law, Italian legislation still showed evident lags compared to the more advanced legislation of other European countries. This spurred the Zanardelli government to pass law no. 242 of 19 June 1902, which established the minimum working age at 12 years. However, once again, the actual implementation of the law was slow and arduous. The reports of the Office for Work, set up at the MAIC, stressed how the law was only enforced in larger, more easily monitored, industrial plants. The number of fines imposed (90 in 1903, 531 in 1904, and 999 in 1905) was, as the ministry inspectors themselves admitted, absolutely inadequate for the scale of the phenomenon (Maic 1909b).

The law was again amended with Consolidation Act no. 818 of 10 November 1907, which, by bringing together all the previous provisions on safeguarding the work of women and children, provided a first example of detailed legislation on the theme. The minimum working age was confirmed at 12 years for work in industrial factories and workshops, in building construction sites, and in (non-underground) quarries, mines, and tunnels; at 13 years for work in underground mines equipped with mechanical traction systems; and at 14 years for work in mines with no mechanical traction systems and for all hazardous jobs. Night work was absolutely prohibited for all women and for males under 15 years of age, as was underground work for all women. However, the law focused only on

---

[7] This did not put an end to the opposition of the free-traders, who stressed their defense of the "unlimited freedom of families," nor to the resistance of the industrialists, who rejected state interference and blamed households for the spreading of child labor. The law was also criticized by the socialists, who felt that the child labor issue could not be dealt with separately from other aspects of the condition of industrial workers. The parliamentary deputy Andrea Costa (1851–1910), for example, argued that there were no financial conditions for actually enforcing the law since it was pointless prohibiting child labor in factories without providing support to households who would have to maintain their unemployed children (Parliamentary Proceedings, *Atti Parlamentari*, 8 February 1886).

industrial employment, while farming continued to be excluded from all forms of regulation and was not even considered in the debate.

With the start of the twentieth century, the international climate changed and the debate on child labor had a significant boost. A series of international conferences was held on the subject, starting with one in Berlin in 1890, followed by those in Berne in 1906 and 1913. They dealt with the safeguarding of physical and moral health, the limitation on working hours and night work, the exclusion of heavy and unhealthy jobs, and the granting of breaks and rest periods. The Washington Convention of 1919, the Genoa Convention of 1920, and the Geneva Conventions of 1921, 1932, and 1937 established minimum working ages and codified rules for various production sectors, even if the attention was solely on industrial jobs: children employed in agriculture continued to be excluded from any form of regulation and from the debate itself.

To align Italian legislation to ILO dispositions, the Fascist regime approved law no. 653 of 26 April 1934, which prohibited the employment of children aged under 14 years in industry and commerce. The sponsor of the bill in the Senate was Mussolini himself, who wanted to highlight the social scope of the provision. The 1934 law also established the concept of "child," meant as a person under 15 years of age. The limitations, however, did not apply to domestic work, to child relatives of an employer up to the third degree, and to farm workers.

2.3 CHILD WORKERS BEYOND COUNT

After World War II, interest for child labor came forcibly to the attention of public opinion, and official inquiries and condemnations by intellectuals and politicians multiplied, all pointing to the widespread phenomenon, especially in the country's southern regions (Bretoni Jovine 1963). The 1934 law was amended by law no. 1325 of 20 November 1961 with regard to the minimum working age, raised from 14 to 15 years, albeit with a series of exceptions depending on the kind of work concerned. Agricultural jobs, once again, remained unregulated.

Child labor legislation received a renewed boost with Law no. 977 of 17 October 1967, which had a much broader scope of application than the previous laws. The law bill was presented by Luigi Gui, the Minister of Education, almost to highlight how one of the fundamental problems linked to child labor was its relation with the world of school education. The obligation to finish compulsory schooling was established as a necessary condition for starting employment.[8] The law extended the regulation also to the agricultural sector, and envisaged

---

[8] In January of the same year, the European Commission had issued Recommendation no. 67-125 inviting European Economic Community (EEC) member states to provide not only for the physical safeguard of minors but also for adequate vocational training in order to further improve youth access to the modern job market.

sanctions not only for employers but also for parents who sent to work their children in school-age, even establishing a safeguard in cases of illegal employment. Moreover, the 1967 law established the separation of legislation regarding child labor from the one on women's employment, thereby recognizing the substantial difference between the two issues. By the start of the 1970s, the legislature considered the child labor issue solved: since 1971, population censuses have no longer looked into the phenomenon of working children in Italy.[9]

3 The Scale of Child Labor

Without any further qualification, the terms "child" or "minor" are ambiguous expressions that vary according to the context and time period they are used in. At what age does one cease to be a "child"? At what age did people cease to be children in the nineteenth century? There are no hard and fast answers (Rodgers and Standing 1981). In the same way, the expression "child labor" is vague. What activities can be considered as "work," and which ones are instead "chores" or simple forms of participation in activities carried out inside the household or within one's family?

It is worth mentioning that there is still no universally accepted definition of "child" or "minor" today. Nor is there a widely shared convention on the age range that can identify the category of "children": today, as in the past, statistical agencies in the world adopt different solutions (ILO 2004). In general, the definitions are adapted to the context and, more specifically, to the availability of data.

We can, however, be more precise with regard to the expression "child labor." The definitions put forward by the ILO distinguish three work categories: "children in employment," "child labor," and "children in hazardous work." The first definition (children in employment) concerns economically active children, as much in the formal economy as in the informal one, who work (even a few hours a week) for a wage or for free outside their own family. The expression "child labor" has a narrower meaning and includes children in the worst forms of child labor conditions and children in employment below the minimum age, excluding children in permissible light work (ILO 2013, 16). The third and final category (children in hazardous work) concerns children involved in very different

---

[9] Law no. 451 of 1997 established a parliamentary commission and a national monitor for children, charged with the coordination, control, and planning of actions for implementing international agreements and national laws concerning the rights of children and teenagers. This law was amended by legislative decree no. 345 of 4 August 1999, implementing the EU directive 94/33/CE concerning the protection of youth in the workplace (Coccia and Righi 2009).

activities from one another, but which all share the fact that they produce negative effects on the child's safety and security (such as long hours; night work;
activities exposed to physical, psychological, or sexual abuse; and underground
or underwater work). For the purposes of the historical reconstruction presented
in this section, the expression "child labor" will be used to mean economically
active individuals aged 10–14 years. The concept of being "economically active"
means "being in an occupational condition" and is the expression used by the
available sources or population censuses.[10] It is difficult to determine the extent
to which the expression "economically active" used in Italian historical sources
can be likened to the same expression used by the ILO. It is plausible that the
expression "economically active" used in demographic censuses lies between the
softer term "children in employment" and the term "child labor," perhaps being
closer to the latter expression.

The Italian population censuses provide indications on the number of economically active children for Italy as a whole, for each region, separately for
boys and girls, and with regard to the economic sector. Contrary to what one
might think, however, the operation of estimating child employment rates is
not merely the consultation of census documentation and diligent transcrip-
tion of the relevant figures. The difficulties in comparing different censuses are
surprising. In the case at hand, for the first twenty years of postunification Italy,
the difficulties even turned out to be insurmountable: the censuses of 1861 and
1871 present such gaps and methodological inconsistencies that they do not
enable a temporal comparison of the figures they report (Vitali 1968; 1970).
For the period after 1961, the censuses have excluded children under 14 years
of age from questions on employment, thereby making it impossible to estimate
the scale of the phenomenon. Thus, what we have is the period 1881–1961, for
which the problems undermining comparisons of statistical data have instead
been resolved (Toniolo and Vecchi 2007).

The first indicator we have constructed is the *child employment rate*. This
measure is defined as the ratio between the number of economically active children and the total number of children of the same age group (10–14 years). The
child employment rate thus tells us how many children work out of every hundred. This is why economists also call it the child labor *incidence rate*. Figure 4.1
reports the estimates of the trend in child labor incidence in Italy, separately for
boys and girls.

The percentage of economically active children in Italy in 1881 was very high
at 64.3 percent, on average; it exceeded 80 percent for boys and approached
50 percent for girls. In the same year, the British censuses recorded a figure
of 22.9 percent for boys and 15.1 percent for girls (Cunningham and Viazzo

[10] For example, according to the population census of 1881, capitalists, property owners, pen-
sioners, prison inmates, prostitutes, and beggars were nonoccupational conditions.

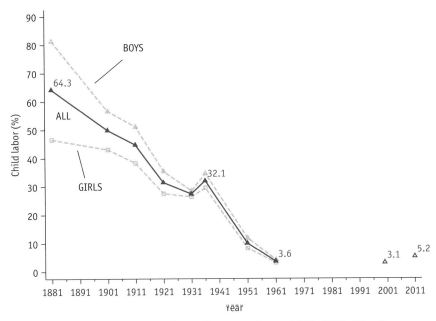

Figure 4.1 THE INCIDENCE OF CHILD LABOR IN ITALY, 1881–2011. The figure shows the trend in the incidence of child labor (vertical axis) over time (horizontal axis). The decreasing trend over time shows that the use of children in economic activities has fallen constantly over time. The data concerning the last decade, even if not strictly comparable with the historical data, suggest that child labor in Italy cannot be considered among the problems resolved since World War II.

1996).[11] Such high percentages as the ones observed in late-nineteenth-century Italy are no longer found in today's world, not even in the poorest countries. The ILO (2008) indicates that the highest percentages of child work are found in sub-Saharan Africa, where the incidence rate is below 30 percent (Box 1).

The second aspect to emerge from Figure 4.1 concerns the trend in the incidence of child labor over time: as Italian economic development progressed and intensified, recourse to child labor decreased. Cunningham and Viazzo (1996) showed how things in other countries went in the opposite direction: the use of child labor increased in the early stages of industrialization and hardly dropped during the more mature stages. De Herdt (1996) documented the case of Belgium and showed how, despite the fact that the country was one of the most industrialized nations of the nineteenth century, it was the last to introduce a law on child labor, in 1889. Until then, the extensive use of child labor probably

---

[11] In 1881 the British had an average per-capita income about two-and-a-half times that of the Italians.

Box 1 Children at Work in the World

Estimating the number of working children in the world is a difficult task for two reasons. Firstly, there is no universally shared definition of what child labor is. Secondly, the relative information is rather delicate and not all countries have reliable statistics. They do not always make the data publicly available and when they do, these statistics are not always consistent with the data from other sources. The case of India is emblematic in this respect. Official estimates put child labor (for children aged 5–14 years) at 2 percent while the data gathered from Demographic and Health Surveys (DHS) studies would suggest 14 percent. On the whole, the data are frustratingly incomplete, and the resulting estimates have the original flaw of being based on substantial measurement errors. The ILO is undoubtedly the international organization that provides the methodologically more sound figures on the scale of child labor in the world. According to the latest estimates, there are around 144 million children (aged 5–14 years) in employment in the world, that is, 12 percent of the total population for that age group (ILO 2013). Boys (51 percent) are slightly more employed than girls (49 percent). In more severe working conditions (child labor proper),

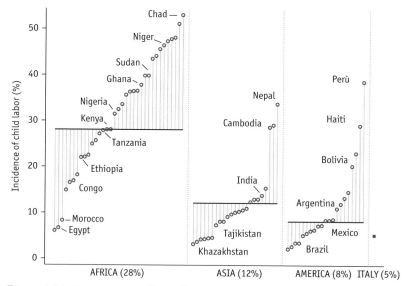

Figure 4.B1 INCIDENCE OF CHILD LABOR AROUND THE WORLD. The graph shows the extent of child labor (measured by horizontal segments along the vertical axis) in Africa, Asia, and Latin America (horizontal axis). The vertical axes describe the scatter of national values around the mean value of each continent.

we find about 120 million children (still with significantly more boys working than girls), that is, around 1 child in 10. Almost 40 million children are employed in *hazardous work*, along with another 50 million older minors (15- to 17-year-olds).

The geography of child labor is heterogeneous. Figure 4.B1 shows the extent of child labor (the second definition, above) in the world with regard to the continents for which we have adequate data. The variations in the incidence of child labor among the continents is marked by horizontal bars while variations of the phenomenon among the countries in each continent is represented by the vertical bars (showing each country's position with regard to the continent's average). Africa has the highest number: on average, 28 percent of African children work, and this figure can exceed 50 percent in some countries such as Chad and the Central African Republic. Asia ranks second (at 12 percent), but we should note the absence of China (for which data are not made public), with Latin America and the Caribbean third (at 8 percent). There are conspicuous absences in the graph: the United States and Canada as well as Europe as a whole and Oceania. Child labor is not monitored in these places.

The distribution of the scale of child labor does *not* correspond to the distribution of children in absolute terms. When we look at the absolute number of the percentage figures, child labor is more concentrated in Asia (almost 130 million children aged 5–17 years), which has over one-and-a-half times the number found in sub-Saharan Africa (83 million), and over seven times the number found in Latina America and the Caribbean (18 million).

characterized all production sectors of the economy, including mining (especially coal mining), a sector in which children aged under 16 years accounted for about 20 percent of the workforce in 1846. Puissant (1976) estimated that this figure increased between 1843 and 1864. Goldin and Sokoloff (1982) showed how the initial stage of industrialization in the Northeastern United States was characterized by a great expansion of manufacturing, which made great use of children and women in the work process. Their view is thus that initial American technological development increased the demand for child labor. However, the number of women and children in employment started to drop by 1840. Horrell and Humphries (1995) studied British household budgets for the period prior to the first censuses (1787–1872) and provided further elements in favor of the view that the initial stages of industrialization led to a rise in the use of child labor. On the basis of a collection of over 600 autobiographies of English workers who lived between the late seventeenth century and the early eighteenth century, Humphries (2012, 6) reached a sententious conclusion: "Child labour was a major contributing factor in Britain's industrialization ... the classic era of industrialization, 1790–1850, saw an upsurge in child labour."

Figure 4.1 shows that the decline in child labor in Italy was a continuous phenomenon, but not homogeneous over time: child employment dropped quite sharply during the first stages of industrialization (1881–1911); it remained fairly stable in the interwar period—where there was a slight increase during the years of the Great Depression (1931–1936); and then it fell sharply again during the years of the Italian "economic miracle" (late 1950s and early 1960s). The data concerning the most recent decade, which are sample-based and thus not directly comparable with the previous data, show beyond any margin of statistical error that child labor was still widespread and perhaps even slightly on the rise. The most striking feature of this process, however, concerns the first period, the one in which the country's socioeconomic structure changed: factories mushroomed, the workforce increased, but the percentage of children in employment fell. In short, Italian industrialization seems to have been relatively benign with children.[12]

If we look carefully at the period 1881–1911, we see that the decreasing trend in child labor slows down between 1901 and 1911—a decade characterized by relatively fast economic growth. This slowdown appears even less explicable if we consider that the period saw the first attempts at regulating compulsory schooling as well as child labor. In the same period we find a decrease in the average number of household members (Livi-Bacci 1993).

As regards the rise in child labor seen in the years 1931–1936, we note that it occurred within a context of rising military spending and the recruitment of part of the adult workforce to meet the needs of the war in Ethiopia (Abyssinia). It is plausible to hypothesize that these factors called for a reallocation of the workforce toward industry and the army. It is thus likely that there were wage incentives spurring children to enter the workforce to replace adult workers. These incentives probably counterbalanced the positive aspect of certain important institutional innovations that occurred in the 1930s with regard to regulating compulsory schooling and the job market.

The application of the laws could instead be behind the drop in the incidence of child labor experienced between 1936 and 1951. It is possible to say that there was a lag between the drafting of legislation in the 1930s and its implementation; and that immediately after World War II the democratically elected governments, in tune with trade unions, created a political and cultural climate favorable to a more effective application of the law. Both the Christian

[12] Saito (1996) reached a similar conclusion with regard to Japan.

Democrats in power and the Left in opposition had cultures and ideologies against the "exploitation" of children.

3.1 ITALY AND THE REST OF THE WORLD

Historical studies and the literature on developing countries all stress that household income plays a crucial role in reducing child labor. The idea is that households can do without the financial contribution of their children once a certain income level is reached enabling them to do so (Edmonds and Pavcnik 2005; Basu and Van 1998). In this section we shall examine the child labor–household income relation by using the census data on child labor made available by the ILO for a set of 104 countries for the period 1881–2004 and the per-capita GDP data provided by Maddison (2001).

Figure 4.2 shows the decline in the incidence of child labor in Italy over time compared to other countries. For each country, the graph shows the level of per-capita GDP (horizontal axis) and the percentage of working children out of

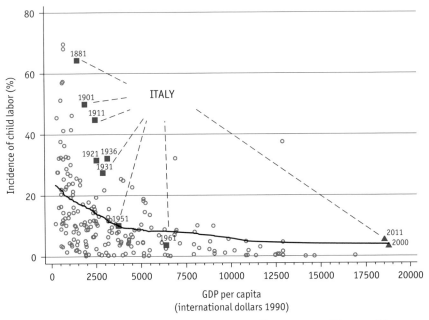

Figure 4.2 CHILD WORKERS IN ITALY AND IN THE REST OF THE WORLD. The graph shows how the incidence of child labor (vertical axis) varies as a function of per-capita GDP (horizontal axis). Each small circle stands for a country; Italy is represented by the small blue squares with the corresponding observation years (triangles refer to survey estimates). Since World War II, Italy has been in line with the average of the other countries. This is shown by the regression curve in the graph.

the total child population (vertical axis). The resulting downward-sloping curve in the graph is obtained by regression analysis and tells us that as per-capita income increased, the incidence of child labor decreased: the shape of the curve suggests that it is a relatively fast decrease when the income level is low, while the decrease slows down as income rises. The graph highlights Italy's position in the international context by labeling the data with the year corresponding to each observation.

Compared to today's poor countries with income levels similar to those of late-nineteenth-century and early-twentieth-century Italy, Figure 4.2 shows that Italy made use of a lot more children. The small squares for the years 1881–1936 are well above the regression curve: this means that, with income being equal, in the years 1881–1936 Italy had higher child labor rates than the ones seen in today's developing countries. We shall return to an explanation of this phenomenon in section 5 of the chapter.

On the other hand, Figure 4.2 also shows that, since World War II, Italy not only fell in line with other countries with regard to child labor but also improved on their experience, as it were: in 1951 the percentage of Italian children in the workforce was within the average, while in 1961 the census figure places Italy among the group of countries that—with income being equal—used a percentage of child labor below the international average. In the symbolic year 2011, when the country celebrated its 150th anniversary since unification, the child employment rate did not disappear, as was hoped, but showed clear signs of being chronic, and perhaps even with a slight rise, in line with the results presented in chapter 1 ("Nutrition") and chapter 9 ("Poverty").

At the contemporary historiographical level, the estimates presented in this section portray a significantly different picture of Italy than the one depicted by the ILO figures (1996) recalled in the introductory section. In the Italy of 1951, children in employment were not one in three, but one in ten; in 1961, working children did not account for 10.9 percent, but 3.6 percent of the total child population. Nor can the Italy of the latter half of the twentieth century be legitimately compared to India, China, Brazil, and Ethiopia (Basu 1999): Italy's use of child labor has been lower in many respects.

3.2 CHILD LABOR IN THE ITALIAN REGIONS

Census data enable us to calculate child labor incidence rates for each region of Italy, separately for boys and girls. In this section we shall summarize the most interesting results emerging from an analysis of the evolution of the child labor incidence with geographical details enabling us to show the different trends for various areas of the country.

Figure 4.3 shows the incidence of child labor for the five geographical macroregions traditionally used: the North-West, North-East, Center, South, and

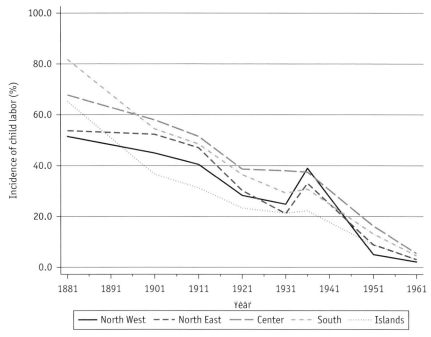

Figure 4.3 Child Labor in Italy according to Macro-area. The figure shows the trend in the number of working children (boys and girls) as a percentage of total children aged 10–14 years (vertical axis) over time (horizontal axis). What emerges is a slow process of convergence over the decades which is characterized by a significant interruption in the country's northern regions in the 1930s.

the Islands (Sicily and Sardinia). The long-term trends of the incidence of child labor in these macroregions are similar to the decreasing trend recorded at the national level. There are, however, significant differences both in the *levels* of child labor rates and in the dynamics of the process reducing the employment of children.

With regard to levels, the southern regions generally have higher child labor incidence rates compared to the central and northern ones. Sardinia is an exception in that, although being a poor region, perhaps the poorest one in the Kingdom at the time, it had lower incidence rates compared to the other southern regions. This was due to a gender gap that was unparalleled in the other regions.

Figure 4.3 clearly shows the convergent trend over the decades: regional differences in child labor incidence rates decreased. The process was a slow one, however, and the reduction in regional differences went ahead in fits and starts. Between 1881 and 1901 the regional differences in child labor incidence rates halved: convergence was very fast. Between 1901 and 1911 the convergence process decelerated visibly and perhaps even came to a halt. A lull characterized the period 1911–1931, during which no significant shift in regional differences was found. The years 1931–1936 saw a period of *divergence*: while the incidence of child labor increased conspicuously in the northern regions, in the central and southern ones there was a lull. This resulted in a broadening of the gap between north and south of the country. Convergence resumed with a formidable boost in the years following 1936, above all, in the decade 1951–1961, with a drop in interregional differences in child labor levels.

We need to analyze the point of arrival of the convergence process shown in Figure 4.3. If we look carefully at the figures concerning the latest year for which we have census estimates, 1961, we see that the regional differences did not disappear: in Liguria and Trentino-Alto Adige, working children accounted for less than 1.5 percent of the total; in Sardinia and Piedmont, the figure was about 3 percent; it was about 4.5 percent in Emilia-Romagna and Tuscany, 6 percent in Umbria, and 8.5 percent in Marche. No clear regional trend emerges, but, on the whole, the geographical disparities that we see in 1961 Italy do not lead us to conclude that the convergence process was complete.

Has this convergence process ever reached completion? If so, when did it happen? There is still no answer to these questions. The available data do not even allow us to hypothesize a possible answer. The Italian statistics agency Istat (2002) and Coccia and Righi (2009) have shown that we do not know all the developments of the child labor phenomenon over the last fifty years of Italian history. The kaleidoscope of studies carried out over the last fifty years do not enable us to draw an overall picture of the evolution of the phenomenon at national or local levels. The methodological, legislative, and regulatory difficulties hindering the measurement of child labor on the basis of the definitions adopted by the international community seem to be quite formidable. The impression is that the answer to our question on the current scale of regional disparities in child labor rates will come—if it ever does—with a lag that cannot be envisaged today.

4 The Role of Technological Development

Karl Marx (1818–1883) had few doubts: the advent of technology would be a bad thing for women and children. "In so far as machinery dispenses with muscular power, it becomes a means of employing laborers of slight muscular strength, and those whose bodily development is incomplete, but whose limbs are all the more supple. The labor of women and children was, therefore, the first thing sought for by capitalists who used machinery" (Marx 1867). So, technology ("the machines" in Marx's words) is evil because it makes women and children an input of the production process, to work alongside or even replace adult male workers. It was not just this, however. Continuing with his reasoning, Marx added that technology, by encouraging child labor, would drive down adult workers' wages, thereby forcing other members of a worker's family, regardless of age and gender, to enter the job market in order to make up for the family's loss in income owing to the reduced wage of the head of the household.

Since Marx's day the relationship between technology and child labor has been the object of careful reflection from both an empirical and theoretical standpoint. This is by no means a mundane relationship. Besides the mechanisms suggested by Marx, there are also others acting in the opposite direction. For example, the so-called endogenous growth theories hypothesize the complementary nature of technological development and human capital: that is, human capital (an educated population) plays a crucial role in technological development because it is a necessary condition for creating new inventions or for adopting existing technologies (Nelson and Phelps 1966; Benhabib and Spiegel 1994). Other growth theories, on the other hand, hypothesize that it was the slow but inexorable technological progress that encouraged investment in human capital: with increased benefits, in wage terms, deriving from greater education, households have invested more in human capital, at the same time decreasing the average number of children born. According to the argument, this process triggered a virtuous circle enabling societies to get out of the centuries-long stagnation typical of preindustrial economies and to embark on the modern era, the one in which technological progress continually feeds per-capita income growth (Galor 2005).

As regards the industrialization process, the most credited theories would appear to adhere to the view that, since the late nineteenth century, technological development has favored the accumulation of human capital because increasingly sophisticated technologies have implicitly required a more educated workforce (Goldin and Katz 2008; Galor 2011). Not everyone agrees with this, given that there are forms of production that, even if technologically advanced, encourage the employment of children. This is the case, for example, with multifunctional electronic sewing machines, which make it feasible and convenient to subcontract work to girls, thereby enabling them to do the work in their own homes (Grootaert and Kanbur 1995; Tuttle 1998; Gratton and Moen 2004). What is the evidence with regard to Italy? What long-term relation emerges between technology and child labor?

The economic sectors that saw the employment of children in Italy were, traditionally, agriculture, building construction, and manufacturing. The census data show a surprising stability of child employment over time with regard to the distribution of children in the various sectors of the economy. Between 1881 and 1951, almost three-quarters of working children were employed in agriculture—with as many boys as girls. Manufacturing, building construction, and mining accounted for 20–25 percent, mostly in the manufacturing sector. The tertiary sector (services) accounted for 5–7 percent. This distribution, which was stable over at least seventy years of postunification Italy, significantly changed between 1951 and 1961—a decade that saw a marked decrease in the number of children employed in agriculture, from 79 percent to 58 percent— and their reallocation in the manufacturing industry.

To assess the connection between technology and child labor, we can construct a different indicator from the one used in the previous section: instead of calculating the number of working children out of the total for the age group, this time we calculate the ratio between the number of economically active children and the total economically active population (including both children and adults). The two indicators are complementary: while the former measures the scale of child labor, the latter measures its *intensity*—in that it grasps the extent to which a given production sector makes use of child labor with respect to adult labor.[13]

The trend in child labor intensity in Italy is illustrated in Figure 4.4, which shows that children have been a decreasing proportion of the total workforce over time. Industrialization and technological development has driven children out of the job market and not the contrary. It is worth remembering that this is a correlation and not a causal effect, but the benefits enjoyed by children with economic development—largely caused by production techniques made more efficient by technological innovation—appear to emerge quite clearly.

Figure 4.4 shows that the percentage of children in the workforce decreased constantly throughout the period concerned. There are two exceptions: (*a*) from 1881 to 1901 the percentage of girls increased, and (*b*) we see a general increase in the intensity of child labor in the period 1931–1936. The graph also shows that the intensity rate is higher for girls than for boys, and that the two measures do not show any convergence until 1936. The characteristics of Figure 4.4 hold for each economic sector with no exception.

The fact that the period 1881–1901 saw a rise in the percentage of working girls out of the total female workforce could mean that technological development in the textile industry—a sector traditionally associated with female employment—in the early stages of industrialization was *not* averse to child labor (Goldin and Sokoloff 1982; Horrell and Humphries 1995). The increase in intensity observed in the latter half of the 1930s is particularly marked in farming, and the previous hypothesis holds true also in this case: that is to say, since war involved the enlistment of a considerable percentage of the adult population, it led to an increase in young workers (also with the employment of child labor being equal).

The changes in child labor intensity over time have been analyzed in greater detail by Toniolo and Vecchi (2007), who concluded that the decrease in labor intensity seen between 1881 and 1961 is only partly due to the fact that, over time, children were reallocated to economic sectors characterized by a lower

---

[13] The term "intensity" is sometimes used in order to indicate the number of hours worked in a day (week or other period of time). This is not how we use it in this chapter.

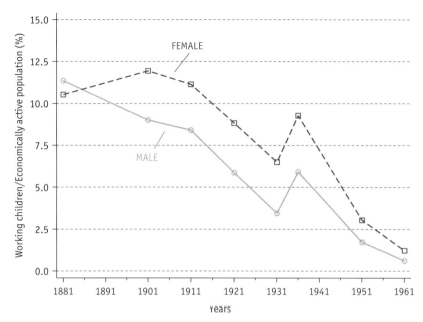

Figure 4.4 THE PERCENTAGE OF WORKING CHILDREN OUT OF THE TOTAL WORKFORCE. The figure shows the trend of the percentage of working children out of the total workforce (vertical axis) over time (horizontal axis). The decreasing trend suggests that technology reduced the employment of children as a production input.

labor intensity: rather, what we see is a decrease in the intensity with which children were employed within each economic sector, from farming to industry and the services. Therefore, on the whole, the story told by Italian census data is one of industrial development substituting away from child labor, reducing its demand in the job market.

5 Why Did the Italians Stop Sending Their Children to Work?

The decrease in the incidence of child labor over the decades that we saw in section 4 leads us to ask what factors were responsible for the decreasing use of child employment in Italian postunification history. We looked at the role of the state as legislator (section 2), which we considered tardy and relatively modest with regard to effectiveness. We then discussed the role of technology (section 4), hypothesizing that it could have favored the decrease in child labor. However, there are many other factors that could "explain" its decrease over the years: the role of the family is certainly the first thing that springs to mind, but the list is a long one and includes demographic, social, economic, and cultural aspects (Cunningham 2000; Humphries 2003; Cigno and Rosati 2005). In this section we illustrate the results of an econometric exercise aimed at identifying the critical factors involved—the ones that contributed to reducing child employment in Italy.

Observing child employment rates in each region of the country for several years enables us to use an econometric technique called "panel analysis". One of the advantages of this technique consists of the possibility of taking each region's specific features into consideration (those that do not change over time, that economists call "fixed individual effects"), and which are presumed to have a (positive or negative) impact on child labor rates. The technique is particularly suitable in our context because some regions—with all other demographic, income, or other characteristics being equal—show a greater child labor "propensity" compared to others. In Veneto, for example, the predominant cultural model seems to be one in which early employment is viewed positively by a broad section of the population.[14] Panel analysis enables us to account for these sociocultural aspects, which are not easily definable or measurable, and to bear them in mind when evaluating the evolution of child labor.[15]

The period examined concerns the years between 1901 and 1961, while the variables we constructed to "explain" the decreasing trend in child labor rates documented in section 3 are the following: (a) the region's average per-capita income, (b) the level of adults' education, (c) the availability of school infrastructures, (d) the distribution of employed workers according to economic sector (agriculture, industry, and the services), (e) the risk of the epidemiological environment in which households live, (f) a measure of the region's predominant "social capital," and (g) the average size of households. The results of this econometric exercise are summarized in Figure 4.5, and the rest of this section will be devoted to our relative comments.

Figure 4.5 compares the contribution made by certain variables (a subset of the a–g list mentioned above) after having "standardized" them, that is, transformed them to make them comparable by using the same unit of measurement. This procedure enables us to compare typically incomparable phenomena. For example, we can establish whether an increase in average household income has a greater impact than a drop in infant mortality caused by improvements in households' epidemiological environment.[16] After standardizing the variables, the results of the regression analysis are shown in Figure 4.5.

[14] Perhaps not surprisingly, the Veneto region tops rankings in high school dropout rates (Megale and Teselli 2006).

[15] The availability of incomplete regional statistics led us to specify an econometrically parsimonious, but sufficiently robust, model to start up the discussion on quantitative grounds. It is worth recalling here that this kind of model does not provide indications on the causal relations between variables, but sheds light on the mechanisms at work in determining the decreasing use made of child labor.

[16] The whole operation is not above criticism (Bring 1994), but it involves a degree of approximation that is negligible in our context. For those interested, the unit of measurement referred to in the text is equal to one standard deviation for each transformed variable.

To understand how to interpret the figure, let's start with the bar concerning "parents' literacy." The length of the bar measures the variation in the extent of child labor associated with one unit change of the level of education of the adult population (put simply, of the parents). The negative value, measured along the horizontal axis, implies that the increase in the percentage of adults able to read and write is associated with a marked decrease in child labor: in particular, an extra unit of education means eight percentage points less in child labor. We shall not go into the details of what we mean by "one unit" of each variable here, because the figure only aims to provide a sense of relative importance of the various factors involved, but these factors are different from one another on both conceptual and empirical levels. The standardization that we mentioned above is for this very purpose: to eliminate from the picture the complication of having to deal with different units of measurement.[17]

The further details provided in the Appendix add a second important component to our picture: they show that the effect of adult education on child labor is significant even when the basic model is extended to include effects common to all the regions and that vary over time. This leads us to rule out the hypothesis that behind the adult education–child labor relation there is really the effect of state legislation introduced in order to regulate the use of child labor and to oblige children to go to school (section 2). On the contrary, the estimates suggest that the mechanism at work is the level of parents' education: as the country's literacy level rises, so too does the households' awareness of the risks and disadvantages of sending their children to work compared to the advantages of sending them to school.

The second bar in Figure 4.5 concerns the role played by the level of average household income, which is approximated here by using the new regional estimates of per-capita GDP (chapter 9, "Poverty"). The estimates show that the increase in regional average income was a crucial factor in explaining the decrease in child labor in these estimates, even if it was of a lower intensity, in importance, compared to adult education.[18] The mechanism at work here is the one envisaged by the model of Basu and Van (1998), suggestively called "the luxury axiom": households send their children to work only when they are forced to by their poverty. The nonworking condition of children, in the historical period dealt with, is a luxury good: as long as parents' incomes are compressed and close to subsistence levels, households cannot afford the luxury of not sending their children to work. The Italian experience is similar to the British one during

---

[17] This result does not change if we adopt more sophisticated measures of the adult population's education level, such as the average number of years of schooling.

[18] An interesting finding emerging from other regressions detailed in the Appendix is the fact that the progress made in average income is particularly significant when we consider the decrease in working girls compared to boys.

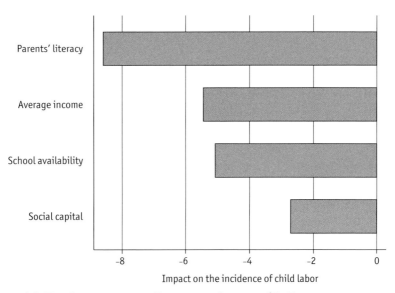

Impact on the incidence of child labor

Figure 4.5 THE IMPORTANCE OF EDUCATING PARENTS (TO EDUCATE THEIR CHILDREN). The figure shows the relative importance that various factors (listed on the vertical axis) have in explaining the decline in child labor seen over time. The longer the horizontal bar (along the horizontal axis), the greater the role played by the corresponding factor. Parents' education turns out to be the most powerful tool in the reduction of child labor in the period 1901–1961. (See Appendix-Sources and Methods, Tables 4.1 and 4.2)

the industrial revolution (Humphries 2013) and confirms the importance of improving household average income in order to decrease child labor.

The third factor considered in Figure 4.5 concerns the role played by the different availability of elementary schools in the territory. As is known, the Kingdom of Italy did not initially have adequate financial resources to enforce the law on compulsory schooling (see chapter 5, "Education"). There was a lack of schools and teachers. Lack of infrastructure is a decisive phenomenon in today's developing countries: the presence and vicinity of schools facilitates access and thus school attendance, thereby making the alternative of work less desirable (Go and Lindert 2010). Figure 4.5 suggests that the increase in the density of schools had a negative and significant impact on the spreading of child labor, regardless of the average income and education levels of individual regions. The availability of schools seems to have been as equally important as regional average income (the relative bars have slightly different lengths, but their difference is not significant). The impact of schools is greater for the labor of girls, for whom the statistical relation is particularly significant. In short, it would appear reasonable to hypothesize that when the state started to build schools, boys, but girls even more so, started to leave the fields.

The fourth factor that, in order of importance, is associated with the decline in child labor is what we have called "social capital," but what we could have called "culture" or "civil consciousness" (Banfield 1958; Putnam 1993; Guiso, Sapienza, and Zingales 2006). It is not easy to adequately measure the civil consciousness of a society (Felice 2012): there is no suitable definition and no data. This said, as a measure of participation in social, civil, and political life, we used the percentage of voters out of the total number of citizens having the right to vote. The results show that, with other factors being equal, in the regions where the number of voters increased over time, child labor—above all, with respect to girls—gradually decreased. One hypothesis is that it might be linked to the gradual granting of the right to vote to women, leading to universal suffrage in 1946. However, if we limit the regression analysis from 1901 to 1936, the impact of the *civil consciousness* variable remains significant. The issue thus deserves further analysis (Go and Lindert 2010).

There are other effects in addition to the ones considered so far and described in Figure 4.5, which likely contributed to determine the decrease in child labor in Italy. As discussed in section 5, technological development may have had a significant impact on child labor, even if economic theory is not clear on whether it encouraged or discouraged it (Goldin and Katz 2008; Galor and Moav 2006). It is not easy to find help on the empirical side because we do not have adequate variables to measure technological progress at the regional level. We have explored the use of census data on the employment structure of the economically active population on the assumption that technology is a crucial factor in determining the distribution of employed workers among economic sectors, namely farming, industry, and commerce. The estimates show how, ceteris paribus, greater industrialization is associated with lower recourse to child labor. The fundamental point concerns the "ceteris paribus" condition: in section 3 we had already hypothesized that development and industrialization were accompanied—in Italy's case—by a conspicuous decrease in the incidence of child labor. The estimates reinforce that hypothesis, ruling out the possibility of attributing to industrialization the effects exerted by other factors (a higher income level, for example, or a better education). The fact that it is an econometrically fragile result (the variable loses strength when we include temporal variables) leads us to be cautious, to consider the possibility that the industrialization process had "simply" accompanied the decrease in child labor over time without suggesting any causal link.

The same caution is necessary when interpreting the results concerning the role of average household size. In this case, the idea is that a greater propensity to invest in one's children's education should also be associated with lower fertility rates, because if children have to go to school and cannot contribute to the family's income, they become more "costly" (Becker, Cinnirella, and Woessmann 2010; Bleakley and Lange 2009).

The estimates given in the Appendix show that the progressive decrease in the average number of children is associated with a decrease in working girls, but not working boys. A possible interpretation of the result for the boys is that as the number of family members increased, a greater number of younger children managed to go to school, seeing that their older brothers were involved in working activities. The result for the girls, despite the fact that it is not statistically significant, is in line with the fact that their work, in many cases, consisted of doing the housework (Humphries 1987). The moment families decided to have fewer children and to improve their "quality" (Becker, Murphy, and Tamura 1990), in the sense of giving them a higher level of education, there was a decrease in the demand for housework, which mostly involved girls.

6 A Story without a Happy Ending

When talking about child labor, the Italians do not have a good reputation. It is an old story. People in Europe were already speaking ill of the Italians in the mid-nineteenth century. We saw this with regard to the "child trading" issue: the French denounced the case of Italian children—literally sold by their parents to sector traders—who wandered the streets of Paris. The news stories coming from the United States were no better. Miriam Cohen (1982, 443) reported the comment of some observers in the late nineteenth century who described the behavior of Italian immigrant families in New York: "The Italian parent is satisfied as soon as his son barely learns to read and write. He, the Italian, waits anxiously for the time his son is able to earn himself a wage." What was striking was the peculiarity of the Italian community compared to those of other nationalities of immigrants.

Other effects would seem to have escaped foreign observers, but were grasped by domestic ones. Francesco Coletti (1866–1940), the author of a splendid essay published in 1911 on Italian emigration, said that the benefits of emigration included not only the effects of remittances on the decline in child labor (the remittances made it less pressing to send children to work) but also "moral benefits." In other words, Coletti observed, even if we do concede that the Italians initially did have a particular propensity for child labor, emigration favored a rapid and widespread evolution toward an appreciation of the benefits associated with being literate and numerate (chapter 6, "Migration"): "One should see the zeal with which lower-class mothers get their children accepted at school and in watching over their every progress! The child is washed, dressed in clean clothes, accompanied to school and warm-heartedly entrusted to the teacher's diligence, because his father writes from America that his son must grow up educated, because only now does he realize the damage of not knowing" (Coletti 1911, 258–259). The process, quite plausibly, continued in the following decades.

In light of the new estimates drafted on the basis of the population censuses, we concluded that most of this reputation is also statistically ungrounded. It is likely that, similarly to what happened in other countries, in the initial stages of industrialization (for example, between 1881 and 1901), the use of child labor in certain sectors (textiles, for instance) did not decrease. However, on the whole, industrialization in Italy, which started in the latter half of the nineteenth century, seems to have been "benevolent" toward children. The new statistical reconstructions presented in section 3 reposition Italy within the international context after World War II: the child labor incidence rates in Italy were in line—if not lower—with the average values of European countries and of those countries with a similar per-capita GDP to Italy's (ILO 1996; Basu 1999).

Census sources do not allow us to go beyond 1961, though: once the legislative framework was completed, Italy stopped counting the number of working children, in the assumption that the problem was solved in view of the existence of adequate laws. In light of the available studies, it is not possible to know how true this was. On the whole, there are many reasons to believe that child labor has not been eradicated, but instead calls for renewed attention on the part of government (Istat 2002; Save the Children 2013).

In the second part of this chapter, we used econometrics to identify the most important factors underlying the decline in child labor. The strongest result concerns the role of literacy in the adult population. This was the most powerful driving force enabling children to avoid entering the workforce—more than household income, more than school buildings themselves (even if still important), and more than the prevalent "social norms" in the various regions of the country.

In view of the improvements in education (chapter 5, "Education"), the temptation is to round off the history of child labor in Italy with a happy ending. If we think about it, illiteracy was eradicated, the average number of years of schooling increased, and access to schools of every type and level increased, along with per-capita income (chapter 7, "Income"). However, we should resist the temptation to do so. Tullio De Mauro recalled the results of a study carried out in 2003 by the *Centro Europeo dell'Educazione* (Cede). According to this study, over two million adult Italians are illiterate (about 5 percent of the adult population); almost fifteen million are semi-illiterate, that is, they are unable to read and understand the text of a questionnaire composed of very elementary phrases; another fifteen million individuals "risk sliding back into semi-illiteracy and are at the lower fringes with regard to numeracy and the ability to comprehend texts necessary in a complex society such as ours" (De Mauro 2010, 23). More recently, an OECD study on twenty-four countries dampened the enthusiasm of many commentators by pointing to Italy's gap with other countries in terms of the competencies of the adult population to understand and use information in order to be active and interact in society and in the economic world (OECD,

2013). According to the rankings drawn up on the basis of the results of the study, Italy lies toward the bottom of the list, behind all those countries taking part in the statistical survey (Hanushek et al. 2013). Perhaps an even more worrying finding concerns the seriousness of the Italian phenomenon, regardless of international comparisons: about 30 percent of the Italian respondents did not even have the *minimum* reading/writing and numeracy skills (OECD 2013, 28). What emerges from the other extreme of the distribution is not very comforting, either: in Italy, only one individual out of every twenty has a *maximum* level of reading/writing skills (ibid.). If what our analysis highlighted is true, that is, the crucial aspect of parents' education in ensuring that their children attend school, then Italian children are forewarned: the risk of being sent out to find a job while still young continues to be great.

Appendix—Sources and Methods

Figure 4.1 The incidence of child labor in Italy, 1881–2011 1881–1961: Toniolo and Vecchi (2007); 2000: Istat (2002); 2011: Associazione Bruno Trentin and Save the Children (2013).

Box 1 Children at work in the world The data refer to children aged 5–14 years, classified as "economically active." The database that the graph is based on was made available to us by the project Understanding Children Work. We particularly wish to thank Furio Camillo Rosati and Lorenzo Guarcello.

Figure 4.2 Child workers in Italy and in the rest of the world The data on the incidence of child labor are from the ILO database (http://www.ilo.org/dyn/clsurvey/lfsurvey.home). The data regarding Italy are our estimates, as in Figure 4.1.

Figure 4.3 Child labor in Italy according to macro-area The sources and methods are described in Toniolo and Vecchi (2007).

Figure 4.4 The percentage of working children out of the total workforce Source: Toniolo and Vecchi (2007).

Figure 4.5 The importance of educating parents (to educate their children) The figure has been constructed on the basis of estimates of the following fixed-effect panel model:

$$L_{it} = \mathbf{x}_{it}\beta + \lambda_i + \tau_t + \varepsilon_{it}$$

Table 4.1 **The determinants of child labor**

	(1)	(2)	(3)	(4)	(5)	(6)	(7)	(8)
Adult male literacy rate	-1.121***	-0.792***	-0.710***	-0.632***	-0.494***	-0.497***	-0.476***	-0.406***
	-0.062	-0.072	-0.063	-0.061	-0.103	-0.106	-0.126	-0.161
Number of schools per 100 children (10–14)		-5.563***	-2.477***	-2.235***	-2.373**	-2.300***	-2.432**	-4.011***
		-1.035	-0.68	-0.736	-0.833	-0.773	-1.076	-1.015
Per-capita GDP			-3.422***	-3.094***	-2.367***	-2.379***	-2.491***	-2.646*
			-0.307	-0.343	-0.528	-0.488	-0.639	-1.297
Percentage of workers in industry				-0.093**	-0.076*	-0.093**	-0.096**	-0.044
				-0.038	-0.043	-0.041	-0.035	-0.063
Percentage of workers in services				-0.483***	-0.373**	-0.477***	-0.486***	0.099
				-0.142	-0.158	-0.159	-0.141	-0.292
Infant mortality (total)					0.072*	0.019	0.023	-0.056
					-0.034	-0.042	-0.046	-0.04
Percentage voters out of electorate						-0.152***	-0.160***	-0.187**
						-0.034	-0.048	-0.084
Average number of household members							-1.195	-0.808
							-4.475	-3.22
Constant	113.389***	105.813***	103.846***	107.150***	84.187***	103.485***	108.240***	100.488***
	-4.715	-3.519	-3.341	-3.774	-11.872	-14.913	-22.829	-34.06
Time dummy variables	no	no	no	no	no	no	no	yes
Observations	120	120	120	120	120	120	120	120
R-squared	0.762	0.804	0.884	0.888	0.891	0.895	0.895	0.953

The three asterisks mean that the estimated coefficients are statistically significant, that is, other tł an zero (with 1% significance).

Table 4.2 The determinants of child labor for boys

	(1)	(2)	(3)	(4)	(5)	(6)	(7)	(8)
Adult male literacy rate	-1.324***	-1.018***	-0.947***	-0.858***	-0.727***	-0.728***	-0.561***	-0.387**
	(0.039)	(0.074)	(0.063)	(0.055)	(0.081)	(0.083)	(0.111)	(0.157)
Number of schools per 100 children (10–14)		-5.184***	-2.504***	-2.222**	-2.361**	-2.301**	-3.321**	-2.446**
		(1.102)	(0.763)	(0.806)	(0.872)	(0.827)	(1.235)	(1.061)
Per-capita GDP			-2.972***	-2.606***	-1.841***	-1.886***	-2.714***	-1.349
			(0.275)	(0.339)	(0.450)	(0.428)	(0.589)	(1.078)
Percentage of workers in industry				-0.099*	-0.086	-0.097	-0.128**	-0.036
				(0.056)	(0.064)	(0.063)	(0.045)	(0.038)
Percentage of workers in services				-0.556***	-0.456**	-0.532**	-0.600***	0.132
				(0.173)	(0.180)	(0.186)	(0.155)	(0.257)
Infant mortality (males)					0.069**	0.029	0.059	-0.046
					(0.029)	(0.038)	(0.035)	(0.034)
Percentage voters out of electorate						-0.117**	-0.176***	-0.118
						(0.050)	(0.059)	(0.073)

	(1)	(2)	(3)	(4)	(5)	(6)	(7)	(8)
Average number of household members							-9.183**	-4.586*
							(3.600)	(2.537)
Constant	131.923***	124.863***	123.155***	126.817***	104.500***	119.389***	155.492***	88.905**
	(2.959)	(3.246)	(2.864)	(3.689)	(9.476)	(13.369)	(17.516)	(30.717)
Time dummy variables	no	no	no	no	no	no	no	yes
Observations	120	120	120	120	120	120	120	120
R-squared	0.831	0.859	0.906	0.911	0.913	0.915	0.920	0.963

The three asterisks mean that the estimated coefficients are statistically significant, that is, other than zero (with 1% significance).

Table 4.3 The determinants of child labor for girls

	(1)	(2)	(3)	(4)	(5)	(6)	(7)	(8)
Adult male literacy rate	-0.907***	-0.554***	-0.461***	-0.394***	-0.262	-0.263	-0.389*	-0.439*
	(0.103)	(0.121)	(0.118)	(0.123)	(0.194)	(0.198)	(0.200)	(0.210)
Number of schools per 100 children (10–14)		-5.971***	-2.456**	-2.655**	-2.375*	-2.299*	-1.530	-5.704***
		(1.217)	(0.998)	(1.053)	(1.168)	(1.134)	(1.270)	(1.555)
Per-capita GDP			-3.897***	-3.605***	-2.987***	-2.909***	-2.221**	-4.099*
			(0.407)	(0.432)	(0.766)	(0.707)	(0.891)	(2.013)
Percentage of workers in industry				-0.089	-0.070	-0.093	-0.071	-0.060
				(0.071)	(0.079)	(0.082)	(0.079)	(0.116)
Percentage of workers in services				-0.411**	-0.301	-0.431*	-0.378	0.034
				(0.159)	(0.221)	(0.244)	(0.248)	(0.476)
Infant mortality (total)					0.069	0.005	-0.016	-0.070
					(0.064)	(0.078)	(0.079)	(0.068)
Percentage voters out of electorate						-0.188***	-0.138**	-0.256*
						(0.062)	(0.063)	(0.132)

	(1)	(2)	(3)	(4)	(5)	(6)	(7)	(8)
Average number of household members							7.014	2.984
							(6.471)	(5.521)
Constant	93.976***	85.845***	83.605***	86.593***	65.157**	87.853***	59.123	116.048**
	(7.767)	(6.687)	(6.707)	(6.750)	(22.967)	(28.431)	(39.063)	(54.752)
Time dummy variables	no	no	no	no	no	no	no	yes
Observations	120	120	120	120	120	120	120	120
R-squared	0.604	0.662	0.787	0.792	0.795	0.802	0.807	0.892

The three asterisks mean that the estimated coefficients are statistically significant, that is, other than zero (with 1% significance).

where L_{it} stands for the child labor rate in region i in year t (1901, 1911, 1921, 1931, 1936, 1951, 1961), λ_i are fixed effects that do not vary over time, and τ_t are the time dummy variables. The covariate **x** vector contains the following variables: the literacy rate of the adult male population aged above 15 years, the number of schools per 100 children aged 10–14 years, the per-capita GDP in euros at 2001 prices, the percentage of employed workers in industry and the services, the average number of household members, and the infant mortality rate. When the years available do not coincide with the census ones of the dependent variable, the data were subjected to linear interpolation. The model was estimated separately for males and females. The results of the Hausman test suggest a preference for the estimates of the fixed effect model rather than of the random effect one.

5

Education

WITH BRIAN A'HEARN

1 The Learning Curve

The Italy that recently celebrated its 150th anniversary is not a highly educated country. According to the latest estimates (Barro and Lee 2013, online appendix), adult Italians had on average completed 9.6 years of education. After completing primary and lower secondary school, the average Italian set aside his or her books and entered the world of work by the age of 16. This level of schooling puts Italy *half a century* behind the world's educational leader, the United States, which surpassed 9.6 years of schooling in the early 1960s, reaching 13.2 by 2010. Of twenty-four advanced economies, Italy's educational attainment surpassed only two (Portugal and Turkey), though in a global context the picture appears rosier. Ranked against sub-Saharan African countries, Italy would place joint second with Botswana (behind South Africa).

Historical estimates place Italy at a similar low ranking in 1870. Late-nineteenth-century Italy stood out as an exceptionally poorly educated society. With an average of less than one year of schooling, Victor Emmanuel II's subjects deserved the dunce's cap and a place in the far corner of the classroom. The country was far behind the leading nations of the day—the United States (5.6 years); Germany (5.5); France and the United Kingdom (4 each); and even other economically backward countries such as Spain (2.4), Japan (1.7), and Greece (1.5). Box 1 explores years of schooling calculations in greater depth, covering the entire period from 1870 to 2015.

International comparisons show an even greater lag when we focus on upper secondary education. At the time of unification, fewer than nine of every thousand children received some form of post-elementary education (De Mauro 1963, 42), while university students constituted a tiny minority of around 6,500, lost—as it were—in a population of over twenty million (Checchi 1997). One hundred fifty years later, 22 percent of young adults (aged 25–34) have a university degree (OECD 2014). This is a small number in absolute terms, but

Box 1 Human Capital in Italy and around the World since 1870

A widely used measure of a country's educational level is average years of schooling. Morrison and Murtin (2009) have recently developed historical estimates that allow us to put Italian achievements in a long-term comparative perspective. On these estimates, Italy has chronically lagged behind the most developed economies and is now half a century behind the United States, and several decades behind European rivals such as the United Kingdom. The trajectories of Japan or, more recently, Malaysia show that, starting from a similar lag, much faster catch-up on educational leaders should have been possible.

Mean years of schooling calculations are difficult and subject to error in the best of circumstances, the more so when estimates are extended away from the information rich environment of modern censuses. In Italy's case, estimates of mean schooling ca. 2010 range from 9.2 (Felice and Vasta 2015) to 11.0 (Cohen and Soto 2007), and Morrison and Murtin (2009)

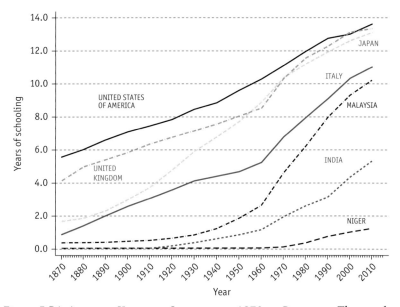

Figure 5.B1 Average Years of Schooling, 1870 to Present. The graph shows the increase in average years of schooling (vertical axis) over time (horizontal axis). Over the 140 years considered here, Italy (blue line) increased its human capital but did not manage to catch up with the more educated countries.

exclude the country from their "core" of highest-reliability estimates. There are also interpretive weaknesses to this measure of education, in particular its silence regarding inequality. Consider a hypothetical system comprising a 5-year elementary school followed by a 5-year secondary school, and a population of 100 school-aged children. Mean years of education are identical when all 100 children complete only primary school (hence, an average in the population of 5 years) or when 50 complete the entire cycle of 10 years, while the rest never set foot in a school.

particularly when compared with figures for other countries. The average for the Organisation for Economic Cooperation and Development (OECD) countries, for example, is 39 percent; Italy is a sidereal distance from the leading countries, where around 60 percent of young people attain tertiary education (e.g., Korea 66 percent, Japan 59 percent, and Canada 57 percent). Nor are comparisons with the "neighbors" much comfort: Spain and France have almost *double* Italy's share of young people completing university (39 percent and 43 percent, respectively).

The quality of education, which is no less important than the quantity, is much harder to measure, but the available data show the scale of Italy's lag. Since the year 2000, the Programme for International Student Assessment (PISA) has conducted international surveys to assess the knowledge and cognitive abilities of fifteen-year-olds. In 2012, PISA assessed nearly 40,000 Italian teenagers on reading comprehension, mathematics, and science: the results were disappointing—below the OECD average in all three disciplinary areas (OECD 2014).

Today's debate on education focuses on higher education, on the quality of teaching, and on the contribution made by "human capital" to productivity and competitiveness (Visco 2008). Historically, the battle for education was, instead, conducted at the elementary school level; it was a question of spreading basic literacy. Acquiring the ability to read, write, and perform basic arithmetical operations (in the nineteenth century), and to access and process information (in more recent times), not only increased productivity and thus income but also directly contributed to an individual's wellbeing, increasing his or her capabilities to understand the environment, to manage health (of the entire family), to take part in political life, and to secure respect for his or her rights (Sen 1985; Hanushek and Woessman 2008). Ultimately, mass literacy and schooling favored individual freedom of action and decreased inequality in the distribution of wellbeing (Checchi 2006; Pope 2009).

To analyze the contribution made by education to the wellbeing of Italians over time, we have constructed a database of key indicators such as school enrollment and attendance, literacy rates, and the number of teachers, at both primary and secondary levels, for the nation as a whole and its regions, for the whole 150 years since unification. The new series tell a story about Italy's achievements that is novel in many respects. It is a story that, as we shall see, has not been easy: increasing the population's schooling and literacy level was accomplished, but painfully slowly and with persisting disparities. According to the data we shall present here, few modern countries have struggled as much as Italy in fighting illiteracy and in getting children into classrooms.

2 Illiteracy Dies Hard

At the proclamation of the Kingdom of Italy in 1861, only 27 percent of the adult population could read—a figure far below that of the most literate countries of the time, such as Sweden (90 percent), Prussia (80 percent), or Britain (67–70 percent). The gap was wide even with respect to France and the Austrian Empire, both with values of around 55–60 percent (Cipolla 1969).

Furthermore, there were considerable differences between the various parts of the country corresponding to the states that existed prior to the country's unification. On the eve of unification, the Italian Peninsula was home to seven separate states: the Kingdom of Sardinia, the Kingdom of Lombardy-Venetia, the Grand Duchy of Tuscany, the Duchy of Modena and Reggio, the Duchy of Parma and Piacenza, the Papal State, and the Kingdom of the Two Sicilies. Figure 5.1 illustrates the stark differences between the territories of these defunct states. With literacy rates above 40 percent—and above 50 percent in some regions— the former kingdoms of Sardinia and Lombardy-Venetia were not far behind France or the Habsburg Empire. In the provinces of the former Kingdom of the Two Sicilies, by contrast, hardly more than one person in ten could read, with the literacy rate failing to reach 20 percent even in the most educated of the southern regions, Campania. The north and south of Italy were two different worlds.

Literacy rates in 1861 were the product, and are now our best evidence, of schooling in the preunification states. In relatively literate Lombardy and Veneto (which would not become part of Italy until 1866), municipalities had been required to set up and maintain elementary schools, and parents obliged to send children aged 6–12 to school. In the Kingdom of Sardinia (Piedmont), schooling had not been compulsory, but education had been firmly in the hands of the state, which by 1848 had imposed a centralized system with detailed regulations covering everything from nursery schools to technical schools and universities, from the training of teachers to their salaries, from curricula to examinations. At the other extreme, in both the Papal State and the Kingdom of the Two Sicilies there had been no obligations of any kind regarding school provision or attendance, nor a recognizable, planned school system. A Neapolitan law of the mid-nineteenth

State	Literacy rate (%)
Kingdom of Sardinia	42.0
Piedmont	50.6
Liguria	34.9
Sardinia	10.8
Kingdom of Lombardy-Venetia	43.2
Lombardy	48.7
Veneto	36.3
Duchy of Parma and Piacenza	22.0
Duchy of Modena and Reggio	25.0
Grand Duchy of Tuscany	27.9
Papal States	24.3
Romagna	24.2
Marche	18.5
Umbria	17.9
Lazio	34.8
Kingdom of the Two Sicilies	14.4
Abruzzi-Molise	13.0
Campania	18.2
Puglia	14.6
Basilicata	11.0
Calabria	12.1
Sicily	12.7
ITALY	27.0

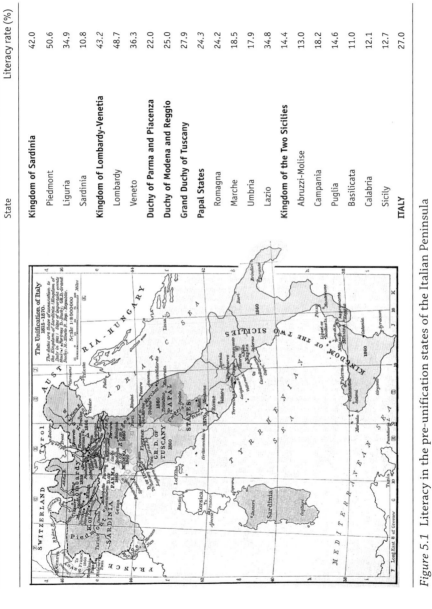

Figure 5.1 Literacy in the pre-unification states of the Italian Peninsula

century "explicitly authorized the entrusting of classes, when necessary, to illiterate schoolmistresses" (De Mauro 1963, 39). Time would reveal how resistant these regions remained to implementing Italian laws on compulsory schooling.

3 The Persistence of Initial Conditions

Having made Italy, we must now make the Italians, D'Azeglio is said to have said.[1] A first step would be to teach them Italian. In a population of over twenty-five million, De Mauro's (1963) estimate is that only 600,000 might have been able to read and write Italian. The remainder were either illiterate or had basic literacy in a language too far removed from Italian for easy comprehension (true of dialects everywhere outside Tuscany and Rome). The new Kingdom's government moved quickly on the legislative front. Piedmont's Casati Law of 1859, which continued the system of detailed and comprehensive regulation of education, was extended to each of the formerly independent states of Italy as they were annexed. The law made basic primary education both free and compulsory. Article 317 stated: "Elementary education is provided free of charge in all municipalities. The latter must provide it in proportion to their capabilities and according to the needs of their inhabitants." Meanwhile, Article 326 declared that parents of both boys and girls who failed to ensure their children received two years of elementary education were punishable by law.

But the difficulty of actually enforcing the Casati Law in the absence of either stick (effective sanctions) or carrot (financial support) soon became clear. Figure 5.2 shows the extraordinary persistence of illiteracy in some regions, even among young people recently of school age (aged 15–19 at the time of the census). In 1911, fifty years and two generations on from unification, youth literacy barely reached 50 percent in the south and islands. The 45-point gap relative to the northwest had not diminished at all since 1861. Southern regions closed the gap significantly only from the 1930s, progressing at a plodding pace while the north ran up against the ceiling of 100 percent literacy. Regional convergence was more by mathematical necessity than by virtue.

4 Money Mattered, up to a Point

The disparate schooling arrangements of the preunification states did share some features. One was a continuing involvement of the Church. In the Kingdom

---

[1] "Fatta l'Italia, bisogna fare gli italiani" is an apocryphal quote attributed to Massimo D'Azeglio (1798–1866), a Piedmontese statesman who played an important role in the Italian *Risorgimento*.

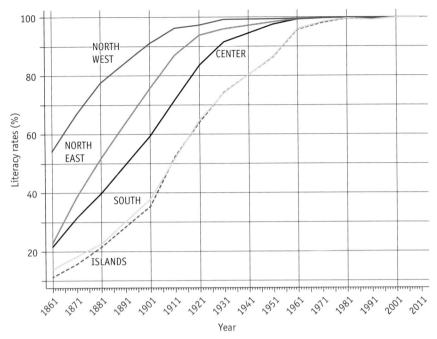

Figure 5.2 YOUTH LITERACY BY REGION, 1861–2011. The figure shows the trend in literacy rates (vertical axis) among young people (ages 15 to 19) in five geographical areas over time (horizontal axis). Southern regions catch up on the North only when the latter bumps into the ceiling of 100 percent literacy.

of the Two Sicilies, bishops could inspect schools and had veto power over the appointment of teachers (who were mostly members of the clergy anyway). In Lombardy-Venetia the parish priest was also the director of the local school, while in Tuscany education was explicitly in the hands of the Piarist fathers. Even in Piedmont, where secularization had probably gone the farthest, a great many teachers remained religious, Catholic moral education was part of the school syllabus, and every school had a spiritual director appointed by the local bishop. Besides being an expression of the society's culture and power relations, this situation had its rationale in the fact that potential teachers—educated people willing to devote themselves to public service—were a rare breed outside the ranks of the clergy (De Fort 1995).

A second common feature of preunification school provision was local finance, which prevailed even where, as in Lombardy-Venetia, it was the state that obliged municipalities to set up and maintain schools—an unfunded mandate, in modern terms. When present, central finance was sporadic, poorly organized, and often tied to particular sponsored schools. Such a system (or perhaps lack of system) was preserved by the new Italian state, and has been the focus of much criticism by Italian historians. It is argued that giving the local authorities the task of providing schooling services was a mistake. Local governments (*comuni*, or municipalities), which were too poor and distracted by other priorities, could not take on the burden of this expenditure; hence, the modest performance of the school indicators for the whole country.

The international literature suggests a different view: in the mid-nineteenth century, decentralized financing was the norm in the most educationally succesful countries such as Prussia and the United States. Lindert (2004) points out that when a consensus in favor of public schools was present in only a few regions, a policy of state-funded, centrally organized education was never going command majority political support at the national level. In the early stages of the diffusion of schooling, a degree of local autonomy helped the process get started. Although Italian historiography maintains the traditional view (meager municipal budgets meant that local governments could not afford anything more than what they provided: little education and of poor quality), data for the year 1881 and summarized in the maps of Figure 5.3 support an alternative interpretation.

The first map shows the distribution of education spending as a percentage of total expenditure (the lighter shade indicates low levels while the darker shade indicates high levels). The data show that the allocation of local resources was more focused on schools in the central and northern regions compared to the southern ones (the same result is obtained when using expenditure in absolute terms instead of as a percentage of total spending).

The second map shows the variation in the relation between two surtaxes—both of them forms of local self-taxation—that the law entrusted to municipal government discretion: the first was a tax on real property, while the second was a tax on consumption. These two kinds of levies roughly correspond to direct taxation, such as an income tax today, and indirect taxation (such as a modern value-added tax). The map shows that the north of the country taxed property more heavily than the south. Because landowners largely made up the ranks of local government, the map suggests that there was a significantly greater willingness on the part of northern landowners to tax themselves in order to provide for local public services than what we find in the south, which opted more for regressive consumption taxes. Battilani (2001) shows that this was a continuation of traditions predating unification. Hence, regardless of average local economic conditions, it would appear that northern municipalities—much more than southern ones—redistributed resources in financing the acquisition of human capital on the part of the less affluent classes. There were also—not infrequent—cases of northern municipalities actually being fined for exceeding the limits established by law for the self-taxation of property.

EDUCATION EXPENDITURE (% OF TOTAL EXPENDITURE)   LAND TAX/CONSUMPTION DUTY

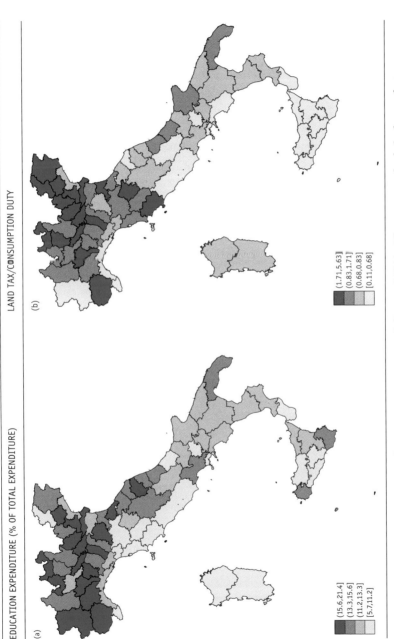

(a)

[15.6,21.4]
[13.3,15.6]
[11.2,13.3]
[5.7,11.2]

(b)

[1.71,5.63]
[0.83,1.71]
[0.68,0.83]
[0.11,0.68]

Figure 5.3 THE QUESTION OF THE "POOR MUNICIPALITIES" (ITALY, 1881). The map on the left shows that education expenditure in the northern regions was significantly greater than in the southern regions: the darker the shade, the greater the percentage of expenditure on education. The map on the right shows the greater propensity to tax land ownership in the north compared to the south. If we take both maps into consideration, we see that promoting schooling was a priority in the north, but not in the south.

5 The Third "R"

The census of 31 December 1861 recorded 17 million illiterates out of a total population of 22 million people: 80 out of every 100 inhabitants were unable to read or write. If we exclude preschool-aged children from the figure, the number of illiterates decreases to 14 million, about three-quarters of the adult population. It was a kingdom of illiterates, then, in the aftermath of unification. A hundred and fifty years later, in the 2011 census, those declaring they were unable to read and write were more than half a million (595,684 people, to be precise) out of a total population of 59 million: that is to say, slightly more than 1 percent of the population are illiterate, according to the National Institute of Statistics.

Figure 5.4 shows the trend in literacy for young people (aged 15–19, in blue) and for the entire adult population (over 15 years of age, in blue).[2] Starting from extremely low levels in 1861, literacy rates increased steadily over the decades. A careful analysis of the series, however, leads us to conclude that these results are rather modest if not downright disappointing. Educating adults is a difficult task requiring, in all likelihood, considerable time. On the other hand, teaching children how to read and write in a free and compul sory state school should lead to substantial and rapid progress in *young people's* literacy levels. When the international community signed the so-called Millennium Development Goals in the year 2000, it was estimated that fifteen years would be enough to achieve universal schooling—that is, for *all* children in every country in the world to complete the entire cycle of primary education.[3] Figure 5.4 shows that Italy had to wait ninety years from the time of unification before achieving literacy rates near 90 percent even among those aged 15–19. (As we shall see in section 6, this was also due to a particularly unbalanced territorial distribution.)

In addition to reading and writing, basic arithmetic is essential for an individual to thrive. If *literacy* is the ability to read and write, we can call basic mathematical ability *numeracy*. Like literacy, numeracy is a cognitive ability contributing to human capital and thus the productivity of an individual and of

[2] The literacy rates in Figure 5.4 are calculated from census data, which tabulate the responses of individuals to questions about ability to read and write. Self-reported literacy will not be accurate when people are reluctant to admit they are illiterate. A'Hearn, Auria, and Vecchi (2011) explore the use of alternative sources including civil marriage records (where the married couple had to sign their names, if they were able to), and the results of informal literacy tests of conscripts: their results confirm the picture outlined in Figure 5.4.

[3] The Millennium Development Goals are eight objectives that member states of the United Nations committed themselves to achieving by 2015, by signing a common declaration. The first goal is to eradicate extreme poverty and hunger, while the second is to guarantee universal primary education. The interested reader is referred to the website: http://www.un.org/millenniumgoals. See also Pritchett (2013).

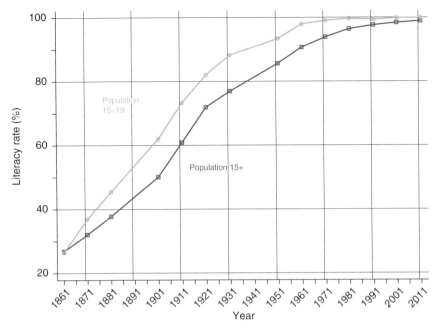

Figure 5.4 LITERACY RATES, 1861–2011. The graph shows the percentage in the population able to read (vertical axis) over time (horizontal axis) for two different groups: the "young" population (pale blue line) and the whole adult population (dark blue line).

the population. Today, there are surveys enabling researchers to measure this ability—for example, the PISA studies mentioned in section 1—but the available data only cover the most recent decades. Economic historians have found a solution to this by drawing on a well-known phenomenon in demography—the tendency to report approximate or rounded ages, or *age-heaping*.

5.1 THE AGE-HEAPING OF ITALIANS

Age-heaping is a common phenomenon that is observed in aggregate data when individuals provide information about their age in round figures, showing a preference for even numbers, multiples of 5 and 10, or other appealing numbers. When a sample of individuals are interviewed and asked for their age, the histogram summarizing the distribution of declared ages usually shows some trace of age-heaping: we see unusually high frequencies (tall bars) for the ages corresponding to appealing numbers, and the opposite for less attractive numbers. This heaping of reported ages on particular numbers makes sample data inaccurate, and creates a real problem for demographers, epidemiologists, and

Box 2 Women and Illiteracy

In Italy today, 27 percent of women aged 25–34 have completed tertiary education; the percentage for men is lower, standing at 17 percent (OECD 2014). This gender gap in favor of women is an epochal role reversal: men have historically always boasted higher educational attainment than women. The same situation is found in developing countries today; according to World Bank data, there are many countries in which men have a 20 percent edge over women with regard to literacy; in Morocco, Tunisia, and other countries in North Africa and in the Middle East, the gender gap lies between 15 percent and 25 percent; in a great many central African countries, the differences are just under 30 percent; in Pakistan it reaches 27 percent, while in Yemen the figure is 36 percent.

Figure 5.B2 shows that, historically, women in Italy too "lagged behind," but not too much. In 1861, for example, the literacy rate was 34 percent among men and 20 percent among women. The 14-point difference is exactly the same as the average for the group of countries with low per-capita incomes today (World Bank 2014), while, from a historical perspective, it may be considered rather small for the times compared to the 21 percent of Spain (the estimate for 1860), 7 percent for France (1872) or 5 percent for Prussia (1871) (Cipolla 1969). The gender gap decreased rapidly for younger generations exposed to public schooling.

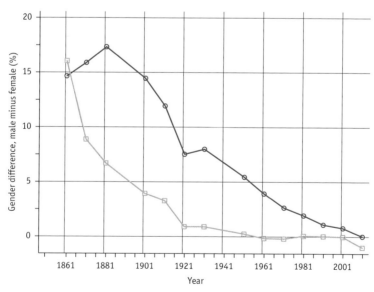

Figure 5.B2 GENDER GAP IN LITERACY RATES, 1861–2001. The graph shows the trend in differences between male and female literacy rates (vertical axis) over time (horizontal axis). The dark blue line refers to the population aged over 15 years, while the light blue line refers to young people aged 15–19 years.

other scholars who need an accurate representation of the population's age distribution.[4]

To illustrate the phenomenon, we shall use data from the Florentine tax registry of 1427 (Herlihy and Klapisch-Zuber 1978). In that year, to raise money for war, the Florentine republic decided to tax its citizens with a levy proportional to their ability to pay. This was no easy task in the fifteenth century. Every citizen was required to declare his or her name, under the city banner, as well as those of his or her family members; the age and occupation of each member; and, naturally, the amount of each source of income (with false declarations punishable by confiscation of the relevant property). Figure 5.5 shows the age distribution in these data.

Economic historians realized that what was a problem for demography could be an opportunity for economic history. The idea is that an individual who does not report his or her age accurately probably does not know it, and is likely to be a poorly educated person with weak numeracy. There is a great deal of evidence in support of this hypothesis; one example is a study carried out in Saudi Arabia in 1976, which showed that individuals reporting ages divisible by 5 (that is, 25, 30, and so on) earned wages 20 percent lower, on average, than the pay of individuals reporting other ages (Myers 1976). Economic historians have thus suggested that the greater the degree of age-heaping observed in a population, the lower the number of educated individuals, in particular with regard to numeracy. According to this interpretation, the presence of age-heaping becomes an indicator of the quantity and, in some respects, the quality of human capital.[5]

Figure 5.6 shows the age frequency distribution for the province of Naples alongside that of Turin for the year 1871. It is a similar graph to Figure 5.5, but for a period almost five hundred years later. If we consider the Naples histogram (in light blue), there is an obvious preference for multiples of five (and, less markedly, multiples of two), which is especially strong among older individuals. Turin (in blue) shows the same patterns, but they are much less pronounced. If we could summarize the degree of age-heaping in a single number, such comparisons would be easier and more precise. The "ABC index" of A'Hearn, Baten, and Crayen (2009) is such a number; it measures age heaping and expresses it in more intuitive terms, as the share of the population that *accurately* reports age, that is, numeracy (Box 3). The ABC index takes values of 93 and 82 in Turin and Naples provinces, respectively. The numeracy gap between the two former

---

[4] Among the first to investigate the phenomenon was an Italian demographer and statistician, Roberto Bachi (1909–1995), in a study of 1951 (Bachi 1951).

[5] Age-heaping has a social side that transcends the individual one; not only does it reveal the individual's cognitive ability, but also that of the environment the individual lives in. In a modern society, individuals need to know their own age to attend school, get a driving license, enlist in the armed forces, get a pension, prove their identity, get a passport, and so on. It was not like this in the past. Many people only had an approximate idea of their age; dates of birth were not recorded—by families or by the registry office.

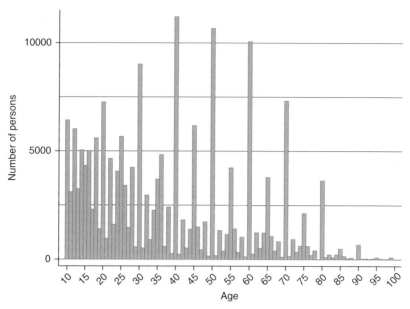

Figure 5.5 AGE-HEAPING IN TUSCANY 1427. The graph shows the frequency distribution (histogram) of the various ages. The peaks we see correspond to the "appealing" numbers, typically multiples of the number five: the unusual frequency of these numbers is not a real phenomenon, but rounding caused by the people's ignorance of their own year of birth.

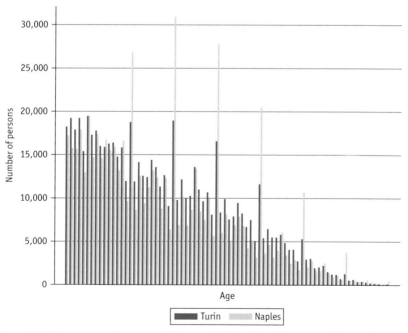

Figure 5.6 NUMERACY, TURIN VS. NAPLES, 1871. The histogram shows the age frequency distribution for the city of Naples (in pale blue) and the city of Turin (in dark blue) in 1871, for the population aged 10 years or over. Age-heaping is more marked in Naples than in Turin, and can be interpreted as a measure of the average differences in education level between the two cities.

Box 3 **The ABC of Women**

The inability to accurately give one's age makes it possible to roughly estimate the different levels of human capital among individuals in a population. An interesting application concerns the comparison between men and
women: the scale of the gender gap is often as difficult to establish as it is
important in order to judge the more or less "inclusive" nature of economic
development. The ABC index that we discussed in the text lends itself well
for the purpose and manages to summarize, in a single number, the degree
of age-heaping in a distribution (A'Hearn, Baten, and Crayen 2009).

The ABC index takes on values from 0 to 100: a value of 75 means that
75 individuals out of 100 accurately stated their age, while 25 could only
give an approximate age, rounding to a multiple of 5; in this case, a young
"thirty-something" who is asked his age will answer 30, or 35, but not one
of the numbers in between.

Figure 5.B3 THE ACTRESS SOPHIA LOREN. The actress Sophia Loren
starred in many films portraying working class women: poor and weak in
arithmetic, but not more than the men were, according to the estimates
discussed here.

The ABC index estimates applied to the year 1871 yield two interesting results. The first refers to the southern question; seen through the lens of the population's arithmetical ability, it confirms the fact that the north of the country had a great advantage over the south. In the southern regions, 80–82 percent of people were able to accurately report their age compared to 91–94 percent in northern regions.

The second result, in line with what we saw when analyzing literacy rates (Box 2), suggests that the gender gap was rather modest, save for some rare exceptions. Nationally, the men had just a slim advantage (90 percent compared to the women's 87 percent); but gender differences were as modest in the southern regions as in the northern ones (2–4 percent). The ABC index would thus appear to tell a different story in which, despite women's lower numeracy compared to men, the gender gaps in the south were no greater than those found in the north.

capitals is thus 11 points, which is smaller but clearly in the same direction as the literacy gap between Piedmont and Campania in Figure 5.1.

For Italy as a whole, the ABC index (among the population over 15) in 1871 was 89. A numeracy rate close to 90 percent portrays the country in rosier hues than does the literacy rate of the same year, close to 25 percent. This impression is deceptive. Age-heaping reflects a very rudimentary cognitive ability—an ability that can be acquired without any formal schooling.[6] Italy's 89 percent estimated numeracy can be compared with figures available for other countries. The ABC index takes on values near 100 percent as early as the late eighteenth century in many European states: over 95 percent in Austria, Belgium, Denmark, France, the Protestant regions of Germany, the Netherlands, Norway, Switzerland, and the United Kingdom. In the aftermath of unification, Italy was not only poorly educated but also little inclined to using numbers.

6 The Italians Go to School

Whether we consider literacy, numeracy, or mean years of schooling, Italy was a relatively backward country in the early years after unification. And subsequent progress was painfully slow: it took a full century for literacy to reach 90 percent

---

[6] A'Hearn and his coauthors established a general tendency towards a much earlier diffusion of numeracy compared to literacy. For example, in fifteenth-century Tuscany, at least 55 percent of the population reported age accurately, while literacy did not exceed 20 percent.

nationwide. Yet the rudimentary abilities to read, write, and count that numeracy and literacy (as measured here) capture are miles from what is required to cope, let alone thrive, in a modern, knowledge-based, technology-driven world. To be sure, this was less true in the past, but we need a better historical measure of human capital than literacy. Mean years of schooling might provide this, but they tell us nothing about the distribution of this schooling (Box 1). In this section we explore the evidence on the extent of participation in the school system (Figure 5.7).

The literature typically considers three indicators: (1) the gross enrollment rate (GER), (2) the net enrollment rate, and (3) the attendance rate. The first indicator is defined as the number of pupils enrolled in elementary schools as a percentage of the school-age population. The ratio can exceed 100 percent when the number of children enrolled includes struggling pupils repeating one or more grades, thus remaining in school outside the normal school ages. The *net* enrollment rate attempts to correct for this problem, considering the number of *school-age* children (only) enrolled relative to the population of the same age group. Net enrollment rates are always between zero and one hundred. Although the net rate is preferable for most purposes, it is uncommon for the historical sources to permit its calculation. The third indicator, as its name indicates, is the ratio of children actually present in school, relative to the school-age population. This third measure is preferable to enrollments (which do not guarantee children actually make it to the schoolhouse on any regular basis), but can rarely be calculated for historical contexts due to the scarcity of data on attendance.

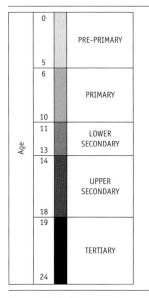

Over the 150 years of Italy's post-unification history, its school system was restructured many times [Cives 1990; D'Amico 2010; Genovesi 2010]. The statistical series reconstructed in this chapter have used the classification shown on the left.

We see four school levels based on student age. The age groups are the ones currently used in the Italian school system:

- Elementary school (age 6–10 years)
- Lower secondary school (age 11–13 years)
- Upper secondary school (age 14–years)
- University (age 19–24 years)

Figure 5.7 Schola Semper Reformanda

In Figure 5.8 we present estimates of gross enrollment rates—the only indicator that has been possible to reconstruct with a certain regularity on the basis of published sources—for Italy's four levels of education: primary, lower and upper secondary, and tertiary. In a sense, this picture tells the whole story of the migration of Italy's children from fields and factories to classrooms over 150 years.

A striking feature of Figure 5.8 is the contrast between enrollment rates in primary school and those for secondary and tertiary education. Taking the latter first, there is an extraordinary lack of progress before World War II. As late as 1931, lower secondary school enrollments were only 6.4 percent of the population aged 11–13. Promising developments such as the expansion of technical education in the early 1900s had been undermined by the famous Gentile reform of 1923. Though raising the school-leaving age to 14, it also eliminated the popular *scuole tecniche* (technical schools) and created new institutions intended to absorb the mass of elementary school leavers, which were "dead ends" in the sense of offering no chance of proceeding to further education. Upper secondary school enrollment rates were an even more disappointing 3.2 percent in 1931. To put this figure in perspective, consider that the enrollment rate for the same age group was 51.1 percent in the United States in the same period (Goldin and Katz 2008, 27).

After World War II, the development of secondary school enrollments presents a very different picture. Particularly for lower secondary schools there is

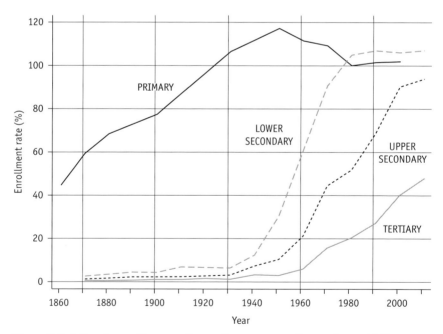

Figure 5.8 A Bird's-eye View of Gross Enrollment Rates, Italy 1861 to present. The graph shows the trend in enrollment rates (vertical axis) over time (horizontal axis) for the four school levels. The curves show the toilsome schooling process of the Italians that is still largely incomplete.

a sudden growth in enrollments, which rapidly reach 100 percent. In addition, the growth of lower secondary schooling seems to have set off a domino or echo effect, with upper secondary rates following at a two- or three-decade lag; university enrollments in turn follow upper secondary with a similar lag. The length of these lags suggests a role for the intergenerational transmission of educational status and aspiration: parents expecting their children to achieve at least the level of schooling they themselves had reached. What triggered the growth of lower secondary enrollment rates? Two salient factors are: first, the transition to a single, common lower secondary school (the *scuola media unica*) begun in 1940 and completed in 1962, which gave access to all forms of further education; and second, a massive increase in educational expenditure and the number of teachers hired by the national government.

7 The Slow, Slow Growth of Primary School Enrollments

Primary school enrollment rates follow a very different trajectory. There is clear, and ultimately significant, progress from the very beginning, but at an extremely slow pace and with no sign of any spillover into secondary enrollments, even of an intergenerational, delayed sort.

At the time of unification, going to primary school was the exception rather than the rule for Italian children: just over 40 percent of those aged 6–10 were enrolled. Fifty years were required, until the eve of World War I, for the enrollment rate to reach (almost) 80 percent. Unfortunately, data on pupils enrolled between 1907 and 1927 were never published, but an acceleration in these years seems quite likely. This period followed the Orlando Law of 1906, which raised the school-leaving age to 12, and saw the implementation of the Daneo-Credaro Law of 1911, which put most aspects of primary school finance into the hands of the national government for the first time. A considerable increase in total expenditure on primary education was also observed in these years (Coccìa and Della Torre 2007).[7]

By the 1920s, gross enrollment rates finally reached 100 percent. In fact, they went on to *exceed* 100 percent for several decades. This arose primarily from the presence of children repeating classes they had failed. In 1949–1950, for example, pupils repeating a grade accounted for 17 percent of total enrollments. This percentage only dropped below the 5 percent mark in the 1970s. Prior to World War II, we lack regular data on the number of "repeaters" (to use the Italian

---

[7] In Italy private education, and particularly education provided by religious institutions, was an important sector in 1861, accounting for about 10 percent of total enrollments. However, private enrollments remained largely stable throughout the nineteenth century and into the interwar period, while public enrollments grew considerably. By 1930, private schools accounted for barely 3 percent of total primary school enrollments.

expression), but can make inferences from evidence on the age distribution of schoolchildren and from their exam pass rates. In 1901, 21 percent of enrolled pupils in the then-compulsory first three years of primary school were outside the "proper" age range (6–8); most of these were aged 9 or more and should have been in a higher grade. Another snapshot, this one from 1926–1927, shows us that 23 percent of the 2.9 million students examined in public elementary schools failed to pass their end-of-year exams for promotion to the next grade (or for their school-leaving certificate). Evidence of this sort indicates that "repeaters" always comprised a significant share of primary school students.[8]

In interpreting gross enrollment rates, it bears reiterating that they are uninformative about the distribution of education. Consider the 60 percent enrollment rate of 1871, for example. This could result, at one extreme, from a situation where 60 of 100 children complete the entire primary school cycle of 5 years, while the remaining 40 never set foot in a classroom. At the other extreme, it could be that all 100 children completed the first three years of school (the so-called lower course, which was made compulsory in 1877 by the Coppino law) and zero proceeded further. This egalitarian hypothesis is not very realistic: first, because of the large number of repeaters; second, due to an initially small but nontrivial number who did continue through all five years (e.g., 8 percent of all primary students in 1881–1882 were in the fourth and fifth grades); third, because of a gender gap in favor of boys, whose gross enrollment rate was 12.5 percent higher in 1861 and 5 percent higher in 1901; and fourth, as a result of dramatic regional differences discussed below. For such reasons, even the rates of 80 percent and more achieved in the last years of Liberal Italy cannot be interpreted as implying most children completed primary school.

7.1 SIGNING UP AND SHOWING UP

Enrollments are not an accurate measure of education if children are not actually in the classroom on a regular basis. Figure 5.9 presents some evidence that enrollment did not always translate into learning. On the assumption that it takes not more than three to four years to learn to read, and if we adopt "egalitarian" distributional assumptions as described in the previous section, we might expect a 60 percent enrollment ratio to produce something like a 60 percent literacy rate among the cohort of children receiving three to four years of schooling. A decade after enrollments are observed, we expect

---

[8] A contributing factor to the gross enrollment rates in excess of 100 in the 1920s is that from 1904 (with the Orlando Law) to 1923, compulsory education comprised four years of "elementary school" followed by two additional years of the "corso popolare." In principle, primary school in this period lasted six years instead of the five years (ages 6–10) valid in all other periods. However, the Gentile reform of 1923 returned primary school to the status quo ante, and in many communities the two-year corso popolare was never established.

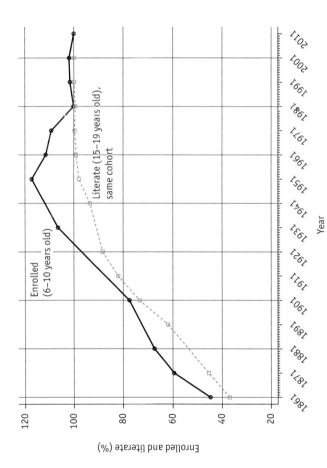

Figure 5.9 THE INEFFECTIVENESS OF SCHOOL ENROLLMENT. The figure compares the enrolment rate of 6–10-year-old children (vertical axis, solid line) with the literacy rate of the same cohort observed ten years later in the census at the ages 15–19 (dashed line). The gap between the two curves measures the ineffectiveness of enrolments.

the literacy rate among 15–20 year olds (the same children now ten years older) to be 60 percent. Literacy in excess of 60 percent would be no surprise, as the alphabet was also learned outside school (at home or during military service, for example).[9]

Figure 5.9 makes exactly this comparison. The solid line depicts elementary school enrollment rates of 6–10 year olds in a given year. The broken line indicates the the literacy rate for this same cohort, when they are observed in the population census ten years later, as 15- to 19-year-olds. To clarify, the literacy rate plotted for 1861 is drawn from the census of 1871. Looking at the vertical gap between the two curves, we see that for each cohort of school-aged children literacy rates were lower than the relevant enrollment rates.

Several explanations suggest themselves. First of all, the assumption of an egalitarian distribution of education is not particularly plausible, as discussed earlier. Second, teaching may have been ineffective, such that many children never properly learned and soon forgot their reading and writing skills. Third, not all those enrolled actually attended school on a regular basis. While absenteeism was a well-known phenomenon (De Mauro 1963), its extent is difficult to measure, for historical data on school attendance are a rare thing. Italy is a partial exception to this pattern, as government concern with the slow diffusion of literacy and schooling led the Ministry of Public Education to collect information on attendance in some periods.

Figure 5.10 presents our estimates of attendance rates, plotting them together with enrollments. The attendance rate is defined relative to the population aged 6–10, not enrolled pupils. The gap between the two is striking. From the mid-1870s to the mid-1880s, some 20 percent of school-aged children were on school rosters but not actually at their lessons when attendance was surveyed (often in March). In the 1882–1883 school year, nearly half a million children who were signed up failed to show up.[10]

7.2 SCHOOL INSPECTORS ON THE JOB

The literature offers a long list of reasons for poor school enrollment and attendance, which are difficult to synthesize, not least because of the tremendous variety of local circumstances across Italy (De Fort 1995; Bosna 1982). We take a new approach here based on the reports of school inspectors.

---

[9] At very low enrollment rates, this reasoning can fail. For example, a 20 percent enrollment rate could, in principle, result from every child going to school for one year, too brief an encounter with education to produce lasting literacy for anyone. Only in 1861 are enrollment rates close to levels that could lead to such an outcome.

[10] Interestingly, we find only a small gender gap in attendance rates, on the order of 5 percent in favor of boys.

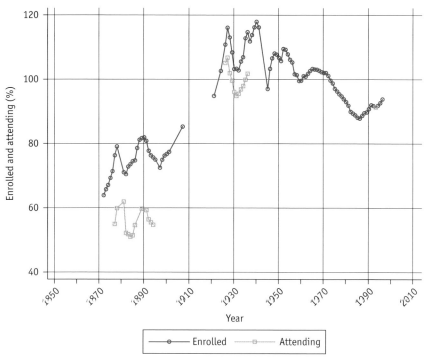

Figure 5.10 ENROLLMENT AND ATTENDANCE, 1861–2011. The vertical axis measures the enrollment (dark blue circles) and attendance rates (light blue boxes) in public elementary schools, relative to the population aged 6-10, showing their variation over time (horizontal axis).

A decade after the enactment of the Coppino Law (1877), which raised compulsory schooling to three years and stiffened the sanctions available to punish noncompliance by local governments and parents alike, the Minister of Education ordered a survey to assess its implementation. The findings of this investigation are kept in the Central Archive of the State in Rome in the form of three large, handwritten registers, with data on the number of teachers, children, and school pupils in every Italian municipality (over 8,000 in number). Of particular interest to us are the comments of the over 200 district school inspectors, who were asked not only to collect data but also to investigate and specify in their report "the reasons why the law on compulsory education has not been completely complied with in the municipality" (Ministero della Pubblica istruzione 1889–1890).

The reasons reported by the inspectors are quite varied, expressed in different ways, and sometimes ambiguous. We have classified these responses into seven categories: (1) the poverty of local families; (2) resistance of parents, for nonfinancial reasons, to sending their children to school; (3) difficulty in reaching schools due to their location and local geography; (4) "poverty" of local

Table 5.1 **Distribution of the reasons for noncompliance with compulsory education legislation, 1890**

	Family poverty	Family resistance	Difficulty of access	Government poverty	Government inaction	Poor-quality schools	Other	Total
Italy	25	9	20	4	28	10	4	100
Center-North	24	8	27	2	24	9	5	100
South	26	10	10	7	35	11	1	100
North-West	27	9	30	3	12	12	8	100
North-East	22	6	26	1	28	11	6	100
Center	24	10	23	1	39	3	1	100
South	29	11	8	5	37	9	1	100
Islands	21	8	14	9	31	15	1	100

Note: The table summarizes the reasons given by school inspectors for incomplete elementary school attendance in 1889-90. Each row gives the share of reasons cited in a geographic area that fall into each category. While poverty appears to have been the greatest hindering factor on the demand side (families), the lack of supply by municipal authorities appears to be due to non-financial reasons.

government; (5) lack of initiative by local government; (6) unsatisfactory quality of schools (concerning school facilities as much as teachers); and (7) other reasons. Table 5.1 summarizes the frequencies with which these various causes were cited by the school inspectors.[11]

The data in the table need to be interpreted with some caution, but they provide some interesting suggestions. Hostility or reluctance on the part of parents was not considered important by many inspectors; more frequently cited was their poverty, which made child labor a crucial component of household income. The poverty of local governments, that is, the inability to muster adequate resources to build and maintain schools (or to rent school premises), and to pay teachers, was not deemed important by many inspectors. What the inspectors did cite frequently was the inaction of local authorities, that is, their noncompliance in tasks such as compiling the lists of school-aged children, their inertia in contacting the parents of habitually absent pupils, or their refusal to impose the relevant sanctions established by law. In short, according to the inspectors, parents could not *afford* to send their children to school, while municipal authorities did not *choose* to enforce or comply with the law.

---

[11] The answers provided by the inspectors are weighted by district populations of school-aged children in order to give an appropriate importance to each observation.

The geographical tabulation of the responses in Table 5.1 highlights regional contrasts. In the center-north, the most frequently declared reasons were the "objective" difficulties that made physical access to schools difficult. Twenty-seven percent of inspectors' responses in the center-north were linked to issues such as a very scattered population far from schools or poor roads in certain seasons. The second most frequent cause cited was the poverty of local families. In the south, by contrast, the inspectors tended to dwell on municipal noncompliance with the law—their lack of initiative was much more often considered a problem than their lack of funds. This diagnosis comprised 35 percent of all cited reasons in the south, as against 24 percent in the center-north. Family poverty was as important in the south as in the north, while the problems of school accessibility amounted to only 10 percent of the total.

Summarizing, it seems fair to say that the inspectors of the center-north were, on the whole, satisfied with the municipalities' efforts and considered the remaining problems as "objective" ones, linked to the physical or economic environment. In the south, on the other hand, the inspectors reported the main problem of the municipalities' action or, rather, inaction.

8 American Lessons

In an influential book, *The Race Between Education and Technology,* Harvard economists Claudia Goldin and Lawrence Katz retrace the path of the United States through what Goldin calls "the human capital century" (Goldin 2001, 264).[12] A remarkable lead in mass secondary schooling ensured that this would also be "the American century" and not the century of industrial pioneer Britain or her rival Germany. Goldin and Katz do not advance a monocausal explanation of America's dynamism in the twentieth century—education is no silver bullet, capable by itself of killing a nation's social and economic woes—but they do assign it the leading role in the story. The American school system had specific traits that fostered mass participation in high schools and later universities, among them its universal, publicly funded, open nature, which contrasted with the elitist, selective systems typical of Europe.

An educated population is able to produce using the most advanced techniques; the abundance of human capital made the most of America's physical and financial capital and thus make a significant contribution to stoking the boilers of American economic growth. It also facilitated American society's capacity to

---

[12] The title alludes to a famous series of lectures prepared (but never delivered, due to the author's untimely death) by Italo Calvino in 1985, entitled *Six Memos for the Next Millennium* (our translation from the Italian).

adapt—necessary to accommodate changes unleashed by various waves of globalization and to make the most of them. The result, on the whole, was that American citizens enjoyed levels of wellbeing unparalleled in the rest of the world.

But America's experience has lessons for the *distribution* of wellbeing too. A negative lesson has to do with inequality of education. Not unlike Italy (section 9), America had persistent regional differences in school participation. In 1930, well into the high school revolution, secondary school enrollment rates ranged from 60 percent in New England to just 31 percent in the East South Central region, a gap that had much to do with the consolidation of racial disparities that continue to plague the United States (Goldin and Katz 2008, 359). A positive lesson has to do with the consequences of technical change. Goldin and Katz identify the twentieth century as an extended period of skill-biased technical change, which increased demand for educated workers more than for unskilled workers. The extra income, or skill premium, earned by educated workers should have grown, worsening inequality. But racing against technological advancement was the progress of schooling, which expanded the supply of educated workers just as demand for them grew. Mass secondary schooling kept inequality in check, and even rolled it back over substantial periods.

These American lessons are of great relevance for Italy. If we acknowledge that schooling plays a leading role in promoting economic growth and progress, then by analyzing the huge lag in schooling rates of Italian schools of every level and type (section 6), we manage to shed light not only on the dynamics of economic growth described in chapter 7 ("Income") but also on those of inequality and poverty (chapters 8 and 9, "Inequality" and "Poverty").

In this section we put the Italian experience in comparative historical perspective. As in sections 6 and 7, we focus on the gross enrollment rate as a measure of school participation. Historical GER estimates should come with a "handle with care" warning, for every country had its own distinct school system. Consider "primary school." In Italy it is natural to identify primary school with the *scuola elementare*, which lasted five years and enrolled children aged 6–10. But in American historical statistics, primary school typically includes everything from kindergarten through eight grade, hence as many as nine years, corresponding approximately to ages 5–13. The French and German systems, and statistics, are not dissimilar to America's, but in Japan "primary school" was just six years (ages 7–12).[13]

---

[13] In addition, school definitions and durations varied over time in the same country. Morrison and Murtin (2009) provide a useful piece of information for interpreting the GERs in Figure 11: the maximal duration historically observed for "primary education". For the countries in Figure 10, they give the following: USA, France (9 years); Germany, Sweden (8 years); United Kingdom, Spain, Greece, Finland (7 years); Japan, Italy (6 years). More typical than these maxima were lower values, e.g., 5 in Italy for much of its history and 8 in France.

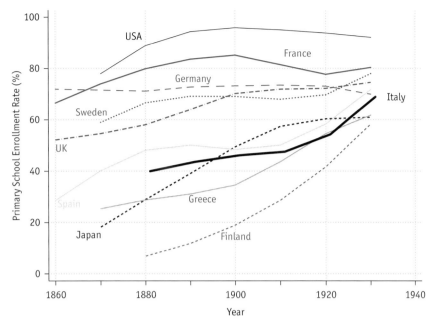

Figure 5.11 PRIMARY SCHOOL GROSS ENROLLMENT RATES, 1860–1930. The graphs show the trend in "primary school" gross enrollment rates for the population aged 5–14 years (vertical axis) over time (horizontal axis).

In Figure 5.11 we have combined Italy's elementary and lower secondary enrollments to create an eight-year "primary school" enrollment total that corresponds approximately to the statistics for the United States, France. or Germany. Enrollments for *all* countries in Figure 5.11 are expressed relative to the population aged 5–14. This ten-year age group implies that even the United States, which was perhaps the world's educational leader in this period, was unlikely to reach a 100 percent enrollment rate. In Italy, if every child completed the full eight years with no repetition of grades, an 80 percent rate would result. On the other hand, it would difficult for Japan to reach 60 percent with only six years of primary education.

In a comparative perspective, Italy's performance is disappointing. By 1880, the United States and France were already near their theoretical limits, while Germany and Sweden fell only slightly short. The United Kingdom was on its way to joining them in fulfilling its primary school potential. Italy's GER of 40 percent was instead at only half its potential value of 80. It is only after 1900, and more particularly during the interwar increase in elementary school enrollments—swollen by pupils repeating grades previously failed, as we have seen—that Italy caught up on these leaders in any significant way.

Meanwhile, other relatively poor, peripheral countries improved their educational performance more quickly, and reached or surpassed Italian GERs. This is in spite of their being disadvantaged relative to Italy in these calculations by having a shorter "primary school" duration. Spain maintains a slender lead; Finland—starting from way back—just about catches up; Greece fully converges; and Japan—also starting from a significant disadvantage—overtakes Italy and reaches its own upper-limit GER by 1910. There is really no reason why Italy should not have been able to catch up with France at 80 percent by 1930, a level her neighbor had reached half a century earlier in 1880.

Figure 5.12 examines GERs at primary, secondary, and tertiary levels from a different perspective. On the horizontal axis is now per-capita GDP instead of the year. We might think of this as measuring "developmental time" instead of calendar time. Each panel presents the historical trajectories of Italy and the United States (the solid lines), against the backdrop of a wide cross-section of countries in 1971 and 2011 (the individual circular markers).

Panel a confirms Italy's lag behind the United States in primary schooling, and reveals that, at a given level of development, it also lagged behind today's poor countries.

Panel b shows that both Italy and the United States lagged behind today's countries in "developmental time." The trajectories of both lie below and to the right of today's countries, indicating lower secondary school enrollments at any given level of GDP. By the late twentieth century, states were much better equipped to tax and spend in support of education, and were impelled to do so by concern with economic competitiveness and pressure from the international community. But there is quite a difference between Italy and America. Very fast growth from 1910 to 1940, a near-vertical segment of the U.S. trajectory, moved the United States quickly from very low secondary GERs to what would later become mainstream values. By 1960, America was near the maximum possible GER. Italy lagged in both calendar and developmental time. In 1940, when U.S. high school enrollments had already reached approximately 70 percent, the country's per-capita GDP was roughly $7,000 (in real terms). Italy did not reach a GER of 70 until 1991, a half-century later. The country followed more quickly in economic terms, reaching a GDP of $7,000 per head in the 1960s, but had a GER of only around 35 at the time.

Panel c shows the gap in tertiary GERs opening up in more recent times and at higher levels of per-capita GDP. In considering the very high enrollment rates achieved by the United States in the most recent data, it bears reiterating that enrollment is not the same as attendance or completion. The OECD data indicate that in 2008 "only" 32 percent of Americans aged 25–34 had completed a four-year university degree (or more), while the enrollment ratio is more than twice that.[14]

---

[14] This reflects the presence of older students from outside the GER age range, of many part-time as well as full-time students, of graduate students, and of students on two-year and vocationally oriented courses. For these reasons, the high GER is a valid reflection of the openness of the American higher education system and the extent of participation in it. On a less positive note, fewer than 60 percent of American students that start a four-year academic program successfully complete it (OECD 2013, 66).

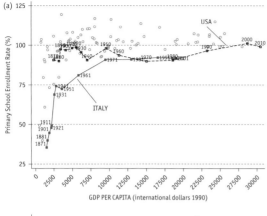

Primary school (6–13 years)
A century behind

Modern primary school enrolments are high even for most of today's poorest countries. The USA achieved such levels from an early date and an early stage of development, while Italy lagged a century behind.

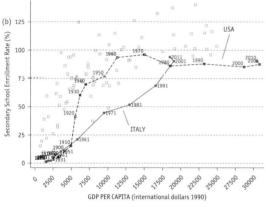

Secondary school (14–18 years)
Painfully slow

The high school revolution between 1910 and 1940 in America brought the country to participation rates typical for a modern country of its income level. Italy instead made steady, but painfully slow progress, and reached a typical enrollment rate for its wealth only in the 21st century.

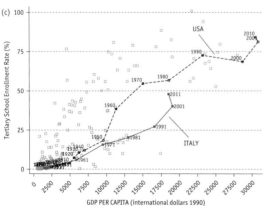

Tertiary school (19–25 years)
In the wrong quadrant

From 1981 to 2011, Italy travels a lonely path through the southeast quadrant of the graph. Only one country had lower university enrolments at a similar level of income (and that was in 1971). Italy underachieved in both GDP growth and enrolment growth.

Figure 5.12 Never the right rate at the right time: education in Italy since 1871. The figure shows the trend in enrolment rates (vertical axis) over time (horizontal axis) for Italy (blue line), the United States (broken line) and a broad set of countries observed in the years 1971 and 2011 (in the cloud of little circles, each represents a country and year).

If we think of education as a component of well-being, we want to read these figures vertically, looking for the amount of education that a country manages to provide at a given level of output. Judged this way, Italy has historically failed to give its citizens the quality of life they should have been able to afford. If we interpret education as human capital, an input into the production process, we might read the graphs horizontally, noting how much education was required to achieve a certain GDP per capita. Depending on the viewpoint, Italy is either surprisingly uneducated or surprisingly prosperous, given the lack of investment in human capital.

9 School Enrollment in the Regions of Italy

In 1861, Italy inherited a diverse set of schooling arrangements from the former pre-unification states, which had produced quite varied literacy rates. Section 2 documented associated differences in youth literacy rates, which took a hundred years to (almost) disappear. The cause of this persistence was a corresponding set of disparities in school enrollment rates.

Figure 5.13, along the horizontal axis, shows the extraordinary variation in elementary school enrollment rates at the time of unification. Piedmont had already achieved 100 percent primary enrollment rates before the battle to "alphabetize" Italians had even begun. In that same moment in Sicily, the enrollment rate was not even quite one in ten. The national rate of 45 percent must therefore be interpreted, in the terminology developed earlier, under the assumption of a highly unequal distribution; Italy was much closer to the extreme of 45 children enrolling for the full five years of primary school, while 55 never saw the inside of a school, than the alternative of 100 children enrolling for just over two years.

The word *enroll* is used deliberately to stress the fact that attendance is another matter altogether. There was some convergence in enrollment rates over time, but as in the case of literacy, this had more to do with the advanced regions bumping up against the ceiling of 100 percent than a strong performance by the educational laggards. In 1901, the gap between Piedmont and Sicily was still over 50 points (117 vs. 53 percent), while the lowest enrollment rate, in Calabria, was only 38 percent.

A century on from 1861, in the heady years of the *miracolo economico*, the battle had shifted to the secondary school front. Figure 5.13, along the vertical axis, shows that here wide gaps in regional attainment *still* prevailed. Enrollments among 11- to 13-year-olds varied from nearly complete (88 percent, in Liguria) to not even half (48 percent, in Calabria).

And of course, as the figure shows, it was largely the *same* regions that had lagged in primary schooling in 1861 that lagged in lower secondary enrollments a century later. Lower secondary school convergence was somewhat

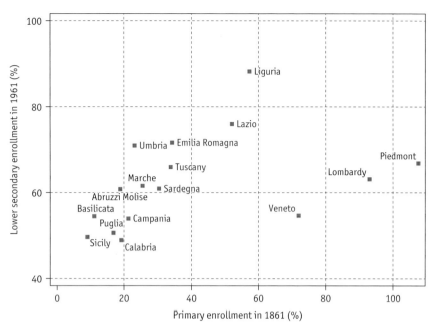

Figure 5.13 A CENTURY OF REGIONAL ENROLLMENT RATES, 1861–1961. The figure displays regional enrollment rates in 1861, at the elementary level (horizontal axis), and in 1961, at lower secondary level (vertical axis). There is great continuity in regional schooling disparities.

quicker than for primary: *all* regions experienced an acceleration in enrollments between 1931 and 1951, and by 1981 all were in the region of 100 percent.[15] But the dominant lesson in the data is the difficulty of quickly overcoming the disadvantages of a poor start in education. This is consistent with the idea of intergenerational transmission of educational aspiration and attainment raised in connection with section 6.

Finally, it is instructive to consider the odd cases of Lombardy, Piedmont, and Veneto in Figure 5.13. Why are these leaders in late-nineteenth-century elementary education so average in late-twentieth-century secondary schooling? Doesn't this contradict the "persistence of initial conditions" interpretation developed here? The answer seems to be that secondary education was the victim of successful industrialization based on low-skilled labor in these regions. Between 1951 and 1961, Lombardy experienced easily the greatest regional increases in total employment, nonagricultural employment, and manufacturing

[15] It is difficult to be precise about the timing of the acceleration in lower secondary enrollments. We have enrollment data for 1941, but no population census, so any estimates for that year involve much conjecture. While enrollments had largely converged by 1981, differences in educational outcomes persisted. The number of pupils successfully passing the lower secondary school leaving exam in 1981 was 30 percent of total enrollments in the north and center, 26 percent in the south and Islands.

employment (Vitali 1970). A booming demand for low-skilled workers in manufacturing and construction raised the opportunity costs of schooling, particularly for poor migrants from other regions. Piedmont was the second or third most dynamic labor market on these same rankings. Liguria, third vertex of the Industrial Triangle, also fits the pattern, in mirror-image fashion, as employment growth was slow, and the region had a precociously large secondary school sector already by 1911 on which it continued to build. Lazio offers a counterexample of a booming region with an economic base in the service sector, with its greater demand for educated workers.[16]

10 The Gloomiest Chapter in Italian Social History

The progress of education in Italy has been disappointing by any standard. The patriots of the Risorgimento meant the school system to provide a common cultural foundation for a new nation. They would surely have been dismayed to discover that it had failed to even make the national language commonplace among their great-great-grandchildren. In the years after World War II, only 18 percent of citizens were habitual Italian-speakers (De Mauro 2014, 41).

Foreign observers were quick to identify education as a weak point of Italian life. British readers were left in no doubt by the 1901 book titled *Italy Today*, by historian Bolton King and his collaborator Thomas Okey. An education expert and author of various books and academic papers on Italy, King had consulted the most informed experts of the time—an array of Italian politicians, academics, journalists, aristocrats, and bankers. The authors did not mince words: "Education is the gloomiest chapter in Italian social history, a chapter of painful advance, of national indifference to a primary need, of a present backwardness, that gives Italy (next to Portugal) the sad primacy of illiteracy in Western Europe" (King and Okey 1901, 233). King and Okey went further, identifying the causes of this failure in Italian institutions: a lack of will rather than a lack of means. "There have been thirty-three Education Ministers since 1860, each eager to distinguish himself by upsetting his predecessor's work. Money has been stinted, and State and communes, lavish in all else, have economized in the most fruitful of national investments" (1901, 233). By and large, the Italian historiography continues to endorse this judgment (Bertola and Sesito 2013).

---

[16] Veneto fits the industrialization hypothesis, as it was one of the more dynamic regional labor markets. But it was less clearly one of the very most rapid growers than Lombardy or Piedmont. Veneto remains to this day a somewhat anomalous case of lowish secondary school enrollments. Its upper secondary enrollment rate in 2011 was 78 percent, by some margin the lowest in Italy.

The historical statistics presented in this chapter are stark. To be sure, over 150 years' childhood was transformed from a norm of no formal instruction for most youngsters in most parts of the country to a situation in which the typical child completes ten years of full-time schooling. But reaching this point was an extraordinarily slow process. Italy required more than 100 years, to 1971 roughly, to reach universal primary (elementary and lower secondary) school participation, something very nearly achieved in the United States, France, or Germany in the nineteenth century.

The spread of upper secondary education to the average Italian got underway only in the 1960s, half a century after America's high school revolution. Even in 2011, only 71 percent of young people had successfully completed upper secondary education (OECD 2013, 36). And only 21 percent of Italians aged 25–34 held any kind of postsecondary degree in the same year. This was barely half the average of the OECD, a club with a number of "impoverished sophisticates" like Chile or Estonia: poorer than Italy but with higher university completion.

Italy's educational attainment, even today, is thus disappointing. But the very recent achievement of "modern" rates of enrollment means that there is considerable intergenerational inequality in education. Today's high upper secondary school participation does little for those over 65, among whom 63 percent have at best an elementary school leaving certificate (ASI 2013, 204). Such individuals are less and less the masters of their destinies in a world where average education levels have left them behind. An OECD study of adult literacy and life skills found that an outsized proportion of Italian adults—59 percent (!) as against at most 28 percent in any other sample country—scored within the lowest achievement level in all four categories tested (OECD 2011). This means competence in finding and processing only the most basic verbal and numerical information: bare functional literacy and numeracy. As we have seen, there is also a geographic element to educational inequality, as regional differences in school participation persisted into recent times.

Much more should have been possible, much earlier. Near-universal primary education was achieved at a per-capita GDP in the range of $2,000–$2,500 in the United States (in the 1870s) or France (in the 1880s) (Grew et al. 1984). In Italy this milestone was reached at roughly $10,000 (ca. 1971).[17] Considering upper secondary school, the story is similar: at a per-capita GDP of roughly $6,000, Italy managed a GER of only 21 percent (in 1961), while the United States had reached 50 percent (in the mid-1920s). Poverty surely did not help, but resource constraints should not have stopped Italians from enjoying much higher levels of education from an earlier date. And, of course,

---

[17] GDP figures are in constant 1990 "international dollars" and are drawn from the Maddison database, downloadable from www.ggdc.net.

more abundant human capital would itself have loosened those constraints by increasing productivity.

In the twenty-first century, education seems to be running out of steam in Italy. The country continues to lag behind the prosperous economies it would like to emulate on measures such as tertiary enrollments or average years of schooling, and shows few signs of catching up. There is growing concern not just about the quantity, but also the *quality* of education. Italian students tend to perform below the rich country average in international comparisons of cognitive ability or financial literacy (OECD 2014). Meanwhile, the university system is plagued by one of the highest dropout rates in Europe. Out of every 100 students enrolled in a three-year *laurea* (degree) course in 2003, only 55 had completed the degree 9 years later in 2012 (while only 23 finished the three-year degree in three years); 38 of 100 had dropped out entirely (Checchi 2014).

The system does not seem to be doing much for social mobility, either. An Italian with poorly educated parents (possessing, at best, a lower secondary school leaving certificate) is very likely to be poorly educated (by the same criterion) himself; the chances are roughly 50 percent in Italy today. His chances of holding a university degree are less than 10 percent (Paolazzi 2014). These probabilities are more than reversed for an individual with university-educated parents; she has a better than 60 percent chance of holding a *laurea* herself, and almost no chance of having stopped at the lower secondary level. The Europe-wide figures for the children of less-educated parents are more favorable: only a 35 percent probability of sharing the parents' low education and a 20 percent chance of completing tertiary-level studies. Italy thus has both a greater share of the older generation with low school attainments and a smaller probability of their children overcoming the handicap.

Italy's schools face several new challenges in the current environment. One is the successful integration of an ever-growing immigrant population. In the context of a negative rate of natural demographic increase, the Italian labor force is increasingly dependent on foreign-born workers. The number of non-Italians in Italian schools has quadrupled in the last decade, reaching three-quarters of a million. Relative to Italians, the children of immigrants are more likely to choose nonacademic secondary school tracks, are less likely to complete secondary school on time, and are less likely to enroll in university.

A second challenge relates to Italy's economic structure. Relative to economies such as Britain, France, or the United States, Italy retains a larger manufacturing sector. Manufacturing accounted for 18 percent of Italian GDP prior to the recent crisis, and more than 20 percent of employment. The education system is not providing much help in the sector's battle for international competitiveness. There is no dual vocational-academic system of apprenticeships on

Box 4 **It's Never Too Late**

In 1961, Italy celebrated the hundredth anniversary of its unification in more sumptuous robes compared to its previous jubilee. The country had embarked on an unprecedented process of modernization, and the Italians had good reason to celebrate: macroeconomic indicators showed virtuous trends (chapter 7, "Income") and social indicators reassured Italians that progress was also reaching the weakest sections of the population (chapters 8 and 9, "Inequality" and "Poverty"). "Not only was Italy made," as Minister Pella proclaimed at the end of a famous celebratory speech, "but even the Italians have been made" (Pella 1961).

In such euphoric times as those of the "economic miracle", it is, however, emblematic that Italian state television (RAI) started the production of a TV program called *Non è mai troppo tardi. Corso di istruzione popolare per il recupero dell'adulto analfabeta* ("It is never too late. A course of people's education for the recovery of the illiterate adult"). The program was broadcast from 1960 to 1968, for a total of 484 episodes. The presenter was Alberto Manzi (1927–1997), a primary school teacher who became an icon for the Italians

Figure 5.B4 IT'S NEVER TOO LATE. In the very years that Italy was experiencing its "economic miracle" there was a popular TV program called "Non è mai troppo tardi" (It's never too late") which took up the challenge against illiteracy. A hundred years after their country's unification, the Italians had overcome poverty, but not their lack of education.

of the time since the program soon became one of the most popular in the country. The program's contents were real distance-education lessons geared to adult literacy. The Italy of 1961 was a place where less than 7 percent of the population had a television set (compared to 27 percent in the United States), but this did not hinder the program's popularity. RAI itself set up over two thousand "viewing stations" in bars and in municipal and parish halls to enable tens of thousands of people to have access to these lessons.

The RAI press office quoted astronomical figures: a million and a half people learned to read and write thanks to the program. Other estimates state that around 35,000 people managed to obtain an elementary education certificate (Grasso 2000, 94). Be that as it may, Italy commemorated its first century as a united country by, implicitly, celebrating the first century of the persistence of illiteracy.

the German model, and enrollments at technical institutes are falling as employers complain that they are in any case increasingly disconnected from the world of work (Confindustria 2014).

The third challenge is dealing with austerity. Italy does not spend an unusually large share of GDP on education; at less than 5 percent, the reverse is closer to the truth. Budget stringency since 2008, however, has meant a 14 percent cut, in real terms, in the resources available to Italian universities. Austerity is not going away any time soon.

Several cautionary tales from economic history seem particularly apt at this juncture. If technical progress continues apace, and continues to favor the skilled, the slowing growth in the relative supply of educated workers in Italy will likely be a source of rising inequality (Goldin and Katz 2008). This will only make the hard choices about economic, and particularly fiscal, policy that lie ahead more difficult.

The most important lesson can be found further back in time. Italy drew little benefit from the technical innovations of the Industrial Revolution such as steam power, coke-fueled metallurgy, or mechanical spinning and weaving (A'Hearn 2014). Developed for the cheap-energy, expensive-labor environment of Britain, they were for many decades unprofitable in the Italian context of scarce natural resources and (super-) abundant manpower (Allen 2009). Later, as falling transport costs made resources increasingly mobile, Italy made a critical blunder in failing to cultivate locally rooted skills by investing in technical training, which could have attracted raw materials and capital. Instead, Italy exported unskilled labor in the form of emigrants (Fenoaltea 2014, 233–235). Italy will always be resource-poor, will always have a location on the periphery of Europe, and cannot determine the direction of global technical change. The foundation of an economically successful future has to be a well-educated population. Failure to nurture talents, develop cognitive abilities, and invest in skills is not an option. Italy dare not miss the skill-biased, knowledge-intensive train now departing.

Appendix—Sources and Methods

General observations In many cases, the regional boundaries have remained the same for the whole postunification period and so no adjustment was necessary. Two exceptions are Valle d'Aosta, (re-)combined with Piedmont, and Molise, similarly reunited with Abruzzo. We did not make changes, instead, for Lazio and its neighboring areas to keep its borders constant (e.g., no effort was made to "undo" the city of Rieti's shift from Abruzzo-Molise to Lazio). Trentino–Alto Adige was simply added to the list of regions from 1921 onward. The north-east of the country had greater problems in this regard: over the decades, the area gained or lost whole areas and a new region, Friuli–Venezia Giulia, was created there. In this case, we combined all the regions with Veneto.

Box 1 Human Capital in Italy and around the World since 1870 The data are drawn from the Morrisson and Murtin (2009) database, are built by perpetual inventory methods before 1960, and include the estimates of Cohen and Soto (2007).

Figure 5.1 Literacy in the pre-unification states of the Italian Peninsula Source: the 1861 population census. For Veneto and Lazio the data were taken from the 1871 census and concern the population aged 15 years and over.

Figure 5.2 Youth literacy by region, 1861–2011 Source: Census of Population, various years.

Figure 5.3 The question of the "poor municipalities" (Italy, 1881) Source: The Ministry of Agriculture, Industry and Commerce (MAIC) published detailed statistics on the revenues and expenditures of Italian local governments (*comuni*). Our numbers are calculated from provincial aggregates of these local figures as published in *Bilanci comunali per l'anno 1882* (MAIC 1884).

Figure 5.4 Literacy rates, 1861–2011 Sources and methods are the same as for Figure 5.2.

Box 2 Women and Illiteracy The sources and methods are the same as for Figure 5.2.

Figure 5.5 Age-heaping in Tuscany 1427 Numeracy is measured by means of the ABC index, which is based on the prevalence of multiples of five in age distributions. Let $p5$ stand for the sample proportion of ages that are multiples of five, expressed in terms relative to the expected proportion, multiplied by 100. The expected proportion is based on the assumption that there is a uniform distribution of all the ages. In the 20–29 age group, for example, we would expect 20 percent of the ages having a 0 or 5 end digit. The formula for the ABC index is:

$$ABC = \left\{1 - \frac{p5 - 100}{400}\right\} \cdot 100$$

for values of $p5$ greater than or equal to 100. The index can be interpreted as the proportion of individuals who accurately declared their own age (A'Hearn, Baten, and Crayen 2009).

Figure 5.6 Numeracy, Turin vs. Naples, 1871 Methods are the same as for Figure 5.5; source: see A'Hearn, Auria, and Vecchi (2011).

Figure 5.8 A bird's-eye view of gross enrollment rates, Italy 1861 to present The gross enrollment rate (GER) is given with respect to the population of the school-age group concerned. As we saw in the chapter, the structure of the Italian school system has changed a great deal over time, and so has the duration of each type of school education and the school starting age. However, in order to establish comparable rates over the 150 years of the country's postunification history, we needed to choose a single definition with regard to both school levels and age groups for a proper comparison. To this end, we used the classification illustrated in Figure 5.7. Hence, for example, the gross elementary school enrollment rate is obtained as the ratio of the number of pupils enrolled in elementary school to the population of the 6–10 age group, that is, those children who had completed their sixth through tenth years of age. Sources. *Elementary*: see A'Hearn, Auria, and Vecchi (2011). *Secondary* and *tertiary*: the resident population in the age groups considered (11–13, 14–18, and 19–24) is obtained from census data. For the years 1891 and 1941, in which no census was carried out, the data are obtained by applying the growth rate occurring between the two closest censuses (1881–1901 and 1931–1951, respectively): estimates obtained using different methods did not yield any significant variations. Because of the variety of school types, as well as several school reforms, it was more difficult to establish the number of students enrolled in lower and upper secondary schools and in universities. The number of students enrolled is provided by the Italian statistical yearbooks (the *Annuari Statistici Italiani*—ASI), which were not always issued on a regular basis. We used the yearbooks published for the years 1878, 1884, 1895, 1905–1907, 1913, 1922–1925, 1932, 1933, 1942, 1951, 1963, 1972, 1983, 1993, 2003, and 2013. All these sources provided the overall number of students enrolled. For tertiary education, we considered all the students enrolled in degree courses—even those not making regular progress toward completion of their course (the *studenti fuori corso*). With regard to upper secondary education for the period until 1941 inclusive, we considered the various types of schools: the *liceo classico, liceo scientifico, ginnasio, scuola normale, scuola complementare, istituto magistrale*, technical and nautical schools and institutes, and *liceo artistico*. Other types of technical education institutes—often under the control of the Ministry of Agriculture, Industry and Commerce (MAIC) rather than the Ministry of Education—were not considered because they were not full-time courses and not directly connected to a specific age group. For the school types included, we often had to impute what percentage of enrollments were to be ascribed to lower secondary schools (11–13 age group) and what percentage to upper secondary schools (14–18 age group). To do so, we used information, where available, on the number of students enrolled in the various school years: this information is contained in occasional publications such as *Statistica dell'Istruzione Media per l'Anno Scolastico 1881–82 e 1891–92, Statistiche sull'Istruzione Elementare 1881–82 e 1891–92* (both published by MAIC); the statistics for lower and upper secondary education for the years 1931–1932, contained in a special issue of the *Annali di Statistica* (Istat, 1936); for the post–World War II years, the *Annuario Statistico dell'Istruzione*, published by the Ministry of Education.

Figure 5.9 The ineffectiveness of school enrollment Source: Update of A'Hearn, Auria, and Vecchi (2011). Note: The answers provided by the inspectors were weighted by district populations of school-aged children in order to give an appropriate weight to each observation.

Figure 5.10 Enrollment and attendance, 1861–2011 Source: A'Hearn, Auria, and Vecchi (2011). The attendance data refer to public schools.

Figure 5.11 Primary school gross enrollment rates, 1860–1930 Sources are as follows. Italy: update of A'Hearn, Auria, and Vecchi (2011). Other countries: Lindert (2007).

Figure 5.12 Never the right rate at the right time: education in Italy since 1871 GDP: the data come from the database of the Maddison-Project, http://www.ggdc.net/maddison/maddison-project/home.htm, 2013 version. GER: the methods and sources for Italy are the same as those described for Figure 5.8. For

both for population and students enrolled, the same sources provided both the overall figure and the regional figures. For the United States, the data come from the Millennial Edition of the *Historical Statistics of the United States*; the data for the remaining countries in the figure come from the database of the Maddison Project for which the UNESCO Institute for Statistics (UIS) provides rates from its own site http://data.uis.unesco.org/. Note: what is here called a "four-year university degree" corresponds to tertiary type A and advanced research programs in the OECD statistics. Tertiary type B programs are shorter (typically two-year), more vocationally oriented courses.

Figure 5.13 A century of regional enrollment rates, 1861–1961 The methods and sources are the same as those described for Figure 5.8. The same sources provided overall and regional figures for population and students enrolled. Note: The figures for Veneto (annexed in 1866) and Lazio (annexed in 1871) are from 1871.

Figure 5B.4 It's never too late Source: Morrison and Murtin (2009).

6

Migration

WITH MATTEO GOMELLINI AND CORMAC Ó GRÁDA

1 Migrants Are Made, Not Born

An economic history of Italy and of the wellbeing of the Italians that omitted an evaluation of the role played by emigration would be incomplete and misleading. The freedom of movement of citizens inside and beyond national borders was an achievement that goes back to the country's unification in 1861 (Sanfilippo 1990). Commenting on the results of the first, bold, and strongly symbolic census of the Italians,[1] the officials of the Kingdom of Italy found it natural to remind the Italians of the previous status quo, that is, the world they had lived in until that moment—a world in which people were not allowed to move around freely, for various reasons:

> Under the governments of a divided Italy there were many obstacles to the free movement of inhabitants from one state to another of the peninsula. The populations were jealously kept within state cloisters, which did not always open to those who, for reasons of convenience or business, had decided to change their place of residence. And it often happened that inhabitants were overcrowding in one state, while they were scarcer in another, nor could a compensation be established nor the necessary balances be maintained for the wellbeing of material and moral life of the masses. Things will be different now that the unification and freedom of the country are happily inaugurated, and the excess of one province can easily go to make up the deficit in another, and all together go to achieve an equal development on which the progress of the entire nation depends. (authors' translation from MAIC 1867, 134)

---

[1] The newborn Kingdom of Italy, officially founded on March 17, 1861, set up its own national statistics service in September and managed to carry out its first general census of the population in December of that very year (Istat 2010).

Once the barriers between the puny preunification kingdoms had fallen, all Italians—not just the economic, political, and artistic elite—were finally free to move up and down as well as beyond the Italian Peninsula. They took to doing so in a tumultuous way, changing abode, province, region, and even continent until they became—as we well know—a people of migrants as no other in the world.

Since emigrating is, essentially, an action geared to seeking improved wellbeing, our aim in this chapter is to identify the features of Italian migration flows in the country's postunification history and to evaluate the overall impacts on the wellbeing of the population. To do all this, we found the usual difficulties linked to the availability of suitable historical data, but this was not our main concern. The difficulty lies, instead, in the attempt to use crude numbers in order to tell a story that is made up of lives, sufferings, sacrifices, losses, farewells, illusions, and disappointments; but also of pride, of enthusiasm for the prospects of a better life, of successes, of the joys of reunions. A huge literature adopts these perspectives, and they feature in an enormous amount of visual works. Specialist studies of Italian emigration are endless.[2] Nevertheless, an analysis focusing on the statistics of the migration flows, both domestic and external ones, will contribute to existing studies and also to the comprehension of such an extremely multifaceted phenomenon.

Italy has constantly faced outflows and inflows of people, at least in her 150-year history as a unified country. Most Italian emigration formed part of two main waves. The first took place during the so-called age of mass migration, the period between the late 1800s and the outbreak of World War I, in which nearly fifty-five million Europeans crossed the ocean to reach the lands of opportunities (Hatton and Williamson 1998). The second took place soon after World War II and lasted until the early 1970s. On the whole, as we shall see, over thirty million Italians emigrated—more than the population in the 1861 census in the aftermath of unification. Migration then changed direction and turned into immigration.

How often have we heard that, in a globalized world, migration can both gradually impoverish sending areas, which are already economically and socially disadvantaged, while also damaging destination countries? We will show that both worries are often exaggerated. There are many countervailing forces, like rises in wages, in per-capita GDP, and in education, that compensate potential emigration-induced losses (linked, for example, to a brain drain). Emigration can be a valuable safety valve that relieves domestic pressures and improves the lot of most (though certainly not all) of those who remain (Ó Gráda and O'Rourke 1997).

---

[2] See Rosoli (1978), Rosoli and Ostuni (1978), Sori (1979), Cinel (1982; 1991), Bevilacqua, De Clementi, and Franzina (2002), Conti and Sanfilippo (2009).

As well as international migration flows, which were the lion's share in Italian historiography, we shall also consider the internal mobility of the Italians—the enormous number of Italian people who moved from the countryside to the towns and cities, from the mountains and hills to the plains, and from inland areas to the coast (Bonifazi and Heins 2000; 2011). Like international emigration, the population's internal movements played a leading role in redesigning the social fabric and in determining the living conditions of the Italians in place and time.

2 Emigrant or Tourist?

Let us begin our "journey" by asking what defined an emigrant. But before focusing on the personal characteristics of the emigrants, we need to briefly describe the data we used and how emigrants were statistically identified.

Our story relies on three main datasets. First, aggregate data for the entire period are available today from an official source, namely, the *Sommario di Statistiche Storiche* of the Italian National Institute of Statistics (Istat), published in 2011. For the years 1862–2005, the book provides us with some basic historical statistics on Italian emigration that we shall use, updating them, in the rest of this chapter. These are essential data, but are insufficient for our purposes for this chapter.

Secondly, for the first wave of emigration (1876–1925), a rich dataset (with numbers, as we shall see, that are not always entirely reliable or consistent) was collected by the Commissariato Generale per l'Emigrazione (CGE), an independent institution that had as its fundamental purpose the welfare of migrants. The achievement of the CGE, whose first commissioner general was Luigi Bodio (1840–1920), a leading figure in Italian statistics at the turn of the century, emerges clearly when one browses through the massive *Statistical Yearbook of Italian Emigration 1876–1925*. This exemplary work of statistical accuracy sheds light on many aspects of migration, including data at the provincial level on emigration and return migration, data on departures from foreign ports, rules of hygiene, health statistics, and the cultural preparation of emigrants.

Besides, we have used microdata coming from various sources such as Italian censuses, ship passenger lists, and anthropometric data that, at least for the first wave of emigration, offer us insights into the demographic structure and human capital content of these outflows. These are secondary and eclectic sources that are irreplaceable when dealing with historiographically important questions, as we shall see in section 5.

In short, what distinguishes the sources and data concerning Italian migration flows is not so much the difficulty in retrieving them (the sources are, instead, abundant) as the complexity required by their use. This is because over the years the procedures for measuring both emigrants and returnees have radically changed with regard to the definition of emigrants as well as calculation methods. This has gone hand in hand with the development of the "measurement culture" and with the state's capacity to gather statistics of its own interest (Marucco 2001). To make good use of Italian statistics on emigration, then, we need to pay particular attention to what statisticians call the "data generating process" (Spanos 1986).

The first ten to fifteen years of the new Kingdom, already the object of intense political and academic debate on the numbers and effects of emigration, laid the groundwork for various experiments for surveying migration flows. In actual fact, no official statistics were produced until 1876, but only reconstructions and estimates that were the fruit of the initiative of individual scholars.[3]

The turning point was in 1877 with publication of the first volume of the Statistics of Emigration, produced "with the ambition to be an official statistic, conducted according to the scientific method (in order to) put a stop to the 'polemic of numbers'" (Marucco 2001, 155). Between 1876 and 1904, data on the number of migrants were gleaned from municipal registers: the authorization to migrate (the so-called green light) was, in fact, granted directly by the municipal authorities. However, only after a clearance by central government was a passport actually issued. The result frequently was a wide disparity between the number of municipal permits and people actually emigrating. In this regard, Carmagnani and Mantelli (1975) stated that the official Italian statistic of the period "does not measure actual emigration, but rather the propensity to emigrate, which in statistical language means it presents a margin of error by excess".

Initially, the distinction between people temporarily emigrating in search of work (temporary migrants) and those who intended to remain abroad permanently was crucial to distinguish the "real" migrant from other travelers. The identification of a migrant thus focused on the mere intention of those who applied for a passport. Bodio himself clearly explained that the emigrant was a person who "departed with the intention of abandoning his own native land; who goes abroad with the deliberate intention of not coming back; he who exits the national border and does not expect to return, or still less can foresee when

---

[3] The most famous is that of Leone Carpi (1810–1898), who gathered a large set of data on emigration from 1869 on (Carpi 1887). Carpi also engaged in a bitter debate with Bodio (Marucco 1998, 153–154).

he will return. He does not need to completely give up the idea of coming back; he just counts on establishing his abode in a foreign country" (Bodio 1877, 25). Inevitably, intentions were not always realized, and this criterion was abandoned: in 1901 there was a change in direction due to the decision to align the statistical definition (based on intentions) with the Law no. 23 of January 31, a fundamental law issued with the primary purpose of providing greater protection to emigrants. Afterwards, Law no. 1075 of August 2, 1913, stiffened the identification criteria of emigrants.

On October 31, 1922 Benito Mussolini became the new prime minister and, as we know, set about the task of turning the country into a one-party dictatorship. The series of laws issued between 1919 and 1925 were largely a continuation of the law of 1913 and restricted the definition of emigrant in official statistics to a person not in a comfortable social condition (Istat 2011, 87).[4] What changed, however, was the underlying rhetoric with regard to the phenomenon: the Fascist regime replaced the term "emigrant" with the expression *Italian abroad* (Villani 2012, 188), while in the official statistics it adopted the term "worker." The reason was explained by Mussolini himself, in a famous speech made in 1925: the Italians abroad, he said, "must be considered in every work of yours and in every moment of your life as pioneers, as missionaries, as bearers of Latin, Roman and Italian civilization."[5] It was, in short, a question of Fascist rhetoric and semantics.

In 1947 Istat adopted a new definition, following the general postwar reorganization of statistics. Emigrants were now defined as those who move abroad for three reasons: *(i)* emigrant workers (moving to pursue a profession or to work); *(ii)* emigrant families (accompanying an emigrant worker or joining one already abroad); *(iii)* other emigrants (those who intended to take up residence abroad for other reasons). The grouping of emigrants according to these three categories has remained, up to more recent times, the main classification for analyzing the phenomenon of foreign migration (Istat 2012).[6]

---

[4] In 1921, when emigration statistics became the responsibility of the Commissariat General of Emigration, an important modification was introduced with the establishment of coupons attached to passports that were detached at the moment of departure. Thus, this coupon-based system of detection (abolished in 1957) helped to more accurately measure the number of those who actually left.

[5] "I compiti dei fasci all'estero" ("The Fasci's duties abroad"), reported by the newspaper *Il Popolo d'Italia*, October 31, 1925.

[6] In 1964 a register of immigrants and migrants abroad was established with the municipalities and finally, with law no. 470 of October 27, 1988, the Register of Italians Residing Abroad (AIRE) was introduced. This contains data on citizens planning to live overseas for a period exceeding twelve months, or who are found to be living abroad (Ministero degli Esteri 1991). It is widely held, however, that the AIRE tends to underestimate the recent flows of European emigration.

3 How Many Italians Set Off?

The collection of official data on emigration began in 1876, when the Divisione Generale di Statistica was founded and began publishing statistics on emigration. The information on aggregate annual emigration flows in the age of European mass migration is by no means perfect. In particular, data on return migration are lacking until 1905 for the United States and until 1921 for Europe, so it is not easy to distinguish temporary from permanent migration.

Italian and U.S. estimates of the number of emigrants to the United States between 1876 and 1913 differ: the ratio between the two rose from 0.6 to 1.4, implying that Italian data tend to underreport outflows before the 1900s and to overreport them thereafter. The pre-1900 underestimation is most likely to stem from the huge numbers of Italian migrants who left for the United States from foreign ports; for example, in 1874 about 17,500 Italians embarked in French ports (Molinari 2001, 238) or clandestinely (CGE 1927, 1701). The high volatility of the ratio in the early 1900s may be linked to the data source: there might be a mismatch between the year in which a passport was requested and the year of actual departure

With these caveats in mind, between 1869 and 2013 nearly 30 million people left Italy. The outflow fluctuated considerably over time and by region. Much of it took place in two great waves, the first between the early 1880s and World War I, and the second between the 1950s and the 1980s (Figure 6.1). Half of those who emigrated (more than 14 million) left the country between 1870 and 1915, in what has been described as the largest human outflow from any single country in recorded history (Choate 2008, 1).

In the first period, migration was largely unfettered (Hatton and Williamson 1998). Then, between 1914 and 1945, many barriers to emigration were raised: attitudes toward immigration hardened in the United States, as we shall see further on; the generalized weakness of economic conditions, in particular in the United States during the Great Depression, reduced job opportunities abroad; and nationalistic politics shaped the geography of alliances and fueled legal and administrative prohibitions in Italy (Cannistrato and Rosoli 1979). All of these obstacles reduced both the size and geographic scope of the flows.

Emigration flows resumed after World War II, and in particular between 1945 and 1973. Even though some of it was spontaneous, postwar emigration was often "managed," the result of bilateral agreements between Italy and European states requiring manpower for reconstruction.

Migration in this period formed part of Italian economic policy; indeed, it was a crucial element in the four-year program proposed by Italy in 1948 to the Organization for European Economic Cooperation (OEEC), the institution charged

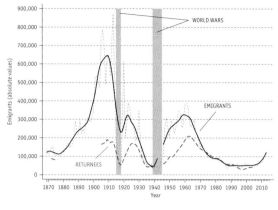

Annual departures

The first statistical surveys indicate over 100,000 departures every year. In the early 20th century the average rose to 600,000–700,000 departures per year, with a peak of 872,000 in 1913. In the same year, to have an idea of the scale of these flows, the most populous city in Italy was Naples, with its 700,000 inhabitants. Milan had slightly over 600,000, followed by Rome (599,000), Turin (427,000) and Palermo (341,000).

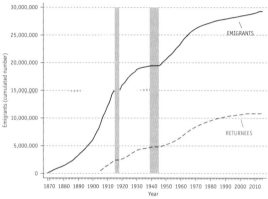

Cumulative departures

Prior to World War I over 15 million Italians had migrated abroad. The S-shaped curve on the left grasps the changes in pace; growth was exponential up to World War I and then slowed down. Another 15 million Italians emigrated in the following 100 years. This makes a total of 30 million people—a multitude unprecedented in history (the slave trade from Africa involved under 10 million people over 300 years [Maddison 2001]).

Figure 6.1 The numbers of Italian emigration, 1870 to date

with the disbursement of Marshall Plan funds in Europe.[7] The flows of population abroad would, on the one hand, ease the unemployment problem; on the other, it would contribute, through remittances, to balancing the balance of payments (Romero 2001, 403). For the years 1952–1953, for example, it was envisaged that remittances would cover at least 10 percent of foreign currency requirements, approximately $205 million. On the basis of the experience of the 1920s, an outflow of 832,000 people was deemed necessary, even if this was not enough to eliminate unemployment: in 1953 there were still at least two million people unemployed.

Figures relating to emigration are usually expressed as emigrants per thousand residents (gross rate). This ratio was about 4.2 in 1870s for Italy; it rose to

[7] In 1961 the OEEC was renamed OECD (Organisation for Economic Cooperation and Development).

a peak of 24.1 per thousand in 1913, with an average of nearly 18 per thousand between 1900 and 1913 (i.e., 1.8 percent of the population emigrated each year). After World War I, until 1929, it was about 7 per thousand; it dropped thereafter and in the 1930s, on average, only 1.4 persons out of every 1,000 residents emigrated each year.

The post–World War II period can be divided into three subperiods with regard to emigration. During the first, from 1945 to 1963, five million people left, implying an annual migration rate of nearly 6 per thousand. Then, up to the collapse of the Bretton Woods international monetary system in 1973, outflows decreased, though remaining substantial nonetheless (two million; an average annual rate of 4 per thousand). In the following three decades, fewer than two million Italians emigrated, with an average emigration rate comparable to interwar levels (1.1 per thousand).

The most recent data issued by Istat are surprising and also worrying. Italians have started to emigrate again and account for the highest number of departures

Table 6.1 **The numbers of Italian emigration**

Decade	Emigrants	Gross rate (per 1,000)	Migration balance
(1)	(2)	(3)	(4)
1869–1880	1,418,037	4.3	–
1881–1890	2,172,832	6.6	–
1891–1900	2,834,726	8.9	–
1901–1910	6,026,690	17.7	–
1911–1920	3,828,065	10.6	–2,672,298
1921–1930	2,405,793	6.8	–1,044,780
1931–1940	702,650	1.6	–112,793
1941–1950	1,144,775	3.5	–698,166
1951–1960	2,937,406	6	–1,613,817
1961–1970	2,646,994	5.1	–778,374
1971–1980	1,082,340	2	39,163
1981–1990	658,292	1.2	45,261
1991–2000	517,095	0.9	–126,071
2001–2013	868,405	1.1	–183,452

Note: The table shows the absolute number of Italian emigrants (col. 2) per decade, the gross emigration rate (col. 3) and net migration balance (col. 4).

in the last decade: 82,000 canceled their residence in Italy in 2013, an increase of 21 percent on the previous year (Istat 2014).[8]

3.1 RETURNEES

Many emigrants return home and do so for many reasons: because the economic or political situation of the country or town of origin has changed, because they have reached their goals, or, on the contrary, because they have not done so and are no longer willing to pay the personal price associated with temporary or seasonal emigration (Cerase 2001). Regardless of the reasons for coming back, the returnees have a significant impact on the society they return to. What is not altogether clear is whether it is a positive or negative impact, and scholars disagree as to the very criteria to be used in assessing the social and economic impact of return migration. Some consider it obvious that a flow of returnees bringing back their savings, new knowledge, and know-how as well as a more open mentality cannot but have a beneficial effect. Others stress some potentially negative effects: "inflation, the decline in economic activities abandoned by temporary emigrants, discontent owing to a less-than-satisfactory experience abroad, and difficulties in readjusting to life in home communities" (Cinel 1991, 2).

Unfortunately, in the case of Italy, data on return migration are only available from 1905 on.[9] In 1905–1914, return migration, as a ratio between returnees and emigrants, was almost 30 percent, on average, and remained at this level up to 1921 (except in 1915 when, due to the outbreak of World War I and military conscription, returnees exceeded outflows). In the interwar period when, as we saw, emigration was severely limited, returnees accounted for two-thirds of total emigration, while in the postwar period up to 1963 the annual return rate was 50 percent. At that point, the average returnees-to-emigrants ratio increased to 0.8, rising further to values higher than 1.0 after 1973.

As usual, aggregate data hide regional heterogeneities. Emigrants from the south in the early twentieth century were more likely to be temporary or seasonal migrants: between 1905 and 1920, well over one-third of migrants in the regions of Lazio, Abruzzo, and further south returned, while the proportion in regions to the north was about one in ten. The outliers were Ligurians (of whom over half returned) and Sardinians, who were very reluctant to migrate but, when they did, mostly left for good.

---

[8] Variations in registry office resident lists tend to underestimate migration flows: although it is compulsory by law to cancel one's name from the registry lists on emigrating, this may actually be done many years after the migrant's departure (Golini 1974, 69).

[9] Giusti (1965) estimates net migration flows from 1876 using census data.

4 Where Did They Come from and Where Did They Go?

The regional origin of emigrants has changed substantially over time (Figure 6.2). In 1876 emigrants from the northwest accounted for half of all emigration. This share swiftly decreased and by 1900 was only 13 percent. By contrast, the share of emigrants from the south and from the islands of Sicily and Sardinia grew from a tiny 5 percent to nearly 50 percent over the same period. During the interwar period, the share of southern emigrants initially decreased in the 1920s and then rose in the following decade. In the first two postwar decades, emigration was definitely a southern matter: the share of southern emigrants (including the two main islands) reached 72 percent in 1963 and stabilized around 40 percent after the mid-1980s.

The fall in emigration from northern Italy at the end of the nineteenth century coincided, as we shall see shortly, with the drop in the share of emigrants bound for Europe. The link between particular sending regions and receiving

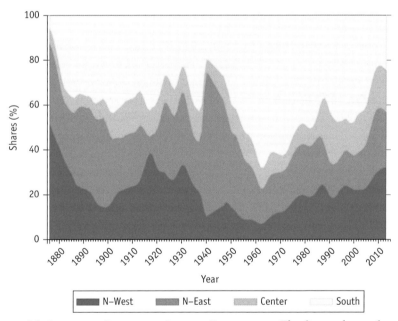

Figure 6.2 REGIONAL ORIGINS OF ITALIAN EMIGRANTS. The figure shows the regional composition of Italian emigrants. If the total of all emigrants (vertical axis) in a given year (horizontal axis) is set at 100, the greater the area of a given color (area of origin), the greater the number of emigrants. From 1876 to 1900 it is the north (in particular, Veneto, Friuli and Piedmont) which accounts for the greatest number of emigrants; from 1901 it is the south (Sicily, Campania and Calabria).

countries is definitely important and highlights the working of so-called network channels. For example, nearly two-fifths of pre-1914 migrants to Brazil were Venetians or Lombards, and the great majority of them settled in the south or southeast of Brazil. Most migrants to Argentina were northerners, with a particularly strong representation from Piedmont, Liguria, and Lombardy. Although the literature reports some cases of "unawareness" about the destination chosen, the emigrant to Australia who declared that she had always thought that "Australia was in America" was unusual (Choate 2008, 23). Path-dependent mechanisms also explain the choice between internal and external migration. According to Golini (1974, 22), with the same social reasons, 58 percent of migrants from the Abruzzo region decided to go abroad whereas 70 percent of migrants from Basilicata (Lucanians) went to northern Italy.

France, Germany, Switzerland, Canada, the United States, Argentina, Brazil, and Australia: over the entire period under consideration, these countries accounted for more than four-fifths of Italian emigration (nine-tenths between 1906 and the mid-1970s). At the outset, Europe accounted for 70 percent of all emigration. This share progressively fell to less than 30 percent in 1890 and then fluctuated around 40 percent up to World War I. In the 1920s and 1930s, Europe's share fluctuated widely between 40 percent and 80 percent, and then stabilized at around 70 percent after World War II (Figure 6.3).

Transoceanic emigration took off toward the end of the nineteenth century, first to Brazil and Argentina and then to the United States, spurred on in part by the ongoing transport revolution that made overseas trips safer and cheaper. The United States matched Europe's share of the total by 1905 (37 percent). Migration to Brazil totaled a little less than one million between the early 1880s and the early 1900s, but declined rapidly thereafter; migration to Argentina reached 0.75 million in the 1900s. The increasing preference for Argentina (where, in 1914, one inhabitant in nine was Italian-born and where about half the population today can claim some Italian ancestry) over Brazil is explained by the relative decline of the latter's economy. The increase in emigration to the United States was responsible for the big surge in the first decade of the twentieth century that lasted until the war. As we have seen, after the war-induced interruption, emigration resumed and was gradually redirected from the Americas to European destinations, in part due to restrictive laws on immigration in the United States.

The redirection of Italian migration flows from the United States to Europe after World War I was also the result of the introduction, in 1917, of literacy tests, which prohibited entry into the United States to those who could not read and write their own language. In 1921 the U.S. Congress voted on the so-called Quota Act that allowed each country to send an annual number of immigrants not exceeding 3 percent of the population of the same nationality recorded in the census of 1911. In 1924, the National Origins Act reduced that percentage

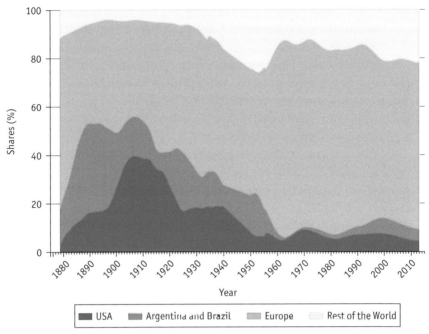

Figure 6.3 WHERE DID ITALIAN EMIGRANTS GO? The figure shows how the distribution of Italian migrant destination countries changed over time (horizontal axis). If the total number of departures (vertical axis) in a given year is set at 100, the greater the area of a given color (geographical area of destination) the higher the number of emigrants. The first wave of emigrants (1876–1915) was fairly evenly distributed between the countries across the Atlantic (the USA and South America) and Europe. After World War II, the percentage of departures for destinations inside Europe increased.

to 2 percent, relating it to the census of 1890. This entailed the virtual exclusion of immigrants from Asia and much of eastern and southern Europe. Finally, in 1927 a further restriction made it almost impossible for those other than British, Irish, and German migrants to enter (Goldin 1994).

Emigration after World War II was emphatically European: the overseas component dropped to about one-tenth on average. Gross flows were nonetheless sustained: 8.5 million people emigrated in this period, 7.3 million of them before 1975.

5 The Best and Brightest. Who Were They?

Visual and literary sources encompassing films, photographs, songs, letters, and novels trace out the profile of the emigrants (Bevilacqua 2011). The general impression we have of Italian migration at the beginning of the twentieth century is quite clear, and it certainly makes sense to think of it as consisting mainly of uneducated and unskilled workers. Italians were often associated with certain niche occupations in the United States, such as picture framers, plaster-figure makers, barbers, fish-and-chip sellers, and tunnelers. Sori (1979) reports data collected by Bodio (1882) on 3,619 Italians who arrived in the United States in 1880 and declared an occupation. About 60 percent were general day laborers, 15 percent farmers, 4 percent musicians, 3.5 percent shopkeepers, and 3 percent servants. The remainder were spread over 55 different occupations. In 1893, a report by the U.S. Commissioner for Labor on conditions in Chicago, based on an analysis of 1,348 "Italian" households, found just over 60 percent were classified as outside the usual industrial and commercial sectors of activity (and thus as irregular or temporary workers) (Auten 1901).

Migrants are not randomly selected from sending country populations (Borjas 1987). In the literature, the early studies claim that migrants are positively selected from the population of the countries of origin (a positive selection, in this sense, means "the best" in terms of ability and motivation). This is in line with data on immigrants' earning, which, in a short time period, exceed the earnings of natives with the same observed socioeconomic characteristics, such as age and education. Not everyone agrees with this view and, on the whole, the nature and direction of selection-bias in migrant populations remains controversial.[10] Were those who departed also better schooled, more self-confident, and less risk-averse than their peers? Where they "the best and brightest"? Across the globe today, the poorer the country of origin, the greater the positive selection.

Aspects related to human capital are not easily identifiable. Literacy is one of the more straightforward measures of human capital. The U.S. Annual Report of the Commissioner-General of Immigration provides data on the literacy rate of immigrants arriving in the late 1890s. We performed some calculations on the data contained in the report and the results are given in Figure 6.4. Italy is last-but-one in the general ranking (ahead of only Portugal): slightly more than half of the Italian migrants who arrived toward the end of the century were unable to read or write. The average educational level of Italian migrants was certainly lower than that of migrants from elsewhere. But what of the comparison between those who migrated and their compatriots who stayed at home? A great deal of information about migrant characteristics in the period of mass migration, 1880–1914, may be inferred from quantitative sources such as census data, official inquiries, and qualitative sources. Among the richest sources is the report of the Dillingham Immigration Commission (U.S. Congress 1911) that

---

[10] See Borjas 1988; Faini 2003; Belot and Hatton 2008; Abramitzky, Platt Boustan, and Eriksson 2010.

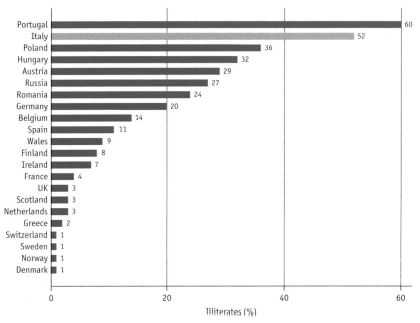

Figure 6.4 PERCENTAGE OF ILLITERATES AMONG EMIGRANTS IN THE
U.S. BY COUNTRY OF ORIGIN. The graph shows the percentage of illiterate
emigrants (horizontal axis) out of total migrants (aged over 10 years) to the
United States in the late nineteenth century for a sample of 22 countries
(vertical axis). The Italian emigrants stand out (along with the Portuguese) for
their inability to read and write.

was a by-product of concerns about the social and economic impact of immigration into the United States. Ship passenger lists offer valuable insight into
the age and gender aspects of migration.[11] For example, they can be used to
compute potential measures of migrants' human capital: their relative ability
in numeracy. Gomellini and Ó Gráda (2013) explored the use of the Whipple
Index, a measurement of numeracy not too different from the ABC index used
in chapter 5 ("Education"), for immigrants arriving between 1880 and 1920 and
for the Italian population as a whole (A'Hearn, Baten, and Crayen 2009). The
results are not conclusive. The comparison indicates *negative* selection bias, that
is, the emigrants were more inclined to age-heap than the population at large.
However, data taken from another source provide a different picture. Data on
nearly twenty thousand passengers on the steamship *Roma*, which plied the
Naples–New York route several times annually, between 1902 and 1905, imply
almost no age-heaping. Cipolla (1969), instead, compared the illiteracy rate of

---

[11] The New York Ellis Island site (http://www.ellisisland.org/) records immigration from 1892
on. It reports names, ages, genders, marital status, and places of origin (but nothing on occupation).

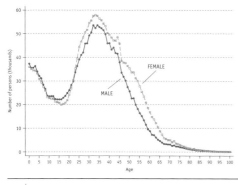

The steamship *Roma*, 1903-05

The 5,000 ton S.S. *Roma*, built in France, plied the Mediterranean-New York route between 1902 and the mid-1920s. It could carry 1,454 passengers (54 of them first-class) at a service speed of 14 knots. These are the age-distributions of the males and females who made the crossing between 1903 and 1905. The modal age group, that is, the most frequent, for both genders is 20-25 years. It is the sons and daughters who left first, before their parents did.

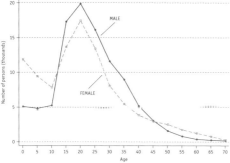

A hundred years later

If we compare the emigration flows of the past (the graph above) with the number of foreign residents in Italy today (graph on the left), we see both similarities and differences. The age of the foreign residents in Italy in 2013 has a higher mode, 30-40 years. It is true, though, that many of these foreigners arrive years before, at a younger age which is perhaps not too different from the age of the Italian emigrants who departed over a century ago. There is a clear gender difference, however: the percentage of women is higher among today's immigrants in Italy than for Italian emigrants a century ago.

Figure 6.5 THE AGE OF MIGRANTS.

Italian emigrants to those of military recruits and found that, in Italy's case, those who migrated were less educated.

Obviously, in some respects, the presence of selection bias is clear: males were much more likely to leave than females, (Box 1); in the period concerned, over seven in ten emigrants were male. Furthermore, emigrants tended to be disproportionately young. One important implication of the gender-age bias is that it entailed a reduction in the labor force's average productivity. This is what happens when it is the "youngest and ablest" who leave, that is, the most productive people in the population: average production thus decreases.

Figure 6.5 (top panel) reports the age and gender distributions of nearly thirty thousand Italian emigrants traveling on the steamship *Roma*. Over half of the males were aged between 15 and 29 years (although there was a significant proportion of older males on board—over three in ten were aged 30 or above). The predominance of male travelers and the small proportion of young males early in the year suggest that family units were more likely to travel in the second half.

Box 1 **The Demographic Impact of Migration**

The effects of migration on population size were sometimes substantial, but varied according to place and time. Caputo (1907), for example, argues that the impact on births, deaths, and marriages in Calabria was temporary and reversed by return migration, but in some small towns in the mountains of Piedmont, the birth rate was reduced by one-third in the last quarter of the nineteenth century. In the demographically overcrowded south, the risk of depopulation was not high even though emigration absorbed nearly two-thirds of the natural increase. Yet, even in 1971 Golini (1974, 72) found that in high emigration regions, such as Molise, 52 percent of the population of the 24–35 age group was "missing" compared to the expected figure based on the 1951 census and the natural mortality rate of the times.

If, on average, emigration did not lead to population decline, it changed other aspects such as gender composition, the number of those living alone (especially women), and the proportion of fatherless households. According to an inquiry into the economic conditions of southern peasants, "during processions you see only women, kids, white heads and bald heads' (Sori 1969, 189). This was how they described the "disappearance" of the adult

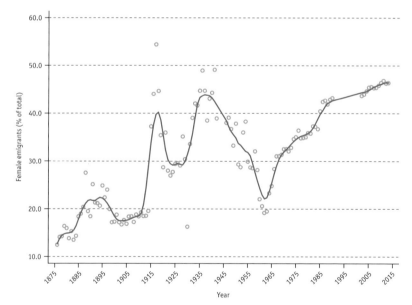

Figure 6.B1 Gender Composition of Italian Migrants, 1875-to date. The figure shows that in the first decade covered by official statistics, the gender imbalance is broad: initially (1876–1885) only 15.2 percent of emigrants were women (there were six men migrants for every woman).

male in places of emigration. Between 1881 and 1911 in many southern regions, the adult male population (19–54) fell by a quarter.

Female emigration accounted for only one-fifth of the total between 1876 and 1914, although men were much more likely to return than women. This evidence is certainly the result of self-selection, but also of the selectivity of the demand for labor abroad. In the United States, men aged over 45 years were dismissed if they could not prove they had family ties, lest they became a burden on public charity (Bosco 1906).

The impact on employment structure was also significant. In the countryside, it was now the women and children who did the tasks normally performed by the men. Hence, male emigration meant a further burden on women's already heavy lot. A parliamentary enquiry promoted in the 1870s by Agostino Bertani (1812–1886), a physician and patriot companion of Mazzini and Garibaldi, documented this vividly: "The women act as beasts of burden, with little care for whether they are pregnant or with young children"; "women cost less than mules" (Bianchi 2001, 258). Furthermore, male emigration provided an opportunity for women's emancipation; with new financial responsibilities "women started going to the post office and to the notary; both money and land began to circulate in their hands. It was up to those left behind to invest the remittances, resort to small loans and satisfy creditors. A condition of autonomy that did not compromise male authority, but replaced it in everyday decisions" (Bianchi 2001; Audenino 1990).

Finally, the mean height of a community or a population is a widely accepted measure of its health and nutritional status—we discussed this at length in chapter 2 ("Height"). At the beginning of the last century, Italian males were much shorter than their Western European peers (e.g., 162.5 centimeters [cm] in Italy compared to 170.4 cm in Norway or 166.8 cm in Germany). Nevertheless, Danubio, Amicone, and Vargiu (2005) studied a sample of 2,140 individuals, mostly southern Italians, who had emigrated to the United States, and offered an indication of *positive* selection in the pre-1914 period. Early-twentieth-century Italian immigrants in the United States were taller than the mean in the regions they left behind: adult males, mainly southern, born after 1880, were 165 cm tall, on average, or 3–4 cm taller than military recruits from the south born around the same time. The outcome is striking, and there is a distinct possibility that the small size of the sample may have been responsible for this overall result. There is also the fact that the result is based on a self-reported measure, which implies a tendency to exaggerate heights (Hatton and Bray 2010).

In conclusion, although Italian emigrants at the beginning of the last century were uneducated and malnourished relative to their European peers, this does not rule out positive selection from the source population insofar as physical strength and motivation were concerned.

The above discussion refers to emigration before 1914. What was the situation during the second post–World War II wave? The 1955 bilateral Italian-German *Gastarbeiter-programm* prompted the migration of over one million low-skilled Italian workers between 1955 and 1973. The findings of a recent analysis of the children of these "guestworkers" who stayed in Germany are consistent with negative selection bias (Dronkers and de Heus 2010). The particularly poor PISA (Programme for International Student Assessment) science scores recorded by the children of Italians may have been partly due to their parents' origin in southern Italy, where scores were strikingly lower than in the north (ranging from 436–450 in the poorest southern regions to 520–540 in the richest northern regions).

6 Why They Left

What are the determinants of Italian emigration? Which forces matter more, *push* (bad economic conditions at home) or *pull* (good opportunities abroad)? Or perhaps something else shaped the magnitudes and directions of migrant flows, such as the progressive formation of a network of former fellow citizens?

The pre-1914 mass migrations from Italy, tsarist Russia, and Central European countries to the United States were surprisingly similar both in size and in short-term fluctuations (Ferenczi and Wilcox 1929). Williamson (2004) showed that migration flows from these countries were fueled by common forces like the relative dynamism of the U.S. economy as well as the increased supply of safe and cheap trips (pull forces). Surely, however, there was a role for push forces, too.

The economic analysis of migration investigates the incentives for an individual to move from a home country (H) to a foreign country (F). The probability of migration is a function of the difference between the two. The investigation analysis is thus a statistical exercise where aggregate migration flows are related to business cycle indicators (like industrial output gaps, unemployment rates) and to measures of relative wages or per-capita incomes.[12] Potential migrants

---

[12] See Hatton and Williamson (1998), O'Rourke and Williamson (1999), Todaro (1969), Hatton (1995), Faini and Venturini (1994a, 1994b), Moretti (1999), and Gomellini and Ó Gráda (2013). Recently, Ardeni and Gentili (2014, 452) maintained that "taking all countries separately and simultaneously, and adopting the most consistent and up-to-date econometric approaches . . . the standard model is only partially confirmed when accounting for heterogeneity of destinations, whereas other relevant hypotheses are not accepted".

Box 2 **Across the Ocean**

Molinari (2001, 237) reports the writings of a farmer from Genoa who made the crossing from Europe to the United States several times. In 1847, the trip from Genoa to New York took as many as 57 days. In 1861, the journey from Liverpool took 17 days. The time taken was halved again (to between 7 and 10 days) by the beginning of the new century. The number of ships specializing in the transport of migrants (and making the crossing several times a year) averaged 82 on the eve of World War I, with peaks of more than 90 between 1902 and 1906. The traffic would resume with eight in 1918 (when the gross emigration of Italians numbered about 28,000), and reached a maximum of 68 in 1921.

Italian ships grew both in numbers and tonnage, i.e., the maximum carrying capacity of the ship in tons. On South American routes, Italian steamers already accounted for 75 percent of the total in the prewar period, while on the North American route the percentage of Italian ships rose from 19 percent in 1901 to 73 percent in 1925. Moreover, all ships of more than 15,000 tons were foreign between 1901 and 1914, but after the war the Italian share reached 53 percent. Average tonnage rose from an initial minimum of 4,231 tons to 10,431 tons in 1925 (Commissariato Generale della Emigrazione Italiana 1927, 1545 et seq.).

How many passengers did the steamers carry? The number of migrants per vessel per trip averaged 744 between 1902 and 1914, but if we consider only trips to North America, the number rises to 978. And how much did the fare cost? Excluding certain landing fees and surcharges for ships undertaking to maintain an average speed of not less than 15 knots, in 1902 the one-way ticket to the United States cost between 150 and 190 lire. Since the average daily wage in agriculture was about 1.8 lire (Fenoaltea 2002) and the work-year was 150–200 days, the cost of the trip was about half an agricultural laborer's annual salary. A substantial, if not prohibitive, sum.

Some mention must be made of two painful issues: health and shipwrecks. Hygienic conditions on board the steamers were very poor; mortality was high and improved only slowly. In 1907 an outbreak of chickenpox on board the steamer *Ravenna* killed 65 children and 15 adults. The boats were dubbed, not unreasonably, "ships of Lazarus" (Molinari 2009, 535). Finally, there were shipwrecks. In this respect, paradoxically, crossings today are more likely to end in tragedy than in the past, as highlighted by Molinari (2009). In the past, shipwrecks and the loss of lives during crossings were the exception; today they are more frequent. Nowadays, some parts of the Mediterranean Sea are real "marine cemeteries" and the phenomenon is considered almost physiological to the dynamics of new migration flows. According to the most careful estimates, there were ten thousand drownings from shipwrecks between North Africa and Southern

Italy in the first decade of the present century, roughly 5 percent of the total (20,000 a year) (Commissariato Generale per l'emigrazione 1927; Hatton and Williamson 1998; Keeling 1999; Molinari 2001; 2009).

Figure 6.B3 THE TRANSOCEANIC TRACK. One of the most interesting aspects of the migration phenomenon is transoceanic shipping, which was subject to dramatic changes, both in technology and turnover. The picture shows the poster of the Italian steamship company "Transatlantica italiana" for the year 1920, featuring the ocean liner *Cesare Battisti*, under construction at the time.

decide whether to leave by comparing expected incomes at home and abroad. In addition, the migrants' decision to leave and where to go can be motivated by the presence in the destination country of a *network* of former fellow citizens.

Aggregate analyses of time-series data show that the level of economic activity in the receiving countries is an important determinant of migration flows in the age of mass migration (Hatton and Williamson 1998). In later periods, by contrast, public policy definitely constrained the size and destinations of migrant flows.[13] Per-capita income differentials (Faini and Venturini 1994a, 80) also mattered, while demographic factors (high birth rates, low population density, the age-structure of the population) do not seem to have influenced migration flows in the Italian case and therefore cannot account for the pattern of Italian migrations. Population pressures counted for little on aggregate.

If we consider the choice of destination across Italian provinces, there is a clear taxonomy: in northern Italy, emigrants from more heavily agricultural provinces were more likely to seek out Brazil than the United States, while southern laborers were more likely to opt for the United States (Hatton and Williamson 1998, 118–120) There is also strong evidence for the persistence of destinations. Furthermore, the aspirations of migrants to the United States and to Argentina differed. The former accumulated no human capital, but saved in order to return home; the latter aspired toward land ownership and permanent residence (Klein 1983).

Finally, using a regional dataset to investigate these aspects, it emerges that differences in wages and network effects (proxied by previous migrants) were crucial. Table 6.2 shows the results of an econometric exercise carried out by extending the estimates in Gomellini and Ó Gráda (2013). The aim of the exercise is to get an indication on the relative importance of many factors at work in determining the migration flows observed in the period 1880–1913. Column (1) reports the gross emigration rate—what the model aims to explain. In Italy's case as a whole, the value of 8.1 indicates that the period 1880–1913 saw an average level of emigration of almost 9 per thousand. Column (2) reports the estimates of the coefficients associated with the "relative wage," defined as the ratio between the domestic wage (in our case, the average wage of each region or macro-area) and the wage of the country of destination. The finding for Italy, for example, is interpreted as follows: a 10 percent increase in the differential between foreign and domestic wages was associated with an increase in emigration rates of

---

[13] Before 1914 and after World War II Italian policy toward emigration was broadly supportive, and the focus was on migrant welfare rather than on discouraging people from leaving (Choate 2008). During the interwar Fascist era, policy was ambivalent, disapproving of although not prohibiting emigration outright (Cannistrato and Rosoli 1979). In that period, as we said, restrictions in the United States, the main host country, exemplified by literacy restrictions and quotas introduced by the Immigration Acts of 1917 and 1921, hit would-be Italian migrants hard in the 1920s.

Table 6.2 **The determinants of emigration in Italy, 1880–1913**

	Migration rate	Relative wage effect	Network effect
	(1)	(2)	(3)
Piedmont	11.9	1.5	75
Veneto	23.0	2.1	85
Liguria	5.5	0.2	66
Lombardy	7.7	0.5	82
Emilia	6.7	0.8	117
Tuscany	7.5	0.8	104
Marche	9.4	0.5	153
Umbria	6.1	0.5	161
Lazio	3.9	0.1	156
Abruzzo	15.7	1.5	108
Calabria	16.2	1.6	119
Campania	11.3	0.9	103
Puglia	4.9	0.3	149
Sicily	9.5	0.8	119
Sardinia	3.1	0.5	157
North and Center	6.8	0.8	111.0
South and Islands	9.6	0.9	123.7
Italy	8.1	0.8	116.9

Note: The table reports average regional migration rates (col. 1), their sensitivity to a change in relative wages (col. 2) and a quantification of the network effect (col. 3).

roughly one person out of every hundred per year (this is how the value of 0.8 in column 2 of the last row of the table is interpreted). Finally, column (3) contains estimates of the magnitude of the network effect, that is, the importance of the chain of solidarity between migrants and the impact of friends and relatives abroad. From their destination countries, immigrants write home with precious information on employment prospects and often foot the bill for the journey through a money transfer or by purchasing a ticket beforehand and then sending it home to the person concerned. Hence, past emigration encourages present emigration, and column (3) provides an estimate of the magnitude of this effect (O'Rourke and Williamson 1999).

All in all, migrants from northern Italy were more reactive to economic incentives (variations in wage differentials) while the decision to leave taken by migrants coming from the center and the south was more network-induced (except Sicily). The estimates in Table 6.2 reveal a powerful network effect: an increase of a thousand people in the stock of population living abroad drew 117 more Italians abroad.

7 The Wellbeing of Those Who Stayed Behind

Emigration has a major economic impact on the economic wellbeing of the countries of origin—an impact that is relatively little studied compared to the impact of immigration in host countries. The sign of the overall impact is not determined ex ante and depends on the interplay between different factors: the effects on the labor force and on real wages; the characteristics of the population outflow in terms of gender, age, and skills; the amount of returnees; and the use of remittances.

There are, in fact, some mechanisms that, at least in part, could compensate for losses of physical and human capital. Migration often acts as a balancing force, fostering convergence between regions and countries, with the effect of offsetting preexisting disparities: thanks to the movements of people, relative prices tend to level off in different countries. In this section we shall focus on four channels that affected the wellbeing of those who stayed behind: wages and per-capita income changes (section 7.1); regional convergence (7.2); remittances (7.3); and the *brain gain* (7.4).

7.1 AND WHAT IF... THE MIGRANTS HAD NOT LEFT?

Taylor and Williamson (1997) estimated that, on the whole, the massive European migration flows in the age of mass migration accounted for 70 percent of the convergence in wages between the Old World and the New World between 1870 and 1914. In Italy's case, Gomellini and Ó Gráda (2013) performed a technically refined exercise of counterfactual history. In Italy, manpower outflows created a relative shortage of workers and a rise in wages. What would have happened to wages without these migration outflows? To answer this question, we evidently need to build a simulation of what could have happened, but did not. This is the meaning of the expression "counterfactual history", which makes it clear that it is an attempt to evaluate what really happened by analyzing what could have happened. Leaving aside the technicalities and the reservations we may have with regard to this kind of analysis, the results obtained are interesting and are worth commenting on.

With zero migration, real wages in 1910 would have been between 13 percent and 22 percent lower compared to their actual value in Italy (Figure 6.6). This

Figure 6.6 ACTUAL AND COUNTERFACTUAL WAGE LEVELS 1870 AND 1914. The graph shows the trend in really observed wages (the solid line, measured along the vertical axis) and the trend in real wages (counterfactual history, the dotted line) if we assume zero migration.

increase in real wages turned into an increase in GDP per head. The calculations of Gomellini and Ó Gráda, reported in Figure 6.6, tell us that per-capita GDP in 1910 would have been between 6 percent and 12 percent lower without emigration. The estimate includes the possible effect of remittances used for investment purposes. Without the emigration of the previous century or so, Italian per-capita GDP in 1973 would have been 4 percent smaller. These estimates may seem "small," given the enormous figure of 30 million emigrants, but "how big is big?" The contribution made by emigration to Italian economic growth matches that of the railway to U.S. economic growth before 1890 or the contribution of the steam engine to British economic history before 1860 (Fogel 1964; van Tunzelmann 1978). Moreover, our calculations leave out the impact on the per-capita GDP of the (hypothetical) descendants of those would have stayed, in the absence of migration. We do not attempt to estimate that impact, but note that people of Italian descent living abroad today greatly outnumber the 30 million who left.

What comes across in this simulation is historiographically significant. Among other things, emigration acted as a safety valve: it induced a reabsorption of excess labor and favored an increase in wages and income, in various ways, thereby improving—in some cases, considerably so—the wellbeing of the Italians who stayed home.

7.2 REGIONAL CONVERGENCE

A particular concern is whether emigration promoted or hampered interregional convergence within Italy in the long run. It could have done so by increasing earnings in regions of heaviest emigration or through the savings made possible by emigrant remittances. Besides this role at the microeconomic level, emigration also plays a macroeconomic role by easing the constraint on the balance of payments.[14]

What can we say about regional convergence in the case of Italy? As we know also from chapters 7 and 14 ("Income" and "The Cost of Living"), spatial convergence in Italy occurred only during the golden age (1950–1973). Did emigration help or hamper this process? We can evaluate the long-run contribution of net migration on per-capita GDP for each region. By performing a simulation similar to the one described in the previous section, this time at a regional level, we get an estimate of the role of emigration on average living conditions (approximated here as per-capita GDP) in the period 1905–1973.

Figure 6.7 summarizes the results, which vary by region, as expected, and range from the very low contribution for Liguria, Lazio, and Sardinia to the very high contribution in Basilicata (where per-capita GDP without emigration would have been 15 percent lower in 1970), Abruzzi, Sicilia, and Calabria. By splitting up the territory into macro-areas, it emerges that international emigration contributed positively to convergence: in the north, net emigration was responsible for 4.1 percent of per-capita GDP growth (Veneto had the highest contribution); 5.1 percent in central Italy (fueled by the strong impact in Marche); and 7.9 percent in the south.

7.3 REMITTANCES

A fantastic rain of gold—that is how the huge flow of remittances into Italy due to the pre-1914 emigration was described at the time—made a significant contribution to economic wellbeing (Massullo 2001, 161).[15] Remittances helped Italy in several ways. Firstly, they directly added to GDP; the most recent reconstructions put their average share of GDP in 1876–1913 at 2.7 percent, ranging from 0.3 percent to 5.8 percent (Balletta 1976; Borghese 2012; Baffigi 2013).

---

[14] See Toniolo (1990, 113), Esteves and Khoudour-Casteras (2009; 2010), Sori (2009), and Balletta (1978).

[15] See also Sori (1969), Stringher (1912), and Borgatta (1933).

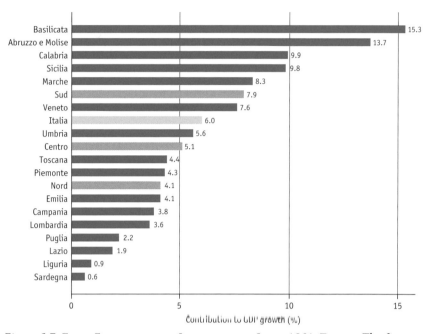

Figure 6.7 FROM EMIGRATION TO IMMIGRATION, ITALY 1861–TODAY. The figure shows the results of a simulation carried out to estimate the contribution made by emigration flows (horizontal axis) to per capita GDP growth in each Italian region (vertical axis). On the whole, emigration was a force acting in favor of the country's economic integration, at least in terms of per capita GDP: the strength of the emigration effect was double in the South compared to the North.

Secondly, as anticipated, their impact was much greater in low-income regions since those were the regions of high emigration, and so remittances helped to dampen regional income disparities.

Remittances found their way back through a variety of channels, both formal and informal ones. The Dillingham Commission reported that Italians remitted money through 2,625 banks in 1907. Remitters from the United States were often subject to systematic exploitation by predatory *banchieri* and this was highlighted in the U.S. press (e.g., "Italian 'Bankers' of New York City," *New York Times*, April 18, 1897). This prompted Italian Treasury Minister Luigi Luzzatti in 1897 to propose a plan to replace the "bankers" by a reliable and low-cost means of transferring remittances. After an intense debate, the state-owned Banco di Napoli was given the privilege in 1901 (de Rosa 1980).

Using information about money remitted through the Banco di Napoli,[16] remittances directed to southern Italy between 1905 and 1913 amounted to

---

[16] The role of the Banco di Napoli in reducing the risk and cost of making transfers was notable, though hardly dominant. In its first year it remitted 9.3 million lire, and it was sending back

60.6 percent of the total, with Sicily, Calabria, and Campania accounting for an average 40 percent (Massullo 2001).

In the previous section we showed the contribution of emigration to the growth of per-capita GDP. In the calculations, remittances were also allowed a role as potential stimuli to investment. But is that justifiable? There is some controversy about how remittances were spent. Although their benefits as a boost to living standards are not in question, the extent to which they boosted the economy is still the object of debate. Macmillen (1982) showed that the unproductive use of remittances could even result in a negative outcome, via an increase in the price level due to consumption and an overvalued exchange rate that dampens exports. The dependence on remittances could also delay appropriate adjustment policies.

True, some qualitative accounts claim that remittances were devoted to "unproductive" purposes, with little effect on per-capita GDP (Sori 1969; Drinkwater et al. 2003; Glytsos 2005). Only a small fraction, around 30 percent,[17] was invested in entrepreneurial activities. Remittances were frequently used to build new houses, increase savings, or repay debts: this can be argued, for example, from the sharp reduction in mortgage debt on peasant properties in Calabria at the turn of the century (Sori 1969, 160; Massullo 2001, 172). Not only this, but Cinel (1991, 226) claimed that "remittances had a marginal impact, at best, in the modernization of the Italian South". The impact of remittances would not have been enough, then, to overcome the backwardness of southern Italy's economic and social structures. In Cinel's words, "The evidence indicates that the return migration and remittances had a more profound impact in those regions, like the Italian Northwest, where a variety of economic dynamics were at work. The impact was less profound in those regions, like the south, where very few economic dynamics were at work" (227). The evidence collected by Cinel only relates to migrants to the United States; once back in Italy, most of them preferred to go back to America for good, "after one or more failed attempts at relocating in home communities, with American money. Returnees who bought land were more likely to become disappointed than returnees who planned to spend the rest of their lives relying on saving" (229).

Nevertheless, there is no doubt that remittances contributed to macroeconomic stability by helping to finance current account deficits and thus

---

nine times that amount, mostly from the United States, by 1914, a share of roughly 10 percent of overall remittances. Boosted by wartime inflation, remittances through the Banco di Napoli peaked at nearly one billion lire in 1920 (20 percent of the total) (Massulo 2001; Choate 2008; U.S. Immigration Commission XXXVII, 271).

[17] Cerase (1967) shows that, in the south, 19 percent returned because their migratory project failed, 40 percent because their savings plans were reached, 26 percent for retirement, and only 16 percent to invest in the area of origin (Sori 1969).

allowing the take-off of the Giolittian age despite the balance of payments constraint (Sori 1969, 160). Remittances sustained a current account surplus between the 1880s and 1900s.[18] Indeed, the data underestimate the contribution of remittances insofar as the savings sent home by letter, or brought in the pockets by the returnees or by the *golondrinas*, those "birds of passage" who traveled seasonally across the Atlantic: they were all excluded from official statistics.

Finally, remittances also had a positive impact on financial development. In the sending regions, savings banks became important hosts for repatriated savings, helping to facilitate the spread of financial know-how. In Italy as a whole, the volume of deposits in post office savings accounts rose from 323 million lire in 1890 to over two billion lire in 1913, while the share of emigrants' savings rose from 0.03 percent to 4.4 percent (Esteves and Khoudour-Castéras 2009; Gomellini and Ó Gráda 2013). Southern savings banks particularly benefited from remittances.

7.4 BRAIN GAIN

When interactions between emigration and human capital are studied, the attention is often directed to the so-called *brain drain*: if people who move out of a country are skilled ones, migration could damage native countries because of human capital depletion. A voluminous literature on this point has shown how a brain drain could hamper the convergence in per-capita income levels across countries.[19] Against this is the possibility of a *brain gain:* emigration can positively influence education levels in source countries by operating through different channels.

We examined the literacy and schooling of the Italians in detail in chapter 5 ("Education"). Despite tragic starting conditions, the Italians made progress as much in statistics on the school-age population as on the adult population. Between 1881 and 1921 the percentage of citizens over 15 years of age who could read and write almost doubled (from 37.8 percent to 72 percent); elementary school enrollment rates rose from 67 percent to 100 percent—that is, enrollment of the entire cohort of children aged 6–10 years. Did emigration influence this process?

The testimonies of Francesco Coletti (1866–1940), a distinguished Italian statistician who contributed to an enquiry into economic conditions of Italian peasants, speak clearly on the subject:

---

[18] See Massulo (2001), Esteves and Khoudour-Castéras (2009), De Rosa (1980), and Del Boca and Venturini (2003).

[19] See Bhagwati and Hamada (1974), Bhagwati and Wilson (1989), Ciriaci (2005), Katseli, Lucas, and Xenogiani (2007), and Piras (2007).

Migration is the best friend of literacy (...). It is the experience of migration that provided strong evidence about the utility of primary education as a powerful tool of an upward social mobility and it is undoubtedly the most persuasive deterrent to drop out of primary school. (...) Migration is the main cause of the rise in school attendance. (Coletti 1911, 257–258)

Three main channels for a brain gain can be identified (Mayr and Peri 2009; Docquier and Rapoport 2009). First, the prospect of emigrating can boost incentives for education in the source country. This is because a basic education can

---

Box 3 **Nice Country, Horrible People?**

"The Italians: the worst rejects of Europe; holders of the record for crime; a horde of vicious, ignorant people; mentally retarded people that lower the American standards; corruptors of judges and politicians; loafers as intrusive as locusts; they call themselves Catholic but are immoral; they can kill their best friend: nicknamed *dagoes* (from dagger)" (Stella 2002). These are just some of the epithets reserved for the Italians by the U.S. press between the late nineteenth century and World War I (La Gumina 1973). No other community was the target of such hostile treatment as that reserved for Italians.

The image we get is certainly an ungenerous one. The 29 million people who emigrated in over a century certainly included delinquents, but not all Italian migrants deserved to be represented by the stereotype of the dishonest and dangerous Italian. Studies carried out in order to set up the Museum of Italian Emigration found that in 1,057 films shot in Hollywood between 1928 and 2000, only 27 percent of the cases gave a positive image of the Italian, who is more frequently portrayed as a criminal (40 percent) or as uncouth, bigoted, stupid, or a buffoon (33 percent).

This perception is certainly influenced by emigration of a political stamp, especially of an anarchic kind, and the (real or presumed) involvement of many Italians in various assassination attempts at the turn of the twentieth century. In the tense climate following World War I, the prejudice turned into a savage hunt of anarchic immigrants, such as the famous case of Nicola Sacco (1891–1927) and Bartolomeo Vanzetti (1888–1927). The two Italians, arrested in 1920 on charges of having committed a bloody robbery, were executed in 1927. They would only be fully rehabilitated in 1977 for not having committed the crime.

The image of the dishonest Italian tarnished that of migrants who faced hunger and prejudice to feed their own children back home in Italy and

Figure 6.B3 ANTONIO MEUCCI (1808–1889). The Italian inventor Antonio Meucci, who emigrated to New York and patented the "electric transfer of the voice". Meucci was one of many who we must remember in order to do justice of the widespread anti-Italian iconography.

also the many success stories. One example among many is that of Amedeo Obici (1878–1947). He left the Veneto region without a cent and became the Peanuts King, giving employment to over six thousand people in the 1930s with his Planters company (today a division of Kraft Foods). Last, but not least, prejudice conceals the contribution made by Italian culture to the American success story. Here, too, we can recall the example of Filippo Mazzei (1730–1816), who inspired the Declaration of Independence and was an intimate friend of the first five presidents of the United States—from George Washington (1732–1799) to Thomas Jefferson (1743–1826)—and also that of Lorenzo Da Ponte (1749–1838), who was called upon in 1819 to found the chair of Italian literature in a college that would later become Columbia University.

help the migrant in various ways (being able to write home, keep track of remittances, reduce the risk of being cheated, receive higher wages linked to schooling). To the extent that leaving was uncertain, some of those who did not emigrate went to school just in case. Second, *return migrants* may promote education to the extent that returnees, thanks to their experience abroad, are more alert to the importance of schooling. Third, *remittances* can play an important role in relaxing a possible budget constraint that prevents people from investing in education.

Taking into account the evolution of the education system, differences in economic conditions, and other factors, Giffoni and Gomellini (2015) estimate that in the first decade of the twentieth century, a 10 percent increase in emigration was associated with a 0.9 percent increase in the school attendance rate. This means that for every 100 additional emigrants, an extra 4 to 7 children were kept at school. Return migration had a stronger impact on primary schooling, though it did not affect the education of adults: 100 additional returnees increased the number of non-dropout pupils in a range from 8 to 11. Differently, migration prospects stimulated schooling responses of adults: 100 more migrants pushed into evening schools from 11 to 14 individuals. Obviously, remittances were also an effective channel for stimulating school attendance.

The relationship between migration and education at the beginning of the twentieth century is even more striking and can best be appreciated at the regional level. Jarach (1877, 57) writes of the Abruzzi, then a region of high emigration, that the benefit of literacy had "penetrated into the consciousness of the population. It rapidly conquered the minds of farmers and shepherds because of the need, once the ocean was crossed, to send news on health and on the accumulation of savings to the families at home, without relying on a stranger".

Wives in Italy received encouragements from U.S.-based spouses to send children to school. In Sicily, enrollments in primary school increased remarkably in the first decade of the twentieth century, rising from 54.5 per thousand inhabitants in 1902 to 73.5 in 1907. Despite the hostile environment in which people lived, and their financial straits, the conviction grew that literacy was an effective weapon against poverty, and "this firm conviction emerged thanks to emigration" (Coletti 1911, 257). In analyzing the high literacy rate of the population living in the Alpine areas on the border with Austria, Switzerland, and France, Cipolla (1969) argued that literacy was triggered by emigration, which forces potential migrants to become literate in order to keep in touch with relatives.

Finally, return migrants were in a good position to see education as a tool to achieving success and prosperity. This may well have induced them to ensure their children attended school. The returned migrant was a human being transformed, bringing new energy and ideas to the village he had left. Emigration, in this sense, was a great school; it was worth "thousands of scholarships. It gets rid of the old rust from the mind, it instills ideas that otherwise would not be able to penetrate" (Coletti 1911, 253). Return migrants were psychologically transformed from the time they left: "Ease, fluency and manner of speaking, style of dress, greater awareness of their own dignity and their rights, no awe of old employers, willingness to participate in municipal affairs, political and general interests". This miracle was all thanks to emigration (Coletti 1911, 251–252).

8 The Welfare of Today's Immigrants

The migration rate is defined as the ratio between the number of persons entering and leaving a country during a given year and the average number of residents in the population in that year, multiplied by a thousand. When it is negative, it means that the number of arrivals is lower than the number of those who migrated abroad (the departures). A negative migration rate is characteristic of a country of emigrants. The curve in Figure 6.8 shows the history of Italian emigration. From being a people of migrants, Italy has turned into a country with a positive and strongly growing migration balance. It is thus clear that the impact of immigration into Italy on the welfare of both the immigrants and the host population should not be forgotten. The issue is of historical and economic importance, which is what we are concerned with here, but it is also politically significant. The former is very useful for the latter, as we shall see shortly.

In 1960 Italy's foreign-born population numbered just 63,000; two decades later it was still only 0.3 million. Since then Italy has become a country of significant net immigration, with the recorded proportion of non-Italians rising from just 0.5 percent of inhabitants in 1980 to 2 percent in 2003 and 7.6 percent (or 4.4 million) in 2013. Non-nationals who entered or are staying on illegally—the so-called *clandestine*—may account for an additional 0.5–0.75 million. While the top three sending countries—Romania, Albania, and Morocco—accounted for one-third of all foreign residents in Italy in 2003 and over two-fifths a decade later, the top twenty sending countries still leave one-fifth of the total stock unaccounted for. With the remainder representing 175 nationalities, the Italian immigration of the recent past has been truly global (Istat 2015; World Bank 2015).

A simple, first-pass way of calculating the benefits to the immigrants themselves would be to compare an estimate of their incomes in Italy with what they might have earned had they remained at home. Lacking comparable wage data, we approximate this for 2013 by multiplying the difference between per-capita GDP in the sending country and in Italy by the number of immigrants from each sending country in that year; adding together; and then reducing the total by two-thirds.[20] Such a measure is intended only as an indication of the massive gains involved, and is subject to some obvious caveats. On the one hand, it ignores the cost of immigration and the psychic cost—if present—of living away from home. On the other hand, it also excludes the gains in terms of better health care in old age and better prospects for the second and third generations.

The gains implied by this yardstick from a sending country perspective are huge. In terms of revenue gained (measured in PPP dollars), the top eight in 2013 were Romania, Albania, Morocco, China, Ukraine, Philippines, Moldova, and

---

[20] For each country i we estimate $N_{i,It}$ $[Y_{It}-Y_i]/3$, where $N_{i,It}$ represents immigration from country i to Italy (It) and Y is per-capita GDP.

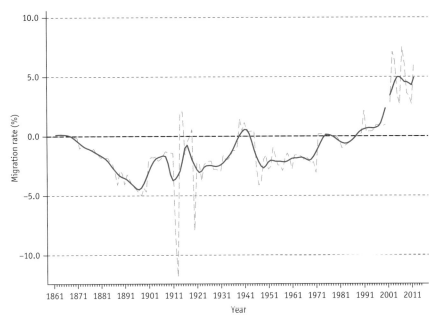

Figure 6.8 LONG RUN CONTRIBUTION OF MIGRATION TO REGIONAL PER CAPITA GDP GROWTH, 1905–1973. The figure shows Italy's transition from a country of emigration to a country of immigration. When the migration rate in a territory is negative, departures exceed arrivals: this is the case with Italy up to the 1970s. Over the last thirty years or so, Italy has become a country with a positive migration rate. Annual values (dashed line) has been smoothed (solid line) to facilitate the identification of the trend.

India. Estimating the gains as a proportion of GDP, by far the biggest beneficiaries were Albania (12 percent) and Moldova (8 percent).[21] Macedonia (2.3 percent), Kosovo (2.3 percent), Morocco (1.6 percent), and Romania (1.3 percent) also gained significantly in this sense. Moreover, still applying the same crude yardstick, the implied contribution of the Italian economy to the wellbeing of migrants was also big: 0.4 percent of Italian GDP in 2003 and 1.6 percent in 2013.

Although Italian public opinion does not take too kindly to the growing immigrant presence—a close replica of U.S. public opinion toward Italians a century ago—immigration has also improved the material wellbeing of the average native Italian in the recent past. Immigrants have concentrated heavily in niches that do not compete with, but rather complement, native labor; this is particularly so in the case of care for the elderly and for children, domestic service generally, and unskilled labor in the agricultural and construction sectors. They

[21] These estimates may be on the low side, given that in the early 2010s emigrant remittances were worth 10 percent of Albanian GDP and over 20 percent of Moldovan GDP (World Bank: World Development Indicators).

Box 4 On the Perils of Misperception

With regard to immigration, the Italians turn out to be the champions of misperception of reality. In the summer of 2014 a survey carried out by IPSOS Mori showed that, out of the 14 countries considered, Italy is the one with the highest overestimation of the number of immigrants in its territory (a perceived figure of 30 percent as against the real figure of 7 percent). The ignorance index, in the words used by of the report, reaches its peak in Italy's case.

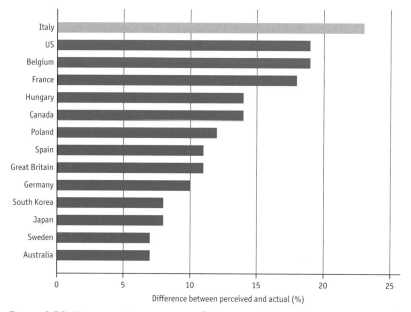

Figure 6.B2 PERILS OF PERCEPTION. "In your opinion, what percentage of the population do you think are immigrants to this country?" The graph shows the difference between the actual figure and the respondents' answers.

have contributed more than they claim from the public purse: according to the OECD (2013) the average immigrant household contributed €12,310 in 2007–2009, while claiming only €3,162 in benefits. And, but for immigrants, Italy's population would by now be almost certainly falling (Giuntella 2012; Boeri et al. 2014). Natives benefit too from any labor market discrimination against immigrant workers (Accetturo and Infante 2013; Coppola et al. 2013).

9 Internal Migration

Alongside international migration flows there were also internal ones, inside the country itself. The earliest statistical reconstructions, somewhat uncertain and fragmented, date back to 1861 and show—contrary to what many people believe—that domestic migration flows were far from negligible: an army of men and women changed their abode, abandoning the countryside in favor of towns and cities, depopulating mountain areas for the hills and plains, and, in particular, leaving the south of the country for the north.

The data we have come from municipal records offices, which, for each year, give us the number of people registered in a different municipality than the one they resided in the year before, and also the number of corresponding cancellations. The first population census of the new Kingdom of Italy does not have a great reputation with historian demographers, but wishing to give it credit, we find that in 1861, 17 percent of the population lived in a different municipality than the one of their birth—a figure not far removed from the one recorded fifty years later (26 percent in 1911). The most distinguishing feature of the first fifty years of postunification Italy was probably the short-range migration that fueled the big Italian cities and particularly Catania, Milan, Rome, Turin, Genoa, and Bari (Golini 1976).

Despite the designs of the Fascist regime, the aftermath of World War I opened up a phase of "vast migration flows" (De Vergottini 1935). The traditional historiographic view depicting Fascist Italy as an immobile country, tied down by the chains of the regime, was overturned by a study published in 1976 by Anna Treves. The idea of hindering the mobility of the population sprang from Mussolini's conviction that strength lay in numbers: "To count for something, Italy must embark on the latter half of this century [1950] with a population of not less than 60 million people", said Mussolini before the Chamber of Deputies, when (it was 1927) the country had just reached 40 million inhabitants. An obsession with demography led to viewing urbanization as the most dangerous enemy; decree after decree, measures were approved restricting the people's movement from the countryside to the city. In 1928 the population was notified of a new clampdown through a newspaper article signed by Mussolini himself: "We must . . . hinder with every means," said the article in *Il Popolo d'Italia*—"even, if necessary, with coercive means, the abandonment of the countryside, prevent with every means the hordes of emigration to the cities" (Treves 1976, 72). At the same time, the prefects up and down the country were given the faculty to enforce this view by acting with the instruments they deemed most appropriate for the purpose. In 1931 a "Commissariat for migrations and internal colonization" was set up with the task of regulating internal migration flows: to move from one province to another, the Italians had

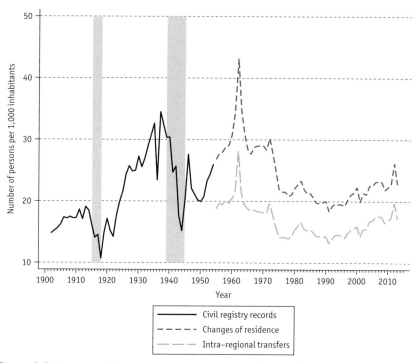

Figure 6.9 INTERNAL MOBILITY, 1900 TO DATE. The graph shows the trend in internal mobility (the vertical axis measures the mobility rate per 1,000 inhabitants) over time (horizontal axis). Not even Fascist policy managed to prevent internal migration flows, a process of huge dimensions, common to European countries in the interwar years.

to apply to the Commissariat for authorization.[22] Treves (1976) showed that, despite the efforts of Fascist policy, internal mobility in the interwar period exploded (Figure 6.9). The regime could do little in view of the great forces unleashed by the country's great economic imbalances and by a huge unemployment rate.

The end of World War II marked the beginning of a new phase. The two distinguishing features of this period are the intensification of internal migration (almost a million and a half people changed abode every year), along with a change in its composition: internal migration changed from intraregional to become increasingly interregional. In the years of the Italian "economic miracle" (1950s–early 1960s), millions of people left the south of the country for the northwestern

---

[22] The peak was reached in 1939 with a law that linked changing one's abode to having a job, despite the fact that another law reserved job placements only to those who already had a residence certificate. This made changing one's abode impossible, in practice, without behaving illegally. It was, as Luigi Einaudi observed some decades later, "the re-establishment of serfdom" in Italy.

regions: Lombardy, Piedmont, and Liguria took in over 110,000 people every year, on average, for fifteen years. Rome received a non-negligible part (Sori 1996).

The series in Figure 6.9 shows a marked peak in the years 1961–1963. It probably reflects the abolition, in 1961, of the Fascist law against urbanization. The peak does not mark a real acceleration of migration flows but a technical rebound due to the emergence of a situation that had remained "clandestine" for decades (Sonnino 1966, 36). In 1961 there were 138,196 new resident registrations in Rome alone, as against the 64,309 registered the previous year. Normality was soon restored: in 1964 the curve shows that the internal migration rate returned to its 1960 level.

Internal migration has similar causes as those underlying international emigration. After World War II a leading role in this form of migration was played by the high demographic pressure caused by Fascist policies: the southern regions were huge reservoirs of underemployed peasant labor (Pugliese and Sabatino 2006). On the other hand, industrial development concentrated in the northwestern regions of the country generated a demand for labor, and this was not just an economic attractor but also a social, cultural, and ideological one (Crainz 2005): internal migration enabled not only an improvement of living conditions but also the achievement of broader aspirations in life (Ginsborg 1989).

10 Conclusions

In the global history of human migration, the emigration out of Italy between the 1860s and 1960s is unique. Its very size means that its impact on welfare was significant both at home and abroad. That is our justification for the length of this chapter. Our main focus has been on the economics and the economic history of Italian migration. Economics is a notoriously dry discipline, but migration remains an emotive topic, from various perspectives. Compare the clinical analysis of economists with the following passage from poet Giovanni Pascoli (1855–1912):

> Don't leave your motherland without wishing her well. If you are poor and forced to seek bread and work in a foreign land, far from your village and your loved ones, love her too, and strongly. Who reneges on one's mother, unless they are poor and she has no bread to give them? Love your homeland which holds the remains of your ancestors and your dear ones. (authors' translation from Pascoli, 1914)

For some migrants, the move abroad is a liberation, but for others—arguably a small minority—it is a separation from which they never quite recover. For some nationalists in the sending countries, migration represents human capital loss and policy failure. For residents of host countries, migration is sometimes seen as a boon, but sometimes, too, as a threat to native employment and culture. All of these sentiments are reflected in the history of Italian migration, and Italians have been at both the giving and receiving ends of them.

The outflow's huge footprint is reflected in the 17.2 million Italian Americans who constitute 5.4 percent of the population of the United States today; the 19.7 million *italo-argentini* who constitute 46 percent of the population of Argentina; and the 27.2 million *italo-brasiliani* who constitute 13 percent of the population of Brazil.[23] Allowing for significant Italian presences in places as far apart as France (4 million, 6 percent), Uruguay (1.2 million, 35 percent), Canada (1.4 million, 4 percent), Australia (0.9 million, 4 percent), Germany (0.7 million, 1 percent), and elsewhere, it emerges that diaspora Italians outnumber those who left by three to one, and they also comfortably outnumber those living in Italy itself.

Elementary economics views emigration as a win-win game. This would imply that those 30 million Italians who emigrated and did not return voted with their feet, whereas those who remained at home gained from the resultant reduced pressure on scarce land and capital. Our analysis broadly corroborates this prediction, despite the human capital losses associated with emigration.

The impact of that emigration on wellbeing where Italians settled is more controversial, as is the impact of immigration today on wellbeing in Italy. But whereas the specialist literature on mass migration to the New World before World War I highlights its negative impact on native wages, the literature on migration into Europe and the United States today tends to emphasize its role in filling niches shunned by native workers, in improving the age composition of the workforce, and in increasing labor market flexibility. And although immigration may have a negative impact on those at the very bottom of the wage distribution scale, it also encourages the upward redeployment of native workers (D'Amuri and Peri 2014; Dustman, Frattini, and Preston 2013). As we have shown above, the gap between perception and reality is significant, and perhaps the study of migration in the past can help to reduce this gap. Of course, knowledge of the economic history of Italian migration flows, the one based on the analysis of historical statistics and the specialist literature, represents a solid bulwark against the rising tide of xenophobic arguments produced in the political-economic debate in recent decades. *On a tous déjà vu ça.*

---

[23] These data are taken from http://it.wikipedia.org/wiki/Emigrazione_italiana (where the original sources are given).

Appendix—Sources and Methods

Figure 6.1 The numbers of Italian emigration, 1870 to date　Source: Istat (2011). The yearly series has been smoothed with a LOWESS filter with bandwidth equal to 0.1.

Figure 6.2 Regional origins of Italian emigrants　Source: Istat (2011).

Figure 6.3 Where did Italian emigrants go?　Source: Istat (2011).

Figure 6.4 Percentage of illiterates among emigrants in the U.S. by country of origin　Sources: Cipolla (2002, 106); Sori (1969, 206). The data refer to 1895, 1897, and 1898.

Figure 6.5 The age of migrants on Steamship *Roma*, 1903–1905　Source: Gomellini and Ó Gráda (2013).

Table 6.2 The determinants of emigration in Italy, 1880–1913　Source: Gomellini and Ó Gráda (2013). The data are from the Commissariato Generale della Emigrazione (1927) on gross emigration for sixteen regions of origin and nine destination countries, from 1876 to 1925 (with a grand total of 10,400 observations). Internationally comparable regional per-capita GDP data are obtained by using Baffigi (2013) and the regional indices are calculated using Daniele and Malanima (2007) and Felice (2013). Internationally comparable regional wages (from 1905) are obtained using Williamson (1995); the indices of regional wages are those proposed in Arcari (1936). Measures of foreign and domestic economic activity are obtained as a deviation of per-capita GDP from the trend (calculated using the Hodrick-Prescott filtering technique). The model used is a standard migration model (Hatton1995; Moretti 1999). It estimates the sensitivity of Italian emigration flows during the period 1876–1913, to changes in relative wages (ratio of Italian vis-à-vis foreign wages), and to changes in the number of people already migrated. We used longitudinal data that allowed us to control for region of departure, country of destination, and time-fixed effects, thereby removing some of the potential biases stemming from omitted variable problems.

Figure 6.6 Actual and counterfactual wage levels 1870 and 1914　Source: Calculations on data from Fenoaltea (2002) and Baffigi (2013). Lire per day on the vertical axis.

Figura 6.7 From emigration to immigration, Italy 1861–today   Source: SSS and Istat website.

Figure 6.8 Long run contribution of migration to regional per-capita GDP growth, 1905–1973   Source: Gomellini and Ó Gráda (2013).

Figure 6.9 Internal mobility, 1900-present   Source: our calculations on data kindly provided by Frank Heins, first used in Bonifazi and Heins (2011).

7

Income

WITH ALESSANDRO BRUNETTI AND EMANUELE FELICE

1 Who Doesn't Know What GDP Is?

Gross domestic product (GDP) was conceived in the United States, in the National Bureau of Economic Research (NBER), a private research institute founded in New York in 1920. Today, the NBER is one of the most important think tanks of North American economists. The first estimates came out in 1934, driven by the need to measure the impact of the Great Depression on economic activity and to monitor the road to recovery (Kuznets 1934). Since then, GDP has become the most famous and widely used macroeconomic indicator in the world. In Italy, the vast majority of primary school textbooks contain a lesson on gross domestic product: even children have to know what GDP is.

The career path of GDP has been spectacular, to say the least. It first became established in national accounting (the set of accounts describing a country's economic activity), receiving much greater attention with respect to consumption (which a great deal of a household's wellbeing depends on), investment (which future economic growth depends on), exports, and public spending. GDP then went on to become an international standard, managing to get countries all over the globe to agree on the methods and definitions necessary to build a homogeneous, shared, and comparable measure. Finally, its last promotion came through a "ratification" by the five main international institutions—the United Nations, the Organisation for Economic Cooperation and Development (OECD), the International Monetary Fund (IMF), the World Bank, and the European Commission—which agreed on the rules for measuring GDP, thereby crowning it as the supreme macroeconomic indicator at both a juridical and practical level (Lequiller and Blades 2006).

The advantage of using GDP probably lies in its aggregate nature: it brings together, within a single number, the value of the final production created by all the economically active agents (private enterprises, public administration, non-profit institutions, and households), both resident and nonresident ones, over a certain period of time. GDP is a number that can be quickly worked out on the basis of easily available macroeconomic data: it has no roots in economic theory, and it is also the fruit of conventions devised to perform a steering function useful to those charged with governing the economy (Fenoaltea 2008).

In more technical terms, GDP measures the overall value—calculated at market prices—of all final goods and services produced within an economic system (a country or a region) over a certain period of time (normally one year). In 2015, Italy's GDP was 1,636,371,669,000 Euros, a figure corresponding about to 60 percent of British GDP, 70 percent of French GDP, 50 percent of German GDP, a little over 40 percent of Japanese GDP, 20 percent of Chinese GDP, and around 10 percent of U.S. GDP. According to IMF estimates (2014), if we set the GDP of the European Union (of 27 member states) to 100, the contribution made by Italy's GDP is 12, while if we set the GDP of the entire planet to 100, the Italian contribution would drop to 3. As we can see, the GDP measure allows us easily to compare national economies.

The value of GDP is often equated to a country's overall income. As the first law of thermodynamics tells us, energy can take various forms, but is not created or destroyed, so a year's value of production can be variously distributed among individuals as income, but these incomes cannot but add up to the total value of the production, that is, to GDP (Box 1).

Other things being equal, the most populous nations have higher levels of GDP. To take this aspect into account when making international comparisons, we can divide GDP by the number of inhabitants to get a new measure—GDP per head or per-capita GDP—which can be interpreted as the national *average* income. Since the Italian population in 2013 was estimated to be 59,685,227 individuals, per-capita GDP for that year was 26,137 Euros per head. Unlike with total GDP, international comparisons based on per-capita GDP take into account the diverse demographic nature of each country. If we look at 2013, GDP per head of the Italians was 96 percent of that of the Germans, 90 percent of the French, 84 percent of the British, and 64 percent of the United States, while it was three times the Chinese figure.

Once we have established that per-capita GDP can be interpreted along the lines of the average income of a population, there may be the temptation to go a step further by considering GDP as a measure of the prevalent wellbeing in a society: per-capita GDP would be to a population's wellbeing what personal income is to individual wellbeing. This apparently harmless and sensible equivalence is incorrect, however. Per-capita GDP is *not* the same thing as wellbeing.

2 GDP and Wellbeing

Although scholars recognize and agree that there is a strong empirical correlation between per-capita GDP and the wellbeing of a population, there is a clear

---

Box 1 1934 AD: GDP Is Born

In January 1934, the National Bureau of Economic Research (NBER) gave Simon Kuznets the task of presenting the first estimates of "national income" of the United States for the years 1929–1932. This was no small news for the experts of the times, especially if we consider that in the early decades of the twentieth century the "empirically oriented" economists were a scant minority (Fogel 2000).

The prose with which Kuznets took to his task is incomparable, managing to combine scrupulous attention to technical details with the desire to put across the underlying ideas. It is worth rereading the passage reproduced above, taken from the original document, the *NBER Bulletin*, published on June 7, 1934. It is a page of economic history and policy that is as important as it is little known.

> Year in, year out the people of this country, assisted by the stock of goods in their possession, render a vast volume of services towards the satisfaction of their wants. Each of these services involves an effort on the part of an individual and an expenditure of some portion of the country's stock of goods. Some of these services eventuate in commodities, such as coal, steel, clothing, furniture, automobiles; others take the form of direct, personal services, such as are rendered by physicians, lawyers, government officials, domestic servants, and the like. If all the commodities produced and all the direct services rendered during the year are added at their market value, and from the resulting total we subtract the value of that part of the nation's stock of goods that was expended (both as raw materials and as capital equipment) in producing this total, then the remainder constitutes the net product of the national economy during the year. It is referred to as national income produced, and may be defined briefly as that part of the economy's end product that results from the efforts of the individuals who comprise a nation.

Figure 7.B1 KUZNETS' "NATIONAL INCOME". In the text above, Kuznets (1929) provides a definition of "national income" which has been accepted ever since [Carson 1975].

distinction between the two terms at a conceptual level. On the one hand, GDP *excludes* aspects that help define wellbeing and that should thus be included. There are many examples of such things, and they typically concern nonmonetary spheres of wellbeing that have no market or even a price with which to evaluate them: for example, health, education, the enjoyment of political and civil freedoms, the availability of free time, clean air, and the quality of affective life. GDP does not take all these aspects into consideration while an ideal measure of wellbeing should. Nor does GDP account for benefits deriving from the possession of durable goods and their quality (things like household appliances and means of transport), many of which significantly affect our everyday lifestyle and thus our wellbeing.

On the other hand, GDP *does include* items that do not generate increases in wellbeing and that should thus be deducted from a measure of wellbeing: amortization (that is, the loss of value incurred by machinery owing to physical wear and tear or obsolescence), profits earned domestically by foreign-owned companies, and the so-called regrettables (expenditures that do not directly contribute to individual wellbeing, but which prevent it from falling, such as spending on defense and on the administration of justice)

GDP *ignores* factors that represent costs—not necessarily pecuniary ones—linked to the production of goods and services, such as pollution or the impoverishment of environmental resources, but even increasing economic insecurity connected to the spreading of atypical and temporary labor contracts. These costs should be deducted from GDP, but they are not.

GDP does not even take other items into account that, although having an economic value, are not monetized. In particular, GDP does not consider unpaid work, and this sometimes has paradoxical effects. An old textbook example of this, which is still found in many economics books today, explains that every time a bachelor marries his own domestic help, the country's GDP falls: this is because the housework performed by the lady of the house without any monetary remuneration is not counted in the GDP accounting, while the same activity performed by a person not belonging to the household, and hired as an employee, contributes to GDP. In the same way, if parents decide to entrust their children's care to a paid babysitter, this leads to a rise in GDP. As in the bachelor's case above, this happens because GDP takes into account the value of paid work, but not of routine housework (Box 2). Both examples describe circumstances where GDP variations do not reflect corresponding variations in the wellbeing of society as a whole: marriages between bachelors and their housekeepers help lead to decreases in GDP as a consequence of accounting conventions, but this does not in any way mean a fall in society's wellbeing as well.

The overall lesson that can be learned from these considerations is as follows. Despite the fact that GDP is not a suitable measure of the living standards of a population, it is still a measure that the analysts of wellbeing look to with

Box 2 **Homemade GDP**

National accounting rules do not consider the value of goods and services produced within the household for GDP purposes. The fact that the sheer scale of this household production in Italy is greater than in other countries led Alberto Alesina, a Harvard economist, and Andrea Ichino, of Bologna University, to reflect on the consequences that this peculiar vocation of Italian households has on GDP. They concluded that international comparisons based on "official" GDP figures *underestimate* the standard of living of the Italians. If the value of "homemade" goods and services were taken into consideration in GDP accounting, then Italy would improve its international ranking. For example, Italy's gap with regard to the United States would narrow from 44 to 36 percent, while the 2 percent deficit with respect to Spain, recorded in "official" GDP, would turn into a 7 percent advantage for the Italians (Alesina and Ichino 2009). The lesson is a universal one: "official" GDP, as calculated by statistics agencies, penalizes the Italians in international comparisons of living standards.

Figure 7.B2 ALBERTO SORDI (1920–2003). The value of homemade spaghetti is not computed in GDP accounting, while the value of the same spaghetti consumed in a restaurant is: "official" GDP does not consider the value of household production. The scene above shows Alberto Sordi (1920–2003) in the 1954 film *Un americano a Roma* (An American in Rome) directed by Steno.

Household production not only brings benefits but also has its costs. In Italy's case, the main costs are the ones borne by women and by the "young elderly" (people aged sixty or so), who in the prime of their productive capacities devote themselves to household chores. In both cases, the people concerned are often involved in less productive tasks than the ones they could perform in the market: the forgone income is the cost of "homemade GDP."

attention because of the instrumental function it plays: an increasing trend in GDP shows that there is economic growth, which is (usually) a necessary condition for promoting the wellbeing of a population. Therefore, it is wrong to deny the importance of GDP in determining the wellbeing of a population, but it is also wrong to confuse the means with the ends and to equate GDP with wellbeing (Anand and Sen 1993). In the rest of this chapter, therefore, GDP will be interpreted for what it is—a market production index of the economic system—but also bearing in mind what it can make possible: an improvement in a population's standard of living.

3 The GDP Factory

Thanks to the reconstruction published in 1957 by the Italian National Institute of Statistics (Istat), Italy was one of the first countries in the world to create its own historical series for GDP.[1] This pioneering work did not really pay in terms of results: judging by what the experts say, the first reconstruction of national GDP had a great many discrepancies along with a relative opacity with regard to sources and methods.[2]

In the following decades, the reconstruction of the historical series of Italian GDP has become an increasingly more practiced activity: new estimates of the same variable have been published at an average rate of one every four years (Vecchi 2003)[3]. Despite the many activities, the "factory" occupied with producing the historical series of national accounting has not managed to assemble its own products to give shape to a system of consistent historical series for

[1] See Istat (1950; 1957; 1958). The system of national accounting was introduced in Italy in the aftermath of World War II, shortly after "the governments of Britain, Canada and the United States had started to use it, during the war, in order to assess compatibility between aims and resources" (Falco 2006, 377; Vanoli 2005).

[2] Nor were they made good by the revision carried out in the 1960s by a group of scholars coordinated by Giorgio Fuà (1919–2000). See Fuà (1968) and Fenoaltea (2003).

[3] Many contributions, however, are variations on the same theme, that is, the estimate published by Istat in 1957 (Cohen and Federico 2001).

the entire 150 years since Italy's unification. Seen from the outside, the "GDP factory" appears to be enlivened by active industrious craftsmen, often extraordinarily qualified and specialised, but with absolutely no desire for coordination: "Each to himself, God for all" (Fenoaltea 2010, 77). This attitude has given users of the historical series a general sense of disorientation: the various series produced soon began to coexist and to compete with one another (Which one to choose? How to reconcile inconsistent overlaps? How to bridge the gaps or discrepancies that have existed and persisted for decades?).

All this is visibly reflected in the current state of the specialized literature, not too different from the situation that one sees with a railroad network when there is no agreement on what standard track gauge to adopt. If railroad track manufacturers were to use different gauges, the final result would be that no train could circulate. In our case of the "GDP factory," this lack of coordination has concerned the scientific community as much as the institutions. Not by chance, until very recently, the only existing long-run reconstruction of Italian GDP had been created outside our factory, by a Briton, Angus Maddison (1926–2010).[4]

The last product of the factory was presented during celebrations marking the 150th anniversary of Italian unification. A study (hereafter referred to as BIT) coordinated by the Bank of Italy, in cooperation with Istat and the 2nd University of Rome "Tor Vergata", reconstructed the national accounts since Italy's unification (Baffigi 2013). On both method and contents, the break with the past was clear-cut: the study managed, for the first time, to coordinate most of the activities inside the GDP factory—it did not just connect all the existing series, but incorporated the results of new studies, thereby yielding historical series covering the whole 150-year history of united Italy.

The following section will present the results of a new estimation exercise performed by updating the BIT series in light of the latest publications on the subject. In keeping with tradition, the work of the GDP factory is never-ending.

4 The Long Leap in the Short Century

For those who have never had the chance to see the century-long trend of per-capita GDP before, Figure 7.1 will certainly be very interesting. It shows the trend of Italian GDP, both total and per head, for the whole postunification period. The series have been calculated "at constant prices", meaning that they allow for variations in the *quantity* of national production rather than variations in its *value*: when the GDP curve in the figure goes up or down, the effect is "real" in that it does not depend on price changes (inflation or deflation), but on

---

[4] See Maddison (1991; 2010) and Conference Board (2012).

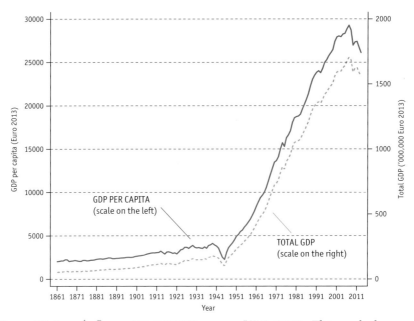

Figure 7.1 ITALY'S GROSS DOMESTIC PRODUCT, 1861–2013. The graph shows
the series for total GDP (broken line, right-hand vertical axis) expressed in
billions of 2013 Euros at today's boundaries and the series of per capita GDP
(unbroken line, left-hand vertical axis) in *thousands* of 2013 Euros.

a higher or lower volume of quantities of goods and services produced and marketed. In this sense, we can say that the GDP trend in Figure 7.1 encapsulates
the entire history of the average income of the Italians.

The estimates show that, on average, Italians today earn thirteen times more
than their ancestors did at the time of unification. Figure 7.1 also shows that
progress in GDP per head is a relatively recent phenomenon, largely coming
about in the latter half of the twentieth century. Since World War II, per-capita
GDP has increased over sevenfold, while in the previous hundred years or so
(1861–1951) it had little more than doubled. In a nutshell, the income of the
Italians made a long leap in a very short time (Toniolo and Vecchi 2010).

The nonlinear nature of the growth can best be grasped by looking at the
trend of per-capita GDP in some symbolic dates. At the time of unification, in
1861, the average income of the Italians has been estimated at around 2,000
Euros *a year* per head, at today's purchasing power, and about two-thirds of
this sum was taken up by food consumption. In 1911, at the peak of the so-
called first globalization, Italy celebrated the 50th anniversary of its unification
with an increased per-capita GDP of around 3,000 Euros per year, 46 percent
of which went to satisfy primary needs. At the third jubilee, in 1961, average
annual income was just over 8,000 Euros—a value almost three times the one

recorded fifty years earlier—and food consumption accounted for about 25 percent of this sum. Today, over a hundred and fifty years since unification, annual per-capita GDP is about 26,000 Euros—more than treble the 1961 figure, with less than 10 percent devoted to food consumption. By managing to triple personal income between the latter two jubilees, the average Italian has become affluent—if not actually "wealthy".

Having gone through the dynamics of per-capita GDP *levels*, we now need to look at the *rate* at which it increased (or decreased) in the various periods considered. The calculations required—concerning GDP growth rates—are reported in Table 7.1. The first growth rate given in the table (column 1) refers to the overall change in GDP in each subperiod. This is a useful figure in that it tells us the magnitude of the change observed between the initial year and the final one, but it is not very useful when we wish to compare periods of different lengths: clearly longer observation periods will tend to show greater total change rates. The problem is easily solved by calculating the *annual* percentage change (rather than the total one) during the period (column 2). The table also includes a third, alternative measure of the GDP growth rate: in column 3, instead of using the change rate, we calculated the number of years it would be necessary to wait before GDP doubled, assuming that it changes at a constant rate from one year to the next, that is, variations of the same percentage (the one given in column 2) every year.[5]

If we wish to schematically summarize the main "facts" emerging in Table 7.1, then we could draw up the following list.

- *1861–1901.* The first two generations of Italians in postunification Italy did not experience high growth rates in per-capita GDP. Indeed, the rate at which GDP increased over the first four decades of the new Kingdom of Italy (0.6–0.7 percent per year) would have required at least a century to double. The political unification of the country did not lead to any "take-off" with regard to the average income of its citizens, but to a slow and gradual increase.[6] However, something changed at the dawning of the twentieth century.

---

[5] The calculation is based on a rule known as the "rule of 70", according to which the number of years needed to double a certain magnitude can be calculated as the ratio between 70 and the annual growth rate of the economic magnitude concerned. For example, if GDP grows at 2 percent a year, the formula tells us that we need to wait 35 years (= 70/2) before it doubles.

[6] Toniolo (2013) identifies a number of reasons for the deadlock of this period. On the one hand, there was the sluggishness *(a)* of the process for creating a single national market (political, administrative, and economic unification did not come about overnight), *(b)* of the formation of an adequate human capital stock (schooling of the population was difficult), and *(c)* in the establishment of the new legal institutions (from the single currency to the approval of the commercial and administrative codes). On the other hand, there were external shocks (two wars of independence, the problem of banditry in the south of the country) and economic policy mistakes with regard to trade and monetary matters.

Table 7.1 **The changeable rate of per capita GDP, Italy 1861–2013**

	Total variation (%)	Average annual variation (%)	Years necessary for the p.c. GDP to double
	(1)	(2)	(3)
Liberal Italy (1861–1913)	59.8	0.91	77
1861–1881	12.9	0.61	115
1881–1901	15.2	0.71	99
1901–1913	22.9	1.73	40
Fascist Italy (1922–1938)	26.1	1.46	48
1922–1929	24.0	3.12	22
1929–1938	1.7	0.19	372
Republican Italy (1948–2011)	609.4	3.16	22
1948–1973	282.3	5.51	13
1973–1992	60.2	2.51	28
1992–2002	16.7	1.56	45
2002–2013	−6.8	−0.64	−109
Italy at 150th (1861–2013)	1187.1	1.70	41

- *1901–1913.* The years of the so-called Giolitti age saw an acceleration in GDP: compared to the previous two decades, the economic growth rate more than doubled (1.7 percent per year). World War I marked a sharp break in this favorable period, but growth would resume rapidly once again in the aftermath of the Treaty of Versailles (1919).
- *1922–1938.* The new estimates describe the interwar period as the combination of two decades that were very different from one another: the 1930s were as bleak (average per-capita GDP growth rate was + 0.2 percent) as the 1920s were rosy (+ 3.1 percent). Such a marked difference between the two decades constitutes a novelty not found in the previous literature.
- *1948–2013.* The republican period shows features that are largely well known: (*a*) in the years 1948–1973 Italy sped along at an unprecedented rate it has not experienced again since (+ 5.5 percent per year); (*b*) the slowdown in the years 1973–1992 is very conspicuous: much like a motorist shifting from a cruising speed on an open highway to a much slower pace on entering a town; (*c*) in the last decade (2002–2013), per-capita GDP actually *fell* by 0.64 percent per year.

Box 3 A Very Long-Term Look, Italy 1300–2011

The graph shows the trend in per-capita GDP (vertical axis) over time (horizontal axis). The stationariness observed from the fourteenth century to the nineteenth century corresponds to the preindustrial economy; modern economic development started in the latter half of the nineteenth century.

Our curiosity of knowing the average income of the Italians in the centuries preceding the country's unification may, at least in part, be fulfilled. Economic historians have actually estimated GDP even for unsuspectingly remote times. The most adventurous estimates refer to the ancient Roman period: according to Maddison (2007), at the time of the death of Emperor Augustus (14 D.C.), the Italic peninsula was (by far) the richest of all the Roman provinces of the Mediterranean basin. Instead, the following centuries were, on the whole, bleak and characterized by a long period of decline, with signs of recovery found only around the tenth century (Lo Cascio and Malanima 2005, 204–205).

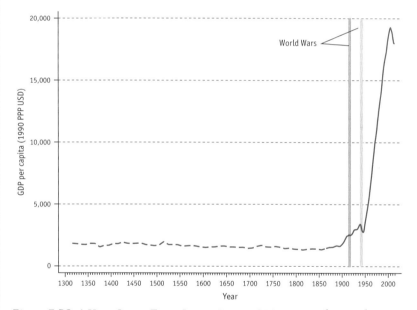

Figure 7.B3 A VERY LONG-TERM LOOK, ITALY 1300–2011. The graph shows the trend in per-capita GDP (vertical axis) over time (horizontal axis). The stationariness observed from the fourteenth century to the nineteenth century corresponds to the pre-industrial economy; modern economic development started in the latter half of the nineteenth century.

The earliest reliable estimates for per-capita GDP of the Italian Peninsula date back to 1300: by connecting the reconstruction made by Malanima

(2006) to the new estimates of the period 1861–2011, we obtain the curve shown in the figure above. This reveals the distinctive features of a preindustrial economy, that is, a centuries-old stagnation of per-capita GDP. The graph's scale hides as much the frequency as the intensity of the annual variations: although the Italian economy of the early Middle Ages had a mastery of the most advanced technology of the times (Cipolla 1952), there were recurring famines, even within the same generation (Livi Bacci 1991, xx; Malanima 2003), with disastrous consequences on the population's standard of living (Ò Grada 2009).

With the start of the Modern Age, say from 1500, the overall GDP of the Italian economy started to rise, but it was accompanied by an even greater increase in the population, with the result shown in the figure: a slow but inexorable decline in per-capita income (Malanima 2006, 21). Despite this downward trend, Italy is still considered to have been one of the most advanced countries until the mid-1700s. After this time, the gap with other western European countries started to increase: "Things changed after 1750. For more than a century, with very short interruptions, the Italian economy experienced a decline which was at once absolute and relative" (Malanima 2006, 111).

As we know, at the close of the 1700s Italy missed out on the first industrial revolution, not being able to adopt British technology based on steam and the railways (Allen 2009). This is reflected in the GDP trend in the figure, which shows a flat trend in continuation of the past. The curve starts to rise in the last decades of the nineteenth century, during the second industrial revolution, based on electricity, oil, and chemicals (Mokyr 1990). This marks an epochal moment in the history of the wellbeing of the Italians—a crossroads in history where Italy took the right road and embarked on the process of "modern economic development" described by Kuznets (1966): rural, backward Italy embarked on a deep transformation that would change its features, on both a qualitative and quantitative level, and turn it into an advanced economy within the space of a century or so.

5 Interpreting the Past

Following the end of World War II, economic historians have put forward various, often conflicting, hypotheses to explain the country's industrialization and modernization processes, summarized in the long-term trend of per-capita GDP (Figure 7.1). In this section, we shall segment Italy's per-capita GDP series into the three periods corresponding to the political periodization of the country over the 150 years since its unification: the Liberal period (1861–1913), the Fascist period (1922–1938), and Republican Italy (since 1946). We shall thus examine each phase in sequence, placing the GDP series within a broader context in which we introduce, albeit superficially, two key factors that explain a country's long-term economic performance—technological progress and the institutional framework.

Technology is behind increases in productivity and thus represents the main determinant in per-capita GDP (Jovanovic and Rosseau 2005; Giannetti 2001). Over the last 150 years, Italy has gone through as many as four technological regimes (Freeman and Perez 1988): *(a)* the first (1861–1875) is the one identified by the three main inventions of the times: the steam engine, the spinning machine, and the railways; *(b)* the second (1875–1908) coincides with the "second industrial revolution", characterized by heavy industry (steel, first and foremost, to which the mechanical industry is connected) and electricity; *(c)* the third (1908–1970s) is defined by the establishment of mass production, such as with Henry Ford, in which petroleum plays a key role and there is the takeoff and affirmation of durable consumer goods, starting with the automobile; *(d)* the fourth and last regime corresponds to the "third industrial revolution" (1970s–today), triggered by the advent of information technology and telecommunications: the industries showing the fastest growth in this phase are linked to electronics and particularly to computer technology (Gordon 2012). The dates marking the shift from one regime to another are obviously approximate and only serve to outline the timeline with which the main innovations have followed each other.

Technology represents a necessary but not sufficient condition for a country to feed its own course toward prosperity: the technological changes must be accompanied by changes in institutions, in the broadest sense, and in society's ideology.[7] Did the new technological paradigms—exogenous factors with regard to the Italian economy—find fertile terrain in the country owing to the fact that institutions and ideologies were favorable to their adoption?

5.1 THE INDUSTRIALIZATION OF THE PENINSULA (1861–1913)

Much has been written on the economic history of Liberal period Italy.[8] The question at the heart of the historiographic debate has often been the following:

---

[7] This is a fundamental point in the speech Simon Kuznets made in Stockholm when he received the Nobel Prize for economics (Kuznets 1971), taken up again in various forms by Abramowitz (1986), and more recently by Acemoglu and Robinson (2012). See also Felice and Vecchi (2015).

[8] Among the more important recent monographs, see Toniolo (1988; 2012), Zamagni (1993), Fenoaltea (2011), Ciocca (2007), and Felice (2015).

when and *why*—from being a rural country, "poor" and backward, as it had been for centuries—did Italy become an industrial country, "wealthy" and modern? The "giant who dominated the Italian debate" after World War II was Alexander Gerschenkron (1904–1979), a U.S.-naturalized Russian economist; it is worth starting from his thesis (Fenoaltea 2007, 352). Gerschenkron identified the "big industrial push" of the country around the mid-1890s and put it down to the creation of *mixed banks*—*Banca Commerciale Italiana* (*Comit*), founded in 1894 with German capital; *Credito Italiano* (*Credit*); *Banco di Roma*; and later on *Banca Italiana di Sconto*. Mixed banks, or universal banks, are so called because they collect capital (the prerogative of commercial banks) and channel it to favor industrial development (the prerogative of investment banks). Through their network of branches, mixed banks collect deposits in the short-term from ordinary citizens and then invest the capital in shares: that is, they turn the capital into long-term credit to industry, precisely what is needed, according to Gerschenkron, to favor the industrialization of a backward country.[9] For Gerschenkron, this was the institutional innovation that acted as the "engine of growth" in Italy and in Germany: it was the mixed banks that managed to compensate for the country's drawbacks (the scarcity of natural resources, the political instability and hesitations of governments during the first decades after unification, the inanity of economic policies) on the path toward Italy's industrialization (Gerschenkron 1955; 1959; and 1962).

The debate following Gerschenkron's work was intense and remained so over the following decades. The common denominator of all the interpretations put forward in successive years was the assumption that economic development followed a stage-by-stage model (Rostow 1960). According to this view, a country develops following an orderly sequence of stages (or phases). Initially, the *prerequisites* for growth must be created (for instance, infrastructure and human capital); the second stage envisages an economic *take-off*—economic growth starts up with a great boost and marks a break with the GDP series trend; the next stage marks a *rise to maturity* (technology opens up new investment opportunities and the economy becomes more complex); and, finally, there is the age of *mass wellbeing*.

It is difficult to establish whether the per-capita GDP series in Figure 7.2 shows a trend in line with the explanation offered by stage-based models. The first two decades of postunification Italy show an uncertain start, and it is only with the beginning of the "Historical Left" and the Depretis Government (1876) that GDP started to grow at an increased rate. The trend does not show any trace

---

[9] In return, the mixed banks typically entered the boards of the firms they financed and obtained access to strategic information. The advantages associated with the presence of a mixed bank must be weighed against the greater fragility of the economic system, due to the interweave that is created between credit capital (banking system) and industrial capital (the real economy).

of the crisis of the 1880s, while the slowdown in the 1890s is clearly visible. On the whole, the terms "take-off" or "big industrial push" are quite inappropriate to describe the trend with regard to the latter half of the 1890s.

An alternative interpretation to the one suggested by the stage-based model was proposed by Fenoaltea (1988; 2006). In this case, the story begins by observing that the new GDP series has an upward trend with no breaks or take-offs, but with fluctuations: these are "economic cycles", mainly caused by the construction industry and more generally by the infrastructure sector. According to Fenoaltea, what decided the various stages of Italian economic growth during the Liberal period was the foreign investment cycle. In this model, what matters is the "willingness of non-Italians to invest in Italy, [that] rose and fell with their willingness to invest in foreign assets in general, without significant peculiarities tied to developments in Italy itself" (Fenoaltea, 2011, p. xx). When foreign investors become inclined to invest their savings abroad, capital flows are set in motion, and facilitate the process that gets the international economy going; when capital flows slow down or cease—then the international economy contracts, and Italy's economy with it. The view of Italy as an "open economy", does not require any stage-based development process and does not envisage any take-off stage: the process is guided by the interweaving of the international economic cycle, investor expectations, and (even if only to a lesser extent) the domestic political cycle. Fenoaltea's interpretation appears largely consistent with cyclical development along an increasing trend (Figure 7.2).[10]

5.2 THE INTERWAR PERIOD (1919–1938)

Compared to the Liberal period, the interwar years have received a lot less attention.[11] This is a shame, because it was a decisive period in which Italy modernized and enhanced the sectors of the second Industrial Revolution (chemicals and heavy industry at the expense of textiles and foodstuffs), and also saw progress at the institutional level by creating the foundations that would accompany the subsequent economic miracle.

Even though it was a rather difficult time, to say the least, at a domestic level and even more so at the international one (two world wars, the Great Crisis of 1929, the Fascist dictatorship and its autarchic turn), in the period 1919–1938 the per-capita GDP growth rate (1.5 percent a year) was significantly higher than the one recorded during the Liberal period (0.9 percent).

---

[10] According to Toniolo (2007; 2012), less convincing is the fact that it overlooks the role played by the national institutional framework and internal political changes. See also A'Hearn (2012).

[11] Among the exceptions: Toniolo (1980), Gualerni (1995), Galimberti and Paolazzi (1998), Petri (2002), Feinstein, Temin, and Toniolo (2004; 2008), and Felice and Carreras (2012).

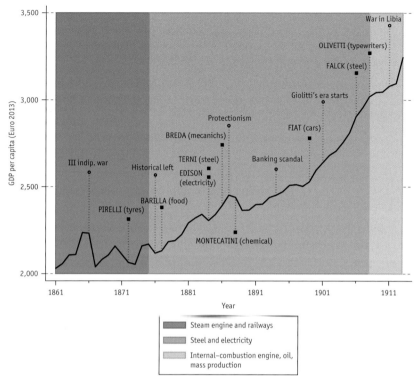

Figure 7.2 PER-CAPITA GDP BETWEEN 1861 AND 1913: NO LULL, NO TAKE-
OFF. The figure shows the per-capita GDP trend against the background of
technological changes (indicated with a different background color intensity),
and the main political and economic innovations.

Behind this overall figure lie very diverse trends that characterized the 1920s
and 1930s (Figure 7.3). The growth during the 1920s was rapid, the result of an
increase in productivity; if the war had any beneficial consequence, then it was
its positive effect on the technological backwardness accumulated during the
conflict—technological progress in the chemical industry, in motor vehicle production, and in aeronautics was greatly stimulated by the war effort (Feinstein,
Temin, and Toniolo 1998, 87). Between 1919 and 1929, Italy grew at a high
rate—over 3 percent a year, on average. The 1920s were really the "Roaring
Twenties" for the Italians, but these were then followed by very difficult years
economically, and even more so politically. The Great Depression of 1929
appears to have had a greater impact than previously thought: between 1929
and 1933 Italy suffered an 8 percent decrease in per-capita GDP compared to the
3.5 percent decrease previously estimated by the "old" series (Vitali 1969). This
is higher than the U.K. figure (–4 percent), and close to the French (–10 percent)
and German (–12 percent) ones, but a long way off from the catastrophic figure
recorded in the United States, where GDP decreased by 27 percent.

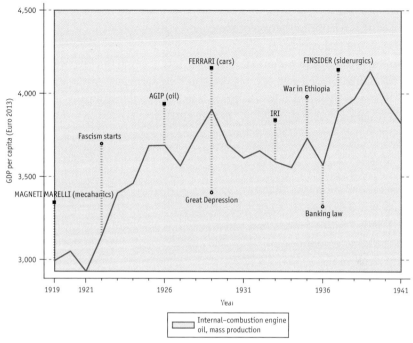

Figure 7.3 PER-CAPITA GDP IN THE INTERWAR YEARS: A CONFLICTING 20-YEAR
PERIOD. The interwar period was characterized by very marked economic
cycles: the graph shows a boom in the decade after the Treaty of Versailles
(1919–1929), the recession following the 1929 crisis and the lively recovery
starting in the latter half of the 1930s.

Paradoxically, but perhaps not so much, it was those very autarchic policies
that steered modernization and thus the expansion of the Italian productive
base: the deflationary turning point of 1926 (with the drastic revaluation of the
Italian lira) made the price of imported materials (e.g., cast iron) and of machinery drop, thereby benefiting industry, which could use inputs at lower prices.
At the same time, however, it made prices rise for traditional Italian exports in
light industries such as textiles, thereby damaging the less-advanced Italian production sectors. The 1929 crisis led to a broad reform of the Italian production
system. On the one hand, it forced the industrial sector to substitute labor (now
more expensive)[12] with capital, and this led to an increase in mechanization; on
the other, the calamitous effects of the crisis on the real economy and on finance
led to the institutional reorganization of the whole edifice of national capitalism. The Institute for Industrial Reconstruction (*Istituto per la Ricostruzione*

---

[12] Deflation, i.e., price decreases, led to a rise in real wages, or to an increase in the labor factor of
production, which became more expensive compared to other goods (Mattesini and Quintieri 1997).

Industriale, IRI) was created in 1933, and in 1936 the banking reform law achieved the separation between banks and industry, that is, between short-term and long-term credit.

On the whole, the prevalent view today in interpreting the interwar period is that the Fascist years were not a break in the long-term path of the Italian economy, but rather a premise for the great leap that would take place after World War II (Gualerni 1995; Petri 2002; De Cecco 2000).

5.3 FROM THE PERIPHERY TO THE CENTER (1946–2013)

The new GDP estimates (Figure 7.4) for the years following World War II do not add much to what we already knew. Once postwar reconstruction was completed, Italy "put on wings" and embarked on a period of growth that history would call the "economic miracle".[13] The new estimates confirm the exceptional performance of the 1950s and 1960s, which emphasize—as we saw in Box 3—an actual break in the centuries-old trend (Malanima 2003; 2006). It is these two decades that saw Italy complete its transition from the "periphery to the center", according to the fortunate definition put forward by Vera Zamagni (1993): the country became a modern industrial one, with a great shift in labor from rural areas to industry, even in Italy's *Mezzogiorno*.[14] There were many reasons for this achievement, starting from some decisions in the geopolitical and international arena: firstly, the Marshall Plan, whose funds were used better in Italy (to renovate the industrial apparatus) than in other countries (Zamagni 1997; Fauri 2010); secondly, the far-seeing anchorage to the European edifice (Fauri 2001; Ciocca 2007). Other factors also moved in the right direction. The fixed exchange-rate system based on the dollar, low prices for oil and other natural resources, and the gradual liberalization of international trade brought benefits to more or less all advanced countries, and particularly to Italy: for example, the decrease in raw material prices in the 1950s and 1960s was particularly advantageous for a country lacking in natural resources.

Among the important elements explaining the country's growth after World War II, there is also the continuity with the past, and particularly with regard to the interwar years. This is the case with the system of *partecipazioni statali* (that is, enterprises indirectly owned by the state through management entities), which was created in the 1930s and made an important contribution to growth in the 1950s and 1960s, becoming the driving force of industrial modernization. There is no counterevidence, obviously, but the idea that has been put forward is that these state-owned companies played a key role

---

[13] In actual fact, GDP showed a miraculous trend in most countries in western Europe: not surprisingly, the period 1950–1973 became known as "Europe's golden age" (Temin 2002).

[14] This is the expression used to define Italy's southern regions.

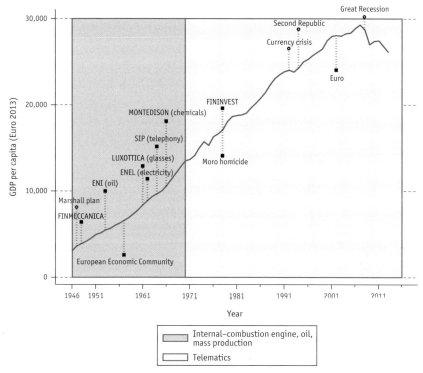

Figure 7.4 PER-CAPITA GDP AFTER WORLD WAR II. GDP in the decades after World War II is characterized by an upward trend—taking Italy from the "periphery to the center"—and by a conspicuous slowdown starting in the 1990s, leading to stagnation with the advent of the new millennium.

in making it possible to devise "far-seeing strategic plans which were instead absent—if we exclude FIAT of Valletta—in large scale private industry" (Barca and Trento 1997, 197).

By the end of the 1960s, Italian industry appeared broadly diversified, even impressive in some respects: the country excelled in the automobile and information technology sector, developed an important chemicals industry, and was at the forefront of the aerospace industry. At the same time, there were also the traditional sectors of products "made in Italy" (particularly textiles, footwear, food, and home furnishings), supported by a widespread network of small and medium-sized enterprises (Amatori 1980; 2011; Colli and Vasta; 2010).

Growth slowed down in the 1970s and 1980s, starting with the first energy crisis in 1973: the system of *partecipazioni statali* degenerated and ended up by obeying clientelistic political demands, which led to setting up manufacturing plants in locations that were far from convenient (Felice 2010). Large-scale enterprises lost ground, and a tertiarization of the economy—that is, a GDP shift from industry to services—took hold in Italy, too.

Box 4 **Words Are Important: Recession and Depression, Crisis and Decline**

Recession, crisis, depression, and economic decline. These are the words that begin to circulate as soon as GDP slows down. If the media do not always pay the necessary attention to them, there are important differences between their everyday meaning and their technical one. It is worth going into their meaning, not for the sake of semantics, but as a premise in order to more clearly deal with the theme of Italy's economic decline.

Recession. In everyday language, periods of positive growth in GDP are called "expansions" while periods of negative growth are called "recessions" (or "contractions"); alternating periods of expansion and contraction of GDP give rise to the so-called *economic cycle*. In economics, the word "recession" is only used when the period of negative growth lasts at least *two consecutive quarters* (Blanchard 1997, 25). There is an alternative definition, used by the U.S. National Bureau for Economic Research (NBER) that, unlike the previous definition, is also sensitive to the scale of the GDP decrease (the idea is that it is worth distinguishing between a 0.1 percent decrease and a 10 percent one) and depends not only on the GDP trend but also on that of other indicators (such as unemployment or sales volume). According to the NBER, "a recession is a significant decline in economic activity spread across the economy, lasting more than a few months, normally visible in real GDP, real income, employment, industrial production, and wholesale-retail sales" (NBER 2008). In practice, the two definitions often coincide, but not always and not necessarily so.

Crisis. There is no single technical or formal definition of the word "crisis". Ironically, the most prestigious Italian encyclopedia, published by the Istituto Treccani, discontinued the volume containing the entry "economic crises" in 1931, right at the height of the most serious crisis of the capitalist economy. The definition underlined the element of surprise and the speed associated with the phenomenon: "The crisis is a shift, often a *sudden* one, from a given equilibrium position to another very different one; the shift is usually a jolting one and *unexpected* by many of the agents, and brusquely leads to *serious* decreases of value and of production activity, a reduction or cessation of remuneration; it is often accompanied by bewilderment, by dramatic episodes" (913, our italics). Since then the international specialist literature has tended to replace the generic term "economic crisis" by distinguishing between a financial crisis (linked to monetary, banking, and exchange-rate matters or to the public debt) and a crisis concerning the real economy. Reinhart and Rogoff (2011) defined the various forms of crisis in quantitative terms: although it is still a little too early to consider the definitions proposed by the two authors as a "standard", they are, undoubtedly, the most authoritative we have available today.

Depression. Likewise for the word "depression", economists still do not have a univocal definition. The new edition of the Palgrave Dictionary of Economics has even removed this entry, while the previous editions attributed an international dimension to the term that is totally missing in the definition of recession: "That term (depression) is reserved for longer periods of more serious adversity on an international scale" (ed. 1987, 809). John Maynard Keynes provided an implicit definition of depression: "a chronic condition of subnormal activity for a considerable period without any marked tendency either towards recovery or towards complete collapse" (Keynes 1936, cap. 18). More recently, Paul Krugman (who won the 2008 Nobel Prize for economics) put forward an informal, but very practical, definition of the term: "depression" describes a situation where the normal medicines (the economic policy tools) administered to the system in order to boost economic activity do not work (Krugman 2012). In short, an economic system would be in a state of depression as soon as economists have repeatedly shown they do not know what to suggest to trigger a recovery.

Figure 7.B4 ITALY ON THE EDGE. Adapted from the front cover of *The Economist*, July 16, 2011.

Decline. Attempting to say what "economic decline" should be taken to mean in the space of a few lines is the hardest task. On the topic of decline, the most interesting reflections are undoubtedly the ones found in economic history. Toniolo (2004) wrote an essay full of reflections from which we can gather the features of an economic decline: *(1)* we must distinguish between an *absolute* decline (when a country cannot manage to maintain the level of wellbeing achieved in the past) and *relative* decline (when a country cannot keep up with the most dynamic economies and, although not experiencing any actual worsening of living conditions, goes down in the international ranking of prosperity); *(2)* a decline has many facets: it concerns the economy, but it is the symptom of a more general malaise involving the institutions, politics, society, and culture, that turns into sclerosis, into a loss of vitality, and into a recalling of past models (22); *(3)* a decline is slow and hardly perceptible: it becomes a political and social problem only when its effects are very widespread and the cost of ignoring them becomes unbearable for the governing elite, sometimes due to shocks such as wars, revolutions, and great financial crises (10); *(4)* about the causes, a decline stems from the inability to adapt an old production model to new circumstances, and this inability to adjust is greater the more successful the older model had been in the past (9).

In any case, the GDP increase in this period still appeared in line with that of the main European competitors, driven by exports and by the country's industrial districts.[15] The latter seem to reflect a new paradigm in the history of enterprise, but some critical observers (De Cecco 2000) noted how their rise owed more to the devaluation of the lira and to a lack of fiscal control, a view confirmed in light of their disappointing performance in recent years.

The years since 1992 have witnessed a decrease in growth, more than halved even with respect to the previous twenty-year period. As Salvatore Rossi (2010, 15) observed, "Adapting to the ICT revolution and globalization (. . .) was, and is, not an easy operation, above all with regard to the change in technological paradigm". What has characterized the last twenty years is, in sum, a hitherto unprecedented inability to adapt to the context—once again exogenously given—that Italy has to operate in (Paolazzi and Sylos Labini 2012). Italy has

---

[15] An industrial district is a system of highly specialized small and medium-sized enterprises geared to export and active in a specific geographical area providing them with the necessary social and economic infrastructure. In synergy with other local institutions, these firms manage to cut transaction costs without requiring a hierarchical structure that is typical of large enterprises (Becattini 1979).

fallen behind, and visibly so, compared to its main European partners, which in turn have lost ground to the United States and even more to emerging Asian countries (as we shall see in section 7). At the turn of the millennium, both the national press and public opinion spoke in terms of an economic decline (194).

6 At Last, the GDP of the Regions

Once Italy's national accounts had been reconstructed, some economic historians began to pursue the aim of replicating the task for each one of the Italian regions. The first attempt on this was made by Vera Zamagni in 1978 by drawing up an income estimation of the Italian regions for the year 1911. Although she was successful, hers was an isolated attempt: silence soon returned, and in the next two decades the measurement of regional differences in GDP remained a poorly researched field.[16] The new millennium heralded new studies enabling, at last, an outline of long-term per-capita GDP development for each of the country's regions. The summary picture we offer in this section is a useful, if not indeed essential, premise for understanding the origins of territorial imbalances today.The trend of regional differences in per-capita GDP for the five large macro-areas of the country is summarized in Figure 7.5.

There are three very interesting results, and they deserve a brief comment. The first concerns the so-called initial conditions. In our baseline year (1871), Italy showed non-negligible per-capita GDP differences: the richest area of the country, the north-west, had around a 25 percent advantage over the poorest area, the south (about 2,000 euros per person a year in the north-west versus 1,600 euros in the south). This is a significant difference, consistent with what emerges in other chapters of this book, considering other social indicators, and with what we know about the distribution of transport and credit infrastructure, which point to a clear advantage for the northern regions (Zamagni 1993, 42; Giuntini 1999b, 597). In order to interpret these differences properly, we must also not overlook the fact that, in 1871, Italy as a whole still had to face the great industrial transformation—the only change that could decisively raise income levels. The situation in other countries was rather similar: new data for Spain (Rosés, Martínez-Galarraga, and Tirado 2011) or for the Austro-Hungarian

---

[16] Official statistics on regional GDP only started to be published in 1970 (Svimez 1993). Esposto (1997) produced estimates for 1871 (macro-regions), 1891, and 1911; Svimez (1961) for 1938 and 1951; Daniele and Malanima (2007; 2011) produced annual estimates from 1861 to 1951, by bringing together estimates made by Federico (2003b), Fenoaltea (2003b), and Felice (2005a; 2005b), in the assumption that, for each sector of economic activity (agriculture, industry, or services), the regional cycles would be the same as the national cycle. This section is based on Felice (2011) and Felice and Vecchi (2015).

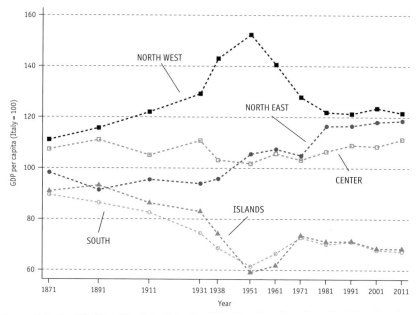

Figure 7.5 THE GREAT ITALIAN DIVIDE, 1871–DATE. The graph shows the per-capita GDP trend (measured along the vertical axis, with Italy = 100) for each macro-region of the country. The long-term trend shows a process of divergence which is interrupted only in the years 1951–1971.

empire (Schulze 2007) indicate a gap in favor of regions with an industrial or services base—Madrid and Catalonia, in the former case, and Vienna, in the latter—but, on the whole, also a relatively modest dispersion of average incomes compared to what would happen as industrialization progressed.

A second comment concerns the spectacular long-term *divergence* process: the north-west regions start from slightly more advantageous baseline conditions, but then proceed at such a pace that in the aftermath of World War II they are a "world apart": in 1951 the citizens of the north-western regions would enjoy a 50 percent higher GDP than the national average. The southern regions, instead, show a diametrically opposite trend, falling behind the rest of the country, such that in the aftermath of World War II they become a sort of second Italy: per-capita GDP in the south is less than half the one of the central-northern regions.

Once again, if Figure 7.5 would not surprise historians—the southern question has been on the scholars' table since the last century—what remains striking is the sheer *scale* of these differences. It is the actual *amounts* emerging in Figure 7.5 that are stunning: in 1951, after 90 years of postunification history, the southern regions had a per-capita GDP of 3,080 Euros a year at today's purchasing power parity (Table 7.A1), a value accounting for barely 40 percent of the north-western regions (where per-capita GDP was 7,335 Euros a year). The average income in Calabria was less than a third (29 percent) of the one in Liguria.

The third result deserving particular attention concerns what occurred in the interwar years: regional differences increased conspicuously. In this period the North-West progressed along the path of industrialization and modernization, while the *Mezzogiorno* remained dramatically still.[17] A factor favoring development in the north-west was the country's great effort in World War I (1915–1918), which steered public procurement toward enterprises of the industrial triangle (Lombardy, Piedmont, and Liguria), the only ones that could deal with the production demands of the war. The north also benefited from deflationary measures and an autarchic policy (section 5.2), which meant an intensification of industrial production toward advanced sectors, mostly located in the north. Instead, the Mezzogiorno suffered from the demographic policies of the Fascist regime, with restrictions to emigration (chapter 6 "Migration"), and this increased demographic pressure on the poorest regions. To this must be added the effect of the "battle of wheat" (in 1925 Mussolini proclaimed the need for Italy to achieve self-sufficiency in food, starting with wheat), which favored cereal growing at the expense of the more profitable crops of Puglia and Sicily (wine, grapes, and citrus fruits), and the immobilism of the social order that guaranteed the rents of great landowners even when the land itself was not productive, thereby hindering modernization in southern agriculture (Bevilacqua 1980; Felice 2007a).

Regional differences greatly decreased from 1951 to 1971. Convergence of the south during the 1950s and 1960s was exceptional and made possible both by the start-up of considerable interregional migration from south to north of the country as well as by a *deus ex machina*—the great public-sector intervention. The *Cassa per il Mezzogiorno* (the Southern Italy Development Fund), set up in 1950, was the instrument through which the state promoted the creation of great infrastructural works in the southern regions—from aqueducts to roads and industrial plants. As well as direct intervention for creating the necessary infrastructure, the *Cassa* also provided for indirect funding of production activities. The initiatives involved public enterprises, which were obliged by law to devote a considerable amount of their investment to the *Mezzogiorno*, but also private ones: both kinds of enterprises received lower interest rate loans and free contributions. It was a top-down action focusing on "heavy", higher added-value sectors such as the chemical, steel, and advanced mechanical industries.[18] In terms of resources allocated in relation to GDP, the investment was on a scale unparalleled in any other western European country (Felice and Lepore 2016).

---

[17] Between 1911 and 1951, the percentage of agricultural labor in southern Italy did not decrease (remaining at around 60 percent), while in the north-west of the country, in the same period, it fell by almost 20 points from 47 percent to 28 percent (Felice 2011).

[18] See Felice (2007a), La Spina (2003), and Lepore (2011).

This convergence of the *Mezzogiorno* turned out to be short-lived, however: the economic policy was not enough to trigger a continuous self-generating process in the south. With the oil crisis of the 1970s, the Ford model based on large energy-intensive factories suffered a setback, and in Italy this was particularly felt by the weaker links of the chain, that is, the plants in southern Italy that had been located there not for market convenience, but because of state incentives or dispositions. At this point, public intervention showed itself to be incapable of reinventing itself and indeed became entangled in a great many welfare or income support trickles, bloating the staff of public administrations and even benefiting organized crime.[19]

Figure 7.5 clearly shows that from the 1970s onward, albeit slowly, the southern regions started to fall behind again. The north-eastern regions instead started to pick up pace in their convergence with the north-western ones, followed by the central regions of the country. The driving force of the north-east was a growing capillary network of export-geared manufacturing firms (Bagnasco 1977; Becattini 1979). The most recent data, of 2009, confirm broad gaps—broader than the ones estimated for the time of Italy's unification. As we shall see better in the next section, economic integration made no real progress.[20]

7 Divided at the Middle

Exactly ten years after Simon Kuznets hypothesized an upside-down U-shaped curve for the relation between income inequality and economic growth (chapter 8, "Inequality"), the economic historian Jeffrey Williamson proposed another upside-down U-shaped curve, this time to describe the trend in the regional income inequalities within the same country (Kuznets 1955; Williamson 1965). Kuznets had concerned himself with the distribution of benefits of economic growth in the population, while Williamson was interested in the sequence with which the various areas of the country managed to bridge the gap with the most successful regions. "Economists have long recognized the existence and stubborn persistence of regional dualism at all levels of national development and throughout the historical experience of almost all presently developed countries", observed Williamson (1965, 3). Despite this awareness,

---

[19] See Bevilacqua (1993, 126–127, 132) and Trigilia (1992). The *Cassa per il Mezzogiorno* was dissolved in 1984.

[20] Per-capita GDP differences between the various geographical macro-regions concerned could be explained by the price differences found in these areas (chapter 14, "The Cost of Living"). This is not the case here. Brunetti, Felice, and Vecchi (2011) showed that by correcting GDP to allow for differences in purchasing power does not change the key features of the historical picture described in Figure 7.5.

however, a convincing explanation for this empirical regularity had still not been found; on the contrary, "one only needs to observe that Frenchmen, Italians, Brazilians, and Americans still tend to treat their North-South problems as unique to their own national experience with economic growth" (Williamson 1965, 3). What must we expect, then, in the course of economic development? The income convergence of regions? If so, in what way and at what pace? If not, why not? Williamson answered by hypothesizing an upside-down U-shaped curve: *(a)* regional inequalities increase in the first stages of industrialization, when the nascent industries tend to concentrate in certain regions rather than in others; and *(b)* they decrease over the following decades owing to a series of mechanisms (labor and capital flows as well as the national government's economic policy actions), which favor the spreading of industrialization in the country, thereby redressing income disparities between regions. The analysis made in this section shows that, in the Italian case, Williamson was right—at least up to a point.

The empirical exercise we shall now illustrate consists of dividing the country into two parts: the center-north and the *Mezzogiorno* (which we shall refer to as "north" and "south" for the sake of brevity). The territorial inequality observed at the national level in a given year may be considered as the result of two very different phenomena: (1) on the one hand, there may be great inequality in per-capita GDP *within* each area (for example, the southern regions could be very different from one another); (2) on the other, it may be that there is a good degree of homogeneity of regional GDPs within the areas concerned, but with a great imbalance *between* the average GDP of the two macro-areas (north and south are homogeneous within themselves, but the north is richer than the south, on average). Both kinds of inequality go to determine total, national inequality, but typically to varying degrees over time. By basing our calculations on the new estimates of regional GDP (section 6), we get the results reported in Figure 7.6, in which we reconstruct how the relative importance of the two components varies over time.

The results emerging in Figure 7.6 are crystal-clear. In the period going from the country's unification to World War II, total inequality (measured by the height of the bars) increases, in full agreement with Williamson's position. In this phase, the effect of the component within the two macro-areas is dominant (the green portion of the bar): in the latter decades of the nineteenth century, over 80 percent of total inequality is explained by the inequality *inside* the north and the south. However, over time, total inequality increases, above all, because it is nurtured by the inequality found between the two macro-areas (the gray portion of the bar). Inequality between north and south proceeds at a fast pace and takes on greater weight from one decade to the next: on the eve of World War I, this component explains about 30 percent of total inequality, while on the eve of World War II, almost 50 percent. Between 1931 and 1951 there is a

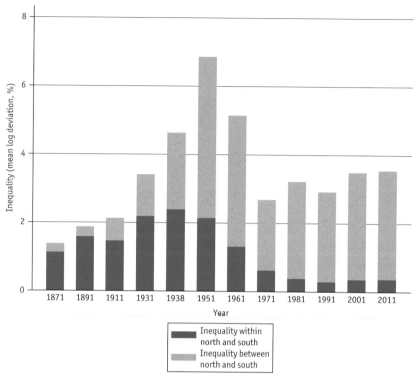

Figure 7.6 THE GREAT POLARIZATION. The graph shows the trend in per-capita GDP inequality of the regions (measured by the height of each bar) over time (horizontal axis). The higher values of the index (the mean log deviation) correspond to greater inequality. The two colors in each bar stand for the two components of total inequality: the light blue portion measures inequality resulting from the average difference in per-capita GDP *between* center-north and south of the country, while the dark blue portion measures the inequality found *inside* each macro-area.

huge break: the north–south divide in terms of per-capita GDP increases and becomes responsible for almost three-quarters of total regional inequality. It is this result that depicts a country which is literally divided at the middle, in terms of per-capita GDP. On the basis of the calculations shown in the figure, this break would never be made good again.

As of 1951, inequality *between* the two macro-areas becomes the key factor—the one explaining the trend in total territorial inequality. Figure 7.6 shows that north and south become relatively homogeneous areas within themselves (the green portion of the bar decreases in absolute terms) and what counts in the dynamics of the north–south divide is the *average* gap that there is between the two macro-areas (the gray portion of the bar increases). The years between 1951 and 1971 are the only ones in which the two extremes of the country come closer, also thanks to the regional development policies we recalled in section 5.

Since 1971 the word that sums up the whole story of regional GDP is *polariza-tion*: as of 1971, the territorial inequality *between* north and south shows high levels and growth over time (which also indicates the simultaneous distancing of the two macro-areas, increasingly more cohesive within themselves, but ever more distant from one another), while inequality inside the two macro-areas shows low levels and a decreasing trend (indicating a great and growing homo-geneity of the regions belonging to each macro-area).

To answer the question posed at the start of this section, we can say that Williamson was right, but only up to a point. In Italy's case, during the ini-tial stages of industrialization we note a growing disparity in average regional incomes. Once industrialization begins to spread, we do indeed find the conver-gence predicted by the model, but this is a singular episode found only in the twenty-year period 1951–1971.[21] This convergence soon disappears, never to return, and it does not even appear on the horizon, judging by the trend over the last forty years: since 1971, regional disparities have increased, albeit in a fluctuating manner.

8 The GDP of the Italians Compared to the Rest of the World

According to the estimates found in the Total Economy Database (TED), between 1870 and 2013 Italy's GDP per head increased twelvefold—a result that is better than the average figure for the twelve countries making up west-ern Europe (whose per-capita GDP increased elevenfold over the same period). Italy managed to do better than the United Kingdom (sevenfold), kept up with France and Germany (twelvefold), but increased its gap with the United States (thirteenfold). It fared worse than Spain and Greece (fourteen- and sixteen-fold, respectively), and with regard to some Scandinavian countries (Norway and Finland increased their incomes twenty-one-fold in the same period, while Sweden increased nineteenfold), not to mention Japan and South Korea (whose per-capita GDP rose thirty- and thirty-seven-fold, respectively). If we look at the long-term picture, Italy has good reason to feel satisfied with its own performance. Rossi, Toniolo, and Vecchi (2011) wondered whether pos-tunification Italy could have done better, but concluded that, at least with regard to GDP, Italy positively surprised many observers, of those times and of today, both Italian and foreign.

---

[21] We must not forget that our analysis here refers to the north–south divide. As we saw in section 6, convergence, instead, continued within the center-north macro-area with regard to the north-eastern and central regions.

Figure 7.7 focuses on the post–World War II years, the years in which Italians, in the space of two generations, completed the country's reconstruction and their road to wellbeing. The question we now ask ourselves is the following: How does Italy's postwar economic growth compare with that of other countries? For example, if we compare Italy's performance with that of the United States, how does our view of the Italian GDP trend change? We can ask the same question if, instead of a single country, we refer to the European Union of 15 countries

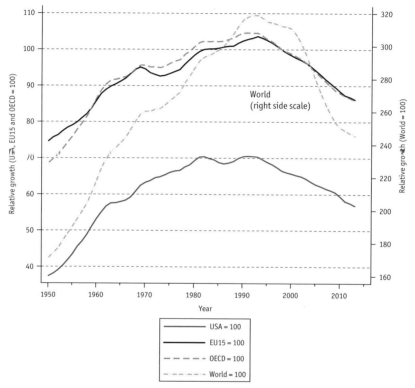

Figure 7.7 THE RISE AND FALL OF PER-CAPITA GDP, 1950–2013. The graph compares Italian per-capita GDP growth with that of the United States (blue unbroken line), with the average figure for the European Union of 15 countries (EU, black line), with the OECD average (blue line) and with the world average (purple line). The curves are interpreted as follows: a value of 100 means that the Italian per-capita GDP is the same as the one of the country or group of countries of reference (for example, this is the case with the EU15 and OECD countries around 1980); values below 100 mean that Italian per-capita GDP is lower than the country or group of countries of reference (this is the case with the United States throughout the period concerned); similarly, values above 100 mean that Italian per-capita GDP is higher than the one of the other country or group of countries considered (this is the case when compared to the world average per-capita GDP).

(EU15), or the 34 countries belonging to the OECD, or even the whole world economy.

The features of Italy's "relative growth" are given in Figure 7.7. Let's start by examining the starting conditions. In 1950 the gap between the average income of the Italians and that of the Americans was huge: per-capita GDP in Italy was a little over a third of the U.S. figure, more or less the same gap separating Italy's current figure with that of, say, Peru or Tunisia. Italy was also significantly poorer than the average of the European countries making up the EU15: by equating the latter's per-capita GDP to 100, Italy's GDP per head did not go beyond 75. Compared to the world average, the Italians instead had a considerable income advantage estimated at 67 percent (in this case, we need to look at the right-hand vertical axis of the figure). The years going from 1950 to 1973 are the "golden years" of western Europe since a general stability of macro-economic indicators (acceptable inflation and limited cyclical fluctuations) went hand in hand with extraordinarily high growth rates (Toniolo 1998, 252). The reconstruction in Figure 7.7 shows that while Europe grew rapidly on the whole, in the same years Italy managed to grow at an even faster rate (this is how to interpret the upward section of the black curve in Figure 7.7). The twenty years concerned, not surprisingly, have gone down in history as the miracle years.[22]

The capacity to catch up with the EU15 (and even more so with the United States) slackened in the latter half of the 1970s, but did not halt: with the start of the 1980s, Italy finally caught up with the EU15 average (the average income of the Italians equaled the EU15 average in 1980). Throughout the 1980s, Italy proceeded at a pace only slightly above that of other countries (European ones and the United States), but starting in 1992 it began to fall behind, firstly imperceptibly so but then at an increasing rate. If we equate the average income of the EU15 countries to 100 in 2011, then the income of the Italians in the same year stood at 87: the Italy-EU15 gap in 2011 was the same as the one recorded in 1961. In just a couple of decades (1992–2013), Italy jumped back fifty years compared to the rest of Europe.

A final remark concerns the growth of the countries making up the "world" group (purple curve, measured along the right-hand axis in Figure 7.7). Figure 7.7 shows an upward trend with a turning point around the years 1991–1992: this means that during the first 40 years (1950–1992), Italian growth was systematically faster than that of the whole world (Italy grew at an average annual rate 3.5 percent faster than the average of the other countries). In the following two decades (1992–2013), not only was there an inverse trend,

[22] According to the calculations made by Crafts and Toniolo (2010, 301), Italy's growth rate in 1950–1973 was significantly higher than that of any other European country except Portugal, Greece and Spain. For an economic history of the "Italian miracle", see Crainz (2005) and Crafts and Magnani (2013).

with Italy growing less rapidly than the rest of the world, but this happened at an increasing rate (every year, on average, Italy grew at a 4.4 percent lower rate than the other countries).[23] Technically, the diagnosis seems to be that of a country in decline.

9 From the Center to the Periphery

Over the one hundred and fifty years or so since the country's unification, Italy managed to bridge the gap—in terms of average national income—with the most advanced European countries of the time of unification (1861)—Britain, France, and Germany. From the periphery, the Italians reached the center, accomplishing a feat that few would have betted on, and on which nobody had ever harbored any expectations. In 1916 Louis Bonnefon Craponne, a brilliant French industrialist and first president of *Confindustria*, published *L'Italie au travail,* a wonderful little book whose very existence was called to our attention by Marcello De Cecco (2013). Craponne tells of French incredulity in learning that the Italians had not only started to produce automobiles, but had even begun taking part in the first car races of the times: "La première apparition de ces machines inconnues avait été accueillie par des sourires passablement ironiques. Quoi? on construisait des autos en Italie? Et ces fabriques—sans importance certainement osaient se mesurer avec nos Renault, nos Panhard nos de Dion? Passe encore l'Allemagne et ses Mercedes, mais l'Italie!" (Craponne 1916, 114).[24] Over fifty years had gone by since the birth of the new Kingdom of Italy, and observers of the day were still unable to update the country's image from the European champion of backwardness to one of a country well on its way to modern economic development.

The GDP estimates presented in this chapter have reconstructed the process with which the country accomplished its transition from a preindustrial rural economy to an advanced economy belonging to the G8, the organization of the eight major industrial powers of the world. Stagnation gradually gave way to growth. The population increased from about 26 million in 1861 to 60 million in 2011; the country's total GDP increased almost thirtyfold. Generation after generation, the children have managed to enjoy better living conditions than

---

[23] This pattern is *not* the consequence of the "China effect". If we compare Italy's relative growth with the rest of the world, after excluding the most dynamic and demographically important countries from the latter (Brazil, India, and China), the conclusions reported in the text do not change: between 1950 and 1992 Italy grew faster than the rest of the world (+ 2.4 percent a year, on average), while between 1992 and 2011 it grew less rapidly (-0.9 percent a year).

[24] "The first appearance of these unknown machines was met with some pretty ironic smiles. What? They produce cars, in Italy? And these insignificant factories dare to compete with our Renault, our Panhard and our de Dion? We can excuse Germany and its Mercedes, but Italy…!" (authors' translation).

those of their parents: today, average per-capita income is almost thirteen times what it was at the time of Italian unification.

The process has been a discontinuous one, however, and the country has remained deeply unequal inside its borders. During the first century of its existence, the economic system grew slowly, to then accelerate after World War II, when it literally leaped ahead. Not surprisingly, there was talk of an "economic miracle". The miracle did not, however, cancel the line dividing the north and south of the country, an original feature of the Kingdom of Italy. The empirical evidence presented in this chapter shows that integration (or convergence, if preferred) has been the exception rather than the rule, and was only seen in the space of two decades (1951–1971); the remaining 170 years were marked by divergence or immobility. The last twenty years have seen Italy's per-capita GDP stop growing, while economic inequalities and the poverty indicators have started to rise. This has naturally nurtured fears of failure and decline (Toniolo and Visco 2004; Tremonti 2008).

Not all analysts share these apprehensions. Some defend irreducibly optimistic theses: "On what principle is it that, when we see nothing but improvement behind us, we are to expect nothing but deterioration before us?" (cited in Supple 1994, 442). The point was made in another context (the British one) and in another time (early nineteenth century), but it expresses a very topical view: is it not, perhaps, the habit of generations of every epoch to look back on the past with nostalgia, to complain about how things are going in their own times, and to paint a black picture of the future? If contemplating the past in order to find comfort with regard to the future is an old and licit activity, it is also an exercise that is quite groundless, scientifically speaking. History does not lend itself to mere extrapolation. The question we thus ask ourselves, as a sort of conclusion, is whether, by analyzing the ultracentennial historical series of Italian GDP, Italy can be considered a country in (relative) decline. The answer that emerges from Figure 7.8 is—without any reasonable doubt—a yes.

Figure 7.8 has the ambitious task of comparing Italy's economic performance with that of *all* the other countries of the world (or, rather, all those countries for which we have reliable per-capita GDP figures) over the 150 years since the country's unification. The figure is rather complex and needs some explanation. Let's start with the first decade considered on the horizontal axis of the graph (1861–1870): after working out the (average annual) growth rate of per-capita GDP for all the countries in the decade concerned, we have indicated (*a*) the growth rate of the country that grew *most* quickly (on average, over the decade); and (*b*) the growth rate of the country that instead wins the wooden spoon for the slowest growth in the same decade. Specifically, the two countries concerned are New Zealand (the best) and China (the worst). Between these two extremes we have shown Italy's position (the small blue circle). By repeating this procedure for all the decades, from first (1861–1870) to last (2010–2013), we get a

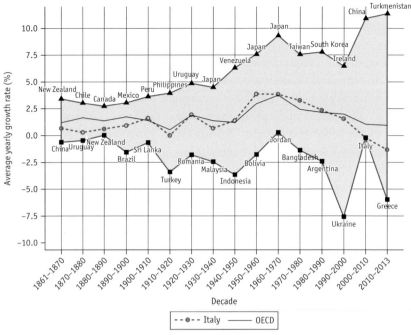

Figure 7.8 FROM THE PERIPHERY TO THE CENTER AND BACK AGAIN. The graph compares per-capita GDP growth rates (average rates in the decades shown on the horizontal axis) for the countries of the whole world (excluding countries of sub-Saharan Africa and the oil-based Middle-Eastern economies). Italy's relative economic decline started in the 1990s, but came out with all its drama in the following decade.

corridor (the gray band) with a floor that represents the frontier of those countries that grew more slowly in each decade (the "laggards' frontier") and a ceiling representing the frontier of those countries that grew the fastest (the "frontrunners' frontier"). The dashed line shows the trend for Italy over the period concerned, which can be compared with the OECD average (black, solid line).

Analyzing Italy through the lens of growth rates gives us all the information we need in order to take a perspective in the debate on the country's relative decline. The main "facts" can be quickly summarized. Firstly, the new Kingdom of Italy, which was born poor in 1861, grew below the OECD average over the following forty years since it was unable to fully exploit the advantages of its own backwardness (Abramovitz and David 1996; Toniolo 2013). Secondly, during the first decade of the 1900s, Italy managed to align its own growth rate with the OECD *average*: growth in the Giolitti years (1900–1910), which was considered exceptional according to domestic standards, was nothing of the kind once we compare the country at an international level. Thirdly, once having reached the growth rate of the OECD countries, for many decades Italy managed to do little more than "grow with the average". This was the case for the whole first half of the twentieth century. Fourthly, we find a real leap in the years 1950–1970: this marks an extraordinary phase in which the country comes closer, albeit not too much, to the front-runners' frontier. For as many as two decades, the country would keep up an annual average growth rate of 5 percent, but would then have to slow down its pace and fall behind. Part of this slowdown is quite normal: it is not easy to "stay at the forefront", while it is easier to grow by starting from a position behind the frontline, having the advantage of being able to emulate the front runners. However, Figure 7.8 does not seem to convey Italy's difficulty in staying close to the frontier of the virtuous countries, but rather its inability to avoid slipping behind toward the frontier of those countries incapable of growing. Since the 1980s the country has embarked on a phase of relative decline: the red line cuts the black line "from above" and enters negative territory: this means that Italy has not only slowed down its GDP pace more markedly than that of the OECD country average, but has actually embarked on a regression process (the per-capita GDP growth rates become negative)—something not found at all with the OECD countries. The decline consolidated in the following decades (in the 1990s the blue line continued to diverge from the black one and headed toward the laggards' frontier) until it shamed the country by coming last in the world ranking: it is Italy that has the worst average growth rate *in the world* for the years 2001–2010.

Although a relative decline is a necessary, but not sufficient, condition for achieving an absolute decline, an analysis of the trend in the per-capita GDP series makes us feel that Italy has embarked on its return journey toward the periphery. Caution is the watchword, here, since we lack a suitable temporal perspective in order to judge whether the malaise is temporary (albeit prolonged), reversible, or irreparable. There is also the hope that the Italians can be capable of an admirable "burst of pride": it has happened before and we cannot exclude it happening again (Toniolo 2013). If, however, the evidence concerning GDP that we have discussed in this chapter is interpreted along with the trend seen in other socioeconomic indicators, and with the whole political system and civil freedoms, then what comes to light is the country's structural weakness, which does away with our many hesitations. It does not take much more to conclude that Italians, by not adjusting to the changing reality, have been in economic decline since the early 1990s—a decline that is only a relative one, for now.

Appendix—Sources and Methods

Figure 7.1 Italy's Gross Domestic Product, 1861–2013 These are the sources: *Industry*: Fenoaltea (2005) for the years 1861–1913, along with estimates by Fenoaltea (1992) for 1911, by Fenoaltea and Bardini (2000) for

1891, 1938, and 1951, by Felice and Carreras (2012) for the years 1911–1951. *Agriculture*: Federico (1992) for 1911, (2000) for 1891, 1938, and 1951, (2003b) 1861–1911. *Services*: Zamagni (1992) for 1911, Zamagni and Battilani (2000) for 1891, 1938, and 1951, Battilani, Felice, and Zamagni (2011) for 1861–1951. *Credit*: De Bonis et al. (2011). For 1970 we used estimates by Picozzi (2012) concerning resource accounting and allocation.

With regard to method, reconstruction of the GDP series was carried out by means of two consecutive steps. Firstly, we calculated the series of the value added of the various economic sectors for the years 1861–1970, on the basis of estimates already available for the benchmark years 1891, 1911, 1938, and 1951, to which we added the new estimates for 1970 produced by Picozzi and those for 1871 worked out by the joint Bank of Italy, Istat, and Tor Vergata research group (BIT, see section 4). The years between the various benchmarks were obtained via interpolation by means of several Istat-Fuà series contained in Vitali (1969) and Istat (1973). The interpolation method is based on correcting the growth factor of existing series in order to guarantee satisfaction of the initial and final condition on the levels of the variables considered: the interpolated series must thus be manipulated so that it can pass through the benchmark years. In more rigorous terms, let $X_0, ..., X_T$ be the series relating to the variable concerned X in the interval $(0, T)$. If $\hat{X}_0$ $\hat{X}_T$ stand for more updated estimates for years 0 and T, the problem is one of reconstructing the trend of X along the entire interval considered, in order for it to be consistent with the new information available. This reconstruction, however it is carried out, involves changing the growth profile of the variable concerned compared to the implicit one of the series $X_0, ..., X_T$. A possible solution consists of applying a time invariant correction coefficient to the growth factor $f_t = X_t/X_{t-1}$ (with $t = 1, ..., T$) of the original series X. In this case, the new series is given by the expression $\hat{X}_t = \hat{X}_{t-1} \cdot f_t \cdot \alpha$, with $\alpha = (\hat{X}_T / \hat{X}_0 \cdot X_0 / X_T)^{1/T}$, and keeps the cyclical trend of the variables used for the interpolation. The method described is applied each time to the reconstruction of the series at current prices, constants, and/or of the implicit deflators, according to the needs posed by the availability and reliability of existing series in the various time intervals lying between the benchmark years. Once the various series of the added value of agriculture, industry, and services are obtained, these will then constitute the basis for calculating GDP for the period 1861–1970. However, since this calculation is based on statistics constructed according to previous accounting rules and conventions to the ones in use since 1974, with the introduction of the European System of Accounts (ESA, the European version of the System of National Accounts), it requires a further step in order to be compatible with the GDP series calculated by Istat for the years 1970–2011. This second step is carried out by interpolation of the benchmark relative to 1951 with official data of 1970 (ESA), by using the cycle of the pre-ESA series from 1951 to 1970. Baffigi (2011) provides greater details on the whole procedure.

Box 3 A Very Long-Term Look, Italy 1300–2013 The series is obtained by bringing together estimates by Malanima (2006) with data from the Conference Board Total Economy Database (2014).

Figure 7.2 Per-capita GDP between 1861 and 1913: no lull, no take-off Our calculations based on the series of Italian GDP 1861–2013, according to the sources and methods described for Figure 7.1.

Figure 7.3 Per-capita GDP in the interwar years: a conflicting 20-year period Our calculations based on the series of Italian GDP 1861–2013, according to the sources and methods described for Figure 7.1.

Figure 7.4 Per-capita GDP after World War II Our calculations based on the series of Italian GDP 1861–2011, according to the sources and methods described for Figure 7.1.

Figure 7.5 The great Italian divide, 1871–date For the years 1871–1951, the regional estimates are obtained by dividing the new estimates of national GDP by regional employment and then correcting the results with the nominal wages per region that approximate the differences in productivity per worker. This procedure, formalized by Geary and Stark (2002), is widely used also internationally and is based on the assumption that capital gains are distributed along the lines of incomes from labor, that is to say, that the elasticity of substitution between capital and labor is equal to one. The method is all the more effective the higher the degree of sector decomposition. In our case, for the four original benchmark years of 1891, 1911, 1938, and 1951, we can refer to an exceptionally high level of detail unparalleled in other countries: the workforce separately considers also data on women and child labor, and is divided by quite a broad number of sectors (for industry and the services, about 130 sectors in 1891, 160 in 1911, 400 in 1938, and 100 in 1951); the wage data have an identical sector decomposition in 1938 and 1951, less detailed but still high in 1891 (30 sectors) and 1911 (34)—Felice (2005a, 2005b).

The estimates for 1871 and 1931 are less detailed, a little over twenty sectors in both cases (Felice 2009a). For 1871, given the lack of data on wages for the tertiary sector, the productivity of services is estimated by assuming that in every region the ratio between the productivity of individual branches of the services and industry as a whole was similar to that of 1891. In all the benchmarks, a different procedure was used with regard to agriculture. This was based on the direct reconstruction of saleable gross production: worked out by Federico (2003) for the years 1891, 1911, 1938, and 1951, or reconstructed from scratch by means of official sources for 1871 (Felice 2009a) and 1931. With regard to a part of the industrial sectors from 1871 to 1911, we used the new estimates produced by Ciccarelli and Fenoaltea (2009), based on employment and wages, but in some cases also on industrial plants and direct production data (for the results of the revision of the estimates of 1891 and 1911, and a comparison of the various hypotheses, see Felice (2009b; 2011)): the latter estimates were also used for revising regional production by sector in 1891, necessary for the 1871 estimate.

Figure 7.6 The great polarization The decomposition of regional income inequality follows the method described in Shorrocks (1980).

Figure 7.8 From the periphery to the center and back again The countries considered are the ones found in the Conference Board Total Economy Database (consulted in February 2015), except for sub-Saharan African countries, the oil-based economies (mostly in the Middle East), and countries with a population below one million people. For certain countries and certain years it became necessary to reconstruct the GDP trend by log-linear interpolation. The title of the graph is an expression taken from De Cecco (2000, 119).

8

Inequality

WITH NICOLA AMENDOLA

1 The Importance of Being Equal

In the collective imagination, economic inequalities are a distinct feature of market economies. There is a great deal of data, no matter how raw, on income and wealth to support this view, and they provide an immediate measure of the economic disparities characterizing today's societies. According to the annual rankings of the American magazine *Forbes,* the richest person on the planet today is the co-founder of Microsoft Bill Gates (b. 1955), whose assets are worth 76.5 billion dollars. This is an astronomical sum, but still lower than the 200 billion dollars amassed by John D. Rockefeller (1839–1937) by the end of the 1930s (Klepper and Gunther 1996). In Italy, first place goes to the Ferrero family, which works in the confectionary industry and whose wealth is estimated at 20 billion dollars—a figure that comes close to the total income produced in one year by the over two million inhabitants of Calabria, a poor region in Southern Italy.

Inequalities are not less glaring if we consider income rather than wealth, and particularly the remunerations of certain categories of professionals. An Italian top manager can earn in one day what a steelworker can earn in a whole year. If the manager is the head of a financial multinational, then the value of one *minute* of his time may be equivalent to a whole year's wages for an unskilled worker. This is the proportion if we compare the over 576 million dollars earned, on average, by the best twenty-five hedge fund managers and the pay packet of an Italian factory worker.

Although acknowledging the pathological nature of the above disparities, the economists who adhere to the most radical version of free-marketeerism—Ludwig Von Mises (1949), Milton Friedman (1962), and Murray Rothbard (1970)—believe that economic inequality is an essential premise for the proper functioning of a market economy. Opportunities for profit and social advancement are what spur firms and individuals to compete with one another and to invest energy and resources in production-process innovation, product diversification, and the conquest of new markets. A forcibly egalitarian distribution of income and wealth would be incompatible with a proper incentive scheme and would end up compromising growth itself and, with it, the wellbeing of the whole community.[1] Even if this extreme view, which goes so far as to attribute a positive valence to inequality, has few supporters today, there are instead many who wonder why people should also worry about inequality rather than focus exclusively on economic growth. After all, to quote John F. Kennedy's famous metaphor, economic growth is like the tide that raises all boats, even the smallest and most rickety ones. According to Martin Feldstein (1999), a growing society must not bother itself with inequality, but rather with absolute poverty, to ensure that no boat gets left behind.

The view of the "irrelevance" of inequality is not a very popular one today. The financial crisis of 2007–2008 and the resulting global recession affecting both the new and the old continent have turned off the engine of growth. A large section of public opinion has started to show open hostility—even through protest movements—toward a growth model that, subjected to the tensions of the crisis, has ended up accentuating rather than tempering the economic and social inequalities (Acemoglu and Robinson 2012). In academic circles, not a few economists have shown that—far from being irrelevant—inequality can actually be an obstacle to growth. We should also consider that the principle of equality is an ethical assumption of any stable social order. In this sense, equality is directly connected to individuals' wellbeing and is independent of its relation with economic growth: the wealth of nations is not solely measured on the basis of the overall value of the social product but also on the basis of the way this product is distributed among citizens.

The general conclusion reasoned out in the following pages is that the theme of economic inequality is a crucial aspect in understanding and evaluating a country's economic history. Any history of the wellbeing of the Italians that ignores the sphere of distribution would thus be incomplete and unsatisfactory. That is why this chapter presents a *quantitative* reconstruction of income inequality in Italy since 1861, the year the Kingdom of Italy was founded.

---

[1] As Von Mises (1949) wrote: "Inequality of wealth and incomes is an essential and necessary feature of the market economy. Its elimination would entirely destroy this type of economy . . . Even those who look upon the inequality of wealth and incomes as a deplorable thing, cannot deny that it makes for progressing capital accumulation. And it is additional capital accumulation alone that brings about technological improvement, rising wage rates, and a higher standard of living" (808 and 819).

1.1 ECONOMIC GROWTH, INEQUALITY, AND WELLBEING

The clear separation of the themes of growth and inequality rests on the assumption that the competition mechanism works properly and without hindrance. When this is the case, the *first fundamental theorem of welfare economics* ensures that the economic system always provides for the efficient allocation of productive resources and implies that distribution of the social product can be handled as a separate issue independently of the determination of the social product itself.[2] Less technically, this means that—under certain conditions—market forces, like an "invisible hand", coordinate individual decisions to spontaneously achieve an efficient outcome in which nobody can improve their own situation without worsening somebody else's. This, in essence, is the theoretical underpinning of the belief that economic growth makes the idea of inequality irrelevant—the idea that the tide will raise all boats regardless. In many concrete situations, however, the conditions of validity of the first fundamental theorem no longer hold. These are the cases where—to use economic theory jargon—the market fails. An example of market failure concerns credit and financial brokerage in general. Regardless of their capacity to pay back loans, the poorest households can be rationed in the credit market because they are unable to provide firm collateral. The problem of having no access to credit can drive families or individuals to invest less than what would be desirable and efficient: parents, for example, may decide to invest less in their children's education, thereby compromising future income-growth opportunities. It is clear that, in situations like these, inequality is no longer an irrelevant factor with regard to growth: great imbalances in the distribution of resources can actually aggravate credit restriction phenomena, thereby hindering economic growth.[3]

There are other mechanisms that lead to the same conclusions. For example, in phases where industrial development calls for the adoption of advanced technologies, it may be necessary to have adequate domestic demand that can support the investment decisions of innovative entrepreneurs. Domestic demand in turn depends on the presence of a robust middle class. A strongly polarized income distribution, with a squeezed middle class, could depress domestic demand to the point of discouraging investment in new technology. This is

---

[2] To complete the first theorem there is the *second fundamental theorem of welfare economics*, which states that any possible distribution of the social product can be obtained through a competitive mechanism, after an appropriate redistribution of initial resources among individuals (Mas-Colell et al. (1995), chap. 16). Taken together, the first and second theorems lead to the conclusion that, even if the competitive mechanism in itself does not bring about a desirable outcome with regard to income distribution, this result can be obtained without giving up efficiency, as long as we agree to a redistribution of the initial resources of economic agents.

[3] See, for example, Aghion and Bolton 1992; 1997; Galor and Zeira (1993); Benabou (1996), and Piketty (1997).

another case in which excessive inequality can compromise growth and thus the wellbeing of a population (Murphy, Shleifer, and Vishny 1989).

The link between growth and inequality can also be explained by mechanisms other than market failure. An important case concerns distortions created by economic policy decisions. For example, a crucial aspect in a democratic system is the votes of "median" voters, that is, of those voters who are in an intermediate position with regard to all the other voters and whose consensus all political parties try to gain. We are referring to the voters of the so-called middle class, to use language that is perhaps more imprecise but less abstract. In an economy characterized by great inequality, in which all the wealth is concentrated in the hands of a few rich individuals, middle-class people try to safeguard their standard of living and thus tend to support political parties that propose redistribution policies, even when these are financed by higher taxes. To the extent that higher taxes distort incentives and hinder growth, inequality will once again have a bearing on economic growth.[4]

The role of economic inequality in determining social wellbeing is not limited to its possible interactions with economic growth. There is ample literature stressing how inequality tends to negatively affect the population's health conditions, regardless of the average wage level in society.[5] The scholars of "happiness economics"—which we shall deal with in chapter 12 ("Human Development")—claim that there is a direct link between inequality and individual wellbeing: marked imbalances in income distribution put social cohesion at risk simply because our "happiness" does not depend on our own income alone, but also on the comparison we make of our income with that of others (Layard 2005). Box 1 goes into more detail on this aspect.

1.2 THE VALUE OF EQUALITY

The economists' interpretations that were briefly outlined in the previous section share an *instrumental* interest in inequality: inequality counts because it conditions economic growth, health, happiness, and social cohesion. However, there is also an *intrinsic* interest in inequality regardless of all the aspects explored so far (Roemer 2009). Human inclination toward equality—with regard not only to rights and opportunities but also to conditions of life—has in many ways been the main distinctive feature of socialist and social democratic movements. More

---

[4] See Alesina and Rodrik (1994), but also Bertola (1993), Perotti (1993), Persson and Tabellini (1994), and Bertola, Foellmi, and Zweimüller (2005).

[5] See Wilkinson 1996, and Wilkinson and Pickett (2006, 2009). Economists have not yet confirmed these views, but show a growing willingness to discuss the matter with colleagues of other disciplines: epidemiologists, sociologists, psychologists, and historians. See Wagstaff and van Doorslaer (2000), and Deaton (2003).

Box 1 Envy, Inequality, and Wellbeing

Having their eyelids sewn up with iron wire to cause a painful blindness. This, according to Dante, is the talion inflicted on the envious who were placed in the second cornice of Purgatory, because in their earthly life they looked on the life of others with jealousy. Apart from the ethical implications of envy, even economists—centuries later—have questioned themselves on the role of envy in economic decision-making. A great many empirical studies have shown that individuals evaluate their own wellbeing not only on the basis of their own income, but also by looking at "the lives of others". If an increase in personal income has positive effects on wellbeing, an increase in the income of one's neighbor instead produces a decrease in personal wellbeing (Easterlin 1995, Luttmer 2005). Studies of experimental economics confirm this feature of individual behavior. Suppose you have to choose between two situations:

Figure 8.B1 Dante Alighieri (1265–1321) by Botticelli (1495). In *The Divine Comedy*, Dante Alighieri placed the envious in Purgatory.

A) Having an annual income of 50,000 euros, while the others earn 25,000 euros;

B) Having an annual income of 100,000 euros, while the others earn 250,000 euros.

Which situation would you rather choose, A or B? In February 1995 this very question was put to a representative sample of students and lecturers of Harvard University. Over 50 percent opted for situation A, that is, preferring a world in which one has lower purchasing power but better "social status", to a world where one has more purchasing power but with lower social status compared to others (Solnick and Hemenway 1998). If this is indeed the case, then the second cornice of Purgatory—should it exist—would appear to be more crowded than even Dante himself had imagined.

Economists have coined the term "social preferences" to indicate the fact that decisions of economic agents are guided not just by what concerns them directly, but also by outcomes concerning others and by the way they are judged by others. Social preferences can take the form of envy, but also of "inequity aversion" (people may be willing to give up a personal gain in return for greater equity in the environment in which they live—Fehr and Schmidt 1999), or of "reciprocity" (people like to help those who are helping them, and to hurt those who are hurting them—Matthew 1993), or even of "social reputation" (people are influenced by the consequences of their actions in terms of social reputation as well as by their self-image—Benabou and Tirole 2006).

generally, it has been a theme crossing the political and philosophical culture of modern Europe, from the time of *What Is the Origin of Inequality among Men, and Is It Authorised by Natural Law?* by Jean-Jacques Rousseau (1712–1778) up to the close of the "short twentieth century" (Hobsbawm 1994) and the current crisis of the welfare state.

The fundamental point is that if equality has any value per se, then income distribution takes on a key role in the very definition of a society's wellbeing. In other words, the distribution aspects become an inseparable part of our judgment on the functioning of the economic system (Dalton 1920; Atkinson 1970). Nobel laureate for economics Amartya Sen showed, for example, how it is possible to achieve a measure of the wellbeing of a society by multiplying per-capita GDP by an income equality index: in this way, an increase in equality would—with no changes in average income—tend to increase social wellbeing. Actually, Sen's reasoning goes beyond this by saying that "a common characteristic of virtually all the approaches to the ethics of social arrangements that have stood the test of time is to want equality of *something* . . . To see the battle as one between those 'in favour of' and those 'against' equality (as the problem is often posed in the literature) is to miss something central to the subject" (Sen 1992, ix). According to Sen, therefore, the preeminent role that the principle of equality has in defining a shared social order is not in question. The underlying issue is instead the choice of specific dimensions of equality that one considers to be more important. In this view, the crucial question is not whether equality is important, but rather to specify what is actually meant by "equality".

2 Inequality of What, Exactly?

To the question "What does economic inequality mean?" many would answer that inequality is simply a measure of the gap between the rich and the poor. This response is not too far from the one we shall give in this section, but it is inadequate from an analytical standpoint. In general terms, what interests economists is the inequality of living conditions, that is, the wellbeing of the population. Wellbeing is, however, a complex, multidimensional concept and is thus difficult to measure. Following a consolidated procedure of economic analysis, in this chapter we shall adopt a drastic simplification by limiting ourselves to using *monetary* indicators of wellbeing, such as income or consumption expenditure. If the limits of this choice lie in the difficulty of grasping the nonmonetary aspects of life conditions (health, education, political freedom and civil rights, and many more besides), the main advantage consists of managing to approximate the level of an individual's wellbeing by summarizing it with a single number that is easily comparable in time and space.

The decision to use a monetary measure does not completely solve the problem. We also need to define the variable to be measured and there are several possible alternatives: we can use income (annual income or an estimation of what an individual earns in a lifetime), or expenditure on consumption, or even an individual's wealth. Although the specialist literature tends to favor the first two measures (income and consumption expenditure), we cannot claim, in general, that any one solution is better than the others.[6] In actual fact, the choice is generally based on considerations of a more practical nature rather than on theory, such as the actual availability and quality of the data. This chapter is no exception to this practice, and it is actually the relative abundance of data on household incomes (chapter 13, "Household Budgets") that led us to measure the inequality of the wellbeing of the Italians on the basis of their household income.

---

[6] See Deaton and Zaidi (2002), Cowell (2011), and Ravallion (1994).

Although we often tend to interpret income as a sort of primitive concept, we must take into consideration that it is actually an aggregate compound that includes various elementary components. It is worth recalling them here, albeit briefly, in order to clarify the definition of the "income" variable for those readers who are not economists. The first component is *income from employment* (wages and salaries): over the last fifty years this component has accounted for over 40 percent of the total income of Italian households. The second component is *income from self-employment*, that is, the remuneration of farmers, tradesmen, merchants, professionals, and all other self-employed people. The definition of income also includes the value of the *production of goods and services for self-consumption* (such as the produce of one's own vegetable garden or cutting one's hair at home—see Box 2 in chapter 7, "Income"). The aggregate compound also includes *income from property*: bank interest payments, dividends and other profits distributed by enterprises to their shareholders, as well as rent from real estate and land. Finally, it also includes *income from transfer payments*, either public ones (pensions and other social payments) or private ones (remittances of migrant workers). The sum of all the aforesaid sources of income goes to make up the *gross income* of a household; if we deduct taxes and social contributions from this sum, we get *disposable income* (or net income). In this chapter the analysis of inequality of the living conditions of the population will be carried out starting from the disposable income of Italian households.

Disposable income has value to the extent that it is turned into purchasing power in order to buy goods and services that are useful in satisfying individual needs. However, a euro does not always purchase the same quantity of goods and services: purchasing power varies geographically (the cost of living is higher in some areas of the country and lower in others) and over time (inflation decreases the purchasing power of a given sum of money). A direct comparison of monetary incomes of Italian households observed in different years or while living in different parts of the country would provide a distorted picture of their real living conditions. To get around this problem, economists adjust monetary incomes (called *nominal* incomes) to turn them into *real* incomes, that is, incomes that have allowed for the effects of inflation and of territorial differences in average price levels.[7] Within certain limits, this makes it technically possible to evaluate the difference between the living conditions of a mid-nineteenth-century Sardinian shepherd and those of a Milanese factory worker today.

A last methodological aspect needs to be specified, concerning the fact that the data available usually refer to households and not to individual members of a household. Since wellbeing is an individual and not collective attribute,

---

[7] The price indices estimated in chapter 14 ("The Cost of Living") are for this precise purpose, and have been applied to the incomes used in the rest of this chapter.

this poses a problem of understanding how household income actually translates into a measure of wellbeing of individual members of the household. Unfortunately, we do not know much about the practices and rules governing the distribution of resources within a household: for simplicity's sake, we shall thus assume that intrahousehold distribution is egalitarian and shall attribute to each member of the household the per-capita household income of the household they belong to.[8]

The reader who has had the patience to follow all the above reasoning on definitions and methodology will now clearly understand the short but technical answer we can give to the question posed at the beginning of this section: by the term "economic inequality" we mean inequality in the distribution of real, annual disposable per-capita income.

3 The Difficult Art of Reconstructing Income Distributions

Reconstructing income distributions over the entire lifetime of the Italian State (since 1861) is a complex task that requires overcoming a fundamental obstacle—the scarcity of reliable data on household incomes or expenditures in the years before the advent of modern statistical surveys (roughly in the 1960s). For the eighty or so years prior to World War II, the problem of data scarcity concerns Italy as it does every other country that has attempted to reconstruct the dynamics of inequality in the long run. There are basically three approaches in the specialist literature: *(a)* using fiscal data on incomes, wages, properties, or inheritances; *(b)* constructing indirect indicators of income; and *(c)* using so-called social tables—summary tables describing average incomes of the classes a society can be organized into (A'Hearn, Amendola, and Vecchi, 2016).

FISCAL DATA

The richest research line is probably the one started up by a group of scholars coordinated by Thomas Piketty, an economist at the Ecole d'économie de Paris.[9]

---

[8] In so doing, we implicitly assume that there are no differences in needs among the various members of the household, nor savings ("economies of scale", in the language of economists) generated by living in a household, such as savings on rent and heating costs. This assumption is not so restrictive if we consider that, in the past, economies of scale were not particularly marked because expenditure on food weighed more heavily on household budgets than the cost of accommodation.

[9] See Piketty (2003), Piketty and Saez (2006), Atkinson and Piketty (2007; 2010), and Atkinson, Piketty, and Saez (2011).

By employing a methodology originally devised by Simon Kuznets (1953), Piketty's research group estimated—as a measure of inequality—the proportion of income of the richest sections of the population (for example, the percentage quota of total income of the richest 5 percent of the population). This approach is based on the idea of using information on taxes paid by individuals supplemented with data on population and on total incomes estimated in the national accounting systems. Although a strength of Piketty's method is that the information necessary is often available for many decades and for many countries, one of the drawbacks—and the most evident—is that fiscal data provide only part of the picture: they do not allow an estimation of the inequality of the whole income distribution, but only reveal—at most—what is happening to the richest segment of the population (Box 2).[10]

Box 2 **The Taxman's Story of the Ups and Downs of the Super-Rich (1901–2011)**

The tax data provided by the Inland Revenue offices of many countries allow a reconstruction of the income trends of the richest segment of the population. Figure 8.B2 shows the trend over time (horizontal axis) of the proportion of income possessed by the richest 5 percent of the population in Italy (vertical axis) and comparing it to that of other countries. In Italy the annual tax on income was introduced as late as in 1951, and publication of the summary tables on tax revenues only started in 1974: for these, the estimates made by Facundo Alvaredo and Elisa Pisano (2010)—and shown in the graph—only refer to the years 1974–2009. For the years 1900–1980, the graph shows a common trend for many of the countries considered, that is, a marked reduction in the percentage income of the richest taxpayers. From the early 1980s, we see a general inverse trend: in Italy the increase is greater than in France, in line with what is observed in Sweden and a lot less marked than in the United Kingdom and United States. If we look at the levels of inequality, the proportion of the richest segment of the population in Italy and France appears in an intermediate position compared to that of Sweden and of the United Kingdom and United States.

---

[10] Fiscal data do not account for nontaxable incomes (which are very important in the less mature stages of market economies), and exclude all those individuals who are exempted from filing a tax return. In France, for instance, the general income tax, introduced in 1914, initially concerned less than 5 percent of French households; in the years between the two world wars, this percentage fluctuated between 10 percent and 15 percent, to reach 50–60 percent in the 1970s (Piketty 2003, 1006).

Figure 8.B2 Top Income Shares, 1900–2010. The graph shows the percentage of income possessed by the richest 5 percent of the population (vertical axis) over time (horizontal axis).

The problem of tax evasion and of tax avoidance, as is easy to imagine, affects tax data and can, at least potentially, compromise their use for an analysis of inequality (Atkinson 2007). Simon Kuznets was well aware of this problem when, as far back as 1953, he devised the estimation method later refined by Piketty: "Some people, of course, evade reporting completely by not filing; others understate their income, or overstate the legally allowed exemptions and deductions" (xxx). Kuznets did not consider this a fatal limitation: "It is as if one tried to paint a fine picture with thick brushes and large blobs of somewhat mixed colors" (xxxi).

INDIRECT INDICATORS

A second research line made use of a variety of statistical materials and analytical methods—as eclectic and ingenious as they are theoretically and empirically fragile. Some examples may be useful to get an idea. For the United States, the researchers explored the use of wage data, in particular the ratio between the average wage of skilled workers (such as office staff) and that of unskilled workers (such as manual laborers). To the extent that both categories of workers are reasonably numerous and can be ranked in an income scale (the former being relatively well-off while the latter much less so), the ratio between their average wages may be interpreted as an indicator of inequality of income distribution: the greater the gap between an office clerk's wage and that of a manual laborer, the greater the inequality.[11] For the United Kingdom, Williamson (1985) constructed an even more ingenious indicator, using window tax data, collected within an Inhabited House Duty (IHD).[12] In this case, the idea is to use the information linked to a tax designed for a particular target (the number of windows) correlated to the value of dwellings and thus to an individual's standard of living (Williamson 1985, 60).

Other researchers, for other countries, have explored the use of other indicators, including body weight and reproductive capacity (Borgerhoff Mulder et al. 2009), but, above all, stature (Soltow 1992; Baten 2000). What all these attempts at reconstructing inequality have in common is the indirect nature of the statistics employed with respect to the reference wellbeing indicator, that is, income. Herein lies the weakness of these approaches: above all, from the standpoint of an analysis of many decades, it is not reasonable to assume that the link between the indirect indicators used and income can remain stable.[13]

SOCIAL TABLES

The third research line we wish to mention includes a number of studies based on "social tables". These are tables providing a quantitative description of the social structure of reference, ranking the classes or social groups according to their average income and to their respective percentages of the population. The first of these tables appeared in the latter half of the fifteenth century. A statistically shrewd use of this material allows making hypotheses on the trend of inequality for historical periods for which alternative sources are unavailable (Soltow 1968; Lindert and Williamson 1982, 1983; Milanovic, Lindert, and Williamson 2011). Here, too, we should not forget that these tables are imperfect sources, and the estimates based on them retain all their limitations and faults

---

[11] The ratio between skilled and unskilled workers' wages (occupational pay ratio) is discussed in Williamson (1985) and criticized in Feinstein (1988) and Morrisson (2000). Many other researchers have used this approach (Brenner, Kaelble, and Thomas 1991). A variation of this consists of using the ratio between land rent and average wage (Lindert, 1986). A second variant is the ratio between per-worker GDP and the average wage of unskilled workers (Williamson 1997), discussed in Prados de la Escosura (2007).

[12] The window tax was a wealth tax employed in Britain and France in the eighteenth and nineteenth centuries: compared to income tax, which was intolerably intrusive for the mentality of the times, the window tax was less intrusive and, at the same time, easy to check. Italy has never had a window tax (a similar idea was perhaps the "balcony tax", introduced by Royal Decree no.1175 of 14 September 1931 and repealed in 1995).

[13] For example, the number of windows of a dwelling is not a good indicator of wellbeing for more modern times. In the same way, the information gleaned from the ratio between wages of skilled and unskilled workers strongly depends on the social and production structure of reference.

In this chapter we shall not use any of the three approaches outlined above. Instead, we shall use an alternative approach based on household budgets—a difficult statistical source, hardly employed so far by the scientific community. Our view is that, despite the difficulties and costs faced in the data-gathering phase, the "household budget" tool is to be preferred, at a technical level, to the ones reviewed above in this section: the arguments in favor of this view are set out briefly in the following section and then in more detail in the chapter dedicated to household budgets (chapter 13, "Household Budgets").

4 Household Budgets in Italy since 1861

The historical reconstruction presented in this chapter regarding income inequality in Italy from the country's unification in 1861 to the end of World War II is based on an archive of household budgets—hereinafter referred to with the acronym IHBD (Italian Household Budget Database)—which contains almost 20,000 observations.[14] Each one of these observations contains information on household incomes and/or expenditures as well as details on the main sociodemographic characteristics of families who lived between 1861 and the outbreak of World War II—a period for which *no* modern sample-based surveys are available. The IHBD is the most innovative element of our research and it is discussed in detail in chapter 13. In this chapter we shall only provide a summary description of the source with a dual aim of understanding its limitations and advantages, and also to assess its potential uses for analyzing inequality in other countries.

In Italy, as elsewhere, household accounts were normally regularly kept only by a very small elite sector of the population, who had substantial wealth to administrate. The studies carried out in the Italian case show with some surprise that there is a fair amount of detailed information also on the accounts of less wealthy segments of the population. Household accounts were found in many spheres, such as in particular inquiries and investigations promoted by governments in order to get an idea of the living conditions of the poorest segments of the population; but also of conditions in the clerical class or the working conditions of certain sectors of the economy. Indeed, almost the entire society left some trace of itself, consigning it to history in the form of household budgets.[15]

The work necessary to build up the IHBD was long and onerous. Gathering the hundreds of sources—kept in libraries and state archives all over the country, and found in the archives of government and ministry offices as well as in the dusty attics of private homes—took almost a decade. This mammoth

---

[14] Section 4 in chapter 13 ("Household Budgets") gives a concrete example taken from the IHBD and concerning a Florentine sharecropper of 1857.

[15] See Stigler (1954), Johnson, Rogers, and Tan (2001), and Deeming (2010).

effort enabled the construction of an impressive archive of Italian household budgets.[16]

From a methodological standpoint, finding these Italian budgets and harmonizing them according to the systems adopted by the Bank of Italy and by Istat, the Italian national statistics agency, is only a first step. The observations contained in the IHBD do not lend themselves to statistical use since they represent a collection—albeit a rich one—of budgets that need to be turned into a representative sample. This is the crucial step to be made in order to improve the quality of the analysis method and to statistically use a set of data that was created and gathered for completely different purposes other than statistical analysis.

Turning the historical data into statistics was performed by means of a procedure that can be described by considering a particular year, such as 1861. Because the households included in the IHBD relative to 1861 are the outcome of archival research instead of a sampling plan, there is no guarantee whatsoever that they will collectively grasp the sociodemographic structure of Italian households in 1861; on the contrary, it may perhaps be more reasonable to expect the income distribution of the sample *not* to provide a reliable representation of the "real" distribution. The IHBD may contain too many urban households or too few large households, or even too many working-class households and not many middle-class ones, so as to provide a distorted view of the actual income distribution of the times. To solve the problem of representativity, we adopted a procedure pivoting on population censuses. The method consists of using census data to build "weights" to be associated with each household contained in the IHBD. Using these weights rebalances the composition of the IHBD sample because they give each household its "proper weight," that is, the weight which that type of household actually had in the population at that time.[17]

For the period after World War II, the IHBD gave way to other sources. For the year 1948 we used a study conducted by the Doxa Institute, the first study on Italian household incomes that was based on a probability sampling procedure.[18] For its times, the study was a real heroic feat: nearly 11,000 households were interviewed, one for every 1,000 households that were thought to reside

---

[16] Also encouraging are the initial results of the research geared to exploring the availability of this kind of source for other countries. See chapter 13 ("Household Budgets"), and A'Hearn, Amendola, and Vecchi (2016).

[17] In the literature, this procedure is known as "poststratification" (Holt and Smith 1979), described in detail by Vecchi (1999) and by Rossi, Toniolo, and Vecchi (2001).

[18] See Luzzatto Fegiz (1949, 1950). The Doxa Institute carried out another two studies in 1955 and in 1958–1959, but unlike Roberti (1971), the data have not been used here for the reasons discussed in Brandolini (1999). The Doxa data are available only in tabular form. This is no insurmountable problem because there is ample literature that developed suitable statistical tools to overcome the drawbacks of this kind of data (Kakwani 1976; Cowell and Mehta 1982).

in Italy at the time. For the years after World War II, the main statistical source on personal income distribution is instead the Survey on the Household Income and Wealth (SHIW) started up by the Bank of Italy in the early 1960s.[19]

In sum, linking the IHBD with later studies, and right up to the current institutional ones conducted by the Bank of Italy, has enabled us to reconstruct—as we shall see in the next section—the trend of the entire income distribution in Italy since 1861.

5 The Anatomy of Italian Income Distribution, 1861–2012

The history of income distribution in Italy since the country's unification in 1861 is largely an unprecedented one: if we make an exception for the estimates of Rossi, Toniolo, and Vecchi (2001), based on consumption expenditures, the studies that remain are few and tell of recent events concerning, at most, the last four or five decades. In this section, we shall start from the suggestive comparison of the "parade of dwarfs and giants," a method of representation that well summarizes the changes in the entire income distribution between 1861 and 2012 (section 5.1). We shall then reconstruct the evolution of inequality, as described by the Gini index (section 5.2) and by the income proportions of quintiles, or fifths, of the population (section 5.3).

5.1 THE PARADE OF DWARFS AND GIANTS

In 1971 the Dutch economist Jan Pen (1921–2010) put forward a method for representing income distribution through a curve that soon became famous in the field with the name "parade of dwarfs (and a few giants)" (Pen 1971). Pen's narrative ploy draws on the adventures of Procrustes (from the Greek word Προκρούστης, meaning "the stretcher"), a rogue bandit of Greek mythology who used to attack and kill travelers along the road connecting Megara to Athens. Before killing them, Procrustes subjected his unfortunate victims to terrible anguish: if the traveler was tall, Procrustes would place the victim on a short bed and then amputate the body parts exceeding the length of the bed; if the traveler

---

[19] The SHIW was conducted annually until 1987 and then every two years since (no study was performed for 1985 and there is a gap of three years between the 1995 study and the 1998 one). Even Istat gathered summary information on personal incomes in a study carried out in 1963–1964, and since 1980 has collected annual data on household consumption; the reliability of this information is discussed in Brandolini (1999). Istat started surveying household incomes in a more detailed manner in the 1990s: from 1993 to 2000 with the European Community Household Panel (ECHP), and since 2003 with the European Statistics on Income and Living Conditions, (EUSILC). These data have not been used here for the brevity of the historical series.

was short, he would place the victim on a long bed and then pull his limbs until the victim's length corresponded to that of the bed. Like Procrustes, but without the cruel vein, Pen had the idea of describing income distribution by giving each member of the population a height proportional to his/her income: in this imaginary world, the poorest people are "dwarfs" and the richest are "giants". At this point, Pen lined up the whole population in ascending order of income in order to start a parade. When the band starts playing, the population starts marching, with the dwarfs at the head and all the others behind, going at the same pace in order to finish the parade in exactly one hour.

The onlookers sitting on the stands placed at the side of the parade would first see some bizarre creatures of microscopic size: these are the poorest individuals. The incomes of these people, measured in the height scale, correspond to perhaps a fraction of a millimeter, and no more.[20] The minutes go by and the procession continues, but what they see is a continuous flow of minuscule creatures. Only after a long time do the actual "dwarfs" that Pen speaks of appear: these are people with a low income, lower than the population average, and especially lower than that of the richest people. As the procession proceeds, the average height of the marchers gets taller, but only very slowly.

Figure 8.1 shows the parade of Italian dwarfs and giants in the year 1861 (unbroken line). The parade proceeds from left to right: the curve starts from levels close to zero and then increases almost imperceptibly. For a long time, we see only uniformly short individuals, and the curve tends to increase in a very slow and monotonous manner for most of the time. Only after 40 minutes do we see people of average height (income); and only after 50 minutes, when over 80 percent of the population has already marched by, do we begin to see a clear increase in the height of the marchers. In the last two or three minutes, when not more than 5 percent of the total population still has to march past, we finally see the first really tall individuals, the richest, who then make way, in the last few seconds, for the very few giants of 1861. The impression that remains in the minds of those who had the patience to sit through the whole parade is one of a very concentrated income distribution: very few giants and a great many dwarfs.

A comparison of Pen's parade for 1861 with that of 2012, also plotted in Figure 8.1 (broken line), summarizes what has happened to income distribution over almost one hundred and fifty years. The microscopic creatures (the extremely poor individuals) have almost disappeared, while the dwarfs are still part of the parade. The overall increase in height of the procession can clearly be seen, as can the increase in the number of giants: not only do the latter account for a greater proportion of the population, but they are clearly also taller than

---

[20] No objection to imagining people—even very tall ones, but upside down: these are people who have recorded negative incomes during the year. For instance, entrepreneurs with balance sheets in the red.

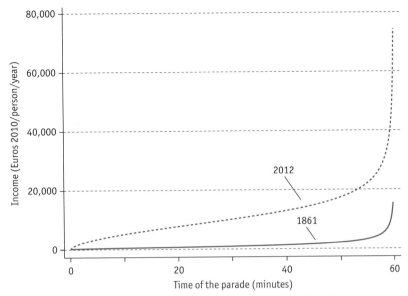

Figure 8.1 THE PARADE OF DWARFS AND GIANTS, 1861 AND 2012. The figure shows the income distribution for the years 1861 and 2012 through the "parade of dwarfs" described in the text.

the giants of the past. A person belonging to the richest 1 percent of the population in 2012 has a real income almost 6 times greater than his/her equivalent in 1861; the height of the richest in 2012 is such that it cannot even be represented.[21] Even greater progress is seen with the dwarfs: the amount of increase in the first part of the parade is one of the most important changes (which we shall come back to in chapter 9, "Poverty"). The average income of the poorest 10 percent of the population in 2012 is almost eight times greater than that of the same segment of the population in 1861. More generally, the inclination of Pen's curve for 2012, a measure of the rate at which the heights increase as the minutes go by, is certainly increased compared to 1861.

In Italy, 150 years after its unification, the dwarfs of the past have almost all disappeared and the giants of 1861 have today become individuals of average height. The estimates of Figure 8.1 tell us that in 1861 the richest 1 percent of the population had a real annual per-capita income of around 10,600 euros (883 euros a month); almost half of the population by now reaches that level of income today. In the century and a half since unification, personal incomes have indeed made giant leaps.

---

[21] The figure excludes individuals with an income greater than 80,000 euros a year in 2010 values: nobody reached an income of this magnitude in 1861, while just under 0.2 percent of the population exceeded it in 2010.

5.2 THE STORY TOLD BY THE GINI INDEX

In an article published in the British periodical *The Economic Journal* in 1920, Hugh Dalton (1887–1962) acknowledged that scholarly preeminence in the analysis of inequality indexes went to the Italians.

> It is generally agreed that, other things being equal, a considerable reduction in the inequality of incomes found in most modern communities would be desirable. But it is not generally agreed how this inequality should be measured. The problem of the measurement of the inequality of incomes has not been much considered by English economists. It has attracted rather more attention in America, but it is in Italy that it has hitherto been most fully discussed. (Dalton 1920, 348)

Dalton was referring to the contribution made by Italian economists and statisticians in the lively debate following the study conducted by Vilfredo Pareto (1848–1923) on the income curve.[22] It is within this context that, in the early 1910s, Corrado Gini (1884–1965) devised the concentration index that bears his name and that condenses, in a single number, the degree of inequality of a distribution (Gini 1912; 1914). The index was created in order to be "applicable not only to income or wealth, but also to every other quantitative phenomenon (economic, demographic, anatomic or physiological)" (Gini 1921, 124). A hundred years later, this index remains the most commonly used income inequality measure in the world.[23]

The Gini index calculates the average gap between each individual's income and that of everyone else, and works out a mean value for it—appropriately rescaled in order to range from 0 (the *minimum* value, in the hypothetical situation in which all individuals in a society have the same income and there is thus perfect equality) to 100 (the *maximum* value, found in the opposite case, that is, where all the income is concentrated in the hands of just one person). For the following discussion, it is useful to bear in mind that low values of the Gini index indicate an income distribution characterized by little inequality, while high values indicate considerable inequality. We cannot precisely establish what high or low means but, on the basis of international evidence, index values ranging from 20 to 25, similar to the ones recorded in northern Europe, indicate

---

[22] See Pareto (1897). Bresciani-Turroni (1939) stressed the importance and primacy of Pareto: "Pareto was the first to conceive the idea of measuring inequality in the distribution of incomes, suggesting a method which, though objectionable, enables comparisons between different places or epochs" (132). See Brandolini (2011).

[23] See Ceriani and Verme (2011) and Milanovic (2005).

Box 3 **Around the World with the Gini Index**

Comparing inequality between countries is something that numerous international research institutes have been doing for many years. The World Bank produces estimates for 160 countries of the world within the project called World Development Indicators (World Bank 2012), with a great many series reconstructed back to the 1960s. According to the latest estimates, the highest Gini index is found in the Seychelles (65.8), while the country with the lowest inequality is Denmark (24.7). All the other countries lie in between these two extremes, with Italy (36.0) appearing in the lower half of the world ranking, but characterized by greater inequality compared to most of the other countries in continental Europe.

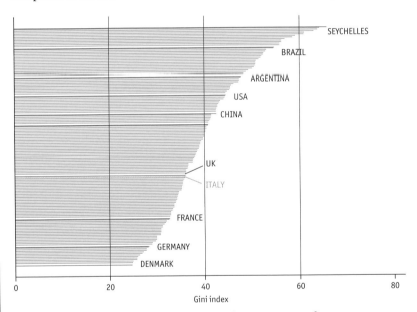

Figure 8.B3 International comparisons of income inequality

The reliability of these rankings is the object of lively debate since it is subject to broad margins of choice with regard to accounting methods and also to a long list of potential measurement pitfalls (Atkinson and Brandolini 2001). There is also no lack of competition between international agencies in producing databanks specifically designed for conducting international comparisons. The statistics office of the Organisation for Economic Cooperation and Development (OECD), for example, has been dealing with inequality for several decades and regularly issues reports on international comparative analyses. In line with the results published by the World Bank, the OECD shows that, out of fifteen member states of the

European Union, Italy has greater inequality values than any of the other countries except Portugal (OECD 2012). Similar results have been obtained by analyzing the data of the Luxembourg Income Study Database (LIS), a database constructed by a research center specializing in international comparative studies on poverty and inequality (http://www.lisdatacenter.org/).

low inequality, while values exceeding 55–60, such as those found in Brazil and South Africa, indicate an extremely high level of inequality (Box 3).[24]

Figure 8.2 presents the history of income inequality in Italy since 1861, as summarized by the Gini index. It is a history that was not fully known until recently, and from which certain "stylized facts" emerge that deserve specific comment.

THE DECREASE IN INEQUALITY OVER THE YEARS

Although taking the statistical error of estimates into due account, in the long run Italian economic growth has been accompanied by a decrease in income inequality. In the latter half of the nineteenth century, the Gini index fluctuated between 45 and 50. Over a century later, it fell by 15–20 points reaching a minimum value of 29.1 in 1991. On the whole, Figure 8.2 shows that in Italian history, modern economic growth has been associated with a decrease in inequality. Only between the early 1980s and early 1990s was there an inverse trend.

The dynamics of the decrease in inequality has not been a linear one. Figure 8.2 shows periods of slow decreases, lulls, and then rapid decreases, along with periods of increasing inequality. Overall, the long-term trend is best described as a sequence of episodes—even long ones—rather than the inexorable coming about of a long-term law linking economic growth to income distribution (Atkinson 1997; Lindert 2000b).

FROM LIBERAL TIMES TO THE FASCIST PERIOD

The first seventy years of postunification Italy were characterized by rather modest changes in the Gini index. Although the index did indeed increase by four points between 1871 and 1901, and then decreased by the same number between 1901 and 1921, the magnitude of the variation—even if not negligible—is quite small on the whole and hardly significant statistically speaking. The country's unification and industrial takeoff marked a doubling of per-capita GDP in the first seventy years of the kingdom, without this making much difference to the level of inequality. Fascism, although constituting a break in the country's political and social history, did not lead to any significant changes in this regard.

[24] See Milanovic (2011), Shorrocks (2005), and Subramanian (2002).

THE EGALITARIAN DRIVE OF THE 1970S

In the two periods of greatest growth of the Italian economy, the Giolitti age (1892–1914) and that of the so-called Italian economic miracle (1950–1963), there prevailed a tendency toward a decrease in inequality, but the greatest decrease occurred during a period of stagnation in the country, between the late 1960s and late 1980s—years in which the Gini index recorded a decrease of as many as 10 points.

As we saw in chapter 7 ("Income"), the intense economic growth of the post-war years led to a great increase in national income, but only part of this increase actually reached the whole population: in the twenty years between 1948 and 1968, per-capita GDP grew threefold while average wages grew only twofold. Despite some progress shown by our estimates, the personal income distribution remained strongly uneven. In this situation, the "hot autumn" of 1969 saw the explosion of social conflict and the start-up of a political phase characterized by a shift in power relations in favor of trade unions and workers, marked by strongly egalitarian demands (Accornero 1992). In 1975 the reform of the wage-indexing mechanism led to adopting the so-called "punto unico di contingenza"—an instrument ensuring that all employees had a wage increase of equal magnitude for every increase in the cost of living index. The equalizing impact of this mechanism was soon amplified by double-digit inflation rates and led to a rapid compression of the structure of wages and salaries, at least until the early 1980s, and this had repercussions on the whole household income distribution.[25]

Much of the fall in inequality levels recorded in the 1970s thus derived from the labor market, but it was also strengthened by the gradual building of the welfare state (chapter 11, "Vulnerability"). What happened at that time was the result of an economic and political conjuncture that was exceptional in many respects, but whose legacy has turned out to be lasting.[26]

INEQUALITY HAS BEEN ON THE RISE IN THE LAST TWO DECADES

Inequality has started to increase again since the early 1990s. According to the data of Figure 8.2, the increase concentrated during the serious economic and foreign exchange crisis of 1992. The sharp increase recorded between 1991 and 1993 pushed the Gini index to 1980 values, and since then it has fluctuated with a slight upward trend. The result is in line with the estimates given in the most recent OECD reports (OECD 2008; 2012). The scale of the phenomenon is smaller compared to other countries, and particularly the English-speaking

[25] See Filosa and Visco (1980), Erickson and Ichino (1995), Brandolini, Cipollone, and Sestito (2002), and Manacorda (2004).

[26] There was no Italian peculiarity in that episode: a qualitatively similar trend—albeit with national diversities—was seen in many other European countries, including Germany, France, Sweden, and Finland (Brandolini and Smeeding 2008).

ones, but the increases in inequality start from levels that are higher, on average, than those of many other European countries and add to the effects caused by prolonged economic stagnation and, more recently, by the so-called Great Recession of 2008–2009. The overall effect of this combination—the lack of growth and increase in inequality—is already visible in the trend in the poverty (chapter 9) and vulnerability to poverty (chapter 11, "Vulnerability") indicators over the last two decades. The barometer of the country's social indexes by now points to a clear worsening of the situation.

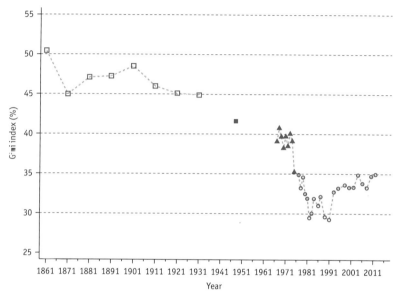

Figure 8.2 INCOME INEQUALITY IN ITALY, 1861–2012. The graph shows the performance of the Gini index (vertical axis) over time (horizontal axis). High values of the index indicate great inequality, while low values indicate low inequality.

Box 4 **There Is a Limit to Everything, Even to Inequality**

There is a limit to everything—even to to the inequality that a country can put up with. On the basis of this consideration, Branko Milanovic, Peter Lindert, and Jeffrey Williamson (2011) devised an indicator for measuring the amount of *actual* inequality (the one that is observed and measured in any given year) compared to *potential* or *maximum* inequality. "Normally, [inequality] measures reach their extreme values when one individual appropriates the entire income (not simply all the surplus). Such extreme values are obviously just theoretical and devoid of any economic content since no society could function in such a state. That one person who appropriated the entire income would soon be all alone (everyone else having

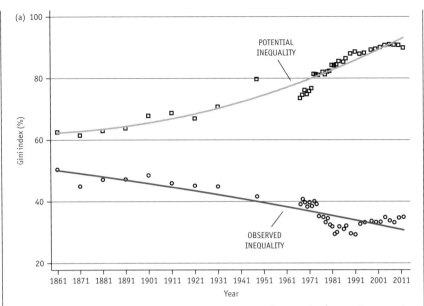

Figure 8.B4a INEQUALITY EXTRACTION RATIO. The graph shows the trend, over time, of observed inequality (dark blue line) and maximum inequality (light blue line): that which would have been observed, each year, if the elite had managed to appropriate the income in excess of the amount necessary to guarantee subsistence to the rest of the population.

died) and after his death inequality would fall to zero and the society would cease to exist" (259). To get around this problem, as a measure of potential inequality they put forward not the value of 100 (the theoretical maximum value of the Gini index), but the value the Gini index would take if income were distributed in such a way as to a) guarantee the mere subsistence of the mass of the population, and b) give a small elite all the part of the social product left over after providing for the subsistence of the masses. It is clear that potential inequality is a historically determined magnitude: the greater the excess of social product with respect to the resources necessary for subsistence, the greater the surplus that the elite can appropriate and thus the greater the potential inequality.

Figure 8.B4b shows the trend of the two kinds of inequality, the one actually observed (dark blueline) and the potential one (light blue line: details of the relative calculation are in the Appendix—Sources and Methods). The fact that the two curves diverge means that the historical series of the Gini index described in Figure 8.2 (and reproduced in stylized manner in the graph in question) provides a misleading picture, in some respects, of the secular evolution of inequality because it *underestimates* the improvements recorded since 1861. If we take into account what could have been the case but actually was not (potential inequality), the judgement on the income distribution

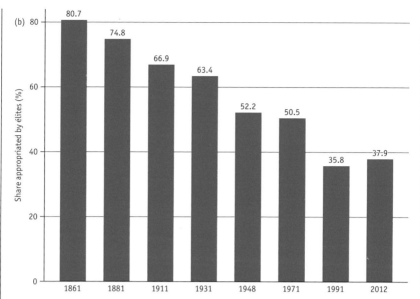

Figure 8.B4b INEQUALITY EXTRACTION RATIO. The graph shows the decrease in the amount of social product that the elite manages to appropriate over the years.

history would be even more positive than the one formulated in the legend to Figure 8.2. We can better understand this point by calculating the ratio between the two curves shown in the graph above: a high value for this ratio (known as the *inequality extraction ratio*, in technical terms) indicates "how powerful, repressive and extractive the ruling groups, their institutions and policies were" (268) in a given year. Figure 8.B4b shows that the "evidence of exploitation of potential inequality" has unequivocally decreased over time, which reveals that throughout Italy's economic history the elite has met with ever greater obstacles to appropriating the surplus deriving from the country's modernisation. In Liberal period Italy, the trend in actual inequality appears largely stable around Gini index values of 40–45 percent (Figure 8.2); in the same years the inequality extraction ratio clearly decreased from 80 percent to just over 60 percent: this means that the liberal elite appropriated a progressively smaller amount of the country's potential inequality. On the whole, the gradient of this measure restores to late-nineteenth-century Italian economic development an even more benevolent feature than the one already emerging from Figure 8.2; a feature that instead worsens in the last twenty years. The inverse trend—albeit a modest one—represents an element of novelty that is unprecedented in the history of postunification Italy: unlike what has happened for the rest of society, the Italian elite of these last two decades has continued to climb the income scale.

5.3 WHERE HAS THE DISTRIBUTION CHANGED?

Like any other summary measure of inequality, the Gini index may be linked to very different changes along income distribution. Therefore, it is worth integrating the analysis by observing how the distribution changes at different points: in the "low tail" containing the poorest individuals, in the central portion of the middle classes, or in the "high tail" where the rich are? An effective way of representing the movements of the whole distribution consists of lining up the population in increasing order of income and then dividing it into fractions of equal size, such as in tenths or fifths. The incomes of all those belonging to each fraction are then summed together to finally calculate their overall proportion with respect to total income. The proportion of the poorest fifth is the amount of total income that goes to the poorest 20 percent of the population and so on. Figure 8.3 shows the trend in the income percentage earned by each fifth of the population. By construction, the sum of the vertical values—that is, for every given year—gives 100. The figure firstly shows that the dynamics of the income proportion of the richest 20 percent of the population closely follows that of the Gini index; between 1861 and the early 1980s the richest fifth of the population lost almost a third of its proportion of income, about 18 points, to the benefit of the rest of the population—and especially to the poorest two-fifths.[27]

In the first seventy years of postunification Italy, the proportion of income of the poorest 40 percent of the population remained largely at the same level. What was seen, instead, was a redistribution of income from the richest fifth of the population to the benefit of the fifth immediately below and, to a lesser extent, to the middle fifth of the population. This redistribution suggests that the consolidation of unified Italy went hand in hand with the strengthening of the middle class—a necessary step in order to sustain a domestic demand for consumption goods that could stimulate growth. Over this long period of time, the proportion of income of the poorest two-fifths of the population peaked in 1921—not at the expense of the richest fifth, but of the two middle fifths. These are small variations that should be taken with some caution, but they are consistent with the rapid increase in wages in the aftermath of World War I, when in just a few months of the so-called red two years, from the street demonstrations against the cost of living in 1919 to the workers' occupation of the factories in August and September 1920, factory workers obtained over 70 percent increases in their daily wages in real terms along with a reduction in working hours to 8 hours per day from the previous 10 or more (Zamagni 1991; Brandolini and Vecchi 2012).

As already noted, most of the action is seen in the 1960s, when there was a clear rebalancing of income proportions from the richest segment of the population to

---

[27] Morrisson (2000) provides tables with estimates of the quantiles for certain European countries and the data are comparable, at least in principle, to the estimates of Figure 8.3.

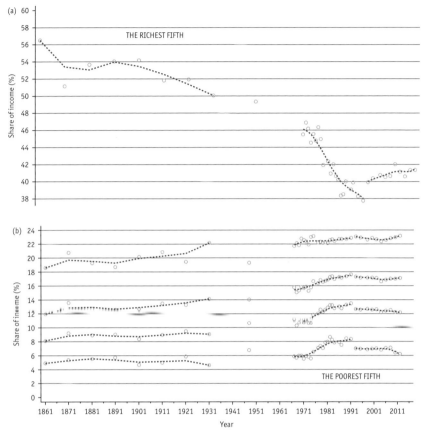

Figure 8.3 Income Proportions of Fifths of the Population,
1861–2012. The figure shows the trend in the proportions of income (vertical
axis) of fifths of the population over time (horizontal axis). The lowest curve
shows the trend for the poorest fifth of the population and is interpreted as
follows: between 1861 and 1931 the sum of the incomes of the poorest 20 percent
of the population fluctuated around 5 percent of the total income. The trend for
the richest fifth of the population is shown by the highest curve in the graph.

the benefit of all the others, and especially to the poorest segment. The last two
decades have seen a partial inversion of this trend—almost exclusively affecting
the richest and poorest fifths of the population. The fraction of income going to
the three middle fifths has changed to a much lesser extent.

Figure 8.4 subdivides the highest fifth even further and shows the proportion
of income earned by the richest 1- and 5-percent segments of the population.
Given the great number of observations available and the many approximate
estimates, these values are more inaccurate than the previous ones, but they still
confirm what was said about the richest fifth of the population. These estimates
are not inconsistent with those obtained for fiscal data by Alvaredo and Pisano

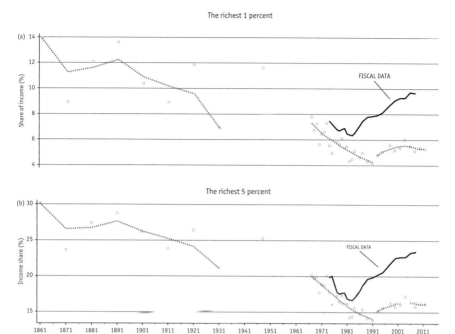

Figure 8.4 PROPORTION OF INCOME (PERCENT) OF THE RICHEST OF THE RICH, 1861–2012. The figure shows the trend in the proportion of income (vertical axis) of the richest 1 percent of the population (upper graph) and of the richest 5 percent of the population (lower graph) over time (horizontal axis). The broken line shows the new estimates, while the unbroken line gives the estimates based on fiscal data.

(2010): the level of the two series is extraordinarily close in the 1970s, even if they tend to diverge from the early 1980s, suggesting that the Bank of Italy's study on household budgets may have underestimated the income growth of the richest segment of the population.

6 The End of Mr. Kuznets's Tyranny

"The Kuznets curve has to some extent tyrannized the literature on inequality trends. Energies that could have moved earlier into exploring the underlying causes of inequality were diverted into a debate over whether there was or was not an inverted U curve, either in history or in postwar international cross-sections" (Lindert 2000a, 173). Kuznets's "inverted U-curve" is the long-term relation between economic growth and income inequality: the upward part of the curve is seen during the initial stages of economic development in which both income per capita and inequality increase, driven up by industrialization and urbanization processes. After a while, the curve levels off and then starts a downward trend as the economy moves towards a more mature development stage. This was what Simon Kuznets (1901–1985) suggested in his presidential speech in December 1954, during the annual meeting of the American Economic Association (Kuznets 1955).

His hypothesis actually rested on little more than circumstantial evidence, as Kuznets himself admitted: "I am acutely conscious of the meagreness of reliable information presented. The paper is perhaps 5 percent empirical information and 95 percent speculation, some of it possibly tainted by wishful thinking" (1955, 26). Nevertheless, Kuznets's speech deservedly brought the issue of the relationship between growth and inequality center-stage in the academic debate. There followed a long and inconclusive debate, involving both economists and economic historians, and this often foundered on the rocks of the lack of suitable data.[28] With regard to Italy, Rossi, Toniolo, and Vecchi (2001) used an early version of the IHBD to show that there was no proof of the existence of a Kuznets curve, although they could not rule it out altogether.

The new GDP estimates of chapter 7 ("Income") and the Gini index of this chapter now enable us to provide a clear, concrete answer: there is no trace of a Kuznets curve in Italy, at least with regard to its postunification history of over 150 years. As Figure 8.5 shows, Italian economic growth in the long run

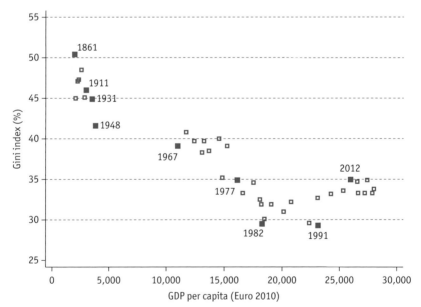

Figure 8.5 AVERAGE INCOME AND INEQUALITY, 1861–2012. The figure shows the trend in income inequality (vertical axis) with changes in per-capita GDP (horizontal axis). Each small square in the graph refers to a year. What emerges is a negative trend (the higher the income, the lower the inequality up to the early 1990s); the last two decades have seen the opposite case: the higher the income, the greater the inequality.

[28] See Brenner, Kaelble, and Thomas (1991), Brandolini (1997), and Kanbur (2000).

has been accompanied by a reduction in the Gini income distribution index, and there is no trace of the initial upward stage envisaged in the Kuznets curve: on average, throughout the period, for every percentage increase in GDP there has been a *decrease* in inequality of 0.16 percent. However, Figure 8.5 does show a clear inverse trend in the final stage of the development process—about 150 years after Italy's unification. After the plateau of the 1980s, what we see is a distinctly new feature in Italian history: income inequality increases parallel with per-capita GDP—a figure of 0.5 percent for every 1 percent of GDP. The paradigm of "the richer, the more equal" has made a U-turn.

7 Economic Growth Is Not the Same for Everybody

If the product of economic growth is not distributed with fairness and does not reach the poorest segment of the population, then that growth is of poor quality— at least with regard to personal wellbeing. In this section we make use of the available data for households in order to better understand the extent to which Italian economic growth has been favorable to the poorest segment of the population.

The literature offers various definitions of "pro–poor growth" (Son 2004; 2007; Ravallion 2004). Here, we shall limit ourselves to using a relatively simple analytical tool called the "growth incidence curve" (Ravallion and Chen 2003). This curve plots the trend in the average growth rate for income over a certain period of time for each *percentile* of the income distribution. Let's look at what the term "percentile" means: let us say we consider a year of reference, such as 2010, and sort in ascending order all the individuals of the population on the basis of their per-capita income (it is a matter of lining up, metaphorically speaking, about 60 million people, from the poorest to the richest). Once the population has been sorted in this way, we single out the person who has an income such that only 1 percent of the population earns a lower income: the income of this person, barely 976 euros a year, is called the first percentile. We can repeat this exercise by asking which person is in the second, third, or fifth percentile, up to the hundredth percentile, corresponding to the annual income earned by the richest individual in the population.

At this point, the interpretation of the curve put forward by Ravallion and Chen should be clear: if growth has been favorable to the poor, the average growth rates of incomes relative to the lowest percentiles of the distribution will be higher than the growth rates of the highest percentiles, and the curve will have a downward trend. We will have the exact opposite when growth is skewed in favor of the richest individuals; in this case, the curve will have an upward trend. Intermediate situations are obviously possible, where the curve goes up in some intervals and then goes down in others, showing that certain sections of the population—not necessarily the richest or poorest—have benefited the most from economic growth.

Figure 8.6 compares the growth incidence curves concerning four subperiods of postunification Italy. The two upper graphs refer to the Liberal and Fascist periods, while the two lower graphs concern two subperiods of Republican Italy—the first from 1977 to the year before the exchange rate crisis of 1992, and the second from that crisis to our times. Unfortunately, the lack of individual data does not allow us to estimate the curves for the period of Italy's reconstruction and economic miracle. To facilitate reading the graphs, the horizontal broken line stands for the average growth rate of income for each subperiod. When the curve lies above this broken line, the percentile of the reference population enjoyed higher than average growth; vice versa, all points on the curve lying below the broken line show the percentiles that had lower than average growth.

At first glance, we immediately see a first fact to emerge from the graphs of Figure 8.6: the growth incidence curves are very different in the four subperiods. The "quality" of growth, that is, the way growth benefits the various segments of the population, varies throughout the country's history—and not always in favor of the poor. In the Liberal period, it appears reasonable to say that growth did not particularly favor either rich or poor. The incidence curve is an inverse U-shape: the income growth rate is higher than the average value only for incomes approximately between the twentieth and eightieth percentiles. It is, above all, the intermediate income groups who benefited from economic growth: this result is consistent with the data presented in Table 9.3 (chapter 9, "Poverty"), which show how, despite the substantial decrease in poverty in this period, the inequality component went against the tide and mitigated the beneficial effects of growth for the less privileged classes.

The situation changed radically in the Fascist period: the growth incidence curve—except for the final part—definitely shows an upward trend. The poorest half of the population did not gain anything from the modest growth—indeed, these people had clear losses. It is the richest households, and particularly the ones lying between the seventieth and eightieth percentiles, who obtained almost all the benefits from economic growth. This confirms the strongly imbalanced nature of the Fascist economy.

Toward the end of the 1970s and throughout the 1980s, economic growth showed its benevolent face, and it was the poor who benefited the most. The growth incidence curve has a definite downward trend and, not surprisingly, these were the years that saw a marked drop in the incidence of poverty. The quality of the impact of economic growth has, instead, seen an inverse trend in the last twenty years. The curve has an upward trend, and the lowest percentile has hardly benefited at all from the albeit modest growth in per-capita income. The trend is paradigmatic: the disposable income of the poor has increased very slowly; the middle class has remained fairly stable; while the income of the richest segment of the population—say, the richest 20 percent—has grown at a higher than average rate.

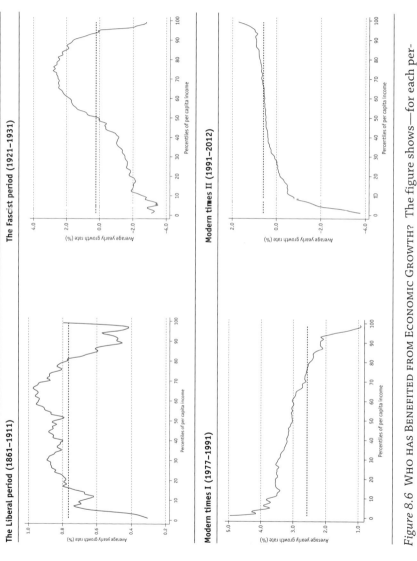

Figure 8.6 WHO HAS BENEFITED FROM ECONOMIC GROWTH? The figure shows—for each per-capita income percentile (horizontal axis)—the average annual growth rate (vertical axis) achieved in each of the sub-periods considered. The horizontal lines in each panel stand for the average growth rates of the period concerned.

8 The Geography of Inequality

Until recently we knew very little—perhaps nothing—about the development of income inequality at a *subnational* level over Italy's 150-year postunification history. Household budgets allow us to take a step forward in this direction, albeit limitedly to the period after World War II.[29] On the basis of the Doxa study that we referred to in paragraph 4, we estimated the inequality of income distribution of Italian regions in 1948.[30]

The figures given in Table 8.1 confirm the existence of a substantial north–south territorial gradient. In the embryonic stage of the Italian republic, the north and south of the country were distant not just in terms of average per-capita income—which was about 15 percent higher in the north—but also with regard to the inequality within each area, with a 4 percent higher Gini index, on average, in the southern regions. If we look at regional data, the differences are even more marked: between the more "unequal" region of Sardinia and the less "unequal" ones of Piedmont and Liguria, there is a difference of about 12 Gini index points. This is roughly the same difference between Sweden and the United Kingdom.

A second exercise consists of jointly analyzing the development of inequality and the average level of living conditions over time. Figure 8.7 compares the country's conditions in the aftermath of World War II—an economy in ruins and the reconstruction process just begun—with a snapshot of Italy in 2012, a century and a half after unification, in a mature phase of the economic development process. The figure has been constructed as follows. In both periods, each region is represented by a small circle whose size is proportional to its demographic weight. Each region is then associated with the average income level per inhabitant (measured along the horizontal axis) and the Gini index (vertical axis). By bringing together both snapshots of the country, the 1948 and 2012 ones, within the same graph, we obtain a sort of "race" with the starting line (represented on the left-hand side of the graph, above the label 1948) and the finishing line (on the right-hand side, under the label 2012).

It is a "race" that saw a clear progress in average incomes in *all* the regions, but this progress appears even more evident in the central-northern regions

---

[29] The statistical method applied to the household budgets contained in the DHBI enables us to produce estimates at a *national* level and thus not suitable for obtaining estimates for regions at a subnational level. In addition to this, inequality indices are notoriously fragile and are particularly sensitive to flaws in the base data (Cowell and Victoria-Feser 1996).

[30] This operation had already been attempted by Kuznets (1963) specifically to corroborate his hypothesis on the relationship between growth and inequality, discussed in section 5. With regard to Kuznets's elaborations, we introduced some concrete improvements: a) the inequality estimates were carried out on per-capita incomes instead of household ones; b) the data were corrected by means of the spatial indexes presented in chapter 14 ("The Cost of Living"), and c) inequality was estimated parametrically (see the under Figure 8.2 in the Appendix–Sources and Methods).

Box 5 **Who Pays the Bill for the Economic Crises?**

The impact of economic crises on households' living conditions is a poorly explored aspect in the economic literature. The economists have, of course, quantified the effects of crises and recessions on the main macroeconomic indicators (the list is a long one and includes GDP, obviously, but also employment, prices, household consumption, credit access, etc.), but rarely have they looked into the distribution of costs associated with a crisis (Atkinson and Morelli 2011): which segments of the population pay the highest price in the face of a systemic negative shock of great proportions like the Great Depression of 1929 and the Great Recession triggered by the financial crisis of 2007–2008 (Crafts and Fearon 2010)? There can be no "single" answer to this question at the empirical or theoretical level: every crisis has different specific causes and consequences depending on the country and historical period concerned. By adopting a research strategy similar to the one used by Jenkins et al. (2011), we can establish the year 2006 as a pre-Great Recession benchmark and then estimate its impact

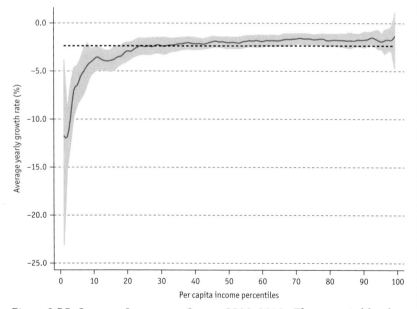

Figure 8.B5 GROWTH INCIDENCE CURVE, 2006–2010. The curve is like the one described in Figure 8.6. The shaded area shows the confidence interval or the breath of marginal error in the estimates. The interpretation is clear: the most penalised households in the Great Recession of 2008–09 were the poorest ones, belonging to the 10–20 lowest percentiles of the income distribution (horizontal axis).

on income distribution with regard to changes taking place in 2006–2012. The result has been plotted in the graph above: the bill for the crisis weighs more heavily on the poorest households—the ones belonging to the first decile of the income distribution. Nor must we overlook the fact that, excluding statistical errors, the only segment to record a positive growth in the four-year period considered is the richest 5 percent of the population.

than in the southern ones (the Italian *Mezzogiorno*). At the starting blocks, the regions appear almost on the same line, albeit in different "lanes" of inequality: the southern regions present a higher degree of inequality compared to the northern regions, which are richer, on average. Instead, at the end of the race, the gap with the southern regions is more marked, even in absolute terms. The level of inequality has decreased in almost all the regions (but not in Lombardy), but, once again, the lowest levels of inequality are found in the center-north of the country, the first to cross the finishing line.

To get a clearer idea of just how much regional differences count in Italy, we can refer to the exercise carried out by Brandolini and Torrini (2010), which compares the Italian situation with those of Germany and Spain, two countries characterized by significant regional differences.[31] The regions of each country are grouped into two distinct geographical areas: a more developed one (the center-north in Italy) and a less developed one (Italy's *Mezzogiorno*). Consider an inequality index that can be broken down into a component that measures inequality *within* the areas and a component measuring the inequality *between* the areas: the former term indicates the level of inequality that would be observed if average income were the same in both areas (in this case, the inequality observed would only be due to the fact that there are income differences within each area); the second term instead represents the level of inequality that would be recorded if disparities within each area were eliminated (that is, if all the inhabitants in the same area had the same income), in which case the only source of inequality would be attributed to differences between average incomes of the two areas. Estimates of the two components for Italy confirm the importance of the gap in average income between the rich regions and poor regions: if this gap could be eliminated, with other conditions being equal, then inequality at the national level would decrease by 18 percent. The same operation carried out in Spain or Germany would lead to a decrease in inequality of 5 and 3 percent, respectively. This means that the income distribution within the Italian areas is about 6 times more unequal than what is found in Germany, and 3.5 times what is observed in Spain.

---

[31] Owing to a lack of information for Germany and Spain, the comparison was made on the basis of nominal incomes and not real incomes.

Table 8.1 **Rich and equal regions, poor and unequal regions, Italy 1948**

Regions (ranked according to the Gini index)	Population	Average real annual income per head	Average real income per head	Gini index
	(%)	(euro 2010)	(Italia = 100)	(%)
Sardinia	2.7	2377	92	44.4
Lucania e Calabria	5.7	2294	89	42.7
Sicily	9.5	2312	90	41.3
Emilia	7.5	2681	104	40.5
Campania	9.2	2371	92	39.0
Puglia	6.8	2306	89	38.4
Veneto e Venezia Tridentina	12.3	2651	103	38.3
Lazio	7.0	2471	96	37.6
Tuscany	6.6	2308	90	35.0
Lombardy	13.8	2930	114	34.0
Abruzzi and Molise	3.6	1924	75	33.5
Marche and Umbria	4.6	1701	66	32.7
Piedmont and Liguria	10.8	3570	138	32.6
North-West	24.6	3211	125	34.0
North-East	19.8	2662	103	39.1
Center	21.7	2170	84	34.7
South	21.7	2330	90	39.4
Sicily and Sardinia	12.2	2326	90	37.9
Center-North	66.2	2705	105	36.1
South-Islands	33.8	2329	90	40.2
Italy	100.0	2578	100	37.4

Source: Our processing of Doxa data (1948).

Even the concentration of incomes within each area is important: if the inequality recorded in the less developed areas were the same as the one found in the more advanced regions, the overall inequality index would fall by 7 percent in Italy and by 5 percent in Spain, while it would increase slightly in Germany (where the more backward eastern *Länder* are the less unequal ones—a likely legacy of the planned economy of their past). In short, if income level and distribution in the poor regions were to match those of the rich regions, total inequality would drop by 25 percent (the sum of the two components discussed above)

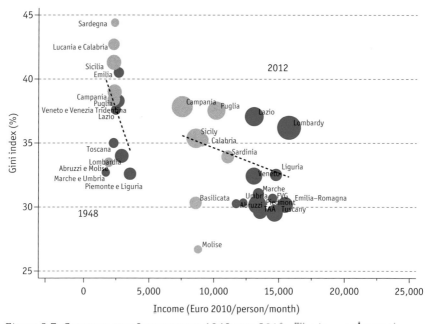

Figure 8.7 GROWTH AND INEQUALITY, 1948 AND 2012. The figure shows the relationship between real income per head (horizontal axis) and the Gini index (vertical axis) at the regional level for the years 1948 and 2010. Each region is represented by a circle in proportion to its population. The regions in the center-north of the country are represented by dark blue circles while the southern regions and islands (Sicily and Sardinia) by light blue ones.

in Italy and by 9 percent in Spain, while it would remain unchanged in Germany. On the whole, these figures show that the magnitude of the regional differences in Italy with regard to inequality is considerably greater than those seen in the other countries considered.

9 The Country of Miracles

Scenes from films like *La Dolce Vita* by Federico Fellini or *Il Sorpasso* (The Easy Life) by Dino Risi, and many other cinematographic masterpieces of "neorealism" and "Italian-style comedy", have managed to vividly and immortally portray the years of the Italian "economic miracle" (Box 6) to audiences all over the world. This short period spanning the late 1950s and early 1960s dragged Italy toward wealth and wellbeing, turning it into one of the most industrialized and economically developed countries in the world.

However, there is a second, longer-term "miracle" that the country experienced and that our estimates enable us to pinpoint: Italy's modern economic development combined growth with greater equity in income distribution. On

Box 6 Of Miracles and Overtakings

The Easy Life is the title under which the Italian film *Il Sorpasso* (literally, "The Overtaking") came out in the United States. Directed by Dino Risi and starring Vittorio Gassman and Jean-Louis Trintignant, this is a precursor "road movie" whose title and story inspired Dennis Hopper and Peter Fonda when they wrote the screenplay for *Easy Rider*. In a similar vein to the famous American masterpiece, Risi's film tells the story of a road trip in a sports car in early 1960s Italy. The characters are Bruno Cortona (Vittorio Gassman) and Roberto Mariani (Jean-Louis Trintignant). Bruno is brash and crass, the image of an unscrupulous Italy living by its wits, while Roberto is shy and an introvert, a projection of the values of the country's productive lower middle classes. The dialogue between the two illustrates the contradictions of a country experiencing the rapid transformations of an economic boom that is well portrayed through the places, people, and situations encountered during the trip. The adventure ends in tragedy in the final sequence when Bruno is egged on by Roberto to overtake yet another vehicle. The car swerves out of control and falls from a cliff. While Bruno gets thrown out of the vehicle and survives, Roberto dies trapped in the wreckage. It is a masterfully symbolic grand finale that lends itself to various interpretations, including a sort of omen on the fragility of the emerging society of wellbeing in Italy.

Figure 8.B6 IL SORPASSO *(1962)* An image from Dino Risi's film *Il sorpasso* (1962) with Vittorio Gassman (right) and Jean-Louis Trintignant (left).

average, over the 150 years of the country's postunification history, the Gini index has decreased by one percentage point every three years. This is by no means a foregone conclusion and makes the country's economic history a very interesting case study for the scientific community. While in the United Kingdom and United States, countries for which we have the best historical reconstructions of income distribution, modernization came about at the cost of greater inequality (at least in the early stages of the process), this is not the case with Italy.

The data on the history of income distribution that have been reconstructed in this chapter show that the Italy's economic growth benefited the working classes in particular: the average income of the poorest decile of the population increased tenfold compared to the sixfold increase of the richest decile. The shift from an essentially agricultural economy, the industrialization process, full participation in the "first globalization," and the final industrial takeoff during the economic miracle years were all accompanied by a decrease in income inequality within the country, at least for the first 130 years of its postunification history. Of course, behind this overall national figure lie broad and persistent regional differences—but the metric of inequality does not seem to be the most significant dividing factor between the north and south of the country.

These positive notes are in stark contrast with the data concerning the last two decades, which are a watershed: as in many other advanced economies, inequality is on the rise again. The scale of this increase is perhaps less alarming than what is seen in other advanced countries (Atkinson 2015; Brandolini 2009), but it is still significant, and with a stagnant economy it negatively affects poverty indicators and households' economic vulnerability—as described in chapters 9 and 11. As Atkinson said when commenting on the sharp rise in inequality in the United Kingdom during the Thatcher years and in the United States under Reagan, "changes in the personal distribution (of income) are large enough to affect our view of aggregate economic performance" (1997, 300). It is still too early to ascertain whether this change will become a lasting inverse trend or if the increase in inequality is destined to peter out with the longed-for end of the critical phase of the crisis. The view ahead is still too short for us to understand what awaits us after the "overtaking".

Appendix—Sources and Methods

This appendix is for readers who wish to consult the sources used and to get further insights into the analytical methods employed. The information is organized in the order of appearance of the graphs and tables in the chapter.

Box 2 Top Income The data used are the ones available in *The World Top Incomes Database*, http://g-mond.parisschoolofeconomics.eu/topincomes (version April 2012).

Figure 8.2 The Gini Index The Gini index estimate is based on three separate types of data associated with three distinct historical periods. For the period concerning Liberal Italy and Fascist Italy, we used the IHBD, described in detail in chapter 13: these figures are *not* of the same quality as modern microdata because they derive from studies that did not have a probability sampling scheme. The information on the period 1948–1975 is available in the form of data grouped into income classes: although individual data are not available, the information comes from probability samples and lends itself to standard analytical techniques. Finally, modern microdata from the Bank of Italy were used for the period 1977–2012.

Each one of the aforesaid three types called for a specific statistical treatment. The non–sample based microdata contained in the IHBD were probably the most difficult to deal with. However much the poststratification technique described in the chapter can correct distortions caused by the nonrandom selection of household budgets, the adjustments are, in any case, incomplete and imperfect. Similarly, the data in the tables have a drawback in the lack of information on income variability within income classes (Kakwani 1976; Cowell and Metha 1982).

In order to estimate inequality indicators on the basis of such heterogeneous data, we decided to *parametrically* estimate individual income distribution. This approach has two advantages. Firstly, it safeguards us from the pitfalls of nineteenth-century data derived from incomplete sources or from distortions that cannot be corrected by poststratification. Secondly, it allows us to compare the pre-1948 estimates (based on the IHBD) with those of the period 1948–1975— the latter also estimated with a parametric method because they are available only in the form of grouped data. The same parametric estimation method was applied to the modern sample–based microdata, even if the high quality of this information enables other techniques to be used. For recent years, the differences between parametric and nonparametric estimates are, in any case, negligible.

The parametric curve used is the generalized Beta type-2 distribution (Bordley, McDonald, and Mantrala 1996; Jenkins 2009), characterized by four parameters and thus sufficiently flexible for our purposes:

$$f(x) = \frac{a x^{ap-1}}{b^{ap} B(p,q)[1+(x/b)^a]^{p+q}}$$

where a, b, p, and q are positive parameters, $B(p, q) = \Gamma(p)\Gamma(q)/\Gamma(p+q)$ is the Beta function and $\Gamma(\cdot)$ is the Gamma function. The formula used in order to estimate the Gini index is contained in McDonald (1984). The estimate used a Stata routine written by Stephen Jenkins, to whom go our thanks for sharing it with us.

Box 5 Inequality Extraction Ratio Potential inequality, that is, the maximum level of income inequality that an economic and social system can sustain in the long run without compromising the system's survival has been calculated as follows. In the equation below, N stands for the total population and ε is the segment of the population to which the country's elite belong. The value of ε is arbitrarily established as 0.001. If the average income of the population is μ, then the maximum average income that the *elite* y_h can appropriate without compromising the survival of the other members of the community is:

$$y_h = \frac{\mu N - sN(1-\varepsilon)}{\varepsilon N}$$

where s stands for the average income guaranteeing a mere subsistence to the $N(1-\varepsilon)$ individuals not belonging to the country's elite. The above equation is the basis for calculating the potential Gini index (Milanovic et al. 2011). Suppose that the overall income of the elite, $y_h \varepsilon N$, is uniformly distributed among all the members of the elite; the same condition must hold for all those living at sub-sistence level, whose income cannot, by construction, be higher or lower than s. The potential Gini index is thus:

$$G^* = \frac{1}{\mu}(y_h - S)\varepsilon(1-\varepsilon) = \frac{\alpha - 1}{\alpha}(1-\varepsilon)$$

where $\alpha = \mu/s$ is average income expressed as a multiple of subsistence income. Unlike Milanovic et al. (2011), we were able to estimate the value of α without needing to exogenously assume it. The estimate of average income μ is easily obtained from each of the statistical sources available for the period 1861–2012. With regard to subsistence income s, we used the estimates of the extreme poverty line PL_{alim} illustrated in chapter 9. The estimate of the potential Gini index for year t is thus:

$$G_t^* = \frac{\hat{y}_t / PL_{alim}(t)^{-1}}{\hat{y}_t / PL_{alim}(t)} \times (1 - 0.001)$$

9

Poverty

WITH NICOLA AMENDOLA AND FERNANDO SALSANO

1 Poverty Is (Not) a Problem That Concerns Us

British Prime Minister Winston Churchill once said, "The inherent vice of capitalism is the unequal sharing of blessings. The inherent virtue of Socialism is the equal sharing of miseries" (Speech in the House of Commons, October 22, 1945). This quotation reflects not only the ideological stance of Churchill, a champion of British liberal conservatism and a proud opponent of the socialist model, but also a widespread interpretation of the links among growth, inequality, and poverty. The most effective weapon to fight poverty is economic growth; if the price we have to pay is an increase in social inequalities, then so be it.

The modern economic theory of growth has more than one point in common with this general view. The standard model (Solow 1956), found in all economics textbooks, simply assumes that growth and distribution are independent phenomena—or, rather, it is not concerned with income distribution and deletes that factor from the analytical picture.[1] No sooner do we leave the realm of economic theory than we realize that the economic growth process is *not* neutral with regard to income distribution. That is to say, it does not involve the citizens of a country in the same measure. History teaches us that growth, especially long-term growth as discussed in this chapter, is a series of deep changes concerning the foundations and structure of society. The interaction between inequality and growth radically characterizes this process.

The latter aspect, as we discuss in chapter 10 ("Wealth"), was taken up by the French economist Thomas Piketty. Piketty gave historical depth and perspective to his arguments, and came to an even more dramatic conclusion: not only are

---

[1] We are referring to personal income distribution and not to the distribution between factors of production, i.e., between labor and capital. The most recent theory of endogenous growth, which starts from the standard model for an in-depth study of the role of technical progress in the dynamics of accumulation, does not make any novel contribution in this regard.

growth and inequality connected to one another, but the forces acting in depth in the capitalist system are such to render the system itself unstable because of a persisting increase in the gap between the "rich" (the owners of capital) and the "non-rich" (the owners of labor). The fact that capital tends to be rewarded at a higher rate than the rate of growth of the economy lies at the heart of this growing divide and of the intrinsic instability of the capitalist economic system.

Hence, if we wish to consider a long-term historical view, our theoretical and analytical edifice must also take into account income distribution or, if you prefer, inequality. Inequality is an inconvenient aspect that complicates the nature of the link between growth and poverty. If the economic development process is accompanied by an increase in inequality, this may prevent the benefits of growth reaching the fringes of the population or may even worsen the conditions of life of less affluent households. The poverty and social exclusion indicators could then remain the same or even worsen. In other words, the idea that greater growth means less absolute poverty may find an obstacle in the dynamics of inequality (Bourguignon, Ferreira, and Lustig 2005). On closer examination, Churchill's argument reveals all its weaknesses.

If the link between growth, inequality, and poverty takes on the features of an analytically complex and historically determined relation, what is crucial then is to consider the secular history of poverty in Italy alongside the reconstruction of the long-term dynamics of gross domestic product (GDP) and of inequality, already dealt with in chapters 7 ("Income") and 8 ("Inequality") of this book. This is, essentially, the aim of this chapter. It is a rather ambitious aim, which obliges us to analyze the matter through the eyes of the quantitative economist and the historian. The economist's eyes are necessary in order to deal with difficulties at the theoretical and empirical levels, linked to measuring absolute poverty over such a long historical period. These difficulties call for data and methods which are not currently available for most countries. The historian's eyes are essential in order to give a historical dimension to the very concept of poverty—to understand not only how it has developed but also how the perception of poverty has changed over time on the part of the Italians and their governing classes. In some respects, this reconstruction is surprising and shows how, until fairly recently, a lack of interest has prevailed—mainly on the part of institutions—with regard to the poverty of the Italians, almost as if the issue does not really concern them. The estimates contained in this chapter offer a different interpretation and also a less optimistic one, unfortunately. While it is true that poverty has decreased drastically, especially after World War II, it is also true that the last twenty years have seen a clear inversion of this trend. The growth-inequality-poverty nexus now looks like a negative spiral. The low growth rate has meant greater inequality and a considerable increase in absolute poverty, now affecting a tenth of the population. Poverty has once more become a problem that concerns us.

2 The "Social Question" in the Liberal Period

The idea that it may be useful to actually count the number of individuals living in poverty has only recently been considered in Italy, in both political and scientific circles. For a long time the governing classes and scientific community did not feel the need to accurately define the condition of poverty: the prevailing concept in the liberal period, over and beyond the ideological connotations, consisted of a *qualitative* judgment based on the direct observation of society through descriptive tools. Hence, politicians, scholars, institutions, and unions did not feel the need to promote surveys to measure the phenomenon.

The principles of classical liberalism, shared by the dominant culture, essentially involved a disengagement of the state in the field of social policymaking. Charity work was considered a private affair, deriving from the individual conscience. According to this view, the institution of any form of "legal charity" would "dry up" the very sources of charity and encourage forms of social parasitism. The main cause of poverty, for centuries identified with the poor's inclination to laziness, would end up being legitimized by public support. The state's intervention was only justified if poverty were to lead to dangerous conflict for the public order and for social stability (Geremek 1986; Woolf 1988; Zamagni 2000). Accordingly, in the first two decades of postunification Italy, the state limited its actions to a mere formal control of the activities conducted by charity institutes and played a "subsidiary" role with regard to the spontaneous initiatives of civil society, such as the mutual assistance societies and the *Opere Pie* (Silei 2003), discussed in chapters 3 ("Health") and 11 ("Vulnerability").

Interest in poverty increased when the emergence of a "social question" drove part of the governing class toward a conservative reformism that aimed to improve the population's living conditions before any destabilizing social conflict could emerge. This was stressed for example by Pasquale Villari (1827–1917): "raising up the lower classes" from "a condition that is shameful for a civilized people [had become] a supreme duty in the interest of rich and poor," if a revolution of the "multitudes," with its unpredictable consequences, was to be avoided (Villari 1885, 430–431).

Starting from the 1880s, the broadening of responsibilities attributed to the state led to greater public commitment also with regard to social policymaking. To improve the population's living conditions, it first became necessary to know them. The governing class of the Kingdom of Italy, over and beyond the literary representations, mostly had no idea of the various social realities present in the country. To overcome this gap between the "legal country" and "real country," the state adopted the instrument of parliamentary enquiries that, starting from field surveys conducted all over the country, had to provide an overall picture of the Italian economic and social structure. Chapter 13 ("Household Budgets") devotes ample space to the main enquiries carried out in liberal-period Italy, from the

Notizie ("News") of 1878–79 to the Faina Enquiry, which ended its print run in 1911. There is thus no need to repeat things here: suffice to recall that none of the inquiries aimed to provide a definition of the living conditions of the "less affluent classes," nor to estimate the number of people actually in poverty conditions.

In Italy, the "Anglo-Saxon" model of social investigation, geared to defining and measuring the poverty phenomenon, was largely ignored by the scientific community.[2] After examining a selection of articles published in some of the most important journals of the times (*Giornale degli economisti, Nuova Antologia, La Riforma Sociale, Annali di statistica*), we find that attention to the "social question" did *not* lead to any search for a method for defining and measuring the poor.[3]

The view that the poverty condition was an indirect datum, deduced from the presence of manifestations typically linked to the phenomenon, also characterized the activity of institutions charged with producing official statistics. The General Statistics Division, entrusted with "taking a snapshot of the Italian population in its territorial distribution, in its demographic elements and in its production activities" (Rondini 2003, 40), did not produce significant results with respect to the measurement of poverty, nor did it develop a systematic reflection on the requirements for establishing whether a part of the population belonged to the ranks of the "poor."

The indeterminateness of the concept of poverty that emerged from the great parliamentary inquiries and from the early official statistics was matched by the uncertainty of defining the status of being poor in the legal system. In 1862 the first law on charity work had used the generic term "less affluent classes" to indicate the beneficiaries of welfare actions. The use of this term enabled philanthropic institutions, mostly ecclesiastic ones, to act with ample discretion without going into the details of a doctrinal distinction between "poverty" and "indigence" that identified poverty as an intermediate condition between straitened circumstances and out-and-out destitution (De Gérando 1867).[4]

---

[2] The lack of any estimates on poverty was not just an Italian peculiarity. Even in other Western countries the surveys and studies carried out tended to identify poverty only indirectly by observing the typical manifestations of indigence such as living in overcrowded dwellings or not consuming enough food and other essential goods. The only country to arrive at devising a method for establishing the number of poor in a given population was Britain. This was not an institutional initiative, however, but the product of research carried out independently by scholars such as Charles Booth and Seebohm Rowntree. See A'Hearn, Amendola, and Vecchi (2016).

[3] On the other hand, there is no lack of attempts to devise new study tracks starting from the problem of poverty. For example, in the tradition of "scientific racism" and the Lombrosian studies, Alfredo Niceforo promoted the development of an *anthropology of the poor classes* in order to find a link between levels of wellbeing and the physical and physiological characteristics of individuals (Niceforo 1906).

[4] The 1890 law on the Opere Pie introduced the status of "poor" as an individual benefiting from welfare activities. However, the adoption of the more explicit concept of "poor" instead of the term "nonaffluent classes" did not match the adoption of any precise criteria for establishing the condition of poverty, despite the fact that the implementing regulation of the law had envisaged the drafting of "lists of poor people beneficiaries" (Law no.6972 of 17 July 1890).

According to the dominant juridical culture in the liberal period, the state's welfare actions were to be distinguished depending on the level of indigence of the beneficiaries. The poor who could not emancipate from their own condition had to limit their own "pretensions" and adapt them to the means they had in order to satisfy their needs (Löning 1892, 563). If, instead, they could not get out of the condition of indigence without external help, then philanthropic assistance was encouraged to avoid the spreading of "pauperism," which was considered dangerous for social stability and an obstacle to economic development (Balocchi 1967, 40).

A first codification of the status of the poor and its connection with the enjoyment of certain rights appeared in the Italian legal system only in 1906, when municipal authorities were given the task of identifying the poor who had a right to free healthcare. In order to enable a more rational organization of medical and obstetric municipal doctors, the municipal council was now obliged to compile an annual "list of the poor" residing in the municipality (Royal Decree of 19 July 1906 no. 466).[5] The discretion granted to local authorities and the differences in criteria adopted for drafting the lists make this source useless today for measuring the historical incidence of poverty in Italy. The legal framework of the welfare and philanthropic activities in liberal-period Italy confirm, on the whole, the lack of a systematic and defined view of the poverty phenomenon already seen in scientific debate and in the role played by institutions.

Indigence as a fault, the disincentive to sloth, and maintenance of the establishment are the main keys for interpreting the phenomenon of poverty shared by the dominant culture of the liberal period. Given these premises, the absence of an interest for a *quantitative* assessment of poverty appears to be a completely rational choice: in liberal-period Italy, the fight against poverty was far from being a tool for promoting social wellbeing, but rather a matter of public order and security, a competence of the Ministry of the Interior.

3 Fascism and the Taboo of Poverty

The Fascist regime maintained an ambivalent attitude toward poverty. The importance accorded to social policies in order to build a "new state" was not matched by any attempt to remove the problem of poverty from the collective imagination. In a context dominated by the political need to present the country's main problems as nearly solved, the incentive to devise scientific methods for defining and estimating poverty decreased. At the same time, the need

---

[5] In actual fact, the municipal authorities had been entrusted with the task of providing for free medical care for citizens as far back as 1865, and these people were put on specific lists called "lists of the poor." In most cases, however, the indication was ignored (Balocchi 1967, 54–55).

to handle and to keep the varied galaxy of welfare institutions under control favored the development of surveys on the number of beneficiaries of social policies.

In the language of the propaganda of the day, one of the mainstays of social policy was overcoming an older concept of charity, to be replaced with the principle of "human, national and Fascist solidarity" as the foundation of a welfare and care activity that was not "humiliating" but "educational" with regard to the working masses. With the creation of many state and state-controlled bodies for the protection of specific categories of people, there was also the progressive construction of a system of social insurance and security (Bertini 2001, 177–313).[6] The beneficiaries of the actions provided by these bodies were mainly employed workers, who were certainly not rich but not too badly off either, and who obtained benefits on payment of statutory contributions. The right to benefit from these new forms of social security stemmed more from working activity and participating in production than from citizenship. Those who still depended on the occasional donations of charity institutions were the people excluded from the process of formation of the Fascist "new man." These were the unemployed, the irregulars, seasonal or temporary workers, beggars, and all those belonging to the social group traditionally identified with the condition of "indigence."

In the years between 1925 and 1932, the newly created National Institute of Statistics, Istat, started up the first surveys explicitly aimed at determining the "number of poor" present in the Kingdom (Istat 1933, 96–100). Although an important novelty, this attempt was in fact a partial and hardly significant effort. The dissimilarity of the criteria adopted for drafting the lists meant that municipal authorities followed criteria that were inconsistently restrictive in assessing the conditions of poverty and in updating these lists. In particular, the size of these lists depended on the actual possibility of providing services that those enrolled in the lists were entitled to, starting with healthcare. Geographical parts of the country that had more resources could, in all likelihood, register a greater number of people in the lists. These survey operations were quickly suspended: the self-representation of the Fascist regime as a project of moral, political, and economic renewal of the "Italic stock" could not coexist with the spreading of news on the presence of about four million Italians registered in the lists of the poor.

At the same time, there was a boost in the so-called fight against beggary—something that had already been forbidden by the Zanardelli code in 1889 and

---

[6] In chapter 3 ("Health") we discussed the insurance schemes against unemployment, workplace accidents, old age and certain diseases—particularly malaria and tuberculosis—which involved a growing number of citizens and acted as a consensus-gathering tool, but also as a way to control the population (Corner 2002, 382–405).

was intolerable for the image of Fascist Italy, so it had to be dealt with from a penal standpoint. The Consolidation Act for laws of public security, besides establishing the prohibition of begging in public places, gave prefects the power to order a compulsory stay in charity institutions for those people who were "incapable of any productive work and who do not have the means of sustenance, nor relatives bound by law to provide alimony and in the condition to do so" (Royal Decree no. 773 of 16 June 1931). Determining the status of being poor was once again delegated to the discretion of an institution with mainly social control aims, without defining any kind of objective criteria to standardize decision-making in this regard.

The indeterminateness of poverty status was confirmed in 1937 by a law establishing the reorganization of the welfare sector that set up municipal assistance agencies (*enti comunali di assistenza* or ECA) to replace charity congregations. The action of the ECAs was geared to all individuals and households who found themselves in "conditions of particular necessity" (law no. 847 of 3 June 1937). Hence, a state of poverty—meant as the absolute lack of all the basics— was not required, but it was enough to be in a "state of need," that is, in a state of temporary impossibility to obtain the minimum necessary "to subsist according to one's social condition" or in a state "of particular necessity in a transitory circumstance."

Unlike the specific action carried out by municipal authorities, the ECA provided *generic assistance* to the poor in order to alleviate them in all possible ways and according to their needs and to the ECAs' financial means. Being registered in the ECA list did not represent an admission, as with the list of the poor, but a mere listing of people assisted or assistable in order to rationalize the management of financial resources and, perhaps, to conduct surveys on the number of households in a state of poverty or need. Enrollment did not create any juridical status of being poor and did not confer any right to the "assistable" individual, who had to be helped in case of need and not because of being on the list (Balocchi 1967, 74–78).[7]

In short, the history of the relationship between Fascism and poverty is characterized by three interacting elements: (1) the increase in the intensity and spheres of state intervention in social policymaking; (2) the creation of a social protection system that tended to safeguard workers, in particular, leaving out the most needy segments of the population; and (3) the regime's tendency to not emphasize, if not to explicitly conceal, the existence of poverty. The tensions among these three points, although a departure from the attitude of indifference

---

[7] Given the indeterminateness of the requirements for registration, the limits of using the ECA lists as a statistical source for measuring poverty are evident: it is not clear whether "many people listed" means "much poverty" or, vice versa, of relative wellbeing of the territory able to assist a broader section of the needy population with greater means.

shown by liberal-period governments, did not enable the state to systematically gather information and data that could provide a complete picture of the extent and development of poverty throughout the country. Eight decades had passed since the country's unification, and official figures on the scale of poverty in the country were still lacking.

4 The Aftermath of World War II: The Poor Begin to be Counted

After World War II the taboo of poverty disappeared. Difficulties in procuring food, growing unemployment, and the material damage caused by the war put poverty squarely on the agenda not only in the daily life of the Italians but also in political debate. "Abolishing poverty" became a cross-party slogan (Rossi 1946; Vigorelli 1948).

Besides discussions on measures to face the emergencies and to lay foundations for the resumption of civilian life, the problem emerged regarding how to take a census of the number of the poor and the tools necessary to obtain reliable figures. During the war, Amintore Fanfani (1908-1999) had already drawn attention to the need to devise a methodology to "quantitatively and qualitatively identify" the poverty phenomenon (Pagani 1960, 23–24). In 1947, speaking in the Constituent Assembly, Luigi Einaudi stressed Italy's lack of "a plan corresponding to the British White Book to tell us how Italian citizens live, what their income is, in which social categories they are divided, how many of them have an income from zero to one hundred thousand lira, how many have an income from a hundred to one hundred and fifty thousand lira, etc." (Fiocco 2004, 97).

The appeals of eminent politicians did not immediately lead to a direct commitment of the state. The first surveys after the war were conducted by state-controlled organizations like the Administration for International Aid (*Amministrazione per gli aiuti internazionali*, AAI) or by private firms like Doxa, founded by Pier Paolo Luzzatto Fegiz (1900–1989).[8] The controversies over the validity of the data that followed the publication of these surveys (Rinauro 2002, 481–486) contributed to raising public awareness on the need for an official survey. The question of a better understanding of social reality also became one of the key themes of political debate (Fiocco 2004, 50–65).

---

[8] The AAI, set up in 1947 to handle the aid coming from the United Nations Relief and Rehabilitation Administration (UNRRA), resumed the surveys of individuals on the municipal lists of the poor, who had not been surveyed since 1932. Since no changes had been made to the way the lists were compiled, the survey had the same faults as the one conducted by Corrado Gini fifteen years earlier (AAI-Istat 1950). As regards the Doxa survey of 1948, it was dealt with extensively in chapter 8 ("Inequality").

A specific parliamentary committee, chaired by Ezio Vigorelli (1892–1964), was set up in 1952 to carry out an inquiry into poverty in Italy and into the means to combat it. The committee charged Istat with the task of carrying out a statistical survey of the living conditions of the population and a survey on the budgets of poor households in order to know and measure differences between the standards of living of various social strata. Poverty was quantified on the basis of the "standard of living," an undefined term at the conceptual level. The committee decided not to calculate an income threshold below which families would be classifies as poor (Braghin 1978). It opted, instead, for an eclectic solution by grading the standard of living into four levels (poor, needy, average, and high) and establishing three indicators: the situation of accommodation (number of people per room), the quality of food (frequency of consumption of meat, sugar, and wine—expensive goods at the time), and conditions of clothing and footwear (Camera dei Deputati 1953). Table 9.1 illustrates some of the main results of the survey.

The inquiry on poverty was a one-off experiment. Starting from the latter half of the 1950s, with the birth of the modern welfare system and the advent of the economic miracle, the poverty issue returned to the fringes of public debate

Table 9.1 **The enquiry on poverty in Italy, 1951–1952**

- 11.8% of the population (about 6.2 million people) live in conditions of extreme poverty.
- The incidence of poverty in the northern regions is 5.8% as against 50.2% for the south and 45.4% for Sicily and Sardinia.
- 85% of households classified as "poor" are in the south; 70% of the "needy" households are in the south.
- 38.2% of households do not consume meat; 28.7% do not consume wine.
- Half the Italian population consume less than a teaspoon (20 grams) of sugar a day.
- 24.4% of the people live in overcrowded dwellings (with over 2 people per room).

The *Enquiry on poverty* decided in October 1951 was the first institutional initiative geared to quantitatively assessing the scale of the phenomenon.

The over 4,000 pages presented the results of the enquiry—the figures, at last—and the general *Report* provided their interpretation. We have summarized some of the more significant figures on the left. Many others are available in the volumes of the enquiry. The data gathered were not used for policymaking to fight poverty. In the analysis of the means to combat poverty, the enquiry underlined the hodgepodge of the legislation and the poor efficiency in using financial resources. Lack of agreement among the various members of the committee prevented the drafting of a reform bill.

(Iorio 2001, 174–175). Italy was becoming a "developed" country, with a relatively modern society and an economic growth that was unexpected in many respects. In this context, poverty appeared to be a "residual" phenomenon destined to fade away as national income increased and the welfare state developed. The persistence of cases of poverty was considered a consequence of the broader issue of income distribution. The attention of political parties, trade unions, and scholars shifted to the theme of inequality, while "poverty" became an outmoded term (Sarpellon 1993, 301).[9]

Only in the latter half of the 1970s did the scientific community's attention, in particular through sociological studies, return to focus on poverty, also in relation to the effects of the oil crisis and the slowdown of the world economy. The first theoretical formulations on "unidimensional," "multidimensional," "objective," and "subjective" poverty, as well as the "new poverties," date back to this period (Guidicini 1991). At the same time, at the international level there was an increasing affirmation of the preference for the concept of "relative" poverty, in which the condition of poverty is linked to the trend in the population's average standard of living[10].

The first institutional estimate of poverty appeared in 1979 with the start of the study funded by the European Economic Community (EEC) within the experimental program "Action against Poverty." The results were published in 1982, edited by Giovanni Sarpellon, who led the group charged with collecting data for Italy. As Sarpellon himself stressed, the definition of poverty adopted by the Italian group was closely connected with the inequality concept: "[I]f, as it seems possible to state, poverty corresponds to the lower rung of the inequality ladder, we may ask at what level does inequality turn into poverty . . . Poverty begins where the distances from the center are such that contact is broken" (Sarpellon 1983, 41).

Given the clear decision in favor of relative poverty, the survey criterion adopted was the so-called *international standard of poverty line*, which classified as poor all those with an income 50 percent lower than the average income in the target country (Beckerman 1978). The indicator of wellbeing normally used at the international level, household disposable income, was indicated as the most suitable by the coordination group of the various national studies. In the Italian case, though, given the poor reliability of income data, it was decided to use the sample study on household consumption carried out by Istat (Sarpellon 1982). According to the results of the study, there were about five million people

---

[9] They mainly talked about *functional* inequality (i.e., about the distribution of the social product among wages, profits, and rent) and not about *personal* inequality, which we dealt with in chapter 8 ("Inequality").

[10] The technical aspects linked to the definition of relative poverty are dealt with in sections 5.1 and 5.2.

in relative poverty conditions in 1978, corresponding to 9 percent of the Italian population.

The figures of Sarpellon's study contributed to increasingly establish the idea that it was necessary to have an institutional action against poverty, if only to find out how far it was rooted in the Italian population. The opportunity to create a body to specifically deal with the phenomenon soon arrived, in 1983, when—within a general functional restructuring of the executive—the then Italian prime minister Bettino Craxi (1934–2000) set up a series of commissions to "check and update" the government's program. One of these commissions dealt with the poverty issue. The chair was entrusted to Ermanno Gorrieri (1920–2004), a leading exponent of the left faction of the Christian Democratic Party, which had long been active on the social policy front (Carattieri, Marchi, and Trionfini 2009, 589–599).

4.1 THE POVERTY COMMISSION

The Poverty Commission for investigating poverty was officially born on 31 January 1984 and saw the participation of statisticians, sociologists, and external consultants with various competencies. The main document drafted by the commission became known as the "Gorrieri Report" and dealt with various aspects of the issue, including the problem of a conceptual definition of the phenomenon and its measurement. Once again, they opted in favor of a definition of relative poverty.

According to the commission's calculations, there were over six million poor people—a finding in line with the EEC survey results. The publication of the Gorrieri Report was accompanied by lively reactions, creating problems within the government itself, which had promoted the survey in the first place. The report, which had become available in May 1985, was "frozen" for some months until it was actually published. During its official presentation, Craxi made sideline statements to the press that reshaped the scale of the problem and was ironic with regard to the commission's conclusions. According to Gorrieri's reconstruction: The journalists asked the prime minister (Craxi) whether he thought it possible that there was still poverty in the fifth industrial power of the world. He replied: "[W]hen I go around I see stores brimming with all sorts of good things, the restaurants crowded, people going on vacation abroad. . . . Well, who knows" (Carattieri, Marchi, and Trionfini 2009, 593n).

A long argument ensued that saw scholars and politicians taking sides on ideological rather than methodological lines in favor of or against the Gorrieri Report (Mioni 1986). The poverty taboo was still, evidently, quite strong. The main result of the whole debate was the decision not to renew the commission's funding and to suspend its activities. After a few months of respite and uncertainty, the work restarted under the chairmanship of Giovanni Sarpellon, who maintained the chair until 1993, when he was replaced by Pierre Carniti. In the meantime, the body's name was changed into the Commission of Investigation into Poverty and Marginalization (1990), without there being any new survey methodologies introduced. The quantitative estimate of poverty was only one of the many tasks of the commission, which was mainly involved in evaluating welfare policies.[11]

In 1996 the commission published the first reconstruction of the historical series of relative poverty indexes starting from 1980.[12] The report was a sort of taking stock of the commission's work on the eve of an important change in its functions. As of the following year it would be Istat's job, assisted by members of the commission, to estimate the scale of poverty in Italy. Every summer since 1997 Istat has issued a short press release outlining the essential features of poverty in Italy compared to the previous year.[13]

The Istat estimates are regularly studied and commented on by the Poverty Commission, which, since 2001, has taken on the title of Commission of Investigation on Social Exclusion (CIES). The Commission published an annual report on policies against poverty and social exclusion (*Rapporto sulle politiche contro la povertà e l'esclusione sociale*) in which the statistics on poverty are related to other socioeconomic indicators (such as job market trends) in order to assess the effects of social policies implemented by the institutions. The commission plays a consultative role and cannot create directives addressed to government bodies. The official production of studies and statistics on poverty and the measures proposed by the commission have not met with any favor at the institutional level, except for the experimentation of a minimum income for integration, which risks becoming an exercise carried on for its own sake.[14] The law setting up the CIES also envisaged a strong steering power of the state

[11] A few years after the publication of the Gorrieri Report, the National Council of the Economy and Employment (CNEL) entered the debate. The first CNEL report was published in 1993 with the title *Rapporto Cnel sulla distribuzione e redistribuzione del reddito in Italia*. The CNEL reports contain estimates of poverty rates for various segments of the population from 1981 to 1991, based on consumption (CNEL 1993; 1994; 1996; 1998; 2000; 2002).

[12] These data were published by the Commission of Investigation on Poverty and Marginalization in 1996. For the sake of continuity, the reconstruction maintained the same methodology used in the previous reports, but it broadened the traditional analysis by introducing two poverty lines obtained by increasing and decreasing the standard threshold by a fifth, and also a "quasi-absolute" evaluation based on a threshold kept constant in real terms at the 1980 value.

[13] From 1994 to 2001, Istat carried out an annual longitudinal study on the population's living conditions within a European project coordinated by Eurostat (European Community Household Panel, ECHP). In 2004 the survey was replaced by the European Union (EU) Statistics on Income and Living Conditions (EU-SILC). The data of the ECHP and the EU-SILC are used by Eurostat as a basis for disseminating the estimates of poverty risk in EU countries.

[14] The minimum income for integration is a support tool ranging from direct monetary transfers to employment or training schemes aimed at people at risk of economic exclusion (Negri and Saraceno 1996; Sacchi 2007).

in social policymaking, while the reform of Title V of the Italian Constitution (Const. law no. 3 of 18 October 2001) gave regional governments exclusive jurisdiction in these matters.

The ups and downs of the Poverty Commission confirm the impression that the "demand" for quantitative-statistical knowledge is still slack: this is an old bad habit, in light of what we have read in this section, which the country has not managed to eliminate. The consequences are self-evident and do not need further comments here: an "institutional" demand, slack in numbers and methods concerning poverty, results in a lack of incentives to produce more detailed information and develop new survey methodologies to the detriment of policymaking for combating poverty.

5 How Poverty Is Estimated

The reconstruction of institutional events connected to the measurement of poverty shows how difficult it is to actually estimate poverty—as much at the conceptual as the empirical level. This section thus aims to simplify the picture by guiding the reader not versed in the art through the maze of socioeconomic literature (to date, scholars still disagree on how poverty should be considered and measured) in order to help him or her emerge with suitable tools to interpret the Italian poverty estimates presented in the last part of this chapter (sections 7–10).

The measurement of poverty is based on three main ingredients. We need an indicator of wellbeing (such as household income or expenditure on consumption); a poverty line (i.e., the lowest income level below which an individual is considered "poor"); and a poverty index (a summary indicator enabling us to summarize the scale of the phenomenon: for example, the percentage of poor individuals out of the total population; or the income necessary, on average, for the poor to get out of their poverty conditions).

These three ingredients are shown in Figure 9.1. The curve indentifies the first ingredient, income distribution per head in a given year: by choosing an income level on the horizontal axis, the corresponding value on the curve indicates the percentage of individuals in the population who earn that level of income. The curve—estimated according to 2012 data of the Bank of Italy—has an asymmetric shape: its long tail on the right shows that there is a relatively low number of people who are very "rich," while most of the population earns closer to values of 10,000 euros per head per year.

The graph shows, in simplified form, the three ingredients necessary to estimate poverty: an indicator of economic wellbeing (individual income or expenditure), a poverty line, and a summary index measuring overall poverty.

The second ingredient, the poverty line (PL), is shown by the vertical line intersecting the horizontal axis at a determined level of income or

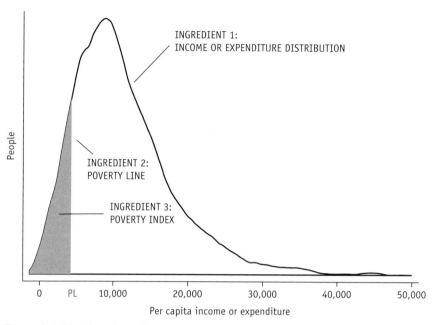

Figure 9.1 The three ingredients for measuring poverty

expenditure: individuals who earn an income lower than PL, or whose expenditure is less than PL, are classified as poor. We shall deal with how this line can be drawn a little further on (section 5.1); what must be stressed here is that identifying the threshold—the poverty line—is an essential premise for any measurement of poverty, absolute or relative poverty, that we wish to take into consideration.

As regards the third ingredient, the indicator of poverty, for our intents and purposes it is enough to observe that faced with a broad choice of indicators (Foster, Greer, and Thorbecke 1984; Zheng 1997), we shall use the simplest one—the *incidence of poverty*—corresponding to the percentage of individuals with an income lower than the poverty line. Geometrically, the incidence of poverty corresponds to the (blue) area to the left of the poverty line PL and below the individual income distribution curve.[15]

To measure poverty over the 150 years of Italy's postunification history, we first need to ask ourselves whether the three ingredients defined above are actually available. With regard to the first one, the indicator of wellbeing, the answer is "yes": the household budgets collected in the IHBD (chapter 13, "Household Budgets"), the Doxa survey, and the data provided by Istat and the Bank of Italy enable us to reconstruct the historical series, but the data also allow us to outline

---

[15] The total area under the income distribution curve is equal to 100. The gray area is thus a fraction of 100 and is interpreted as the percentage of poor people in the population.

the profile of poverty for the whole time period, precisely as we did in chapter 8 ("Inequality"). We have already talked about the third ingredient, the indicator of poverty: we shall use the incidence of poverty. The faults of this indicator are well known (Watts 1968; Sen 1976a), but it is a natural starting point and offers the advantage of simplicity of interpretation[16]. The second ingredient—the poverty line—is the more important and difficult challenge because it means facing and solving the underlying question which we recalled in the introductory section: What is poverty? Not only this, but in view of the long time frame we are dealing with, we must realize that the answer to this question may not always be the same: poverty takes on different features over time and is different now from what it used to be.

5.1 POVERTY IS NOT WHAT IT USED TO BE

To deal with the consequences of the accommodation problem afflicting the city of Rome right from when it was proclaimed the capital of the Kingdom of Italy, in the early 1930s the Fascist government started an experiment combining welfare and control of the population. The inhabitants of the city's illegal shacks, part of the people evicted from the historical center—the temporary workers, irregulars, and those excluded from the process of forming the Fascist "new man"—were all accommodated in "shelters" or in the peripheral suburban *borgate* (housing estates) being built in those years. Some of these, like the *borgata* Gordiani, were supposed to be a temporary solution with a view to moving these residents somewhere else later (Salsano 2010).

Twenty years later, as we can see in the Enquiry into Poverty (*Inchiesta sulla miseria*) of 1951–1952, the shacks of the *borgata* Gordiani were still standing:

> [T]housands of men live there . . .) in the worst conditions for living their physical and moral life . . . . Only the main street, Via dei Gordiani, is asphalted. Both sides of the street are uniformly lined with low shacks, creating a heavy and monotonously gray atmosphere. Not a tree in sight, nor a tuft of green. Every now and then, in the side streets, you see small square concrete buildings, a few meters long on each side: these are the 25 toilets built for a population of over 5 thousand people. These constructions, built in the utmost haste at a low budget, are deteriorated by use and by the elements: the walls are dirty and decayed, the window panes either missing or broken, the doors and windows disjointed; the roofs cannot stop the water

---

[16] The incidence of poverty does not take into account such things as the distance separating each poor individual from the poverty line: that is, it does not tell us *how* poor the poor actually are (Baldini and Toso 2004).

filtering down indoors, generating a ruinous dampness, made worse by the water rising from the floor—given the lack of any proper stone foundations—and which seeps in from the walls making everything damp: the household objects and bed linen. (authors' translation from Camera dei Deputati 1953, 106–107)

This long preamble, seemingly superfluous at the analytical level, is instead useful to understand the basic problem faced when trying to define the poverty line: the criterion adopted must grasp the progress made in the living conditions of the Italians over the country's history, but it must also identify new forms of poverty still present today, in the outlying areas of Rome as in many other cities and places in Italy. Today's poverty does not have the same features as yesterday's.

While there is broad consensus on the fact that the *notion* of poverty cannot be defined independently of the historical and social context of reference (Citro and Michael 1995), scholars, specialists, and institutions that deal with these issues in various ways instead tend to have their differences on the more specific question of *measuring* poverty. Some call for the need to estimate a measurement of *absolute poverty* while others favor the measurement of *relative poverty* (Foster 1998). This terminological choice well defines the problem, but it is inappropriate because it gives the idea that measuring absolute poverty is detached from the context people live in. This is untrue and misleading.

The *relative poverty line*, which we shall indicate with PL_r, is defined as a fraction of the average level of income of the target social group (Townsend 1962; Atkinson 1998):

$$PL_r = k\overline{Y}$$

where $\overline{Y}$ stands for the average income per head of the target group and k stands for the *share* of this income that the individuals must earn so as not to be classified as poor. The underlying idea is that the condition of poverty is like a notion of social exclusion, measured from the relative position of the poor person compared to the average condition of the population. For example, if average individual income is 20,000 Euros per year and $k = 50$ percent, the poverty line PL_r is 10,000 euros per year. As we can see, the criterion for measuring relative poverty is based on a direct link between the poverty line and the average resources available in the target society: this connection is made formally explicit in the algebraic relation linking PL_r to $\overline{Y}$.

The *absolute poverty line*, which we shall indicate as PL_a, is instead defined *regardless* of the average value of incomes of other individuals. Typically, this line is identified by the value of minimum resources necessary to purchase a set of goods and services considered "essential." It is often useful to assume that PL_a

Box 1 **Where Do the *Kids of Life* Live?**

The difficult living conditions the households of the *borgata* Gordiani had to put up with are now something of the past. The last remains of the *borgata* were knocked down in the early 1980s and the squalid shacks there live on only in some film sequences such as in *Accattone* (1961), where Pier Paolo Pasolini—Italian film director, poet, and writer, among the most important of the twentieth century—recounts the adventures of the *ragazzi di vita* (literally "boys of life", meaning "hustlers") born and raised there. The boys of life have not disappeared, however. Some have probably escaped the condition of the urban subproletariat, but others today live in the Roman suburbs of Tor Bella Monaca, Spinaceto, and Laurentino 38. Although these neighborhoods have running water, electricity, and sanitation in every home, they still have conditions that go to define poverty today. An effective and well-constructed measure of poverty has the arduous task of grasping the features that the first and second picture below have in common, but without overlooking the elements of undoubted progress that characterized the urban reclaiming schemes implemented in Rome in the 1970s and 1980s.

Figure 9.B1a Pier Paolo Pasolini (1922–1975) on the Set. The picture shows Pasolini on the set of his film *Accattone* (1961) while strolling along the mud roads of Rome's Gordiani neighborhood.

Figure 9.B1b ET IN TERRA PAX (2010). The photograph, taken in Rome's Corviale neighborhood, shows a scene of the film *Et in terra pax*, shot in 2010, which tells stories of crime and violence in today's outlying Roman suburbs.

derives from the sum of two components: the cost of a basket of *foodstuffs* and the cost of a set of *nonfood* goods and services:

$$PL_a = PL_f + PL_{nf}$$

The food component (PL_f) can be thought of as a measure of the minimum cost of a food basket that can satisfy the average calorie needs of individuals, bearing in mind their lifestyle.[17] The nonfood component (PL_{nf}) instead includes expenditure on clothing, accommodation, healthcare, and other things related to our basic needs. The definition of PL_a clearly shows that the absolute poverty measurement criterion does not directly depend on the population's average standard of living: unlike with PL_r, changes in average income $\bar{Y}$ do not have any direct impact on the absolute poverty line PL_a.

5.2 THE PROS AND CONS OF POVERTY LINES

The measurement method based on the relative poverty line has an evident advantage: its simplicity. Once we have chosen the indicator of wellbeing, let's say income, and once we know the average income of individuals, all we have to do is establish a specific value for k, that is, that fraction of the population's average income deemed acceptable so as not to be considered poor. Given the choice of k, we can determine the poverty line and the ground is set for estimating any poverty measurement we like.

[17] In chapter 1 ("Nutrition") the average energy requirement was estimated, year by year, bearing in mind not only lifestyle but also the development of the structure by gender and age of the population.

Besides the simplicity of calculation and the few data needed to implement the method, there is another advantage of a theoretical nature. The measurement of relative poverty may easily be compared over time and space as long as these comparisons are made on the basis of the same value *k* of reference. It is choosing the same value for *k* that makes it possible for us to compare poverty measurements calculated for different countries or for the same country in different time periods.

Despite the aforesaid advantages, the relative poverty measurement does have a fundamental drawback: it is both a measurement of poverty and a measurement of inequality, and these two aspects are inseparable. This analytical ambiguity has two important implications: (1) it is possible to see an increase in poverty even when *everybody's* wellbeing increases; and (2) poverty is interpreted as a structural element of modern societies that, in practice, is difficult to eliminate.

To clarify the first point, let's use a virtual exercise illustrated in Table 9.2. Let's consider a hypothetical country where, according to the international standard of poverty line, there is a 40 percent incidence of poverty. Let's now suppose that the country is experiencing a year of steady economic growth that benefits *everyone*, nobody excluded; let's also imagine that the gains from this growth are not uniformly distributed, but are proportionately more for the "rich" than for the "poor." However much the economic growth leads to the increased wellbeing of all the population (the incomes in the second row of the table are greater than the ones in the first row), the indicator of relative poverty records a substantial increase, reaching the 60 percent mark; everybody is better off but the number of poor people increases. This result may not be paradoxical, but it is certainly counterintuitive. It is also self-explanatory, bearing in mind the possible redistribution effects of growth: greater average income shifts the poverty line up, but individual incomes do not all grow in the same proportion. In order not to be considered poor now, individuals have to earn more because the *average* level of wellbeing has increased. However,

Table 9.2 **The paradox of relative poverty**

Persons	A	B	C	D	E	Total	Mean	Poverty line	Poor (%)
Before	2	2	16	20	60	100	20	10	40
After	3	3	24	170	300	500	100	50	60

Note: The first row of the table shows the income distribution of a (hypothetical) population of five individuals, indicated by the letters A, B, C, D and E. Suppose we adopt a relative poverty line and we calculate it by means of a value k of 50%, we thus get a poverty line of 10: on this basis, 2 individuals out of 5 (A and B) are considered poor. In the second row we see the hypothetical distribution after a period of economic growth that has benefitted all the individuals. With the new poverty line, however, now individual C is also classified as poor, and thus 3 out of 5 are now poor. Everyone is now better off than before, but relative poverty has increased!

households with lower incomes have benefited proportionately less than richer households. As a result, some individuals who were not poor previously are now relatively more distant from the standard of living of the whole population and find themselves in a new condition of poverty.

The second implication concerns the structural nature of the phenomenon and is a direct consequence of the fact that *relative poverty is none other than a measure of social inequality*. Poverty eradication policies implemented through income support are thus doomed to fail if they do not also envisage the elimination of social inequalities—a much more ambitious goal than what is normally envisaged in programs of social spending and the fight against poverty (Ruggles 1990).[18]

Empirically, the measurement of relative poverty has always turned out to be an indicator that has little sensitivity to the growth in collective wellbeing.[19] In Italy's case, for example, the incidence of relative poverty calculated by Istat for the years 1978 through 2009 remained almost stable, fluctuating around a value of 11 percent. It is thus legitimate to question the usefulness of having a poverty indicator based on a figure that is essentially invariable.

In view of all these criticisms, advocates of relative poverty lament the inadequacy of the alternative measure of absolute poverty in grasping the evolution of poverty over time and its specificity compared to the social context of reference. That is to say, it is not a measure that can tell us where the "kids of life" of the *borgata* Gordiani live today. Despite its limits, then, the measure of relative poverty seems to be the only option available to coherently analyze the trend in poverty over time and space. But is that really true?

The concept of absolute poverty differs from that of relative poverty because it identifies the poverty conditions of each individual regardless of other people's living conditions. The poverty line is determined by the value of minimum resources necessary to satisfy a set of essential needs and so does not depend on the way income and consumption are distributed among individuals: the money a household must earn to steer clear of poverty does not increase if their neighbors win the lottery.

Given this distinction, it would not be proper to draw the conclusion that the absolute poverty line must be—after allowing for variations in purchasing power—constant over time or independent of the social context of reference. There are, indeed, three elements that change over time and that must be taken

---

[18] Indeed, and this is another way to highlight the critical points in the definition of relative poverty, a general policy of "impoverishment" accompanied by a radical redistribution in an egalitarian sense could lead to a drastic decrease in poverty.

[19] As Sarpellon (1982) observed with reference to Italy and with regard to a measure of relative poverty: "[W]e can say that in all epochs of our history about 15–20 percent of the population can be considered poor." More generally, the standard measures of relative poverty are "homogeneous of grade zero with respect to average income," that is, they do not change when a population's average income changes (Ravallion 1994).

Box 2 **The Relative Poverty That Europe Likes**

While most developing countries adopt absolute poverty lines, the OECD countries, as well as those belonging to the European Union, prefer relative poverty lines. The latter preference is base on the idea of having to take into account the context and, in particular, the cost of *social exclusion*, or the resources necessary to lead a life that guarantees not only an adequate quantity of basic goods and services but also everything a person needs in order to live with full dignity in his or her own society (Ravallion 2014).

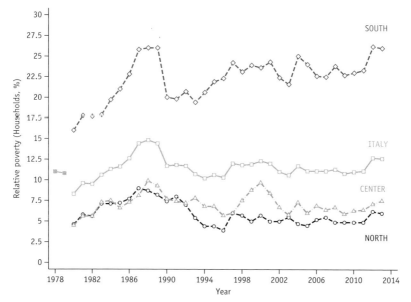

Figure 9.B2 RELATIVE POVERTY BASED ON HOUSEHOLD EXPENDITURE BY MACRO REGION (1978–2014). The figure shows the trend of relative poverty measured on the basis of household expenditure (the vertical axis measures the quota of population with an expenditure below half of average expenditure) over time (horizontal axis). In addition to the national trend, the figure shows also the trend for the three Italian macro regions: North, Center and South.

into account. These are: (*a*) the level and nature of essential needs; (*b*) the basket of goods and services that satisfy these essential needs; and (*c*) the minimum cost of this basket. It is thus correct to say that the absolute poverty line depends on the particular circumstances that help determine these three factors. We are thus dealing with a *relatively* absolute poverty line: it is absolute in the sense that it is constructed starting from the cost of a basket of "essential" goods and services, but it is also relative because what defines the essential evidently depends on the context we are referring to.[20]

Hence, the characteristic that distinguishes the absolute line from the relative one is not so much independence from the historical and social context of reference, but independence from individual income distribution. Paradoxes such as the one illustrated in Table 9.2 are not possible when measuring absolute poverty: if all the individuals are better off (i.e., if we get what economists call a "Paretian improvement"), then absolute poverty necessarily decreases. In other words, social inequality remains, conceptually and analytically, a separate aspect from the criterion of defining absolute poverty.

For some, the clear-cut distinction between inequality and poverty is an unacceptable fault. In our view, this separation is instead a strength. By this we do not mean to say that the poverty phenomenon is independent of inequality. As we shall see, absolute poverty is sensitive to changes in income distribution. Instead, it is the *criterion* for defining poverty that must be independent of the characteristics of the distribution of the chosen wellbeing indicator. If this were not the case, the poverty line would end up being a sort of "moving target" that would not allow us to grasp whether the impact of growth and inequality on poverty is due to a real change in the population's living conditions or to a change in the very criterion for establishing the state of poverty. This is the basic reason that led us to prefer adopting a measure of absolute poverty.

6 Constructing a Poverty Line

Once having taken the fundamental decision, that of measuring absolute poverty, then, on a practical level, we need to select the most suitable method— among the various ones found in the literature (Ravallion 1994; 1998; Kakwani 2003)—in order to determine a poverty line to be applied to the 150-year history of postunification Italy.

---

[20] An example will help to clarify this point. In modern industrialized Italy the average calorie requirement is different from what it used to be in nineteenth-century rural Italy owing to the different demographic structure of the population (the number of children compared to the number of adults, their body weight, and their height) as well as the different lifestyles. The average minimum cost necessary to satisfy nutritional needs has changed thanks to a different production structure and different composition of demand. The nature of essential needs has also changed: the percentage of nonfood needs definable as essential has grown over the decades and the value of goods and services that can satisfy these needs has increased with respect to the value of foodstuffs. It would thus be totally misleading to identify the absolute poverty line of modern Italy by means of the same criteria adopted for determining Italy's absolute poverty line on the eve of the country's unification.

Given our intents and purposes, we opted for a procedure based on the method devised by Molly Orshansky for the United States in the 1960s (Orshansky 1963; 1965). The Orshansky method has a dual advantage: on the one hand, it requires a limited amount of information, which is important given the difficulty in obtaining nineteenth-century data; on the other, given the scarcity of statistics, it allows us to efficiently incorporate the main elements that determine changes in the poverty line over time (Citro and Michael 1995, 104, 110–114). These advantages more than outweigh the well-known limitations of the method that are extensively stressed in the literature.

The Orshansky method is an indirect estimation procedure based on the consumer behavior of the poorest households and enables us to measure the non-food component of the poverty line without having to reconstruct its underlying basket of goods and services. We assume we know the individual average calorie requirement and also the minimum cost of a calorie. This information is rather complex to reconstruct along such a long time frame, but it is not an impossible task (see chapter 1, "Nutrition"). If we multiply the minimum cost of a calorie by the average calorie requirement we, evidently, get an estimation of the food component of the poverty line, that is, of the minimum cost an individual must face to satisfy his or her nutritional needs. Unfortunately, it is not possible to use the same procedure for estimating the nonfood component. An equivalent of the calorie requirement for nonfood needs does not exist. The alternative proposed by Orshansky is to use the amount of poor households' expenditure on food. In theory, the total spending of the poor coincides with the poverty line. Hence, for example, if a poor household devotes 60 percent of its total consumption to food, on average, then we can deduce that the food component of the absolute poverty line will account for 60 percent of the total poverty line. To estimate the nonfood component, then, all we have to do is know what poor households spend on food.

It is important to stress that the three elements necessary to estimate the poverty line according to the Orshansky method—namely the average calorie requirement, the minimum cost of a calorie, and the proportion of poor households' average expenditure on food—grasp in quite a simple manner the factors *a*, *b*, and *c* discussed in the previous section,[21] which are responsible for the variation of the poverty line over time. By means of the historical series of calorie requirements, we can estimate the variations over time of the nutritional needs linked to the population's physiological and demographic changes, and to changes in work and life habits. The trend in the minimum cost of a calorie tells us not only of the variations in conditions of production and distribution of foodstuffs and their quality, but also of the variation in relative value of these

---

[21] For the reader's benefit, we recall here that (*a*) is the level and nature of essential needs, (*b*) the basket of goods and services satisfying these needs, and (*c*) the minimum cost of this basket.

Mollie Orshansky, an American statistician and economist, devised the method for calculating the poverty line that was adopted by the United States government. She was born in 1915 to a Jewish Ukrainian family who had emigrated to the Bronx to escape poverty. She worked for thirteen years in the Agricultural Department, gathering and analyzing data on household budgets and food consumption. In 1958 she started working for the Social Security Administration. Between 1964 and 1965 she developed her method for calculating the poverty line. Immediately after publishing her study, the federal agency charged with implementing the "war on poverty" declared by President Johnson officially adopted the Orshansky index for measuring poverty. The first to be amazed was Orshansky herself, who had thought of her index "only" as a research tool without imagining it could be used to determine the criteria for accessing welfare policies. Her name later became one of the most cited in the specialist literature—so much so that she was referred to as "the ubiquitous footnote" [Fisher 2008]. She died in 2006, at the age of 91.

Figure 9.2 Mollie Orshansky (1915–2006).

goods with respect to nonfood items. The proportion of expenditure on food grasps the variation of essential needs and of the basket of goods and services to satisfy them, as well as the change in the relative value of foodstuffs compared to other consumer goods.

The method described above thus allows us to estimate an absolute poverty line that is updated every time to account for changes that determine the level and nature of essential needs as well as the expenditure necessary to satisfy them.[22] Figure 9.3 shows our estimations, that is, the trend in absolute poverty line since 1861, expressed as 2010 euros. The dashed line is the estimation of the minimum cost of just the food need: this threshold is a sort of "extreme" poverty line, below which we find households that do not have a sufficient total income to buy the basket of essential foodstuffs. The total poverty line (blue line) is obviously above the food poverty line because it includes a component of minimum expenditure on nonfood goods and services.

---

[22] The constraints imposed by the availability of data have required some adjustments with respect to the procedure for estimating the absolute poverty line illustrated in this section. The specific methodology adopted is described more thoroughly in the further analysis section at the end of this chapter.

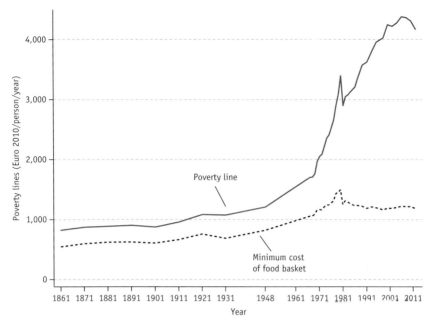

Figure 9.3 THE POVERTY LINES. The graph shows the development of the total and food poverty lines (vertical axis, the unbroken and dashed line, respectively) over time (horizontal axis).

In line with expectations, the estimated poverty line is not constant over time. It is an "absolute" line that varies over time according to the referenced social context; the poor of 1861 are those whose income was enough to purchase a basket of goods and services—food and nonfood items—considered essential in 1861. Today's poor are those whose income is enough to purchase a different basket of goods and services than the one of 1861—a basket that is adapted and suitable for modern Italy. These changes are evident in the graph: in 1861 the food poverty line was about 550 euros per person per year at current purchasing power (Euros 2010). This means about 1.5 euros a day to satisfy the basic need for food—a result close to the threshold of "a dollar a day" introduced by the World Bank in the early 1990s to conduct international comparisons of poverty (Ravallion, Datt, and Van de Walle 1991).[23] In the same year the total poverty line is estimated at 821 euros per person per year, that is, 2.25 euros a day; essential nonfood consumption accounted for about 33 percent of the total poverty line. About 150 years later, the estimations establish the food poverty line at 1,186 euros per person per year, that is, 3.25 euros a day, while the total

[23] The "dollar a day" poverty line was used by the World Bank as a tool for monitoring poverty on a world scale. The line has recently been updated to 1.25 dollars a day (Ravallion, Chen, and Sangraula 2008).

poverty line is around 4,172 euros per person per year (you are considered poor if you do not have 12 euros a day to meet all your basic needs). Today, nonfood items account for about 72 percent of the overall poverty line.

If we compare the start and end point, we see how the extreme poverty line, that is the minimum expenditure necessary to satisfy one's food requirements, has not changed much over the years of Italy's postunification history. Instead, what has been responsible for shifts in the poverty line is the nonfood component, owing not only to new essential needs emerging over the years but also to the increased economic value of essential nonfood needs.

7 The Vanquishing of Poverty

In this section we shall present the estimations of absolute poverty in Italy for the whole postunification period. This is an important, hitherto unwritten, page of Italy's economic history. To properly interpret the figures we are presenting, it is worth recalling that the poverty being measured here, although classifiable in the "absolute poverty" category, is *not* the same thing as extreme poverty; nor is it a measure based on unchanging parameters in time and space. The poverty we are measuring is at the same time "relative," because it refers to a precise historical context, and "absolute" because the value of essential goods does not depend on the population's average income. The two aspects—the relative and the absolute—cohabit in the poverty concept and are difficult to separate from one another.

Figure 9.4 summarizes the dynamic nature of the *incidence* of absolute poverty in postunification Italy. The graph clearly shows how the rise in per-capita GDP documented in chapter 7 ("Income") along with the development of the social inequalities examined in chapter 7 have led to greater wellbeing for the Italian population, and in particular for its more disadvantaged segments. The long time-frame illustrated in the figure thus attests to the vanquishing of absolute poverty. The most interesting question, however, concerns the time and way this happened—an aspect we shall now turn our attention to.

Italy was born poor (in 1861 about 44 percent of the Italians did not have a sufficient income to cope with everyday needs), but it managed to drastically reduce indigence by decreasing the percentage of the poor population to around 7 percent in 2012. In the 150 years of the country's postunification history, the poverty rate decreased tenfold. The progress is staggering, above all, if we consider the fact that we are not counting just the "extreme" poor, but more generally all those who do not manage to reach a minimum standard of living that is updated with regard to the standards of every period.

During the 150 years examined, the population more than doubled: there were just over 26 million Italians in 1861, and there were just under 60 million

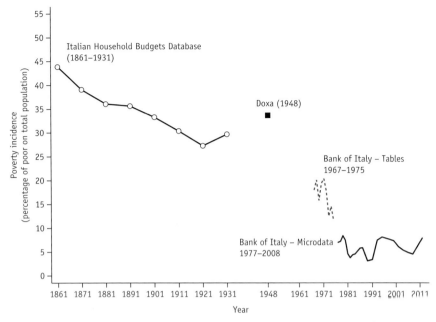

Figure 9.4 THE PERCENTAGE OF POOR PEOPLE IN ITALY, 1861–2012. The graph shows the trend in the incidence of poverty (vertical axis) over time (horizontal axis).

in 2012. The demographic growth implies that absolute poverty decreased, but less spectacularly than what we find in the analysis of poverty rates. In 1861 there were 11.5 million poor compared to 4.7 million in 2012. Hence, if poverty were measured by means of a "head count," then we would have to say that in 150 years, poverty in Italy dropped twofold instead of tenfold.

A second important aspect concerns the structure of the poverty reduction process. The poverty trend over the decades has not been a linear one, and there have even been episodes of an inverse trend (an increase in poverty). In the Liberal period, for example, there was a very gradual decrease in the poverty rate. In 1911, at the time of the fiftieth anniversary of the country's unification, Italy saw a decrease in the incidence of poverty from 44 percent to 33 percent but, owing to a growth in population, the number of the poor remained largely the same: there were 11 million in 1861 and 11 million in 1911. What is the conclusion if the percentage of the poor population decreases, but the actual number of poor people remains the same? Can we say that poverty has decreased? Most economists would instinctively say yes; others, though, the ones working "in the field," would say that what counts for eradicating poverty (financial resources) depends on the number of people involved—on the absolute number of the poor rather than on poverty rates. Both sides are partly right, and the issue is not easy to solve (Chakravarty, Kanbur, and Mukherjee 2006).

In the interwar period, poverty increased, albeit slightly, as much percentage-wise as in absolute terms. The figures for 1931 show that 30 percent of the Italians—over 12 million individuals—were technically in poverty conditions. If we use a head count as our measurement, we conclude that in the first seventy years of the country's postunification history, poverty in Italy *increased* by about 5 percent; if we look at the incidence, though, we conclude that poverty *decreased* by over 20 percent.

The figures for poverty for 1948 depict a country on its knees, with poverty levels last seen in the nineteenth century. Mountains of books have been written on the miserable conditions of the Italian population in the aftermath of World War II. What our estimations add is the scale of the phenomenon. According to our calculations, at least 15.5 million Italians were poor—that is to say, one Italian out of every three. To find a similar figure in the country's history we have to go back half a century before, to the 33.5 percent estimated for 1901.

The years of reconstruction and of the "economic miracle" do *not* seem to be so miraculous as regards poverty. Unfortunately, the figures to confirm what appears to have happened in the 1950s are lacking: the enquiry into poverty of 1952 does not offer data that can be compared with ours, and there are no alternative sources for producing credible estimations. The first reliable data available are for 1967, and they show that poverty decreased compared to the immediate postwar years, but without drastic accelerations: in 1967, one Italian out of every five was still poor, for a total of about 10 million people. Poverty reduction was thus rapid, but not very much so, and the scale of the phenomenon remained significant. Despite this (as we documented in sections 2–4), politics, the institutions and scientific debate have devoted little attention to this phenomenon.

If we wish to talk in terms of miracles, then that of the "vanquishing" of poverty must be placed in the 1970s, when there was a drastic reduction in the incidence and number of absolute poor in the space of a decade: from 20 percent (10 million poor people) in 1970 to about 5 percent (4 million people) in 1980. The poverty reduction rate in the 1970s was approximately three times the one recorded during the 1950s and 1960s (3 percent and 1 percent, respectively). This is an interesting finding in view of the fact that the 1970s are traditionally described as "difficult years": those were the years of "stagflation," where high inflation went hand in hand with economic stagnation, and where per-capita GDP increased but at a significantly lower rate compared to the previous twenty years (2.9 percent in the decade 1972–1982 compared to an average annual rate of 4.7 percent between 1949 and 1972). The decade saw two oil crises (the first in 1973 and the second in 1979–1980), and the climate was made difficult by political instability and terrorism. The great drop in poverty observed in these years is open to a dual interpretation. On the one hand, there is the fact that economic growth may, per se, not be enough—or may not be the most effective way to eradicate poverty: what counts is the *quality* of that growth, its social stratification. On the other, it could herald the advent of an imbalanced process of public financing that has led to the current crisis of the welfare state. Between 1969 and 1980 the Italian public debt rose from 40 percent to 60 percent of GDP, to then take off in the following years. In other words, even under the pressure of growing social conflict, the country chose to drastically reduce poverty in those years and not think too much about the repercussions of this strategy over time: that is, it chose an easy shortcut whose cost would be paid by future generations (Rossi 1997).[24]

The incidence of poverty remained at record low levels (3–5 percent) throughout the 1980s and into the early 1990s. The incomes policy implemented in that very decade was an epochal innovation that probably also goes to explain the result we see in the poverty incidence data. Starting in 1993, the year after a strong devaluation of the Italian lira that led to Italy leaving the European Monetary System (EMS), there was a considerable increase in poverty: the incidence rate reached 8 percent in 1995 (as many as 4.6 million Italians were classified as poor). In the last decade there has been a decreasing trend in poverty, in line with what we will see in chapter 11 ("Vulnerability").

Finally, we wish to underline the consistency of our results with those obtained in a recent study on absolute poverty carried out by Istat (Istat 2010b). Istat's estimation procedure is based on an expenditure indicator recorded in the survey on consumption carried out by the statistics institute itself. Our estimates, on the other hand, are based on the disposable income recorded for the most recent years on the basis of the survey carried out by the Bank of Italy. Like us, Istat adopted a measure of absolute poverty, but calculated a poverty line by means of a *cost of basic needs* approach (Ravallion 1994), while our poverty line follows an Orshansky-type method. Whereas Istat used the household as the unit of analysis, we chose the individual (assuming that each member of a household receives the same share of total household income). Despite all these differences, the final estimations are surprisingly close. The national poverty incidence calculated by Istat for 2012 is 6.8 percent compared to our 7.9 percent, calculated on Bank of Italy data.

To conclude this section, it is interesting to also focus on the "hardest" forms of poverty more directly linked to the concept of survival. We have already mentioned that hunger was a normal sight in the newly constituted Kingdom of Italy. According to the estimates presented in the first chapter of this book, in around 1861, 40–60 percent of the population had an insufficient diet with regard to calorie intake. The country's development and industrialization process enabled it to

---

[24] Hence, in the 1970s the boost in social spending, which grew rapidly right from the previous decade (chapter 11, "Vulnerability"), and the impact of legislative innovations in that decade were strongly felt (Ferrera 1984, 41–42).

largely solve the problem of undernutrition but, in the aftermath of World War II, the lack of food again became a concrete issue for a broad section of the population.

Figure 9.5 shows the estimates for the incidence of "extreme poverty," meant as the percentage of individuals in the population who cannot—over a year—afford to purchase a suitable basket of foodstuffs not just for survival, but also for performing all normal everyday activities, work-related or not. Bearing in mind the margins of error associated with estimates, it turns out that between 1861 and 1871, 20–25 percent of the population did not have the financial means necessary for a suitable diet.

Since the poorest households are normally the ones forced to sacrifice their spending on food, even if necessary, in order to buy nonfood goods and services that are also essential for survival in good health (Bidani and Ravallion 1994), the data in Figure 9.5 seem to be consistent with the estimates of undernutrition presented in chapter 1 ("Nutrition"). The fact that the two results are in agreement despite their being based on independent sources and different estimation methods is reassuring for the overall robustness of the picture we are depicting.

As with the general measure of poverty, Figure 9.5 shows that the trend of the incidence of extreme poverty over time is decreasing and that this fall is not rapid, but interrupted, on more than one occasion, by episodes where extreme poverty stagnates or actually increases, albeit slightly. In 1948, 12.5 percent

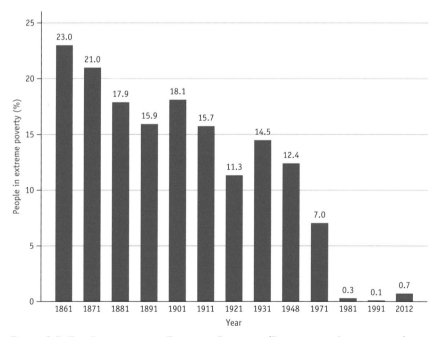

Figure 9.5 THE INCIDENCE OF EXTREME POVERTY (PERCENT OF INDIVIDUALS), 1861–2012. The figure shows the trend over time of the percentage of the population with an insufficient income to purchase a basket of essential foodstuffs.

of the Italian population did not have enough resources to guarantee a proper diet.[25] After over twenty years, in 1971, the percentage almost halved (dropping to 7 percent), but the absolute figure indicates that the scale of the phenomenon was still significant: over 4 million Italians lived in conditions of extreme poverty. Extreme poverty actually disappeared in the 1970s, with the acceleration we saw earlier, with regard to the data on general poverty (Istat 2010b).

8 Poverty, North and South

After examining the incidence of poverty at a national level, we shall now turn to analyzing the figures in more detail with regard to different parts of the country. For most of the period considered, we must firstly say that the data do not enable us to obtain regional estimates as reliable as the national ones (section 7).[26] With due caution, we can, however, outline the fundamental traits of the trend in poverty within the two macro-geographical areas of the center-north and the south. It is, in any case, a very interesting analysis given the preeminent role of the "southern question" in Italian history.

As we can see in Figure 9.6, at the time of the country's unification, 52 percent of the population in southern Italy is classified as poor, accounting for about 5 million people. The poverty incidence was lower in the central and northern regions: there were about 4.8 million poor people corresponding to 37 percent of the population. The north–south gap is quite large: at the time of unification, Italy thus had a clear-cut territorial divide. The southern population was poorer than the northern one. This finding confirms what we observed, from various angles, in the first part of this book and does not depend on the differences in cost of living between north and south. The estimates in Figure 9.6 are obtained by using a single national poverty line, but household incomes have been adjusted by means of the spatial deflators presented in chapter 14 ("The Cost of Living") to account for the territorial differences with regard to the cost of living.

The fifty years after the country's unification mark overall progress: absolute poverty dropped everywhere. The decrease is not uniform, however: the fall in poverty was faster and more marked in the northern regions. Hence, while unification brought wellbeing throughout the country, the people living in the center-north were the ones who managed to reduce poverty more quickly.

---

[25] The figure is in line with the one obtained by the *Enquiry into Poverty*, which estimated that 11.8 percent of the population lived in conditions of extreme poverty (Table 9.1).

[26] For example, a system of weights was applied to the household budgets contained in the IHBD (1861–1931) in order to produce estimates at national level, but not for subnational units. In the case of the Bank of Italy's tabular data (1966–1975), there is significantly lower information regarding the regional level compared to the data provided for Italy as a whole. Even the regional estimates for more recent years (1977–2012) should be used with some caution.

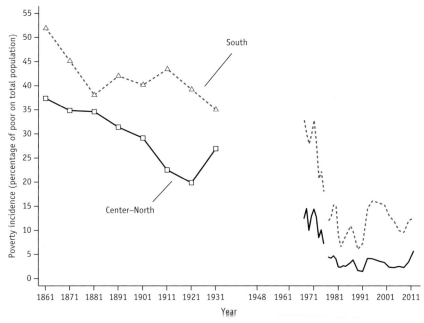

Figure 9.6 THE POVERTY INCIDENCE IN THE CENTER-NORTH AND SOUTH, 1861–2012. The graph shows the trend in poverty incidence (vertical axis) over time (horizontal axis) for the central-northern regions and southern ones. The poverty line used is reported in the Statistical Appendix at the end of this book. The estimates allow for differences in cost of living between the two macro-areas since incomes are in real terms (Chapter 14, "The Cost of Living").

The interwar years recorded a resurgence of poverty, especially in the north, where its incidence rose from 20 percent to 27 percent. In the south, instead, the percentage of poor people continued to fall, albeit more slowly (from 39 percent to 35 percent). The data probably grasp the impact of the greatest economic crisis the modern world has experienced, between 1929 and 1931, as well as migration flows from the rural areas of the south to the cities of the north (Sori 1979).

Unfortunately, we do not know what happened in the aftermath of World War II. The Doxa survey of 1948 provides a precious snapshot of the Italy that came out of the war, but does not allow us to comparably estimate the poverty in the north and south of the country.[27] The first data available for our purposes relate to the late 1960s and show a considerable widening of the poverty gap between north and south, even if absolute poverty began to fall sharply: from 1967 to 1977 the poverty incidence in the center-north fell threefold (from 12.5 percent

[27] The geographical gap emerging from the *Enquiry into Poverty* of 1951–1952 is broad, whatever the poverty indicator used: the percentage of households living in conditions of extreme overcrowding was 2.9 percent in the north as against 15.5 percent in the south; households with "nonexistent, low, or very low" meat, sugar, and wine consumption accounted for 6.9 percent of the total in the north compared to 58.9 percent in the south; households with footwear in shabby conditions were 2.4 percent in the north as against 10.6 percent in the south.

to 4.4 percent), followed also by the south, which saw absolute poverty drop from 33 percent to 12 percent. The decrease continued at a brisk pace during the 1980s.

After the currency crisis of the early 1990s, the poverty incidence began to rise again. In the southern regions, the 1993 survey shows a doubling (*sic*) of the poverty incidence compared to 1991 (in absolute terms, the poor increased from 1.5 to 3 million people); in the center-north the poverty incidence almost tripled (the number of poor people rose from 0.5 to 1.5 million). Poverty decreased throughout the decade, albeit slowly, in the north (from 4.1 to 3.1 percent between 1993 and 2000) while it remained high and stable in the south. On the eve of the new millennium, the poverty incidence in the southern regions stood at about 15 percent: to find a similar percentage in the north, we need to go back over thirty years before.

Another more explicit way to describe the dynamics of poverty incidence between north and south is to interpret the incidence itself in terms of "poverty risk." For example, if we observe that the poverty incidence in a country is 20 percent, this means that a child born in that country will, a priori, have a 1 in 5 chance of growing up in poverty. Let us now consider the likelihood of being poor in the two macro-areas of the north and south, the relation between these two areas probably provides a measure of how much greater the risk is of being poor in one area compared to the other. In other words, if the likelihood of being

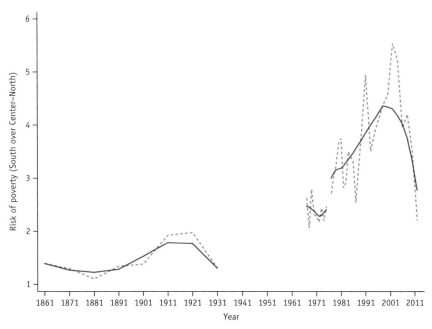

Figure 9.7 HOW MUCH DOES POVERTY RISK INCREASE IF WE MIGRATE FROM NORTH TO SOUTH? The graph shows the trend in the relation between the poverty incidence rate in the South and that of the Center-North (vertical axis; the unbroken line approximates the real trend of the curve). This relation can be interpreted as the extra risk of being poor if you live in the South instead of the North. Living in the South has always implied a greater poverty risk; in the last thirty years this risk has approximately doubled.

poor is 10 percent in the north and 20 percent in the south, we can conclude that the *risk* of being poor in the north is half that for the south or, conversely, that the risk of poverty in the south is double that of the north.

In Figure 9.7 we estimated the difference in poverty risk between the north and south of the country. The figure shows that the center-north has systematically lower risk levels than the south, for the whole postunification period. That is, there is an "extra risk" of poverty associated with the southern regions. The gap is considerable and growing over time: in the first seventy years, the greater risk of poverty in the south compared to the north gravitated in the range of around 40–50 percent; a hundred years after unification, the extra-risk component approximately doubled, with a sharply rising trend. A child born south of the 42nd parallel in 2010 in Italy has over a 300 percent risk of living in poverty compared to a child born to the north of this imaginary line. However, in the past few years the increasing trend started reverting, and in 2012 the poverty risk in the south is around two times higher than in the north. The dynamics of the poverty risk differential helps us to further qualify the evaluation of the way the benefits of growth have spread in the country. While it is true that absolute poverty has dropped sharply over the country's postunification history, it is also fair to say that the magnitude of this progress has differed greatly between regions.

9 The Trickle-Down Theorem

The idea that economic growth is not only a necessary condition, but also a sufficient one, to reduce poverty has been deeply rooted in the traditional theory of economic development. As a result, the redistribution implications of growth have long remained in the background, playing a secondary analytical role (Kakwani and Pernia 2000). The belief has been that once growth is assured, the benefits of the increase in production and income, however different the times and intensity, would reach everyone (Rosenstein-Rodan 1943): like a mountain spring divides into a thousand rivulets along its course down to the valley, so the greater income generated by economic growth would reach all segments of the population. According to the "trickle-down" theorem, growth solves the problem of poverty virtually automatically. This view seems to have received some empirical support in the work of Dollar and Kraay (2002), where it is estimated that the income elasticity of the poor with respect to the population's average income is equal to one: one more percentage point of economic growth would mean a one percent reduction in poverty.

The trickle-down theorem is not actually a theorem at all. Not only is there no rigorous demonstration of it, but, on the contrary, there are many clues and counterexamples that show how growth is not enough, in itself, to eradicate poverty. The theoretical reasoning that invalidates the trickle-down theorem is rather mundane: what can break down the virtuous growth-wellbeing mechanism is the increase in inequality. If growth is accompanied by greater inequality, not all people will have an equal share in the resulting wellbeing. The system may expand on the whole, but the poor will remain poor, and may even increase in numbers. The lack of any automatic connection between economic growth and absolute poverty is also amply highlighted at the factual level.

Without going into the details of the theoretical and empirical debate, we shall just limit ourselves to observing how, over the last twenty years, the literature on developing countries suggests the following conclusion: economic growth is normally accompanied by an increase in inequality, but the net effect on absolute poverty is positive. The growth effect prevails over the redistribution effect (Kanbur 2000). What does this mean for Italian economic history? Which forces have mostly contributed to determine the decreasing trend in absolute poverty over the decades, documented in Figure 9.4?

For the years we have microdata available, we can accurately identify and quantify the role played by economic growth and by income inequality. The idea is as follows. Imagine we have the income distribution of a given year and the poverty line marking the threshold below which all individuals are classified as poor. The variation in the poverty rate observed during a certain time period may be interpreted as the result of two effects. The first is the effect we would observe if the incomes of all the individuals increased by an amount equal to the average growth rate observed in the period concerned. In this case, we would get a new distribution with the same shape as the previous (inequality does not change because the increase has benefited all in the same proportion), but it has "shifted forward" as a result of the fact that each person's income has increased. Since the poverty line has not changed, the generalized rise in incomes involves a decrease in absolute poverty. We shall call this first variation the "growth effect." The second effect, which we shall call the "inequality effect," measures the variation in poverty we would get if the only change in income distribution were the one due to variations in people's relative incomes in the period concerned. The variation in poverty that we would see in this hypothetical case should be attributed not to the variation of average income, assumed to be zero, but exclusively to the variation in income inequality. Datt and Ravallion (1992) demonstrated that the variation *observed* in the poverty incidence in a certain time interval may be broken down into the two aforesaid effects—the growth effect and inequality effect.

Table 9.3 shows the results of this breakdown, considering four subperiods of the time interval concerned. To understand the meaning of the estimates given, we shall consider the first sub-period, corresponding to the years 1861–1911. The data in the table show that the decrease in poverty observed in this period (−14.5 percent, first row) may be obtained by summing the growth effect (−19.3 percent, second row) to the inequality effect (+ 4.8 percent, third row). The interpretation is as follows: if there had been no change in income inequality between 1861 and 1911, poverty would have decreased by 19.3 percent (it was 43.9 percent in 1861, and would have become 24.4 percent in 1911, instead of the value actually observed of 30.4 percent). However, the value in the third

Table 9.3 **Growth, Poverty, and Inequality, 1861–2012**

	1861–1911	*1921–1931*	*1977–1991*	*1991–2012*
Italy				
Observed variation in poverty	−14.5	7.6	−3.8	4.5
Growth effect	−19.3	−0.8	−6.3	−2.1
Inequality effect	4.8	8.4	2.5	6.6
Center-North				
Observed variation in poverty	−15.6	14.5	−2.9	4.2
Growth effect	−17.0	0	−4.3	−1.4
Inequality effect	1.4	14.5	1.4	5.6
South				
Observed variation in poverty	−10.3	−3.7	−5.4	5.1
Growth effect	−21.1	−3.1	−9.7	−3.3
Inequality effect	10.8	−0.5	4.3	8.4

Note: The table breaks down the variation observed in poverty incidence rates (first row) for four sub-periods (columns). In each period, the variation in observed poverty is equal to the sum of the "growth effect" (second row) and the "inequality effect" (third row). The first is interpreted as the variation in poverty that would be observed if there were no variation in income distribution during the period concerned; the second effect is interpreted as the variation in poverty that would be observed if average income did not vary during the period.

row of the table tells us that income inequality has changed and has moved in the opposite direction to the growth effect, slowing down its beneficial effects. If there had not been economic growth, the change in inequality between 1861 and 1911 would have caused a 4.8 percent increase in poverty (the poverty incidence was 43.9 percent in 1861, and would have become 53.4 percent in 1911). The columns of the other subperiods are interpreted in much the same way.

Once we understand how to read Table 9.3, the overall figure that emerges is clear. Over the 150 years of Italy's postunification history, the growth effect has normally dominated the inequality effect: a result in line with what we observe in today's developing countries. As expected, economic growth has favored a reduction in poverty. Inequality, instead, has gone against the grain: the variations in income redistribution have always had an adverse effect on absolute poverty (this is how we interpret the positive sign in the third row of Table 9.3). Despite this, growth has almost always offset the inequality effect thereby producing, as a net result, a decrease in the absolute poverty incidence. There are two exceptions: the first concerns the interwar period (1921–1931), while the second a more recent twenty-year period (1991–2012). In these periods the inequality effect prevailed over the growth effect and not only slowed down the decades-long decrease in absolute poverty, but even made it rise.

The idea that the interwar years were difficult times is nothing new. However, our analysis allows us to identify the profile of the causes of the lack of progress in the fight against poverty, namely slack growth associated with increasing income inequality. It is the same profile as the one we can link to the dynamics of poverty in more recent years.

If we look at figures disaggregated by macro-areas, in both the center-north and the south the growth effect dominates the inequality effect; from this standpoint, there are no surprises. There are, however, two aspects worth commenting on. In the interwar period, the quality of economic growth is very different between north and south (second column). While the north had an increase in poverty entirely driven by the inequality effect, in the south the inequality effect is negligible, and even the modest decrease in poverty should be attributed to the growth effect. The figure for the two more recent decades (fourth column) is also interesting: poverty grew in both north and south. In both cases this increase can be explained by the inequality effect, but in the south the magnitude of this effect seems to be greater.

10 Poor Italy?

No country in the world can probably boast an estimate of the absolute poverty trend along such a long time-frame. The data presented in this chapter tell a new story of the country and, above all, establish certain still unknown "facts" about its economic development. This knowledge enables us to evaluate how the economic progress of the country—the spectacular increase in per-capita GDP documented in chapter 7 ("Income")—has been distributed among the Italians and whether it reached the poorest segment of the population.

We should, however, make good use of these figures, interpreting them properly. The reader who has been patient enough to follow us until now will have understood that establishing a coherent absolute poverty line for the whole time period of Italy's postunification history is a complex exercise both conceptually and empirically speaking. The solution involves value judgments and some discretion. To be more explicit, any analyst of wellbeing would be willing to admit, even if only privately, that setting a poverty line is actually a political process. This is not to say that the incidence estimates are not solidly grounded, but more simply that the teachings we can draw from them derive especially from the comparisons of the poverty incidence in time and space: from an interpretational standpoint, what counts is not the poverty *levels*, but rather the *variations* on poverty and its territorial and social structure.

In this view, the results presented in this chapter convey two fundamental messages: one positive, the other negative. The positive message is that, regardless of current levels, the incidence of absolute poverty in Italy has decreased throughout its postunification history. It has not been a linear process and there have been moments showing an inverse trend, but these have been short-lived.

The negative message is similar to one that is common to many chapters of this book and concerns the territorial distribution of poverty. Once again, the country is divided. During Italy's *Risorgimento*, Garibaldi's "Thousand" (volunteers) landed in Sicily—a region that was poorer than the one they had sailed from (Liguria). One hundred and fifty years later, his "Thousand" (*Mille*) would find a south still more distant from the north of the country. Despite the generalized decrease in poverty incidence rates, the gap between north and south has widened over time, with a great acceleration in the last few decades.

The analysis of the dynamics of absolute poverty is not limited to taking a snapshot of a divided Italy, but also of a country that has progressed at two speeds. The dynamics of the relative risk of poverty is, in this sense, quite eloquent: in 1861 an inhabitant of the south had a 50 percent higher probability of being poor than a citizen of the north. Today, this very same relative probability has increased 200 percent. The poverty incidence in the north is close to the line of extinction (2.2 percent), while in the south it still concerns almost 10 percent of the population.

The magnitude and persistence of these territorial differences poses many questions. There is, firstly, an underlying problem: can an advanced democracy like Italy put up with the existence of such broad pockets of poverty in its territory? Added to this ethical issue is also the question of whether the persistence of such large territorial imbalances in wellbeing will compromise Italy's social cohesion, stability, and future growth prospects.

The recent drives toward fiscal reforms of a federalist nature call for a rapid solution. In the light of these reforms, it seems crucial to have analytical and monitoring tools to assess the income redistribution effects and the impact in terms of wellbeing. What is ultimately needed is a political class that is sensitive to the issue and determined to innovate in view of the decades of indolence we have documented in the first part of this chapter. The meshes of the institutional framework must be closed and harmonized, and responsibilities must be attributed: no country wishing to be considered civilized can allow its poor to be poor forever.

Appendix—Sources and Methods

In this section we shall describe the method followed to estimate the poverty lines. It is an adaptation of the procedure suggested in Orshansky (1963; 1965; 1969) to the availability of Italian data over the 150 years concerned.

The Orshansky method defines the incidence of poverty $H(t)$ in year t as follows:

$$H(t) = prob\left\{c_i(t) \leq \frac{F_{kal}(t)\ \beta C_{kal}(t)}{W_{food}(t)} = PL(t)\right\}$$

where $c_i(t)$ is the daily per-capita consumption of the i-th household in year t and β is a correction factor allowing for the difference between the minimum cost of a calorie and the corresponding average cost C_{kal}, $F_{kal}(t)$ is the yearly individual minimum caloric requirement and $W_{food}(t)$ is the average food expenditure of the poor households. In our estimation procedure, we assume $\beta = 0.8$ on an empirical basis. The probability of the i-th household falling below the poverty line coincides with the percentage of the population whose per-capita consumption is lower than the absolute poverty line $PL(t)$. If we take $s_i(t)$ to stand for the savings rate, then income is given by $y_i(t) = c_i/([1 - s_i(t)])$. This enables us to rewrite the previous equation as follows:

$$H(t) = prob\left\{ y_i(t) \le \frac{F_{kal}(t)\beta C_{kal}(t)}{W_{food}(t)[1 - s_i(t)]} \right\}$$

This new relation defines the incidence of poverty in an income framework rather than a consumption one. The poverty line is now given by:

$$PL'(t) = \frac{F_{kal}(t)\beta C_{kal}(t)}{W_{food}(t)[1 - s_i(t)]}$$

$PL'(t)$ is relatively easy to estimate. In the numerator, $F_{kal}(t)$ is available for each year of the postunification period (chapter 1, "Nutrition"); $C_{kal}(t)$ can easily be estimated. With regard to estimating the denominator, one needs to know the households' average propensity to save. Since our aim is to measure poverty, we can focus on the subset of poor households, for which we can assume that $s_i(t) = 0$. Poor households do not save, on average. If this is true, then $PL'(t) = PL(t)$.

For some periods we do not have an estimate of $W_{food}(t)$, or of the proportion of the poor households' spending on food. Instead, we do have the *average* amount of food spending $W_{food}(t)$, with regard to the whole population. We have thus hypothesized that:

$$W_{food}(t) = \gamma(t)(t)\overline{W}_{food}(t)$$

where parameter $\gamma(t)$ increases from 1 to 1.3 at a constant average annual rate. The formula used in order to estimate the incidence of poverty is given by:

$$\widehat{H}(t) = prob\left\{ y_i(t) \le \frac{F_{kal}(t)\beta C_{kal}(t)}{\gamma(t)\overline{W}_{food}(t)} \right\}$$

where the estimation of the absolute poverty line for year t is given by:

$$\widehat{PL}(t) = \frac{F_{kal}(t)\beta C_{kal}(t)}{\gamma(t)\overline{W}_{food}(t)}$$

Figure 9.1 The three ingredients for measuring poverty Source: Authors' own elaboration.

Figure 9.B2 Relative poverty based on household expenditure by macro-region (1978–2014) The figure shows the trend of relative poverty measured on the basis of household expenditure (the vertical axis measures the quota of population with an expenditure below half of average expenditure) over time (horizontal axis). In addition to the national trend, the figure shows also the trend for the three Italian macro-regions: north, center, and south.

Figure 9.2 Mollie Orshansky (1915–2006) Source: https://upload.wikimedia. org/wikipedia/commons/e/e6/Mollie_Orshansky_1967.jpg.

Figure 9.3 The poverty lines The graph shows the development of the total and food poverty lines (vertical axis, the unbroken and dashed line, respectively) over time (horizontal axis). Source for the data: Vecchi 2011: 314–317.

Figure 9.4 The percentage of poor people in Italy, 1861–2012 The graph shows the trend in the incidence of poverty (vertical axis) over time (horizontal axis). Source: Authors' own estimates.

Figure 9.5 The incidence of extreme poverty (percent of individuals), 1861–2012 The figure shows the trend over time of the percentage of the population with an insufficient income to purchase a basket of essential foodstuffs. Source: Authors' own estimates.

Figure 9.6 The poverty incidence in the center-north and south, 1861–2012 Source: Authors' own estimates.

Figure 9.7 How much does poverty risk increase if we migrate from north to south? Source: Authors' own estimates.

10

Wealth

WITH LUIGI CANNARI AND GIOVANNI D'ALESSIO

1 Wealth and Wellbeing

In 1665, around Christmas time, a booklet was published with the title "*Verbum Sapienti*, and the Value of People". The author, Sir William Petty (1623–1687), was deeply concerned with the unfairness of taxation in the realm of King Charles II who called upon his people to finance a war against the Dutch. Petty denounced the operation of the tax system, writing "According to the present ways, some pay four times as much more as they ought or needed" (Petty 1899, 103). Bent on correcting this aberration in the tax burden, Petty decided to investigate the financial affairs of his country: "just Accounts might be kept of the People, with the respective Increases and Decreases of them, their Wealth and Foreign Trade" (104). And that is exactly what he did: the pages of *Verbum Sapienti*, only known to a few today, are a milestone in the history of social sciences in that they contain the first estimates we know of a nation's accounts (Stone 1984, 117).

Petty's work circulated widely and had a significant impact, both in England and in other countries. It is no accident that Adam Smith inquired into the nature and the causes of the *wealth*, not income, of nations. In France, several carried out exercises in calculating the wealth of nations, but for the whole of the eighteenth century and much of the nineteenth they were only a minority. It was at this point in history, in the latter half of the nineteenth century, that "being an economist meant first and foremost being able to estimate the national capital of one's country: this was almost a rite of initiation" (Piketty 2014, 57). The names of those who devoted themselves to calculating national wealth in this period were already famous in their day and have remained so in the economic literature ever since: Robert Giffen (1837–1910) for Britain, Alfred de Foville (1842–1913) for France, and Maffeo Pantaleoni (1857–1924) for Italy. The countries that were about to embark on the greatest process of globalization in history were very interested in measuring themselves against other countries. That is the reason for the great success in 1884 of the *Dictionary of Statistics*, edited by M. G. Mulhall (1836–1900), "the first Statistical Dictionary ever published in any language" (Mulhall 1884, vii). In that volume, Mulhall produced wealth estimates for about twenty countries, and the figures placed Italy behind *all* the nations of the Old World.

2 Some Good Reasons for Studying Household Wealth

Unlike their predecessors, modern economists choose income as the main measure of wellbeing. Taken singly, however, neither income nor wealth does a good job in measuring the standard of living of an individual or population. Economists explain that income is a *flow*, which tells us how things went over a period of time—a month, year, or lifetime—whereas wealth is a *stock*, a *cumulation* of past flows and starting point for future developments.

Even taken together, income and wealth fail to provide a complete picture of a population's wellbeing. Income, consumer spending, gross domestic product (GDP), and wealth are variables that are open to a fundamental criticism regarding the importance of nonmonetary aspects of wellbeing. This point was made by Robert F. Kennedy, brother of the U.S. president, in his famous speech of March 1968: they are variables that measure everything "except that which makes life worthwhile" (Kennedy 1968).

Although the limitations of GDP hold equally for wealth, the latter does provide additional insights compared to income. When an entrepreneur has a "bad year", for example, or an employee is unemployed for a period, income ceases to be a good indicator of their standard of living. It is possible that the entrepreneur and the unemployed worker manage to maintain their standard of living by drawing on the savings they accumulated in the past. In this case, wealth is a better indicator of wellbeing. More broadly, we can identify at least four distinct ways that wealth is connected to wellbeing.

Firstly, wealth can generate wellbeing directly. A textbook case is the homeowner who benefits directly from the wealth possessed: accommodation. In the same way, owners of durable consumer goods (such as automobiles, household appliances, or valuable artworks) enjoy a "service" from using these goods (Wolff 1998). In both cases, the nonmonetary benefit can be expressed in monetary terms, as a hypothetical *imputed income*. For homeowners, the imputed income is the rent they would have to pay if they were to rent their own home. For the owners of automobile other durable goods, the imputed income corresponds to the cost of renting that good. Besides hypothetical imputed income, wealth typically generates real monetary income. As the savings that produce wealth represent income not consumed, the interest income generated by wealth is a reward for not consuming immediately, thereby making resources available that can be used by the production system in order to generate other income.

Secondly, wealth creates wellbeing when it is turned into current consumption. If, for any reason, a household wishes to enjoy a (temporarily) higher standard of living, it can achieve this by liquidating part of its wealth on the market. The level of wellbeing can thus be modulated by using savings, according to decisions that may or may not have been planned. In old age, for instance, when the capacity to generate income is lower than in the central years of the life cycle, wealth enables us to provide for our needs even with an inadequate income (Deaton 1992). More generally, those who have wealth have a greater capacity to stabilize their consumption flow in the face of life's uncertainties. For those who do not have any wealth, any adversity (or shock) that reduces or eliminates their capacity to generate income (losing one's job, having a serious illness, or even an earthquake or flood) can mean a terrible deterioration of their living conditions. In this case, wealth plays an insurance function with regard to unforeseeable events and contributes to an individual's wellbeing by reducing his/her economic vulnerability (Dercon 2005). Chapter 11 ("Vulnerability") is completely dedicated to this topic.

Thirdly, personal wealth may facilitate access to credit, thereby making it easier for individuals to obtain bank loans to start a business compared to those who do not have any personal wealth (Evans and Jovanovic 1989; Hurst and Lusardi 2004). In this case, personal wealth acts as a guarantee (collateral) and overcomes what economists call a "liquidity constraint", that is, the need for cash to undertake immediate expenditures.

A fourth link between wealth and wellbeing goes beyond consumption, both real and potential consumption: the power, influence, and prestige accorded to those who possess wealth—especially in considerable amounts. Wealth conveys power, particularly in the context of widespread corruption, but also more generally (Rowbottom 2010).

All these reasons make the study of Italians' wealth, and its development over time—with regard to both size and composition—a very interesting thing indeed. This chapter aims to complement the story of income (chapter 7) with that of wealth. This means addressing the issue of *inequality* of wealth, which is connected to the *origin* of wealth and its *equity*. Historically speaking, a non-negligible portion of wealth did not arise as a reward to labor and individual ability, but was inherited. In the end, we shall have a basis for evaluating the role of the so-called starting conditions.

3 What Goes to Define the Wealth of the Italians

What do we actually mean by the "wealth of the Italians"? And how do we go about measuring it? Wealth—no matter whether we refer to an individual, a household, a society, or the whole world—is defined as the stock of material and immaterial goods that have a market value and can thus be traded for money or for other goods. It includes both real assets (such as land, buildings, machinery, infrastructure, patents, etc.) and financial assets (such as bank deposits, stocks and shares, bonds, pension funds, etc.). From the value of these assets we must deduct financial liabilities, that is, total debt.

Wealth can be estimated for various categories of individuals. The pioneers of wealth measurement, in the seventeenth century, were only concerned with *national wealth*. This was the variable that could guarantee security and prosperity for the nation, at a time when the capacity to finance war was a precondition for national survival. Today, the national accounting rules envisage the assignment of national wealth to several constituent *institutional sectors*.[1] Among these, at the heart of this chapter, is the household sector.

A recurrent distinction divides national wealth into two components: private and public. The first, *private wealth*, is the set of assets (net of debts and including the value of enterprises) that are directly or indirectly owned by Italian households, while *public wealth* is that which is possessed by the state and its various emanations (regional, provincial, and municipal authorities as well as other public administration bodies). Estimating public wealth is a very complex task, especially when we wish to measure the value of the country's environmental assets and artistic and cultural heritage: What value can we attribute to the beaches of Sardinia or to the Colosseum in Rome? We shall not venture into this territory; rather, in this chapter we shall exclusively focus on "private wealth", a term we shall use as a synonym for "household wealth".

If the aforesaid definitions seem sufficiently clear, there are more than a few difficulties in reconciling the theoretical level with the practical one. We briefly discuss three important examples. First, from the financial standpoint, a public pension that an individual will receive in the future has every right to be included in the definition of wealth: the flow of future resources (i.e., the pension) is, to all effects, a form of wealth (Beltrametti and Della Valle 2011). In practice, however, future pensions are excluded from the definition of private wealth because of the technical difficulties arising when measuring their value: this omission is of no small importance when we wish to compare countries that have different pension systems.

The second example concerns education, that is, "human capital". It is universally acknowledged that expenditure on education and on vocational training is an investment that can generate a return in terms of future income. The difference in the educational attainment of two individuals may thus be considered

---

[1] The European accounting system distinguishes five sectors: (a) nonfinancial corporations (e.g., industrial or commercial enterprises); (b) financial corporations (e.g., banks or mutual investment funds); (c) general government; (d) households; (e) nonprofit institutions serving households (e.g., sports associations). The five sectors together make up the total domestic economy.

Box 1　The Public Debt of the Italians, 1861–2014

In Italy's case, years characterized by a high public debt have been the rule rather than the exception (Figure 10.B1). The national debt was higher than GDP in 67 of the 155 years considered here. In 87 years the debt/GDP ratio exceeded 90 percent, which some consider critical threshold beyond which the pace of a country's economic growth is compromised (Reinhart and Rogoff 2010). That is a prediction that must be taken with a grain of salt, but it is beyond doubt that high debt at least puts at risk financial stability and growth. In 115 years, the debt was higher than 60 percent of GDP—a middle-to-high value by international standards. Only in the period following World War II, with the so-called economic miracle (from the early 1950s to mid-1960s), was the burden of the debt close to 30 percent of GDP.

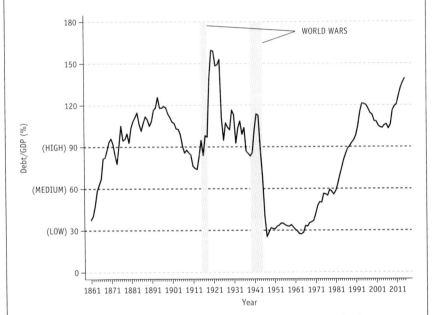

Figure 10.B1 THE ITALIAN PUBLIC DEBT, 1861–2014. The graph shows the trend of the ratio between the public debt and GDP (vertical axis) over time (horizontal axis). A high public debt—above 90–100 percent of GDP— has been a feature of Italian economic development since the birth of the Kingdom of Italy.

In Italy's case, not including the public debt when calculating the private wealth of households does not significantly alter the temporal profile of the process of wealth accumulation (D'Alessio 2012). The convention adopted thus does not impose any significant distortions on our picture of wealth trends. The exclusion of the public debt in the calculation of household wealth remains a very delicate issue because the two variables are strictly interconnected – with important consequences for the population's living conditions. The increase in the debt stems from excess government spending relative to revenues. This expenditure includes services for and transfers to households (such as pensions, health, and education). If the government were to pursue a policy of balancing the budget through lower spending and higher taxes, there would be fewer resources for households (household disposable income would be lower and/or households would have to spend part of their income to purchase services formerly provided by the state). Hence, although not included in the calculation, the public debt does affect the capacity to accumulate wealth.

a difference in wealth: other things being equal, a more educated individual has greater human capital and is thus "wealthier". As with pension wealth, the value of this form of wealth is subject to considerable uncertainty since it depends on many factors beyond the individual's control (job opportunities, luck, health conditions, etc.), and is therefore excluded from household wealth. When dealing with economic history, however, leaving out human capital has significant consequences. This point was grasped by Deirdre McCloskey (2014): "Since 1848 the world has been transformed by what's between the workers' ears". In other words, if the definition of wealth were to take human capital into account, as theory suggests it should, then the amount of wealth and also its composition would be very different from what we see in current estimates. This must be borne in mind, particularly in consideration of what we saw in chapter 5 ("Education"): over the last two centuries, there has been a spectacular increase in human capital, becoming perhaps the most important component of the capital of a nation (Goldin and Katz 2008).

A final point that deserves attention when evaluating private wealth concerns how *public* assets and liabilities are dealt with, particularly with regard to the national debt (Box 1). The state's debts are indirectly the debts of its citizens. If we agree that the public debt must be settled sooner or later, it will be honored through future taxation: the public debt is thus a debt of the country's households, and as such should be deducted from their total wealth. The usual definitions of household wealth, however, do *not* deduct the amount of public debt.[2]

---

[2] There are two basic reasons for this. The first is of a practical nature and is due to the fact that we cannot accurately know who will be called upon to settle the debt. Hence, if it may be correct to deduct the overall public debt from the overall amount of wealth of the country's households, this

4 The Measurement Challenge

The total wealth of households can be evaluated through two main types of sources. The first are the *national accounts* (macroeconomic data), where wealth is measured starting from administrative or census information. The second type of sources consists of *sample surveys* of households (microeconomic data). The data are obtained by interviewing the households themselves. In Italy the Survey on Household Income and Wealth (SHIW) conducted by the Bank of Italy is the main microeconomic source for information on wealth.

Macroeconomic data are probably more accurate for estimating the overall value of assets (to the extent that data collection is reasonably precise). On the other hand, the aggregate nature of the data does not make it possible to go beyond the average value, that is, it does not enable us to relate information on wealth to the characteristics of its owners.

Microdata, instead, offer a much more varied possibility of analysis as a function of the detailed information that can be collected in surveys—but they do have some flaws with regard to quality. In Italy as in other countries, the more affluent households tend to refuse to participate in these surveys more frequently than other households. Moreover, even when households do agree to take part, in some cases they are more reticent and declare less than what they actually own. Despite reassurances on the confidentiality of the data and of their use, the respondents show lingering concerns in disclosing sensitive information. The stronger this resistance, the less accurate the reconstruction of household wealth, and so sample estimates tend to underestimate the real magnitude of wealth possessed.

We do not have fully reliable statistics for a large part of Italy's postunification history. Italian official statistics—historically very attentive to the profile of income (chapter 7) and of consumption (chapter 9)—started dealing with wealth much later. The economic historian is thus obliged to venture into a literature that is full of ad hoc estimates constructed from disparate and not always reliaable sources. Needless to say, it is an operation that requires some compromise: much as the early measurers likened the difficulties in estimating national wealth to that of evaluating the height of St. Peter's Dome without having a suitable measurement tool (Box 2), in the same way the creation of a long-term

operation is impossible at the individual level: it is up to future fiscal policies to determine which individuals, in which generation, will have the burden of settling this debt. The second reason is of a logical nature and stems from the consideration that the same reasoning with regard to debts can also be applied to the state's assets. The state is the owner of enterprises, property, and other assets (beaches, forests, etc.), which are a form of wealth for society. It would thus be logical to count them in, when calculating the wealth of households. Aside from the measurement problems, that is, the fact that the estimates of these components are somewhat arbitrary (again, what price can you put on the beaches of Sardinia or on the Colosseum?), this broader definition involves a substantial distortion of the concept of household wealth, and leads us closer to national than private wealth.

Box 2 On Maffeo Pantaleoni, Corrado Gini, and Measuring the Dome of St. Peter's Church in Rome

In Italy it was the economist Maffeo Pantaleoni (1857–1924) who first produced a documented estimate of the wealth of the Italians. In 1884, at the end of a study taking up almost 250 pages of calculations, Pantaleoni concluded that private wealth probably amounted to 48 billion, 107 million lire (about 1,776 billion euros today). In concluding his study, Pantaleoni warned that, despite the enormous efforts, it was an approximate calculation, "almost like what an individual would do if they had to measure the height of the dome of St. Peter's Church in Rome without the necessary instruments. Instead of jumping into the task blindly, the person would most likely search for terms of comparison with nearby buildings of known height, and would approximately count the rows of stone blocks of equal size, and also count, perhaps through the number of paces, the length of the shadow cast, and would do other such things in order to have a certain number of criteria to approximate the

Figure 10.B2 Corrado Gini (1884–1965).

reality better than he could do without the criteria. This is nothing short of what I have tried to do here, and I do not wish to be understood in any other way" (Pantaleoni 1884, 220). The sincerity with which Pantaleoni stressed the wide margins of error associated with estimates of national wealth is not a ritual warning; on the contrary, it is an attitude taken up systematically in the following decades by other authors who have set about calculating wealth.

If Pantaleoni was the first to deal with the wealth of the Italians, the foremost authority in the matter was, right up to the advent of modern survey systems, Corrado Gini (1884–1965), an unrivaled master. At the age of 25, Gini started a study that took him five years to complete, in which he examined wealth as much in its conceptual foundations as in its measurement aspects. The work, entitled *L'ammontare e la composizione della ricchezza delle Nazioni* ("The Amount and Composition of the Wealth of Nations"), published in 1914, republished and extended in 1962, was a labor that earned Gini immediate academic fame as well as prestigious appointments in Italy and abroad.

After that, Gini produced over 800 publications, combining his genius with an unusual capacity for work (Giorgi 1996, 13). Those who had the opportunity to know him remember that he used to work until 8 p.m. as president of Istat (a post he kept from 1926 to 1932), to then go to the university to work until midnight, expecting the presence of his entire staff: assistants, clerks, and attendants. Next morning, his working day would start at 6.30 a.m., when he would start telephoning his assistants at their homes (Giorgi 2001, 365).

Writing in 1947, Gini got off the mark before anyone else—from Kennedy, who we quoted in our introductory section, to Sen—in reflecting on the gap separating wealth from wellbeing and from happiness: "The original purpose of studies (. . .) on wealth was to increase the happiness of populations. The oldest treatises on the subject make explicit reference to this. If the sensation of this has disappeared from modern ones, it depends not only on external factors that are, in some respects, of a physical nature, and to which we refer when speaking of income (. . .), but also, and essentially, on internal factors, and namely health, self-confidence, nervous balance, the purity of conscience and so on, which it would be pointless to attempt to measure. Every day we see examples of people who, although swimming in abundance, are unhappy, sometimes to such an extent that they take their own life, and it is among the upper classes, and not the lower ones, that suicides are more frequent. We cannot expect a measure of happiness from income" (Gini 1950, cited in Gnesutta [2000]). The lesson, which remained a dead letter for many decades, is today on everyone's minds—scholars and policymakers alike.

(over a century) historical series of the stock of wealth implies decisions that are not always devoid of personal discretion.

5 The Likely Amount of the Wealth of the Italians

In Figure 10.1 we illustrate the hitherto unpublished story of the process of accumulation of the Italians' wealth. The figure shows the trend of per-capita wealth at 2013 prices, that is, corrected for purchasing power changes.

A first comment concerns the dynamics of the series, the pace with which savings set aside by households turned into wealth, year by year. On closer inspection, it was a very slow process: for seventy years, growth never exceeded 1 percent per year (on average). At this pace, per-capita wealth doubled within a space of over seventy years: not the children or grandchildren, but only the third generation managed to have double the resources of their ancestors. Starting in the aftermath of World War II, the pace increases but does not take off, in the way that GDP does (chapter 7, "Income"): during the years that have gone down

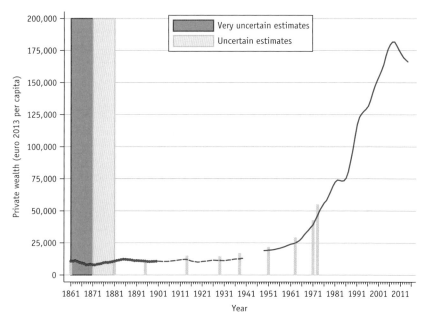

Figure 10.1 THE PRIVATE WEALTH OF THE ITALIANS, 1861–2012. The graph shows the development of the stock of per capita wealth of Italian households (along the vertical axis) over time (horizontal axis). The different forms of the curve indicate the changes in the underlying sources of the estimates, discussed in the appendix. The vertical bars are the estimates of Goldsmith and Zecchini (1999) used here as a benchmark.

in history as those of the "economic miracle" (in terms of GDP, 1950–1963), the growth rate of wealth was appreciable (+ 3 percent), but less than half what would be recorded in the 1970s. This was the decade that had an unprecedented growth of wealth (over 7 percent per annum, on average). After a peak in the 1970s there was a progressive deceleration that became more marked in the 1990s (during which wealth was accumulated at + 1.5 percent per year), and eventually gave way to the inverse trend we see today.

The above trends took the average level of per-capita wealth today to a level 21 times higher than that seen in 1871 (briefly reaching 23 in 2007, on the eve of the Great Recession). The wealth multiplier (equal to 21) is thus more powerful than the one of GDP (equal to 13), and is the result of an even faster leap. The Italians became affluent in the space of around thirty years.

What still remains to be analyzed is the negative trend recorded in the recent economic crisis. According to our statistical reconstruction, this trend inversion is unprecedented in its duration and intensity. Between late 2007, when net wealth reached a peak (over 185 thousand euros per head, including newborn babies), and 2013 there was a 10 percent fall, on the whole. A decisive influence on this trend was the fall in house prices in the late 2000s. It is a negative variation unparalleled since World War II, but with an even graver precedent in the late 1920s. Prices for newly-constructed buildings fell from an index value of 100 in 1927, to a low point of just 66 in 1934, recovering to 1927 levels only in 1941.[3] Since the late 1920s, house prices have tended to increase much more rapidly than other prices: between the late 1960s (1969 marking a low point for the real estate market) and 2007 (a peak), house prices increased by over two-and-a-half times, in real terms. We shall discuss this more extensively in section 7.

5.1 REGIONAL WEALTH

A fundamental aspect of Italian history, not just with regard to wellbeing, is the dualism between the country's north and south. The first studies carried out by Italian economists on regional wealth go back to the earliest decades of the new Kingdom and, although not providing an accurate picture, do at least give us a sense of the attention that contemporaries devoted to the issue. The first accurate estimates were provided by Guido Sensini in a book that had little luck at the time, and is still not much known today, but that received praise from one of the most authoritative economists of the day, Vilfredo Pareto (Pareto 1984, 434).[4]

---

[3] The fall in the price of existing buildings over the same period was even greater, to a low of 62. Recovery was incomplete as of 1941, when the index stood at only 85.

[4] Pareto wrote to Pantaleoni in December 1904: "Guido Sensini has sent me a book of his which seems excellent in every way. I presume he was one of your disciples" (authors' translation). Actually, Pantaleoni detested Sensini and did everything he could—successfully so—to hinder his academic career (Magnani 2004).

According to Sensini's (1904) reconstruction, in the latter half of the nine-teenth century (1879–1883) the per-capita wealth of the northern regions was 90 percent greater than that of the southern ones. The estimates of Corrado Gini for the early twentieth century showed that mean household wealth in northern regions was 60 percent higher than that of southern regions. At the start of the twenty-first century, per-capita wealth in the north was about 80 percent greater than in the south. These are largely incomparable evaluations owing to differences in the methods and data used, but what appears beyond doubt is that the dualism of the Italian economy, going back centuries, has never been bridged and is still very significant.

Aside from some fragmentary evidence, it is still not possible to tell the his-tory of the wealth of Italy's regions.[5] There are still no reliable statistical recon-structions for the whole period. In Figure 10.2 we present our elaboration of results published by several scholars, which provide benchmarks for certain years. Caution in interpreting these estimates is a must, because of the uncer-tainty associated with the calculations and the heterogeneous nature of the methods used by different scholars. With regard to the regions, this caveat is no pro forma ritual: Gini stressed it emphatically. A particularly important cause of error, for example, lay in regional differences with regard to the so-called eva-sion coefficients (that is, the percentage of inherited wealth not declared to tax authorities): "[T]he Veneti [the people of the Veneto region], a little for their character, a little out of habit, acquired during the Austrian domination, are par-ticularly inclined to defraud the tax authorities" (Gini 1959, 89). The extent to which each region had its own inclination to cheat the taxman makes regional rankings based on wealth fallacious—at least in the earlier years, estimates for which were based on fiscal sources.[6]

The general lesson to be learned from these considerations concerns mea-surement and methodological aspects. The estimates currently available, at least the ones based on tax sources, do not pass the requirements of robustness and transparency expected by the scientific community—they did not at the time Gini was writing, and nothing significant for our purposes has been done since. Our comments on the estimates in Figure 10.2 will thus be limited to those aspects that appear the most robust.

According to the earliest data, at the start of the twentieth century the high-est levels of per-capita wealth were found in four regions: Liguria, Lombardy,

[5] Vera Zamagni (1980) wrote an interesting review on "wealth and the wealthy in modern times" that is particularly of note for the space dedicated to the years leading up to Italy's unification (1861).

[6] Gini's warning leads us to a head-on criticism of the numbers shown in the left-hand panel of Figure 10.2: "Many with me will refuse to believe that the mean per capita wealth, in Veneto, is not only lower than the mean wealth of Italy, (. . .) but also lower than that of Puglia and Sicily, and almost the same as the one of Basilicata. These were the same results as those of Nitti who applied the same evasion coefficients to all these regions" (Gini 1959, 90).

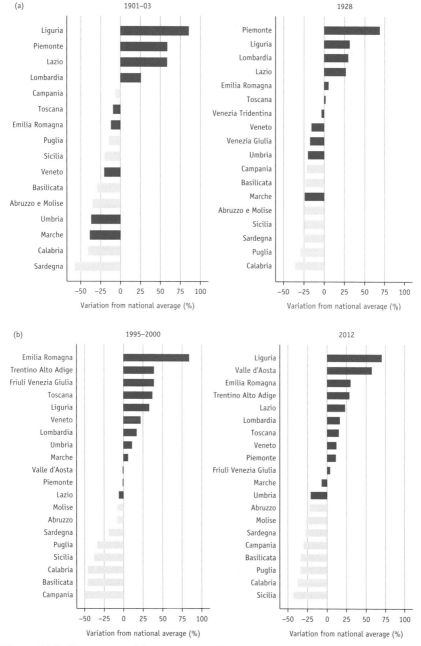

Figure 10.2 HOUSEHOLD WEALTH IN THE REGIONS, 1901–2012. The figure shows the development of the regional rankings established on the basis of household per capita net wealth. Each bar shows how much each region differs from the national mean wealth: if the bar is in positive territory (right of 0 on the horizontal axis), the region is richer than the national average (e.g., in 1901-03, Lombardy had a mean wealth 86 percent higher than the national average). If the bar lies in negative territory, the region has a lower wealth than the national average (in 1901-03 Sardinia was the poorest region, with a value 42 percent of the national average). The northern regions have dark bars while the southern regions have lighter bars.

Piedmont, and Lazio; the lowest in Sardinia, Calabria, Umbria, and Marche. In the richest region, Liguria, net per-capita wealth was four to five times higher than in the poorest region, Sardinia. Over time, the gap between these two extremes has narrowed, but not too much. According to Bank of Italy estimates (2014a), the wealthiest region in the country is still Liguria, while the poorest region is now Sicily, still with a broad gap: for every euro of Sicilian household savings, Ligurian families have three.

The polarization of wealth between north and south depends crucially on the composition and dynamics of its components over time. For example, in 2012 the share of net wealth held in domestic shares and stocks was 12 percent in Lombardy and 2 percent in Calabria; a variation in share prices thus tends to have a greater impact on the per-capita wealth of the Lombards compared to the Calabrians. A homogeneous increase in the price of real estate would be reflected in a more marked growth in the wealth of regions where this form of asset's share is the greatest.

Today's per-capita wealth is also influenced by regions' capacity to save in past times, and is thus affected by determinants such as the level of economic development and the population's age structure. The regions with the oldest tradition of development show higher levels of wealth relative to income because saving operated for a longer period. This is probably the case for many northern regions, Piedmont, Liguria, and Lombardy, first and foremost (chapter 7, "Income"). As regards age structure, the regions more skewed toward younger sections of the population, who have had less time to accumulate wealth, show lower values of these indicators, on average.[7] The case of Liguria—the region with the greatest life expectancy in the country (chapter 3, "Health")—is probably an emblematic one. Wealth indicators are also affected by the degree of urbanization and by the incidence of metropolitan areas, where higher quotations of the real estate market prevail (e.g., in Campania, Lazio, and Lombardy).

Cannari and D'Alessio (2006) showed that the regions differ not only with regard to levels of wealth but also in their *composition*, and we see the traditional dualism of the Italian economy confirmed here, too. Since long historical series of the composition of regional wealth are unavailable, we cannot but look at the most recent data. In 2012 in the southern regions, the share of wealth held in real assets exceeded that of the northern regions (by about 10 percent). Differences between north and south are also found in the composition of financial assets. The financial portfolios of southern households show a higher incidence of deposits (particularly postal ones) and cash, and a lower incidence of

---

[7] Some analyses, using SHIW data, show that if the distribution of socio-demographic variables in all Italian regions were the same as the national average, the differences between the regional averages in terms of per-capita wealth would decrease by about 10 percent (Cannari and D'Alessio 2002).

bonds, mutual funds, and shares. Portfolio composition in the south is thus less geared to risk. These differences are due to many factors, including (a) the economic and social conditions of the regions (higher unemployment rates, greater uncertainty about future incomes, and a more fragile production structure push the residents of southern regions to invest in less risky assets); (b) the level of "social capital" (Nuzzo 2006; Felice 2012), meant as civicness and a degree of mutual trust among economic agents (where social capital is low, as in southern Italy, the attitude towards risky financial instruments is affected by generalized mistrust, causing individuals to invest less in shares and more in deposits and liquid assets); (c) the overall wealth level (when it increases, it leads to a rise in the share of risky assets); (d) the average level of household education (the evaluation of risk profiles and the yield of more sophisticated financial instruments calls for greater knowledge); (e) the relative prices of the various assets (since house prices are higher in central and northern regions compared to southern ones, including Sicily and Sardinia, the possibility to access this form of asset, with overall wealth being equal, is higher for southern households); and (f) the supply structure (the lower coverage of the banking system in the south favors choices such as investing wealth in post office savings instruments).

What do we know about the above factors historically? Very little. In Italy's case, the historical analysis of the regional dynamics of household wealth is a largely unexplored field; this is an important gap in light of the scale of territorial differences we have documented in this section. In a context where informal social protection mechanisms prevail (the extended household), the net wealth of households plays a key role in absorbing the negative shocks that jeopardize individuals' living conditions (Brugiavini and Weber 2014). The availability of long-term regional data, then, is fundamental to a full appreciation of the dynamics of territorial disparities of wellbeing.

6. The Composition of Wealth

As the composition of a family's diet tells us something about their standard of living (chapter 1), so the composition of household wealth gives us clues as to the wellbeing they enjoy. In sections 6.1 and 6.2 we therefore investigate the types of assets owned by families, focusing on durable goods and the family home, respectively. But there are other reasons to examine the composition of wealth. A clear picture of the composition of wealth is essential to implement redistribution policies—to have greater impact on some sections of the population and less on others. Already in the nineteenth century Pantaleoni (1890) denounced the fact that movable wealth easily escaped the inheritance tax, as did Corrado Gini (1962) decades later: "[T]he exchange of real estate, securities and other movables requires a different regulation by the law. . . . Depending on the prevalently movable or immovable nature of wealth, different taxation systems may be appropriate for the tax authorities". In general, a shift toward more movable assets makes it more difficult for tax authorities to reach wealth, subject it to taxation, and thus perform a redistributive action (Zucman 2014).

We can also see the traces of structural change in the composition of national wealth. Gini (1962) documented Italy's backwardness relative to the United Kingdom or France in just the way. In the early twentieth century Italy could be judged rural and backward with almost 70 percent of total wealth in land and real estate, only 30 in financial or other assets, whereas the United Kingdom already had a modern wealth structure, in which real assets accounted for less than 25 percent of the total. Quirino (1962) updated Gini's calculations by documenting the metamorphosis of Italian wealth underway towards mid-century: the percentage in movables was on the rise compared to real estate assets—the "indication of a transformation of the economic system from a predominantly agricultural one to . . . an increasingly . . . industrial and commercial nature" (402). It is the wealth of landowners that declined in favor of industrial and financial capital. All this is in line with the data provided by Goldsmith and Zecchini (1999) that document the gradual disappearance of "agricultural" capital.

More precise and reliable data for Italy are found for the years after World War II. Figure 10.3 shows that real assets continue to account for a high percentage of total wealth. Over half, sometimes two-thirds, of the wealth of Italian households is constituted by real estate, which is not very liquid when drawing down one's wealth to face a rainy day is required.

For welfare analysts, a limitation of Figure 10.3 is that it gives an incomplete picture of the role played by particular components of wealth with regard to the population's standard of living. There are qualitative aspects that escape any monetary measurement. We cannot even rule out the possibility that the share of consumer durables is misleading if used as an indicator of wellbeing. The figure shows a slow decline in the percentage of durables in total wealth, despite the enormous effect that the automobile, refrigerator, and washing machine, or even the radio and television, have had on the daily life of the population. The durables curve in Figure 10.3 fails to represent the role of these assets in contributing to the wellbeing of the Italians. We shall analyze this in greater detail in the next section.

6.1 DURABLE GOODS

Durable items such as automobiles, household appliances, and furniture have a positive and significant impact on living standards, despite the fact that expenditure on these goods often takes up only a modest percentage of disposable income. Bowden and Offer (1994) showed that in the United States, for example,

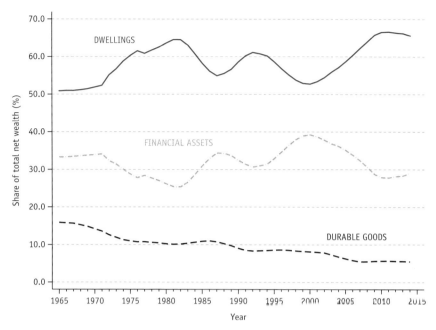

Figure 10.3 The Composition of Wealth, Since 1965. The graph shows the three main categories which go to make up the private wealth of households: real estate (homes), financial assets, and wealth held in the form of durable consumer goods.

the expenditure on domestic appliances accounted for 0.5 percent of disposable income in 1920, and barely 2 percent in 1980. Yet, durable goods changed the lifestyles of individuals, either by saving their time—as in the case of household appliances—or by facilitating their enjoyment of their time, as with entertainment appliances (Offer 2005). Either way, consumer durable goods clearly matter to the wellbeing of individuals, much more than we can see from the monetary measurements used by economists (Slesnik 2001).[8]

When consumerism suddenly hit Italy after World War II, a leading role was played by consumer durable goods such as household appliances, automobiles, and motorcycles. These were the objects of desire of the Italians in the two or three decades that brought Italian society out of generations of enforced parsimony.

If we were to ask women of at least two generations, those born in the 1920s and 1940s, which consumer good had contributed the most to their personal

---

[8] For economists, a durable good is "a consumption good that can deliver useful services to a consumer through repeated use over an extended period of time" (Diewert 2009, 447). The important characteristic of a durable good is less its physical durability than its ability, like capital goods, to be productive more than one period (Amendola and Vecchi 2014).

wellbeing, we would probably get a single answer: the washing machine. The washing machine freed women from their most tiresome chore: doing the washing. "Before the introduction of running water, gas and electricity, people had to spend two days to do the washing: you first had to make a fire to boil the clothes, to then wash them, rinse them, wring them, at times blue them, put them out to dry and, finally, iron them" (Paoloni 2013). Before World War II, even in the economically most advanced countries, affording a washing machine was within the means of only few: in 1916 only one in 100 American famiies had a washing machine; in the United Kingdom, even in 1934 the figure was just one household out of every 100.

In Italy the first washing machine was produced by the Officine Meccaniche Eden Fumagalli of Monza, manufacturers of precision machine tools. In 1945 they created the Candy Model 50, advertising it as the first wholly Italian-made washing machine. In 1952, in Milan—the country's most "modern" city—only 2.3 percent of households had one. If only 6 percent of households declared they had a washing machine in 1961, from the latter half of the 1960s there was a real boom in demand for this product, and Italian manufacturers rose to the challenge (and also exported their washing machines, taking advantage of the economies of scale generated by domestic demand) (Castellano 1965). In 1970 over half of Italian households had a washing machine, and in 1980 only 15 percent still lacked one.

The uptake of refrigerators also started in the early 1950s, slightly predating the demand for washing machines, but taking a very different direction (Figure 10.4).[9] The spread of the refrigerator was rapid. The population's migration from the countryside to the city left women, at least initially, the time for domestic chores since they no longer worked in the fields. While a refrigerator was essential for preserving food in an urban context, owning a washing machine could wait: women's domestic work was still "cheap" and women still carried out household chores, resignedly.

We still need to say something about automobiles. The Italian company FIAT (Fabbrica Italiana Automobili Torino), destined to shape a non-negligible part of Italy's industrial history and to provide the object of desire—perhaps still the most important—of young male consumers, was founded in 1899. Five years later, automobiles were still very rare. The first issue of the statistical yearbook *Annuario statistico delle città italiane*, published in 1906, recorded the number of automobiles in the provincial capital cities. In 1904, out of a total of 52 provincial capitals, 16 of them did not have a single car. Milan, with 445 vehicles (less than one for every thousand inhabitants), topped the list. Genoa had 0.5

---

[9] The first electric washing machine was developed in 1907 by Alva Fisher. The first domestic refrigerator was marketed in the United States in 1913.

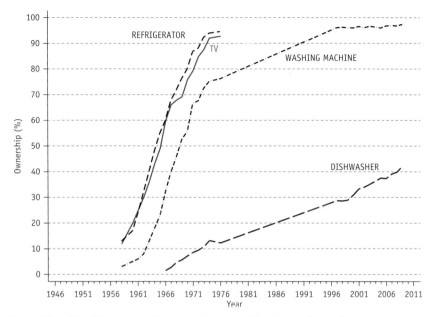

Figure 10.4 THE UPTAKE OF DURABLE GOODS. The figure shows the percentage of households who owned the domestic appliances indicated in the graph (vertical axis).

cars per 1,000 inhabitants; Turin, the hometown of FIAT, had 0.3, Rome and Florence 0.2, while Naples and Palermo had 0.1. Venice had as many gondolas, very expensive and destined only for the richest nobility, per 1,000 inhabitants as there were cars in Milan. Automobiles were, and remained for many years, a great luxury good—the conspicuous consumption of the highest income groups (Toniolo and Vecchi 2010).

Even on the eve of World War II, only 0.7 percent of Italians owned a car: the south had roughly half the number of the north. Then the 1950s arrived: in a decade the number of vehicles per 1,000 inhabitants quintupled. In the 1960s they quadrupled again, reaching one car for every five inhabitants in 1971. The growing popularity of the motor car was favored by public policies on infrastructure: work proceeded briskly on modernizing old roads, widening, and asphalting them, thereby privileging the development of the road network over the railway network (Cannari and Chiri 2006). Italy amazed itself and the whole world by completing the *Autostrada del Sole* ("Highway of the Sun")—750 kilometers of motorway—designed and built between 1956 and 1964. Before its construction, it took about two days to travel from Naples to Milan. Nowadays, with one car for every 1.5

inhabitants, also counting children, Italy ranks among the leading countries for the degree of motorization.

6.2 THE HOME

The classic durable good—the most durable of all—is the home. Once our primary needs—food and clothing—are satisfied, then possessing a comfortable home has always been an absolute must for every individual.

A crude but effective indicator for evaluating the suitability of a home is the crowding index. This measure can be defined in various ways, such as the number of persons per room or the number of persons per bedroom, but the overall picture we get by looking at the long-term evolution of crowding is not significantly altered by the choice of indicator. The point is that the presence of too many people per room favors the spreading of infectious diseases and increases the likelihood of domestic accidents; it has negative effects on mental wellbeing, increases the probability of family breakup, and is, from any perspective, a factor that negatively affected the wellbeing of the Italians.

The historical data needed to reconstruct the progress achieved on this front are scant. The censuses of the Italian population have, since 1861, gathered information on the number of homes and the average number of people per home, but they do not enable us to make methodologically sound intertemporal comparisons.[10] Although we do not have a measure of the degree of crowding in nineteenth-century Italy, we do have abundant sources providing qualitative descriptions. If we randomly choose one of the preparatory manuscripts of the far-reaching Jacini Enquiry into the conditions of agriculture and the rural population, whose proceedings were published between 1881 and 1890, we find accounts like the following:

> The peasants' dwellings are horrid hovels consisting of one ground-floor room with walls of earth and stone with an average length and width of 5 meters, and height of 3 meters. ... The walls unplastered and the floor unpaved. All the furnishings in this miserable hovel consist of a paltry bed in which all the family slept, even as many as five people. A table, a large chest and two or three primitively shaped wooden chairs, a saucepan and a large frying pan. ... Since the donkey, pig and ... chickens all live in the same hovel, it is easy to deduce whether those dwellings can be healthy. (Archivio Centrale di Stato 1877–1895)

---

[10] The reason for this is the variety of definitions adopted to define the target of the survey, definitions which changed at every census: first they targeted "the house" and then "the dwelling", and then "the premises", so that, in the end, comparisons are impractical until the 1931 census (Istat 2014).

"Five people to a bed"—it is, in all likelihood, a condition concerning the poorest segment of the population, and thus not representative of the average conditions of the whole population. Nevertheless, they are still useful indications to appreciate the intensity and speed of deep change that would, in the following decades, transform the living conditions of the Italians inside their homes.

The first census concerning both the population and their homes dates back to 1951, and started the era of modern statistics on the matter. This did not occur by chance. At the end of the war, the estimated damage to dwellings was great. Millions of Italians were in search of a home, particularly in the cities hit the hardest by bombings (Genoa, Turin, and Milan, but also Naples and Messina), where the urbanization of the rural population made the situation even more difficult.

In 1951 the Italians had homes of modest size: about 40 percent of the dwellings used as the main residence had one or at most two rooms. On average, there were 3.3 rooms per home, with large differences throughout the country: in the south the index fluctuated between 2.1 of Basilicata and 2.5 of Campania and Sicily. In the center-north, Liguria, Tuscany, and the Marche, there were 4.3 rooms per dwelling.

Figure 10.5 shows that in 1951 the crowding index of Italian homes was 1.31 people per room, a value not far removed from the one of twenty years earlier (1.36). Almost fourteen million people—30 percent of the population—lived in

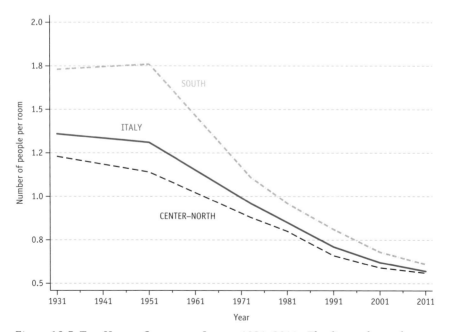

Figure 10.5 THE HOUSE CROWDING INDEX, 1931–2011. The figure shows the house crowding index (vertical axis) over time (horizontal axis).

overcrowded homes. Of these, a little under four million lived in critical conditions, with almost six people per room. These were mostly southern families
(such as 950,000 Campanians, 800,000 Apulians, and about the same number
of Sicilians, as against 100,000 Lombards and 60,000 Veneti).

The reconstruction that took place in the following decades thus had to meet
a strong need to rebuild all the housing destroyed by the war and to provide
homes to a growing number of individuals that economic development had made
more affluent. The investments in housing rose from 3.3 percent of GDP in
1951 to about 8 percent in 1964; between 1951 and 1961 the number of homes
increased by almost three million. In meeting this demand, however, quality was
largely neglected, in a context where there was a lack of town-planning instruments for safeguarding the territory.

Despite the increase in supply, there were still enormous tensions in the housing market, especially for the less privileged living in the big cities. To address
these problems, it was decided to freeze rents. In 1978 a fair rent law was passed
that established rent on the basis of the characteristics of the dwelling; it also
provided a series of rules on the duration of the tenancy contract, and so on. The
law turned out to be excessively rigid and contributed to reducing the supply of
homes on the market. As a result, many homes remained vacant, and the law
also stimulated a parallel private-rental housing market. This encouraged people
to purchase their own homes. The number of homes continued to grow in the
1970s and 1980s, also as a result of unauthorized building—especially in southern Italy, where three quarters of the homes built between 1971 and 1981 had
various forms of irregularities, as against 14 percent in the north and 10 percent
in the center of the country.

In 1971 the crowding index dropped to 0.95, corresponding to about one
room per person. The average household in 1971 was composed of 3.3 people
who lived in a home of 3.5 rooms. The most recent census of 2011 showed
that the crowding index dropped to 0.57. In the same year, the average size
of an Italian household fell to 2.4 members, and the average size of a home
increased to 4.3 rooms. Today, the problem of house crowding concerns a relatively small section of the population; according to the standards established
by the Commission for the Study of Poverty—set up at the Office of the Prime
Minister—in a study of housing poverty in Italy, 10 percent of households still
had problems of overcrowding (Ricci 1997).

Figure 10.5 also shows the different living conditions in the center-north and
south of the country. In the north, the crowding index is always lower than that
of the south, but the gap narrows over time. In the years 1931–1951, all central and northern regions show a tendency to improvement in living conditions
of the population, while those of the south (except for the regions of Abruzzi
and Molise, and Sardinia) show an increase in the average number of people per
room. Starting from 1951, the crowding index dropped rapidly in southern Italy.

Box 3 The Trial of Purchasing a Home

How has the ease of buying a house changed over time? The answer to this question is more complex than one might imagine, depending on the factors taken into account in the comparison. Over time, besides changes in house prices and wages, there have also been changes in the quality of dwellings, household composition, and ease of access to credit. According to one of the first studies carried out by the Bank of Italy, the value of a primary residence in 1966 was almost 5 million lire, on average; the equivalent of 45,000 euros today. In absolute terms, the average value of homes then grew more than fourfold in constant prices, reaching about 190,000 euros in 2014.

A simple indicator that takes into account not just prices but also the growth of incomes in the period relates the value of a dwelling to annual household income. That is, it expresses the number of income years necessary for the average household to purchase an average home. Figure 10. B2 shows historical estimates of this ratio, starting from 1966. According to this index, between 1966 and 2014 the cost of purchasing a home more than doubled in terms of household income. Geographically, the ratio shows higher values for the larger cities.

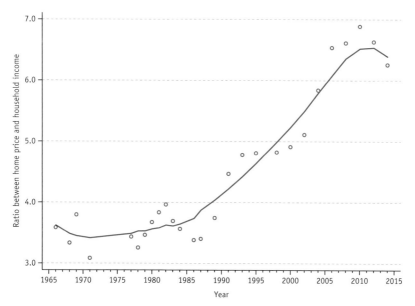

Figure 10.B3 THE EFFORT OF PURCHASING A HOME. The figure shows the number of income years necessary, on average, to purchase a home in Italy between 1966 and 2012. The estimates show that, in the space of one generation, people must work double the years compared to their parents.

In conclusion, the greater difficulties of acquiring a main dwelling signaled by a simple price increase are attenuated if we consider that household incomes also rose, that fewer people live in the household, on average, that there is thus need for less space, on average, and that homes today are of much better quality than they used to be. Nevertheless, even in view of all these aspects, purchasing a home in 2014 seems to be more onerous in terms of income years than in the mid 1960s.

A comparison with other European countries shows that the crowding index in Italy is higher than in France, Germany, and the United Kingdom, and similar to that of Greece, Spain, and Portugal. According to the first European Quality of Life Survey (EQLS), carried out by the European Union (EU) agency Eurofond, in 2003 a hypothetical household of 4 people could have a 6-room home in Italy, but the figure was 7.6 rooms in Germany, 8 in France, and as many as 10.4 in the United Kingdom.

The average Italian dwelling has also changed a great deal with regard to aspects other than size. In 1948 a bathroom was a luxury that only 27 percent of homes had. Even a toilet with running water was the privilege of only 60 percent of households. If electricity was by now universal, only one home in ten had a telephone. Two households out of three had a wood or coal-fired stove. Central heating was a luxury only found in 10 percent of homes.

7 The Distribution of Wealth

"In Italy, the 10 richest individuals own a quantity of wealth that is equivalent to that possessed by the poorest 3 million Italians" (Cannari and D'Alessio 2006). Although this statement effectively conveys a sense of the gap between rich and poor even in a developed country like Italy, it still deserves some clarification.

Inequality in wealth tends to be much more marked than inequality in income. If we take 2014, the last year for which we have estimates, the Gini index of net wealth is about 0.61 as against the 0.35 we see for income; the richest 10 percent of households own 43.7 percent of all net wealth, while the 10 percent of households with the highest incomes instead receive only 25.3 percent of overall income.

The greater inequality we find for wealth compared to income can be explained in various ways. Firstly, inequality in wealth tends to reflect variation across individuals in stage of the life cycle. If all members of a population had identical incomes and saving behaviors (ignoring inheritance, for the sake of simplicity), they would have different levels of wealth depending on their age; wealth needs time to be accumulated. In actual fact, we know that there is a typical age-profile for both income and wealth.

In addition to differences in lifetime earning capacity, inequality in wealth reflects other individual characteristics besides. Different preferences with regard to deferring consumption over time, that is patience, can cause people to devote correspondingly more or less resources to immediate consumption compared to saving. Risk aversion affects both the savings rate—since it changes the wealth level desired as a precautionary measure—and the type of investment chosen. The presence and number of children may, finally, affect the ability to accumluate wealth, the need to save for old age, and the goal of leaving an inheritance. Significant effects on wealth distribution can be attributed to capital gains (i.e., to changes in the value of assets) or to particular household experiences, such as a costly health problems, unemployment, and so on. Inherited wealth and gifts are also of particular importance in determining levels of wealth inequality.

But how has wealth inequality changed in Italy over recent decades? The answer to this question is more difficult than it appears at first glance, owing to the limited availability of sample data and the poor quality of what is available. According to the reconstruction put forward by D'Alessio (2012), inequality in wealth was decreasing between the late 1970s and early 1990s, increasing during the 1990s, and again slightly decreasing in the early 2000s; the microdata also show that inequality since 2008 has started to rise. Although these results call for some caution, inequality in 2012 was lower than the values recorded at the end of the 1970s.

What makes interpreting these indices tricky is the fact that trends in inequality are influenced by trends in asset prices, reflecting the diffusion of different types of asset among the various strata of the population. In general, a rise in share prices tends to increase levels of inequality (because wealthier people tend to own these assets), while the opposite happens when there is a fall in share prices. Since most Italians own their homes, house prices tend to have an opposite effect: their increase tends to reduce inequality, while the opposite happens when house prices fall. Trends in house prices and in share prices often tend to move in opposite directions (the correlation is -0.6 [D'Alessio 2012, 11]). Therefore, the two effects tend to work together and generate a cyclical movement.

But how do wealth levels and wealth inequality in Italy compare with other countries? According to estimates reported in the Global Wealth Report of the Credit Suisse Research Institute, in mid-2014 Italian households held about 4.8 percent of global net wealth, while Italy accounted for about 3 percent of world GDP and 0.8 percent of world population. According to the data of this

Box 4 **Mean Wealth and Median Wealth: But What Difference Does It Make? The Story of the Poor Germans**

There is no more insidious exercise than attempting to draw methodologically robust conclusions about which in a group of countries is the wealthiest. The inherent danger is of not taking due account of the "details" and getting hold of the wrong end of the stick.

A interesting example emerged in the Great Recession, which is worth recalling here. As we all know, at a certain moment in their history the Europeans decided to build a common home—the European Union (EU)—and to give themselves a common currency, the euro, issued by the European Central Bank (ECB). When deciding on economic policy, it is essential to have clear picture of the economic conditions of individual member states. This is a necessary condition to—directly or indirectly—avoid transfers going the wrong way: people becoming lenders when they should be borrowers and vice versa. In this regard, general amazement was created by an ECB report (2013) showing that the *median* wealth of German households was lower than that of Italian and Spanish households—and even of Portuguese and Greek ones (left-hand panel in the graph). Can the Germans really be the poorest (or least affluent) of

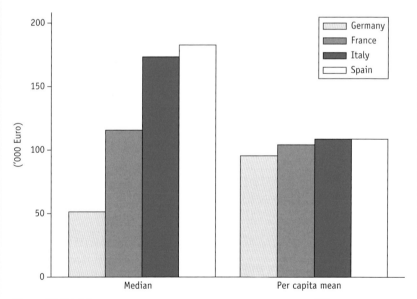

Figure 10.B4 MEAN WEALTH AND MEDIAN WEALTH IN SOME EU COUNTRIES, 2013

all the Europeans? The publication of these statistics triggered a media storm branding it as unacceptable that the "the poor Germans have to pay for the rescue of the much richer Greeks, Spaniards and Portuguese" (De Grauwe and Ji 2013).

To understand this, we must delve into the details. If we use the *mean* value of household wealth instead of the median value, and use per-capita instead of total household wealth, we get what is shown in the right-hand panel of the graph: the differences of the left-hand side disappear and the minimal variation we still see is not statistically significant. The reasons for this distortion lie in the fact that: 1) when the difference between the mean and the median is large, it means that the inequality of the wealth distribution is particularly high, and 2) the different demographic structure of the countries concerned must be taken into account (which, in part, happens when we take household size into account).

The choice of indicator (the mean instead of the median) and of the unit of analysis (the individual instead of the household) shows a much better economic condition of German households—and this is even more marked when we consider wealth net of the public debt.

report, mean wealth per adult in Italy ranks 14th in the world, and this rises to 5th place when median wealth per adult is considered.

As regards the distribution of wealth, the indications we glean from international studies are not always convergent. The levels of inequality found in Italy are lower than those of most other developed countries, such as Canada, Finland, Germany, Sweden, the United Kingdom, and the United States (Sierminska, Brandolini, and Smeeding 2007; Davies, Sandstrom, Shorrocks, and Wolff 2009). Recent estimates based on data from the HFCS (Households Finance and Consumption Survey) studies carried out by the central banks of the Eurozone countries (Fessler et al. 2014) confirm that the level of inequality in wealth in Italy is comparatively modest; higher values are found in 7 out of the 14 countries considered, including Austria, France, Germany, the Netherlands, and Portugal, while only 4 countries have lower inequality (Greece, Slovakia, Slovenia, and Spain).

Hence, although the estimates are not always consistent, as we said, and should be taken with a grain of salt, the indications for Italy would seem to converge in indicating relatively moderate levels of wealth inequality. In an accounting sense, this result is largely attributable to widespread home ownership in Italy—much higher than in many other European countries.

8 Wealth and GDP, a Dangerous Relationship

Over the last few years there has been renewed interest in measuring the wealth of nations. Particularly salient have been the studies published by Thomas Piketty and a host of collaborators of high academic caliber. Piketty and Zucman (2013), for example, managed to reconstruct historical estimates of the national wealth of France, the United Kingdom, and the Unites States back to the eighteenth century. Ohlsson, Roine, and Waldenström (2014) added the case of Sweden since the early nineteenth century.

Unlike past scholars, who were interested in wealth in order to establish a ranking of nations on the basis of their "power", today's studies are motivated by a concern that has begun to haunt academic circles and is attracting increasing attention on the part of the general public. The tendency for wealth to increase disproportionately with respect to income, and to concentrate in the hands of a small group of individuals, risks making modern capitalist systems explode. Bang!

The point is explained by Piketty in the conclusion to his monumental work *Capital in the Twenty-First Century,* judged by many as one of the best works of economics written "in the last several decades" (Milanovic 2014, 519):

> The overall conclusion of this study is that a market economy based on private property, if left to itself, ... contains powerful forces of divergence, which are potentially threatening to democratic societies and to the values of social justice on which they are based. ... The principal destabilizing force has to do with the fact that ... wealth accumulated in the past grows more rapidly than output and wages. The entrepreneur inevitably tends to become a rentier, more and more dominant over those who own nothing but their labor. Once constituted, capital reproduces itself faster than output increases. The past devours the future. (Piketty 2014, 571)

The idea of a past that devours the future is a suggestive image, which earned Piketty the epithet "the new Karl Marx". Marx considered the capitalist system to be an intermediate step in the history of humankind. Other organizational forms (slavery, feudalism) had preceded it and others would follow: first socialism and then communism. To grasp how one organizational form gives way to another, Marx studied the "laws of motion of capitalism", becoming convinced that capitalist societies had an inbuilt tendency towards social polarization—to concentration of wealth (in capitalists' hands) and impoverishment of the masses (the proletariat). In Marx's view, economic development would exacerbate the imbalance between the former—a set of economically strong, but numerically weak individuals—and the latter, an economically weak, but numerically predominant mass. Revolution, in which the proletariat expropriated the wealth of the capitalists, would liquidate the historical stage of capitalism and open up a new era: Communism (Roncaglia 2006).

History, as we know, did not prove Marx right. Society did not polarize into the two extremes predicted by Marx, and Italy witnessed the creation of a broad middle class (Sylos Labini 1974). However, winds can change, even suddenly, and history offers numerous examples of this. The changeability of the wind nurtures a more or less latent disquiet.

Piketty deals with the problem on the opening page of his book: "When the rate of return on capital exceeds the rate of growth of output and income, as it did in the nineteenth century and seems quite likely to do so again in the twenty-first, capitalism automatically generates arbitrary and unsustainable inequalities that radically undermine the meritocratic values on which democratic societies are based" (Piketty 2014, 1). In other words, what if Marx got it wrong only with regard to the when? What if the apocalypse (the revolution, that is) is just around the corner?

To deal with the specter of Communism, Piketty studied the relation between wealth in a given year and the income produced in the nation during that same year—a ratio that he denotes with the Greek letter β. If we let W stand for households' wealth and Y for their income (which we can approximate, for the sake of convenience, by GDP), the relation is: $\beta = W / Y$.

This indicator has many advantages, including the facts that it lends itself to simple interpretation and is an analytical as well as descriptive tool. Let us start from the first point. If, in a country, wealth (how much households have inherited and managed to save over their lifetimes: what is shown in Figure 10.1)[11] is six times GDP (how much households produce during a year, a proxy for income), then $\beta = 6$. This number tells us nothing about the *distribution* of wealth among households within the country—what Marx was interested in—but gives us a measure of the relative importance of wealth compared to income, or "how intensely capitalistic the society is" (Piketty 2014), and nothing more. Nevertheless, β plays a leading role because it determines the movements of another Greek letter α, with which Piketty denotes the share of income that goes into the capitalists' pockets (that is, of the individuals who possess wealth)—precisely what Marx was interested in. The formula linking the two Greek letters α and has β been called the "first fundamental law of capitalism":

$$\alpha = r \times \beta$$

[11] Note that we are using household wealth, which is not quite the same as Piketty's definition of capital; see Milanovic (2014, 521).

where r is the interest rate. If, for example, $\beta = 6$ (i.e., if wealth is the equivalent of six years of GDP) and the return on wealth is 5 percent ($r = 5\%$), then the amount of national income that goes to the capitalists is 30 percent ($=5\% \times 6$) of the country's total product).

It is perhaps a little pretentious to call this equation a "law" because it is a simple accounting identity, but it is certainly useful for understanding the impact of β, the relationship between wealth and GDP; the equation says that when β increases, α also increases, that is, the concentration of income flowing into the hands of capital holders rises. In the formula, the link between α and β is the interest rater, which we shall deal with shortly. The fundamental point is that β determines the motion of the capitalist system: it is β that nurtures the inequalities and the social polarization described by Marx; and it is β that can tell us the distribution of wellbeing in the long run. If β increased indefinitely, α would approach 100 percent, implying a society in which almost all income goes to the capitalists, in which the impoverishment of the proletariat would be so great as to bring about a revolution.[12] So much for theory; what do we know about β historically?

For France, the United Kingdom, and the United States, Piketty's historical studies reconstruct the trend of β and conclude that in the time frame considered, roughly since the French Revolution, β has had a U-shaped trend. The values of β were high in the late-nineteenth century (more in Europe, where it was 6 or 7, than in the United States, where it was 4 or 5) and then decrease, almost halving in the space of half a century. From this low point, but they began to grow again, reaching a level of 6 in Europe and a slightly lower value of 4 in the United States. In other words, the dynamic of β in recent decades has been sufficiently strong as to reach values not too different from those recorded in the late-nineteenth century. By the "first law of capitalism" the movements of β are necessarily accompanied by those of α, that is, by an increasing share of the total product that goes to reward the capitalists; the specter of the past—the social tensions if not outright revolutionary actions—come back to haunt the modern world, which thought it had achieved high and generalized levels of wellbeing forever.

How does Italy fare in all this? Having estimated household wealth in section 4, and having a GDP series, it is easy to calculate β, the ratio of wealth to GDP, for Italy. The result is reported in Figure 10.6.

Discounting the estimates relating to the first twenty years, characterized by considerable uncertainty, the trend of β throughout the history of postunification Italy is in line with the U-shaped pattern characterizing other European countries (more similar to Italy with regard to social and economic structure), although some exceptions can be seen. In the late nineteenth century, the

---

[12] There must be the condition that $r > g$, where g is the rate of growth of total income.

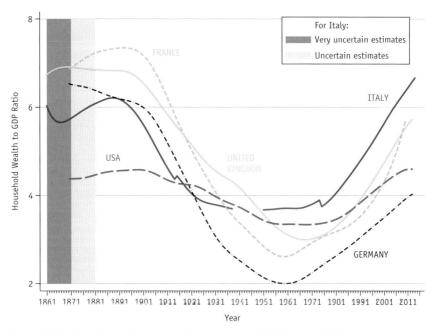

Figure 10.6 THE RATIO BETWEEN WEALTH AND GDP, SINCE 1861. The figure shows the trend of the ratio between wealth and income (vertical axis) over time (horizontal axis) for a set of countries. The U-shaped trend found by Piketty is common to all the countries considered in the graph—including Italy.

"capitalistic intensity" of the Italians was not too different from that of the Germans, the French, or the British.

However, it appears that World War I did not have such a strong impact in Italy. If what Gini said about the material destruction of the war is true, a role here can be played by net foreign assets. The wealthiest families and firms of Britain, France, and Germany were hit by the loss of investments in government bonds and shares in holdings abroad or in the colonies: depending on the case, the war or its associated political upheavals led to the loss or irrecoverableness of investments (Cameron and Neal 2002; Francese and Pace 2012). As we have seen, the composition of Italy's wealth in these years was still that of an underdeveloped country, where the lion's share went to the real components of wealth (land and buildings, which accounted for over two-thirds of total wealth), while the financial component is incomparably smaller than what we find in France or in the United Kingdom. Italy, then, had less to lose, and hence lost less. Mutatis mutandis, similar mechanisms explain the fact that, after the Great Depression, the fall in β was more modest in Italy than elsewhere. In this circumstance we should add Italy's lower international exposure: the Fascist autarchic policies probably lessened the direct impact on household wealth.

The dynamic of β after World War II shows an initial trend where the wealth-GDP ratio decreased as a result of the "economic miracle", which acted on the income of the Italians to such an extent that it dragged β down. As impetuous economic growth subsided during the last three to four decades, the combination of stagnating real income and growing private wealth, boosted from time to time by increases in house prices, make Italy the group champion as regards the speed of growth of β: today, Italy ranks first among the countries with long historical records, with a β of level 6, a value greater than the starting point over 150 years ago.

The U-shaped trend we see in Italy reflects a deep transformation of the Italian economic system and of the power relations within society, and thus deserves an explanation. What factors are at play in determining the trend of β?

9 Tracing the Origins of Wealth

The history of Italy and of its wealth (Figure 10.6) would seem to confirm Piketty's disquieting claim that the past has started to devour the present, and with it the future. For some decades now in Italy, we have seen an increase in the relative weight of wealth (the past) with respect to income (the present) at a pace that is unprecedented in the country's history, and unparalleled even in other countries for which we have reliable data. Hence, we may well ask ourselves what lies behind the growth in wealth of the Italians over the last two centuries: its origins and whether it is in line with the predictions of Piketty's theoretical framework. In this section we shall examine the role of two important factors: saved wealth and inherited wealth.

9.1 SAVED WEALTH

Is a high saving rate a good or bad thing? The question is not easy to answer and depends on one's point of view, that is, if we look at the effects or the determinants of saving. Household saving is the main domestic source of financing for investment and is thus important for long-term economic growth. It must also be recognized that saving enables us to cope with unexpected circumstances. Other things being equal, a high savings rate may mean less economic vulnerability, enabling greater household protection against adverse events.

As regards determinants, the interpretation is rather more complex, as highlighted by the "life cycle theory" devised in the 1950s by the economists Modigliani and Brumberg (1954). The premise is that individuals have a net preference for maintaining consumption at a stable level over time instead of letting it fluctuate with income. To achieve this, households save in the phase of life when income is high (this means sacrificing consumption in the stage when

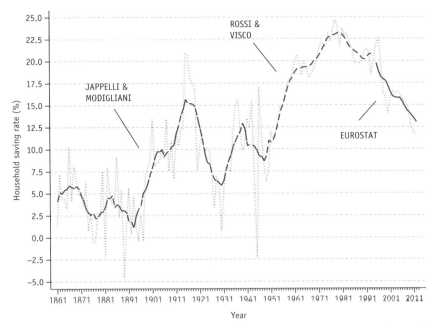

Figure 10.7 THE SAVINGS RATE OF ITALIAN HOUSEHOLDS, 1861–2013. The graph shows the household saving rate (vertical axis) over time (horizontal axis). The annual data (dotted lines) have been smoothed to facilitate identification of the trends.

they are economically active) and use their savings at a later stage, say, during old age, when their income is less. In so doing, households manage to stabilize their standard of living over time. However, a high saving rate may also be due to the fact that households expect their income to fall in the future; just as a decrease in saving may reflect the expectation of greater future income. Hence, it is not always true that savings mean a healthy financial situation; people may save when they fear adverse events in the future—saving for a rainy day, as they say (Deaton 1992; Jappelli and Pistaferri 2006).

In Figure 10.7, we have reconstructed the long-term trend of the saving rate of the Italian families. The series firstly shows that the Italians, far from being born savers, have become so in the course of time. Up until the turn of the twentieth century, the Italians did not manage to save more than 5 percent of their income. This is an obvious thing when we consider that, in a country as poor as postunification Italy, the leeway for savings was quite slim. Less obvious is the fact that the Italians have remained a people of savers even when they might not have been. Saving rates have continued to rise—except in the immediate aftermaths of the two world wars—reaching a peak at the end of the 1970s, when the savings rate approached 25 percent. Since then there has been a decline in which the savings rate has fallen to about 10 percent, just as it was on the eve of World War I.

The decreasing trend seen in the past thirty years can be explained in various ways (Ando, Guiso, and Visco 1994; Bassanetti et al. 2011): the development of insurance markets has reduced the need to save for precautionary reasons; the progress achieved by financial markets has led to greater ease of access to credit and lower interest rates; and a relatively generous pension system, despite recent reforms, has made saving for old age less necessary at a time when increasing life expectancy and a drop in fertility rates have led to a great increase in the percentage of elderly people in the population.[13] The decrease in the number of children may also have mitigated the need to save in order to leave an inheritance. In more recent years, the economic-financial crisis has contributed to the drop in the savings rate: with falling incomes, many households have tried to avoid cutting back their consumption by drawing on their savings.

Today, the savings rate of Italian households is no longer unusually high compared to other countries as it was in the past. In 2011, according to OECD data, household saving as a percentage of disposable income was lower in value than the Eurozone average.

Saving also plays a role in Piketty's theoretical framework—indeed, a key role. Piketty calls it the "second fundamental law of capitalism" (Piketty 2014, 166). The formula expressing this law is as simple as the "first law of capitalism", examined in the previous section:

$$\beta = s / g$$

where s stands for the household saving rate and g is the annual growth rate of GDP. If, for example, s = 10 percent (i.e., households save 10 percent of their incomes) and GDP rises at the rate of 2 percent ($g = 2\%$), then $\beta = 5$. The formula expresses a very intuitive economic logic: with other things being equal, a country in which households save a great deal (a high s) accumulates a large stock of wealth; if, while this is happening, the economy hardly grows or stagnates, that is, if GDP goes up very slightly or not at all (a low g), then the s/g ratio increases and the section of the population that owns the wealth increases its own economic importance in an increasingly disproportionate manner. Living in such a society, where wealth (and the income it generates for capitalists) has such a prevalent role compared to income (especially income arising as a reward for labor), may have its advantages. Ultimately, wealth can turn into productive capital, into investment, and thus can feed economic growth; growth can potentially benefit the whole population—probably not all citizens in the same measure, but it does not matter if this means getting out of economic stagnation.

---

[13] Recall that our definition of private wealth does not include pension entitlements.

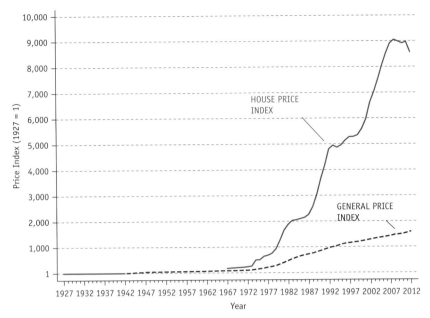

Figure 10.8 THE HISTORICAL TREND IN HOUSE PRICES, SINCE 1966. The graph compares the trend of the general price index (broken line) with that of house prices (blue line). In both cases, the year 1927 has been set at 1: the vertical axis thus measures the multiple with respect to 1927.

However, if the disproportion between wealth and income becomes excessive (if β is too high), there may be adverse effects in society owing to the fact that an increasing share of resources is controlled by those who own the wealth. The economic repercussions can easily turn into political ones.

Before rounding off, it is worth making a technical comment that will enable us to illustrate another aspect of the accumulation of wealth by the Italians. Piketty relies on the assumption that the prices of what constitutes wealth move, on average, at the same pace as the general price trend. If this were not the case, for example, if the prices of real assets increased more rapidly than average prices, then the β ratio could increase independently of the savings rate. As an example of this, consider the price trend for houses, which are the most important component of household wealth. Knoll, Schularick, and Steger (2014) managed to construct long historical series (since 1870) of house prices for fourteen countries, not including Italy. For Italy, we have reconstructed an index that starts in 1927 and leads to the present day. From 1966 to 2012, house prices in Italy rose almost 50 times compared to the increase in the general price index of almost 20 times (Figure 10.8). In the past fifty years the trend in wealth has thus been considerably affected by the real estate cycle, and this has influenced the wealth/income ratio β.

Other calculations for other countries, which we have not reported here for the sake of space, show a strong statistical correlation between wealth and house price trends (Bonnet et al. 2014). This is an important result that we shall come back to in the final section because, if it is true that house prices guide the trend of β, then given the widespread home ownership in Italy, the idea that a rising β heralds revolutionary social tensions is weakened.

9.2 INHERITED WEALTH

Another way of acquiring wealth is through inheritance, and this is at the heart of disputes today, not just with regard to theory. It is commonly held that transfers of wealth between generations are frequent and important. The most important reason for these intergenerational transfers is probably altruism, that is, the parents' joy in making their sons' and daughters' lives easier. These transfers partly depend on uncertainty with regard to life expectancy: even hypothesizing a *Homo economicus* totally focused on himself and who wishes to consume everything and leave nothing behind, uncertainty about the date of death prevents him from planning to have zero income and zero wealth on the eve of his death; what is left turns into an involuntary legacy. Bequests can also reflect strategic or gift-exchange motives: elderly parents may, for example, encourage assistance from their sons and daughters by promising them an inheritance.

From a macroeconomic perspective, inherited wealth plays an important role, even if little discussed outside academic and expert circles. So long as the interest rate r is sufficiently high (in particular, higher than the rate g of GDP growth), what happens is that inherited wealth (a sum which is the expression of all that has been accumulated in the past) tends to prevail over the wealth that the economically active generation is producing in the present (savings).[14] The fact that, with $r > g$ inherited wealth grows automatically and at a greater pace than wealth that is set aside out of income earned through one's own labor inexorably increases the role of inequalities that originate in the past—even the remote past. Again, it is the past that devours the future.

Estimating the portion of wealth handed down by bequest is not an easy thing to do. We can gain some insights from a snapshot made by the Bank of Italy (2002). In 2002 about a third of households had received a transfer from their parents, and the values of such transfers accounted for about a quarter of household net wealth.

---

[14] One might expect the return on capital (r) to be low in a stagnant economy with a low growth rate (g). Why should the condition that $r > g$ prevail? Cannari and D'Alessio (2006) suggest an answer for today's developed countries, including Italy: "The chance to invest in virtually any part of the world, in search of the best profit opportunities, tends to sustain the return on wealth, even in countries where growth is low. If the growth rates of the Italian economy remained low as in the last few years, inherited wealth could increasingly become the premise for individual wellbeing compared to the capacity to generate income through one's own work" (15).

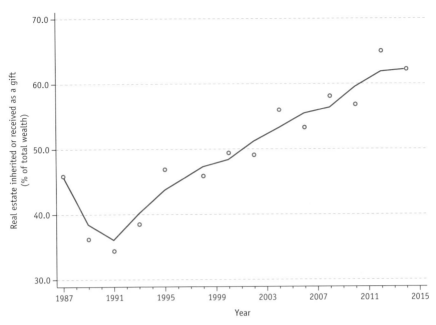

Figure 10.9 VALUE OF REAL ESTATE INHERITED OR RECEIVED AS A GIFT, 1987–2014. The figure shows the increase of inherited wealth (vertical axis), expressed as a percentage of total wealth, over time (horizontal axis). Italians face increasing obstacles in getting rich by their own work and effort.

We must bear in mind that the people receiving a transfer also benefit from the returns to capital, as well as from potential capital gains. This comes about by means of the mechanism involving the interest rate r, which we talked about before. If, for example, an individual inherits a sum of money from his parents and decides to invest it in real estate, after ten years he will have a greater wealth than what he received; the value of what he inherited grows not only due to inflation but also due to the real yield of his investment (a flow of rent on the property purchased, in this case). If we also attribute the part of wealth thus generated to his inheritance, that is, if besides the monetary revaluation we also take into account the flow of income and associated saving generated by this transferred wealth (assuming a real rate of return of 2 percent), the portion of wealth due to inheritance in the Bank of Italy survey exceeds 50 percent. These calculations show how intergenerational transfers are an important part of households' net wealth and thus of their wellbeing.

Going back into time and assessing how the weight of inherited wealth has changed over the years is not an easy thing to do because of the lack of data. Cannari and D'Alessio (2007) find that in the period 1991–2002 the relative weight of inherited wealth in total wealth tended to rise. By adopting the procedure proposed by Barca, Cannari, and Guiso (1994), we have estimated the share of inheritance specifically in real estate wealth (Figure 10.9), thanks to a question posed in a survey on household budgets carried out by the Bank of Italy. That survey asked households how they had acquired their real estate and, in particular, if it had been inherited. Our calculations using these data yield an assessment of the importance of inherited real estate assets as a wealth transmission mechanism. What clearly emerges is the increasing importance of inherited wealth over time.

The slowdown in GDP growth and in the scale of capital gains have contributed to increasing the relative importance of inherited wealth. If we still lack solid empirical grounds for accurately measuring the phenomenon, we can still say that for some decades now, the conditions of wellbeing of the Italian population tend to depend less on one's labor and initiative and more on the quirks of fate and on the past—in short, from inherited wealth.

10 In the Wealth Trap?

The wealth of the Italians took its time in coming, but once it did, the accumulation mechanism then proceeded at a rapid pace. The Italians have become so rich that some have voiced concerns that Italy, like France, the United Kingdom, and the United States, could fall prey to the so-called central contradiction of capitalism. Too much wealth may have destabilizing effects—it may trigger forces that lacerate the socioeconomic fabric, thereby jeopardizing democracy (Piketty 2014, 571). Can too much wealth really conceal a pitfall for the wellbeing of the Italians?

Let us proceed step by step. The initial sluggishness of the saving process was, in some respects, healthy; in a poor country as Italy was in the mid-nineteenth century, the capacity to save sums of a certain size was simply unthinkable for most of the population. In a hundred years the Italians followed a path leading them eventually to save over a quarter of the income produced every year, on average. At the end of the 1970s the propensity to save in Italy was higher than in any other country in the world, except Japan. The fall in saving that started in the 1980s has been interpreted as a sign of modernity. The greater security of the economic environment of the last two generations of Italians has demanded less prudence of them, less self-insurance, less saving. The slowdown in economic growth and the economic-financial crisis in recent years have had an influence as well.

The estimates presented in section 9.1 documented the speed with which annual saving turned into wealth. We indicated the moment of takeoff in the early 1970s; no other economic indicator examined in this book shows such a rapid and persistent rise. The record high was achieved in 2006–2007, before the start of the Great Recession: the wealth of the average Italian was 185,000 Euros (at 2013 prices), a value corresponding to more than 6 times the average income (approximated here as per-capita GDP). Such a high wealth–income ratio can be worrying: this is the thesis put forward by Thomas Piketty and discussed at length in section 8. If wealth—the inheritance that comes from the past, typically concentrated in a few hands—increases too much compared to income, that is, what is produced with one's own labor and initiative, then the tension between the (few) holders of wealth and the (many) workers can reach such levels as to shake the entire economic system, its laws, and its order. If, with reference to France, Piketty could say that the past (wealth) has started to devour the future (income), the same can be said for Italy. The estimates show that the wealth–income ratio is higher today in Italy than in France, with values close to those recorded in the late nineteenth century. The specter of Balzac's *Le Père Goriot*, evoked by Piketty to disturb the dreams of modern French society, could—in view of the estimates presented in this chapter—also plausibly upset the nights of twenty-first-century Italians.

On a more in-depth analysis, the worries of the Italians have solid grounds, but for reasons only in part related to the personal distribution of wealth. The dynamic of Italian wealth since World War II has been determined to a significant degree by the trend in house prices. The price of homes (the most important component of household wealth) has shown a systematically faster increase than the general price index. The Italy of 1951 already had 40 percent of the homes inhabited by their owners, while the percentage was almost 80 percent in 2012. In a country where home ownership is so widespread, an increase in house prices does not generate excessive tensions in the wealth distribution. What is certain, though, is that the accommodation problem worsens for those, such as the younger generations, who do not own a house and wish to purchase one—a problem affecting about 20 percent of the population today (about 12 million citizens).

An important implication emerging from this analysis is that in Italy Piketty's disequilibrium between wealth and income is more to do with the *functional* distribution of income, (i.e., with the increasing proportion relating to capital compared to labor), rather than with the *personal* distribution, (i.e., the proportion going to rich and poor). This ties in with the relationship between generational lines, for example. But this is, evidently, a topic of a different nature and scope compared to that of the intrinsic instability of the capitalist system.

A more serious concern stems from the direction taken by household wealth (falling in the last five years or so) and income. On the whole, Italy is not keeping pace—not a very fast one, at that—with the other European countries. As we saw in chapter 7 ("Income"), the problem is not only due to the serious economic and financial crisis of recent years but has more distant and complex roots going back 20 or 25 years.

The point had already been grasped by Toniolo (2004), for example, well before the onset of the Great Recession: "there is not a day that passes without seeing the *structural* weaknesses of our system highlighted by this or that" (17, our italics): among the factors responsible for the slow income growth of the Italians, Toniolo mentions Italy's loss of international market share, lower employment rates, inadequate infrastructure, low education levels of the workforce, a production structure too skewed toward small firms, weak spending on research and development, and a high public debt. This list of structural weaknesses can also be extended by adding such things as questions of legality, which is especially lacking in some areas of the country. This aggravates the economic conditions of the areas concerned, driving the more capable local entrepreneurs to move their operations away from their area and discouraging outside people from starting any form of business there. These difficulties have been exacerbated by three great changes that have characterized the world's economy over the last few decades: a new technological paradigm based on information and communication technologies (ICT) (Felice and Vecchi 2015); an acceleration of globalization and the integration of the world's financial markets; and the progress of European integration, culminating with the introduction of the single currency, the euro. These changes have quickly increased the competitive pressures on the Italian production system, which has not been able to react properly, unlike in the past: structural problems within industry have not helped matters either (a sectoral composition too dependent on traditional, "low-tech" production and the fragmentation of production), nor have factors external to enterprises (the poor efficiency of public administration and an inadequate legislative framework). These traits illustrate "the poor capacity of adjustment of a successful model to conditions different from the ones that gave rise to the actual success. The economic decline stems from a social, cultural and institutional sclerosis" (Toniolo 2004, 8). Hence, the recent history of Italian wealth is a vivid representation of the persisting difficulties of the Italian economy.

Appendix—Sources and Methods

Box 1 The public debt of the Italians, 1861–2014 For the years 1861–2012 we used Balassone, Francese, and Pace (2013). For the years 2013–2015 we used Bank of Italy (2016).

Figure 10.1 The private wealth of the Italians, 1871–2012 The statistical reconstruction of the series proceeded backward from 2014 to 1871. For the years *2014–2005* we used Istat (2015); for the years *2005–1995* we used the official estimates of the Bank of Italy's Statistical Bulletin (https://www.banca-ditalia.it/pubblicazioni/bollettino-statistico), combined with the value of durable goods. For the years *1995–1965* the growth rates implicit in the series of Brandolini et al. (2004) were applied backward to the value of the 1995 series. For the years *1965–1951*, we started from the series of Marotta and Rossi (1992) and reestimated the levels of the series concerning dwellings by referring to Goldsmith and Zecchini (1999). Assuming that the estimates of the latter provide the correct value of the value of dwellings for the benchmark year 1951, we corrected (rounding down) Marotta and Rossi's series. For the period *1950–1939*, adequate statistical information is lacking; this is mostly with regard to the war years during which the Italian state had to reorganize after the devastations and social and political upheavals. For the years *1938–1901*, we used the estimates of Retti-Marsani (1936; 1937), which are the most reliable today (Zamagni 1980; Baffigi 2009). Retti-Marsani covered the years between 1901 and 1934, but De Vita (1941) updated the series to 1938. For the years *1900–1861*, we constructed an intertemporal projector on the basis of the flows of inheritance, donations, and various bequeathments, calculated by Tivaroni (1926). In the graph, the series thus obtained is compared with Goldsmith and Zecchini's estimates (1999), available only for benchmark years. In relation to the period before World War I, the choice could have been for other "quality" estimates: one is Baffigi's (2008), another is Sensini's (1904). However, in both cases, the series focus on the same statistical material of Tivaroni, but they use methods that are more difficult to defend.

Figure 10.2 Household wealth in the regions, 1901–2012 For 1901–1903: Nitti (1905). For 1928: De Vita (1933). For 1995–2000: Cannari and D'Alessio (2002). For 2012: Bank of Italy (2014a).

Figure 10.3 The composition of wealth, since 1966 Source: our calculations based on Brandolini et al. (2004) and Banca d'Italia (2012).

Figure 10.4 The uptake of durable goods Sources: Refrigerator, dishwasher and washing machine: from 1957 to 1964: Luzzato Fegiz; from 1965 to 1976: Banca d'Italia, *Reddito, risparmio e struttura della ricchezza delle famiglie italiane*, taken from *Bollettino,* various years; from 1997 to 2009: Istat, *Il possesso e l'acquisto dei beni durevoli (1997–2004)*, available at www3.istat.it/istat/audizioni/171005/H-Dossier7.pdf, and later updates; Television: *International Historical Statistics: Europe, 1750–1993* (Mitchell). Population data are from Istat, *Serie Storiche.*

Figure 10.5 The house crowding index, 1931–2011 Source: Capodiferro (1965) for the years 1931 and 1951; our calculations on data from "I consumi delle famiglie," Istat (various years) for the years 1973–2001.

Box 3 The Trial of Purchasing a Home Source: D'Alessio and Gambacorta (2007), updated with calculations on SHIW data.

Box 4 Mean Wealth and Median Wealth: But What Difference Does It Make? The Story of the Poor Germans Sources: our calculations based on European Central Bank (2013).

Figure 10.6 The ratio between wealth and GDP, since 1861 The series relative to Italy is calculated as the ratio between household wealth (see Figure 10.2) and GDP (within the borders of the times) estimated in Baffigi (2013). For the other countries in the figure the source is Piketty and Zucman (2014). The series are smoothed by means of a LOWESS filter, with bandwidth = 0.3.

Figure 10.7 The saving rate of Italian households, 1861–2012 For 1861–1950: our calculations on data provided by Jappelli and Modigliani (1987); 1951–1994: Rossi and Visco (1995); 1995–2012: Eurostat (2014), the version available in July 2014. The dotted line corresponds to the annual values of household gross savings; the thick line corresponds to a nine-point moving average.

Figure 10.8 The historical trend in house prices The source for the general price index is Istat (value of currency). The source used for house prices from 1927 to 1941 is the Fascist Federation of Builders, whose data are reported in Istat's statistical yearbook of those years. For 1941–1942 we used Istat data (1943), which contain the real estate market prices in the main Italian cities. The data on the level of prices per room in the eight main Italian cities of 1942 have been combined, city by city, with those reported in the review *Il consulente immobiliare* of 1966, which reports prices per square meter, using the estimates of the average size in square meters of rooms based on land registry statistics.

Figure 10.9 Value of real estate inherited or received as a gift, 1987–2014 Source: our estimates based on the update of Cannari and D'Alessio (2008).

11

Vulnerability

WITH MARIACRISTINA ROSSI AND LUCIA LATINO

1 An Ugly September Sunday

> In short, an ugly September Sunday dawned—a Sunday in false September which lets loose a tempest on one between the cup and the lip, like a shot from behind a prickly-pear.... The poor little thing, who did not even know she was a widow, went on crying: "Oh Blessed Virgin! Oh Blessed Virgin! Oh Virgin Mary!" ... The house by the medlar was full of people. "Sad is the house where there is the 'visit' for the husband." Everybody passing and seeing the poor little orphaned Malavoglia at the door, with dirty faces, and hands in their pockets, shook their heads, saying: "Poor Cousin Maruzza, now her hard times are beginning". (Verga 1881, chapter III, English trans., *The House by the Medlar Tree*, 1890)

This passage, taken from the novel *I Malavoglia* by Giovanni Verga (1840–1922), tells of the epilogue of a tragedy at sea in which Bastianazzo Malavoglia loses his life. Following the shipwreck of the *Provvidenza*, the Malavoglia family faces a triple tragedy: the death of the head of the family, the debt for the shipload of lupin beans lost at sea, and the cost of repairing the ship. Overwhelmed by this dramatic event, the family suddenly falls into dire straits and the future holds only one prospect: poverty.

The shipwreck of the *Provvidenza* has something in common with Coupeau's accident in *L'Assommoir* by Émile Zola (1840–1902); and also the dismissal of Johannes Pinnenberg in *Little Man, What Now?* by Hans Fallada (1893–1947). Coupeau falls to the ground while mounting an eaves gutter and remains bedridden for months on end; the family's savings go to care for him, but then, exhausted by the disease, he takes to drinking, thereby marking the beginning of the end. Johannes, instead, is fired unjustly from his job, and this forces him to live in the anxiety of precariousness and unemployment.

These are all examples of what the economists call "the realization of a negative idiosyncratic shock", that is, a risk that, by materializing, strikes an individual or a family and may lead to a worsening of their wellbeing. These are mainly risks linked to health (illness, disability, old age, death) or to occupational hardships (dismissal, unemployment) (Gollier 2001).[1]

To these idiosyncratic risks must be added other kinds of risks. Going back to Fallada's novel, Johannes Pinnenberg's life is conditioned not only by the loss of his job, but more generally by the economic crisis overwhelming Germany in the 1930s. Similarly, the change in the macroeconomic climate (the German hyper-inflation of the 1920s) strained Ludwig Bodmer in *The Black Obelisk* by Erich Maria Remarque (1898–1970): the money that would have been enough to buy a gravestone the day before was no longer enough to buy a loaf of bread the day after. In the novel *La Ciociara* (published in English as *Two Women*) by Alberto Moravia (1907–1990), Cesira (the widow played by Sophia Loren in the film version, directed by Vittorio De Sica) is forced to abandon everything—home, shop, and every other belonging—in order to flee Rome when the Germans occupy the city in September 1943. Even Louis Roubieu in Émile Zola's *The Flood* loses everything. He is the wealthiest farmer in the village, but in just one night the river Garonne breaks its banks and sweeps away the money and affections of a lifetime. The experiences of Johannes, Ludwig, Cesira, and Louis, although different, are all the result of a "negative systemic shock" (Dercon 2001, 26). Economic and financial crises, social unrest, wars, and natural disasters are risks that threaten all the households of an entire community or nation. In a population, not all the individuals are exposed to the same risks with the same likelihood, but it is easy to see that an all-around evaluation of an individual's wellbeing cannot be devoid of the presence of risk. If the risk materializes and strikes the individual, the consequences can entail a (temporary or permanent) decrease in income and, more generally, a worsening of living conditions. That is why scholars of poverty know that they must assess not only the poverty *observed* at a given moment in time but also future *potential* poverty.

On this premise, the task we have undertaken in this chapter is that of assessing how the living conditions of the Italians have been—and are still—conditioned by the presence of risk and uncertainty. We shall consider the time frame of the whole postunification period. This means comparing very heterogeneous situations, since the degree of complexity and risk of society have changed over time and coping mechanisms capable of neutralizing the occurrence of negative events have increased. While the former factor influences the likelihood of experiencing a negative event, the latter one affects the magnitude of the damage it produces.

The Malavoglia family in Giovanni Verga's novel (mentioned at the beginning of the chapter) belongs to the "cycle of the losers". Verga tells the tale of a

---

[1] The risk may also involve positive shocks, of course, such as an unexpected gain (winning the lottery). In this chapter we shall focus on potentially damaging risks to families' wellbeing.

family that is structurally unable to get over a shock. Despite the family's initial determination to quickly get back on its feet after the shock, and despite the pity and solidarity shown by their community, the family breaks up in the end, with the downfall of all its members. Do families still exist today who are as exposed to risk as they are helpless to prevent it or to cope with its consequences? What risks have jeopardized and/or jeopardize the serenity of Italian families? What instruments and rules could have been used in order to safeguard the wellbeing of those who have been exposed to the risk of becoming poor over the 150 years of postunification Italy? Have these instruments, institutions, and rules been effective in protecting the wellbeing achieved by the Italians over this period? This chapter will provide answers to these questions.

In the first part (sections 2–4) we shall examine the role played by the main actors—the Church and state—in dealing with the population's economic vulnerability. We shall consider the nature and scope of the "safety nets" that these institutions developed over time (Zamagni 2000). The underlying idea—not above criticism—is that of interpreting the scale of these safety nets as an inverse measure of vulnerability: a net that becomes larger over time, and whose meshes become smaller, suggests a greater capacity of society to protect its members from the risk of negative events.

The first net we shall consider is the one offered by religious institutions. Although it is not within our power to assess or estimate the "economic" role played by the Church in assisting the poorest segments of the population, we shall use some statistics that can portray the scale of welfare actions in the early decades of postunification Italy. The second net taken into consideration is that of the state. We shall run through history, from the nineteenth-century welfare system to the modern welfare state, highlighting the methods and rules giving rise to its structure.[2] The role of systemic shocks, largely overlooked by historiographic literature, is examined in section 5.

The second part of this chapter narrows the time frame of reference to the period 1980–2010: this enables us to use more sophisticated econometric tools to estimate the evolution of the probability with which Italian households, both poor and nonpoor ones, are exposed to the risk of future poverty. The results of our analysis are surprising in some respects: Italy appears to be a country in which a relatively modest segment of the population can be classified as "poor",

---

[2] For reasons of space, we shall not deal with other aspects that are also worthy of attention. The market offers protection through a broad range of insurance instruments. There are—and were—safety nets linked to one's occupation: the mutual aid associations, for example, or the cooperative societies of production. The role of the community of affection that the individual lives in is also of great importance, and particularly the household. Saving and the resulting accumulation of wealth is the main form of self-insurance against future risks (Keynes 1936; Kotlikoff 1989). The saving rate of households since the time of unification and data on household wealth are analyzed in chapter 10 ("Wealth").

while an unexpectedly broad segment turns out to be at risk of poverty in the future. If this is so, it would be unwise to consider the level of wellbeing achieved by the Italians over the past 150 years or so as a given once and for all: the analysis of the last few decades shows that the country urgently needs to reflect on the best way to reduce the population's vulnerability to poverty. On the basis of the estimates presented in section 7, we find many citizens who, without any proper social safety net, could—just like the Malavoglia family in Verga's novel—experience an "ugly September Sunday".

2 Church Support

The little church of Pio Monte della Misericordia in Naples houses an oil painting by Michelangelo Merisi, better known as Caravaggio, on the seven corporal works of mercy. Painted between 1606 and 1607, the work masterfully summarizes the charity and welfare mission of the Church. Caravaggio resorts to the personification of the acts of mercy by depicting the tender story of Cimon and Pero, who are father and daughter. Cimon, who is condemned to death by starvation, is kept alive by the milk that is secretly breastfed to him by his daughter. She is allowed to visit her father on condition that she does not take him any food. This personifies the merciful acts of feeding the hungry and going to visit convicts. Caravaggio depicts other figures in this work, including Samson drinking from the jawbone of an ass (refreshing the thirsty), a young wealthy man giving part of his cloak to a naked beggar on the ground (clothing the naked), an innkeeper welcoming a pilgrim (giving shelter to pilgrims), and many others. This is the way Caravaggio tells of the works that the Church has carried on for centuries: taking care of the poor, widows, orphans, and people living on the fringes of society.

The Pio Monte della Misericordia is only one of the many welfare institutions operating at the time of Italy's unification. There was a plethora of religious organizations (oratories, brotherhoods, hospitals, religious organizations, pawnshops,[3] etc.) that played a crucial social role, given the repressive attitude that the new Italian state showed toward the poor from the very beginning. According to the liberal ideology of the House of Savoy and of the new Italian State, the poor were not only unworthy of any aid but also represented a threat to the social order and to public hygiene.

---

[3] The pawnshops, called *Monti di Pietà*, founded thanks to the work of the Franciscan friars, were institutions that received public and private donations, and granted small loans in exchange for some collateral. By charging a modest interest rate, they tried to combat the usury of the times. In 1862 they were taken over by the *Opere Pie*.

A good approximation of the extent of the social safety net established by the Church can be gained from a national study of 1862, carried out to assess the assets and activities of the charity organizations called the *Opere Pie* ("Pious Works"). These were public institutions created over the centuries under the Church's "civil authority" and were run by the clergy (Caravaggio 1911). They dealt with welfare in all its forms, from providing hospital care and other health services to organizing maternity hospices; mental asylums and shelters for people of all ages: institutes for foundlings and orphanages; homes for the deaf and dumb, the blind, and "unruly youngsters or youngsters exiting prison"; and old people's homes called *ricoveri di mendicità* ("beggary shelters"). They provided a money-lending service through a widespread network of pawnshops and also provided many other services of an educational, child nursing, dotal, and alms kind.

At the time of unification, the *Opere Pie* were huge financial organizations. They were numerous (almost 18,000 by December 31, 1861) and owned enormous assets, estimated in 1861 at 20 percent of the GDP (Lepre 1988). They were widespread across the country, even if not ovenly distributed. This enabled the *Opere Pie* to reach almost one citizen out of four, from simply providing a meal to outright hospitalization, but the data show just how solid and far-reaching the Church's safety net was with respect to the nature and extent of the noninsurable risks.

The average value of the welfare services at the time was around 16 lire (62 euros today). If we consider that an unskilled worker of the times could earn between 1 and 1.5 lire a day while a skilled worker could earn between 2.5 and 3.5 lire a day (Bandettini 1960; Aleati 1961; Di Rollo 1965), we see that, on average, one welfare action covered the equivalent of ten to fifteen workdays of an unskilled worker, and not more than a week's work for a skilled worker. If we try to imagine the worker's family, perhaps composed of two adults and three children, we see that the 16 lire received by the *Opere Pie* in 1861 in the event of an accident, say, would have been barely enough to provide the whole family with a subsistence diet for a period of ten or eleven days at the very most.[4]

The data examined above conceal the coexistence of two very different welfare systems in 1861 Italy. In the south of the country, despite the fact that 92 percent of the population lived in municipalities with at least one charity institution, the percentage of the beneficiaries was a lot lower than for the north; for every beneficiary in the south there were five in the north (Conte, Rossi, and Vecchi 2011). On the other hand, the average value of assistance per

---

[4] The calculation, purely an indicative one, assumes a requirement of 10,000 calories per household; if we hypothesize a bread-only diet (with an energy content of 2,800 calories per kilogram) and assume a price for bread of 0.4 lire per kilo (Istat 1958), we obtain a daily expenditure for bread of 1.43 lire, which leads to the result commented in the text.

beneficiary in the south was far greater (120 euros per person, in current terms) than in the north-east (70 euros). Giovanna Farrel-Vinay (1997) suggested that some of these differences can be attributed to the different management of the *Opere Pie*: in the north they were run by the regular clergy, while in the south they were run by brotherhoods who tended to perform a function similar to the one of mutual aid associations, that is, they catered "only" to people who were members.

In the decades after 1861, the number of welfare institutions continued to grow, increasing from 17,897 in 1861 to 21,866 in 1880 and 27,078 in 1900. The annexation of Lazio to the Kingdom of Italy in 1870 justifies most of the increase in these numbers. The exceptional nature of the Lazio figure did not actually astonish observers of the times: as early as 1850, Cardinal Carlo Luigi Morichini observed how in Rome "there were more dowries to be handed out than spinsters to marry" (Lepre 1988, 11).[5]

A significant turning point came in 1890 with the so-called Crispi Law, which transformed the *Opere Pie* into public institutions of welfare and charity (*Istituzioni Pubbliche di Assistenza e Beneficienza*, IPAB), under the supervision of provincial and municipal authorities. The lawmakers' intention was that of reorganizing all charity organizations, which were mostly of a religious nature, and it reflected the penetration in Italy of a more modern view of welfare: assistance to the poor started to become part of the tasks of the state. The Church interpreted the new legislation as being anticlerical and usurping in its intent—the fear was that the state was changing the original aim of the *Opere Pie* and that the poor would be used as pawns for political ends (Fiori 2005).

It was only during the Fascist period that the Church regained ground. A 1926 law allowed clergymen to be part of the IPAB governing boards. Then, in 1929 the Lateran Pacts marked the reconciliation of the Italian state with the Roman Catholic Church of Pope Pius XI after over half a century of "cold war." The Pacts acknowledged full autonomy for a series of institutions run by the Church, on the sole condition that they would not be funded in any way by the Italian state (Iannitto 1990).

Although the advent of the modern welfare state has progressively reduced the Church's role in providing for the poor, at least in comparison with previous centuries, the Church is still a leading actor. According to Ranci (1999), at the end of the twentieth century, the organizations linked to the Church accounted for 70 percent of private residential institutions, 50 percent of private hospitals, 60 percent of privately run vocational training centers, 75 percent of

---

[5] Given the high concentration in Lazio, and especially in Rome, of organizations geared to providing hospitality for religious reasons, it is fair to imagine that the impoverished sections of the population who suffered a shock would leave their community in order to find refuge in and around Rome (Fiori 2005).

private elementary schools, and 48 percent of private secondary schools.[6] More recently, the Italian Episcopal Conference (CEI) showed that the social services linked to the Catholic Church have tripled, from 4,089 in 1988 to 14,246 in 2010 (Sarpellon 2002; CEI 2012). This trend is in line with those of other industrialized countries. In Germany, for instance, the two major Christian churches operate through Caritas and Diakonie, and have a number of employees second only to the public sector. Around 50–60 percent of the services they provide are linked to caring for the elderly and the disabled. In Sweden, too, where the welfare state had relegated the Church to a mere complementary role, the Church is becoming increasingly involved in forms of "direct welfare production" (Petterson et al. 2004).

Even if we turn our attention beyond Europe, we find religious organizations as the main actors in the welfare field. In Australia, at the end of the twentieth century, the six main social welfare providers were organizations linked to the ecclesiastic domain (Winkworth and Camilleri 2004). In the United States, the principle of religious freedom and the separation of Church and state had spurred the Supreme Court, between 1947 and 1980, to a series of decisions limiting the government's possibility of supporting religious organizations even if for secular activities, but since 1996 a series of reforms have encouraged the involvement of religious organizations in providing social welfare services to the poor (Scheitle 2010).

On the whole, there seems to be a substitution effect between Church and state.[7] The shrinking of the welfare state and a return to privatizations has created a vacuum that is being filled in the old manner, by religious institutions.

3 The Unbearable Lightness of the State

In line with classic liberalism thought that considers every individual responsible for his/her own condition, the Italian Liberal state did not take on any welfare obligations. The task of assisting the needy was delegated to local charity institutions, both private and religious ones. Although these institutions were autonomous in their management, they were under the surveillance of the Ministry of Interior. The prefect, as the official representative of the central government, had to preside over the welfare territory with the sole task of "guaranteeing freedom", that is, of creating the conditions through which those who wanted to take care of the poor (and had the money to do it) could do so in the forms most suitable to local customs and needs. The scope and quality of the welfare service was of no interest to the government or to parliament: this

---

[6] These estimates are rounded down and we must also add the work of Caritas, of nonjuridically autonomous religious institutions, and of informal activities carried on by parishes.

[7] See Hungerman (2005), Gruber and Hungerman (2007), and Kersbergen and Manow (2010).

meant that, in practice, "a shelter for beggars could provide meat and wine to these people every day, once a week, or twice a year. It could provide activities in the open air or keep them indoors all the time" (Farrel-Vinay 1997, 160). The term "lightweight state" thus often meant a discretional kind of social welfare not tailored to actual needs.

Very little happened in the first two or three decades of the Liberal period in Italy. The difficulties of the public coffers of the newly unified state were obvious. To this must be added the insufficient staffing, the lack of grounding of administrative cadres, and the few technical means necessary to oppose local powerbases, which were often riotous or defaulting (Romanelli 1995, 138).

The Crispi Law of 1890 (mentioned above) marked the start of a shift from a regime based on *private charity* to another based on *legal charity*; this is the time frame in which the state started up a gradual process of extending its own competencies with regard to *welfare*. This was followed some years later (1898) by the introduction of *statutory* accident insurance as well as the possibility (not statutory) for workers to register with the national social security fund for worker disability and old age (*Cassa nazionale di previdenza per l'invalidità e la vecchiaia degli operai*). Although the actual number of people benefiting from this protection was low (farm workers were excluded, for example), the principle introduced was still a clear, significant break with the past. An accident was compensated regardless of its chance or of employer or even worker responsibility. For the very first time in the country's history, it was possible to prevent indigence by public means.

The sequence with which social insurance initiatives were introduced in Italy is in line with the more general trend found in many countries, in Europe and beyond. A study by Peter Flora and Jens Alber (1981) on twelve European countries highlights that the first form of insurance introduced normally concerned work-related accidents, while the last was the development of insurance forms against unemployment. The country that was the forerunner in social security legislation was the Germany of Otto von Bismarck (1815–1898): it was Bismarck who set up the first welfare state in the world. In six years he introduced statutory insurance systems for the safeguarding of *all* workers of the German Empire against sickness (1883), work-related accidents (1884), and invalidity and old age (1889). This was a top-down decision inspired more by the desire to earn workers' loyalty and to lure them away from the destabilizing influence of socialist ideas, but it was an epochal turning point. It marked a move away from the liberal view postulating the lightness of the state, and broadened the state's sphere of interest to all the main social issues (education, hygiene, health, worker safety, and so on). Hence, we had a state that was no longer light, at least not as much as tradition and custom demanded (Kuhnle and Sander 2010).

Emulation of the German welfare state was gradual, nonlinear, but unstoppable. By the end of World War I, 32 countries in the world had already introduced insurance against work accidents, while only 7 countries provided

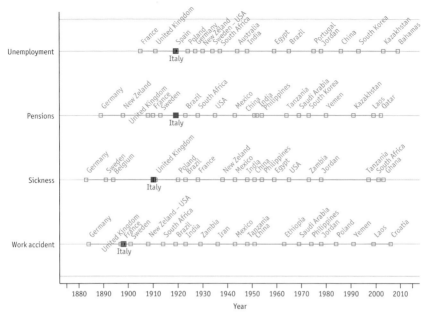

Figure 11.1 The Introduction of Insurance Against Certain Life Risks, Since the 1880s. Each horizontal line refers to a different type of insurance (given on the vertical axis); on each line, the small blue square shows the year in which the insurance form was introduced in Italy, which is, on the whole, among the early adopters.

unemployment benefit. Figure 11.1 summarizes the history of how the main forms of insurance spread in the five continents.[8] We have examined four kinds of insurance: unemployment, accident, sickness, and old age. For those countries on which we managed to obtain data, we have indicated the date on which a *statutory* insurance system was introduced: the far left of each line shows the precursor country, while the far right gives the biggest laggard. If we take unemployment, for example, the figure shows that the first country to introduce a statutory insurance scheme was France (1905), while the last was the Bahamas (2009). Italy's case can be assessed through the small blue squares: on the whole, for the risks considered here, Italy is among the precursor countries.[9]

---

[8] A summary of the introduction of various forms of insurance in the world is found in Kangas (2010).

[9] Outside Europe there emerges a significant delay in introducing insurance against unemployment and sickness. Almost half the countries in Asia (47 percent) have still not introduced statutory unemployment benefits. The relative figure is 69 percent for the American continent and 89 percent for Africa, while the only countries to provide unemployment benefit in Oceania are Australia and New Zealand. The same can be said for insurance against sickness: there is no insurance obligation for 24 percent of Asian countries, 36 percent of African countries, and 73 percent of those in Oceania.

In Italy, World War I accelerated the reforms for statutory pension and unemployment insurance. In the aftermath, in 1919, *statutory invalidity and pension insurance* was extended to all employees, including farm workers. The same year saw the introduction of *statutory unemployment insurance* for industrial workers (and it was extended to farm workers in 1923), with equal contributions by employer and employee: this marked the completion of the cycle of reforms started up in 1898. Insurance against the risk of job loss was an important addition to the Italian social security system; in this regard, Italy (like Spain) did not take too long, all told, to follow the example set by France (1905), some northern countries like Norway and Denmark (1906, 1907), and the United Kingdom (1911).

The interwar years saw a strengthening of the welfare state in the world, both with regard to the number of countries involved and in terms of the number of beneficiaries. In Italy, the advent of the Fascist regime opened up a phase characterized by great institutional innovations, both positive and negative ones. The regime started rather badly, in 1923: all farm workers were excluded from unemployment insurance; the state also took away the right to pension and accident insurance for sharecroppers, settlers, and farmers (Ferrera 1984, 33). In 1925 the government decided to dissolve the Italian federation of mutual aid associations, but at the same time created the national organization for maternity and childhood (*Opera nazionale maternità e infanzia*—ONMI), the first state body dedicated to the social welfare of mothers and children.

In 1927 the emanation of the *Labor Charter* marked a turning point in the way of perceiving public intervention.[10] The Fascist state "elevated" the social security system to become the main instrument for achieving cooperation between capitalists and workers (Girotti 2004). The Charter never became law and remained a declaration of principles, but the importance of this step must not be underestimated since it laid the foundations for the welfare state after World War II.

In the 1930s there was a proliferation of mutual aid associations at trade, company, and local levels (Ferrera 1984). At the same time, the state proceeded to the administrative centralization of the social security system, which was organized within three large organizations: *INPS* (*Istituto Nazionale della Previdenza Sociale*, the National Institute for Social Security) for pension, invalidity and unemployment insurance, family allowances and tuberculosis insurance), *INAIL* (*Istituto Nazionale Assicurazione Infortuni sul Lavoro*, the National

---

[10] Clause XVII of the Charter reads: The Fascist State proposes: 1. the refinement of accident insurance; 2. the improvement and extension of maternity insurance; 3. the insurance against work-related illnesses and against tuberculosis as a path towards a general insurance against all illnesses; 4. the refinement of insurance against involuntary unemployment; 5. the adoption of special dotal insurance forms for young workers.

Institute for Insurance on Occupational Accidents) for work-related accidents and illnesses), and, finally, *INAM* (*Istituto Nazionale per l'Assicurazione contro le Malattie*, National Institute for Insurance against Illness), also for maternity. However, many commentators stress that the order was only apparent and that the management of these institutions was not so much geared to social security as to maintaining social consensus and the popularity of the regime: according to this interpretation, the system had developed those "particularistic-patronage" features that remained in the postwar period.

In the aftermath of World War II, the debate on social security was first conducted in the Constituent Assembly and led to the establishment of *every* citizen's *right* to the safeguarding of health.[11] Article 38 is emblematic in its establishment of the right to social welfare. The "lightweight" state of the Liberal period finally gave way to the Republican state: social welfare became a constitutional law.

The latter half of the 1950s saw the beginning of a series of actions in line with article 38. The most important of these concerns family allowances (already introduced in 1934, but extended to all workers in 1955) and the redundancy fund (*cassa integrazione*) (1945), a mechanism geared to safeguarding not so much the individual worker (as with unemployment insurance), but the entire workforce of a certain company. The "Rubinacci reform" (1952) introduced the so-called *minimum treatment*: when the calculated pension could not guarantee a dignified standard of living, the pension would be supplemented in order to reach a minimum threshold.

The reforms with which the state tried to pave the way to a *universalistic* system go from the 1962 reform of compulsory schooling to the creation of the national health system in 1978, by way of introduction of the *social pension* in 1969: the Italian welfare state held the principle that an elderly person (over 65 years of age) had a right to economic support by the community even if the person had not earned this right through his/her own work.

Universalism and generosity are the two features of the welfare state we need to bear in mind when evaluating the effectiveness of the safety net established by the state to protect its citizens. The first term, *universalism*, refers to the degree of coverage of the population. In principle, all citizens are entitled to the services of the welfare state: there must be no privileging of particular social groups or certain categories of workers. In practice, this is not always the case: some citizens obtain insurance coverage owing to their employment status,

---

[11] June 2, 1946 saw the first free elections after more than twenty years of Fascist dictatorship. The electors were given two cards: one to choose between a monarchy and a republic, and the other to elect the deputies for the Constituent Assembly, which would have the task of drawing up the text of the new Italian Constitution. The Italians voted in favor of a republic, 12.7 million as against 10.7 million who preferred a monarchy.

while others do not have any coverage whatsoever. On the other hand, the term *generosity* refers to the adequacy of the provision to the individual's need (Greve 2013). Typically, the generosity of a social provision is measured by calculating the ratio between the amount of the transfer and the value of the need to be satisfied. The simplest example is that of an unemployment benefit: to assess its generosity, one normally calculates the ratio between the transfer payment (the unemployment benefit) and the forgone income, what the worker does not earn after losing his/her job (Scruggs 2007). This is the so-called replacement ratio, in technical terms.

The different welfare state systems of various countries in the world have been developing and differentiating to the extent that they have promoted the spheres of universalism and generosity. In Figure 11.2 we have reconstructed this process for the years 1930–2005, a time frame established by the availability of the necessary data (Korpi and Palme 2008).

The figure shows that, between 1930 and 2005, Italy made great progress as much with regard to insurance coverage (universalism) as to generosity. What emerges, in particular, is the generosity of the Italian welfare system with regard to pensions, which is higher than in any other OECD country. In 1965, law no. 903 introduced the retirement age pension and established a minimum of 35 years of contributions for retirement, without establishing an age limit. Italy became the only western country where a person who started working at 14 years of age could retire at 49. This was, evidently, a real form of actuarial largesse to citizens since the sum they paid in contributions was considerably lower than the pension treatment received later. In other words, the foundations were laid for the nonsustainability of the entire pension system. In the following years, a series of other reforms spurred the state to field a growing quantity of resources, with a strong acceleration toward the end of the 1970s.[12] "We [Italy] spend more than everyone else on pensions", as documented by Boeri and Perotti (2002). On the whole, the Italian pension system has long ignored the equivalence between costs borne and benefits received by households, in the name of equity. Hence, we have a system characterized (until recently) by a marked "generosity" concealing regressive mechanisms—all to the advantage of more affluent households.

---

[12] In 1968, Italy changed from a contribution-based system to a wage-based one: the pension no longer depended on the contributions actually paid into the system, but now corresponded to 65 percent of the salary earned in the last three years of employment. In 1969 the "Brodolini reform" linked pensions to the cost of living (the index-linking of pensions, in economists' language). In 1973 the government introduced the so-called baby pension for public-sector workers, who were now entitled to retire after only 14 years and 6 months of contributions for women with children, 20 years for men, and 25 for workers of local public bodies.

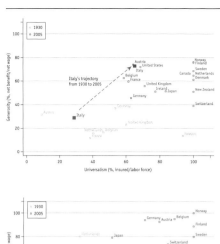

Pensions

Italy is generous, but with a few

The generosity of the Italian pension system enables an average pensioner today to enjoy a pension amounting to 73% of his/her income. This generosity often hides marked disparities in treatment. However, considering just minimum insurance pensions, 65% of the workforce has this minimum assistance. While the progress made since 1930 is evident, Italy remains far removed from the universalism guaranteed in the Scandinavian countries, in Canada and in New Zealand.

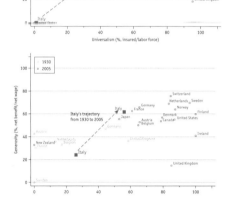

Sickness

The Italians are bottom of the class

In 1930 Italy the percentage of workers with sickness insurance was negligible. There has been great progress over the years, but in international comparisons, Italy remains bottom of the class in terms of insurance coverage (65%), ranking only better than Japan.

Unemployment

The last European country in the race to universalism

In absolute terms, between 1930 and 2005, Italy improved in both spheres: universalism and generosity. Compared to other countries, though, it loses ground: second only to Germany and the United Kingdom in 1930, in 2005 it ranked last in Europe in the race to universalism. Unemployment benefit is guaranteed to less than 60% of the working age population.

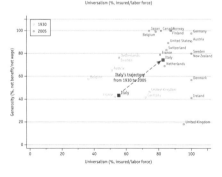

Work accidents

The primacy among the four insurance types

The work accident insurance of the Italians shows the highest coverage (number of insured out of the total workforce) among the insurance forms considered, but we are still far from the universalism guaranteed by a third of the countries. As regards generosity, in 2005 a third of the countries guaranteed benefits higher than 90% of income while Italy only managed 74%. This finding is alarming if considered along with the data on work accidents in Italy that are significantly above the European average.

Figure 11.2 THE ACHIEVEMENT OF PROTECTION AGAINST CERTAIN LIFE RISKS, 1930s–2005. The figure examines four insurable risks (old-age/pensions, sickness, unemployment and work accidents) and compares the insurance systems of a broad set of countries in 1930 (the light-colored squares) and in 2005 (the blue squares). Each graph shows the percentage of insured people (horizontal axis, universalism) and the ratio between net benefit and net wage (vertical axis, generosity). In absolute terms, Italy made progress in all four spheres, but in relative terms the balance is less praiseworthy.

The generosity of the pension system is countered by the weakness of what the sector experts call "social assistance" or the "social safety-net".[13] Like other southern European countries (Greece, Spain, and Portugal), Italy has traditionally relegated social assistance to a marginal role. Maurizio Ferrera's view in this regard is clear: "The so-called safety-net evolved slowly, through a sequence of fragmented and mainly categorical additions (orphans, widows, disabled, poor elderly, etc.), with disparate rules, low integration between cash benefits, (generally underdeveloped) services, and wide holes" (Ferrera 2010, 622). Along with Spain and Portugal, Italy stands out for particularly low levels of expenditure on childcare (Del Boca and Wetzels 2010).

The social pension itself, which was supposed to be an instrument in the fight against poverty,[14] never actually achieved its goal because of the small sum concerned (Ascoli 2002). Attempts to introduce a minimum wage systematically failed. There are, locally, various forms of income support, but each administration adopts its own weights and measures. Unlike what we find in the rest of Europe, a core universal minimum wage does not actually exist in Italy (Monti and Pelizzari 2010).

The factors hindering this arm of the welfare state are several. On the one hand, the strong role of the family as a "social shock absorber" and the shadow economy as an alternative source of earnings have lowered the demand for measures of social assistance against poverty; on the other, the incapacity and weakness of the administrative apparatus have acted from the supply side. In particular, in Italy "fears of triggering or exacerbating 'welfare patronage' have been often evoked as politico-institutional justifications for limiting the scope of targeted schemes" (Ferrera 2010).[15] Moreover, concerns for fairness (Rossi 1997) and the effectiveness of the current system (Boeri 2000; Fornero and Castellino 2001) are not lacking.

---

[13] Social safety nets are instruments used in the fight against poverty and include such things as food or money allowances, or social housing. The common denominator of these benefits is universality. They are not given to select groups of workers or to those entitled to a certain form of insurance benefit, but are given to all those whose income is below a certain threshold (means- or income-tested benefits). They are thus a kind of last resort of benefits destined to protect families at risk of sliding into poverty (Bahle et al. 2010).

[14] Imagine what would happen in the absence of a social security system, if an individual planned his/her own savings on the basis of the wrong time horizon: if life, for example, turned out to be longer than expected, this would mean having to cut down on consumption during the senile period, with negative effects on the person's wellbeing. The statutory pension system prevents, and eliminates, this source of uncertainty by transforming the number of contributions into a flow of payments in the form of annuities that continue until the pensioner's death.

[15] Over the last 20 years, boosted by European integration, there has been an attempt to recalibrate the system in order to guarantee a more homogeneous social security system along with more effective and universal safety nets (Ferrera 2010).

4 Social Expenditure

At the end of the first decade of unification, public spending in the new Kingdom of Italy was considerable if compared with that of other countries: about 15–20 percent of GDP (Brosio and Marchese 1986). In some European countries, such as Germany, the United Kingdom, and Norway, it did not exceed 10 percent, while in the United States it was 7 percent (Tanzi and Schuknecht 2000). Public expenditure included military spending, expenditure for running the public administration, expenditure for public works and also for servicing the public debt, that is, for paying interest on the public debt inherited from the pre-unification states and consolidated in the "Great Book of the Public Debt". Subordinate to the priorities that emerged in the early years of the Kingdom, the state's intervention in social security matters began to intensify. In this section we pose the problem of *measurement*: How big was the state's involvement in this sphere?

In the absence of a universally agreed definition, we have reconstructed the historical series of social expenditure by calculating an indicator that includes the public spending components characterized by at least one of two fundamental traits: the redistributive nature, and the aim of increasing social security of the weakest segments of the population. Operatively, we have calculated social expenditure by summing six components: *a*) spending on basic assistance to poor families; *b*) unemployment benefit; *c*) spending on pensions (including the so-called social pensions);[16] *d*) housing allowances; *e*) spending on public health; *f*) spending on education.[17]

Of these expenditures, the one on pensions is probably the least redistributive in nature, followed by spending on education, which also has a modest redistributive function (Wilensky 1975). If we deduct spending on pensions and on education from total social expenditure, we obtain an aggregate that we shall call "social transfers" that is useful to grasp the extent to which the state's intervention safeguards citizens in difficulty.

The statistical reconstruction of social expenditure required an operation connecting the existing series—none of which, if taken individually, are able to cover the entire period from unification to date. The result is shown in Figure 11.3.

---

[16] On this point the decision is not in line with Lindert (1994; 2004). In the "Anglo-Saxon" system that Lindert refers to, social security expenditure does not include assistance elements as in Italy. Hence, in a system where a pension corresponds almost exactly to the contributions paid, the redistributive element is missing. Finally, note that the definition of social expenditure does *not* include spending on public works.

[17] The choice to include spending in education is supported by our finding in section 7 as the increase in year of schooling is identified as one of the elements that has mostly contributed to increase households' resilience.

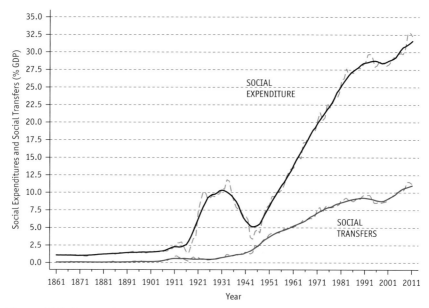

Figure 11.3 Social Expenditure and Transfers in Italy (Percent of GDP),
1861–2011. The graph shows the trend in social expenditure expressed as a
percentage of GDP (vertical axis, values smoothed by means of a 9-period moving
average) over time (horizontal axis). The definition of social expenditure includes
spending on basic assistance, unemployment benefit, housing allowance, pensions,
health, and education. Social transfer expenditure, which is obtained by deducting
spending on pensions and education from social expenditure, measures the
redistribution effect—from rich to poor—borne by the state.

A first observation concerns the level of expenditure. Over the first fifty years,
social expenditure was quantitatively modest, fluctuating at around 1 percent of
GDP. Looking at the figures, the Liberal Italian state was rather lightweight and
invested few resources in the "social question". It also provided a lot less in redistribution from the richer segments of the population to the poorest ones: social
transfer expenditure accounted for a negligible portion of GDP, always below
0.5 percent throughout the nineteenth century.

In the interwar period there was a growth in social expenditure owing to a
positive evaluation of public intervention and also because of the emergency
needs dictated by the crisis of the late 1920s, the bleakest one of modern times
(Feinstein, Temin, and Toniolo 2004). "The Depression was seen by many as a
monumental failure of the market economy and of laissez-faire, a failure that
justified governmental intervention.... By 1937, the minimal state committed to laissez-faire policies was on the way out" (Tanzi and Schuknecht 2000,
9–10). In the Fascist period, social expenditure not only increased, but it deeply
changed its composition: the social security component soared and accounted
for most of the welfare expenditure.

Social expenditure accelerated after World War II: a hundred years after unification, it accounted for 10 percent of GDP, twenty times the percentage reported for the start of the period (over the same period, GDP increased about ninefold compared to the initial values). This growth showed signs of slowing down only around the mid-1980s. In particular, Figure 11.3 highlights that if we exclude spending on pensions and on education, the series of social transfers decreased slightly after the 1980s: per-capita GDP slackened and the economy became more fragile, which increased the vulnerability of the less affluent. The state, however, decreased its support instead of increasing it, by lightening up on the percentage of GDP destined for social expenditure. It is the "Robin Hood paradox": redistribution from rich to poor is less present when and where it is needed the most (Lindert 2004).

International comparisons (Figure 11.4) show that Italy has always ranked in an intermediate position: a lighter welfare state than the one found in Scandinavian countries (Denmark, Sweden, and Finland), traditionally generous,

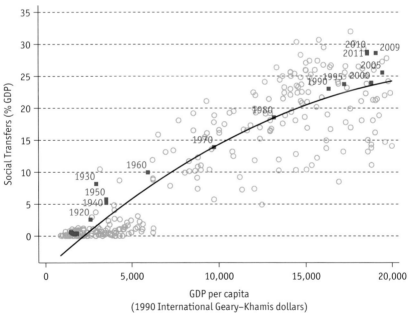

Figure 11.4 Social transfers in Italy and in some OECD Countries (Percent of GDP). Each circle in the graph stands for a country in a certain year (Italy is instead represented by blue squares); the regression curve shows how social transfers (vertical axis, as a percentage of GDP) vary as per capita GDP varies (horizontal axis). The positive slope means that, on average, as income increases, the percentage of social expenditure also increases. Over the hundred and fifty years considered in the graph, Italy systematically ranks close to (and slightly above) the mean.

but heavier than the one found in other countries such as Switzerland, Japan, and the United States.

If the trend in expenditure reveals the *quantity* of government intervention, we learn a great deal about the *quality* of public action by looking at how its composition has changed over time. "The budget is a sort of fingerprint of government.... Tracing the budget composition over time illustrates the changing role played by the state in society" (Obinger and Wagschal 2010). Figure 11.5 shows the results obtained by equating total social expenditure to 100 and then observing how it is distributed within the six functions that make it up: education, health, pensions, assistance, unemployment benefit, and housing allowance.

A joint analysis of Figures 11.3 and 11.5 allows us to trace the long-run development of the social system. In the Liberal period, the government spent little: what spending there was went mostly on basic education and health services, as well as on pensions, through assistance-type payments and benefits. Government decision-making in this regard was obviously conditioned by the lack of proper financial means, but it was also the result of an underlying, precise and conscious, criterion of the governing class of the times: the state did not recognize a citizen's right to assistance, but the freedom to assist others for those who wished to.

The twentieth century saw the development of two fundamental ideas in the conception of a social security system: the centrality of employment and social security. In Italy, spending on social security gained greater importance in terms of resources employed and became the predominant item of all social expenditure. The increase in this component, very marked in the aftermath of World War I, was not sustainable after the crisis of the 1930s and it was significantly reduced.

In the aftermath of World War II, the institutional changes were accompanied by demographic changes that played a leading role in explaining the trends in the composition of social expenditure in the last fifty years: spending on pensions soared and healthcare expenditure had a steady growth.[18] Who lost out in all these changes? That is to say, which component of social expenditure was less safeguarded in absolute terms (i.e., with regard to the amount of expenditure allocated) and in relative terms (i.e., increasing less compared to other components)? In the losers' ranking, the top positions see knowledge ("youth") and the needy ("the poor"). The former constitutes "human capital" and is the essential engine of economic growth: it represents the country's main hope to maintain future high levels of wellbeing (chapter 5, "Education"). The second aspect,

---

[18] As Boeri and Perotti (2002) observed, it is extremely difficult to assess the redistribution effects of pensions. The authors show how the Italian system contains elements of iniquity, privileging the more affluent segment of the population much more than what is found in other European countries.

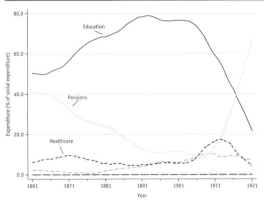

LIBERAL ITALY (1861–1921)
Assistance

Social expenditure with redistribution effects was at a bare minimum: 50-80% of spending was on education. Expenditure on assistance – mostly on healthcare – accounted for only 5% of the total. World War I and male universal suffrage gave most citizens the opportunity to decide on the rules. This led to an increase (in absolute terms) in spending on education and on pensions (multiplied by 20): the change in relative weight of these two components is conspicuous.

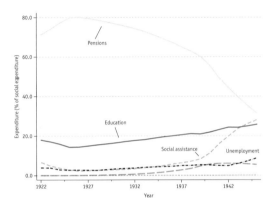

FASCIST ITALY (1922–1945)
Social security

Social expenditure was mostly on pensions. The government increased its spending on voluntary social security schemes and extended the protection through agencies, corporative bodies and professional associations. Expenditure on health and family protection increased significantly from the late 1920s. Unemployment benefit was introduced.

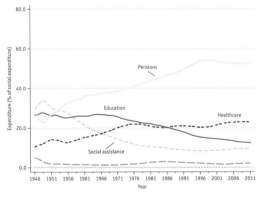

REPUBLICAN ITALY (SINCE 1946)
Social assistance

The country managed to overcome poverty and the population began to live longer. The result – greater income and an ageing population – is visible in the gap that opens up between spending on pensions (strongly rising) and expenditure on social assistance and education (decreasing, percentage-wise). As the graph shows, an ageing population needs more healthcare. On the other hand, spending on assistance has fallen.

Figure 11.5 SOCIAL EXPENDITURE COMPOSITION BY FUNCTION, 1861–2011. The figure shows the change in composition of social expenditure for three sub-periods of Italy's post-unification history.

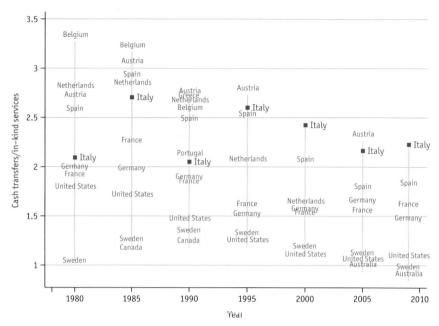

Figure 11.6 NEW SOCIAL RISKS, 1980–2011. The figure shows how the relation between expenditure for cash transfers and spending on social services (vertical axis) changed between 1980 and 2010. When the relation has a "high" value (e.g., Belgium in the 1980s), the interpretation is that the country pays little attention to new social risks. Italy followed the general trend in reducing money transfers, thus paying increasing attention to new social risks, but ranking as the country with the highest relation in 2010.

the poor, has to do with equity and the principles of article 38 of the Italian Constitution, recalled in section 3. Sacrificing growth and equity is not strategic and does not respect the principles underlying the country's civil cohabitation, but favors the political class and government consensus. It is *political economy*. In other words, who votes? Certainly not school-age youth.

To conclude, we wish to turn our attention to recent developments in the literature on new social risks (Taylor-Gobby 2004). The welfare state faces new risks linked to the new demographic dynamics and new work-family balances: the lengthening of average life expectancy with a consequent growing demand for healthcare services, the extinction of the household model based on the "male breadwinner" (Lewis 2001; Pascall 2008), and the huge influx of women in the job market have created new needs. If the old welfare state mainly worried about compensating loss of income, from sickness, unemployment, or old age, by means of cash transfers, the new challenges today stem from the impossibility of combining maternity or elderly care with one's job, or from the spreading of atypical labor contracts generally not envisaging forms of social security. These risks affect the same group of people—youth, families with young children or with elderly members who are not self-sufficient, and working women—and call for a welfare state that places greater emphasis on services (Esping-Andersen 2002; Castles 2006).

For the period 1980–2010, the data of 18 OECD countries show a gradual change underway: we see a fall in the cash transfer component in the relation between cash transfers and in-kind service expenditures. This indicates an increase in forms of protection against new social risks, typically benefiting women, younger segments of the population, and less skilled workers (Bonoli 2005). Does this confirm a change in direction? Perhaps, but not for Italy, where the old welfare state has still not been scrapped: along with the other southern European countries, Italy still allocates a considerable portion of social expenditure to cash transfers, ranking as the country with the highest cash transfer/in-kind services ratio in 2010 (Figure 11.6).

5 Disasters

Over the 150 years since Italy's unification, Pandora's box has poured out its ills onto the country, wreaking immense economic havoc with millions of victims. If the Italians have gained the upper hand in many of these ills, managing to drive them back into the box over the years, others still remain and are a continuous threat looming over the citizens' wellbeing. This is mostly the case with systemic—and not always insurable—risks affecting a broad set of individuals, such as wars, economic crises, and natural disasters. Estimates that have been cobbled together, but not overly so, indicate that since 1900 the economic damage caused only by natural and technological disasters could amount to 180 billion dollars (at 2014 prices)—three times the damage caused in France and Spain (57 and 52 billion, respectively).[19]

It is not easy to gain a sense of proportion with regard to how these systemic risks have conditioned the population's wellbeing, and how the economic and social impact has developed over time. Emanuela Guidoboni, a historian, and Gianluca Valensise, a geophysicist, have completed a mammoth study on earthquake activity in Italy, documenting the intensity and extent of all the earthquakes that have hit the country since its unification (Guidoboni and Valensise 2011). The study is supported by data gathered over 25 years of research, and offers interesting food for thought for the history we are dealing with. There are two main lessons to be learned in our context here.

---

[19] The calculation is based on figures retrieved in August 2014 from the International Disaster Database (http://www.emdat.be).

Box 1 **The *New York Times* and Sicily, 1908**

On December 31, 1908 the *New York Times* devoted four pages to the news of the terrible earthquake that hit the city of Messina, in Sicily, in the morning of December 28. The 37 seconds that shook that stretch of land which separates the tip of Italy's boot from the eastern coast of Sicily, and the subsequent waves—two to nine meters high—irreversibly changed the fate of that city. The tragedy was immense: the earthquake killed 40–60 percent of the city's population. The *New York Times* states that when the news reached the *Anchor Line Italia*, a ship full of migrants on the Naples–Sicily–New York route, the ship's pilot made the following comment to the captain: "The worst you have ever heard in your life. For every vestige of one of your biggest ports has been wiped off the face of the earth". This negative shock had permanent effects because Messina lost its role as a great port city and became the center of opportunistic business activity for the city's reconstruction.

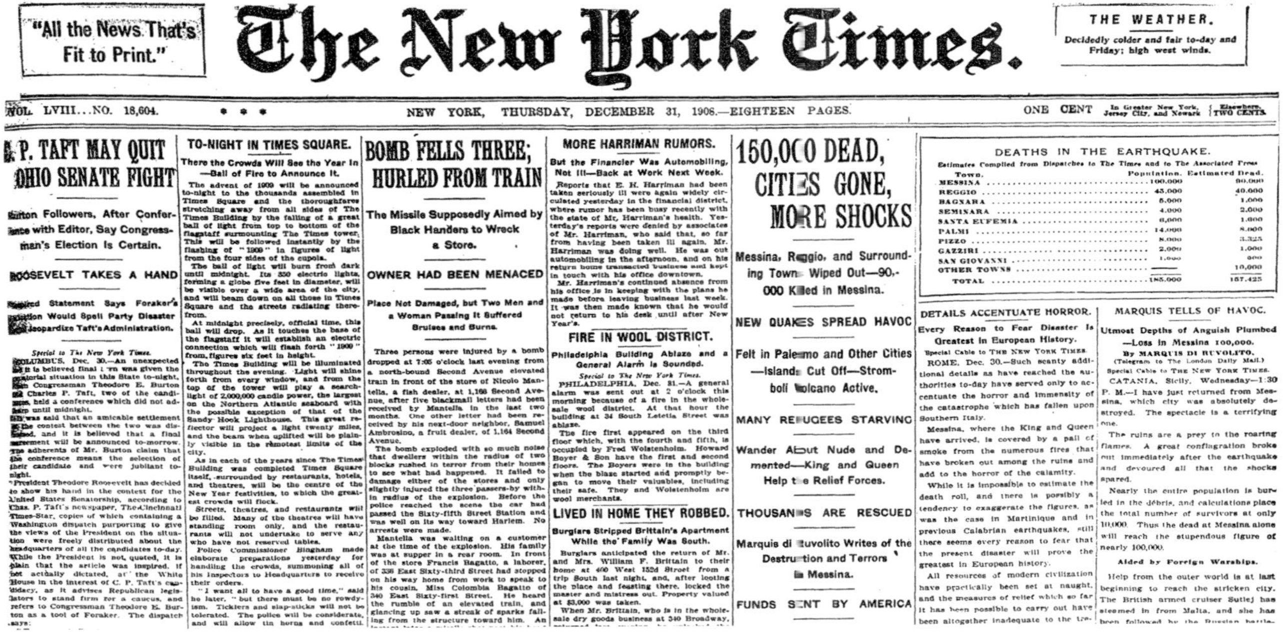

"All the News That's Fit to Print."

The New York Times.

THE WEATHER. Decidedly colder and fair to-day and Friday; high west winds.

VOL. LVIII...NO. 18,604. NEW YORK, THURSDAY, DECEMBER 31, 1908.—EIGHTEEN PAGES. ONE CENT In Greater New York, Jersey City, and Newark | Elsewhere, TWO CENTS.

C. P. TAFT MAY QUIT OHIO SENATE FIGHT

Burton Followers, After Conference with Editor, Say Congressman's Election Is Certain.

ROOSEVELT TAKES A HAND

Signed Statement Says Foraker's Election Would Spell Party Disaster and Jeopardize Taft's Administration.

TO-NIGHT IN TIMES SQUARE.

There the Crowds Will See the Year In —Ball of Fire to Announce It.

BOMB FELLS THREE; HURLED FROM TRAIN

The Missile Supposedly Aimed by Black Handers to Wreck a Store.

OWNER HAD BEEN MENACED

Place Not Damaged, but Two Men and a Woman Passing It Suffered Bruises and Burns.

MORE HARRIMAN RUMORS.

But the Financier Was Automobiling, Not Ill—Back at Work Next Week.

FIRE IN WOOL DISTRICT.

Philadelphia Building Ablaze and a General Alarm Is Sounded.

LIVED IN HOME THEY ROBBED.

Burglars Stripped Brittain's Apartment While the Family Was South.

150,000 DEAD, CITIES GONE, MORE SHOCKS

Messina, Reggio, and Surrounding Towns Wiped Out—90,000 Killed in Messina.

NEW QUAKES SPREAD HAVOC

Felt in Palermo and Other Cities —Islands Cut Off—Stromboli Volcano Active.

MANY REFUGEES STARVING

Wander About Nude and Demented—King and Queen Help the Relief Forces.

THOUSANDS ARE RESCUED

Marquis di Ruvolito Writes of the Destruction and Terrors in Messina.

FUNDS SENT BY AMERICA

DEATHS IN THE EARTHQUAKE.

Estimates Compiled from Dispatches to The Times and to The Associated Press.

Town.	Population.	Estimated Dead.
MESSINA	100,000	90,000
REGGIO	45,000	40,000
BAGNARA	6,000	1,000
SEMINARA	4,000	2,000
SANTA EUFEMIA	6,000	1,000
PALMI	14,000	8,000
PIZZO	8,000	3,325
GAZZIRI	2,000	1,000
SAN GIOVANNI	1,000	900
OTHER TOWNS	—	10,000
TOTAL	185,000	157,425

DETAILS ACCENTUATE HORROR.

Every Reason to Fear Disaster Is Greatest in European History.

MARQUIS TELLS OF HAVOC.

Utmost Depths of Anguish Plumbed —Loss in Messina 100,000.

By MARQUIS DI RUVOLITO.

Aided by Foreign Warships.

Figure 11.B1 THE 1908 MESSINA EARTHQUAKE. The figure shows the front page of *The New York Times* of December 31, 1908. Among the various headings we read: "160,000 DEAD, CITIES GONE, MORE SHOCKS—Messina Reggio, and Surrounding Towns Wiped Out—90,000 Killed in Messina—MANY REFUGEES STARVING—Wander About Nude and Demented—FUNDS SENT BY AMERICA—J.P. Morgan gives $10,000." At today's values, the check made out by the American magnate J.P. Morgan (1837–1913) would amount to about 210,000 euros.

The first lesson is the fact that the new Kingdom of Italy was born at a time of four important earthquakes, all situated in the central and southern regions between 1851 and 1859. Just the earthquake of 1857, three devastating tremors in the space of an hour, caused over eleven thousand deaths and affected a huge area from the region of Basilicata to the lower part of Campania. "The earthquake of December, 1857, by almost the first notices that reached England"—wrote Robert Mallet (1810–1881), one of the founding fathers of modern seismology— "revealed itself as the third greatest in extent and severity of which there is any record as having occurred in Europe" (vii).[20] Interestingly, Guidoboni and Valensise observe that "these earthquakes lacerated not only the buildings, but also the social fabric and confidence of the inhabitants: the miserly and bureaucratic administrative machine of the Bourbon state, in a context of police control of the public order for political reasons, left those lands desolated and almost devoid of resources for their reconstruction—and even without any rules and regulations" (15). The lands of the Umbria region, at that time part of the Papal State, suffered the same fate.

The birth of the new Kingdom did not reduce the delays in reconstruction— something that was certainly not facilitated by the great backwardness of the infrastructure in the south, where out of 1,848 municipalities in 1860, 1,321 did not have any road connections. To the extent that the management of the operations for the (non-) reconstruction of the earthquake areas reflects the nature of the political institutions and governing classes of the times, the picture that emerges on examining the documentation leaves little doubt on their "extractive" nature (Acemoglu and Robinson 2012). Nor did the demise of the Bourbon Kingdom of the Two Sicilies and its absorption into the new Savoy Kingdom of Italy change anything from the point of view of the citizens hit by the earthquakes: the political line remained that of looking away from the ruins. For decades, the government had a single focus, with or without earthquakes: the maintenance of public order in a context marked by rebellions, which was alarming to say the least. Guidoboni and Valensise go further and suggest that the way the government handled the damage caused by pre-unification earthquakes may have played a non-negligible role—or even a key role—in nurturing the *questione meridionale* (the "southern question"), that is, in broadening the gap between north and south of the country (27).

The second lesson that emerges when examining the long history of earthquakes in Italy still concerns the country's institutions. The data tell us that the most devastating earthquakes—those unleashing enormous energy—were quite rare in Italy: one or two per century and not more. On the other hand,

---

[20] On behalf of the London Royal Society, Mallet documented the aftermath of the earthquake with a mission approved and financed at lightning speed. The documentation, including photographic material, gathered by Mallet (1862) is described in Guidoboni and Ferrari (1987) and Ferrari (2004–2009), and shows the extraordinary backwardness of the country's southern regions.

earthquakes of high destructive power occurred with greater frequency, "almost with metronome regularity", one every 4–5 years, on average, and hit over 1,500 places (Figure 11.7). Despite this centuries-old seismic risk, Italy has never managed to react rationally: instead of becoming part of the national culture and triggering an institutional response (as in other countries), earthquakes remained for too long outside the political-economic agenda. If the scarcity of resources may, at least in part, justify the inaction of nineteenth-century Italian governments, and even the pre-Republican ones, for the more recent decades we can certainly denounce an obstinate myopia in territorial programming as well

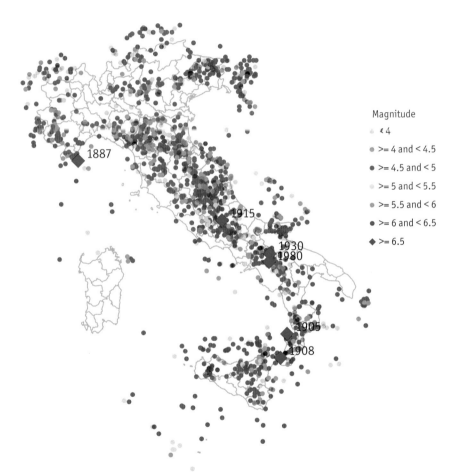

Figure 11.7 ITALIAN EARTHQUAKES (1861–2011). The figure shows the location and intensity of the earthquakes that have hit Italy since 1861. The colors indicate the extent of earthquake damage. Although there have been relatively few really devastating earthquakes, Italy's position along the "collision line" between the African plate and Eurasian one makes it one of the most dangerous places for earthquakes in Europe. The areas mostly at risk are the Friuli region (in the north-east), the Apennine mountain chain, Calabria and eastern Sicily.

as a structural weakness in applying the laws (Guidoboni and Valensise 2013, 414–415). It is a trait that delineates and characterizes the country's entire pos-tunification history—a figure that evidently has meta-economic roots.

Since what determines the vulnerability of a community is the combined effect of the ex-ante risks and the effectiveness of the mechanisms available for absorbing the shocks (Strömberg 2007; Chen, Luo, and Pan 2013), it would be reasonable to expect Italy's economic growth in its history to have been accompanied by less vulnerability to damage caused by natural disasters. The data of the Centre for Research on the Epidemiology of Disaster (CRED) do not appear in line with this expectation: earthquakes in Italy have not only caused considerable economic damage, but they have, above all, not highlighted any tendency to reduce the scale of the damage over time.[21]

Furthermore, while earthquakes account for a great loss of life and economic damage when compared to other natural disasters, we must not forget that the Italian territory is also exposed to a high degree of risk of landslides and floods. According to data of the Istituto Superiore per la Protezione e la Ricerca Ambientale (ISPRA), in 2012 almost 40 percent of the municipalities were exposed to a high landslide risk and 45 percent to a high flood risk (as against a figure of 36 percent for areas with high earthquake risk).

There is, on the other hand, a low perception of the risk of natural disasters. This is certainly due to the low frequency of catastrophic events, but also it may be due to the government's tendency to provide financial aid after a natural disaster. This may explain the gap between Italy and the other advanced countries with regard to insurance coverage. The government's action may, in particular, encourage crowding-out: knowing that the state will intervene (ex-post, after the event, but even ex-ante, in the assumption that state engineers are able to protect more than what happens in reality) encourages the individual to take on moral hazard behavior entailing a disincentive to self-protection (Boustan, Kanh, and Rhode 2012).

In Italy there are no statutory insurance policies for these events, unlike what is found in France and Spain, and nonstatutory policies (widespread in the United Kingdom and in the United States) are not very popular. This low insurance penetration in Italy may indicate low financial knowledge that—erroneously—leads

---

[21] There are many reasons for these tragedies and they include the inadequacy of the measures adopted for proper protection against risk. Economic factors (the post-earthquake reports of technical experts have always talked of the fragility of building constructions owing to the poor quality of materials and of the techniques used) must also include a lack of proper prevention policies and inadequate enforcement of existing laws. There is also a low perception of the risk of natural disasters: individuals tend to, irrationally, refuse to abandon the devastated locations (Guidoboni 2011). In San Fratello, Sicily, after a ruinous landslide in 1922, part of the inhabitants went to live on the coast, but many of them gradually went back to the site of the disaster after World War II. They were hit by another landslide in 2010 and the state had to step in to guarantee the survival of the built-up area in view of the population's firm resolve not to "abandon their native land" (Cafiso 2012).

people to perceive insurance as a cost with no real benefit. Households seem to prefer a sort of "self-insurance" through savings—a hypothesis that is confirmed in the Italians' high propensity to save, even if it is currently falling (chapter 10, "Wealth").

According to a study by the Joint Research Centre of the European Commission, the insurance penetration rate for natural disasters (that is, the percentage of insurance premiums with regard to GDP) is less than 10 percent in Italy: the worst of the EU15 countries along with Greece (Maccaferri, Cariboni, and Campolongo 2012). The result is a dog chasing its tail: the high ratio between damage caused and damages insured intensifies the state's reparatory action, which, from the population's standpoint, may be perceived as a form of public insurance that discourages citizens from resorting to private insurance policies themselves. The combination of these factors (high danger and lack of suitable strategies to face risk) makes Italy a more vulnerable place than it would be if there were greater commitment with regard to risk management tools. Nor is this analysis of events comforting in that we find a persistent absence of learning mechanisms.

6 Vulnerability to Poverty

In this section we shall focus on the concept of *vulnerability to poverty*. The term "vulnerability" is popular not just in everyday language but also in the scientific literature. It is an expression that has proliferated in the social sciences and also in other disciplines such as environmental sciences, disaster management, and health and nutrition sciences (Alwang, Siegel, and Jørgensen 2001). Because of its popularity, the term has taken on an elusive feature over time: different people use it in different ways.

In this section we shall adopt the definition of vulnerability that is becoming popular in development economics (Dercon 2001). The reason why scholars have gone beyond the concept of poverty and have introduced the idea of vulnerability to poverty springs from the fact that the measurement of poverty grasps a circumstance that inevitably belongs to the past: the poor are "counted" as such when they already are such. Economists resort to Latin to describe this circumstance by saying that poverty is an *ex-post* measure (that is, measured after it happens): why not try to devise an *ex-ante* measure, that is, an indicator that can predict who could become poor in the future? Since uncertainty plays a key role in determining the wellbeing of households, economists have defined vulnerability to poverty as "the likelihood of becoming poor in the future" (Zhang and Wan 2009), "the magnitude of the *threat* of poverty, measured ex-ante, before the veil of uncertainty has been lifted" (Calvo and Dercon 2005). Vulnerability is thus a condition associated with possible future poverty—it is a latent, potential form of poverty. It is not just those who are already poor who are vulnerable, but also those at risk of becoming poor.

Let us take the case of two households that are identical in everything except for the working condition of the head of the household. Let us suppose, in particular, that the head of one of the households is an employee while the other is self-employed. Suppose also that the two households expect identical future incomes in their working life; the *variability* of future incomes of the two households will be different, however, in that income from self-employment is typically subject to greater variability compared to the one from subordinate employment. The likelihood of experiencing a period of future poverty will thus be different for the two households: the one with a more variable income will have greater poverty risk (with expected income and every other household characteristic being equal). The variability of future incomes is a significant component in establishing poverty risk.

In more general terms, the concept of vulnerability entails two interrelated aspects: on the one hand, it explicitly introduces the role of *risk*; on the other, the *response to risk*. It is common knowledge that households have a different degree of exposure to risk that depends on the environment and on household characteristics. For example, a household with more economically active adults will have a low risk of sliding into poverty because it can implement a broader number of strategies to deal with negative events (such as by increasing its supply of labor).

If we accept the fact that, besides income level, it is important to account for the future variability of income, and if we assume that it is possible, with sufficient accuracy, to estimate the likelihood of becoming poor in the future for each individual of the population, then we can achieve three objectives: *a)* identifying the types of subjects who are more vulnerable, *b)* understanding which mechanisms make them vulnerable, and *c)* intervening ex-ante with support policies to prevent these subjects from becoming poor. It is, conceptually, a revolution with respect to the traditional approach of measuring poverty: vulnerability is an ex-ante measure instead of an ex-post one; that is, it can prevent as well as treat the poverty phenomenon.

The obvious question at this stage is the following: where do we get the crystal ball for measuring the likelihood of becoming poor in the future? Unlike poverty, vulnerability is a condition that can *never* be observed, but only estimated. That is, it can be predicted with some margin of error that always accompanies estimates. Vulnerability is an intrinsically stochastic concept because it reflects a condition of *future* poverty that depends on whether uncertain events occur or not. Who do we turn to, then, for our crystal ball?

Economists and econometricians have for several years now been working on producing crystal balls for this very purpose.[22] There are thus various prototypes

---

[22] See, for example, Ravallion 1988; 1996; Morduch 1994; Chaudhuri, Jalan, and Suryahadi (2002); Ligon and Schechter 2003; Christiaensen and Subbarao 2005; Dercon 2007. More recently, Dang and Lanjouw (2014) explored the use of vulnerability lines.

available—some do produce images similar to, although not perfectly like, the future (Bourguignon, Goh, and Kim 2004). Before turning to the construction of such a tool and its application in the Italian historical case (which we shall deal with in section 7), we shall go into more depth on what we mean *operatively* by "vulnerability to poverty".

We shall start by recalling that a household's poverty in a given year is measured by assessing whether the household's consumption in that year is below a certain minimum threshold, the poverty line. The outcome of this operation is a dichotomous variable: if the observed consumption is below the poverty line, the household is classified as "poor", otherwise it is "not poor".[23] To calculate vulnerability to poverty, we proceed in a similar way by estimating the household's consumption in the following year. It is not too difficult to estimate future consumption as long as suitable data are available. For example, if there is a sample survey on household budgets that is repeated over time, it is easy to formulate a model assessing household consumption behavior. It is also easy to estimate this on the basis of the available data and then to use the results to make forecasts. Once these forecasts are obtained, we can proceed in similar fashion as for poverty: a given household is classified as "vulnerable" if the model has estimated that the household has a high likelihood of not remaining above the poverty line in the following year; otherwise, the household is classified as "not vulnerable".

There are thus four possible combinations for classifying each household: *a)* poor and vulnerable (i.e., with a high likelihood of remaining poor), *b)* poor but not vulnerable, *c)* not poor but vulnerable, and *d)* not poor and not vulnerable. Case *d)* is the least interesting one because it essentially concerns the "well off", those households that are not poor today and have a low probability of becoming so tomorrow. Point *c)*, instead, defines a very interesting case, that of a household which is not poor today but is at a high risk (i.e., above average risk) of becoming poor tomorrow (and, hence, is vulnerable to poverty): this kind of household is of great interest for policymakers because it represents a primary objective of *prevention* policies for the fight against poverty. Case *a)*—a poor and vulnerable household—is also interesting because it indicates a situation of *chronicity* of poverty. In this case the policymaker is dealing with households that require a radically different form of action than with case *c)*: while insurance

---

[23] A reflection on observed consumption rather than potential consumption is necessary here. Household consumption can be a good measure of the wellbeing of the household's members as long as the observed consumption coincides with the household's potential consumption. In actual fact, many households—especially more elderly ones—have higher potential consumption values than the ones observed: a difference largely justified by their stock of wealth. Using observed consumption instead of potential consumption may, in such cases, classify some households as vulnerable to poverty when they really are not (Brandolini, Magri, and Smeeding 2010). In a country like Italy, where the decumulation of wealth is practically nonexistent in the elderly, this evidence may suggest new strategies for combating poverty (Borella and Rossi 2014).

instruments may be effective for the latter, chronic households require actions to enhance their capacity to generate income. Finally, case *b*) concerns households that are temporarily but not chronically poor.

In the next section we shall place Italian households within the four aforesaid categories and we shall follow them over time. We shall thus distinguish the various types of poverty—the chronic and the temporary, the observed one and the potential one. The analysis is useful not so much for examining what has happened in the 150 years of Italy's postunification history (we do not have enough data for the whole period), but to contribute to policymaking after this long period: the idea of vulnerability to poverty is precisely that of looking ahead by learning from the past.

7 Italy, a Country with a High Poverty Risk

In the preceding section we highlighted the innovative nature of the "vulnerability to poverty" concept when the term is used in its technical meaning of the "likelihood of becoming poor in the future". The innovative feature essentially lies in the fact that the measurement of vulnerability simultaneously takes into account the current *level* of household consumption and the *risk* of this decreasing in the future owing to uncertainties of the economic environment.

The theme of vulnerability is particularly important in our context, which strives to grasp the trends of the past 150 years of Italy's postunification history. We have seen how vulnerability to poverty has changed significantly over time as the welfare state was created and households became more affluent—not all to the same extent, but such that there is no doubt on the advantages associated with being born today rather than 150 years ago. The population is still exposed to uninsurable risks today, probably more to systemic risks than to idiosyncratic ones (section 5). Nevertheless, there are also more subtle, more microeconomic risks that are less talked about: a child that does not find a place in a public daycare does not make the economic headlines as a negative shock, but that is what it actually is. At the national level, public and private daycare cover only 12 percent of potential demand (Istat 2010): this means that the decrease in household income—in terms of direct cost (if the household turns to the market) or of "opportunity cost" (the parent caring for the children cannot enter the job market and thus forgoes income and aspirations)—is huge and equal to a third of the total (Altroconsumo 2010).

Uncertainty makes the Italians restless and limits their capacity to enjoy the levels of wellbeing achieved over their postunification history. To what extent are these perceptions detached from reality? We can check the facts with reference to the last three or four decades. The exercise carried out and illustrated in this section makes use of the survey on household budgets conducted by Istat. By grouping together the data gathered by the survey on household consumption

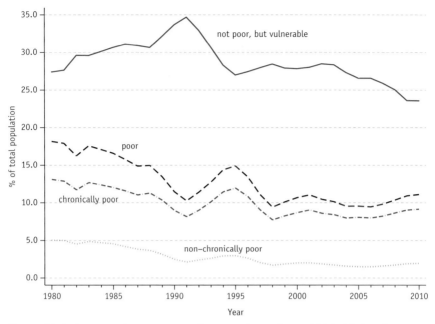

Figure 11.8 CHRONIC POVERTY AND POVERTY RISK, ITALY 1980–2010. The figure shows the trends of the percentage of the Italian population classified as poor (broken black line), chronically poor (broken blue line) and temporarily poor (dotted line). The figure also shows the percentage of the population that is not poor, but at risk of poverty in each year (23–36 percent, solid blue line).

for the years 1980–2010, we obtain a sample of over 800,000 households, corresponding to over 2.4 million people for whom we have a detailed knowledge of expenditure on consumption of goods and services, as well as their main sociodemographic characteristics. By adapting the methodology devised by Christiaensen and Subbarao (2005), we measured the Italian population's vulnerability to poverty and followed up its development over time. The main result is reported in Figure 11.8.

The first result contained in Figure 11.8 concerns the trend of absolute poverty in the country, which shows an overall decrease from 1980 to 2010 (chapter 9, "Poverty"). Nevertheless, the currency crises in 1992 pushed a significant number of Italians into poverty: institutional reforms brought uncertainty and households reacted with a contraction in consumption. In the late 1990s, Italy was able to recover, but the positive trend of poverty reduction lost pace, showing a worsening scenario when the 2008 financial crises hit. In 2010, the poverty rate went back to its value at the beginning of the new millennium (11 percent)[24]. What is even more alarming, is the nature of the poverty, which is

---

[24] The percentage does not include illegal migrants and homeless people.

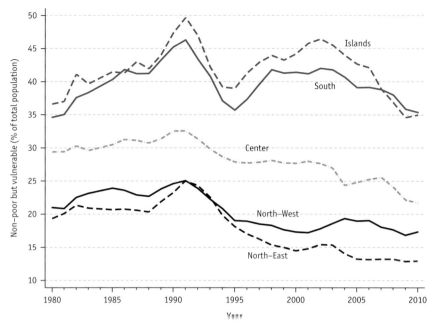

Figure 11.9 Vulnerability in the 5 Macro-areas, 1980–2010. The figure shows the trend over time of the percentage of the non-poor but vulnerable Italian population, that is, the population at poverty risk.

largely *chronic* (this is how the closeness of the line of the chronically poor to the one of the total poor is interpreted): the proportion of vulnerable households, among the poor, increases from 72 percent in 1980 to 81 percent in 2010 (see Table 11.A1 in the Statistical Appendix). Chronic poverty is probably the most hideous form of poverty, the one in which the suffering caused by extreme deprivation is aggravated by social exclusion and the lack of hope of ever getting out of the poverty trap.

The second result concerns the population's vulnerability. Figure 11.8 shows that the population with an above-average likelihood of sliding into poverty in the future makes a very high percentage: between 1980 and 2010 this percentage fluctuated steadily from 23 percent to 36 percent, but remained below 30 percent from the mid-1990s.[25] What emerges, all told, is thus the latent fragility of the economic health of Italian households over the period concerned. While all this may not be new to scholars of the field, the scale of the phenomenon probably is. However, data reveal how Italians have built resilience. In fact, if the crisis in the 1990s pushed the average probability of becoming poor from 11.6 percent in 1991 to 16.5 percent in 1995, the vulnerability level increased only by

[25] The average probability of becoming poor has fluctuated between 17 percent in the 1980s and 11 percent in the last decade.

1.2 percentage points between 2007 and 2009,[26] and it started decreasing again in 2010 (11 percent). The recent financial crises hit less severely Italian families compared to the crises in the early 1990s. The National Statistical Office confirms our results: "Italy paid a high price in terms of production and employment because of the recession, but *limited the social impact and avoided systemic crises* that instead took place in other countries" (Istat 2010). However, the crisis is not over yet. Although, we did not have data on 2011–2014, official statistics report that the fall in private consumption was the worst in 2012 and 2013.

For the vulnerable households, their expenditure on consumption does not classify them as poor, but the margin with respect to the poverty line is slight, such to deprive these households of suitable instruments to face any negative shocks. On the basis of the estimates of our econometric model, wealth plays a primary role, and the households use it to keep their consumption above the critical threshold. It is thanks to the wealth accumulated over the years that, from the early 1990s, a growing percentage of households managed to maintain their standard of living. In this case, sector experts talk in terms of a mere "coping scheme", but cutting down on one's wealth cannot, evidently, be a sustainable strategy. Furthermore, our model sees the increase in average education as one of the elements that have mostly contributed to enhancing the resilience of households, by exerting a positive and significant impact on consumption levels. The progress recorded in chapter 5 ("Education"), although not praiseworthy when compared to other countries, is still important to build up the households' defenses against adversity.

Still more eloquent is the data on vulnerability to poverty when disaggregated by geographical region. In Figure 11.9 we see that the gap between southern Italy and the central and northern regions shows no real sign of narrowing. The northeastern regions are quite successful in reducing the financial fragility of households, more than any other region in the country has managed to do. Even the north-western regions have managed to reduce their citizens' vulnerability to poverty, but with an inverse trend in the last decade, revealing a greater latent fragility persisting over time. We also see an improvement of the southern regions and the main islands, along with a particularly virtuous trajectory of the central regions of the country.

8 Fragile Italy

Life has its risks and uncertainties, with events whose probability of occurring is in some way measurable; but there are also conditions that cannot be evaluated

---

[26] The average probability of becoming poor was 10.5 percent in 2007 and 11.7 percent in 2009.

beforehand. This holds true today as it did at the time of Italy's unification. What has changed over time is the nature, extent, and range of the risks. At the same time, the strategies possible to neutralize these risks have also increased. Science and technology, on one side, and demography, on the other, have eliminated certain risks, but have created others.

Over the hundred and fifty years examined, different risks have called for different safeguards. As we saw, the actors and roles have changed. Alongside households and the Church there is the increasing role of the state and the market. The forms of protection have become less episodic and arbitrary and increasingly governed by law. What were once informal bonds of solidarity have turned into guarantees and then into rights.

The quantitative information presented in this section leaves little room for doubt: the protection of households' standard of living in the face of risk and uncertainty pervading the environment in which they live has made giant leaps forward over the hundred and fifty years of the country's postunification history. The nineteenth-century Welfare State, born poor and uncaring of the basic functions performed by modern systems (reducing poverty and inequality, encouraging participation in the job market), has changed deeply over time, as much with regard to social legislation as to the resources provided. In the same way, the extraordinary enrichment of citizens (chapter 7, "Income") has enabled forms of self-insurance that have extended the network of protection created by the state. Today's Italians are incomparably more protected, on average, than their ancestors in the face of every kind of risk—whether idiosyncratic (an illness) or systemic (an earthquake).

The development of safety nets over time does not, however, lend itself to an easy interpretation. Reconstructing the development of social expenditure, with its dimensions compared to GDP and its composition, reveals indicative secular trends: the increase in the capacity to spend (and, we should stress, of corresponding private expenditure) to cover the individual against risks that would otherwise not be insurable; and the capacity of protection networks to focus on risks caused by the context in which households and enterprises operate. From this standpoint, the history of protection networks over the last century and a half of Italian life is certainly an achievement.

What the indicators examined do not reveal concerns the existing networks, the ones we see today—an evolution of past ones. The many protection networks, which are by now formalized and bureaucratized, have produced their own constituencies in that they have enabled disparate interests to organize to defend the networks themselves, thereby transforming social institutions generally well-disposed to change into institutions ever-less capable of accompanying the different forms of being of markets, enterprises, and households. This phenomenon is visible, documented, and denounced by many observers (Rossi 1997; Boeri 2000; Boeri and Perotti 2002).

Over and beyond the increasing tendencies of one or another indicator, a long time since the country's unification, the indicator concerning the adequacy of protection remains an open issue. This is highlighted—almost in brutal terms— by the quantitative estimates of the *vulnerability to poverty*. The analysis carried out in section 7 highlighted the existence of two different but coexisting phenomena: on the one hand, a "hard core" of chronic poverty and, on the other, *potential* poverty—that is, a broad section of the population that is not poor, but has a significant probability of becoming poor in the future.

This chronicity must not be confused with the physiologicity; there is no reason to believe that the poor must always be with us, that they will always exist (chapter 9, "Poverty"). The fact that over 80 percent of the poverty observed is chronic means that there is no turnover among the poor: in Italy the poor are the "usual faces", and have well-identified household typologies. Society knows the features of domestic poverty, but it has so far not been able to implement effective policies to eradicate it.

Nor should poverty risk be considered ineluctable—and certainly not on the scale suggested by the estimates presented in this chapter. All this gives us a lesson, if not a warning: the current concentration of public policies in the fields of health and social security—spheres where more modern risks are *not* concentrated—leads us to think that we would do well not to fool ourselves. After years of decline, absolute poverty has stalled, while the risk of sliding into poverty remains high, as always in the south more than in the north. In 1974, Giuseppe Prezzolini (1882–1982), an untiring critic of the Italians, put together a collection of writings in a book entitled *Italia fragile* ("Fragile Italy"). Commenting on the austerity imposed on the Italians by the first oil shock, Prezzolini did not hesitate to unleash yet another scathing rebuke and to reaffirm his thesis: "Italy is fragile thanks to its governing class. (...) The governing classes, Liberal, Fascist, Christian Democrat, [however], cannot have duped the Italians for a century without the Italians being a little willing to be duped. Lincoln once said that you can fool all the people some of the time, and some of the people all the time, but you cannot fool all the people all the time. Who knows? He didn't know the Italians" (Prezzolini 1974, 33–36).

Appendix—Sources and Methods

Figure 11.1 The introduction of insurance against certain life risks, since the 1880s Our processing on the basis of SSA 2012, 2013.

Figure 11.2 The achievement of protection against certain life risks 1930s– 2005 Our processing from the Social Citizenship Indicators Programme (Korpi and Palme 2008).

Figure 11.3 Social expenditure and transfers in Italy (percent of GDP), 1861-2011. Education: 1980–today: www.istat.it, 2011 and Checchi [1997]; 1979–1866: Brosio and Marchese [1986]; 1865–1861: the series has been retropolated using growth rates from Ragioneria Generale dello Stato [1969].

- Pensions: 1990–2008: www.istat.it, 2011; 1981–1989: retropolation with growth rates from Oecd [1999]; 1951–1980: Ferrera [1984]. For the years 1935–1950 retropolation based on Repaci [1962]; finally for the years 1861–1934: Ragioneria Generale dello Stato [1969].
- Health: 1990–2009: www.istat.it, 2011; 1989–1981: «Annuario statistico italiano», various years; 1951–1980: Ferrera [1984]; 1861–1950: retropolation with growth rates from Ragioneria Generale dello Stato [1969]. Similar results are obtained by Atella and Cincotti [2008] for the years 1963–2006.
- Unemployment subsidies:1990–2009: www.istat.it, 2011; 1981–1989: retropolation with growth rates from Oecd [1999]; 1951–1980: Ferrera [1984]; for the years 1919–1951 we have hypothesied a constant growth rate that, when applied to the year 1951, brings to zero the expenses for the year 1919, when the unemployment subsidy was introduced.
- Housing subsidies: 1990–2008: www.istat.it, 2011; 1989–1981: retropolation with growth rates from Oecd [1999]; 1980–1954: Ferrera [1984]; 1953–1913: retropolation with growth rates from Repaci [1962]; 1862–1912: retropolation with data from Ragioneria Generale dello Stato [1969].
- Basic assistance: 1990–2008: www.istat.it, 2011; 1980–1989: retropolation with data from Oecd [1999]; 1979–1954: Ferrera [1984]; 1953–1913: retropolation with data from Repaci [1962]; 1912–1861: retropolation with data from Ragioneria Generale dello Stato [1969].

Figure 11.4 Social transfers in Italy and in some OECD countries (percent of GDP). Source: Lindert (2007), our estimates, and the Social Expenditure Database (SOCX) consulted on Aug. 28, 2014 from OECD.Stat. In this graph the social transfers also include spending on pensions.

Figure 11.5 Social expenditure composition by function, 1861–2011 Sources: same as in Figure 11.3.

Figure 11.6 The new social risks, 1980–2011 Our processing from the Social Expenditure Database (SOCX) data, consulted on Sept. 7, 2014 from OECD.Stat.

Box 1 *The New York Times* and Sicily, 1908. Source: Times Machine, The New York Times Company 2014 (http://timesmachine.nytimes.com/).

Figure 11.7 Italian earthquakes (1861–2011) The map was constructed on the basis of the Database Macrosismico Italiano (DBMI11 version), accessible at: http://emidius.mi.ingv.it/DBMI11, care of the Istituto Nazionale di Geofisica e Vulcanologia (Rovida et al. 2011).

Figure 11.8 Chronic poverty and poverty risk, Italy 1980–2010 The method adopted follows the one indicated by Chaudhuri (2003) and Christiaensen and Subbarao (2005). The level of vulnerability of a household i at time t is given by

$$v_{it} = Pr\left(c_{i,t+1} \leq z\right) \tag{1}$$

Estimating equation (1) means estimating consumption at time $t + 1$, and this can be easily obtained when at least two consecutive waves of observation are present for the same household. This is possible only when we have longitudinal data. However, given the cross-sectional nature of the Istat data, we aggregated the households belonging to a similar group as if they represented a pseudo-household. This approach enables us to convert the available data—which have a very long temporal dimension—into pseudo-longitudinal data (Deaton, 1985). After all the households are grouped into cohorts on the basis of the head of the household's year of birth, gender, and region of residence, the first step consists of estimating a consumption equation at cohort level:

$$\ln c_{j,t} = \alpha + X_{j,t}\beta + u_{j,t} \tag{2}$$

where j identifies the cohort and t is time. $c_{j,t}$ and $X_{j,t}$, respectively, stand for mean consumption (c) and the average of a series of demographic and socio-economic characteristics of all households i belonging to cohort j at time t. The stochastic term $u_{j,t}$ is not homoscedastic, and is defined by:

$$u_{j,t} = \theta_{j,t} + \left[\exp\left(X_{j,t}\gamma\right)\right]^{\frac{1}{2}} \times e_{j,t} \tag{3}$$

where $e_{j,t} \sim N(0, \sigma^2)$ and $\theta_{j,t}$ are household characteristics that cannot be observed. Although these characteristics do not change over time; the nature of the non-longitudinal data and the aggregation of households at the cohort level make this term variable over time. The term $u_{j,t}$, after removing the fixed effects, includes the idiosyncratic shocks.

The heteroscedastic component is common to all households belonging to the same cohort for each year, but differs from one cohort to another. The specificity given by equations (2) and (3) makes it possible for the regressors themselves to have a different effect on the mean and variance (Just and Pope 1978). Hence:

$$E\left(\ln c_{i,t} \mid \mathbf{X}_{i,t}\right) = \alpha + \mathbf{X}_{i,t}\beta \tag{4}$$

$$V\left(\ln c_{i,t} \mid \mathbf{X}_{i,t}\right) = \sigma_{\theta}^2 + h\left(\mathbf{X}_{i,t}; \gamma\right) \times \sigma_e^2 \tag{5}$$

Let us consider an explicative variable such as wealth. Wealth will correlate positively with consumption but it will have a reduction effect on its variability. We thus expect wealth to affect mean consumption positively (the positive sign in equation [4]) and consumption variability negatively (the negative sign in equation [5]). The coefficients α, β, γ of the model are estimated by a three-step heteroskedastic correction procedure (Judge et al. 1985). In the first stage, a least squares regression (2) at the cohort level produces consistent estimates of β, and the square of the residues represents a consistent estimate of the error variance. Subsequently, we generate the weights to be used in the third stage by regressing $\ln(\hat{u}^2_{j,t})$ on $\mathbf{X}_{i,t}$ and obtaining consistent estimates of parameter γ. The third stage consists of estimating (2) which is weighted to account for the heteroscedasticity (hence, $\ln c_{j,t} \times [\exp(\mathbf{X}_{j,t}\,\hat{\gamma})]^{-0.5}$ regressed on $\mathbf{X}_{j,t}\beta \times [\exp(\mathbf{X}_{j,t}\,\hat{\gamma})]^{-0.5}$). This enables us to obtain consistent and efficient estimates of α and β. At this point, by combining the characteristics of each household with the coefficients estimated in the third stage, we can obtain the consumption value (as a log) and its variance.

These estimates are used in order to construct the vulnerability index as follows:

$$v_{it} = \Pr(\ln c_{i,t+1} \leq \ln z \mid \mathbf{X}_{i,j,t}, \hat{\alpha}, \hat{\beta}, \hat{\gamma}) = \phi\left(\frac{\ln z - \left(\hat{\alpha} + \mathbf{X}_{i,j,t}\hat{\beta}\right)}{\hat{\sigma}_{j,t}}\right) \tag{6}$$

where z is the poverty line (estimated in chapter 9, "Poverty") and ϕ stands for the cumulative density of a normal distribution. Note that v can obtain a value between zero and one. Given v, which is estimated for each household of the sample, in order to obtain a dichotomous variable that indicates whether the household is considered at vulnerability risk or not, we need to establish a threshold above which the likelihood of becoming poor associated with an individual is considered high. To this end, we used the sample mean of the number of poor in each year. Hence, an individual (or household) is considered vulnerable if the probability of becoming poor is greater than the percentage of poor people in the population (interpretable as the mean probability of sliding into poverty).

12

Human Development

WITH NICOLA AMENDOLA AND GIACOMO GABBUTI

1 The Challenge of Complexity and the Temptation of Simplicity

Income, wealth, longevity, health, education, child labor: each chapter of this book has tried to tell the story of the progress made by the Italians with regard to wellbeing since the day the Kingdom of Italy was created. What emerges is a number of stories, which do not always concur with one another. At this point, is it possible to join the various threads together? Is it possible to summarize the complex picture and to clearly reconstruct the dynamics of the wellbeing of the Italians?

One possible way to summarize the whole picture and to face the challenge of complexity—more technically, to manage the "multidimensionality" of wellbeing—consists of constructing a single statistical measure, a "composite indicator", that can bring together various pieces of information contained in the social indicators reconstructed so far. It is, besides, an approach in line with the widespread tendency of searching for a single, simple measure that can grasp the scale of the improvements, and evaluating society's adherence to different ideals of "progress" (Engerman 1997).

Nevertheless, building a composite indicator is not a "harmless" operation or one that is conceptually free of difficulties. Selecting the more relevant dimensions of wellbeing and reducing it to a single measure involves making a value judgment on the importance and relative weight of these dimensions. The analyst can choose to combine income, life expectancy, and knowledge; but why not, say, income, life expectancy, and freedom? Even if we do agree on a set of dimensions, what weight should be accorded to each? What counts more: life expectancy or freedom? Do they count the same? Ultimately, and this is the point we want to make clear to the reader, the construction of a composite index directly reflects the preferences of its creator, that is, of the person wishing to measure collective wellbeing.

Despite the conceptual and interpretational limitations, composite indices have found fertile terrain in the field of economic history. Leading scholars such as Nicholas Crafts (1997) and Leandro Prados de la Escosura (2010, 2013), for example, have produced estimates of the most popular of these indices, the Human Development Index (HDI), for many countries, covering the whole period since the Industrial Revolution. The HDI is constructed as a simple arithmetical mean of three elementary social indicators: average income, life expectancy at birth, and average schooling (UNDP 2013b). The idea is that of using HDI to analyze global convergence in *development*, rather than convergence in economic growth, as captured by GDP dynamics. This is, clearly, a tempting analytical perspective that implies the possibility of answering questions like "How has the wellbeing of the Italians changed since the country's unification?" with a single graph instead of the dozens of tables and diagrams contained in this book. At the same time, the extensive use of the HDI in long-run convergence analysis risks obscuring and making us underestimate the scope of the methodological issues posed by these types of indices. But, as Oscar Wilde said, "The only way to get rid of a temptation is to yield to it". Therefore, in this chapter we shall present a series of the HDI, and of the extension of the HDI, for Italy since its unification, and we shall ask ourselves what lessons can be learned from a historical and methodological standpoint.

At the end, this exercise makes us clearly see the fact that composite indices should be handled with great care. Depending on the solutions adopted by the analyst, composite indices can give rise to radically different interpretations of Italian history. For instance, a crucial decision is whether or not to include a social wellbeing dimension such as "freedom"—a slippery but important concept for a country that over the 150 years of its postunification history has experienced regimes reflecting almost the entire political spectrum from "dictatorship" to "democracy".

The general conclusion we offer the reader is as simple as it is apparently disappointing: the composite indices applied to economic history are a false lead that does not solve the problem of a synthetic definition of "wellbeing", able to unambiguously capture all the aspects of this complex phenomenon (Sen 2005, 158). If composite indices are not the desired solution, they are not a pointless exercise in any case. As we shall see, the reasons for being dissatisfied with composite indices are the very ones that must help us to understand how much the history of wellbeing we are telling is sensitive to arbitrary decisions and ethical judgments.

2 Composite Indices: A Simple or a Simplistic Solution?

Wellbeing is a complex, *multidimensional* phenomenon, but policymaking and even the general audience require simple, comprehensive measures for describing it. There is clearly a tension between these two aspects. As noted by Brandolini (2007, 5), the various strategies that can be adopted to solve this tension are essentially distinguished by the degree of processing and manipulation of the original data. Some authors straightaway relinquished the simplicity, thereby maintaining the complexity of the "wellbeing" phenomenon intact and describing it through batteries of non-aggregated social indicators. One of these authors, among the most important, is certainly Amartya Sen (1985), the Indian Nobel Prize–winning economist. The degree of processing of the starting data is, in this case, at a bare minimum if not nonexistent. Other authors have followed different roads (Hicks and Streeten 1979). In the wake of Nordhaus and Tobin (1972), when measuring income some economists have tried to include the value of goods and services that, although affecting a person's wellbeing, do not have a market and are thus not included when measuring GDP. The classic example of this is offered by Usher (1973), who incorporated in the GDP index improvements in a population's life expectancy, attributing a monetary value to it (Box 1). There is also a third possibility that is apparently simpler than the others and hinges on composite indices.

In general, the construction of a single indicator of wellbeing, a composite index, can be broken down into two easier subproblems. The first is *identifying* the spheres to be taken into consideration: What aspects must be considered simultaneously in order to define the level of wellbeing of a society? The list is necessarily a long one and, besides the classic spheres (such as income, health, and education), may also include other dimensions such as freedom, the enjoyment of civil or political rights, personal safety, and the quality of the environment. The second problem concerns the *aggregation* of the dimensions: once they have been identified, what remains to be understood is whether and how it is possible to put them together into a single number, a "composite index" in statistical language, that summarizes the level of a country's wellbeing, like a thermometer gives a person's body temperature.

We should recall here that there is no lack of head-on criticism of a methodological nature with regard to composite indices. As noted by the Princeton economist Marc Fleurbaey (2009), "Discussing the theory underlying such indicators can be done shortly because there is little theory".[1] As we said before, the choice of the elementary indicators to be included in the index is totally arbitrary; and also totally arbitrary is the rule used to aggregate such indicators in a single number. Moreover, these indices suffer from what economists would define as a lack of "microfoundations". The point, as subtle and slippery as it is important, is the following: the dimensions of wellbeing included in the index are clearly dimensions of *individual* wellbeing; however, the unit of reference

---

[1] Martin Ravallion (2013b) has noted how composite indices are completely devoid of theory and can thus be called "mashup indices".

Box 1 **Man does not live on GDP alone: the development of the Italians between income and life expectancy, 1873–2013**

"If you ask a man whether he prefers economic conditions as they are today to those of fifty or a hundred years ago, he would probably say that he prefers conditions as they are today, and his preference might have less to do with the material things we possess than with the fact that we live longer" (Usher 1973, 193–194). Starting from this consideration, Dan Usher constructed a very particular indicator obtained by combining GDP and information contained in mortality demographic tables. The idea is that by having an appropriate "conversion rate" representing the value that citizens ascribe to greater life expectancy, it then becomes possible to add to national income the monetary value of changes (generally increases) in life expectancy. The result, in Italy's case, is reported in Figure 12.B1 below.

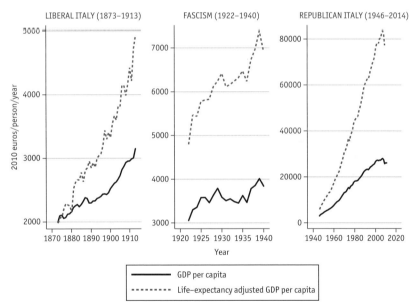

Figure 12.B1 THE DEVELOPMENT OF THE ITALIANS BETWEEN INCOME AND LONGEVITY, 1872–2013. The figure shows the per capita GDP series (black line) and the per capita life expectancy adjusted GDP series; that is, evaluating—in monetary terms—the value of the increase in the population's life expectancy (blue line).

The blue line represents a new index—the Life-Expectancy Adjusted GDP (LEA-GDP), obtained by summing per-capita GDP with the estimated value of progress (or regression) in life expectancy, while the black line plots per-capita GDP. The comparison changes—and actually quite appreciably improves—the views on progress in the Italians' wellbeing. The impact is particularly significant in the first period of Italy's postunification history, when the increase in life expectancy is more marked (from 29 years, at the time of the country's unification, to almost 50 years on the eve of World War I) and income relatively stagnant: while GDP increased at a rate of 1.1 percent per annum, wellbeing—measured following Usher—rose at more than double the rate (+ 2.3 percent).

Besides enabling us to assess the increase in life expectancy of the Italians after the country's unification from a different angle, Usher's experiment suggests two further reflections. Firstly, if it is true that life expectancy is probably the most important social indicator, any index that only adjusts GDP for the latter remains incomplete, that is, lacking in other fundamental aspects of wellbeing. Why include life expectancy and not also education, environmental quality, or the enjoyment of civil rights? A second consideration concerns the very fact of attributing a monetary value to the increase in life expectancy. Giving a price to human life is not just an arbitrary operation (different individuals will give a different value to life), but also questionable at a conceptual level. While it may be a necessity for insurance companies, it is hardly justifiable for economists and scholars of economic history.

of a composite index is not the individual, but the "society". For instance, the value obtained by combining the average income, life expectancy at birth, and average schooling of a society, as is the case with the HDI, is obtained by aggregating average indicators and not the wellbeing of every individual in that society. The relative value of an extra year of life with respect to average income, implicitly defined by the HDI, must never be interpreted with individuals in mind, but with the whole of society. In other words, the relative value of life, according to the HDI, is not the outcome of the value that every single individual attributes to life.

Despite the theoretical flimsiness, the simplicity of composite indices has been their key to success. One of the first examples of a composite index introduced in the literature was the Physical Quality of Life Index (PQLI) (Morris 1979). This index is a simple arithmetical mean of the literacy rate, the infant mortality rate, and life expectancy at birth, appropriately placed on a common scale from 0 to 100. The index immediately showed its effectiveness in enabling a direct comparison of different countries: in this form it was also taken up by Giovanni Federico and Gianni Toniolo (1991) to describe the progress of wellbeing of the Italians in the Liberal period (1861–1913) (Table 12.1).

The creators of the PQLI believed more in the method than in the indicator, that is, they firmly believed in the usefulness of alternative indices to GDP—not to replace it, but rather to supplement it in order to better grasp the dynamics of

Table 12.1 **PQLI: Selected European countries and three main Italian regions, 1870–1910**

Year	Country				Italian regions		
	England & Wales	France	Belgium	Italy	North-west	North-east	South & island
1870	62.9	62.2	n.a.	26.9	40.5	27.1	17.6
1880	70.8	64.4	n.a.	36.9	47.0	41.2	28.4
1890	71.3	67.7	65.5	n.a.	n.a.	n.a.	n.a.
1900	78.9	73.7	75.9	56.7	66.8	62.1	46.0
1910	n.a.	84.0	82.4	62.0	70.5	68.9	49.4

Note: The adoption of a composite index, as Morris' PQLI, is able to represent—by means of a simple table—both cross-country comparisons and time-evolution of "material wellbeing" in some European countries and regions during the "Liberal Age" (1870–1910). Italy clearly emerges as a backward country, even though the extent of the backwardness greatly increases moving from the North-west to the South. Source: Federico and Toniolo [1991: 201], table 10.2.

social progress: economic progress, but also progress in human development.[2] Time has proved this intuition true; the very same international institutions that had encouraged the use of alternative indicators to GDP soon developed the most famous of composite indicators, the HDI, launched by the United Nations Development Program (UNDP) in 1990, which we shall start dealing with in section 3. Right from the start, the stated aim of the HDI was to focus attention by constructing an index that would have the same impact that GDP had on public opinion (Streeten 1994, 235). In the words of Mahbub ul Haq, a Pakistani economist and politician working in the UNDP and "father" of the HDI, this index had to be "of the same level of vulgarity as GNP—just one number—but a measure that is not as blind to social aspects of human lives as GNP is" (UNDP 1999, 23).[3] In the last twenty-five years the HDI has spread its domain over and beyond development economics. Among the various people who have embraced the cause of the HDI or, more generally, of composite indices we can find, not surprisingly, scholars of economic history. Having an index of wellbeing could provide a univocal answer to the century-old debate on standards of living during the Industrial Revolution (Floud and Harris 1997, 114), or it could help put the macroeconomic

---

[2] In the monograph that launched the PQLI on the international scene, Morris affirmed it with great clarity: "While there is no special reason to keep the PQLI functioning—it's present usefulness does not depend on its ability to work forever—the index suggests the potential value in developing other measures with limited objectives" (1979, 105).

[3] GNP stands for *gross national product*, a variant of GDP. It is defined as the value of all the goods and services produced in one year by labor and capital services supplied by the *citizens* of a country—both living abroad and in the country's territory—thus focusing on ownership instead of geographical location (Blanchard 1997, 149).

study of global convergence onto a more complete metric footing than is currently the case, being limited to income indicators (Sala-i-Martin 2002).

3 Wellbeing and Human Development

In the late 1980s the UNDP called together a group of the most renowned developmental economists of the day to practically implement a new approach to the economics of wellbeing developed by Amartya Sen some years previously and now known as the *capability approach* (Sen 1979; 1985). Sen presented this new idea in 1979 within the Tanner Lectures series held at Stanford University. According to Sen, the wellbeing of individuals should not be based on what they possess, but on what they are actually able to achieve. Let's consider the purchase of a bicycle. The traditional economist resorts to the market price of the bicycle to evaluate the utility it gives the owner: the higher the price, the greater the benefit to the rider. Sen is, instead, interested in the "functionings" or the set of activities that the bicycle's owner can now do having bought the new bicycle. These "functionings" do not solely depend on the object itself, but also on the individual and on the context: what you can do with a bicycle will not only be different for able-bodied individuals compared to those with motor disabilities, but will also depend on the condition of roads, the degree of safety in the rider's neighborhood, and other environmental factors. The set of all these "functionings" that an individual is able to acquire—from the most basic (adequate nutrition, access to health care, etc.) to the more complex ones (having self-esteem, being able to actively participate in the life of one's community, etc.)—will measure his or her "capabilities." It is these capabilities that will, ultimately, determine the person's wellbeing. As we can see, Sen shifts attention from the more limited sphere of goods and services possessed to a broader one in which we evaluate not just what people are or do (the "functionings"), but also—and especially—what people may want to be or do (the "capabilities"). At the heart are "the freedoms or valuable opportunities to lead the kind of lives they want to lead, to do what they want to do and be the person they want to be" (Robeyns 2005, 95). In this view, human development is seen as a process capable of "enlarging people's choices" (UNDP 1990, 10)— sometimes also expressed as "empowerment".

Turning such a fascinating and abstract concept into an index useful for designing and implementing social policies is evidently a big challenge. However, the UNDP put forward a solution surprisingly quickly. As early as July 1990, within the first Human Development Report, it presented the first Human Development Index (HDI). It was immediately apparent that this was not just another index among the many around. According to its creators, the HDI had to be "an index potentially capable of answering the central questions: when has human development occurred; to what level or extent; and what has caused it?"

(Kelley 1991, 316). Not only this, but the HDI proposed to do so by combining solid methodological grounding, simplicity (by considering just a small number of variables), and practicality (including them within a single composite index) (Haq 2003, 127–128). In short, it was an index explicitly created to challenge the leadership of GDP in the universe of measures of wellbeing.

3.1 THE STORY OF THE HDI

Right from the start, the HDI was conceived as a composite index combining three elementary indices relating to three spheres of wellbeing: life expectancy, knowledge, and income. In the creators' view, these were the essential spheres of development, the premise for subsequent expansions of the set of individual "capabilities." While life expectancy and knowledge are clearly part of a well-lived life, income was included with an explicitly instrumental role: they chose income (in practice, per-capita GDP) not so much in acknowledgment of the intrinsic role played by the availability of money in producing wellbeing, but rather because they needed a "residual catch-all," that is, a term able to take into account all the "capabilities" not directly included in the indicator (Anand and Sen 2000, 86). In its original form, the HDI was a simple arithmetic mean:

$$HDI = \frac{1}{3}I_E + \frac{1}{3}I_S + \frac{1}{3}L_Y \qquad (1)$$

where the terms on the right-hand side stand for life expectancy at birth (I_E), a schooling index (I_S), and income (L_Y). The different notation used for the latter recalls the fact that GDP enters the equation after being transformed through the logarithmic function. As GDP increases, its natural logarithm grows less proportionately. As an instance, Italian per-capita GDP in 1861 was 1,970 euros, less than 8 percent of the value in 2013 (26,064 euros): when we move to the logarithmic scale, the difference shrinks—log(1,970) = 3.29, that is the 75 percent of log(26,064) = 4.41. This kind of transformation conveys the idea that wealthier individuals obtain less satisfaction from an extra dollar than poorer individuals do (UNDP 1990).

The HDI has quickly progressed since its introduction in the early 1990s. The new UNDP reports, published annually and arriving at their 24th edition in 2015, have received a great deal of criticism from academia, leading to a progressive refinement of the index.[4] The latest and most important revision is the one contained in the report issued in 2010. On the occasion of the twentieth

---

[4] Among the most significant contributions, see Srinivasan (1994), Ravallion (1997; 2012a; 2012b) and Klugman et al. (2011); for a review, see M. Kovacevic (2010).

anniversary of the birth of the HDI, it was decided to change the HDI formula by introducing a geometric mean instead of the simple arithmetic mean:

$$HDI = I_E^{1/3} \times I_S^{1/3} \times L_Y^{1/3} \tag{2}$$

The main reason for being dissatisfied with the original formula given in equation (1) is that the latter implicitly assumes a *perfect substitutability* between arguments. In the "old" HDI, one year less of life expectancy is perfectly compensated by an increase of equal magnitude in the schooling index (Desai 1991). Paradoxically, the human development of a modern industrialized economy may be made equivalent to the degree of human development of a population with a null life expectancy, as long as its citizens—who have not even had the time to go beyond the cradle—are sufficiently educated or sufficiently wealthy. Perfect substitutability appears hardly desirable when the components of the index are considered *essential* dimensions of wellbeing: by definition, that which is essential cannot be replaced (Sagar and Najam 1998). The formula in equation (2) solves the problem: the substitutability is *imperfect*[5] and a null life expectancy makes the value of the HDI null: knowledge is worthless if we do not have the chance to live (and vice versa). In concrete terms, shifting from the old formula to the new one, a country with high life expectancy but not so high schooling as Italy lost 5 positions in the HDI ranking: in UNDP (2009), it was 18th—above the United Kingdom and Germany, while in UNDP (2010) it was 23rd—just below Greece, which presented more "balanced" value among the three dimensions.[6]

One need hardly say that the new formula has also aroused criticism. The HDI does not express an "engineering" sort of relation between the dimensions of wellbeing: there is no straightforward relation between human development as a function of "life expectancy", "education", and "income". Even if we assume that development only consists of these three ingredients, it is a cake with more than one recipe. The HDI is rather a preference system of a hypothetical individual who, faced with different social "menus" (or different combinations of the three dimensions of wellbeing considered by the HDI), makes a specific order—albeit a subjective one. While it is obvious to say that, choosing between two countries, it is preferable to live in the one with the higher life expectancy, it is more difficult to make a preference when there is more than one indicator. In

---

[5] The formula in equation (2) is none other than a Cobb-Douglas-type utility function that is well known to economists and has many desirable analytical properties.

[6] Actually, the UNDP (2010) changed not only the HDI formula but also the indicators to be included to represent two dimensions: GDP is replaced by GNI—Gross National Income; literacy by average and expected years of schooling. Therefore, part of the reranking also depends on these changes. However, the historical applications of the HDI applied the new formula to old indicators, since the new ones are rarely available in long time-series (Gidwitz et al. 2010).

this case, ranking the two countries is a more complex and controversial operation. The HDI solves the problem by reducing the complexity to a single number, and enables us to conclude that we are better off in the place with the higher life expectancy.[7] It is understood that the order underlying the HDI is not an objective one, nor is it derived from the value systems of the individuals making up society,[8] but exclusively depends on the preferences of those who observe and judge them. Different preferences correspond to different formulas of the index and thus different orders. Behind an apparently technical decision such as choosing between a simple arithmetic mean (equation 1) and a geometric mean (equation 2), there are actually different preferences (Decancq and Lugo 2013).

3.2 THE HDI AND HISTORY

The birth of the HDI in economic history may be traced back to the work of Nicholas Crafts in the latter half of the 1990s. Crafts, at the time a professor of economic history at the London School of Economics, had provided in the 1980s an influential reinterpretation of the British Industrial Revolution. Crafts (1997) adopted the HDI in order to bring a new perspective into one of the most lively debates in the discipline, that of the impact of the Industrial Revolution on living conditions of the British people. With reference to the sixteen industrialized countries for which data were available, Crafts constructed a historical series of the HDI in order to complement the traditional national income series. A comparison between the dynamics of the HDI and GDP would enable "a new angle on comparisons of economic progress in different economic eras" (Crafts 1997, 301).

After such a noble entrance, the HDI has earned its place in economic history books (Broadberry and O'Rourke 2010; Persson 2010), but also in the historiography of every continent. Leaving aside for the moment the Italian case, Astorga, Berges, and Valpy Fitzgerald constructed the series for Latin America (2005), while the HDI for Africa was studied by Leandro Prados de la Escosura (2013a). The latter then extended the series to the whole world in a later work (2013b).

The works of Prados de la Escosura deserve particular mention because, by taking up an idea of the Indian development economist Nanak Kakwani, already in 1993, he introduced a new composite index. According to Kakwani: "[A]s the standard of living reaches progressively higher limits, incremental improvement should require much greater resources than similar incremental improvements

---

[7] *De facto*, for those more versed in the foundations of economics, the HDI can be interpreted as an ordinal utility function describing the preferences of a hypothetical observer with respect to the aggregated dimensions of wellbeing included in the HDI itself.

[8] There is also good reason to believe that reconstructing a social preference system starting from individual preferences is an arduous task, if not an impossible one (see Arrow 1951).

from a lower base" (Kakwani 1993, 308). If we agree with Kakwani, we should give greater weight to increases that are, in some respects, more difficult to achieve, such as increasing life expectancy to 90 years when it is already 89, compared to increases that are easier to achieve through vaccination and prevention campaigns in countries characterized by low life expectancies. If the HDI must reflect this nonlinearity, or this different evaluation of the relative weight of increases in social dimensions of wellbeing, then we need to reward the improvements that are more difficult to achieve than the easier ones. Hence the need to create a new composite index, which Prados de la Escosura (2013) called the "Historical Index of Human Development" (HIHD):

$$HIHD = F_E^{1/3} \times F_S^{1/3} \times L_Y^{1/3} \tag{3}$$

In equation (3), F stands for the transformation proposed by Kakwani and applied to the two social indices other than income. Such a transformation attributes increasing weight to marginal increases that are often costlier to achieve. At the same time, the decreasing marginal benefits of income are guaranteed by the logarithmic transformation L_Y.

What may appear to be reasonable, however, may not be acceptable. For example, it is enough to note that income and the two other dimensions are treated in the opposite ways: while in the HDI an increase in per-capita GDP is somehow "reduced" by the logarithm, the HIHD gives an increasing weight to education and longevity indicators. What we wish to stress here, once again, is not the greater or lesser reasonability of the various indices, as the fact that both the original HDI and the HIHD involve preferences that are completely subjective.

Ours is not a "technical" crux—the stuff of economists. The risk that a historian runs by adopting one of the various formulas of the HDI is quite serious and concrete: the fact that opinions may become historiography. Figure 12.1 compares two different HDI formulas for Italy and the OECD countries, and helps to clarify this point. The idea is to show the implications at the interpretative level that can derive from using one formula rather than another.

As we can see in Figure 12.1, the choice of formula changes not just the level of the index (using a geometric mean systematically shifts the index values downward compared to the arithmetic mean), but also its dynamics. Let us first look at levels. If, when commenting on his series reported in Table 12.2, Crafts noted that in 1870 the values of the main industrialized countries such as the United Kingdom are comparable with the ones found in today's developing countries (around 0.4), by using the new HDI formula even the industrialized countries of the day would fare worse than Niger, the country with the lowest HDI in the world today (0.348), according to the Human Development Report of 2015. If we consider the dynamics, according

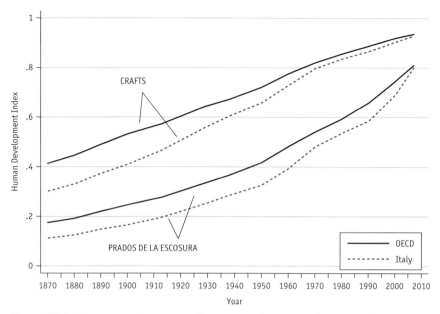

Figure 12.1 DIFFERENT FORMULAS, DIFFERENT STORIES. The figure shows the Human Development Index for Italy (broken line) and for the OECD countries (unbroken line) plotted along the vertical axis, over time (horizontal axis). The comparison between the two formulas used—by Crafts (1997a) and Prados de la Escosura (2010)—shows broad differences in levels and dynamics.

to Crafts's series, Italy achieves a level of wellbeing comparable to the average of the industrialized countries already in the early 1970s. That is to say, the moment of great convergence coincided with the economic boom years, and GDP and wellbeing had very similar underlying dynamics. If we use the formula put forward by Prados de la Escosura, instead, the lesson to be drawn is the exact opposite: Italy progressed for almost 130 years along a parallel trend to that of the other western European economies, and only in the last twenty years of its history managed to recover and to fully align with the standards of wellbeing found in the other OECD countries. In light of our discussion, the problem of which composite index formula to choose means deciding on which preference system to adopt, and the answer can only be one: it all depends on our own preferences.

3.3 WHAT COUNTS IS THE ORDER, JUST THE ORDER

Figure 12.1 offers us the opportunity to discuss a second problem, as important as the one on the subjectivity of preferences discussed so far. The graphs comparing the HDI series for various countries over time have been created, typically, in order to study their variations over time—the growth rates and

Table 12.2 **Crafts' Human Development Index, 1870–1992**

Country	1870	1913	1950	1973	1992
Australia	0.539	0.781	0.853	0.885	0.927
Austria	0.261	0.501	0.731	0.876	0.925
Belgium	0.429	0.621	0.833	0.88	0.926
Canada	0.411	0.682	0.842	0.903	0.95
Denmark	0.448	0.677	0.857	0.89	0.92
Finland	0.151	0.389	0.74	0.873	0.934
France	0.4	0.611	0.818	0.881	0.93
Germany	0.397	0.632	0.787	0.876	0.921
Italy	0.187	0.441	0.666	0.862	0.912
Japan	0.16	0.381	0.607	0.891	0.937
Netherlands	0.45	0.676	0.867	0.899	0.936
Norway	0.367	0.575	0.85	0.897	0.932
Sweden	0.412	0.628	0.858	0.9	0.929
Switzerland	0.457	0.679	0.843	0.882	0.925
UK	0.496	0.73	0.844	0.883	0.916
USA	0.466	0.733	0.866	0.9	0.937

convergence between the various areas.[9] This analytical exercise calls for a clear interpretation of the *absolute value* of the index, an interpretation that appears in stark contrast with the ordinal nature of the index itself. Can we say that the HDI increased by 30 percent, for instance, from one year to the next? If, during a certain time period, the HDI of a country increases more quickly than that of another country, can we conclude that the former is approaching the second in terms of wellbeing? According to the creators of the HDI, the answer is negative.

The HDI was created explicitly to *rank* the *relative* performances of the various countries in a given moment in time (UNDP 1993, 110). Anand and Sen

---

[9] Crafts used the HDI to measure "the speed of development in different eras" (1997a, 310); Prados de la Escosura asked "whether the human development gap between the 'core' and the 'periphery' deepened over time" (2010, 850) and, in his last work, commented on the "absolute gap" and "rate of variations" (2014, 12); Astorga et al., explained that the wellbeing of Latin Americans "almost doubled between 1900 and 1939, and more than doubled to 1980" (2005, 775). With regard to Europe, Millward and Baten wrote that "HDI showed signs of convergence within Europe during the interwar period" (2010, 253), while for Baines et al. (2010, 399) "The average HDI score for Europe rose by almost 30 percent between 1950 and 2003 (0.699→0.905)", despite the fact that they consider the HDI to be a *relative* measure.

(1994) did not overlook the possibility of constructing a historical series of the index, but came to the conclusion that "no special significance is attached to the absolute value of the index, the entire analysis being conducted in terms of the ranking of countries relative to one another" (8). The HDI is thus a purely *ordinal* index.

When we can dispose of an ordinal measure, all we can do is to create a ranking or establish the position that a certain country has within a list of countries. An ordinal index such as the HDI does enable us to see whether a country improves its ranking but, by using a sports metaphor, does not tell us whether it does so because of a series of wins or because the other competitors are going through a bad patch of results. The same limitation is found when the HDI is placed within a historical context, that is, when looking at the progress made by a country over time. The only thing we can do is compare the relative positions of the country over time, but we cannot say anything regarding the extent of the progress made or the magnitude of the crises it has experienced.

Judging by the historiographic literature, it seems that few have taken this consideration seriously. If the ordinal nature of the HDI had been respected fully, we would have understood that its variations over time can give us two—and only two—kinds of lessons. The first concerns the compilation of rankings in space: still with reference to Figure 12.1, the fact that Italy shows a lower level of human development than the OECD average—in every year considered during the period 1870–2007—allows us to conclude that, over the whole period considered, the Italians enjoyed a lower wellbeing, on average, than their contemporaries in northern Europe or in North America. The second lesson concerns the compilation of rankings over time. Because by taking any year into consideration, the index for the subsequent year has always been greater than for the preceding one, we may conclude that the Italians have "always" improved their wellbeing. What we cannot, in any way, infer from the figure is by *how much*. When indices are ordinal ones, the vertical spaces between the two curves in Figure 12.1 have no interpretation whatsoever. Nor does the graph enable us to see the pace with which the Italians have achieved the growth: an ordinal measure does not allow us to analyze growth rates because the very definition of "growth rate" should be based on a cardinal interpretation of the HDI.

The general lesson, of a methodological kind, is that the nature of the HDI poses serious limits to historiographic analysis. These limitations are found at various levels. A first limit concerns the decision to ignore individual preferences (Fleurbaey 2009) by constructing an index directly based on social aggregates. This limit must be borne in mind, especially for its implications, as we stressed in section 1, when dealing with interpreting the variations of the index. There is also the arbitrariness of determining the decision by the various formulas available: it is a choice that filters history by imposing the analyst's preferences on the data. Much as this represents a common trait in any historiographic operation, it is particularly limiting, if not paradoxical, when referred to a tool that we use in order to provide a quantitative and apparently objective solution to the problem of measuring human development. There is, finally, a problem linked not so much to the already discussed analytical limitations of the HDI as to a frequent and persisting bad habit in interpretation that drives many to attribute a cardinal feature to the HDI where its nature is clearly an ordinal one. This is not a purely academic issue, as we shall see in the next section.

3.4 THE HDI, MADE IN ITALY

The employment of the HDI in economic history has also involved Italian scholars. The first Italian estimates started to circulate in economics departments in more or less the same years in which Crafts introduced the HDI in the discipline. The first works were made by Conte, Della Torre, and Vasta (2001), to be taken up and then disaggregated at a regional level by Felice (2007), up to the latest series by Brandolini and Vecchi (2013) and Felice and Vasta (2015).

In the wake of this tradition, in this section we shall explore the use of a new index that attempts to capitalize on the main points discussed in the previous sections. The index we propose aggregates the three "usual" components with a geometric mean, but standardizes all three elementary indices without resorting to any transformation: be it a logarithmic transformation of GDP, which does not consider the fact that income has been included as a "residual catch-all" and, as such, should not be distinguished from other indicators of human development,[10] or the transformations suggested by Kakwani and taken up by Prados de la Escosura,[11] which meet a "cost" criterion (the difficulty for policymakers to achieve new objectives) rather than any actual social benefit:[12]

$$HDI = I_E^{1/3} \times I_S^{1/3} \times I_Y^{1/3} \qquad \textbf{(4)}$$

Our index does not, evidently, escape the limitations of the HDI that we have discussed so far: it is directly based on aggregate social indicators, reflects our preferences, and is limited to creating a ranking among the possible social

---

[10] The point was grasped by Gormely (1995, 264), Sagar and Najam (1998, 253–254), and Crafts (1997, 304).

[11] From this angle, the index is as neutral as possible. The substitutability between components is imperfect, but totally symmetrical between the components themselves. It is, in effect, a Cobb-Douglas-type function directly defined on the standardized indicators.

[12] The different angle may lead to exactly the opposite conclusions. As observed by Noorbakhsh (1998) and Chakravarty (2003), basic skills like reading and writing transform life in a marginally greater manner than a university degree or Ph.D., which are certainly more difficult and expensive to obtain.

arrangements. However, it does have the virtue of simplicity and transparency: the trade-off between the various HDI dimensions is wholly explicit where, in the previous formulations, owing to the stratification of the various transformations, it remained implicit and not easy to decipher (Box 2).

What new things do we learn from the new index? Not very much, all told. The ordinal nature of the index enables us to see how, in the Liberal period, human development—although rising—shows some regressions: in this new series, the index sometimes remains stable for a couple of years (even three, in the period 1878–1880), but sometimes decreases (1892, 1902, and 1908). The increase was more continuous during the Fascist regime and has also been so since World War II: the only interruptions reflect great external shocks (the Great Recession in 1930, the first oil crisis in 1973, and the currency crisis of 1992). On the whole, we can say that the Italians enjoy greater wellbeing today compared to the time of the country's unification (Figure 12.2). The conclusion, although not completely mundane historically speaking (history does not necessarily coincide with a drive toward better conditions of wellbeing), is the most we can say, given the ordinal nature of the HDI.

More interesting, from the interpretative side, is the exercise of breaking down the HDI that is shown in Figure 12.3, which illustrates the separate contribution made by each one of the three dimensions—life expectancy, education (split between literacy and enrollment), and income—to human development.

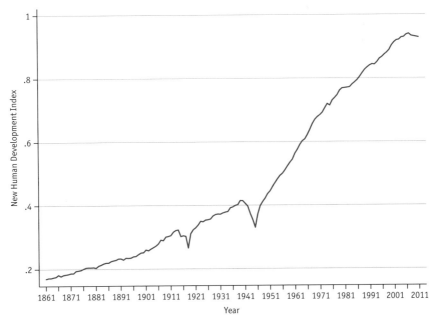

Figure 12.2 ITALIAN HUMAN DEVELOPMENT SINCE ITALY'S UNIFICATION. This figure shows the trend of the new series of the Italian HDI since Italy's unification.

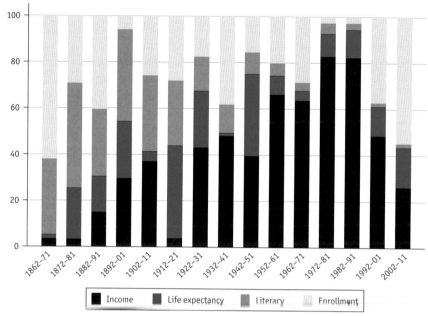

Figure 12.3 THE DRIVING FORCES OF ITALIAN HUMAN DEVELOPMENT,
1861–2011. For each decade considered (horizontal axis), the graph shows
how much the change in HDI (vertical axis) is due to each of its constitutive
components. For example, in the period 1862–71, over half the HDI variation is
ascribable to the increase in schooling (light gray bar) compared to the value of
over 30 percent due to better literacy (dark gray bar). The contribution made by life
expectancy (blue bar) and income (black bar) is marginal in this decade.

It is a particularly simple breakdown in the case of our new HDI index, thanks
to the explicit nature of the link between the social indicators making up the
index itself.

Although there are many results emerging from Figure 12.3, we shall only
focus on the most interesting ones. The first concerns the Liberal period in which
it was the increase in education that raised the HDI, whereas life expectancy,
which also rose steadily over time, did not play a significant role, thereby partly
contradicting the centrality that emerged in Usher's analysis (Box 1). During the
Fascist period it was GDP that took on a progressively more important role since
it began to rise more markedly. In the 1950s and 1960s two factors contributed
most to the HDI: the economic boom and the increased access to secondary and
university education. GDP and school enrollment accounted for 70 percent of
the increase in the HDI. Unlike GDP, which stagnated in the last decade, the
HDI continued to rise until 2007 and then came to a halt. In 2008, the last year
considered in the graph, the contribution of income slowed down and lost—in
just one year—double the contribution made over a whole decade. The impact of
this sharp decrease offset the slight increases in other indicators, and the index

Box 2 **My kingdom for a horse. Or perhaps two?**

In his famous textbook which has educated generations of economists, Paul Samuelson explained that "there is nothing intrinsically reprehensible in working with (...) aggregate concepts", but that it is, however, important to understand their limits by analyzing "the nature of their construction" (1983, 44). This observation is all the more relevant for the HDI. The tool needed to achieve the understanding that Samuelson hoped for is the study of marginal rates of substitution (MRS). Supposing an individual consumes a certain combination of food and clothing. The MRS between food and clothes represents the quantity of clothing that the individual is willing to give up in order to have an extra unit of food. The MRS measures the subjective reasons of exchange between food and clothing. In the HDI

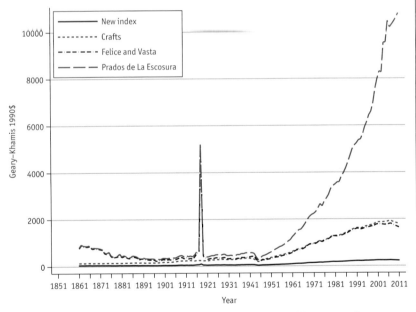

Figure 12.B2 THE VALUE OF ONE EXTRA YEAR OF LIFE: MARGINAL RATES OF SUBSTITUTION OF HDI. The figure shows the marginal rate of substitution (MRS) of life expectancy for income—i.e., the value in dollars of an extra year of life, on average, for society. The different series show how this varies among the various indices considered in the text. As we can see, the results are rather different: if the formulas using an arithmetical mean, for example, do not record such a marked drop in life expectancy after World War I and the worsened conditions of health, the formula put forward by Prados de la Escosura gives exponential weight to further increases in life expectancy when the average value approaches the upper limit.

context, the MRS of life expectancy E_t with respect to per-capita GDO Y_t is the amount of per-capita dollars we are willing to give up in order to increase life expectancy by one year. The MRS is thus, to all intents and purposes, the "weight" or the relative importance of the population's average life expectancy compared to average per-capita income. Anand and Sen's call for making the judgments inherent in formulating the index (1994, 6) clear and comprehensible to the general public means revealing the MRS implied in each of the formulas proposed for the HDI. Faced with different HDI formulations, the MRS makes it easier to understand which one is more consistent with our preferences. Moreover, since the MRS is a relative magnitude, a sort of relative price, it means that it can, unlike the HDI, have a *cardinal* interpretation.

To put the discussion on a more concrete footing, we have produced Figure 12.B2 which shows the development, over time, of the MRS for life expectancy compared to per-capita income. To begin with, let's consider the new index we proposed (black line, equation 4 in the text). One extra year of life would be worth around $50 in 1861. Not much, admittedly. The graph shows that for as much as a century after unification, the MRS remained close to this value. It is only with the economic boom of the 1960s that our HDI formula makes the MRS rise, to a peak of $240 in 2007. The indices used by other authors show a very different trend: even though they start from a higher MRS (above $140 in the case of the index calculated by Crafts; over $750 for the index put forward by Felice and Vasta), they shoot up in the aftermath of World War II. Crafts's formulation assumes that in 2007 a year of life can be worth around $2,000—a value that is not too far removed from the one assumed by Felice and Vasta (about $1,800). The index created by Prados de la Escosura exceeds all: since 1861 the value of one additional year of life rises from $800 to beyond $10,000 (over 12 times more). These discrepancies stem from using a geometric mean. The point was well grasped by Martin Ravallion, on the occasion of the introduction of the new HDI formulation: the HDI "puts a higher value to an extra year of life for people in rich countries than poor ones," with the "unacceptable implication that rich people, or residents of rich nations, are worth more than the poor" (2012a, 206). Ravallion's observation also naturally applies to interperiod comparisons or to economic history. As the above calculations show, the historical series of the Italian HDI attribute a (very!) different weight to life expectancy in different periods of history: this evaluation may be legitimate, but it is never transparent. Although it is reasonable to question the decision made by Richard III in Shakespeare's famous play, to do so, however, the reader has every right to know just how many horses the historian would demand in exchange for his kingdom.

showed a fall for the first time since 1993, almost returning to 2005 levels. In this sense, then, the HDI confirms an Italian decline in the last decade: indeed, it also allows us to say that this decline is not limited to the capacity for expenditure, but also affects people's "capabilities" in the broadest sense, as measured by the HDI itself. Hence, extending our horizon does not change the scene: social indices that increase only slightly do not compensate the Italians for the more negative income component of the western world (chapter 7, "Income").

3.5 THE ITALIAN LACK OF DEVELOPMENT

While the HDI can give us a first overall picture of long-term development processes, the Italian case is particularly interesting because it allows us to reason not only on the choice of a more appropriate formula but also on the "minimalist" choice of including only life expectancy, education, and income in the index. Narrowing the field of HDI definition to just these three social indicators has become common practice as much in international comparative studies as in long-term historical-economic analyses. In this section we shall argue that, at least in the Italian context, this is not a best practice.

To start up the discussion, the most emblematic case is perhaps the one concerning the interwar years: while the idea that wellbeing increased during the Fascist period should not be rejected a priori, the conclusion—based on the HDI in Figure 12.2—that people were better off under this regime than during the Liberal period is, at the very least, a "problematic" one. However much descriptions of the Fascist period are often rosier compared to the savageness of the Nazi dictatorship, we are still talking about a totalitarian regime involving an intolerable suspension of political and civil rights. Sen himself recalled the case of Antonio Gramsci, one of the most important Italian intellectuals and politicians and a leader of the Communist opposition to Fascism, who was sentenced to twenty years imprisonment in 1926. In his final address, public prosecutor Michele Isgrò spoke of the need to "prevent this brain from functioning" (Sen 2003, 1244). Only a few years earlier, more summary treatment had been meted out to the leader of the reformist socialists, Giacomo Matteotti: after speaking in Parliament on the violence that marred the elections of April 6, 1924, that gave Mussolini's party the absolute majority of seats, Matteotti was kidnapped and killed by a group of Fascists on June 10, 1924. While they were still searching for his body, the Socialist, Catholic, and Liberal parliamentary oppositions, led by Giovanni Amendola,[13] abandoned Parliament

[13] Amendola would also die two years later, after the beatings suffered in a Fascist assault. The same fate would be reserved to Piero Gobetti, a young Liberal intellectual. The list of illustrious victims of the Fascist regime sadly exceeds the space allowed in this chapter.

(the Montecitorio Palace)[14] in a symbol of protest. Mussolini's government quickly took advantage of this to abolish freedom of the press and stepped up its authoritarian stance in the country. That same year saw the abolition of the right to strike and even to migrate within the country, in a crescendo that, by way of the official birth of the dictatorship with the creation of the Fascist Grand Council in 1928, continued up to the infamy of the Race Laws that emanated in 1938. Among the many measures envisaged, mixed marriages were now forbidden as was education for Jewish children. This marked the darkest moment for the young Italian state, which would lead to the tragic epilogue of war and Nazi occupation.

This short description of the Fascist years does not obviously purport to be a historical reconstruction, but rather aims to show just how much the political and civil freedoms of the Italians deteriorated in that dramatic period of postunification history. If all this appears obvious to the reader who is familiar with the Italian history between the two world wars, it is not apparent for the HDI. Italian human development increased throughout the Fascist period.[15] Something, evidently, escapes the HDI—something that the dynamics of income, life expectancy, and knowledge do not manage to grasp.

If the triad of life expectancy, knowledge, and income is not enough to grasp what the collective conscious does not fail to understand, the question we should ask ourselves is whether and how it is possible to produce composite indices of human development that can do better, by including some measure of a country's civil and political rights.

4 Beyond the HDI

The need to extend the sphere covered by the index to also include political rights and personal freedoms was clearly felt by the creators of the HDI: "[H]uman development is incomplete without human freedom" (UNDP 1990, 15). However, they considered this sphere too important and complex to be aggregated and "mixed up" with the others. Paul Streeten, one of the members of the original group of experts, explained that the degree of arbitrariness that would inevitably accompany any measure of political and civil liberty would compromise the reliability of the index (1994, 236). The solution they finally adopted was that of supplementing the HDI with the Human Freedom Index (a

---

[14] The Montecitorio Palace is still the seat of the Italian Parliament today.

[15] Ivanov and Peleah (2010) reconstructed the HDI series for the Soviet Union and found that, even more than Italy, the Soviet Union's care to spread education and to satisfy the primary needs of the population led to the greatest performance in human development in history. Here, too, it is reasonable to have some doubts.

second composite index introduced in the second Human Development Report of 1991), and then the Political Freedom Index (1992).

The first ones to try to build a bridge between socioeconomic research and studies made in political science were the economists Partha Dasgupta and Martin Weale in a famous essay of 1992. The two development economists constructed a new index by combining literacy, life expectancy at birth, income, the infant mortality rate, and—a novelty—two indices constructed to incorporate international differences in the enjoyment of civil and political rights. These five indicators were aggregated by means of "Borda's rule",[16] a weighting system already around in ancient Roman times and formalized by the French admiral Jean-Charles de Borda in the late eighteenth century. This new index was called, by their names, the "Dasgupta-Weale Index" (DWI).

The question that Dasgupta and Weale (1992) posed concerned the connection between civil and political rights and economic growth: "Do 'authoritarian' governments achieve better economic results? Or, to put it bluntly: are civil and political liberties a 'luxury' poor countries cannot afford, in that they act as a drag on economic performance?" (124). The historiographical significance of this question did not escape Nicholas Crafts who, in his first experiments of applying the HDI to historical analysis, provided a first estimate for the DWI for 1860, concerning the United Kingdom, Belgium, the Netherlands, the United States, Denmark, Germany, Austria, France, Sweden, Spain, Norway, and also Italy (Crafts 1997b). His contribution was undoubtedly precious for placing at the heart of historical-economic quantitative analysis the role of noneconomic factors, institutions and their capacity to guarantee civil and political liberties and, through this, the wellbeing of the population. With hindsight, Crafts's pioneering estimates of the two indices of civil and political freedoms appear summary and arbitrary at the methodological level, but not at the conceptual level. Analytical frailty prevailed, however, over conceptual innovation: the idea of importing the DWI into historiography was, *de facto*, hardly followed.

4.1 POLITICAL RIGHTS AND CIVIL LIBERTIES

Dasgupta and Weale (1992) adopted two separate indices: a first index of political rights ("R1"), constructed to measure the real possibility for citizens to participate in determining their country's government, policies, and laws; and a

---

[16] Borda's rule works as follows: the results of the various years considered are ranked from best to worst for each one of the five indicators. Hence, we give a value to each year according to its ranking: i.e., a value of 1 to the highest, 2 to the second, and so on. The higher the ranking—that is, the lower the score—the better the performance. The same exercise is repeated for all five spheres of the index. The five results are then summed up, and the years ranked according to their overall score (the lowest score being the best year).

second index concerning civil liberties ("R2"), meant as the possibility to give one's own opinion (such as, but not only, through freedom of the press) without fear of state repression (Taylor and Jodice 1983, 58–68).

Both indices are provided by Freedom House (2013), a U.S. nongovernmental organization that has published a report on freedom in the world since 1972. For each country, the analysts working with Freedom House answer a list of 25 questions (10 for R1 and 15 for R2) concerning aspects of the electoral process, freedom of expression, the judiciary, and the government, and they answer each question with a score ranging from 0 (noncompliance) to 4 (full *de jure* protection and *de facto* application). The sum of the scores of both indices is converted into a scale from 1 to 7, where 1 expresses the maximum level of rights and liberties, while 7 represents the lowest level (Gastil 1986). When the mean of the two indices is below 2.5, the country is considered "free," while it is only partly so with a mean score of up to 5.5. Table 12.3 provides some examples.

Some examples will illustrate this: North Korea, which scores a 7 on both R1 and R2, is considered "not free", as is China (7 for R1 and 6 for R2), Afghanistan, Iraq, and Iran (scores of 6 and 6 for all three countries), but also Russia (6 and 5). Only 6 percent of the countries in North Africa and the Middle East are considered "free", as are 22 percent of the ones in sub-Saharan Africa, while almost all western Europe is considered free (96 percent). The Anglo-Saxon world has a mean score of 1.

Although any measurement of democracy is necessarily discretional, Freedom House's method offers certain non-negligible advantages: the scoring guidelines

Table 12.3 **Freedom House Index: some examples for the year 2010**

Country	R1 Index (political freedom)	R2 Index (civil rights)	FH Index	Label
North Korea	7	7	7	Not Free
China	7	6	6.5	Not Free
Iran	6	6	6	Not Free
Russia	6	5	5.5	Not Free
Venezuela	5	5	5	Partially Free
Lebanon	5	3	4	Partially Free
Kenya	4	3	3.5	Partially Free
Italy	1	2	1.5	Free
United Kindgom	1	1	1	Free
United States	1	1	1	Free

Note: The table reports some example of the index. Only 6% of the countries in North Africa and the Middle East are considered "free", as are 22% of the ones in Sub-Saharan Africa, while almost all western Europe is considered free (96%). The "Anglo-Saxon" world has a mean score of 1. Source: Freedom House [2013].

for each question are well defined, the questions concern many aspects of social and political life, and the scale from 1 to 7 is able to grasp the differences not only between democracy and dictatorship, but also between an absolute monarchy and constitutional monarchy, and among formally democratic regimes that pose heavy restrictions in some spheres of rights. A further advantage, useful for historical analysis, is the relative replicability of the method: on the basis of the Freedom House criteria, it is possible to reconstruct the index backward even in light of the institutional and political innovations that have characterized the past of states and nations. While the Freedom House experts use news reports to formulate their index, the historian can call on the vast secondary production concerning Italy's social, juridical, and political history. We attempted to reconstruct both indicators for Italy's postunification history: the results are shown in Figure 12.4.

In the aftermath of unification, Italy was a monarchy: it was the king who had the power to appoint the government and could push it to resign; the Senate

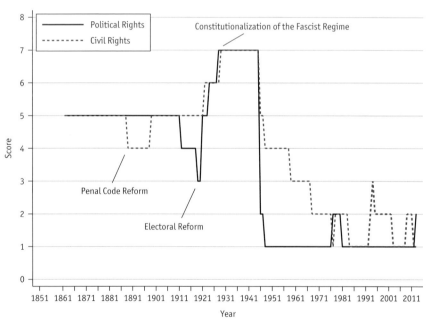

Figure 12.4 CIVIL AND POLITICAL RIGHTS IN ITALY, 1861–2013. The graph shows the trend of political rights (unbroken line) and civil rights (broken line) over time (horizontal axis). The series, measured along the vertical axis, range from 1 (which stands for the full enjoyment of rights) to 7 (indicating serious and substantial deprivations). The two series have a non-linear trend: the modest freedom enjoyed during the Liberal period vanished with the advent of Fascism, which curtailed both political and civil rights. Even with the return to democracy after World War II, the latter rights needed more time to be fully established.

was an unelected body; and under 2 percent of the population had the right to vote, on the basis of the census. On the whole, the political initiative of the lower classes was very limited (Rodotà 2011, 7–9) to the extent that the Italy of the times has been called a "mono-class" state that was still not formally democratic (Giannini 1970, 46). If we also add an inclination to little transparency and the scandals of the Italian governing class right from the dawning of the new kingdom (Toniolo 2013, 35), we can justify the score of 5 obtained (the starting point of line R1 in Figure 12.4), which places Italy slightly above a completely autocratic State with regard to political freedoms. Crafts (1997b) had already assigned the same score, and it corresponds to the score given in the latest report of Freedom House (2013) to Venezuela (see Table 12.3). The electoral reforms of the years 1912–1919 would introduce proportional representation and "almost" universal suffrage, improving R2 up to a peak of 3 on the eve of World War I.

With regard to civil rights, the Albertine Statute—the fundamental law granted by the House of Savoy (the Italian royal family) in 1848 and later applied to the whole of the Kingdom of Italy—could not be considered as a sort of a modern constitution: article 1 declared "The Roman, Catholic and Apostolic Religion the sole Religion of the State," and did not provide any safeguards with regard to the omnipotence of the legislator (Allegretti 1989, 407–411), nor did it safeguard freedom of the press, of association, and of gatherings. All were further restricted by the prime minister, General Luigi Pelloux, after some riots in 1899 (the so-called Pelloux Law). Freedom of teaching was nonexistent, and the jurist Attilio Brunialti called the judiciary "nothing but a delegate of the Government" (Brunialti 1870); in the absence of any well-codified labor law, the factory was a sort of "absolute monarchy" (Merli 1972, 147) and workers could be fired simply for their ideas (Rodotà 2011). In response to the first claims for social rights, there were the so-called *eccidi proletari* (proletarian massacres), started by General Bava-Beccaris: the order to open fire on a Milanese crowd in May 1898 caused 80 deaths and guaranteed a senatorial seat for the General. Despite the term "Liberal", monarchical Italy was thus a country that safeguarded civil rights in a very partial way: the R2 index for civil rights gives 5 in 1861 (3, according to Crafts [1997b]), and then 4 after the Penal Code reform of 1889.

The fragility of the "formally democratic" Italian state would soon be revealed in the violence of the Fascist gangs against press offices, political party headquarters, and trade union offices that characterized the "black two years" of 1921–1922—correspondingly, R1 is declassed to 5. With the Fascist march on Rome (October 28, 1922), which led to Benito Mussolini's appointment as prime minister (October 31), R1 (the political rights indicator) is further declassed to 6. The Fascist regime soon consolidated itself in a few years, with the known consequences on citizens' liberties: the 1924 elections gave Fascism an over-whelming majority thanks to the intimidations and violence denounced by Matteotti, but especially because of a new electoral law, the so-called Acerbo Law, which abolished proportional representation and assigned two-thirds of the parliamentary seats to the party receiving barely 25 percent of the votes. The same year saw the abolition of the freedom of the press and the right to strike. Both indices, R1 and R2, decrease from 6 to 7 with the constitutionaliza-tion of the Fascist Regime on December 9, 1928.

From the ruins of World War II, Italy emerged with a new Constitution that women also had a hand in drafting. The elections of 1946—first the local elections of March and then the institutional referendum of June 2 to decide whether to remain a monarchy or to become a republic—were the first to see a determinant participation of women. The new Republican Constitution was adopted in 1948: we give the highest score on the R1 index (political rights) already in this very year. However, it would take some decades for the full implementation of the Constitution with regard to civil rights. Only in 1959, with the creation of the High Council of the Judiciary, were the foundations laid making it possible for the first time to establish the liberal principle of independence of the judiciary from political power. The Italians had to pursue an even longer road to obtain a complete affirmation of civil rights and free-dom of expression. As late as 1960, after seeing Federico Fellini's masterpiece *La Dolce Vita,* the then Minister of Culture Umberto Tupini sent a letter to the president of the Italian industrial cinematographic association recommending the censorship of all those "scandalous subjects, negative for the formation of the Italians' civil conscience". The "hot autumn" of 1968 heralded a tormented decade that brought new social and civil achievements, however: the Fortuna-Baslini Law of 1970, to mention a significant example, introduced—for the first time—the possibility of divorce in Italian law. An attempt to repeal this law four years later through a referendum strongly supported by the Catholic hierarchies failed.

On the whole and despite their stylized and approximate manner, the indi-ces R1 and R2, for political rights and civil liberties respectively, do manage to describe the difficult, nonlinear road of the Italians toward political democracy and respect for civil liberties. These indices are purely ordinal ones—the differ-ence between 1 and 2 in each index cannot be compared to the difference, say, between 6 and 7—but they still allow us to obtain a trend in the overall phe-nomenon in order to include it within a composite index of wellbeing. While it is true that R1 and R2 do not add anything new to historiography, their adoption within a composite index of development has an important effect, enabling us to have a more detailed account of the development of the living conditions—not just material ones—of the Italians.

4.2 WE WERE WORSE OFF WHEN WE WERE WORSE OFF

Can the improvement in living conditions of the Italians during the Fascist period that is seen in almost all the indicators presented in this book, as well as in the summary of this chapter on the HDI, compensate for the loss of freedom in Mussolini's autocratic regime? A popular Italian saying with reference to the Fascist period is, "We were better off when we were worse off": is that really true? The availability of a series of indices measuring civil and political rights such as the one presented in the previous section allows us to provide an answer, albeit a debatable one, by means of the conceptual framework and methodological apparatus of the HDI.

A first possible strategy consists of combining R1 and R2 with the other series making up the DWI, which means ranking the years by means of the Borda Rule. For instance, if we consider per-capita GDP, the highest value is found in 2007 while the lowest is in 1867. Hence, we give a value to each year according to its ranking: that is, a value of 1 to 2007 (the highest), 2 to 2006, and so on up to 138 for 1867 (the years of the two world wars are excluded). The same operation is repeated for all five spheres of the index. Having done this, the years are then ranked according to their overall score: we find that 2007 was the best year for the Italians, while 1867 ranks 134th. Figure 12.5 shows the complete ranking for all the 150 years of the country's postunification history.

The story of the Italians told by the DWI is different from the one told by the HDI. The former index records a tendency toward improvement for the whole Liberal period, which is then followed by an almost vertical drop from 69th place in 1921 to 110th place in 1924. The loss of wellbeing during the Fascist period following the lack of fundamental liberties of the Italian population is fully reflected. It would take the end of the Fascist regime and of World War II (shown in the data for 1946) to get back to the levels of wellbeing recorded before the advent of the dictatorship.

We can achieve similar results with another approach. We constructed an alternative index by including R1 (political rights) and R2 (civil liberties) directly in the HDI we saw in formula (2)—a sort of "extended" human development index (EHDI) covering the sphere of political and civil liberties, as follows:

$$EHDI = I_E^{1/4} \times I_S^{1/4} \times I_Y^{1/4} \times I_F^{1/4} \qquad (5)$$

where I_F stands for the index of freedom obtained by summing the scores of the responses to the 25 items of R1 and R2, and has a range of 0 to 100. The procedure, certainly open to refinement, allows us to see whether the inclusion of an added variable within the HDI can produce similar effects to those emerging

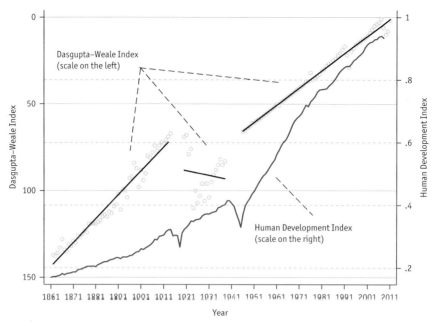

Figure 12.5 ACCOUNTING FOR FREEDOM: THE DASGUPTA-WEALE INDEX, 1861–2013. The figure shows the trend over time (horizontal axis) of the Dasgupta-Weale index (left-hand vertical axis) and of the HDI (blue line, right-hand vertical axis). The first index also includes R1 (a measure of political rights) and R2 (civil liberties). The inclusion of these two spheres radically changes the historical judgment of the Fascist period. While the wellbeing of the Italians shows continuous progress in the Liberal period and Republican period, the interwar years show a clear decrease of the index.

when directly using the Dasgupta-Weale index. Figure 12.6 shows the EHDI (dotted line) compared to the HDI (bold line).

When we take civil and political rights into consideration as an integral part of human development, the history of the wellbeing of the Italians reveals novel aspects that are largely overlooked by the historiography based on the HDI. Improvements in material life are summed—with a positive or negative valence—to the possibility of self-determination offered by the political, institutional, and social system in general. This is a fundamental aspect that Sen had in mind when talking about "capabilities". The human development process of the Italians thus no longer has a linear trend but comes to a sharp halt, an inversion in trend, just when Italy started to equip itself with the state tools necessary to combat the centuries-old blight of illiteracy and to spread the benefits of the health revolution to the whole population.

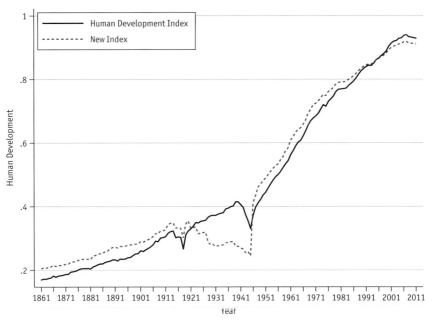

Figure 12.6 Human Development and Freedom, 1861–2013. The figure
compares the HDI (unbroken line) with the "extended" HDI (broken line) which
includes a fourth dimension of wellbeing, "freedom", obtained by combining the R1
index (political rights) and R2 index (civil freedoms). As with the Dasgupta-Weale
index, the effect of this redefinition changes the long-term trends in the wellbeing
of the Italians, sweeping away any nostalgia for the Fascist period.

5 Who Is the Judge: History or Historians?

In judging the processes and transformations experienced by peoples and
nations we often appeal to the tribunal of history. It is history itself that, as it
unfolds, attributes rights and wrongs, offering a solution to debates enliven-
ing the community of social science scholars and, more generally, the world of
academia. Things are not that simple, however. History is filtered by those who
write it, and historians very often get their own back by donning the judge's
robes. In this sense, the HDI is an emblematic case where the judgment of historians replaces that of history.

As we amply discussed in the previous pages, the HDI has many drawbacks
in all its varieties. Although it does have the advantage of condensing the many
spheres of wellbeing into a single number, it is still an index based on scanty or
no theoretical foundations. Added to this is the fact that the choice of dimensions of wellbeing to be included in the index is quite arbitrary; and, despite the
interpretations in a cardinal sense that abound in the literature, especially in
economic history, the HDI is a purely ordinal tool.

Box 3 The Italians' search for happiness, 1947–2013

In 1974 the American economist Richard Easterlin wrote an essay of great impact. By placing per-capita GDP and the percentage of American citizens who declared being happy on the same graph, Easterlin concluded that "there has been no improvement in happiness in the US over almost a half century in which real GDP per-capita more than doubled" (Easterlin 1974, updated in 1995, 38). The weak link between mean income and happiness surprised more or less everyone—to the extent that the result was immediately referred to as "Easterlin's paradox": what typically holds for an individual (a higher income means greater happiness) does not seem to be true for a country as a whole (an increase in per-capita GDP does not lead to an improvement in the happiness of the entire population).

Over the following decades, attempts to measure *happiness* (or *life satisfaction*) increased and are now too numerous to mention: since 1973 the

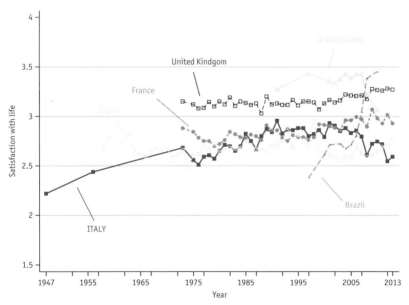

Figure 12.B3 THE ITALIANS' SEARCH FOR HAPPINESS, 1947–2013. The graph shows the trend of life satisfaction (World Happines Database; vertical axis) over time (horizontal axis) for various countries. In 2013 the Italians ranked unhappier than their French neighbors, but also with regard to the Japanese, British, Americans and Brazilians. However, more recent years show that the happiness of the Italians is probably greater than the one recorded for the decade after World War II (1948-1956), but lower than the one found forty years ago (1973).

European Commission has conducted the Eurobarometer, a survey system started up to monitor not just European Union citizens' opinions on political and social issues but also their happiness. The same thing is performed by the Latinobaròmetro (since 1995) and Asian Barometer (since 2001). In 2012, even the United Nations launched the first World Happiness Report, drawing the world's attention to the case of Bhutan, a country of under one million inhabitants at the foot of the Himalayas. The country's constitution imposes a calculation of the Gross National Happiness (GNH) index—a composite index based on both objective indicators (e.g., income) and subjective ones (e.g., happiness). If we build a hospital, we must also measure the psychological perception its users have of it: if the hospital does not increase the happiness *perceived* by the population, then the hospital does not improve the wellbeing of the citizens of Bhutan (Ura et al. 2012).

There are various international databases available today that can satisfy our every curiosity on the measures proposed for ranking countries of the world according to their happiness—from the World Database of Happiness (WDH) (Veenhoven 2014) to datasets produced by the World Values Survey (2008). We constructed the figure by starting from the WDH itself. The figure compares the average happiness of the Italians (in blue) with that of the United States, the United Kingdom, Japan, France, and Brazil. In absolute terms, the Italians seem to be stably among the "unhappiest" or the least satisfied of our sample. On the other hand, the happiness of the Italians does show an inverse trend from the mid-1990s. There is certainly no trace of a paradox, in Easterlin's sense: Italy's decline in per-capita GDP (first in relative and then in absolute terms) actually started in the 1990s (see chapter 7, "Income"), and this increased inequality in income distribution (see chapter 8, "Inequality"), leading to a rise in absolute poverty (see chapter 9, "Poverty"). On the whole, at least in Italy's case, the subjective measures of happiness are in line with what GDP and, in part, the HDI have already revealed (Cannari and D'Alessio 2012).

In light of these trends, there is the temptation to give credit to the happiness index and to see it as a sort of composite index of subjective wellbeing. Ultimately, when people make their own judgment, they assess the spheres relevant to their own wellbeing, attribute a relative weight to each of these spheres, and come to a bottom line. If we were to do this here, however, we would be victims of a classic example of a "fallacy of composition": what holds for an individual may not necessarily be true for society as a whole. As we saw, the HDI is not constructed on the basis of individual preferences, but is instead defined directly on aggregate social indicators. It is thus not a suitable tool for shifting from individual rankings to social rankings that are consistent with the latter. To this we must add an even more elementary problem: the notion of happiness does not necessarily coincide with the notion of wellbeing. It may be different from one individual to another and, in general, may be conditioned by the context people live in (Fleurbaey et al. 2009, 11).

But the aspect we wish to stress more, in our conclusions, is that the HDI largely reflects the preferences of its creators. If the person who uses it is a historian, then the HDI will largely reflect his/her own judgment of history. There is nothing actually wrong with this as it is often the case and is the reason why the judgment of the tribunal of history is never unappealable, but we should be conscious of this fact. Hence, if the creators of the HDI aimed to win the challenge of complexity by constructing an objective aggregate measure of social wellbeing, then the challenge can be considered lost. The HDI only gives a ranking of wellbeing consistent with the value system associated with the particular specification of the HDI we are using.

If that is the case, then we should ask ourselves why we have obliged the reader to bear with us for so many pages. The answer lies in the very simple fact that we can learn a lot from a lost challenge. The fragility of history told by the HDI makes us understand just how questionable the story told by other, more consolidated, indicators is. For a better understanding of this point let's consider a particular specification of the HDI that we have not dealt with before. Supposing that the HDI has the generic form:

$$ISU = I_E^{w_E} \times I_S^{w_S} \times I_Y^{w_Y} \qquad (6)$$

where we recall that I_E, I_S, and I_Y stand for the social indicators of education, health and per-capita GDP, respectively. Unlike the HDI illustrated in the previous sections, here we assume that the system of weights of the geometric mean making up the HDI, given by the values w_E, w_S, w_Y, is not necessarily symmetrical. Supposing also that we decide to give little or no weight to the population's average life expectancy I_S, and that we consider education, as measured by I_E, not to be a significant factor of growth and wellbeing. This decision may be one that few people would agree with, but it is still a judgment, and, as such, must be accepted. From a formal standpoint, this ethical system leads to the hypothesis that we have $w_E = w_S = 0$ and $w_Y = 1$. Only per-capita GDP is given a positive weight, and thus is equal to one. But, in this case, the HDI is identified with per-capita GDP, which is, as we know, a widely used and commonly accepted indicator. The HDI will thus help us to understand also how the decision to rely on a monodimensional and monetary indicator like GDP is a value judgment and, what is more, a value judgment that not many, if they had a clear perception of it, would be willing to subscribe to.

What we have illustrated is only an example, a rhetorical artifice, but it is useful to enable us to understand that if the HDI is not a satisfactory solution to grasp the many dimensions of wellbeing, giving up the challenge of multidimensionality from the start is also an equally unsatisfactory solution, if not more so.

Appendix—Sources and Methods

Figure 12.B1 The development of the Italians between income and longevity, 1872–2013 The graph extends the calculations made by Brandolini and Vecchi (2011). The per-capita GDP curve corrected for life expectancy is the one proposed by Usher (1973; 1980): $LEA_t = GDP_t \left(L_t / L_0 \right)^{1/\beta}$, where $L_t = \pounds_j p_{j0} L_{jt}$ is mean life expectancy among all the cohorts of age j ($j = 1, 2, \ldots, 110 +$), weighted with respect to the base year 0. The relation in brackets is the growth rate of overall life expectancy between a generic year t and base year 0 adjusted according to a discount rate β (assumed to be 0.25 in the figure), which actually reflects the relative importance given to life expectancy: "small" values of β correspond to high evaluations of the benefits of an extra year of life expectancy and involve a greater gap between "simple" GDP (GDP_t) and the adjusted one (LEA_t). Sources: the GDP series is the one estimated in chapter 7 ("Income"); the life tables used are the ones available in the Human Mortality Database (consulted in March 2014).

Figure 12.1 Different formulas, different stories The series in the figure are obtained by means of the basic formula of the HDI (UNDP 1990, given in the text by equation 1). Each component I_x is standardized in the following way: $I_x = (x_t - \underline{x})/(\bar{x} - \underline{x})$, where $\bar{x}$ and $\underline{x}$ stand for the maximum and minimum value of variable x, respectively. In the case of per-capita GDP (L_y), the variable is transformed by applying the natural logarithm to x_t, $\bar{x}$ and $\underline{x}$. The dotted series are constructed on the basis of data kindly made available by Leandro Prados de la Escosura, and refer to equation 3 in the text, introduced in Prados de la Escosura (2010). In this case, the income component is maintained as before, but the following convex transformation is applied to the nonmonetary variables: $F_x = \log(\bar{x} - \underline{x}) - \log(\bar{x} - x_t)/\log(\bar{x} - \underline{x})$.

Figure 12.2 Italian human development since Italy's unification The series is obtained by applying a new formula of the HDI proposed in the text (equation 4). In its extended form, it is as follows:

$$HDI_t = \left\{ \left(\frac{e_t - \underline{e}}{\overline{e} - \underline{e}} \right) \times \left(\frac{y_t - \underline{y}}{\overline{y} - \underline{y}} \right) \times \left[\frac{1}{2} \left(\frac{l_t - \underline{l}}{\overline{l} - \underline{l}} \right) + \frac{1}{2} \left(\frac{g_t - \underline{g}}{\overline{g} - \underline{g}} \right) \right] \right\}^{\frac{1}{3}},$$

where e stands for the population's average life expectancy, y is per-capita GDP, and the schooling index is obtained through the simple average of l, the literacy rate, and gross enrollment rates (g). For all indices, the value of $\underline{x}$ has been set at 0 (a less arbitrary decision than any other since it is a "natural" minimum value), with the result of eliminating this component from the calculation of marginal rates of substitution (MRS). For the maximum values ($\overline{x}$), we opted, where possible, for the "natural" maximum (that is to say, 100 for l and g); for y, we adopted the value of $20,000 Geary-Khamis (base year: 1990). Even if this decision is an arbitrary one, it does not change the overall ranking: by adopting a maximum value of, say, $40,000, we obtain the effect of "rescaling" the series downward, without altering the ranking. The sources are as follows: the per-capita GDP series are the ones described in chapter 7 ("Income"); life expectancy is the one estimated in chapter 3 ("Health"); for the literacy rate and gross enrollment rates, the sources are those of chapter 5 ("Education").

Figure 12.3 The driving forces of Italian human development, 1861–2011 The graph is obtained by cumulating—for ten-year periods—the marginal contributions of the four simple indices (per-capita GDP, mean life expectancy, literacy rate, and gross enrollment rates) to the variations of the HDI series shown in Figure 12.3. Since the index is obtained by means of a geometric mean, it is not possible to break down its components in a precise manner, as it is instead possible to do for the HDI proposed by Crafts (1997a). Hence, we calculated the marginal contribution made by each elementary index to the overall index in the following way: $\partial ISU_t / \partial x_t = ISU_t / 3(x_t - \underline{x})$. In the case of the two education indices, division by 3 is the overall contribution, while it becomes $ISU_t / 6(x_t - \underline{x})$ for the single indicator. We can see that the maximum value does not come into this formula, nor does the minimum value (which disappears because it is established as zero for all the indices), eliminating a source of arbitrariness in the index ranking.

Figure 12.B2 The value of one extra year of life: marginal rates of substitution of HDI The four HDI formulas used by Crafts (1997a), Felice and Vasta (2015), Prados de la Escosura (2010), and the one in equation 4 in the text imply different MRS between the elementary indices. The figure considers the MRS between life expectancy at birth (e) and per-capita income (y); given the definition of $SMS_{e,y} = \dfrac{\partial ISU_t}{\partial e_t} \Big/ \dfrac{\partial ISU_t}{\partial y_t}$, it is clear that it varies as a function of t, and that it takes on different expressions and values depending on the HDI concerned. The graph shows the various series of $SMS_{e,y}$, calculated by means of the following formulas: $SMS_{Cr.} = y_t (\log \bar{y} - \log \underline{y}) / (\bar{e} - \underline{e})$; $SMS_{F\&V} = y_t (\log y_t - \log \underline{y}) / (e_t - \underline{e})$; $SMS_{PDLE} = y_t (\log y_t - \log \underline{y}) / [\log(\bar{e} - \underline{e}) - \log(\bar{e} - e_t)](\bar{e} - e_t)$; $SMS_{AGV} = (y_t - \underline{y}) / (e_t - \underline{e})$. The latter formula, with $\underline{e} = \underline{y} = 0$, simplifies as $SMS_{AGV} = y_t / e_t$.

Figure 12.4 Civil and political rights in Italy, 1861–2013 The series concerning political rights and civil liberties were developed by means of the method used by Freedom House (2013). By using secondary historical sources, we gave a score ranging from 0 to 4 to each item envisaged in the Freedom House method. With respect to *political rights*, these concern: a) the electoral process (3 items); b) political pluralism and participation (4 items); and c) government functioning (3 items). For *civil liberties* the items concerned a) freedom of expression and thought (4 items); b) the rights of association and organization (3 items); c) the state of law (4 items), and d) the person's autonomy and individual rights (4 items). For each year, the score given certifies the level of the country's compliance: a value of 0 means "lack of good practices"; 1, little or a few good practices, but lack of good legislation; 2, some/many good practices, but few good laws; 3, many/all good practices as well as some good laws; 4, good practices and good corresponding laws. If it is true that this method is not completely devoid of analyst discretion, it is still a well-established method. To clarify this, we shall enter the scores for Italy for the years 1862, 1922, and 1948 in Table 12.4. The letters correspond to the categories listed above (thus, for instance, "A" in the first column means "electoral process), and the classification of the items is the one we find on Freedom House's website. The annual series with the scores given for the period 1862–1971 is available from the authors on request; for the years 1972–present, the data are in Freedom House (1972–2013).

Once the scores have been expressed, their sums yield two indices that are defined, respectively, on the scales 0–40 (DP) and 0–60 (LC). For the three years of our example above, they are given in the two "Total" columns. Starting from these scores, the Freedom House procedure envisages assigning a value on a scale 1–7, where 1 is the worst result and 7 is the best. In the case of political rights,

Table 12.4 Scores for political rights and civil liberties in Italy, detail for the years 1862, 1928, and 1948

Year	A 1	A 2	A 3	B 1	B 2	B 3	B 4	C 1	C 2	C 3	Total	PR	D 1	D 2	D 3	D 4	E 1	E 2	E 3	F 1	F 2	F 3	F 4	G 1	G 2	G 3	G 4	Total	CL
1862	0	1	0	1	1	4	4	0	2	2	15	5	2	1	1	3	1	3	1	0	1	1	1	2	3	1	0	21	5
1928	0	0	0	0	0	0	3	0	2	0	5	7	0	2	1	1	0	0	0	0	0	0	0	0	3	1	1	9	6
1948	4	4	4	4	4	4	4	4	2	3	37	1	2	2	3	3	1	2	3	1	2	1	1	0	3	1	3	28	4

the minimum score (6) is given to values between 0 and 5; between 6 and 11 it is 2; between 12 and 17 the score is 5; 4 up to 23; from 24 and 29 we give a 3; 2 between 30 and 35; 1, the best score, above 26. For civil liberties, 1 is obtained at 53; from 44 to 52, 2; from 35 to 43, 3; 4 for 26–34; 5 for 17–25; 6 for 8–16; the score of 7 is obtained under 7. The above operation leads to the results of columns PR and CL: with a score of 15, for example, in 1862 Italy has a middling to low result (5) in terms of political rights; this result drops to 7, the minimum, in 1928, to then reach the maximum (1) in 1948. By combining the two indices of PR and CL, we get a mean value, adopted by Freedom House as the summary indicator: if this average lies between 1 and 2.5 (for example, when both indices give 2), the country is indicated as "free" (see 1948, for example, with a mean of 2.5); if the average is between 3 and 5, instead, the country is classified as "partly free" (Italy in the aftermath of unification is barely in this category). Below this, that is, with an average from 5.5 to 7, the country has very low scores in both indices and is considered "not free." This is Italy's case for 1928.

The main sources consulted for compiling the annual series that we have given an example of in Table 12.4 are Allegretti (1989) and Giannini (1970) with regard to the institutional framework; Pombeni (1995) on the development of parliamentary representation; Piretti (1996) and Corbetta and Piretti (2009) on the results and number of voters in the elections; Merli (1972) and Rodotà (1995) on worker's conditions and trade union rights; Guarnieri (1995) on the autonomy of the judiciary and the police. An overview of the sphere of rights over the 150 years concerned is provided by Rodotà (2013).

Figure 12.5 Accounting for freedom: the Dasgupta-Weale Index, 1861–2013 The figure presents the Dasgupta-Weale index for Italy, after excluding the years 1915–1919 and 1939–1945 for their exceptionality. The index is obtained by combining per-capita GDP (Y), literacy rate (L), life expectancy at birth (E), and infant mortality rate (M) for the two indices of political rights (PR) and civil liberties (CL) by means of the Borda method (Goodman and Markowitz 1952; Smith 1973; and Fine and Fine 1974). To illustrate this, we have constructed Table 12.5, where we consider the same years as in Table 12.4.

Table 12.5 **The Dasgupta-Weale Index (DWI) for Italy, detail for the years 1862, 1928, and 1948**

Year	Y	E	M	L	DP	LC	Total	DWI
1862	132	139	137	138	71	75	692	137
1928	70	77	78	77	128	122	552	96
1948	69	65	63	64	1	54	316	64

The year starting our series, 1862, is a time of great backwardness not only with regard to the economy, but also with respect to health (the country ranks last for life expectancy, and last but two for infant mortality) and education (literacy is the second-worst result). The situation is only partly redressed by the indices of freedom. On the other hand, in 1928 both PR and CL pull down the country's ranking in the DWI. Finally, PR has a maximum value in 1948—and this value is maintained, with few exceptions, throughout the Republican period.

Figure 12.6 Human development and freedom, 1861–2013 The series is obtained by adding the "freedom" dimension (equation 5 in the text) to the HDI series of Figure 12.3. Component I_F is obtained by summing the totals of PR and CL, as shown in Table 12.4: for example, $F_{1862} = 15 + 21 = 36$, $F_{1928} = 5 + 9 = 14$ and $F_{1948} = 37 + 28 = 65$. Since the F series thus obtained naturally ranges between 0 and 100, these are the minimum and maximum values adopted.

Figure 12.B3 The Italians' search for happiness, 1947–2013 The graph is constructed on the basis of the World Happiness Database (WHD) (Veenhoven 2014). For the years 1947 and 1956, the data are our processing of Doxa statistics (Luzzatto Fegiz 1949; Doxa 1966). The data collected by the WHD and used here are obtained through answers to the following question: "How satisfied are you with the life you lead?" "Not at all" is scored as 1; "not very satisfied" as 2; "fairly satisfied" as 3; and "very satisfied" as 4. The Doxa questionnaire had a slightly different approach: instead of using satisfaction, the item used was: "At the present time, do you feel happy or unhappy?". The concepts are thus not completely the same. The possible answers were: very happy; fairly happy; neither happy nor unhappy; rather/very unhappy; I don't know. The same study was replicated in 1956, this time separating "rather" from "very unhappy" in the possible answers. By excluding the "don't know" response, we have kept the "rather/very unhappy" response, attributing a score of 1 to it, and then upwards to 4, indicating "very happy".

13

Household Budgets

WITH STEFANO CHIANESE

1 The Accounts of a King and Those of a Laborer

> In the past historians could be accused of wanting to know only about "the great deeds of kings," but today this is certainly no longer true. More and more they are turning toward what their predecessors passed over in silence, discarded, or simply ignored. "Who built Thebes of the seven gates?" Bertold Brecht's "literate worker" was already asking. The sources tell us nothing about these anonymous masons, but the question retains all its significance. (our translation from Ginzburg 1976, xi)

The quotation above, taken from *The Cheese and the Worms: The Cosmos of a Sixteenth Century Miller* by Carlo Ginzburg, accurately illustrates the aim of this chapter. In order to reconstruct the development of the Italian population's living conditions over time, we need data that can objectively document the consumption behaviors and standard of living of the *whole* population, mostly consisting of ordinary men and women rather than of kings, poets, heroes, and navigators. As we know, history abounds with materials on the latter people, but it is scant when it comes to revealing what we really need for our purposes: data and information on the households of "anonymous masons".

We have thus decided to devote this chapter to describing a process of long, painstaking archival and bibliographical research focusing on retrieving household budgets—accounting statements recording a household's incomes and expenditures—from the foundation of the united Kingdom of Italy (1861) up to the birth of modern sample surveys (1960s). The roughly 20,000 household budgets collected were reprocessed and entered into a database that we have called the "IHBD" (Italian Household Budgets Database). As we shall see further on, it is an innovative tool from a historiographic standpoint as well as an essential instrument in order to estimate income inequality (chapter 8) and absolute poverty (chapter 9) on the basis of modern scientific standards.

This chapter is more descriptive than analytical. The main aim is to give the reader an account of the kind of sources used in other parts of this book. The focus is not solely on Italy's case. Indeed, we shall show how it is possible to raise the level of research and analyze household budgets in order to explore the living conditions of populations of other countries, or even of entire continents. We are exploring, for example, the possibility of creating an international Historical Household Budgets Database (HHBD), with the purpose of reconstructing the development of the distribution of living conditions on a world scale, à la Bourguignon and Morrisson (2002). This is the potential of household budgets: telling the story of wellbeing of all the citizens in the world (A'Hearn, Amendola, and Vecchi 2016).

2 What Are Household Budgets and What Are They For?

A household budget is an accounting schedule that briefly sets out the incomes and expenditures of a household, with reference to a given period of time. Many people today, as in the past, note down their household accounts, often in an informal way, in order to keep the family's incomes and expenditures under control. In the past, these accounts were kept in a simple jotter that listed the various daily expenditures to then sum up at the end of the month. Today, the jotters have been replaced by modern information and computing technology (ICT) but, in substance, the aims and methods for keeping the family's accounts are the same as those of our forebears.

Besides being a domestic tool pertaining to a citizen's private life, for some decades now household budgets have also been a public tool—a fundamental element of national statistics. Interviewers of Istat, the Italian national statistics institute, visit the homes of tens of thousands of Italians every year to gather information on their incomes and expenditures. The data is then processed, rendered anonymous, and made available to institutions and the scientific community. In Italy's case, the official system for surveying household budgets was devised in the 1960s. After some preliminary trials, Istat carried out its first large-scale sample survey on household budgets in 1968. Around 27,000 households (out of a total of about fifteen million) were interviewed in that year, and for each one the researchers recorded expenditures on goods and services purchased during the survey period, taking care to distinguish over 130 categories of items of expenditure. In the subsequent decades Istat has continued to collect household budget data on an annual basis for a representative sample of the whole Italian population.

Parallel to Istat, even the Bank of Italy conducts its own sample survey on household budgets. Since 1965 the Italian central bank has gathered thousands of household budgets—on an annual basis until 1987 and then every two years thereafter (they started with fewer than 4,000 interviews in 1965 to then reach about 8,000 households interviewed in 2010). Unlike the Istat survey, which focuses on consumption expenditure, the Bank of Italy's survey has traditionally focused on household *income* and savings (Brandolini 1999).[1]

What are all these data on household budgets for and who uses them? The scientific community and institutions use household budgets because they are essential in economic analysis. Household budgets can be analyzed to estimate private consumption of households, the most important component of national accounting systems (for 2011, about 60 percent of Italian gross domestic product (GDP) was accounted for by household consumption). Economic statisticians use household expenditure to construct a general retail price index (the tool for measuring inflation) as well as spatial indexes of the cost of living (in order to determine such things as differences in average prices levels between the north and south of the country, or between the town and countryside). Indeed, it is household budgets that reveal the basket of goods consumed and that provide the system with the weighting of prices necessary to construct these indexes. The composition of household expenditure and its development over time also, naturally, interests the production sector, because it reveals the development lines of consumer tastes and preferences or of the markets that producers turn to. Knowledge of household income and expenditure also serves to devise social policies, as much in mature economies as in the so-called developing countries. The most important international agencies—from the United Nations to the World Bank—provide assistance to countries requesting it in order to design and implement surveys on household budgets: a key element for establishing development plans and for gaining access to international financing (Deaton 1997).

The difficulty faced in this chapter stems from the fact that we are dealing with around 150 years of Italy's postunification history while the household budgets collected in sample surveys are a product of the post–World War II era. What can we say for the approximately first hundred years of Italian postunification history? Are there household budgets available for the period prior to World War II? If so, which sources can we get them from? What is the substance, quality, and reliability of these data? Some scholars have already answered these questions, suggesting that household budgets in the years before sample surveys constitute relatively abundant material.[2] The fundamental question is thus

---

[1] Over time, interest has also extended to wealth, credit, and other aspects concerning household financial behavior (Cannari and D'Alessio 2003).

[2] See Niceforo (1933), Somogyi (1959), and Vecchi (1994; 1999).

another: Can household budgets previous to the modern era of sample surveys be considered historical material (i.e., capable of documenting the living conditions of certain families from a qualitative standpoint) or in the same way as statistics? Although the usefulness of historical-qualitative documents is self-evident, in this book we are interested in the second kind of materials. In other words, must we limit ourselves to using the household budgets available in order to *deduce* the development of the living conditions of the Italian population or can we go beyond the analysis of individual cases and *infer*, in statistical terms, the development of the population's wellbeing over the 150 years of postunification Italy? We believe it is possible to conduct the latter kind of exercise. The wealth of materials kept in the country's public and private libraries and archives is a mine of household budgets and of sources, enabling an accurate reconstruction of the trend in living conditions of the Italian population right from the time of Italy's unification. Once we get over the difficulties of digging and extracting, we will show how it is possible to transform the retrieved household budgets—which are very different from one another since they were produced by different hands and for different purposes—and to organize them in a useful way for statistical and economic analysis.

3 A Short History of Household Budgets

Establishing a precise moment in time when interest for households' living conditions began is no easy task. The oldest economics treatise we have today, the *Oeconomicus* by Xenophon (about 425–355 B.C.), acknowledged that "the economy is in its foundations the study of the family order, which is implemented by its incomes and expenditures" (Vinci 1940, 335). Cicero tells us that in ancient Rome the Roman citizens habitually kept two kinds of accounts: a sort of first entry (called *adversaria*) in which they hurriedly jotted down their everyday transactions, and a real book of expenditures (the *codex accepti et expensi*) in which these first entry notes were then properly organized on a monthly basis (Smith, Wayte, and Marindin 1890). None of these documents has come down to us, if not in an indirect form, such as the descriptions in the letters by Cicero or other Latin writers.

The documents kept in the Italian archives turn out to be richer in evidence on the population's living conditions beginning from the late Middle Ages. Although this material is still largely unexplored, the studies carried out have brought to light household budgets dating back to the fourteenth century (Somogyi 1959). However, up to the seventeenth century, the literature is dominated by studies devoid of numbers but full of "comparatives, superlatives and intellectual arguments" (Hull 1963–1964). This is why almost all the information we have on the population's standard of living has long remained of a *qualitative* kind—as much in Italy as elsewhere.

In economics the introduction of the description of social phenomena in quantitative terms is part of the broader methodological revolution that started in the natural sciences with Galileo, Hobbes, and Bacon. With regard to household living conditions, quantitative studies were the exception rather than the rule up to most of the nineteenth century. It is only in the eighteenth century that the first social-economic studies appeared geared toward *measuring* the population's standard of living.

3.1 PREHISTORY (CA. 1750–1850)

Who first introduced household budgets as a tool of economic analysis is still an open question. We can only very briefly recall some of the main theses in this regard here. Like Higgs (1893; 1899), Stigler (1954) attributed the first use of budgetary data to the English reverend David Davies (1741–1819) and to the sociologist Frederick Morton Eden (1766–1809). Davies collected 127 household budgets of his parishioners (Davies 1795), while Eden published a study on poverty in which he included 86 budgets (Box 1). Edoardo Evangelista, who wrote a short note in Istat (1968a), attributed this primacy to Antonio Genovesi (1712–1769), an Italian priest and author of *Lezioni sul commercio* ("Lessons on Commerce," 1766–1767), while the economist Alfred Marshall (1842–1924) suggested the name of Richard Cantillon in his most famous work, *Principles of Economics*: "whose lost Supplement seems to have contained some workmen's budgets" (Marshall 1890; 9th ed. 1961, 115). The dispute thus involves two Britons (Stigler's thesis), an Italian (Evangelista's thesis), and a Frenchman (Marshall's thesis). Pending further documentary evidence, the attribution remains a controversial one.

Gathering household budgets remained an episodic phenomenon from the latter half of the eighteenth century until the mid-nineteenth century—a hundred years that have been called the "prehistory" of household budgets (Del Vecchio 1912). For this first period, the existing material is not enough to conduct any real quantitative analysis of the living conditions of the Italian population.

3.2 FROM CHRONICLES TO INVESTIGATION TOOLS
   (CA. 1850–1950)

Household budgets became an established tool of political, social, and economic analysis during the latter half of the nineteenth century. The bonds that had structured the society of the ancien régime were crumbling under the drive of new social models stemming from industrialization, causing the rise of new phenomena bearing a destructive and disaggregating potential. Knowing the population's real living conditions became an ever-pressing need for governments, and getting proper information became a priority of the political agenda.

Box 1   Budgets of Well-to-Do Families: Oxford, UK, 1795

From the work *The State of the Poor* by Sir Frederick Morton Eden, an important social researcher of his time, we have reproduced a detail of a page with the budgets of six households residing in Oxfordshire. The year is 1795, which is in the initial stage of the British Industrial Revolution.

For each household, Eden collected details of weekly and annual expenditures as well as the incomes of each household member. The figures may be difficult to comprehend by the modern reader because they use the monetary system used in Britain before 1971, when the current decimal system was introduced. In 1795 Oxfordshire, one *pound* (abbreviated with the "£" sign.) was worth 20 *shillings* (abbreviated with an "s.") and a shilling was worth 12 *pennies* (abbreviated with a "d.").

Eden made some short comments (not shown here for lack of space) on each family, at the bottom of the table. Thus, for example, he considered the first family to be "a decent family", the second "a negligent idle family", and the third "an industrious cleanly family". Giving moral judgments to explain household budgets was a typical and widespread practice of the times.

OXFORDSHIRE.—BANBURY.

EXPENCES.

	£.	s.	d.
This family ufes 4½ half-peck loaves in a week, or 234 annually, which fell at prefent for 22d. each, £.21. 9s.; but taking the average price of laft year, 1s. 2d. ; they coft annually	13	13	0
Tea and fugar, about	2	10	0
Butter and lard	1	10	0
Beer and milk	1	0	0
Bacon, and other meat; about	1	10	0
Soap, candles, &c. about	0	15	0
Houfe-rent	3	0	0
Coals	2	10	0
Shoes and fhirts	3	0	0
Other cloaths, &c.	2	0	0
Total expences	£.31	8	0

Figure 13.B1 THE STATE OF THE POOR (1797). The picture shows part of page cccxlviii, contained in Eden's third volume (1797). Of the six families of agricultural laborers, only two had positive savings at the end of the year.

Thus, scientists, politicians, and philosophers, public and private institutions, and sociologists and economists took to the field. In *The Condition of the Working Class in England*, Friedrich Engels (1820–1895) documented the living conditions of English laborers and stated that the industrialization process had worsened their standard of living and that this would necessarily lead to a violent revolution. Three years later, in February 1848, Marx and Engels brought out the *Manifesto of the Communist Party*, the publication of which coincided with the revolts that enflamed many parts of Europe. The opening sentence of this little book—"A spectre is haunting Europe—the spectre of communism. All the powers of old Europe have entered into a holy alliance to exorcise this spectre: Pope and Tsar" (Marx and Engels 1848)—eloquently summarizes the incentives that led governments to deal with the population's living conditions.

The institutions countered by adopting new analytical tools to monitor a complex reality that had considerable regional and local differences. As we shall see with Italy's case further on, large-scale investigations were commissioned in order to document the population's living conditions in part by using household budgets. The surveys of these decades were not, however, conducted on a regular basis or by means of modern-type probabilistic samples, but instead households were selected in a subjective manner and the procedure itself was imperfect in many ways. Nevertheless, they were still "grand surveys" and, as such, were an epochal novelty. They were "grand" investigations in that they involved a large number of households, were carried out all over the country, and dealt with a broad range of themes (not only economic, health, and demographic conditions but also moral and political aspects).

With some exceptions, the nineteenth-century-type surveys of the early twentieth century did not fail in their aim of providing useful elements for evaluating the population's living conditions (Bulmer, Bales, and Sklar 1991). The reasons for this success include the work of the French engineer and sociologist Pierre Guillaume Frédéric Le Play (1806–1882).

3.3 MONSIEUR LE PLAY'S LEGACY

Le Play was a mining engineer who developed his passion for the social sciences when attending the École des Mines of the polytechnic institute of Paris. During the academic year 1828–1829, Le Play embarked on a trip for a mining analysis of the territory. He set off in the company of a friend, Jean Reynaud (1806–1863), a future undersecretary of state, and walked for 4,200 miles (6,800 kilometers) from May to November across the regions of Central and Eastern Europe. The notes he took on his travels enabled him to graduate as a mining engineer, but they were also crammed with observations on the way of life of the people he met.

In the winter of 1830, Le Play set about publishing his travel log when a terrible accident interrupted his work. This episode is an important step in our story because it was a turning point in Le Play's life—he was barely 24 years old at the time—and the accident sidetracked him from his mining studies in favor of economic and social studies. The story is told by Eugène De Fourcy (1812–1889), one of Le Play's colleagues at the Polytechnic: "Dans une préparation de potassium, une violente projection de cette dangereuse substance l'atteignit aux avant bras. Accourus à ses cris, les élèves du laboratoire eurent à peine le temps de lui arracher ses vêtements en flammes. Les deux mains étaient horriblement dépouillées et calcinées" (De Fourcy 1883, 33).[3] Forced to stay in bed due to a long convalescence, Le Play recounted how it was in those long nights of suffering that he matured the will to dedicate himself to the study of social issues: "Je fis voeu de consacrer, chaque année, six mois de voyages à mes études de métallurgie, menées de front avec celles des familles et des sociétés" (Le Play 1879, 41)[4]. From that moment on, Le Play never lost sight of social studies and systematically gathered household budgets. True to his resolve, in the years 1833–1838 he visited Spain, Belgium, England, Scotland, Ireland, Austria, and southern Russia. It was in these travels that he devised what would become his research method, based on a rigorous, patient, and scientific analysis in the field. Le Play drew up an extremely detailed *cadre*, a scheme, for gathering information on the households examined. It was on the basis of this *cadre* that Le Play drafted the first *family monographs*: he lived with the target families for long periods, recording even the minutest detail of their lifestyle, and compiled the sections of each monograph according to the same procedure. Le Play's idea was simple: families, like minerals, have a finite number of varieties (typologies), which can be fully described provided you follow a scientific protocol. Once the functioning of the type of family was studied, then, as the Latin poet Virgil said, *ab uno disce omnes* (from one example, learn all).

Le Play's method was an instant international success. In 1855 he published the first collection of thirty-six family monographs, *Les Ouvriers Européens*, which in January 1856 received the prestigious *Grand prix de statistique* of the Académie des Sciences of Paris. Two years later Le Play was encouraged to continue his studies by Napoleon III, who was working on plans for social reform. This domestic, institutional acknowledgment was followed by an international one, promoted—in the implementation of its own statute—by the Société d'Économie Sociale. The affirmation of Le Play's method came about through

---

[3] "From a potassium preparation, a violent projection of this hazardous substance reached his forearms. Recalled by his screamss, the lab students barely had time to tear his clothes in flames. The two hands were horribly unskinned and incinerated" (authors' translation).

[4] "I have decided to dedicate, every year, six months to traveling for my studies of metallurgy, conducted simultaneously with those on families and on businesses" (authors' translation).

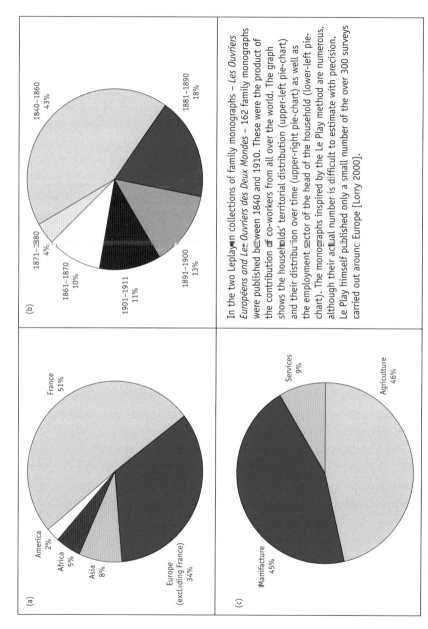

(a)

America 2%
Africa 5%
Asia 8%
Europe (excluding France) 34%
France 51%

(b)

1840–1860 43%
1881–1890 18%
1871–1880 4%
1861–1870 10%
1901–1911 11%
1891–1900 13%

In the two Leplaysian collections of family monographs – *Les Ouvriers Européens* and *Les Ouvriers des Deux Mondes* – 162 family monographs were published between 1840 and 1910. These were the product of the contribution of co-workers from all over the world. The graph shows the households' territorial distribution (upper-left pie-chart) and their distribution over time (upper-right pie-chart) as well as the employment sector of the head of the household (lower-left pie-chart). The monographs inspired by the Le Play method are numerous, although their actual number is difficult to estimate with precision. Le Play himself published only a small number of the over 300 surveys carried out around Europe [Lorry 2000].

(c)

Services 9%
Agriculture 46%
Manifacture 45%

Figure 13.1 Le Play's family monographs

the bulletin *Les Ouvriers des Deux Mondes*, which published dozens of monographs distributed in four continents, and they all followed Le Play's *cadre*. His method rapidly made converts in international institutional and scientific circles (Figure 13.1). Italy, as we shall see in section 4, was no exception: the first Italian household budgets were actually collected on the initiative of Le Play's Société Internationale.

3.4 MODERN SAMPLE SURVEYS (SINCE 1950)

There was a single standard procedure for conducting social surveys from biblical times up to the end of the nineteenth century: the census. To find out a certain characteristic of the population, for instance, the families' standard of living, the census method involved compiling a list of *all* members of the population and then gathering information useful for the purpose—a task that was often prohibitive in terms of economic and human resources.

With the dawning of the twentieth century came a revolutionary idea put forward by Anders Nicolai Kiaer (1838–1919), then just over fifty years old and the director of the Norwegian statistics office. Kiaer "put forward the idea that a partial investigation (*i.e.* a sample) based on what he called the 'representative method' could provide useful information. The aim of his representative method, the new paradigm in statistical investigations, was that the sample should be an approximate miniature of the population" (Bellhouse 1988, 2). Kiaer's idea, however, met with the fiercest opposition: "No calculations when observations can be made", was the response of the old guard in defense of the census method (Kruskal and Mosteller 1980, 175). It took another thirty years before the use of the "representative sample" became an accepted and respected practice by statisticians: at the conference of the International Statistics Institute, held in Rome in 1925, the debate ended with the adoption of an official resolution that recommended using the sample method. The issue was no longer *whether* to use sample surveys but *how*.

The ideas that developed in academic circles took, as is normal, more time before they found an application in the sample surveys carried out by national statistics agencies (Stephan 1948; Seng 1951). In the aftermath of World War II, times were at last ripe not only from a technical-scientific standpoint, but also from a practical one. The conduction of sample investigations was made possible by adequate budgetary allocations. The result was an "institutionalization" of household budgets: central statistics institutes of countries all over the world started implementing, either sooner or later, sample surveys on household budgets (Table 13.1). The era of occasional investigations, linked to specific survey needs, gave way to systematic surveys—institutional ones.

In Italy, today, household budget surveys are considered statistics of public interest and are included in the "National Statistics Program". This means,

Table 13.1 **Sample surveys on household budgets: precursors and laggards**

Country	Year of first survey	Sample (no. of households)	Sample (% pop.)	Income	Consumption
(1)	(2)	(3)	(4)	(5)	(6)
India	1951	10870	0.03		X
Austria	1954	4039	0.58	X	X
Francia	1956	20000	0.45		X
UK	1957	6500	0.13	X	X
Sweden	1958	3000	0.40		X
Spain	1958	4200	0.14	X	X
Greece	1958	2500	0.31		X
Germany	1963	60000	0.81	X	X
Italy	1965	3343	0.06	X	
Brazil	1967	115000	1.31	X	
Italy	1968	27000	0.51		X
USA	1968	4800	0.02		X
Portugal	1968	9643	1.06		X
Denmark	1976	1500	0.30		X
Mexico	1984	4650	0.06	X	X

Note: the table shows the years (column 2) in which household budget surveys were started up in some countries (column 1), as well as the sample size in absolute terms (column 3) and in relation to population size (column 4). Columns 5 and 6 show whether the surveys also assessed incomes or household consumption (or both); "X" stands for inclusion.

among other things, that the households randomly extracted from municipal records cannot refuse to take part in the statistical survey and must keep a log of their domestic incomes and expenditures. This is what the relevant law states: "Those who, on being requested to provide data and news … do not comply or who provide scientifically flawed or incomplete information, shall be subject to a monetary fine" (Legislative Decree 322, 6 September 1989, art. 7, par. 3). The inclusion of household budget investigations in national statistical surveys evidently marks the final shift of responsibility from the private sector to the public one. Private initiatives geared to the acquisition of household budgets are still carried out by a plethora of subjects in Italy today, but they have played only a secondary, if not marginal, role in the last few decades, and their results are not even comparable in terms of statistical accuracy to those obtained by the institutions, firstly and foremost by Istat and the Bank of Italy.

4 In Search of Sources

Reconstructing the centuries-old history of the living conditions of the Italian population by means of household budgets is an ambitious goal that required a great effort in terms of study and creativity. The material examined is imposing indeed. The sources include both printed works and manuscripts, jealously kept in libraries and archives, public and private, all over the country.

The first household budget to be included in the IHBD concerns the family of Giuseppe O., a sharecropper of Bagno a Ripoli, located in the hills around Florence. It was conducted on the initiative of Ubaldino Peruzzi de' Medici (1822–1891), who was the first mayor in the history of Florence and also the Minister of Public Works in the Cavour and Ricasoli governments (1861–1862), the first two after the unification. Peruzzi zealously compiled what represents the first monograph of an Italian family published in Le Play's work. The first section of the monograph summarizes the history, activities, and habits of Giuseppe's family, while the second section displays the tables of the family's income and wealth statements. The wealth of information provided was probably unexpected by those who had the opportunity to browse through the monograph. For instance, we learn that the family's home, about 350 square meters (m²) on two floors, was furnished with 6 beds, 15 chairs, 3 tables, 2 bedside tables, 3 wardrobes, 2 dressing tables, and 2 kitchen worktables, for a total value of 697 lire of the times (worth 3,300 euros today). Each household object, from the pots and cutlery to the glasses and pitchers, is associated with an estimation of value, as are the garments of each household member (the whole wardrobe of the lady of the house was worth 150 lire—little more than 700 euros today).

Finally, we learn of the family's earnings and expenses throughout the year. The detail of the information gathered is, once again, surprisingly accurate: the expenses are divided into 52 items, but a note was made even of the *quantity* of food consumed. The household's income (1,975 lire per year, equivalent to about 9,500 euros today) is a little higher than their consumption expenditure (1,717 lire, or 8,200 euros today). A comparison—rather daring at a methodological level—with households today would place this Florentine sharecropper's family in the lower part of the income distribution, probably within the fourth income decile (that is to say, in the group accounting for 30–40 percent of the poorer sections of the population).

The structure of the expenditure reveals the family's standard of living. Giuseppe's family spent two-thirds of their total expenditure on foodstuffs and the remaining third had to cover all the other needs of the family, from rent to heating, and from clothes to medical bills (Figure 13.2, upper bar of the graph). Today, 150 years later, a family the size of Giuseppe's would divide their expenditures in the opposite manner: only 21 percent on food and 79 percent on all the rest (lower bar). Perhaps the most eloquent finding of Figure 13.2 concerns the

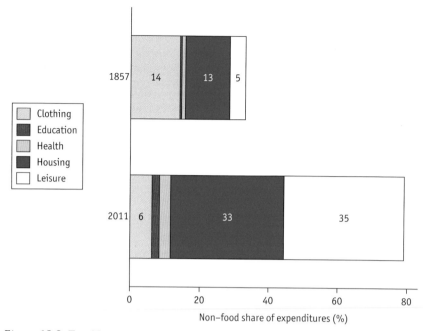

Figure 13.2 THE NONFOOD EXPENDITURES OF GIUSEPPE, A FLORENTINE SHARECROPPER, 1857. The graph compares the structure of non-food expenditure for Giuseppe's family (upper bar), observed in 1857, with that of a modern family (lower bar).

increase in resources devoted to "free time"—an entry that includes expenses on transportation, communication (telephone and the Internet), personal care, trips and holidays, and so on—things that accounted for less than 5 percent of Giuseppe's total family expenditures, but accounting for 35 percent today.

Although other family monographs would later be added to Giuseppe's one, on the whole, the number of Italian authors who got involved in the art of drawing up family monographs was rather low. This must not be misleading: over and beyond the purely numerical datum, the importance of Le Play's method lies in having given a sort of—direct or indirect—imprint on the whole production of household budgets for the next hundred years.

4.1 ENQUIRY AFTER ENQUIRY, BUDGETS IN THE LIBERAL PERIOD (1861–1920)

Like all modern nation-states, even the newborn Italian state needed to equip itself with new survey tools to determine the real conditions of the country and of its citizens. The large-scale investigations on the population's living conditions, extended to all the national territory, appeared in the last quarter of the nineteenth century. The technical people called upon to coordinate and devise the surveys of this period were often well versed in, and admirers of, Le Play's monographic methodology and tried, not always successfully, to implement its survey criteria.

Over the four-year-period 1876–1879, the Ministry of Agriculture, Industry and Commerce published a report on the conditions of agriculture, "the first serious attempt at an overall investigation of the conditions of Italian agriculture" (Caracciolo 1958, 26). Although it does not contain information on agricultural household budgets, the report was the start of an important project geared to the periodical publication of news on the state of agriculture and of its workers (Maic 1882).

In subsequent years, enquiry after enquiry, the household budgets multiplied and confirmed their usefulness as a survey tool for assessing living conditions. The three most important initiatives were, briefly, the following. The first was the *Jacini enquiry*, which was started up in 1881 to investigate the conditions of farmers in southern Italy and in Sicily; the second, the *Montemartini enquiry*, published in 1909 with 149 budgets of farming households, for the years 1905–1907, all residing in the Puglia region of southern Italy; and the third, the *Faina enquiry*, published in 1911, was of a monumental scale, but actually yielded a very limited number of household budgets (Somogyi 1959, 164).

These large-scale official enquiries are an essential source of household budgets in the first sixty years of Italy's postunification history. However, although being of a large scale compared to the standards of the times, these enquiries yielded a rather low number of household budgets. To broaden the database, we necessarily had to embark upon new and more particular research paths (Chianese and Vecchi, 2011).

4.2 BUDGETS IN THE INTERWAR YEARS (1921–1940)

The period between the two world wars saw Mussolini's rise to power and the establishment of the Fascist regime, an international crisis that severely damaged the Italian economy, wars fought for imperialistic pipedreams, and a world conflict the country was dragged into until its final collapse. In September 1943 Italy was effectively divided into two, with the king and the allies in the south, and the German troops and Mussolini's Social Republic in the north. Dramatic events caused heavy effects on the production of official statistics, and it is not difficult to see the negative consequences also with regard to the collecting of household budgets (Fracassi 1961).

In this context, the Istituto Nazionale di Economia Agraria (INEA) had a considerable monopoly with regard to investigations on the living conditions

Box 2 **Small Failures: Household Budgets and the Civil Code**

Of the sources used for the IHBD, probably the most unusual consists of bankruptcy proceedings. These often contain the household budgets of the owners of the bankrupt firms, typically small and medium-sized artisan and commercial enterprises.

In Italy bankruptcy has been regulated within the reforms made over the years to the Code of Commerce. Article 686 of the Code of 1882 reads: "Within three days of the cessation of payments, including the one in which they ceased, the bankrupt must declare such in the chancellery of the commercial court designated in the previous article. The declaration must be accompanied by the filing of the true certified balance sheet, dated and undersigned by the bankrupt, and by its trading books in the state in which they are. The balance sheet must contain the indication and approximate estimation of all the bankrupt's real estate, a list of all his debts and credits . . . the profit and loss account as well as a list of expenditures". In the generic definition of "expenditures", according to the most common interpretation, the legislator wished to include not only those of business activity but also those concerning the maintenance of the bankrupt's family (Vidari 1886, 39). According to the law and its interpretation, therefore, every trader, craftsman, or entrepreneur in general, at the time of his bankruptcy, had to present a detailed account of his domestic expenses. The State Archive of Naples alone houses about 7,000 records for the years 1871–1920 on bankruptcies of various kinds of Neapolitan enterprises. Expanding the finding to the national level gives us tens of thousands of potential expenditure balances of the same number of Italian households. In actual fact, the bankrupt people who compiled a detailed balance sheet useful for our purposes were perhaps the exception rather than the rule; examining the funds of around forty State Archives, however, we collected about 900 household budgets, mainly concentrated in the years 1881–1921.

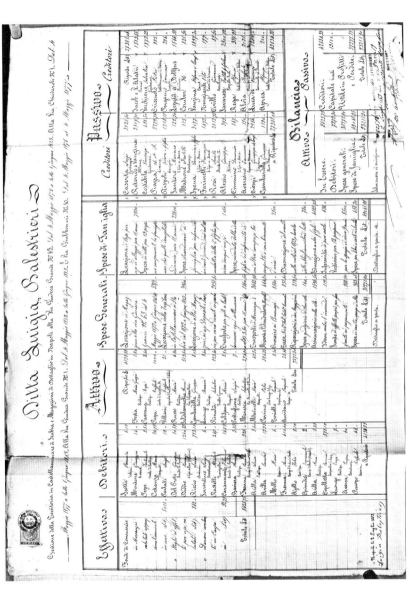

Figure 13.B2 THE BUDGET OF A BANKRUPT FAMILY. The picture shows the balance sheet of a Neapolitan textile firm owned by Luigia Balestrieri that failed in 1882. The central part shows the family's expenditures divided into six categories (food, clothing, dwelling, health, education and other expenses). Source: Naples State Archives. Tribunale di Commercio, Fallimenti, Fascicolo 2563 bis. Italy, 1882.

The distribution of households studied by the INEA from a territorial perspective appears skewed in favor of the central and northern regions, and the distribution of the occupation of the head of the household shows that some of the poorer categories are underrepresented: tenants and day workers. The selection criterion used by the INEA to select the households to be studied is an example of "judgmental" or "expert choice" sampling: this is, naturally, the main reason for the unbalanced distribution of the INEA sample. Some authors have put forward a more radical criticism: that the choice of households was conditioned or, rather, flawed by the ideological views of Arrigo Serpieri and Ugo Giusti, who had promoted the study (Favero 2007). According to these authors, the INEA investigation did not collect budgets of "typical" households but rather of "ideal" households (Section 4.5), in line with the Fascist ruralization plan.

Figure 13.3 THE GEOGRAPHIC DISTRIBUTION OF HOUSEHOLDS IN THE INEA SURVEY (1925–1936)

in the agricultural and rural sectors of Italy in the interwar years. The mission of the institute, founded in 1928, was indeed that of promoting and coordinating studies on the rural economy that were until then discordant and disconnected. Under the supervision of Arrigo Serpieri (1877–1960), one of the most important Italian agrarian economists as well as the undersecretary for agriculture in the 1920s, the INEA started up a series of large-scale surveys making great use of household budgets. The main one of these surveys was published with the title *Monografie di famiglie agricole* (Monographs of Agricultural Families) and contains over 100 monographs with household budgets collected between 1931 and 1938, making it the most important source for the study of the economic conditions of farmers in the 1930s (Figure 13.3).

The wealth of information gathered by the INEA for agricultural households is not matched by the equally abundant documentation for nonagricultural households. With reference to the interwar years, the household budgets we managed to retrieve are mostly from company archives or records of public administrations that we will talk about in section 4.4.[5]

___

[5] Indeed, there is no lack of investigations on nonagricultural households, but we did not always manage to glean useful data from them. As regards sheer numbers, the most important survey seems to be the one carried out in 1937 by the Fascist Confederation of Industrial Workers on the budgets of 744 blue-collar workers' families (Costanzo 1940, 229). We found no trace of it in the archives we examined.

4.3 THE BUDGETS OF ITALIAN HOUSEHOLDS
GO TO PULP (1948–1965)

The aftermath of World War II marked the decline of the household mono-graph. This kind of survey started in the latter half of the nineteenth century and peaked in the interwar years, to then quickly decline to extinction. The progressive disappearance of monograph-based surveys was mirrored by that of Le Play's *cadre*, part of a broader trend (examined in section 3.4) linked to the revolutionary idea of replacing the census method with the "representative sample". What distinguished the years immediately after World War II was the conduction of sample surveys on thousands of households. The ones carried out in Italy in the 1950s and 1960s are reported in Table 13.2.

Many of the surveys listed in Table 13.2 are well known, and the original publications for most of them are as easily accessible as the literature they stim-ulated. However, we did not manage to recover original data for any of them in any form: the booklets compiled by the families, the tabular version of the data that was normally made available by the surveying organization, the punch cards that fed the earliest computers, or the magnetic tapes on which the data were recorded. The reasons for such a "mass disappearance" are many, even if every survey is a case in itself. We know, for instance, that the materials of the Istat surveys were sent to be pulped and the proceeds donated to the Italian Red Cross: this was a common practice in post–World War II Italy and lasted perhaps two or three decades, even if not always documentable.[6] On the disappearance of the original data of the other surveys, though, we only have rumors.

The review of the sources carried out so far summarizes the more traditional part of the materials used in order to construct the IHBD, but there is more. For example, there are hundreds of bibliographic or archival references that yield budgets of individual households. There are the papers of family archives that contain domestic accounts, often for long periods of time, of families that are mostly aristocratic or of the propertied class.[7] There are inquiries made by trade union movements, chambers of commerce, cultural institutes, trade asso-ciations, or even individual scholars. There is the national and local press, or the publications linked to specific production sectors, which devote attention to the living conditions of their own workers and in so doing make frequent use of household budgets.

---

[6] This is based on oral exchanges made during the years of this research.

[7] For instance, the IHBD contains the household budgets kept for over 25 years by the family of the second President of the Italian Republic, Luigi Einaudi (1874–1961). The examples are many and include the accounts of members of the nobility, whose accounts were often kept by the bookkeeper in the family's service.

Table 13.2 **The first sample surveys in Italy**

Organization	Year	Sample (no. of households)	Households (coverage)
(1)	(2)	(3)	(4)
Doxa	1947–48	10940	All
Camera dei Deputati	1952	1847	Poor
Camera dei Deputati	1952	1026	Matera
Camera dei Deputati	1952	1322	All
Comune di Trieste	1952–61	2164	Trieste
Doxa	1953	1599	All
Istat	1953	8207	Non agriculture
Isce	1956–57	350	Miners
Istat	1963–64	13235	All
Isce	1963–64	9000	Almost all

Note: For each agency or institution concerned (column 1), the table shows the year in which the survey was carried out (column 2), the number of households (column 3), and their type or origin (column 4). "Doxa" is the first private firm that carried out sample surveys in Italy; "Istat" is the National Institute of Statistics; "Isce" stands for the Statistics Institute of the European Communities.

4.4 PUBLIC AND PRIVATE EMPLOYEES

Among the sources that contributed to the IHBD, there were the personnel records of public institutions and of private enterprises. In this case, we are dealing with an original and innovative source for studying the population's living conditions, even if it is an extremely variable one with regard to the information it contains.

First, it is worth recalling that keeping personnel records was an administrative task of the personnel department. For each new employee, the department had to create a new record in which to note information on the person's family members (age and sex), any other dependents, as well as a reconstruction of the *overall income* that took not only the employee's own wages into account but also other earnings (production bonuses, family allowances).[8] Frequently, but not always, the records also contain a short description of the employee's assets (for instance, whether the employees owned the house in which they lived).

---

[8] The most complex case concerns situations where besides the employee there are other members of the family who are economically active, but for whom information on earnings is not given. In such situations, it was decided to make ad hoc hypotheses on the basis of the available information, evaluated case by case. These cases were not frequent.

A second strength of this source is that it concerns workers with very different skills, responsibilities, and wage levels. The household budgets collected concern families of senior directors of ministries, but also of teachers, forestry guards, police officers, archivists, caretakers, and porters. The characteristic of covering the whole spectrum of clerical staff thus assured the presence in the IHBD of a social segment that was usually absent in nineteenth-century enquiries and often even ignored by surveys conducted up to the 1960s.

With regard to the funds of personnel of private enterprises, the study turned out to be more complex. Sensitiveness toward the conservation of company archives turned out to be generally low. Unfortunately, the materials kept in company archives were very often considered of little interest and thus were dispersed or simply destroyed. Fortunately, there are some exceptions: the archives consulted more successfully were those of Ansaldo (Genoa), Birra Peroni (Rome), Banco di Napoli, Ilva (Naples), and Manifattura Cotoniera Meridionale (Salerno).[9]

4.5 BEYOND ROYAL FAMILIES

Despite the abundance of sources described in the preceding pages, some family typologies escape the surveys or are significantly underrepresented. This naturally creates some difficulty that must be overcome if we wish to use the IHBD as a representative sample of the population. We adopted two solutions in these cases. The first consists of using the "typical household" from which we obtain a "typical budget", while the second solution resorts to "hypothetical households" from which we obtain "hypothetical budgets".[10]

A *typical budget* may be defined as one containing "what is needed, in terms of material goods and services, by a particular type of family in order to achieve a particular standard of living in a particular place at a particular time" (Saunders 1998, 2).[11] Unlike the traditional household budget, the typical budget does not

---

[9] The financial and industrial enterprises mentioned are among the most important in Italian entrepreneurial history. Ansaldo is the leading Italian metallurgical company. Founded in 1854 by the Genoese engineer Giovanni Ansaldo, under the encouragement of Cavour, who wanted an enterprise capable of producing steam locomotives for Piedmont's nascent railroad network; in 1934 it became a state enterprise and has remained so ever since. The Peroni mark was born in 1846 and produces one of the most famous beers in Italy. The Banco di Napoli is the most important credit institute in southern Italy, with origins dating back to the sixteenth century. Ilva is the first and most important southern Italian steel firm, founded in 1905. Manifattura Cotoniera Meridionale was created in 1829 by Swiss industrialists and closed down in the early 1980s.

[10] Both of these types of budgets can be somehow linked to the concept of "standard budget" (see Orshansky 1959; Innes 1990).

[11] Note that in no way must we assume that the reference standard of living corresponds to a *minimum* level (Johnson, Rogers, and Tan 2001, 29–30).

result from a field survey, but is usually created by an "expert". An example of this, which was frequent in the early twentieth century, concerns the habit of local administrations to monitor the cost of living. To carry out this task, the municipal office concerned started by outlining the traits of a typical household (also called the "average" or "representative" household) by establishing its main demographic characteristics (also with the cooperation of the registry office) as well as its "typical" consumption and income (defined on the basis of familiarity with the prevailing customs and traditions in the territory of reference). Once the household traits were established in this way, the next step was to estimate the expenses necessary (or, alternatively, the income necessary) for that household to lead a "normal life", given the prices prevailing in the local market.

If the typical household cannot be equated with a real household, the data used for constructing the monthly income and expenditure account are based on objective and informed surveys in the territory. Some of the decisions underlying these calculations are discretional, but they have some important advantages: specificity (the elementary data refer to the local reality they aim to represent), replicability, and transparency (the calculus underlying the typical budgets is—as a rule—illustrated in every detail).

We shall now turn to the second solution, the one about *hypothetical budgets* (Zimmerman 1935, 14). By this term we mean the budgets reconstructed on the basis of a plethora of information, often a combination of wage data, retail prices of goods and services, and demographic data. In the case of the IHBD, we included the hypothetical budgets created starting from sources reporting the hourly remunerations actually paid to workers of specific firms (mainly industrial plants), and with them also the number of hours and days actually worked in a year. The data are differentiated according to the category, sex, and age of each worker. With similar information, we can easily reconstruct the annual wages earned by individual workers in different working fields. To shift from individual incomes to household ones, we thus need to hypothesize household composition and the employment situation of its members by means of additional, often qualitative, sources. The combined use of all this information enables us to give form to a hypothetical budget.

Note that using hypothetical budgets is not a short cut: on the contrary, it is a difficult, time-consuming operation because it means using many external, detailed, and local sources that must be assembled with great skill. With respect to the discretionary aspect that inevitably accompanies certain steps in the process, the main advantage from a historical as well as statistical standpoint is that, despite their name, "hypothetical budgets", the information used for their construction is absolutely real and genuine. Indeed, we can say that, in some cases, these hypothetical budgets are of a higher quality than the data obtained by interviewers or given by households themselves. Without doubt, they contribute to the proper specification of the collection of data on which statistical analysis will be based (Spanos 1986).[12]

What the hypothetical budget and typical budget have in common is the fact that in both cases their data are not obtained by means of the usual methods (interviews, questionnaires, keeping a diary), but gained, at least in part, through many sources that, combined together, actually yield household budgets. What differentiates one type of budget from the other, however, is the technology used in their construction. With the typical budget, the data are gathered and combined by a contemporary observer, while with the hypothetical budget the data are composed by a modern analyst. The IHBD makes use of both types of household budgets discussed in this section, inaugurating a methodology that requires more in-depth analysis on both historiographic and statistical levels, but which—as we shall see in the next section—produces encouraging results.

5 Many Budgets Do Not Make a Sample

The material on household budgets has been called "a kaleidoscopic mosaic" (Somogyi 1973, 841). In effect, although research into the sources described in the previous section has brought to light the availability of a suitable number of household budgets, this is not enough to put together the pieces of the whole mosaic and to interpret it. The main problem is that a collection of household budgets, however large it may be, does not constitute a statistical sample representative of the population, and thus cannot be used for conducting statistically based economic analyses. The risk lies in creating a distorted view of reality.

The first step for constructing household budgets properly consists of creating a database in order to place the data within the same scheme, reclassifying them to make the income and expenditure items homogeneous and thus possible to compare in both space and time. This operation led to creating the IHBD. The second step is the most difficult one and consists of transmuting the IHBD: that is, promoting the "collection" of budgets to the rank of statistical "sample". There is, in fact, no reason to assume that the households present in the IHBD are representative of the Italian population. Indeed, we may perhaps claim that the absence of one sampling scheme makes the IHBD more likely *not* to be representative of the population. The solution to this problem has been devised and described elsewhere;[13] it is thus not necessary here to illustrate the technique used, but we can briefly summarize it.

---

[12] Hypothetical budgets are an alternative to using "pseudo-observations", a purely statistical solution explored in Rossi, Toniolo, and Vecchi (2001).

[13] See Vecchi (1999; 2011) and Rossi, Toniolo, and Vecchi (2001).

It is worth starting from the IHBD and describing its structure. For the years prior to modern surveys (1861–1961), the IHBD is nothing but a large table consisting of about 20,000 rows (as many as the household budgets it contains) and about 200 columns, as many as the variables in which we gathered the information on each household. The variables were arranged into three sections.

The first concerns the *socio-demographic characteristics*: for each household we recorded the number of family members, their age and gender, as well as other data on the head of the household's education and employment status (whether employed and, if so, the sector of economic activity concerned).

The second section concerns the household's *earnings*. In this case, the IHBD has almost slavishly adopted the structure of the survey on household budgets conducted by the Bank of Italy. We thus distinguished the various sources of income into four main categories: earnings from salaries and wages, earnings from self-employment, income from capital, and income from transfer payments. This decision was made in view of the need to connect the "old" data contained in the IHBD (the pre-1965 period, that is, prior to the Bank of Italy survey) with the "modern" data (the post-1965 period). In so doing, we manage to create a collection of incomes of Italian households in order to cover the whole 150 years of Italy's post-unification history.

The third and last section of the IHBD concerns the households' *expenses*. The data on household expenditure were organized according to the survey scheme used by Istat's current investigation on household consumption in order to link the older part of the IHBD (pre-1968, that is, prior to the Istat survey) with the more modern one (the post-1968 years). In this case, 148 items of expenditure were established, distinguishing the traditional commodity groups: expenditures on food (in turn divided into more detailed categories of expenditure: bread and pasta, meat, fish, cheese, fruit and vegetables, drinks, etc.), the home, heating and lighting, clothing and footwear, education and health, and many other categories.

Table 13.3 summarizes the substance of the database. The overall scale of the IHBD is noteworthy: a collection of almost 20,000 household budgets is undoubtedly a large "sample". Of course, we must bear in mind that the period the households refer to covers over one hundred years: if we divide the period concerned into decades, the size of the samples is in the region of 2,000 households per decade.[14] As we saw in chapter 8 ("Inequality") and chapter 9 ("Poverty"), it is a suitable sample size for estimating, with sufficient accuracy, the income inequality and poverty characterizing each decade.

Over and beyond the numerical substance of the IHBD, it assesses the representativeness of households of the Italian population. A very large sample

---

[14] The firms that conduct so-called opinion surveys today use samples that rarely exceed 1,500 respondents, and on this basis obtain estimates that are statistically representative of the whole Italian population.

The ideal household (Superman with Superwoman) and the average household (Average Man with Average Woman). The "average" households may—deliberately or by mistake—be very far removed from the typical case and may instead portray "ideal" ones.

The cartoon on the left ironically summarizes the main risk associated with using "typical budgets". The issue is an old one, at least as old as Le Play's method which we saw in Section 4.1. Le Play selected households he considered "typical" or "average", and, on the basis of these few observations, aimed to study the entire population (Kruskal and Mosteller 1979: 253–54). The problem that may arise, naturally, is that of proper specification: if the household chosen by the expert is not a "typical" one (Average Man and Average Woman) but instead an "ideal" one (Superman and Superwoman), this would prejudice the analysis. The main message to bear in mind, here, is of a methodological kind: "typical budgets" are a source of precious information for historiographic analysis, but they cannot be used in the same way as modern household budgets extracted by means of probability methods.

Figure 13.4 TYPICAL HOUSEHOLDS OR IDEAL HOUSEHOLDS?

can be of little use if the households it includes have been badly selected, for example, if they exclude certain types of households or include an excessive number of other types. It is easy to see how within each decade in which Table 13.3 is organized, the household distribution does not always reflect that of the population, as deduced from censuses. For instance, if we consider the first row of the table, we see an overrepresentation of northern households (42 percent in the IHBD compared to the 35 percent we see in the data of the 1871 census) and an underrepresentation of households residing in the central and southern regions.

The fact that the IHBD shows a flawed representation of the population in a given year is a serious problem, but not a fatal one. The solution adopted here is based on a simple idea. The idea consists of using the population censuses (conducted every ten years since 1861) to construct "weights" to be given to each household contained in the IHBD; giving households relative weights makes the IHBD composition more similar to that of the Italian population it aims to represent. A concrete example will help to explain this better. If, in a given year, the IHBD contains a much smaller number of blue-collar households than the ones that actually existed in the population at that time, then, on the basis of the population census, we can construct a variable (which statisticians call a "weight") enabling us to adjust, that is, increase the weight of blue-collar

Table 13.3 IHBD: The Italian Household Budgets Database

	North			Center			South and Islands			Italy
	Agriculture	Industry	Services	Agriculture	Industry	Services	Agriculture	Industry	Services	Total
1855–1871	446	454	209	154	150	101	652	235	242	2643
1872–1881	263	489	88	78	25	160	158	497	338	2096
1882–1891	95	314	85	23	317	116	883	334	289	2456
1892–1901	93	167	125	136	29	83	89	167	275	1164
1902–1911	368	946	211	129	336	110	499	245	278	3122
1912–1921	148	30	118	71	605	92	174	93	240	1571
1922–1931	321	954	128	114	295	82	70	262	309	2535
1932–1941	149	64	22	294	57	65	241	101	59	1052
1942–1951	106	26	22	1	24	40	80	8	49	356
1952–1965	29	899	1276	3	16	21	616	10	3	2873
1855–1965	2018	4343	2284	1003	1854	870	3462	1952	2082	19868

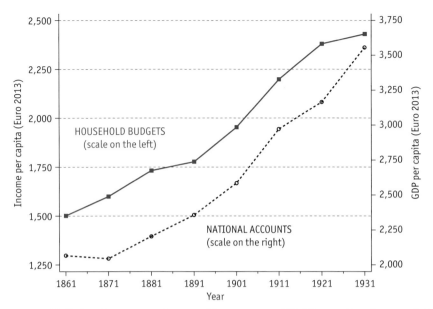

Figure 13.5 THE INCOME OF ITALIAN HOUSEHOLDS (IHBD) AND PER CAPITA GDP, 1861–1931. The figure compares the trend over time (horizontal axis) of average income per head, estimated on the basis of household budgets (left-hand vertical axis), with that of GDP per head (right-hand vertical axis). The two sources agree in outlining the long-term trend of average income of the Italians.

households in the IHBD. Similarly, if the IHBD contains too many households of a given type (such as ministry staff of a certain region), we can adjust this overrepresentation by creating a variable that decreases its weight. Hence, the weight of each IHBD household will be different depending on the need: this weighting corrects—at least to a certain extent—the flaws in IHBD representativeness, enabling us to conduct the economic analysis on the basis of a proper statistical methodology.[15]

The effectiveness of the method just described may be appreciated by comparing average income per head, estimated on the basis of the household budgets contained in the IHBD, with GDP per head. There are important conceptual differences between the two variables, including the fact that not all the product of a country becomes income that can be spent by households, but we can expect the temporal evolution of the two variables to be similar if the post-stratification procedure has been effective. As Figure 13.5 shows, there is an underlying consistency between the IHBD data and those of the national accounts. Since they are independent sources, this evidence offers a significant statistical validation of the IHBD data.

---

[15] The technique described in this section is referred to as "post-stratification" by statisticians (Holt and Smith 1979).

6 Different Countries, Different Budgets

The question we ask in concluding this chapter is whether the abundance of household budgets documented for Italy is a peculiar case. Is there any reason to believe that Italy is a country unusually rich in household budgets and is thus peculiar in this regard? We still do not have any certain answers, but the thesis we are putting forward is that the analysis carried out for Italy can be replicated for other countries, probably for entire continents, and perhaps even for the whole world.

We can start our story in Honolulu, Hawaii, in August 1928. Within the first Pan-Pacific Women's Conference—an event dedicated to promoting equal opportunities in the Pacific region (Hinder 1928)—it was decided to conduct a survey of the studies on household living conditions. In view of the subsequent edition of the conference, envisaged for 1930, a commission was appointed in order "to collect precise information on what had been done, what was in course of investigation at that time, and what might be done in the near future in the fields of standards of living and dietary studies" (Handman 1935, 2). The first report—solely limited to the United States—brought to light such a large amount of materials that it was decided, without too much hesitation, to strengthen the work team in order to extend the research to other countries.

The most important publication appeared in 1935, when the U.S. Department of Agriculture brought out a monumental work titled *Studies of Family Living in the United States and Other Countries: An Analysis of Material and Method* (hereafter referred to as "the Williams-Zimmerman report"). The research was coordinated by Carle C. Zimmerman (1897–1983), a Harvard professor of sociology, and Faith M. Williams (1893–1958), an economist at the Bureau of Home Economics, supported by a committee of fifteen professors and researchers of the most prestigious American universities. The figures of their study are impressive: covering a time horizon from the latter half of the nineteenth century to the early 1930s, they found around 1,500 printed works containing quantitative information on the standard of living of households of 52 countries of five continents.[16] For each country, the Williams-Zimmerman report provides a profile with a short but accurate bibliography illustrating the information available on households' living conditions. Not all, but most of the documents cited lead to household budgets (real or "typical" ones, according to the definition given in section 4.5).

The "great catalogue" created by Zimmerman and Williams was the starting point and inspiration for broadening the scope of our research. The picture emerging from our research is an incomplete one (the study is still at an embryonic stage), but the results point to the existence of hundreds of thousands of

---

[16] Nor is there a lack of references to budgets of families who lived in Elizabethan England, late Medieval France, or even imperial Rome.

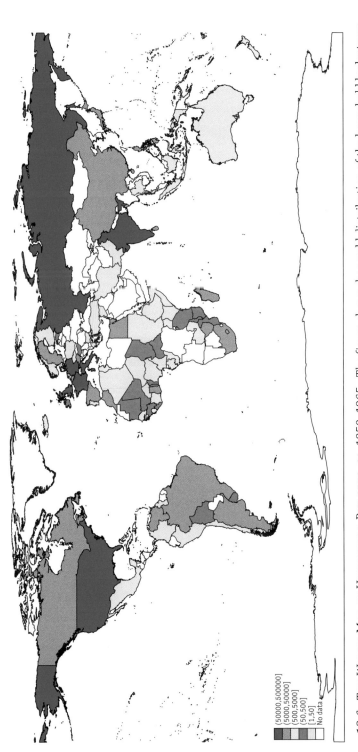

Figure 13.6. THE WORLD MAP OF HOUSEHOLD BUDGETS, CA. 1850–1965. The figure shows the world distribution of the household budgets we found information on. The lighter shade indicates a low number of data available, while a darker shade indicates an abundance of household budgets.

[50000,500000]
[5000,50000]
[500,5000]
[50,500]
[1,50]
No data

household budgets.[17] An overall picture is provided by Figure 13.6, which shows how the territorial distribution of budgets is broad (the countries covered account for 98 percent of the world population), if not homogeneous: around two thirds of the households are located in Europe, 10 percent in Asia, and 23 percent in the Americas. It turned out to be more difficult to find household budgets in Africa and Oceania. With regard to the temporal distribution of budgets, the median year—the one dividing the observations into two groups of the same size—is 1928: the retrieved household budgets are thus strongly concentrated in the first decades of the twentieth century rather than the second half of the nineteenth century.

At this stage, we must ask ourselves whether it is wise to invest time and resources in the research and processing of tens of thousands of domestic budgets scattered all over the globe. We believe it is, with the advantages that we shall discuss in the next section. The data summarized in Figure 13.6 are preliminary ones; in many respects, Figure 13.6 is nothing more than a "core-sampling" of just the surface of the whole terrain of sources. However, we must bear in mind the variety of forms that household budgets can often take in local contexts. The experience of Italy, documented in this chapter, shows that large scale collections à la Williams and Zimmerman, however imposing they may be, are but the tip of the iceberg. The real scale of the "household budgets" source is seen only when, on starting up our research, we get down to actual business.

7 In Praise of Household Budgets

In January 1956, at the price of 300 lire (not even 5 euros in today's currency), it was possible to purchase the first of six booklets making up the *Prediche Inutili* (Useless Sermons), a collection of "articles and paragraphs" penned by President Luigi Einaudi. In the first "sermon", Einaudi observed: "Is deciding without knowing of any use? And decisions must, in truth, be followed by actions. One decides when one knows one is able to implement; one does not decide for the sake of sterile fanciful ostentation. (...) Hasty laws beget new laws meant to amend and to perfect; but these new laws, because they have been dictated by

---

[17] It is quite difficult, at this stage, to accurately estimate the real availability of household budgets. To do so means retrieving and consulting the bibliographic references currently scattered in libraries and archives all over the world. To get an idea of the sheer scale of the task, the total number of budgets that can be retrieved exceeds 2.0 million observations, most of which are probably available only in the form of grouped data. This is not a fatal obstacle with a view to reconstructing the income distribution (Cowell 2012; Shorrocks and Wan 2008).

the urgency to remedy the flaws of the badly designed ones, are inapplicable, if not at the cost of subterfuges, and they need to be perfected again, so that very soon everything becomes an inextricable muddle, which no-one can ever get out of" (10). The interesting thing about Einaudi's thinking is not so much the question from which it moves (can we take decisions without proper data?)—the answer to which is, in many respects, obvious—but rather the frankness of his denunciation of a common practice, that of deciding without knowing. Much of past economic history, in Italy as elsewhere, has described conditions of life and distributions of income, wealth, and poverty of families, without having suitable data and rigorous methods, at least not according to modern international scientific standards. In other words, it was decided without bothering too much about knowing.

It is not even a peculiarly Italian habit. In his 1954 presidential address to the American Economic Association, Simon Kuznets observed how the study of households' living conditions and their distribution was a field of study "plagued by looseness in definitions, unusual scarcity of data and pressures of strongly held opinions" (Kuznets 1955, 1). The contents of Kuznets's observation are in total syntony with those of Einaudi's preaching.

It is these considerations that inspired the research described in this chapter. Since the wellbeing of households and of their members is to be found within the folds of their domestic budgets, the first concern was to check whether the historical sources were able to produce sufficient materials to investigate the development of the standard of living of the Italians over the long run. The research—which lasted almost twenty years, but is summarized in just a few pages here—has shown that household budgets are a relatively abundant resource in Italy and probably in many other countries of the world as well. The sources enable us to reconstruct the accounts of kings and, to a great extent, even those of the "anonymous masons" we recalled in the introduction.

The second step consisted of confuting a widespread, deep-rooted belief in academic circles. This point can be illustrated by again citing Einaudi, who wrote an important essay in 1936 that appeared in the second issue of the *Rivista di Storia Economica*. In Einaudi's words, "I too believe that Le Play's method is unusable from a statistical point of view. I can add that it does not at all diminish the value of household budgets, which are compiled by statistics offices today, if we say that Le Play's budgets are and must remain another thing. Le Play's budgets are thus a historical document and not a statistical one ... Le Play thought he was creating a statistical work and instead he wrote stories". Well, if Einaudi's reasoning is completely correct at the methodological level, we have arrived at quite the opposite conclusion: household budgets can transmute their own nature of historical data into that of statistical data. To make this come about, one should not underestimate empirical difficulties or even statistical ones. With regard to empirical difficulties, we experimented with the combined use of real household budgets, "typical budgets" (constructed after having defined a "typical household") and "hypothetical budgets" (conjectural budgets constructed on the basis of secondary sources). The result—the IHBD or Italian Household Budgets Database—was combined with the data of population censuses by means of a statistical technique known as post-stratification. In so doing, we obtained statistically grounded, empirically solid, and historically plausible results. This is the best praise one could make in favor of historical household budgets and their use in modern economic history analysis (A'Hearn, Amendola and Vecchi, 2016). To future research we entrust the task of broadening the horizons and extending that analysis beyond the national borders of Italy: *per aspera ad astra* (the sky is the limit).

Appendix—Sources and Methods

Figure 13.1 Le Play's family monographs Our processing of Le Play's data (1855, 1877–1879), Société d'economie sociale (1857–1862); Société d'économie sociale (1885–1913).

Table 13.1 Sample surveys on household budgets: precursor countries and laggards The sources are as follows (according to country, in alphabetical order). *Austria*: Statistik Austria (1956); *Brazil*: IBGE (1967); *Denmark*: Danmarks Statistik (1976); *France*: Insee (1958); *Germany*: Statistisches Bundesamt (1963); *Greece*: NSSG (1958); *India*: NSS (1951); *Italy*: Banca d'Italia for 1965 (1965) and Istat for 1968 (1968); *Mexico*: INEGI (1984); *Portugal*: Instituto Nacional de Estadística Statistics Portugal (1968); *Spain*: Ine (1958); *Sweden*: SCB (1958); *United Kingdom*: Office for National Statistics (1957); *United States*: Survey Research Centre, University of Michigan (1968).

Picture 13.2 The budget of a bankrupt family Source: Archivio di Stato di Napoli, Tribunale di Commercio, Fallimenti, Fascicolo 2563 bis.

Figure 13.3 The geographical distribution of households in the INEA survey (1925–1936) Our processing of INEA data (1925–1936).

Table 13.2 The first sample surveys in Italy The sources, according to row, are as follows: *1)* Doxa (1951); *2)* Camera dei Deputati (1953–54); *3)* Ambrico (1954); *4)* Camera dei Deputati (1953); *5)* Unpublished material of the Comune di Trieste; *6*) Cao Pinna (1958); *7*) Istat (1960); *8*) Isce (1960); *9*) Istat (1968); *10*) Isce (1966).

Figure 13.4 Typical households or ideal households? The cartoon is from Kruskal and Mosteller (1980), 170.

Table 13.3 IHBD: the Italian Household Budgets Database The sources have been described in Chianese and Vecchi (2011).

Figure 13.5 The income of Italian households (IHBD) and GDP per head, 1861–1931 The "Household budgets" curve is obtained by calculating, for each decade, the average income per person on the basis of IHBD data. These values are transformed into Euro 2013 by means of the Istat coefficients (2014). The "National accounts" curve is obtained by combining the ten-year averages calculated on the per-capita GDP estimates given in chapter 7 ("Income") and reported in the statistical appendix.

14

The Cost of Living

WITH NICOLA AMENDOLA

1 Everything Depends on Price

In April 2008, one U.S. dollar was worth 62 eurocents. With such a favourable exchange rate, many Italians jumped at the chance to spend their holidays in the United States, not just to experience magnificent landscapes or the vibrant atmosphere of the big cities but also, and more prosaically, to go shopping. It was as if the Italians suddenly had a 40–50 percent discount on a wide range of consumer goods—from clothes to electronics—to fill their suitcases before going home. Back in Italy, the price of these commodities would have been higher and, in some cases, well beyond what they could afford.

According to economic theory, price differences cannot last for very long. The arbitrage mechanism would inevitably tend to eliminate them: consumer demand would turn to the market with the lowest price, thereby making it rise, while producers' supply would concentrate in markets with the highest price, thereby causing it to fall. In theory, therefore, the free movement of supply and demand should ensure that the same commodity sold in different markets has the same price—this is the so-called law of one price. However, reality contradicts theory, at least in its strictest formulation.[1] In the late 1970s, in collaboration with the United Nations, a group of scholars of the University of Pennsylvania started up a world-scale research program in order to estimate purchasing-power differences of national currencies for 189 countries (the Penn project).[2] The data they gathered were organized into the Penn World Table and

---

[1] In actual fact, because of various barriers, the arbitrage mechanisms cannot always guarantee the validity of the law of one price. Traders do not have perfect information on commodities and their sales price, and this means that the same commodity can be sold at different prices (Stigler 1961; Burdett and Judd 1983). Moreover, transport costs are often significant, firms can have a non-negligible market power, and there are various restrictions to the mobility of goods and factors of production (Lamont and Thaler 2003).

[2] See Kravis et al. (1975), and Kravis, Heston, and Summers (1978; 1982).

confirmed the existence and persistence of territorial price differences. Despite the forces of arbitrage, prices tend to systematically remain higher in richer or relatively more developed countries (Summers and Heston 1991).

The differences found by the Penn project are not solely linked to exchange rate fluctuations: price differences for the same commodity can also be found within more homogeneous currency areas such as the "euro zone" (Goldberg and Verboven 2005), as well as within individual countries themselves. Italy is an excellent example of this. If you travel around the country, you would see that in the south many goods and services are cheaper compared to the north, and these differences are not negligible. For our intents and purposes, the most important implication of the failure of the law of one price, regardless of its causes, is that interpersonal comparisons of the Italians' wellbeing cannot be analyzed without considering the existence of territorial differences in prices.

Prices do not just vary in space but also over time. In comparisons with regard to wellbeing, inflation (increases in prices over time) and deflation (decreases in prices over time) count as much as territorial variations in prices, especially if we compare prices in distant years. Let's take the case of a Fiat 600, the economy car that became the symbol of the Italian economic miracle. In 1960 its list price was about 600,000 Italian lira; with the same amount, corresponding to 310 euros, we could at most buy a bicycle today. If we simply used the official euro/lira conversion rate to convert the 600,000 lira of 1960 into today's equivalent sum, we would get a totally distorted measure of the purchasing power that 600,000 lira had in the 1960s.

Finally, there is another aspect to take into account. Even when there is no inflation and there are no territorial differences in the cost of living, there may still be changes in price structure. This is what happens when some goods become more expensive and others cheaper. From the individual's point of view, price changes may have positive or negative effects depending on his or her consumption preferences or habits. If the price of the commodity that I most desire and consume rises, while the price of a commodity that I do not want and usually do not consume decreases, the effect of the change in price structure on my standard of living will be negative, while it would be positive in the opposite case.

The general conclusion is that if we adopt monetary incomes to measure wellbeing without considering differences in average prices in the various parts of the country, inflation and deflation, or even changes in price structure, we run the risk of getting a distorted view of the living conditions of Italian households. The main problem is that while the history of inflation in Italy is largely well known, that of the territorial dynamics of prices in Italy over the 150 years since the country's unification is still a largely unexplored field. In this chapter we shall try to bridge this gap in order to arrive at a proper comparison of household incomes with regard to different times and places.

2 What Are Price Indexes and What Are They For?

In economics some research fields are fatally tedious while others, however challenging, may be rather inconvenient. The field of price indexes is one that probably deserves both attributes: tedious and inconvenient. Let's recall here that a price index is nothing but a tool to measure the overall level of prices in different periods of time or in different places.[3] That the study of price indexes constitutes a tough and tedious subject is well known to experts in the field and depends on technical aspects that our reader would probably find rather uninteresting. The idea that the field is an inconvenient one stems from the fact that although our knowledge of price movements can help us to understand and solve problems, it can sometimes increase them by creating the premises for political or social conflict: in recording price variations, price indexes highlight and certify the accompanying redistribution of purchasing power.[4]

Price indexes, however, deserve a third attribute: they are indispensable. This is because, as we saw in the opening paragraph, they are used in order to properly measure the living conditions of households. But they are also essential in order to plan a country's economic policy, to arbitrate industrial relations, and to analyze changes in production and social structure. To achieve these goals, we need both kinds of price indexes available today: temporal indexes and spatial indexes.

Temporal price indexes are, without doubt, the ones that are more familiar to the reader. They record inflation and deflation phenomena: the value of the index is established at 100 for any given year of reference (called "base year"), and the gap between the price index and the value of 100 in a different year represents the variation of the general level of prices up to that year. For example, if we establish 1995 as the base year and the value of the index in 2010 is 138, this means that prices increased by 38 percent between 1995 and

---

[3] In this chapter the terms "price index" and "cost of living index" are used with the same meaning. Technically this is wrong. A "price index" is a statistical indicator measuring the average level of prices, while the "cost of living index" (or "real index of the cost of living") is a measure—deriving from economic theory rather than statistics—of the minimum average cost to achieve an established level of utility (Deaton and Muellbauer 1980). In this chapter we have decided to use these terms interchangeably for clarity of exposition, without there being any significant side effects.

[4] As far back as the 1830s, Joseph Lowe, the pioneer of price indexes, lamented how slowly their use was spreading. Lowe gave two reasons for this: the poor political economy skills of the governing classes ("the unfortunate neglect of political economy in the education of our public men") and the desire not to make the population at large aware of the scale of the problem ("the interest of government, the greatest of all debtors, to prevent the public from fixing its attention on the gradual depreciation of money") (Lowe 1823, 346).

2010. The effects of inflation are well known: when prices rise and incomes do not keep pace, the purchasing power of households decreases along with their wellbeing.

Spatial price indexes (also known as *purchasing power parity indexes*) are perhaps less well known. A spatial price index measures differences in the average level of prices between different geographical areas. The interpretation of a spatial price index is the same as for a temporal one, except for the fact that we are not comparing price variations over time but between different localities. If we establish the average price level in Italy at 100, then differences with regard to 100 measure the price level differences in different parts of the country.

An example can clarify this point and help us to understand the importance of using spatial price indexes. Let's consider two workers and imagine that one of them lives in Milan, the principal city of one of the richest regions in Italy (Lombardy), while the other lives in Naples, the principal city of one of the poorest regions (Campania). Suppose that both earn 2,000 euros a month and that prices in Milan are 15 percent higher than the national average, while prices in Naples are 10 percent lower than the national average. This means that the spatial price index would give Milan a value of 115 and Naples a value of 90: these are artificial values but, as we shall see, not too far removed from reality. The two workers' wages of 2,000 euros is something that economists call a *nominal wage*. In order to compare two people's purchasing power, we need to divide their nominal wage by the spatial price index (and then multiply by 100): for the Milanese worker this gives a sum of 1,739 euros, while for the Neapolitan worker it is 2,222 euros. These two sums are their *real wages*, which provide a measure of the two workers' actual purchasing power. With other things being equal, the Neapolitan worker's purchasing power is about 28 percent greater than the Milanese worker's one. The above example shows the fundamental economic principle which states that, with territorial differences in price levels, the use of nominal sums (how much we get in our pay packet) distorts comparisons of purchasing power, and thus of wellbeing, between individuals, households, and social groups. Appropriate comparisons must be made by means of real amounts, that is to say, sums that have been corrected through spatial price indexes.

3 Money, Inflation, and Deflation

A shared currency and the stability of its value constitute a fundamental element for the birth of a national economy and the development of the living conditions of its citizens. That is why, once Italy was created in March 1861, it was soon decided to create a currency for the Italians. This was no small task if we consider that, at the time of unification, there were about 270 different currencies in circulation within the new kingdom—a legacy of the complex monetary history of the pre-unification period (De Mattia 1959, 14). The Italian lira was created in July 1861, but took almost a quarter of a century to overcome the resistance on the part of various vested interests and to become established, *de facto* as well as *de jure*, finally replacing the other currencies (Toniolo, Conte, and Vecchi 2003). The lira would continue in circulation, as an autonomous currency, with all its ups and downs, until 1998, when Italy joined the European Monetary Union, thereby giving up its national monetary sovereignty. At the stroke of midnight on 28 February 2002, the Italian lira ceased to exist and was handed over to the euro.[5]

Contrary to what common sense would suggest, money is not necessarily the best way to keep your savings: stashing your money under the mattress may be a very bad strategy. The monetary value of goods and services vary over time, sometimes quite sharply, and so does the value of money itself. It makes no sense, for instance, to compare the wellbeing of a household of 1960 with one of today by just looking at their monetary incomes. Changes in prices over the years have been such that the sum needed for a household in 1960 to lead a decent life for a whole year would hardly cover the expenses of just one week today.[6]

Figure 14.1 summarizes the trend in prices in Italy since 1861. The first finding to emerge is the prevalence of inflationary periods: in Italian history, for each year of deflation we see four of inflation. The overall rise in prices experienced in Italy since the country's unification (1861–2014) has been above the one recorded in many of the most important industrialized economies in the world (Table 14.1); Italian inflation, however, has never been serious enough to trigger hyperinflation or lead to a total loss of the value of money (Box 1). If we use a 20 percent threshold per year to identify periods of "high inflation" (Reinhart and Rogoff 2011, 5), then the historical series of Italian inflation shows only one crisis, in 1980, at the peak of the inflationary process triggered by the first oil shock of 1973. The 1970s and 1980s represent a peculiar period in the whole of Italy's postunification history. Fratianni and Spinelli (2001), the authors of an important monetary history of Italy, came to the conclusion that, if we exclude the turbulent period between the two world wars, the inflationary processes recorded in Italy in its Liberal period (1861–1913) and in the first twenty years of the Republic (1950–1972) are completely in line with what is seen abroad, while the 1970s and 1980s are an "Italian peculiarity": in those two decades the Italian inflationary process was more intense than the one abroad. In the years following the Maastricht Treaty (1992), which established the European Union, Italy embarked on a process of convergence with the inflationary dynamics seen in the countries of the European Union.

---

[5] January 1, 2002 saw the introduction of euro banknotes and coins in dual circulation with the lira. On February 28, 2002, lira banknotes and coins ceased to be legal tender.

[6] A proper comparison requires turning the 1960 lira into current values. This operation is quite simple, thanks to the availability of coefficients published by Istat, the Italian national institute of statistics (Istat 2012).

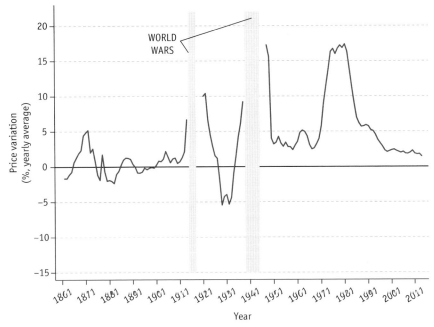

Figure 14.1 INFLATION AND DEFLATION RATES, 1861–2014. The figure shows the annual trend in prices (vertical axis) over the 150 years of post-unification Italy (horizontal axis). Values above the horizontal line show periods of inflation (rise in prices), those below instead correspond to periods of deflation (years in which prices fell). The two world war years (gray areas) are excluded since they historically record greater values of inflation owing to war and military spending. Annual fluctuations of the series have been smoothed out in order to better grasp the long term trend.

The international data in Table 14.1 are not easy to interpret. Both theoretically and empirically, it is indeed difficult to identify an ideal long-term inflation level that would minimize any social costs due to the gradual loss of monetary value (Gale 1982; Walsh 2010). That is to say, it is difficult to establish whether, given the fundamental characteristics of the country and its place within the international economic context, Italian price variations since unification have been at a too high or too low rate. However, there is general agreement on the fact that the instability of prices, that is, the volatility of inflation rates, in any case creates negative effects, distorting decision-making in production, investment, and consumption on the part of households and firms. From this standpoint, Italy is a virtuous case. If we measure the variability of inflation rates over the 150 years since unification, we see a low variability of inflation in the country compared to what is found in many other countries (Table 14.1, column 8), and also a decrease in price volatility.[7]

[7] The decrease in the variability of inflation over time is not given in Table 14.1, but may be deduced from the data reported in Table 14.A1 in the statistical appendix.

Table 14.1 **Inflation and deflation in the five continents, 1861–2014**

Country	Beginning of period covered	Average inflation rate	Share of years in which inflation exceeded			Number of years of hyperinfl.	Variability of inflation
			10%	20%	40%		
Europe							
Austria	1861	25.6	17	12	8	1	0.12
Denmark	1861	2.9	11	1	0	0	0.50
France	1861	5.7	20	8	3	0	0.53
Germany	1861	$1.4 \cdot 10^9$	19	9	5	2	0.08
Greece	1861	13.8	33	12	5	1	0.23
Italy	1862	8	18	6	3	0	0.26
Netherlands	1861	2.1	7	1	1	0	0.30
Russia	1861	25.5	19	9	3	1	0.23
Spain	1861	4.3	19	2	0	0	0.64
Sweden	1861	3.2	11	2	0	0	0.46
Turkey	1861	15.9	34	23	17	0	0.51
UK	1861	3.1	12	3	0	0	0.42
Africa							
Algeria	1870	5.8	20	10	3	0	0.48
Egypt	1861	4.8	30	9	1	0	0.43
South Africa	1896	5	21	1	0	0	0.81
Zimbabwe	1921	304	33	20	11	2	0.12
Latin America							
Argentina	1861	69	43	25	15	4	0.21
Brazil	1861	85.6	44	27	17	6	0.24
Chile	1861	22.5	42	26	7	1	0.33
Mexico	1878	11	32	14	5	0	0.52
Peru	1861	88.6	28	15	11	3	0.13
North America							
Canada	1868	2.4	7	1	0	0	0.49
USA	1861	2.3	9	1	0	0	0.43

(continued)

Table 14.1 **Continued**

Country	Beginning of period covered	Average inflation rate	Share of years in which inflation exceeded			Number of years of hyperinfl.	Variability of inflation
Asia							
China	1861	37	17	11	9	3	0.20
India	1861	4.7	20	5	1	0	0.43
Indonesia	1861	21.2	38	21	12	1	0.23
Japan	1861	13.2	20	11	5	1	0.16
Thailand	1861	3.9	17	9	3	0	0.23
Oceania							
Australia	1861	2.6	9	1	0	0	0.45
New Zealand	1861	2.9	11	0	0	0	0.54

Note: For each country in the list, the table gives the average annual inflation rate (column 3) since the year given in column 2. Columns 4, 5 and 6 give the fraction of years in which inflation was higher than 10, 20 and 30%, respectively, while column 7 shows the years of hyperinflation experienced in each country. Finally, column 8 contains a measure of the variability of inflation (the coefficient of variation) of the various countries in the period considered.

Apart from the problem of uncertainty linked to price volatility, it is worth recalling that, in the short run, inflation and deflation both lead to a redistribution of national product and wealth, and in this way directly affect households' living conditions. Let's consider the case of inflation. If the erosion of the purchasing power of money is damaging to some people, it may be beneficial to others. For creditors or people on a fixed wage, a currency devaluation means lower purchasing power, which will persist for as long as income does not increase to keep pace or the credit position runs out. For debtors, instead, inflation is welcomed because it lowers the real value of the credit, that is, the sums of money to be paid back in the future. In the same way, in times of inflation, firms see the value of expected revenues rise against their already incurred costs, thereby experiencing a temporary increase in profit. On the inflation side, therefore, we inevitably find both winners and losers.

The same holds for deflation, but in the opposite direction: a decrease in prices improves the position of creditors, but worsens that of debtors. A recurring example of this in the history of capitalist economies is the one of real estate bubbles, like the one many consider triggered the financial crisis of 2007. When the bubble burst and house prices plummeted, it affected many households in the United States, Ireland and Spain—countries that had experienced particularly sharp increases in real estate prices—and they now find themselves having to pay back thirty-year house loans on properties worth much less than before, in some cases as much as 50 percent less. The net wealth of these households has

Box 1 The specter of hyperinflation

When the increase in the general level of prices is higher than 40–50 per-cent a *month*, then we no longer talk in terms of inflation but of "hyper-inflation" (Cagan 1956; Reinhart and Rogoff 2011, 5). At this rate, the purchasing power of money halves within a month and a half or so, with

Figure 14.B1 HYPERINFLATION IN GERMANY, 1923. The photograph shows a young woman stoking the home fire with a heap of banknotes: owing to hyperinflation, the national currency was worth less than the paper it was printed on.

the result that money itself rapidly loses the characteristics underlying its keeping and use.

There are people who will never forget the devastating effects associated with hyperinflation. In the aftermath of World War I, hyperinflation in Germany not only destroyed its economic foundations—wiping out the savings of most of the country's population—but also paved the way to the worst disaster on a global scale of modern times: "Hitler is the foster-child of inflation", observed the British economist Lionel Robbins (1898–1984) (Bresciani-Turroni 1937, x). The problem was triggered by the devaluation of the German currency: in January 1919, a few months after the Treaty of Versailles was signed, an ounce of gold cost 170 Marks; in November 1923 it cost an incredible 87 thousand billion Marks. Such a devaluation rapidly affected the internal price mechanism and led to inflation rates of over 300 percent per *month* (Feinstein, Temin, and Toniolo 2007).

Although the German case is perhaps the most-cited example in history, the highest hyperinflation ever recorded was actually in Hungary: in July 1946 the general level of prices in the country increased by 4.19×10^{16} (the scientific notation means that 4.19 is multiplied by a multiple of 10 containing 16 zeros, that is, 4 million billion times). During that month, the prices of Hungarian commodities doubled every 15 hours nonstop.

It is worth recalling, here, that hyperinflation is not something confined to history books. Between 1980 and 2012, Hanke and Krusk (2012) counted as many as 38 episodes of hyperinflation, recorded all over the world: in Europe (above all, in Eastern European countries in the early 1990s, that is, during their transition toward a market economy), in Africa, and in many Latin American states.

dropped drastically and with it their leverage capacity, making them particularly vulnerable to the effects of the economic crisis.

The effects of deflation are not completely the same as the ones of inflation. While it is true that deflation means an increase in the purchasing power of wages and incomes, that is, of the sources of income earned in a fixed amount, it is also true that falling prices reduce the profits expected by firms and the value of their assets, which, as a form of collateral, allow them regular access to credit. A worsening in expected profits and credit restrictions means that, sooner or later, there will be a fall in production and an increase in unemployment. The increase in the purchasing power of wages and incomes may thus be more than offset by the specter of redundancies and recession. As John Maynard Keynes (1883–1946) wrote: "[I]nflation is unjust and deflation is inexpedient. Of the two perhaps deflation is, if we rule out exaggerated inflations such as that of Germany, the worse; because it is worse, in an impoverished world, to provoke unemployment than to disappoint the rentier" (Keynes 1923, 40).

4 Figures That We Know

Although the first works on price indices were developed in the early eighteenth century and the corpus of theoretical and methodological knowledge became consolidated as far back as the late nineteenth century, the actual century of the price index is, to all effects, the twentieth century.[8] It was World War I, especially, that boosted the production of price statistics. The inflationary flare-ups and resulting internal social tensions drove most western countries to adopt the necessary tools to survey retail prices on a nationwide scale (Stapleford 2009).

Italy was no exception, and 1927 marked a turning point in this respect. Very soon after its founding (1926), the national statistics agency, Istat, was charged with creating a national index for the cost of living, to replace the local indexes calculated by some large municipalities. The statistics institute quickly took to its task: the first booklet of the *Bollettino dei prezzi* (the "Price Bulletin") appeared on July 22, 1927 and was thereafter issued on a bimonthly and later monthly basis in the following years. Today, we have an official series of price indexes[9] enabling us to convert into current values any monetary sum of any year of Italian postunification history (Istat 2012).

Although the problem of measuring inflation was satisfactorily solved already in the late 1920s, that of measuring price differences between various provinces and geographical areas still remains an open question today, and it has received little or no attention. There are no official long-term estimates of territorial differences with regard to the cost of living. It is, evidently, a gap that is difficult to make good—requiring information on the prices of hundreds of

---

[8] William Fleetwood (1656–1723), a British economist and statistician, presented the first rudimentary estimate of temporal price indices in the treatise *Chronicon Preciosum* of 1707 (Ferger 1946; Kendall 1969; Diewert 1993).

[9] The price index calculated by Istat is based on the value of a basket of goods and services typically consumed by the Italian population. Basket composition is systematically reviewed over time in order to allow for changes in the target population's consumption habits. The first consumption basket, used in Italy for the period 1928–1938, contained just 55 items: 20 general foodstuffs, a dozen items of clothing, rent, 8 items for domestic heating and lighting, plus 18 "sundries"—paper and pens, plates and glasses, cod liver oil and castor oil, as well as other widely consumed items of the times. The latest basket—updated in 2012—reflects the consumption structure of a modern affluent society and includes almost 1,400 items, 200 of which concern foodstuffs; almost 600,000 price quotations are sent to Istat headquarters every month by the municipal statistics offices (D'Acunto 2006; Istat 2012).

goods and services of homogeneous quality, with surveying points located all over the country. Faced with such a daunting task, some have even suggested scrapping the whole idea altogether because the "cure is worse than the disease" (Vaccaro 1999).

Among the first to take up the challenge was Campiglio (1986; 1996). Campiglio compared the cost of the same basket of goods and services in some of the main cities in Italy. By simulating the effects of moving from one city to another on the cost of living, Campiglio found considerable differences in the average level of prices. For example, "the increase in income necessary to enable a worker from Palermo, the regional capital of Sicily, to maintain the same standard of living in Milan, the main city of northern Italy, is estimated at around 30 percent" (Campiglio 1996, 64–65). Alesina, Danninger, and Rostagno (2001) extended the degree of coverage of the estimates at regional level by using a projection model similar to the one we shall use in section 5. According to their study, in 1995 the average difference in prices between north and south of the country was 14.3 percent.[10] A third attempt was the one made by Declich and Polin (2005). This is based on a comparison of the minimum expenditure needed to purchase the same basket of essential goods in different places: this time, the reference year is 2002, and the results show that the cost of foodstuffs in the north is 17–20 percent higher than in the south, while the gap in the overall cost of living index shows differences of 38–44 percent.[11]

On the institutional side, the production of spatial price indexes is a sore point. In April 2008, Istat reported a study on territorial price levels showing broad differences—even if not directly comparable with the figures seen above. We can mention two examples: with reference to just foodstuffs, the difference in the average level of prices recorded in 2006 between Bolzano—a city near the border with Austria, in the far north of the country—and Naples turned out to be 25.3 percent; with regard to home furnishings, the difference between Milan (the affluent big city in the north-west) and Campobasso (a small province in the south) exceeded 50 percent. In July 2010, Istat published a complete index of purchasing power parities, which, however, did not take imputed rents into consideration when calculating the cost of living: that is to say, the rents that households would pay if they did not own their homes. By neglecting this item, which is not very sensitive to the rebalancing mechanisms

[10] This is an average gap between the cost of living of two large areas of the country, and does not make the result immediately comparable with Campiglio's estimates: the latter refer to Italy's provinces, which are more heterogeneous in themselves and thus show greater differences.

[11] The consumption basket considered by the authors refers to only less privileged households instead of the whole population, and this makes comparisons with the other studies mentioned less clear-cut. Bertozzi and Espa (2005) obtained similar results on the basis of independent data and methods.

of arbitrage, the Istat index underestimates the actual scale of the territorial gap. Hence, if we limit ourselves to just foodstuffs, the new data referring to 2009 reduce the territorial divide between north and south of the country: between Bolzano and Naples, the gap in prices of a basket of foodstuffs is 18.5 percent.

The most reliable estimates of the territorial differences in the cost of living in Italy are, in our view, the ones produced by Cannari and Iuzzolino (2009). The two authors integrated the Istat estimates (2008a) with a great deal of additional information—taken from various sources—on house prices, energy products, and other services, and constructed econometrically robust estimates of the general level of prices for the Italian regions. For 2006, average prices in southern Italy were confirmed as 18–19 percent lower compared to those of other areas of the country. Regional differences are even more marked: the most expensive regions are found in the north-west of the country (Lombardy and Liguria), which have average prices that are 28–29 percent higher than the ones in the southern regions, where the cost of living is lower, such as Basilicata, Molise, and Calabria.

The numbers thus far are the ones that we know, summarized in Figure 14.2. But our investigation also has a historical side; we are not just interested in finding out current territorial differences in the cost of living, but also the differences

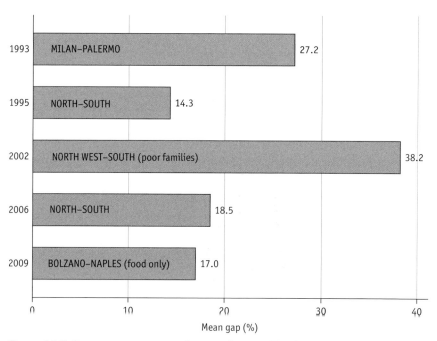

Figure 14.2 DIFFERENCES IN THE COST OF LIVING: THE NUMBERS THAT WE KNOW. The figure summarizes the scale of the territorial differences in average prices for certain geographical areas and certain years. The sources are given in the appendix.

characterizing the country in the past. The usefulness of this kind of reconstruction is twofold: on the one hand, it allows us to see whether long-term trends point to a process of territorial integration or divergence in prices and, on the other, it provides us with a necessary tool (the series of spatial price indexes) with which we can fully compare monetary indicators of individual wellbeing.

5 Italian Prices since 1861

We do not know whether, in the period from Italian unification (1861) to just before World War I (1913), the cost of living was higher, on average, in the northern regions of the country compared to the south or vice versa. The information available allows us, at most, to put forward some "informed hypothesis". Something may be learned by studying the *relative dynamics* of prices of foodstuffs between north and south of the country, that is, by analyzing the trend over time of the relation between inflation rates in the north and south.

Figure 14.3, plotted on the basis of a heterogeneous collection of sources, shows that the relationship between the price changes of foodstuffs in the north and south fluctuates with great frequency around the value of 1. This means that, although there are subperiods in which the cost of a basket of foodstuffs grows more quickly in the north than in the south (the relation is greater than 1), these periods are relatively short and they almost systematically alternate with periods, again short, in which the exact opposite happens. The first fifty years of postunification Italy would thus not appear to be characterized by price convergence or divergence phenomena; this is an empirical finding in line with the results obtained by Federico (2007b) and compatible with the hypothesis that the markets of the main foodstuffs were already relatively integrated from the birth of the Kingdom of Italy to the outbreak of the Great War.

The sources available for the period after World War I are more numerous and enable us to calculate a real cost of living index. For the years 1922–1938, we were able to use hitherto unpublished data found in some handwritten registers kept in the premises of Istat's Price Division,[12] while for the years following World War II (since 1947), we extended the estimates published in Amendola, Vecchi, and Al Kiswani (2009), based on a projection procedure similar to the one proposed by Alesina, Danninger, and Rostagno (2001). The results of our statistical reconstruction are summarized in Figure 14.4, which compares the dynamics of the cost of living in the central-northern regions and in the southern ones

---

[12] These registers provide a monthly account of expenditures in 51 Italian cities with regard to a homogeneous consumption basket including not only foodstuffs but also other goods and services such as clothes, accommodation, heating, and medical fees.

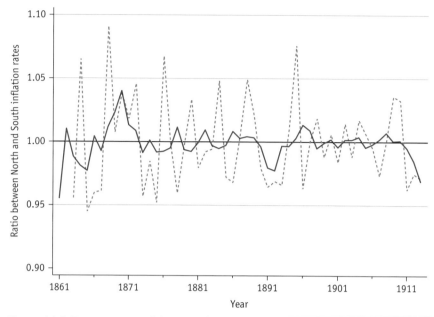

Figure 14.3 LIBERAL ITALY (1861–1913). NEITHER CONVERGENCE NOR
DIVERGENCE OF PRICES. The graph shows how the relationship between the
inflation rate of foodstuffs in the northern and southern regions of the country
varies over time. The blue line is obtained by smoothing out the annual values
(broken line), which are sensitive to measurement errors. If the relation is greater
than 1, it means that prices are rising more rapidly in the north compared to the
south, while a value lower than 1 shows a price trend in the south which is more
accelerated compared to the trend in the north of the country.

of the country since the end of World War I.[13] These are hitherto unpublished
historical series showing certain new facts that deserve a short comment.

THE LACK OF CONVERGENCE IN THE INTERWAR PERIOD

The year 1922 marked the end of the liberal state in Italy and the start of the totalitarian Fascist state. The break with the institutions of the past was very clear-
cut: in line with the idea of totalitarianism, the Fascist state entered every aspect
of the country's life, including the economy. The state introduced price ceilings
for certain foodstuffs in order to safeguard consumers' purchasing power, and
a great many informal initiatives were taken—including coercive practices—to
enforce the government's measures (Toniolo 1980; Zamagni 1981); in the latter

---

[13] The statistical appendix gives the estimates underlying Figure 14.4, but also the estimates of
the cost of living for all 20 regions of Italy and the five administrative macro-areas. It also contains
estimates of territorial price differences for just foodstuffs.

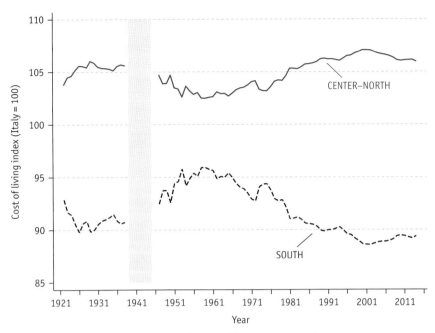

Figure 14.4 THE COST OF LIVING: CENTER-NORTH VERSUS SOUTH,
SINCE 1922. The figure shows the trend in the cost of living (vertical axis) over
time (horizontal axis). The gray area corresponds to the war years. On average,
households in the central-northern regions (unbroken line) have always had higher
prices than southern ones (broken line).

half of the 1930s there was even an attempt to carry out a general administrative control of prices and quantities (Zamagni 1993). Judging from Figure 14.4,
the government's direct and active role in the economy of the Fascist period did
not make for greater integration, however coercive, between north and south,
at least with regard to differences in the cost of living. On average, throughout
the period concerned, consuming the same basket of commodities in the north
was 15 percent more expensive than in the south. It may be that the establishment of a corporative system that hindered competition thwarted any action in
favor of southern Italian development and integration (Ciocca 2007). Or perhaps, more simply, the persistence of a gap between north and south was due to
the lack of any real development policy for the south. However, Figure 14.4 does
show a turning point—already observed in chapter 7 ("Income")—at the end of
the 1920s: while the north–south gap in prices *increased* (by about 5 percentage
points) between 1922 and 1929, during the 1930s it stabilized at around 15 percent. One hypothesis to explain this trend is that postwar recovery led to greater
inflationary pressure in the north than in the south, as a result of the greater concentration of industry in the northern regions that had to face a rapidly expanding internal and external demand after the world war (Zamagni 1993).

ITALY AFTER WORLD WAR II MARKED BY DIVERGENCE

Postwar reconstruction marked the start of a phase of convergence between north and south of the country. However, it did not last long because it brusquely came to a halt at the beginning of the 1960s, when the cost of living in the central-northern regions was 10 percent higher than what was prevalently found in the southern ones. The subsequent decades were characterized by a continuous period of divergence that doubled the gap in the average level of prices between north and south. In 2011 the gap between the cost of living in the north and south of the country has been estimated at 18 percent.

At this stage, it is reasonable to ask whether the territorial differences in the cost of living observed in Italy are within the norm or are instead an exception when compared to other countries. A first term of comparison is given by the price differences between Germany's eastern and western regions in 1994, just four years after the official date of reunification of East and West Germany. Cannari and Iuzzolino (2009) reported—for just foodstuffs—a price level in East Germany that was 5 percent lower, on average, than the one in West Germany. In comparison, the difference in cost of the foodstuff basket between northern and southern Italy in the same year is 18.3 percent, according to our estimates (Table 14.A2). The differences in the overall cost of living index between East and West Germany in 1994 has been estimated at 11.4 percent, compared to the 17.7 percent estimated for Italy. Johnston, McKinney, and Stark (1996) reported estimates of price differentials for twelve regions of the United Kingdom for the years 1979–1993. For 1993, the greatest gap was found between the south-east and the north of the country, and stood at 7.9 percent: in Italy, in the same year, the gap between north-east and south was 21 percent. The comparison for 1979 is similar: the greatest gap recorded in the United Kingdom was 7.9 percent (the highest prices being in Northern Ireland, and the lowest in the northern regions of Britain), while in Italy it was 23.2 percent (the highest prices being in the central regions, and the lowest in the south).[14] If there were a Guinness World Record for territorial price differences, then Italy would be the European champion outright.

6 Waiting for Godot

North-south convergence with regard to the cost of living plays the part of Godot in the script of Italian economic history: someone that everybody is waiting for, but who never actually turns up. The statistical reconstruction presented in this

---

[14] The comparison with the United Kingdom is flawed by the different number of regions compared: 12 in Britain and only 5 in Italy. The greater aggregation of the Italian estimates leads to underestimating the scale of regional disparities compared to the British case.

chapter shows that the gap in the average level of prices between north and south of the country is a permanent feature of Italian economic development (Rossi and Toniolo 1994), which not only shows no sign of possible solution but actually appears to have worsened over the last few decades. The law of one price has found no application in Italian history.

From an empirical perspective, the failure of the law of one price is nothing new. International data show the presence of systematic price differences on a world scale, and identify a particular phenomenon, referred to as the "Penn effect" in the literature: high-income countries have higher prices compared to low-income ones. On a national level, Italy offers a robust empirical confirmation of the Penn effect. At a more domestic level, the north of the country may be likened to the richest countries while the south to the poorest ones. Even within a picture of a widespread increasing trend in GDP, the positions of the two macro-areas of the country have not changed over the 150 years since unification: the north has always had a higher per-capita income than the south and, in line with the Penn effect, a higher overall price level. Why? The most widely known theoretical explanation of the Penn effect was put forward by Balassa (1964) and Samuelson (1964; 1994), who attributed international differences of average prices to differences in productivity found in the various countries. In the richest countries we normally see greater labor productivity, which in turn means higher average wages compared to those earned by workers in the poorest countries. However, while for goods open to international competition the wage differences are not reflected in price differences in the same direction (owing to competition among producers), the same is *not* true for many domestic goods and services. In most cases, domestic goods are not subject to the discipline of competition,[15] and the prices of these goods tend to be higher in those countries that pay the highest salaries, that is to say, the richest countries.

Although we do not have sufficient elements to come to any final conclusion on the causes of this territorial divergence in prices in Italy, the Balassa-Samuelson effect, that is, the divergence in productivity between the north and south of the country, is an important clue.[16] Estimates by Felice (2011) show that, in effect, differences in labor productivity between the northern and southern regions are a permanent feature of the Italian economy. If the

[15] A hairdresser in Milan must not worry about the prices established by hairdressers in Naples, and the same applies for those who wish to rent an apartment or, more generally, those who have to establish a price for nontradable goods and services.

[16] The role of the Balassa-Samuelson effect with reference to the Italian context was discussed in Nenna (2001). Daniele and Malanima (2007) documented the dualistic nature of Italian development since World War II and its links with productivity differences on the basis of regional estimates of per-capita GDP; Fenoaltea (2007) provides an explanation attributing the cause to the combined effects of economic policy mistakes and a poor discernment of economic historiography.

Balassa-Samuelson hypothesis turns out to be true, the persistence of territorial differences in prices would not just have consequences on the measurement and distribution of individual wellbeing (aspects that are key to this book), but would also point to the more general problem of the country's economic integration and growth prospects.

The divergence observed over the decades since World War II has brought to us a country in which the average differential in the cost of living between north and south is 18–20 percent, with peaks of 30 percent if we compare actual regions rather than macro-areas. In interpreting these figures, we may be tempted to conclude that—with income being equal—the southern Italian households enjoy greater levels of wellbeing compared to northern households. The risk is, in this case, to confuse the symptom with the disease. More correctly, we should ask ourselves why, despite the fact that there is an average 20 percent "bonus" for those who decide to live in southern Italy, northern families decide *not* to move south. What should be investigated are the reasons for this lack of mobility which, once again, is a clear sign of a lack of economic integration and, at the same time, is part of the mechanism that maintains this persistence of territorial differences.

The more evident explanation for why a 20 percent reduction in the cost of living, with income being equal, does not constitute a sufficient incentive to move south lies in the fact that many aspects of wellbeing escape monetary comparisons. A couple of examples can clarify this point. The first concerns citizens' access to basic services, particularly health and education. The territorial imbalances between north and south, not only in terms of access, but also—and above all—in terms of the quality of the services available, have been talked about in national newspapers for years. These differences are an additional burden to southern households and should be taken into account in order to compare their wellbeing with other areas of the country where services are present, accessible, and of a higher standard. The second example concerns services which go to the benefit of the whole community: defense, law, and order. The Bank of Italy (2009) provides a great deal of data documenting the territorial differences in this regard, showing systematically unfavorable conditions in the south: we should also take these factors into account when measuring wellbeing. In view of all these aspects, the lower cost of living in the south—far from being an advantage for southern households—reflects a condition of economic backwardness that market mechanisms and political actions have not managed to deal with effectively.

Appendix—Sources and Methods

Figure 14.1 Inflation and deflation rates, Italy 1861–2014 Source: Istat (2014). The figures in the original series have been transformed with a moving average of 5 periods.

Table 14.1 Inflation and deflation in the five continents, 1861–2014 The database of reference for all countries, except Italy, is the one constructed by Reinhart and Rogoff (2012), available at http://www.reinhartandrogoff.com/data/ (accessed November 2012). Inflation rates for 2011–2014 years are taken from the World Economic Outlook Database (2014) available at http://www.imf.org/external/pubs/ft/weo/2014/02/weodata/download.aspx.

Figure 14.2 The numbers that we know Sources: 1993: Campiglio (1996), 63 and Table A.3b, 168. 1995: Alesina et al. (2001), 22. 2002: our computations of data by Declich and Polin (2005), Table 6, 288. 2006: Cannari and Iuzzolino (2009), Table A2.1, 34, col. 9. 2009: Istat (2010), Table 2, 4.

Figure 14.3 Liberal Italy (1861–1913): neither convergence, nor divergence of prices Let us begin with the sources. For the years 1890–1913: the enquiry into the prices of consumption goods paid by national boarding schools from 1890 to 1913 (*Inchiesta sui prezzi dei generi di consumo pagati dai convitti nazionali dal 1890 al 1913*). The investigation surveyed retail prices at national boarding schools, but it is reasonable to suspect that they were determined within long- or medium-run procurement contracts, and thus show greater stickiness compared to market prices. We cannot even rule out that, besides the real territorial differences in the cost of living, the prices paid reflected the different levels of efficiency and bargaining power in the territory of the boarding schools. For the years 1874–1889: the weekly bulletin of the prices of certain major foodstuffs and bread (*Bollettino settimanale dei prezzi di alcuni principali beni alimentari e del pane*), published by the Ministry of Agriculture, Industry and Commerce (MAIC) in 1886. The source covers the period 1874–1889 and contains wholesale prices for 6 foodstuffs (wheat of first and second quality, maize, rice, olive oil, and wine) in 77 markets scattered throughout the country. It is an excellent source as regards territorial coverage, but with evident limitations with regard to the number of foodstuffs concerned (Federico 2007a). For the years 1862–1885: the movement of prices of certain foodstuffs from 1862 to 1885 (*Movimento dei prezzi di alcuni generi alimentari dal 1862 al 1885*), a MAIC publication, gathering the prices at production of five foodstuffs (wheat, maize, wine, olive oil, and rice) in 23 markets. Let us now look at the calculus methodology. The procedure used hinged on the source that presents the broadest territorial coverage, that is, the MAIC data for the years 1874–1896; for the previous years, we projected the indexes backward, making the most of the MAIC survey of 1886, while for the later years we used the price data contained in the survey on national boarding schools.

Figure 14.4 The cost of living: Center-North versus South, since 1922 For the years 1947–2014, the reconstruction of the series of spatial indexes for the

Italian macro-areas is based on a procedure of projection of the spatial indexes estimated for the year 2006 by Cannari and Iuzzolino (2009), by means of annual inflation rates on a provincial basis. This method was already experimented by Alesina, Danninger, and Rostagno (2001), and is based on the hypothesis that the information contained in local price documentation can be usefully exploited to reconstruct the trend in the structure of purchasing power parities at a regional or macro-area level, starting from a reference year in which this structure is known. In formal terms, let L_t^s be the spatial price index of region s in year t. For simplicity's sake, we assume that L_t^s is a Laspeyres-type index:

$$L_t^S = \frac{\sum_j p_{j,t}^s q_{j,t}^n}{\sum_j p_{j,t}^n q_{j,t}^n} = \sum_j w_{j,t}^n \frac{p_{j,t}^s}{p_{j,t}^n}$$

where $p_{j,t}^s$ stands for the average price of commodity j in year t and in region s, and $q_{j,t}^n$ stands for the quantity consumed of commodity j in year t and in the reference region n identified, in our case, with the national aggregate. The right-hand side of the equation shows how the index L_t^s can be expressed in terms of a weighted average of relative regional prices with respect to average national prices, where the weighting system is given by the expenditure components at national level $w_{j,t}^n$. Suppose we now backdate the index by a period:

$$L_{t-1}^S = \sum_j w_{j,t-1}^n \frac{p_{j,t-1}^s}{p_{j,t-1}^n}$$

Supposing the structure of relative prices within the regions, and also the structure of national consumption, are stable over time, we can easily demonstrate that:

$$\frac{p_{j,t-1}^s}{p_{j,t-1}^n} = \frac{P_t^n}{P_{t-1}^n} \frac{P_{t-1}^S}{P_t^S}$$

where P_t^s is the temporal price index of region s in year t with respect to an arbitrary base year t_0. Assuming stability in the structure of relative prices within the regions, the dynamics of relative regional prices compared to average national prices is entirely identified by the dynamics of regional deflators. Recalling the assumption of invariance of the national expenditure components, we can write:

$$L_{t-1}^S = \frac{P_t^n}{P_{t-1}^n} \frac{P_{t-1}^S}{P_t^S} L_t^S$$

from which we see the recursive structure of the method concerned: by applying this equation iteratively, and hinging on the *spatial* price index available for a reference year, we can reconstruct the trend in spatial indexes for an arbitrary period of time.

For the years 1927–1938, we used the unpublished data contained in the registers kept at the Rome Price Division of Istat. The provincial inflation rates used for projecting the 1927 index back in time to 1922 were taken from the *Annuario statistico* (statistical yearbook) of the statistics and studies office of the Milan municipal council. The yearbook contains useful information on 16 provincial capital cities (Comune di Milano 1928).

Statistical Appendix

Chapter 1

Table 1.A1 **Calorie availability and requirements (daily, per capita)**

| Year | Per-capita calorie availability | | Calorie requirements |
	Total	*Without alcohol*	
1861	2497	2323	2259
1871	2462	2301	2262
1881	2587	2410	2259
1891	2622	2436	2227
1901	2839	2631	2213
1911	2909	2726	2198
1921	2987	2727	2207
1931	2859	2667	2150
1941	2642	2514	2149
1951	2401	2235	2131
1961	2706	2955	2087
1971	3438	3196	2026
1981	3512	3316	2030
1991	3640	3484	1996
2001	3674	3528	1964
2011	3539	3436	1978
2014	3488	3385	1978

See chapter 1 ("Nutrition") for sources and methods.

Table 1.A2 **Available macronutrients (daily, per capita)**

Year	Carbohydrate	Protein animal	Protein vegetal	Protein total	Lipid animal	Lipid vegetal	Lipid total
1861	443.6	13.8	73.9	87.7			44.1
1871	425.1	12.2	70.2	82.4			48.0
1881	433.1	14.1	70.7	84.8			57.3
1891	443.1	14.7	71.6	86.3			56.0
1901	475.4	17.2	75.9	93.2			62.8
1911	490.9	19.7	78.1	97.8	28.2	33.3	61.6
1921	509.1	20.1	75.2	95.3	28.2	35.1	63.2
1931	489.0	22.0	72.5	94.5	30.8	27.5	58.3
1941	464.1	20.3	65.6	85.9	28.6	20.6	49.2
1951	414.7	19.8	59.1	78.9	23.4	24.1	47.4
1961	482.6	30.1	50.9	82.5	33.1	43.7	77.2
1971	506.1	43.1	54.8	98.0	48.8	64.6	113.5
1981	483.1	52.9	51.8	104.9	61.4	67.3	128.9
1991	455.0	60.8	51.3	112.3	69.9	81.9	152.3
2001	455.6	62.7	51.5	113.7	71.7	85.5	155.2
2011	423.0	59.9	50.0	109.9	68.7	87.7	156.4

See chapter 1 ("Nutrition") for sources and methods.

Chapter 2

Table 2.A1 **Average height of conscripts in the draft at age 20 years, Italy 1855–1980**

Year	Height	Year	Height	Year	Height	Year	Height
1855	162.7	1892	164.4	1929	167.4	1966	
1856	162.6	1893	164.6	**1930**	167.5	1967	173.7
1857	162.7	1894	164.7	1931	167.6	1968	
1858	162.8	1895	164.8	1932	167.6	1969	173.8
1859	162.9	1896	165.0	1933	167.6	**1970**	
1860	162.7	1897	165.0	1934	167.8	1971	
1861	162.9	1898	165.0	1935	168.0	1972	174.0
1862	163.0	1899	165.0	1936	168.0	1973	174.1
1863	163.0	**1900**	164.5	1937	168.2	1974	174.2
1864	163.1	1901	164.9	1938	168.4	1975	174.3
1865	163.3	1902	164.9	1939	168.4	1976	174.4
1866	163.3	1903	165.0	**1940**	168.7	1977	174.4
1867	163.5	1904	165.2	1941	168.8	1978	174.4
1868	163.5	1905	165.3	1942	169.0	1979	174.5
1869	163.5	1906	165.4	1943	169.0	**1980**	174.6
1870	163.3	1907	165.5	1944	169.1		
1871	163.3	1908	165.6	1945	168.7		
1872	163.4	1909	165.7	1946	169.5		
1873	163.4	**1910**	165.8	1947	169.8		
1874	163.6	1911	166.0	1948	169.7		
1875	163.6	1912	166.1	1949	169.8		
1876	163.8	1913	166.2	**1950**	169.9		
1877	163.9	1914	166.3	1951	170.1		
1878	164.0	1915	166.2	1952	170.1		
1879	163.9	1916	166.2	1953	171.1		
1880	163.9	1917	166.3	1954	171.1		
1881	163.9	1918	166.4	1955	171.5		
1882	163.9	1919	166.8	1956	171.9		
1883	164.0	**1920**	167.2	1957	172.2		

(continued)

Table 2.A1 **Continued**

Year	Height	Year	Height	Year	Height	Year	Height
1884	163.9	1921		1958	172.2		
1885	163.9	1922		1959	172.4		
1886	164.0	1923		**1960**	172.7		
1887	164.1	1924		1961	172.8		
1888	164.2	1925		1962	172.8		
1889	164.3	1926		1963	173.0		
1890	164.3	1927	166.8	1964	173.2		
1891	164.4	1928	167.2	1965	173.4		

See chapter 2 ("Height") for sources and methods.

Table 2.A2 Average height of military draft conscripts at age 20 years, according to region and geographical area, Italy 1855–1980

Region	1861	1871	1881	1891	1901	1910	1931	1941	1951	1961	1971	1980
Abruzzi and Molise	161.0	161.5	162.3	162.8	162.7	163.7	165.5	166.9	169.2	171.9	173.4	174.7
Basilicata	159.6	159.7	160.9	161.5	161.3	161.9	162.6	163.9	166.3	169.7	172.2	173.4
Calabria	159.7	160.7	161.6	161.9	161.6	163.3	162.9	165.1	167.2	169.5	171.4	172.4
Campania	161.5	162.1	162.9	162.9	163.1	163.6	165.1	165.8	168.2	171.0	172.7	173.1
Emilia-Romagna	164.5	164.5	165.1	165.2	165.9	167.0	169.6	170.6	172.1	174.5	175.0	175.4
Friuli	166.3	166.8	167.0	166.1	167.3	168.7	171.5	172.9	174.1	176.2	177.2	178.0
Lazio	162.7	163.0	163.9	164.8	165.3	165.2	168.0	170.4	170.8	173.9	174.2	175.4
Liguria	164.2	164.5	165.5	166.1	166.6	167.8	169.9	171.2	172.1	174.2	174.6	175.1
Lombardy	163.9	164.3	164.9	165.6	165.6	167.1	169.0	169.9	171.2	173.8	174.6	175.2
Marche	162.7	163.2	163.6	163.4	163.8	164.8	167.8	169.0	171.1	173.4	174.4	175.2
Piedmont	163.4	163.9	164.6	165.3	166.0	167.4	169.8	170.9	171.6	174.2	174.4	174.9
Puglia	161.1	161.9	162.1	162.9	162.2	163.4	164.7	166.1	168.4	171.3	172.7	173.4
Sardegna	159.2	159.8	160.5	160.8	161.1	161.3	163.5	165.1	166.2	169.2	170.6	171.5
Sicily	161.1	161.8	162.0	161.9	162.6	163.8	164.9	165.8	167.6	170.4	171.8	172.6
Tuscany	164.7	164.6	165.0	165.9	166.0	167.0	170.2	171.1	172.5	174.8	175.1	175.8

(continued)

Table 2.A2 Continued

Region	1861	1871	1881	1891	1901	1910	1931	1941	1951	1961	1971	1980
Trentino							169.5	171.2	172.7	175.3	175.8	177.1
Umbria	162.6	163.1	163.8	163.7	164.2	165.2	167.3	168.4	171.4	173.6	174.6	175.6
Veneto	165.6	165.9	166.8	166.5	167.1	167.9	169.9	171.1	172.4	174.8	176.0	177.0
North-West	163.7	164.1	164.8	165.5	165.8	167.2	169.4	170.5	171.5	174.1	174.6	175.3
North-East	165.2	165.4	166.0	165.9	166.7	167.6	170.0	171.2	172.5	174.9	175.8	176.5
Center	163.7	163.8	164.3	164.9	165.2	165.9	168.8	170.2	171.5	174.1	174.5	175.5
South	160.9	161.5	162.3	162.6	162.5	163.4	164.7	165.8	168.1	170.9	172.6	173.3
Islands	160.8	161.4	161.7	161.6	162.3	163.3	164.6	165.7	167.3	170.1	171.5	172.3
Center-North	164.1	164.4	165.0	165.5	165.9	167.0	169.4	170.6	171.8	174.3	174.9	175.7
South	160.9	161.5	162.1	162.3	162.4	163.4	164.7	165.8	167.9	170.6	172.2	172.9
ITALY	162.9	163.3	163.9	164.4	164.8	165.8	167.6	168.9	170.0	172.8	174.0	174.5

See chapter 2 ("Height") for sources and methods.

Chapter 3

Table 3.A1 **Life expectancy at birth, 1961–2012**

Year	Male	Female	Total
1861	26.0	26.9	26.4
1871	28.8	29.7	29.2
1881	34.0	34.4	34.2
1891	38.5	38.5	38.5
1901	43.3	43.8	43.5
1911	44.5	45.0	44.8
1921	48.5	50.0	49.3
1931	53.7	55.8	54.8
1941	51.3	58.2	54.6
1951	63.5	67.0	65.3
1961	67.2	72.5	69.9
1971	68.9	74.9	71.9
1981	71.1	77.8	74.5
1991	73.6	80.3	77.1
2001	76.8	82.8	80.0
2011	79.5	84.4	81.9
2012	79.6	84.4	81.9

See chapter 3 ("Health") for sources and methods.

Table 3.A2 **Probability of death at different ages**

Age	1872	1881	1891	1901	1911	1921	1931	1941	1951	1961	1971	1981	1991	2001	2006	Total
0	220	212	186	167	144	135	109	106	64	43	28	14	8	4	4	96
1	107	98	73	59	65	56	39	31	11	4	2	1	0	0	0	36
2	84	66	53	42	29	24	14	10	4	2	1	0	0	0	0	22
3	57	42	36	28	16	14	7	5	2	1	1	0	0	0	0	14
4	35	28	24	18	11	10	5	4	2	1	1	0	0	0	0	9
5	23	21	17	12	8	7	4	3	1	1	0	0	0	0	0	6
10	6	6	4	3	3	3	2	2	1	0	0	0	0	0	0	2
15	6	6	5	4	4	4	2	2	1	1	1	0	0	0	0	3
20	9	8	8	6	6	7	4	9	1	1	1	1	1	1	0	4
30	10	9	8	7	6	9	5	6	2	1	1	1	1	1	1	5
40	13	12	10	9	8	8	6	6	3	2	2	2	1	1	1	6
50	18	18	14	13	11	11	10	10	7	6	5	5	3	3	2	9
60	36	35	27	26	23	22	20	19	15	15	13	12	9	7	6	19
70	82	85	66	67	62	56	52	51	41	37	34	30	23	18	16	48
80	151	159	150	144	144	144	138	141	116	102	93	84	65	53	47	115
90	275	269	299	294	268	285	263	302	263	244	223	212	182	159	146	246
100	417	360	457	448	427	456	461	495	441	430	407	402	376	361	342	419
105	480	415	519	503	489	520	528	559	515	509	491	490	474	467	451	494

See chapter 3 ("Health") for sources and methods.

Table 3.A3 Life expectancy at birth by region (total male and female), 1861–2011.

Region	1861	1871	1881	1891	1901	1911	1921	1931	1941	1951	1961	1971	1981	1991	2001	2011
Abruzzi	32.1	33.4	34.2	36.3	40.8	42.6	46.6	54.5	55.4	64.1	69.4	71.6	73.7	77.4	80.3	81.7
Basilicata	28.5	27.6	31.3	30.9	36.8	41.9	41.4	48.8	50.5	60.4	68	71.8	75.3	77.7	79.8	81.4
Calabria	31.2	31.9	33.7	36.8	42.1	45.2	47.7	54.2	54.6	64.4	69.8	73	75.6	78	79.8	81.7
Campania	29.5	31.2	34.4	36.1	40.8	43.7	45.4	53	52.8	63.2	67.2	69.1	72	75.7	78.4	80.2
Emilia-R.	32	32.9	34.7	38.5	43.9	48.1	49.9	57.4	59	66.1	69.5	71	73.8	77.6	80.3	81.9
Friuli-V.G.							53.5	55.5	59.4	70.4	71.1	71.9	73.4	76.6	79.6	81.9
Lazio	36	27.8	32.4	38.5	43.4	47.5	49	53.7	55.5	64.4	69.1	73.1	77.4	78.9	79.6	81.7
Liguria		37.2	37.6	40	45	48.2	51.3	59.7	60.3	67.4	70.5	72.4	75.2	78.5	79.7	81.7
Lombardy	31.5	32.4	35.6	38.8	42	44.9	45.9	52.5	55.9	63.6	67.6	70.3	74.4	78.4	79.7	81.8
Marche	33	35.9	36.5	39.7	43.7	47.3	49.1	58	59.6	66.8	70.8	72.7	74.8	78.4	80.9	82.6
Molise	32.1	33.4	34.2	36.3	40.8	42.6	46.6	54.5	55.4	64.1	69.4	71.6	73.7	77.4	80.3	82
Piedmont	33.5	35.4	37.6	40.5	44.9	48.7	50.8	57.9	58.7	64.7	67.9	70.4	74.9	78.7	79.5	81.5
Puglia	34.9	31.4	34.1	33.4	36.2	40.9	41.4	50.1	52	62	67.1	70.5	73.9	77.6	80	81.7
Sardinia	31	31.4	34.4	37	41.3	44.4	44.4	52.8	54	64.1	69.4	70.9	73.9	77.1	79.8	81.7
Sicily	34.4	32.1	35.8	38.1	40.8	42.3	47	54.1	55.1	66.3	71	72.8	74.5	76.9	79.1	80.8
Tuscany	32.1	33.4	34.2	36.3	40.8	42.6	49.2	59.7	60.1	67.1	70	72	74.3	78.2	80.5	82.4

(continued)

Table 3.A3 Continued

Region	1861	1871	1881	1891	1901	1911	1921	1931	1941	1951	1961	1971	1981	1991	2001	2011
Trentino AA							49.9	53.9	57.6	64.4	68.8	71.9	75.2	78.6	80.4	82.2
Umbria	34.7	36.4	37.1	41.3	44.7	48.8	50.7	59.6	61.3	68.3	71	72.3	73.8	77.6	80.5	82.2
Valle d'Aosta	33.5	35.4	37.6	40.5	44.9	48.7	50.8	57.9	58.7	64.7	67.9	70.4	74.9	78.6	79.1	81.3
Veneto		34.5	37.2	42.4	48.4	49.8	50	57.3	60.9	66	68.4	70	72.1	76.9	80.3	82.2
Northwest	32.9	34.2	36.6	39.6	43.5	46.7	48.3	55.3	57.4	64.5	68.1	70.6	74.7	78.5	79.7	81.7
Northeast	32	33.7	35.9	40.5	46.2	49	50.5	56.8	56.7	66.5	69.2	70.8	73.2	77.3	80.2	82.1
Center	32.6	32.9	34.4	37.8	42.2	45	48.9	57	58	65.9	69.8	72.5	75.6	78.4	80.1	82
South	31.2	31.2	33.9	35.1	39.5	43	44.5	52.2	52.8	62.9	67.8	70.4	73.4	76.8	79.2	81
Islands	33.7	31.9	35.6	37.9	40.9	42.7	46.6	53.8	54.9	65.8	70.6	72.4	74.3	76.9	79.2	81.1
Center-North	32.6	33.7	35.8	39.2	43.7	46.8	49.2	56.3	58.3	65.5	68.9	71.2	74.5	78.1	80	81.9
South	32	31.5	34.5	36.1	40.1	42.9	45.3	52.8	53.6	63.9	68.8	71.1	73.7	76.8	79.2	81
ITALY	29.1	30.4	34.7	38.4	43.2	45.4	45	54.5	55	65	69.4	71.9	74.6	77.3	80	81.5

See chapter 3 ("Health") for sources and methods.

Table 3.A4 **Infant mortality rate by region (total male and female), 1861–2011**

Region	1861	1871	1881	1891	1901	1911	1921	1931	1941	1951	1961	1971	1981	1991	2001	2011
Abruzzi											31.7	23	13.7	8.7	4.4	3.4
Basilicata	234.2	255.8	219.5	212.5	183.1	155.4	160.1	150.3	160.9	104.4	63.6	35.1	14.8	7.9	3.3	4.7
Calabria	213.3	220.1	212.2	189.9	161.8	134.7	130.6	114.7	130.2	77.1	53.7	33	15.5	8.9	5.3	5.4
Campania	195.3	213.7	202.3	189.5	160.6	140.2	135.5	119.9	128.5	76.3	56.7	41.7	17.1	9.8	5.3	4.3
Emilia-Romagna	259.6	254.5	230.5	221.5	182.3	151.8	131.4	92.1	77.6	48.7	31.3	23.3	11.6	6.8	4.2	3.5
Friuli–Venezia Giulia							137.5	116	39.4	47.9	30	20.9	8.8	4.3	2.8	3.7
Lazio		222.3	190.6	161.8	140.6	122.2	106.5	91.3	91.6	52.6	35.3	24.1	12.6	7.9	5.5	4.2
Liguria	209.8	195.9	179.6	165.4	141.5	120.1	102.6	71.3	72.9	44.3	31.9	22.9	12.6	7.8	5.3	2.6
Lombardy	261.4	227.3	202.5	199.4	183.9	165.9	155.8	131.4	111.6	64.3	36.6	23.6	11.8	6.5	3.9	3.3
Marche	253.1	242.6	217.6	199.8	162.2	140.3	130.7	87.4	81.9	49	30.8	19.2	11.5	8.2	4.5	3.1
Molise											45.7	26.3	12.2	7.7	2.3	2
Piedmont	234.7	208.2	188	177.8	157.8	129.6	112.1	88.6	81.4	50.6	37.4	28.1	13.3	6.6	3.6	2.9
Puglia	209.1	224.4	200.1	195.3	180.4	159.3	172.9	139.3	142	87.5	58.1	32.8	16.7	9.3	5.8	4.6
Sardinia	203.9	190.4	166.5	155.2	148.2	125.2	134.8	106.1	106.7	68	44.2	29.1	13.3	7	3.6	2.6
Sicily	219.6	225.7	212.8	201.2	188.3	162.7	156.9	132.4	134.1	72.1	48	33.4	16.6	9.8	6.3	5.1
Tuscany	232.1	212.2	184.6	172.6	145.4	120.8	106.6	74.8	70	44.4	28.5	20.9	11.6	7	3.6	2.6
Trentino–Alto Adige							137.3	114.5	91.3	58.1	35.5	22	9.3	5.8	3.2	3.1
Umbria	249.4	240.2	208.8	192.5	161.7	136.4	125.5	91.3	81.5	47.7	32.5	21	10.1	6.6	3.4	3.1
Valle d'Aosta									112.9	66.8	35.5	29.1	12.6	6	2.6	3.9
Veneto		235.7	199.8	181.6	149.2	137.2	130	89.8	77.3	49.7	30.7	19.9	11.1	5.9	3.4	2.8
ITALY	228.7	223.4	202.3	188.7	166.8	144.5	137.2	110.5	107.1	65.2	42.5	28	13.8	7.9	4.6	3.6

See chapter 3 ("Health") for sources and methods.

Chapter 4

Table 4.A1 **Incidence of child labor, 1881–1961 (percent working children aged 10–14 years out of total children)**

Boys and girls	1881	1901	1911	1921	1931	1936	1951	1961
Piedmont	46.3	46.1	46.5	34.5	30.3	49.3	8.4	3.1
Lombardy	55.5	50.3	43.4	28.7	25.7	36.1	3.9	2.1
Trentino AA	—	52.8	48	32.2	11	34.9	3.5	1.3
Veneto	52.8	51.2	49.2	29	27.3	28.6	12.3	4.2
Friuli VG	—	49	41.3	24.3	13.3	32.9	6.8	2
Liguria	52.7	38.5	31.6	21.6	18.4	31.7	2.8	1.1
Emilia Romagna	55.2	56.1	49.5	35	32.7	35.6	12.7	4.4
Tuscany	66.3	55.8	52.2	35.6	32.6	37.4	13.3	4.4
Umbria	67.4	63.5	54.8	46.2	49.9	41.4	22	6.1
Marche	78.6	65.4	58.4	44.6	45.1	41.9	23.3	8.5
Lazio	60.8	47.1	40.4	27.9	23.8	29	6.1	2.4
Abruzzo e Molise	83.8	61.8	52.3	40.4	32.1	38.4	12.7	4.1
Campania	70.2	48.2	42.4	30.7	24.5	24.7	8.9	3.5
Puglia	76.9	47.9	43.7	31	24	23.5	13.5	5.6
Basilicata	86.1	56.9	51.8	41	37.4	37	18.9	5.1
Calabria	92.7	57.5	52.6	39.6	28	30	11.5	4
Sicily	74.4	39	31.9	24.5	21.5	20.6	9.7	3.4
Sardinia	57.5	35.2	31.5	22.8	21.7	24.3	8.2	2.9
Italy	*64.3*	*49.9*	*44.8*	*31.5*	*27.4*	*32.1*	*10*	*3.6*
Boys								
Piedmont	54	47.1	47.2	34.1	27.3	48.5	9.2	3.5
Lombardy	67.2	51.2	44.4	29.5	25.4	36.1	4.2	2.2
Trentino AA		52.7	49.8	34.1	10.7	38.4	3.9	1.5
Veneto	75.5	55.4	54.1	30.6	25.5	30.1	11.6	4
Friuli VG		52.7	46	24.5	11.3	34.8	5.9	1.8
Liguria	70.7	41.9	35	23.5	18.6	36.4	3.5	1.3
Emilia Romagna	77.5	56.3	50.1	33.9	29.3	37.6	13.3	4.5
Tuscany	88.8	56.5	50.9	34.1	26.1	37.8	12	4.2
Umbria	90	63.2	54.1	40.1	33.9	40	19	5.4
Marche	94.6	67.7	61.9	43.6	37.8	38	22.2	8.1

(continued)

Table 4.A1 **Continued**

Boys and girls	1881	1901	1911	1921	1931	1936	1951	1961
Lazio	82.7	52.5	47.4	31.1	22.9	29.7	6.9	2.7
Abruzzo e Molise	97	68.9	59.9	46.9	32.7	36.8	15.9	4.8
Campania	83.9	56.5	48.4	35.7	26.6	26	10.7	4
Puglia	94.9	66.1	61.5	42.8	33.2	32.7	18.2	6.5
Basilicata	99.6	67	61.3	48.9	43.1	36.6	24.6	6
Calabria	97.3	61	61.7	47.3	34	30.3	14.5	4.7
Sicily	96.8	62.5	51.6	40.1	35.5	33.3	16.9	5.5
Sardinia	94	59.4	52.8	37.6	34.6	38.1	13.3	4.4
Italy	*81.3*	*56.6*	*51.1*	*35.4*	*28.5*	*34.6*	*11.8*	*4.1*
Girls								
Piedmont	38.6	45.1	45.8	34.9	33.5	50.1	7.5	2.8
Lombardy	43.6	49.4	42.4	28	26	36.1	3.5	1.9
Trentino AA		52.8	46	30.4	11.2	31.4	3.1	1.1
Veneto	29.1	46.9	44	27.4	29.3	27.1	13	4.4
Friuli VG		45.3	36.9	24.1	15.1	31	7.7	2.3
Liguria	34.6	35	28.1	19.6	18.2	26.8	2.1	1
Emilia Romagna	32	55.8	48.8	36	36.3	33.6	12.1	4.3
Tuscany	42.6	55	53.5	37.1	39.3	36.9	14.7	4.6
Umbria	42.8	63.8	55.5	52.7	66.8	42.7	25.1	6.8
Marche	61.7	63	54.9	45.6	52.5	46	24.4	9
Lazio	37	41.4	33.3	24.5	24.9	28.3	5.2	1.9
Abruzzo e Molise	70.3	54.5	44.4	33.7	31.4	40	9.4	3.4
Campania	55.9	39.7	36	25.4	22.3	23.5	7.1	2.9
Puglia	57.7	29.1	25.4	18.7	14.6	14	8.8	4.7
Basilicata	72.2	46.7	42	32.8	31.5	37.5	13	4.2
Calabria	87.7	53.8	43.1	31.5	21.8	29.7	8.4	3.2
Sicily	51	13.9	10.5	7.6	6.5	7.3	2.1	1.1
Sardinia	17.9	9.7	9	7.3	8.2	9.9	2.9	1.3
Italy	*46.6*	*43.1*	*38.3*	*27.5*	*26.4*	*29.5*	*8.2*	*3.1*

See chapter 4 ("Child Labor") for sources and methods.

Table 4.A2 Intensity of child labor, 1881–1961 (percent working children aged 10–14 years out of total economically active population)

Boys and Girls	Agriculture	Construction	Manufacture	Commerce	Transports	Credits	Government	Total
1881	12.6	11.7	11.6	4.6	4.6	5.3	4.5	11.0
1901	11.9	9.0	10.6	2.9	2.4	3.8	3.3	10.1
1911	11.5	7.5	9.3	3.2	2.5	4.0	2.8	9.4
1921	8.6	5.3	6.7	2.1	1.8	2.7	2.1	6.9
1931	5.9	3.3	4.1	1.3	1.1	1.8	1.2	4.4
1936	9.8	4.2	6.0	2.2	2.0	2.6	2.2	7.1
1951	3.7	1.1	1.1	0.5	0.4	0.6	0.5	2.1
1961	1.4	0.5	0.6	0.3	0.3	0.3	0.3	0.8
Boys								
1881	13.5	11.8	11.4	4.4	4.6	4.6	4.5	11.4
1901	11.3	9.0	8.7	2.4	2.4	2.4	3.0	9.0
1911	11.1	7.5	7.5	2.5	2.5	2.5	2.4	8.4
1921	7.8	5.3	5.3	1.7	1.7	1.7	1.7	5.9
1931	4.8	3.3	3.3	1.0	1.0	1.0	1.0	3.4
1936	8.8	4.2	4.2	1.9	1.9	1.9	1.9	5.9
1951	3.1	1.1	0.8	0.4	0.4	0.4	0.4	1.7
1961	1.2	0.5	0.4	0.2	0.2	0.2	0.2	0.6

Girls

1881	11.0	11.3	11.9	5.3	5.7	5.9	4.9	10.5
1901	12.9	11.8	13.4	4.9	4.5	5.0	5.1	11.9
1911	12.0	10.6	12.3	5.5	5.4	5.5	5.3	11.1
1921	9.9	8.7	9.3	3.5	3.5	3.7	3.9	8.8
1931	7.8	5.9	5.9	2.5	2.5	2.5	2.5	6.5
1936	11.5	9.5	9.5	3.1	3.1	3.1	3.1	9.3
1951	4.9	2.4	1.7	0.8	0.8	0.8	0.9	3.0
1961	1.9	1.7	1.3	0.4	0.4	0.5	0.5	1.2

See chapter 4 ("Child Labor") for sources and methods.

Chapter 5

Table 5.A1 Literacy rates, population between 15 and 19 years old

	1861	1871	1881	1901	1911	1921	1931	1951	1961	1971	1981	1991	2001
Piedmont	55.7	71.6	83.0	93.9	97.3	98.4	99.3	99.4	99.5	99.7	99.8	99.7	99.9
Liguria	55.7	55.4	70.4	86.4	94.3	97.8	98.7	99.3	99.5	99.7	99.8	99.7	99.9
Lombardy	52.4	65.6	74.7	90.0	95.9	96.3	99.2	99.3	99.6	99.7	99.8	99.7	99.9
Trentino AA						99.2	99.6	99.7	99.7	99.8	99.7	99.8	99.9
Veneto		42.0	57.0	80.3	88.7	93.6	95.8	98.1	99.4	99.6	99.8	99.7	99.9
Emilia-Romagna	22.9	34.3	45.1	69.7	84.7	93.0	95.6	98.4	99.4	99.7	99.8	99.7	99.9
Tuscany	25.7	37.5	45.0	63.2	74.9	85.1	93.4	98.4	99.4	99.7	99.8	99.6	99.9
Umbria	14.7	21.9	30.2	52.1	65.7	80.1	89.5	97.0	99.2	99.6	99.8	99.7	99.9
Marche	16.8	24.5	30.4	48.3	62.5	81.6	91.3	98.0	99.4	99.7	99.8	99.6	99.9
Lazio		30.7	43.0	64.6	76.0	83.7	89.9	96.6	99.2	99.6	99.8	99.4	99.9
Abruzzi-Molise	13.8	17.5	22.5	39.5	57.2	69.6	83.3	93.4	98.8	99.5	99.7	99.5	99.9
Campania	13.8	22.4	27.4	43.2	56.8	68.1	75.9	86.9	95.7	97.9	99.5	99.0	99.8
Puglia	13.8	16.4	21.4	37.6	50.2	62.6	73.3	85.7	95.5	98.4	99.6	99.3	99.9
Basilicata	13.8	13.0	16.3	30.5	45.3	59.5	66.7	84.2	96.5	99.0	99.7	99.4	99.9
Calabria	13.8	14.1	15.4	25.9	38.5	56.9	65.0	81.2	94.6	98.3	99.5	98.6	99.8

Sicily	11.3	15.6	21.4	35.2	53.1	64.4	74.1	85.6	95.1	97.6	99.4	99.0	99.8
Sardinia	11.0	16.0	21.9	35.8	49.3	62.4	75.1	88.6	97.7	99.3	99.7	99.5	99.9
Northwest	52.4	66.8	77.5	91.0	96.2	97.2	99.2	99.4	99.5	99.7	99.8	99.7	99.9
Northeast	22.9	38.5	51.7	75.6	87.0	93.8	96.0	98.3	99.5	99.7	99.8	99.7	99.9
Center	21.6	31.5	40.0	59.3	71.8	83.6	91.5	97.5	99.3	99.6	99.8	99.5	99.9
South	13.8	18.2	22.5	37.7	51.5	64.7	73.9	86.3	95.8	98.3	99.5	99.1	99.8
Islands	11.2	15.7	21.5	35.3	52.4	64.1	74.3	86.3	95.8	98.1	99.5	99.1	99.8
Center-North	33.8	49.6	59.8	78.1	86.9	92.7	96.0	98.4	99.4	99.7	99.8	99.6	99.9
South	13.0	17.4	22.2	36.9	51.8	64.5	74.0	86.3	95.8	98.3	99.5	99.1	99.8
Italy	26.5	37.0	45.4	61.9	73.4	82.0	88.2	93.4	97.9	99.1	99.7	99.4	99.9

See chapter 5 ("Education") for sources and methods.

Table 5.A2 Literacy rates, population 15 years old and older

	1861	1871	1881	1901	1911	1921	1931	1951	1961	1971	1981	1991	2001
Piedmont	50.6	58.0	66.2	79.9	88.3	93.2	95.8	97.4	98.0	98.3	98.8	99.0	99.2
Liguria	34.9	43.8	54.1	71.3	82.1	89.9	92.4	95.5	97.2	98.1	98.9	99.2	99.4
Lombardy	48.7	56.1	62.2	76.4	85.9	91.3	95.1	97.2	98.3	98.8	99.2	99.4	99.5
Trentino AA						98.4	98.9	99.2	99.5	99.6	99.7	99.7	99.7
Veneto		36.3	44.6	62.0	73.2	84.8	87.2	93.4	96.1	98.0	98.9	99.3	99.5
Emilia-Romagna	24.1	28.5	34.9	50.6	64.0	76.9	82.6	90.9	94.5	96.9	98.3	99.0	99.3
Tuscany	27.9	34.2	39.9	52.2	62.2	71.8	79.6	87.7	92.2	95.3	97.5	98.6	99.1
Umbria	17.9	21.0	26.6	38.3	48.5	61.5	69.7	83.7	89.4	93.5	96.4	98.0	98.8
Marche	18.5	21.8	26.0	36.2	46.2	62.0	69.5	84.0	89.8	93.8	97.0	98.3	99.1
Lazio		34.8	42.8	55.4	66.2	74.4	78.4	88.4	92.8	95.6	97.5	98.5	99.0
Abruzzi-Molise	13.0	15.6	19.4	28.7	39.1	53.6	60.4	77.4	84.7	89.6	94.0	96.3	97.9
Campania	18.2	20.9	25.0	34.2	45.2	58.8	60.7	73.6	82.4	87.7	93.1	95.2	96.9
Puglia	14.6	16.3	20.0	29.7	38.9	49.1	55.7	72.4	81.6	87.9	93.0	96.0	97.0
Basilicata	11.0	12.7	14.7	22.8	32.2	45.6	48.3	66.3	75.8	83.1	89.3	92.5	95.4
Calabria	12.1	13.5	15.7	21.1	29.7	45.3	46.0	63.3	74.1	81.2	88.4	91.8	94.7
Sicily	12.7	15.1	19.1	28.3	40.3	48.8	55.4	72.2	81.4	87.1	92.6	95.2	96.8
Sardinia	10.8	14.7	20.8	31.4	40.0	51.0	59.4	74.0	83.2	89.0	93.9	96.4	97.9

Northwest	47.9	55.4	62.9	77.1	86.3	91.8	95.0	97.0	98.1	98.6	99.1	99.2	99.4
Northeast	24.1	32.8	40.3	56.9	69.1	83.1	86.4	92.8	95.7	97.7	98.7	99.2	99.4
Center	23.9	30.1	36.0	48.1	58.5	69.5	76.7	87.0	91.9	95.1	97.4	98.5	99.0
South	15.0	17.2	20.8	29.5	39.6	52.8	56.2	71.7	80.8	86.8	92.3	95.0	96.6
Islands	12.3	15.0	19.4	28.9	40.3	49.2	56.2	72.6	81.8	87.6	92.9	95.5	97.1
Center-North	37.1	41.9	49.0	63.4	73.9	83.3	87.4	92.9	95.6	97.3	98.5	99.0	99.3
South	14.2	16.6	20.3	29.3	39.8	51.6	56.2	72.0	81.1	87.0	92.5	95.1	96.8
Italy	26.9	32.1	37.8	50.1	60.9	72.0	77.0	85.6	90.7	93.9	96.5	97.7	98.4

See chapter 5 ("Education") for sources and methods.

Table 5.A3 Gross primary enrollment rates, population between 6 and 10 years old

	1861	1871	1881	1901	1931	1951	1961	1971	1981	1991	2001
Piedmont	107.7	116.0	110.3	117.0	119.1	120.5	115.2	111.2	101.3	101.5	102.5
Liguria	57.3	78.5	92.5	102.9	117.0	118.1	114.6	109.0	99.9	101.7	104.4
Lombardy	92.9	93.3	100.1	104.2	118.7	118.2	110.3	109.9	100.2	101.3	101.7
Trentino–Alto Adige					125.9	104.4	111.7	108.9	99.8	100.1	99.0
Veneto		72.0	88.5	95.0	116.3	124.8	113.1	107.7	100.2	100.8	101.0
Emilia-Romagna	34.2	50.9	68.5	87.6	114.7	120.9	110.6	107.3	100.1	101.2	102.1
Tuscany	33.8	52.0	51.3	71.3	110.0	118.2	111.1	108.9	100.2	101.3	102.8
Umbria	23.2	40.1	61.6	68.0	103.0	120.6	112.9	107.2	99.2	100.6	102.9
Marche	25.5	39.8	48.8	62.5	104.3	118.7	108.1	106.3	100.1	100.9	100.8
Lazio		52.1	65.8	84.2	107.0	120.1	110.9	108.1	101.1	104.6	106.0
Abruzzi-Molise	18.9	41.8	50.6	56.7	103.4	128.7	112.6	107.2	99.2	99.2	101.1
Campania	21.3	45.6	53.1	57.9	93.0	114.1	109.1	110.8	97.4	102.3	101.2
Puglia	16.9	31.4	36.3	51.0	86.4	104.2	107.1	107.9	100.8	99.9	101.3
Basilicata	11.5	37.0	37.5	45.4	81.5	117.0	113.2	106.5	96.3	101.7	99.2
Calabria	19.2	27.8	36.6	37.9	79.2	119.2	118.8	109.6	97.9	97.2	97.4
Sicily	9.5	23.7	33.3	53.1	89.7	110.1	110.3	111.2	101.6	103.3	102.9
Sardinia	30.3	40.1	53.2	58.3	104.3	123.1	118.0	111.7	102.2	102.4	101.2

Northwest	94.7	100.8	103.4	108.9	118.6	118.8	112.2	110.2	100.5	101.4	102.1
Northeast	34.2	62.6	80.2	91.8	116.7	121.0	112.1	107.7	100.1	100.8	101.2
Center	30.0	48.0	54.8	71.8	107.3	119.3	110.7	108.0	100.6	102.9	104.2
South	18.9	38.3	45.1	51.9	89.8	114.0	110.8	109.2	98.6	100.5	100.6
Islands	13.4	26.8	37.0	54.0	92.6	113.6	112.2	111.4	101.8	103.1	102.5
Center-North	67.2	75.4	84.2	93.7	114.7	119.7	111.7	108.8	100.4	101.7	102.5
South	17.1	34.6	42.4	52.6	90.7	113.9	111.3	109.9	99.6	101.3	101.2
Italy	44.7	59.5	67.4	77.5	106.5	117.2	111.5	109.3	100.1	101.5	101.9

See chapter 5 ("Education") for sources and methods.

Table 5.A4 **Number of students per teacher, Italy 1861–2001**

Year	Students per teacher
1861	35.8
1871	39.6
1881	41.0
1889	40.9
1901	41.6
1907	47.5
1931	44.4
1941	39.6
1951	26.2
1961	22.0
1971	20.7
1982	15.2
1991	10.6
2001	9.6

See chapter 5 ("Education") for sources and methods.

Chapter 6

Table 6.A1　**Emigrants, Returnees and Migration Rate, 1871–2013**

Year	Emigrants	Returnees	Net Balance	Migration Rate
1871	122,479			4.6
1881	135,832			4.7
1891	293,631			9.5
1901	533,245			16.2
1911	533,844	2,02,435	−331,409	15.0
1921	201,291	1,23,999	−77,292	5.5
1931	165,860	1,07,730	−58,130	4.0
1941	8,809	46,066	37,257	0.2
1951	293,057	91,904	−201,153	6.2
1961	387,123	2,10,196	−176,927	7.7
1971	167,721	1,28,572	−39,149	3.1
1981	89,221	88,886	−335	1.6
1991	51,478	56,004	4,526	0.9
2001	46,901	35,416	−11,485	0.8
2011	82,461	31,466	−50,995	2.7
2013	125,735	28,433	−97,302	19.7

See chapter 6 ("Migration") for sources and methods.

Table 6.A2 **Destination of Italian Emigrants (percent), 1881–2013**

Year	US	Argentina	Brazil	Australia	Europe	Rest of the world
1881	0.08	0.12	0.05	0.00	0.68	0.07
1891	0.15	0.08	0.37	0.00	0.35	0.04
1901	0.23	0.11	0.15	0.00	0.46	0.05
1911	0.36	0.06	0.04	0.00	0.49	0.04
1921	0.34	0.17	0.04	0.01	0.40	0.05
1931	0.10	0.11	0.01	0.00	0.68	0.10
1940	0.05	0.01	0.00	0.01	0.91	0.01
1951	0.03	0.19	0.03	0.06	0.51	0.18
1961	0.04	0.01	0.01	0.04	0.85	0.05
1971	0.09	0.01	0.00	0.04	0.79	0.07
1981	0.05	0.01	0.01	0.02	0.77	0.15
1991	0.08	0.03	0.01	0.02	0.76	0.10
2001	0.07	0.05	0.02	0.01	0.64	0.21
2011	0.05	0.02	0.03	0.01	0.67	0.22
2013	0.04	0.01	0.03	0.01	0.70	0.19

See chapter 6 ("Migration") for sources and methods.

Table 6.A3 **Origin of Italian Emigrants (percent), 1881–2013**

Year	North West	North East	Center	South and Islands
1881	0.39	0.25	0.07	0.29
1891	0.18	0.45	0.04	0.32
1901	0.16	0.28	0.12	0.44
1911	0.25	0.27	0.16	0.32
1921	0.30	0.23	0.11	0.35
1931	0.36	0.32	0.12	0.20
1941	0.04	0.90	0.03	0.03
1951	0.15	0.35	0.12	0.38
1961	0.07	0.17	0.10	0.66
1971	0.12	0.18	0.07	0.63
1981	0.18	0.23	0.08	0.51
1991	0.17	0.15	0.19	0.49
2001	0.22	0.16	0.14	0.49
2011	0.32	0.27	0.19	0.23
2013	0.32	0.25	0.19	0.24

See chapter 6 ("Migration") for sources and methods.

Table 6.A4 **Italian Internal Migration Rates, 1901–2013**

Year	Total flow (from civil registry records)	Total flow (declared changes of residence)	Interregional flows
1902	14.8		
1911	18.6		
1921	15.2		
1931	25.6		
1941	24.7		
1951	20.8		
1961		34.4	21.4
1971		28.3	18.0
1981		22.8	16.0
1991		18.3	13.2
2001		19.9	14.3
2011		22.8	17.3
2013		22.8	17.2

See chapter 6 ("Migration") for sources and methods.

Chapter 7

Table 7.A1 Per-capita GDP, Italy 1861–2013

GDP per capita			GDP per capita			GDP per capita			GDP per capita		
Year	Current prices	Constant prices (2013)	Year	Current prices	Constant prices (2013)	Year	Current prices	Constant prices (2013)	Year	Current prices	Constant prices (2013)
	(Euro)	(Euro)		(Euro)	(Euro)		(Euro)	(Euro)		(Euro)	(Euro)
1861	0.170	2031	1901	0.217	2640	1941	2.916	3821	1981	4329	18756
1862	0.171	2057	1902	0.216	2682	1942	3.621	3585	1982	5106	18822
1863	0.167	2107	1903	0.224	2706	1943	4.914	3029	1983	5943	19030
1864	0.166	2110	1904	0.225	2754	1944	9.779	2497	1984	6795	19643
1865	0.176	2237	1905	0.233	2810	1945	18.217	2263	1985	7623	20184
1866	0.186	2233	1906	0.254	2905	1946	40.921	3080	1986	8428	20758
1867	0.177	2039	1907	0.271	2957	1947	78.223	3634	1987	9220	21421
1868	0.187	2080	1908	0.267	3020	1948	92.288	3925	1988	10244	22309
1869	0.179	2107	1909	0.275	3044	1949	95.619	4195	1989	11238	23047
1870	0.181	2159	1910	0.285	3047	1950	107.720	4541	1990	12426	23503
1871	0.182	2111	1911	0.313	3080	1951	127.097	4959	1991	13560	23845

1872	0.193	2064	1912	0.328	3096	1952	136.659	5158	1992	14260	24028
1873	0.214	2053	1913	0.342	3245	1953	150.879	5500	1993	14676	23803
1874	0.217	2160	1914	0.323	3078	1954	160.171	5668	1994	15517	24306
1875	0.186	2171	1915	0.354	2911	1955	175.501	6015	1995	16750	25007
1876	0.182	2118	1916	0.500	3147	1956	190.379	6272	1996	17753	25290
1877	0.203	2131	1917	0.719	3165	1957	203.797	6592	1997	18537	25748
1878	0.200	2185	1918	0.999	3097	1958	218.482	6925	1998	19297	26108
1879	0.191	2191	1919	1.103	2994	1959	230.983	7368	1999	19926	26484
1880	0.202	2225	1920	1.544	3050	1960	249.522	7837	2000	21051	27445
1881	0.199	2292	1921	1.538	2930	1961	278.501	8406	2001	22046	27938
1882	0.203	2320	1922	1.622	3148	1962	310.950	8913	2002	22845	28051
1883	0.194	2342	1923	1.735	3400	1963	355.178	9388	2003	23487	27968
1884	0.186	2306	1924	1.748	3459	1964	388.005	9672	2004	24310	28271
1885	0.198	2340	1925	2.157	3686	1965	414.837	10020	2005	24819	28348
1886	0.207	2391	1926	2.294	3688	1966	449.203	10605	2006	25713	28876
1887	0.199	2452	1927	1.987	3566	1967	494.879	11339	2007	26694	29282
1888	0.196	2439	1928	1.985	3746	1968	533.484	12083	2008	26855	28732

(continued)

Table 7.A1 Continued

	GDP per capita			GDP per capita			GDP per capita			GDP per capita	
	Current prices	Constant prices (2013)	Year	Current prices	Constant prices (2013)	Year	Current prices	Constant prices (2013)	Year	Current prices	Constant prices (2013)
Year	(Euro)	(Euro)		(Euro)	(Euro)		(Euro)	(Euro)		(Euro)	(Euro)
1889	0.203	2365	1929	2.008	3904	1969	586.452	12799	2009	25757	26993
1890	0.211	2366	1930	1.753	3694	1970	659.094	13495	2010	26219	27369
1891	0.210	2398	1931	1.545	3612	1971	715.734	13672	2011	26614	27424
1892	0.196	2401	1932	1.438	3656	1972	780.744	14112	2012	26382	26762
1893	0.193	2438	1933	1.307	3590	1973	935.983	15003	2013	26138	26138
1894	0.188	2452	1934	1.300	3557	1974	1179.142	15724			
1895	0.198	2472	1935	1.434	3732	1975	1342.484	15299			
1896	0.200	2509	1936	1.476	3571	1976	1679.032	16291			
1897	0.200	2513	1937	1.844	3894	1977	2031.034	16629			
1898	0.203	2503	1938	1.992	3970	1978	2380.602	17101			
1899	0.209	2531	1939	2.152	4133	1979	2902.668	18056			
1900	0.213	2597	1940	2.478	3954	1980	3618.073	18625			

See chapter 7 ("Income") for sources and methods.

Table 7.A2 The pace of growth in Italy and elsewhere, 1861–2013

Years	ITALY	France	Germany	Spain	Sweden	United Kingdom	United States	Canada	Brazil	Argentina	China	India	EU15	OCSE
1861–1870	0.68	0.65	1.68		1.55	1.13	1.16	1.57	0.20		-0.62	0.00	1.10	1.20
1870–1880	0.30	1.23	0.80		1.13	0.86	2.68	0.69	0.54	2.51	0.10	0.23	1.14	1.65
1880–1890	0.62	1.14	2.00		1.53	1.43	0.63	2.74	0.54	2.51	0.10	0.69	1.41	1.37
1890–1900	0.94	1.93	2.09	0.96	2.25	1.14	1.89	2.04	-1.55	2.50	0.09	0.25	1.58	1.73
1900–1910	1.61	0.31	1.15	0.59	2.31	0.26	1.95	3.40	1.26	3.32	0.10	1.52	0.73	1.39
1910–1920	0.01	0.85		1.40	1.15	-0.14	1.13	-0.51	2.28	-0.95	0.11	-0.92	-0.35	0.54
1920–1930	1.93	3.45	3.58	1.87	3.30	1.81	1.13	2.22	0.85	1.62	0.19	1.34	2.80	1.88
1930–1940	0.68	-1.14	3.12	-2.28	1.87	2.34	1.21	1.10	1.77	0.20	-0.47	-0.56	1.21	1.37
1940–1950	1.39	2.52	-3.25	0.51	2.71	0.12	3.15	3.11	2.95	1.83	-1.88	-1.03	-0.10	1.21
1950–1960	5.61	3.62	7.05	3.45	2.57	2.22	1.71	1.84	3.40	1.09	3.98	1.98	3.89	2.96
1960–1970	5.59	4.43	3.50	7.48	3.88	2.22	2.87	3.25	2.73	2.76	1.63	1.43	3.85	3.76
1970–1980	3.27	2.61	2.56	3.83	1.62	1.85	2.14	2.59	5.45	1.17	3.15	0.78	2.51	2.42
1980–1990	2.35	1.80	1.93	2.74	1.66	2.42	2.25	1.55	-0.54	-2.40	5.84	3.38	2.08	2.13
1990–2000	1.56	1.46	1.58	2.69	1.71	2.23	2.15	1.77	0.97	2.72	6.22	3.70	2.07	1.96
2000–2010	-0.21	0.55	1.00	0.69	1.88	0.88	0.66	1.04	2.26	2.00	10.82	5.98	0.92	1.06
2010–2013	-1.32	0.23	1.67	-1.63	1.63	0.30	1.39	1.08	0.98	2.12	7.64	3.73	-0.09	0.94

See chapter 7 ("Income") for sources and methods.

Table 7.A3 **Per-capita GDP of the regions, Italy 1871–2011 (Euro 2013)**

	1871	1891	1911	1931	1938	1951	1961	1971	1981	1991	2001	2011
Piedmont	2181	2592	3551	4487	5511	7275	11096	16543	21926	27279	32073	29893
Valle d'Aosta						7836	14912	18511	23464	28901	34615	36941
Liguria	2930	3451	4737	5939	6666	8014	11003	15886	20463	27684	30397	29152
Lombardy	2341	2762	3674	4451	5519	7593	12357	18293	24458	29997	36292	35515
Trentino–Alto Adige				3309	3776	5247	9784	13849	21063	28614	36152	35103
Veneto	2134	1921	2658	2695	3335	4865	8826	13549	20238	26850	31598	31483
Friuli–Venezia Giulia				4559	4713	5525	7733	13713	20444	27684	31291	30825
Emilia-Romagna	2004	2535	3323	3948	4133	5545	9515	15586	24177	28710	34252	33567
Tuscany	2217	2448	3000	3833	4006	5212	8927	14382	20650	25252	30425	29838
Marche	1733	2105	2495	2572	3129	4250	7347	12427	19731	24394	27687	27781
Umbria	2096	2434	2843	3605	3800	4468	7162	12674	18325	22343	26709	25477
Lazio	3089	3755	4595	5050	4725	5302	9692	14601	19563	27565	31514	31812
Abruzzo	1685	1621	2094	2290	2307	2881	5632	11320	16243	21151	23664	23448
Molise							5111	9529	13936	17407	23189	21254
Campania	2263	2324	2901	2941	3256	3432	6002	9734	12529	16787	18244	17360
Puglia	1883	2439	2621	3078	2851	3224	5741	10267	13561	17622	18746	18320
Basilicata	1412	1774	2261	2536	2251	2336	4943	10240	12829	14307	20339	19362

Calabria	1461	1599	2159	2027	1941	2326	4598	9119	12060	14236	17964	17908
Sicily	1987	2225	2621	2973	2851	2881	4334	9584	12717	16620	18439	17936
Sardinia	1647	2247	2827	3089	3279	3124	6061	11593	13336	18242	21289	21199
North West	2346	2774	3757	4667	5677	7558	11319	17486	22864	28924	34504	33348
North East	2075	2192	2941	3392	3803	5237	9036	14355	21851	27804	32995	32525
Center	2267	2664	3237	4003	4097	5049	8885	14109	19975	25991	30313	30523
South	1889	2072	2544	2695	2728	3050	5590	9953	13148	16954	18970	18457
Sicily and Sardinia	1919	2235	2658	2998	2950	2931	5195	10062	13354	17026	19138	18758
Center-North	2246	2578	3378	4057	4613	6100	10121	15599	21720	27732	32799	32333
South	1898	2127	2581	2796	2803	3010	5455	9980	13223	16978	19026	18539
ITALY	2111	2398	3080	3612	3970	4959	8406	13672	18756	23845	27938	27424

See chapter 7 ("Income") for sources and methods.

Table 7.A4 Per-capita GDP of the regions corrected for purchasing power parities, Italy

	1931	1938	1951	1961	1971	1981	1991	2001	2011
Piedmont	3597	4523	7528	11169	15590	21564	26539	30913	29093
Valle d'Aosta	5080	5813	7499	15002	18529	22437	26402	32175	35203
Liguria	5080	5813	7364	9950	14047	18153	23744	26652	26469
Lombardy	4030	4901	6793	11353	16043	21763	25731	31097	32090
Trentino–Alto Adige	2825	3423	5068	9473	13014	18203	26040	32133	31454
Veneto	2825	3423	5253	9718	14092	20951	27500	31102	32237
Friuli–Venezia Giulia	4332	4614	5615	8204	14042	19704	26078	29049	29217
Emilia-Romagna	3691	3823	5290	9387	14028	22250	26008	30885	31862
Tuscany	4181	4460	4340	7729	12000	17559	21766	26504	31696
Marche	2656	3313	4002	6886	11603	20397	25084	28259	25793
Umbria	3714	4066	3576	6193	10031	15955	20437	24870	24472
Lazio	3599	3392	4632	8119	12029	17174	24930	27942	28971
Abruzzo	2433	2467	2814	5576	11057	16270	22188	25543	25667
Molise				4948	9009	14186	19459	26682	23370
Campania	3076	3267	3729	6490	10046	14117	18797	20171	20942
Puglia	3211	2982	3449	6065	11054	14747	18720	20224	20518
Basilicata	3038	2863	1995	4572	9008	13369	15733	23698	22650

Calabria	3372		2705	5039	9892	13724	16374	20832	21315
Sicily		3295	2719	4545	8978	12594	16954	19622	19859
Sardinia	3288	3634	3149	5999	11817	13820	19708	23340	23938
North West	4028	4905	7092	11142	16259	20953	25737	30656	30786
North East	3349	3712	5309	9391	14669	21126	26658	30944	31713
Center	3744	3859	4350	7672	12103	17715	23556	27334	28652
South	2849	2846	3244	5901	10854	14446	18647	20991	20641
Sicily and Sardinia	3358	3380	2807	4866	9619	13374	17617	20516	18758
Center-North	3734	4241	5721	9571	14553	20015	25349	29736	30484
South	2997	2998	3094	5536	10423	14098	18309	20839	20733
ITALY	3506	3853	4813	8158	13263	18202	23141	27113	25740

See chapter 7 ("Income") for sources and methods

Chapter 8

Table 8.A1 Inequality in Italy, 1861–2012

Year	Gini	S1	S2	S3	S4	S5	Top10	Top5	Top1	Q1	Q2	Q3	Q4	Q5
1861	50.4	4.9	8.1	11.9	18.6	56.5	41.5	30.1	13.9	511.4	762.8	921.8	1127.3	1893.3
1871	45.0	5.4	9.2	13.6	20.7	51.1	35.2	23.7	8.9	585.3	886.0	1070.3	1301.8	2110.4
1881	47.1	5.5	8.9	12.7	19.2	53.7	38.6	27.5	12.1	652.0	946.8	1130.2	1364.2	2217.6
1891	47.3	5.7	9.0	12.6	18.7	54.0	39.6	28.8	13.5	682.5	968.6	1143.6	1366.0	2180.5
1901	48.5	4.6	8.4	12.7	20.1	54.2	38.1	26.2	10.4	638.7	1000.9	1228.1	1518.0	2559.9
1911	46.0	5.0	8.9	13.4	20.8	51.8	35.6	23.9	8.3	750.5	1167.1	1423.1	1744.8	2867.0
1921	45.1	5.9	9.5	13.3	19.4	51.9	37.2	26.4	11.3	939.0	1341.5	1581.2	1880.5	2944.7
1931	44.9	4.6	9.0	14.1	22.2	50.1	33.1	21.1	6.9	829.4	1361.8	1686.0	2087.4	3427.4
1948	41.6	6.8	10.6	14.0	19.3	49.3	35.3	25.3	11.6	972.5	1314.6	1502.5	1731.8	2549.7
1967	39.1	5.9	11.2	15.7	21.7	45.5	30.4	20.2	7.8	1802.1	2703.2	3159.9	3678.2	5287.3
1968	40.8	5.6	10.3	15.0	22.1	46.9	30.8	19.8	6.8	1701.9	2602.3	3119.3	3740.7	5745.3
1969	39.7	6.0	10.7	15.3	21.8	46.1	30.5	19.9	7.3	1975.9	2947.0	3484.0	4119.2	6147.9
1970	38.3	6.0	10.9	15.8	22.8	44.5	28.4	17.7	5.7	1996.8	3035.0	3615.4	4299.5	6422.4
1971	39.7	5.5	10.7	15.7	22.6	45.5	29.5	18.9	6.5	2026.2	3158.6	3774.4	4490.6	6697.8
1972	38.5	5.9	11.1	15.9	22.3	44.8	29.1	18.8	6.6	2220.2	3362.4	3969.0	4668.3	6817.8

1973	40.0	5.8	10.7	15.3	21.9	46.3	30.7	20.0	7.3	2794.0	4212.2	4993.6	5915.4	8848.1
1974	39.1	5.6	10.7	15.8	23.0	45.0	28.6	17.7	5.6	2789.8	4363.7	5244.4	6280.0	9467.8
1975	35.2	6.5	11.8	16.7	23.1	41.9	26.1	16.0	5.0	3130.6	4661.0	5474.2	6404.0	9159.5
1977	34.9	7.1	12.0	16.3	22.2	42.3	27.2	17.3	5.9	3641.6	5174.4	5982.5	6913.2	9770.3
1978	33.3	7.3	12.6	16.8	22.3	40.9	26.1	16.5	5.7	3980.4	5590.8	6399.5	7309.1	10038.6
1979	34.6	7.0	12.2	16.5	22.2	42.0	27.1	17.3	6.1	4075.3	5786.4	6654.9	7638.6	10629.3
1980	32.5	7.8	12.6	16.7	22.2	40.7	25.8	16.2	5.4	4424.5	6077.5	6945.6	7943.4	10990.0
1981	31.9	8.0	12.8	16.8	22.1	40.2	25.5	16.1	5.5	4325.4	5899.0	6702.7	7616.2	10390.4
1982	29.5	8.6	13.2	17.2	22.6	38.3	23.5	14.2	4.3	4675.0	6274.7	7117.9	8081.9	10951.8
1983	30.1	8.3	13.2	17.3	22.7	38.5	23.7	14.4	4.5	4672.8	6368.3	7234.8	8210.7	11074.4
1984	31.9	7.8	12.8	16.9	22.4	40.0	25.1	15.6	5.1	4731.9	6521.9	7446.7	8498.4	11655.5
1986	31.0	7.9	13.0	17.3	22.7	39.1	24.2	14.8	4.7	4566.7	6327.4	7221.9	8226.5	11167.3
1987	32.2	7.5	12.8	17.1	22.7	39.9	24.9	15.4	5.0	4874.8	6856.9	7857.3	8978.3	12270.3
1989	29.6	8.5	13.3	17.3	22.7	38.2	23.4	14.2	4.3	5762.2	7800.8	8859.9	10061.0	13595.8
1991	29.3	8.3	13.5	17.6	22.9	37.8	23.0	13.9	4.2	5911.0	8057.2	9137.8	10342.8	13814.5
1993	32.7	7.0	12.7	17.3	23.1	39.9	24.8	15.2	4.8	5220.5	7563.8	8725.7	10009.1	13686.1
1995	33.2	6.9	12.6	17.2	22.9	40.4	25.2	15.6	5.1	5245.1	7602.7	8773.8	10071.2	13821.8
1998	33.6	6.8	12.6	17.1	22.6	40.8	25.8	16.3	5.6	5606.1	8136.0	9346.0	10666.0	14494.0

(continued)

Table 8.A1 Continued

Year	Gini	S1	S2	S3	S4	S5	Top10	Top5	Top1	Q1	Q2	Q3	Q4	Q5
2000	33.3	6.9	12.6	17.1	22.8	40.5	25.4	15.8	5.2	5864.4	8489.6	9789.2	11228.0	15398.6
2002	33.3	7.0	12.6	17.1	22.7	40.6	25.6	16.0	5.4	6196.7	8918.2	10256.4	11736.8	16056.2
2004	34.9	6.8	12.2	16.6	22.3	42.0	27.0	17.2	6.0	6450.4	9304.6	10739.2	12351.7	17191.7
2006	33.8	7.1	12.4	16.8	22.5	41.2	26.1	16.4	5.5	6869.1	9828.9	11324.1	13004.1	17996.1
2008	33.3	7.1	12.5	17.0	22.8	40.6	25.4	15.8	5.1	6858.2	9834.0	11345.6	13042.6	18027.5
2010	34.7	6.4	12.2	17.0	23.0	41.3	26.0	16.2	5.4	6502.6	9696.8	11279.1	13026.5	18067.1
2012	35.0	6.2	12.2	17.1	23.2	41.4	25.9	16.1	5.3	5727.7	8686.4	10140.0	11732.4	16264.7

See chapter 8 ("Inequality") for sources and methods.

Chapter 9

Table 9.A1 **Absolute poverty lines (Euro2010/person/year), 1861–2012**

Year	Food poverty line	Total poverty line
1861	546.4	820.7
1871	598.4	869.9
1881	622.9	884.3
1891	626.1	901.5
1901	608.4	872.2
1911	665.9	956.0
1921	759.4	1080.8
1931	688.5	1071.9
1948	821.0	1205.9
1967	1054.9	1699.8
1968	1056.0	1705.4
1969	1086.6	1760.2
1970	1153.2	1965.1
1971	1165.4	2047.8
1972	1161.1	2085.6
1973	1207.4	2215.6
1974	1243.8	2350.6
1975	1241.6	2405.9
1977	1310.1	2656.0
1978	1431.8	2897.8
1979	1450.4	3083.5
1980	1495.8	3392.2
1981	1250.1	2897.0
1982	1313.5	3046.5
1983	1293.8	3073.6
1984	1266.6	3121.5
1986	1229.5	3206.7
1987	1234.1	3341.7
1989	1221.9	3568.8
1991	1184.6	3622.3

(*continued*)

Table 9.A1 **Continued**

Year	Food poverty line	Total poverty line
1993	1210.5	3793.4
1995	1194.6	3950.3
1998	1162.8	4022.7
2000	1187.1	4245.2
2002	1185.3	4218.8
2004	1202.6	4276.0
2006	1220.7	4377.7
2008	1215.9	4363.7
2010	1214.6	4308.6
2012	1185.7	4171.6

See chapter 9 ("Poverty") for sources and methods.

Table 9.A2 **Absolute poverty incidence (percent of the population), 1861–2012**

Year	Italy	Center-North	South
1861	43.9	37.4	51.9
1871	39.1	34.8	45.1
1881	36.1	34.6	38.1
1891	35.6	31.4	42.0
1901	33.3	29.1	40.2
1911	30.4	22.5	43.4
1921	27.3	19.8	39.2
1931	29.7	26.9	35.0
1948	33.7		
1967	18.0	12.5	32.8
1968	20.1	14.5	29.9
1969	15.8	10	27.9
1970	19.4	12.9	29.9
1971	20.4	14.4	32.8
1972	17.8	12.8	27.8

(continued)

Table 9.A2 **Continued**

Year	Italy	Center-North	South
1973	12.5	8.5	20.7
1974	14.6	10.1	22.2
1975	11.6	7.3	18
1977	7.0	4.4	12
1978	7.2	4.2	12.8
1979	8.4	4.7	15.3
1980	7.5	4.1	14.9
1981	4.6	2.4	9
1982	3.8	2.3	6.6
1983	4.4	2.7	7.7
1984	4.5	2.5	8.9
1986	5.8	3.3	10.0
1987	5.8	3.8	9.8
1989	3.1	1.7	6.1
1991	3.4	1.5	7.3
1993	7.5	4.2	14.6
1995	8.1	4.1	16.1
1998	7.7	3.6	15.6
2000	7.4	3.3	15.2
2002	6.1	2.3	13.0
2004	5.3	2.3	11.9
2006	4.9	2.5	9.9
2008	4.5	2.3	9.6
2010	6.2	3.4	12.0
2012	7.9	5.7	12.5

See chapter 9 ("Poverty") for sources and methods.

Chapter 10

Table 10.A1 **Private Wealth and Saving Rates in Italy, 1861–2011**

Year	Private Wealth (billion €)	Private Wealth, costant prices (billion 2013 €)	Wealth Per Capita (2013 €)	Beta Ratio (W/Y)	Saving rate
1861	0.02	232.04	10461	6.62	1.39
1871	0.02	216.52	7930	4.94	5.28
1881	0.04	297.12	10262	6.25	-2.18
1891	0.04	336.28	10792	6.26	5.63
1901	0.04	346.54	10445	5.58	13.39
1911	0.05	416.05	11566	4.77	11.84
1921	0.20	364.79	9479	3.42	10.38
1931	0.24	467.85	11169	3.70	5.27
1938	0.31	552.34	12491	2.60	12.20
1951	27.00	892.28	18769	4.49	12.00
1961	48.67	1215.06	23966	3.50	19.81
1971	123.07	2058.19	37982	3.19	21.19
1981	1092.47	4348.05	76924	4.47	23.73
1991	3784.09	6686.49	117776	4.92	21.39
2001	6848.43	8738.60	153326	5.45	16.69

See chapter 10 ("Wealth") for sources and methods.

Chapter 11

Table 11.A1 Vulnerability and poverty in Italy, 1980–2010

	1980			1990			2000			2010		
	Poor	Not poor	Total	Poor	Not poor	Total	Poor	Not poor	Total	Poor	Not poor	Total
Vulnerable	39.61	60.39	100	18.63	81.37	100	25.10	74.90	100	27.89	72.11	100
Not vulnerable	10.37	89.63	100	3.55	96.45	100	3.27	96.73	100	3.05	96.96	100
Total	22.12	77.88	100	10.21	89.79	100	11.29	88.71	100	10.99	89.01	100
Vulnerable	71.94	31.15	40.17	80.57	40.00	44.14	81.70	31.03	36.75	81.15	25.91	31.98
Not vulnerable	28.06	68.85	59.83	19.43	60.00	55.86	18.30	68.97	63.25	18.85	74.09	68.02
Total	100	100	100	100	100	100	100	100	100	100	100	100

See chapter 11 ("Vulnerability") for sources and methods.

Chapter 12

Table 12.A1 Some Indices of Human Development in Italy, 1861–2013

Year	New HDI	HDI + democracy	MRS between Life Expectancy and GDP	Political Rights	Civil Liberties	Life Satisfaction
1861	0.170	0.205	49.9			
1871	0.187	0.219	50.9	5	5	
1881	0.204	0.233	42.9	5	5	
1891	0.232	0.273	42.9	5	4	
1901	0.261	0.290	43.4	5	5	
1911	0.305	0.327	54.9	5	5	
1921	0.330	0.332	48.2	5	5	
1931	0.372	0.274	52.5	7	7	
1941	0.406	0.270	62.9	7	7	
1951	0.444	0.489	57.3	1	4	
1961	0.563	0.609	91.2	1	3	
1971	0.684	0.724	136.8	1	2	
1981	0.769	0.791	177.2	1	2	5.72
1991	0.840	0.845	214.8	1	1	6.39
2001	0.913	0.899	237.9	1	2	6.32
2011	0.929	0.910	222.8	1	2	5.72
2013				2	1	5.38

See chapter 12 ("Human Development") for sources an methods.

Chapter 14

Table 14.A1   **Inflation and deflation, Italy 1861–2014**

Year	% Variation	Year	% Variation	Year	% Variation	Year	% Variation
1862	0.6	1912	0.9	1962	5.1	2012	3.1
1863	−2.9	1913	0.2	1963	7.5	2013	1.1
1864	−2.7	1914	0	1964	5.9	2014	0.2
1865	−1.7	1915	7	1965	4.3		
1866	1	1916	25.1	1966	2		
1867	2.5	1917	41.4	1967	2		
1868	4	1918	39.4	1968	1.3		
1869	0.6	1919	1.5	1969	2.8		
1870	1.4	1920	31.4	1970	5.1		
1871	0.1	1921	18.3	1971	5		
1872	13	1922	−0.6	1972	5.6		
1873	6	1923	−0.6	1973	10.4		
1874	2.4	1924	3.5	1974	19.4		
1875	−14.4	1925	12.3	1975	17.2		
1876	5.8	1926	7.9	1976	16.5		
1877	4	1927	−8.6	1977	18.1		
1878	−3.7	1928	−7.3	1978	12.4		
1879	−1.2	1929	1.6	1979	15.7		
1880	3.7	1930	−3.2	1980	21.1		
1881	−6.5	1931	−9.7	1981	18.7		
1882	−2.4	1932	−2.6	1982	16.3		
1883	−3.2	1933	−5.9	1983	15		
1884	−1.9	1934	−5.2	1984	10.6		
1885	2.2	1935	1.4	1985	8.6		
1886	−0.1	1936	7.6	1986	6.1		
1887	−0.2	1937	9.5	1987	4.6		
1888	1.3	1938	7.7	1988	5		
1889	1.7	1939	4.4	1989	6.6		
1890	3.6	1940	16.7	1990	6.1		
1891	−0.3	1941	15.7	1991	6.4		

(continued)

Table 14.A1 **Continued**

Year	% Variation	Year	% Variation	Year	% Variation	Year	% Variation
1892	−0.9	1942	15.6	1992	5.4		
1893	−2.2	1943	67.7	1993	4.2		
1894	−0.4	1944	344.4	1994	3.9		
1895	−0.6	1945	97	1995	5.4		
1896	−0.4	1946	18	1996	3.9		
1897	−0.2	1947	62.1	1997	1.7		
1898	0.7	1948	5.9	1998	1.8		
1899	−1.6	1949	1.5	1999	1.6		
1900	0.5	1950	−1.3	2000	2.6		
1901	0.1	**1951**	9.7	**2001**	2.7		
1902	−0.7	1952	4.2	2002	2.4		
1903	3	1953	1.9	2003	2.5		
1904	1.2	1954	2.7	2004	2		
1905	0.1	1955	2.8	2005	1.7		
1906	1.9	1956	5	2006	2		
1907	4.7	1957	1.9	2007	1.7		
1908	−1	1958	4.8	2008	3.2		
1909	−2.8	1959	−0.4	2009	0.7		
1910	2.8	1960	2.7	2010	1.6		
1911	2.5	**1961**	2.9	**2011**	2.8		

See chapter 14 ("Cost of Living") for sources and methods.

Table 14.A2 Spatial index of the cost of living per region and macro-area, Italy 1951–2014

	1951	1961	1971	1981	1991	2001	2011	2014
Piedmont	93.8	96.4	96.8	98.7	99.8	100.7	102.7	102.8
Valle d'Aosta	101.4	96.5	96.4	101.5	106.2	104.4	104.9	104.8
Liguria	105.6	107.3	107.5	109.4	113.2	110.7	110.1	111.8
Lombardy	108.5	105.6	108.0	109.1	113.1	113.3	110.7	109.9
Trentino–Alto Adige	100.5	100.2	100.9	112.3	106.6	109.2	111.6	114.1
Veneto	89.9	88.1	88.9	93.7	94.8	98.6	97.7	97.9
Friuli–Venezia Giulia	95.5	91.5	90.9	100.7	103.0	104.5	105.5	105.2
Emilia-Romagna	101.7	98.4	102.0	105.5	107.1	107.6	105.4	105.1
Marche	103.1	103.5	103.9	93.9	94.4	95.1	94.1	94.3
Tuscany	116.5	112.1	113.5	114.1	112.6	111.4	107.7	106.8
Umbria	121.3	112.2	112.0	111.5	106.1	104.2	104.1	104.0
Lazio	111.1	115.8	115.9	110.5	107.3	109.5	109.8	109.9
Campania	89.3	89.7	86.3	86.1	86.7	87.8	91.4	91.1
Abruzzo	99.4	98.0	96.7	96.9	92.5	89.9	90.9	89.7
Molise	102.2	100.2	96.1	95.3	86.8	84.3	82.9	83.0
Puglia	90.7	91.9	87.7	89.2	91.4	90.0	89.3	89.7
Basilicata	113.6	104.9	100.9	93.1	88.2	83.3	85.5	85.0

(continued)

Table 14.A2 Continued

	1951	1961	1971	1981	1991	2001	2011	2014
Calabria	83.5	88.5	89.5	85.3	84.4	83.7	84.0	85.6
Sicily	102.8	105.3	103.6	98.0	95.1	91.2	90.3	89.8
Sardinia	96.3	98.0	95.2	93.6	89.8	88.5	88.6	88.7
North west	103.4	102.9	104.4	105.9	109.1	109.2	108.3	108.0
North east	95.7	93.4	95.0	100.4	101.2	103.5	102.6	102.8
Center	112.6	112.4	113.1	109.4	107.1	107.6	106.5	106.3
South	91.2	91.9	89.0	88.3	88.2	87.7	89.4	89.4
Islands	101.3	103.6	101.5	96.9	93.8	90.5	100.0	100.0
Central-North	103.5	102.6	104.0	105.3	106.2	107.0	106.1	106.0
South-Islands	94.4	95.6	92.9	91.0	90.0	88.6	89.4	89.4
Italy	100.0	100.0	100.0	100.0	100.0	100.0	100.0	100.0
Standard deviation	9.4	7.9	8.5	8.7	9.4	10.1	9.6	9.8
Regional range	37.8	27.7	29.6	28.9	28.8	30.0	28.7	31.1
Macro-area range	21.4	20.5	24.1	21.1	20.8	21.5	18.9	18.6
CN vs. South	10%	7%	12%	16%	18%	21%	19%	19%

See chapter 14 ("Cost of Living") for sources and methods.

References

A'Hearn, B. 2003. "Anthropometric Evidence on Living Standards in Northern Italy, 1730–1860." *Journal of European Economic History* 63, no. 2: 351–381.

A'Hearn, B. 2014. "The British Industrial Revolution in a European Mirror." In R. Floud, J. Humphries, and P. Johnson (eds.), *The Cambridge Economic History of Modern Britain*. Cambridge: Cambridge University Press, 1–52.

A'Hearn, B., J. Baten, and D. Crayen. 2009. "Quantifying Quantitative Literacy: Age Heaping and the History of Human Capital." *Journal of Economic History* 69, no. 3: 783–808.

A'Hearn, B., F. Peracchi, and G. Vecchi. 2009. "Height and the Normal Distribution: Evidence from Italian Military Data." *Demography* 46, no. 1: 1–25.

A'Hearn, B., C. Auria, and G. Vecchi. 2011. "*Istruzione*." In G. Vecchi, *In ricchezza e in povertà. Il benessere degli italiani dall'Unità ad oggi*. Bologna: Il Mulino, 159–208.

A'Hearn, B., N. Amendola, and G. Vecchi. 2016. "On Historical Household Budgets", Rivista di Storia Economica, no. 2: 137–176.

AAI (Amministrazione per le attività assistenziali italiane e internazionali). 1950. *Rivista di Storia Economica. Indagine sugli istituti di ricovero, i refettori, gli iscritti negli elenchi comunali dei poveri al 31 maggio 1948*. Rome: Tipografia Failli.

AAI (Amministrazione per le attività assistenziali italiane e internazionali). 1952–1953. *Organi ed Enti di assistenza pubblica e privata in Italia*. Rome: Aai.

AAI. 1949. *L'attività assistenziale dell'Amministrazione per gli aiuti internazionali nel quadriennio 1945–48*. Rome: Poligrafico dello Stato.

Abramitzky, R., L. P. Boustan, and K. Eriksson. 2012. "Europe's Tired, Poor, Huddled Masses: Self-Selection and Economic Outcomes in the Age of Mass Migration." *American Economic Review* 102, no. 5: 1832–1856.

Abramovitz, M. 1986. "Catching UP, forging ahead, and falling behind." *The Journal of Economic History* 46, no. 2: 385–406.

Abramovitz, M. A., and P. A. David. 1996. *Convergence and Deferred Catch-up: Productivity Leadership and the Waning of American Exceptionalism*. CEPR Publication, no. 401. Stanford: Stanford University Press.

Accetturo, A., and L. Infante. 2013. "Skills or Culture? An Analysis of the Decision to Work by Immigrant Women in Italy." *IZA Journal of Migration* 2: 2.

Accornero, A. 1992. *La parabola del sindacato*. Bologna: Il Mulino.

Acemoglu, D., and J. Robinson. 2012. *Why Nations Fail: The Origins of Power, Prosperity, and Poverty*. New York: Crown Business.

Aghion, P., and P. Bolton. 1992. "Distribution and Growth in Models of Imperfect Capital Markets." *European Economic Review* 36: 603–611.

Aghion, P., and P. Bolton. 1997. "A Theory of Trickle-Down Growth and Development." *Review of Economic Studies* 64: 151–172.

AIRTum Working Group. 2010. *I tumori in Italia, Rapporto 2010: La prevalenza dei tumori in Italia*. Epidemiologia e prevenzione, supplemento 2 (September–December).

Alderman, H., and M. Garcia. 1994. "Food Security and Health Security: Explaining the Levels of Nutritional Status in Pakistan." *Economic Development and Cultural Change* 42, no. 3: 485–507.

Aleati, G. 1961. "Le retribuzioni dei lavoratori edili in Milano, Pavia e nei rispettivi territori dal 1819 al 1890." *Archivio economico della unificazione italiana*, s. I, vol. XI, fasc. 1. Turin: Ilte.

Alesina, R., S. Danninger, and M. Rostagno. 2001. "Redistribution through Public Employment: The Case of Italy." *International Monetary Fund Staff Papers* 48, no. 3: 447–473.

Alesina, A., and D. Rodrik. 1994. "Distributive Politics and Economic Growth." *Quarterly Journal of Economics* 109: 465–490.

Alesina, A., and A. Ichino. 2009. *L'Italia fatta in casa*. Milan: Mondadori.

Allen, R. C. 2009. *The British Industrial Revolution in Global Perspective*. Cambridge: Cambridge University Press.

Allegretti, U. 1989. *Profilo di storia costituzionale italiana. Individualismo e assolutismo nello stato liberale*. Bologna: Il Mulino.

Altroconsumo. 2010. www.altroconsumo.it/scuola/20100301/nidi-pochi-posti-a-peso-d-oro-Attach_s268203.pdf

Alvaredo, F., and E. Pisano. 2010. "Top Incomes in Italy 1974–2004." In A. B. Atkinson and T. Piketty (eds.), *Top Incomes: A Global Perspective*. Oxford: Oxford University Press, 625–663.

Alwang, J., P. B. Siegel, and S. L. Jørgensen. 2001. *Vulnerability: A View from Different Disciplines*. World Bank Social Protection Discussion Paper, no. 115.

Amatori, F. 1980. "Entrepreneurial Typologies in the History of Industrial Italy (1880–1960): A Review Article." *Business History Review* 54, no. 3: 359–186.

Amatori, F. 2011. "Entrepreneurial Typologies in the History of Industrial Italy: Reconsiderations." *Business History Review* 85, no. 1: 151–180.

Ambrico, G. 1954. "Inchiesta a carattere comunitario. Risultati e orientamento. Relazione: povertà e storia nella comunità di Grassano. Indagine sperimentale sulla civiltà contadina", *Atti della Commissione parlamentare d'inchiesta sulla miseria in Italia e sui mezzi per combatterla*, vol. 14, tomo 1. Rome: Camera dei deputati.

Amendola, N., and G. Vecchi. 2014. *Durable Goods and Poverty Measurement*. World Bank Policy Research Working Paper (7105).

Amendola, N., G. Vecchi, and B. Al Kiswani. 2010. "Il costo della vita al Nord e al Sud d'Italia, dal dopoguerra a oggi. Stime di prima generazione." *Rivista di politica economica* 70, nos. 4–6: 3–34.

Anand, S., and A. Sen. 1993. *Human Development Index: Methodology and Measurement*. United Nations Development Programme Occasional Paper, no. 8.

Ando, A., L. Guiso, and I. Visco. 1994. *Saving and the Accumulation of Wealth*. New York: Cambridge University Press.

Angelini, M. 1996. "Mestieri girovaghi e moralismo storiografico. Studio sulla "tratta dei fanciulli" nell'Appennino settentrionale (XIX secolo)." *il Risorgimento* 48, no. 3: 425–437.

Arcaleni, E. 1998. "La statura dei coscritti italiani delle generazioni 1854–1976, 'Bollettino di Demografia Storica.'" *Società Italiana di Demografia Storica* 29: 23–59.

Arcari, P. M. 1936. *Le variazioni dei salari agricoli in Italia dalla fondazione del Regno, "ISTAT, Annali di Statistica.".* Serie VI—Vol. XXXVI. Rome: Tipografia Failli.

Archivio Centrale dello Stato. 1877–1885. *Giunta per l'inchiesta agraria e sulle condizioni della classe agricola in Italia (Inchiesta Jacini)*. Rome: Forzani e C.

Arrow, K. J. 1951 *Social Choice and Individual Values*. New York: Wiley.

Arru, A., (ed.). 2003. *Pater Familias*. Rome: Biblink.

Asian Barometer. 2015. http://www.asianbarometer.org/.

Ascoli, U. 2002. "Le caratteristiche fondamentali del Welfare State italiano, 'Cittadinanza. Individui, diritti sociali, collettività nella storia contemporanea.'" In C. Sorba (ed.), *Proceedings from the annual SISSCO Padova conference 1999*. Quaderni della rassegna degli Archivi di Stato.

Astorga, P., A. R. Bergés, and V. FitzGerald. 2005. "The standard of living in Latin America during the twentieth century." *Economic History Review* 58, no. 4: 765–796.

Atella, V. e F. Cincotti. 2008. "La spesa sanitaria ed il quadro macroeconomico." In Fondazione Farmafactoring (ed.), *La sanità in controluce*. Rome: Franco Angeli.

Atkinson A. B. 1970. "On the Measurement of Inequality." *Journal of Economic Theory* 2: 244–263.

Atkinson, A. B. 1997. "Bringing Income Distribution in From the Cold." *Economic Journal* 107, no. 441: 297–321.

Atkinson, A. B. 1998. *Poverty in Europe*. Oxford: Blackwell.

Atkinson, A. B. 2007. Measuring Top Incomes: Methodological Issues. In Atkinson, A.B., and T. Piketty (eds.). 2007. Top Incomes over the 20th Century: A Contrast between Continental European and English- Speaking Countries. Oxford: Oxford University Press.

Atkinson, A. B. 2015. *Inequality: What Can be Done?* Cambridge, MA: Harvard University Press.

Atkinson, A. B., and A. Brandolini. 2001. "Promise and Pitfalls in the Use of 'Secondary' Data-Sets: Income Inequality in OECD Countries as a Case Study." *Journal of Economic Literature* 39: 771–799.

Atkinson A. B., and S. Morelli. 2011. "Economic Crisis and Inequality," UNDP Human Development Research Paper, 2011/06.

Atkinson, A. B., and T. Piketty (eds.). 2007. *Top Incomes over the 20th Century: A Contrast between Continental European and English-Speaking Countries*. Oxford: Oxford University Press.

Atkinson, A. B., and T. Piketty (eds.). 2010. *Top Incomes. A Global Perspective*. Oxford: Oxford University Press.

Atkinson, A. B., B. Cantillon, E. Marlier, and B. Nolan, 2002. *Social Indicators: The EU and Social Inclusion*. Oxford: Oxford University Press.

Atkinson, A. D., T. Piketty, and E. Saez. 2011. "Top Incomes in the Long Run of History." *Journal of Economic Literature* 49: 3–71.

Auten, N. M. 1901. "Some Phases in the Sweating System of the Garment Phase of Chicago." *American Journal of Sociology* 6, no. 5: 602–645.

Avveduto, S. (ed.). 2011. *Italia 150 anni: popolazione, welfare, scienza e società*. Rome: Gangemi.

Bachi, R. 1951. "The Tendency to Round Off Age Returns: Measurement and Correction." *Bulletin of the International Statistical Institute* 33: 195–221.

Baffigi, A. 2013. "National Accounts." In G. Toniolo (ed.), *The Oxford Handbook of the Italian Economy since Unification*. Oxford: Oxford University Press, 157–186.

Baffigi, A. 2011. "La contabilità nazionale dell'Italia, 1861–2011." *Quaderni di Storia Economica* no. 18. Rome: Bank of Italy.

Bagnasco, A. 1977. *Tre Italie. La problematica territoriale dello sviluppo italiano*. Bologna: Il Mulino.

Bahle, T., M. Pfeifer, and C. Wendt. 2010. "Social Assistance." In F. Castles, S. Leibfried, J. Lewis, H. Obinger, and C. Pierson (eds.), *The Oxford Handbook of The Welfare State*. Oxford: Oxford University Press.

Baili, P., R. De Angelis, I. Casella, E. Grande, R. Inghelmann, S. Francisci, A. Verdecchia, R. Capocaccia, E. Meneghini, and A. Micheli. 2007. "Italian Cancer Burden by Broad Geographical Area." *Tumori* 93: 398–407.

Baines, D., N. Cummins, and M. S. Schulze. 2010. "Population and Living Standards, 1945–2000." In S. Broadberry and K. O'Rourke (eds.), *The Cambridge Economic History of Modern Europe. Volume 2: 1870 to the Present*. Cambridge: Cambridge University Press.

Balassa, B. 1964. "The Purchasing Power Parity Doctrine: A Reappraisal." *Journal of Political Economy* 72, no. 6: 584–596.

Balassone, F., M. Francese, and A. Pace. 2013. "Public Debt and Economic Growth: Italy's First 150 Years." In G. Toniolo (ed.), *The Oxford Handbook of the Italian Economy since Unification*. Oxford: Oxford University Press.

Balderas, J. U., and M. J. Greenwood. 2010. "From Europe to the Americas: A Comparative Panel-Data Analysis of Migration to Argentina, Brazil, and the United States, 1870–1910." *Journal of Population Economics* 23, no. 4: 1301–1328.

Baldini, G. F. 1939. *Monografie di famiglie agricole. Tre famiglie di braccianti del ravennate*. Faenza: Fratelli Lega.

Baldini, M., and S. Toso. 2004. *Diseguaglianza, povertà e politiche pubbliche*. Bologna: Il Mulino.

Balestrieri, M. 1925. *I consumi alimentari della popolazione italiana dal 1910 al 1921*. Padova: Metron.

Balk, B. M. 2008. *Price and Quantity Index Numbers*. Cambridge: Cambridge University Press.

Balletta, F. 1978. "Emigrazione Italiana, cicli economici e rimesse, 1876–1976." In F. Balletta (ed.), *Un secolo di emigrazione italiana 1876–1976*. Rome: Centro Studi Emigrazione.

Balocchi, E. 1967. *La qualificazione di povertà nel diritto amministrativo*. Milan: A. Giuffrè.

Bank of Italy. 2009. "Mezzogiorno e politiche regionali." *Seminari e Convegni* 2. Rome.

Bank of Italy. 2013. "La ricchezza delle famiglie italiane nell'anno 2012." *Supplementi al Bollettino Statistico—Indicatori monetari e finanziari* 65. Rome: Bank of Italy.

Bank of Italy. 2014a. "L'economia delle regioni italiane." *Economie regionali* 21.

Bank of Italy. 2014b. "La ricchezza delle famiglie italiane." *Supplementi al Bollettino Statistico—Indicatori monetari e finanziari* 69. Rome: Bank of Italy.

Bandettini, B .F. 1960. "Le retribuzioni dei lavoratori edili a Firenze dal 1819 al 1890."0 *Archivio economico dell'unificazione italiana*" s. I, vol. X, fasc. 3. Turin: Ilte.

Bandiera, O., I. Rasul, and M. Viarengo. 2012. "The Making of Modern America: Migratory fFlows in the Age of Mass Migration." *Journal of Development Economics* 102, no. C: 23–47.

Banfield, E. C. 1958. *The Moral Basis of a Backward Society*. Chicago: Free Press.

Barberi, B. 1961. *I consumi nel primo secolo dell'Unità d'Italia, 1861–1960*. Milano: A. Giuffrè.

Barca, F., L. Cannari, and L. Guiso. 1992. *Bequests and Saving for Retirement: What Impels the Accumulation of Wealth*. Papers 165. Banca Italia: Servizio di Studi.

Barca, F., and S. Trento. 1997. "State Ownership and the Evolution of Italian Corporate Governance." *Industrial and Corporate Change* 6: 533–560.

Barro, R. J., and J. W. Lee. 2013. "A New Data Set of Educational Attainment in the World, 1950–2010." *Journal of Development Economics* 104, no. C: 184–198. http:// dx.doi.org/ 10.1016/j.jdeveco.2012.10.001.

Bassanetti, A., C. Rondinelli, and F. Scoccianti. 2012. *The Decline of the Italian Saving Rate*. Mimeo, Rome: Bank of Italy.

Basu, K. 1999. "Child Labor: Cause, Consequence, and Cure, with Remarks on International Labor Standards." *Journal of Economic Literature* 37: 1083–1119.

Basu, K., and P. H. Van. 1998. "The Economics of Child Labor." *American Economic Review* 88, no. 3: 412–427.

Baten, J. 2000. "Economic Development and the Distribution of Nutritional Resources in Bavaria, 1797–1839: An Anthropometric Study." *Journal of Income Distribution* 9: 89–106.

Baten, J., and Murray, J. E. 2000. "*Heights of Men and Women in 19th-century Bavaria: Economic, Nutritional, and Disease Influences*." *Explorations in Economic History 37,* no. 4: 351–369.

Battilani, P. 2000. "I protagonisti dello Stato sociale italiano prima e dopo la legge Crispi." In V. Zamagni (ed.), *Povertà e innovazioni istituzionali in Italia. Dal Medioevo ad oggi*. Bologna: Il Mulino. 587–610.

Battilani, P. 2001. "Decentramento o accentramento: obiettivi e limiti del sistema amministrativo locale scelto con l'Unità del paese." *Rivista di storia economica* 3: 313–357.

Battilani, P., E. Felice, and V. Zamagni. 2011. *Il valore aggiunto dei servizi a prezzi correnti (1861–1951)*. Mimeo, Rome: Bank of Italy.

Becattini, G. 1979. "Dal 'settore' industriale al 'distretto' industriale. Alcune considerazioni sull'unità di indagine dell'economia industriale." *Rivista di economia e politica industriale* 5, no. 1: 7–21.

Becker, G. S., K. M. Murphy, and R. Tamura. 1990. "Human Capital, Fertility, and Economic Growth." *Journal of Political Economy* 98, no. 5: 12–37.

Becker, S., F. Cinnirella, and L. Woessmann. 2010. "The Trade-off between Fertility and Education: Evidence from before the Demographic Transition." *Journal of Economic Growth* 15, no. 3: 177–204.

Beckerman, W. 1978. *Estimates of Poverty in Italy in 1975*. ILO Working Papers, no. 70.

Behrman, J. R., and A. B. Deolalikar. 1987. "Will Developing Country Nutrition Improve with Income? A Case Study for Rural South India." *Journal of Political Economy* 95, no. 3: 492–507.

Bekaert, G. 1991. "Caloric Consumption in Industrializing Belgium." *Journal of Economic History* 51: 633–655.

Belot, M. V. K., and T. J. Hatton. 2008. *Immigrant Selection in the OECD*. ANU Centre for Economic Policy Research DP, no. 571.

Beltrametti, L., and M. Della Valle. 2011. *Does the implicit pension debt mean anything after all?* CeRP Working Papers 118. Turin: Center for Research on Pensions and Welfare Policies.

Benhabib, J., and M. Spiegel. 1994. "The Role of Human Capital in Economic Development: Evidence from Aggregate Cross-country Data." *Journal of Monetary Economics* 34, no. 2: 143–173.

Bellhouse, D. R. 1988. "A Brief History of Random Sampling Methods." In P. R. Krishnaiah and C. R. Rao (eds.), *Handbook of Statistics.* vol. 6, 1–14. Amsterdam and New York: North-Holland Pub. Co.

Benabou, R. J. 1996. *NBER Macroeconomics Annual 1996.* Vol. 11, 11–92.

Benabou, R. J., and J. Tirole. 2006. "Incentives and Prosocial Behavior." *American Economic Review* 5: 1652–1678.

Bennett, M., and R. Peirce. 1961. "Change in the American National Diet, 1879–1959." *Food Research Institute Studies* 2: 95–119.

Berentsen, W. H. 1987. "German Infant Mortality, 1960–1980." *Geographical Review* 77, no. 2: 151–170.

Bertini, F. 2001. "Il fascismo dalle assicurazioni per i lavoratori allo Stato sociale." In M. Palla (ed.), *Lo Stato fascista.* Milan: La Nuova Italia, 177–313.

Bertola, G. 1993. "Factor Shares and Savings in Endogenous Growth." *American Economic Review* 83: 1184–1198.

Bertola, G., R. Foellmi, and J. Zweimüller. 2005. *Income Distribution in Macroeconomic Models.* Princeton: Princeton University Press.

Bertola, G., and P. Sestito. 2013. "Human Capital." In G. Toniolo (ed.), *The Oxford Handbook of the Italian Economy since Unification.* Oxford: Oxford University Press, 249–270.

Bertoldi, S. 1993. *Dopoguerra. Da Piazzale Loreto alla Dolce Vita.* Milan: Rizzoli.

Bertoni Jovine, D. 1967. *La scuola italiana dal 1870 ad oggi.* Rome: Editori Riuniti.

Bertozzi, V., and G. Espa. 2005. "La comparazione del livello assoluto dei prezzi nelle città capoluogo di regione." *Quaderni dell'osservatorio del commercio, Provincia Autonoma di Trento*, October.

Bevilacqua, P. 1980. *Le campagne del Mezzogiorno tra fascismo e dopoguerra: il caso della Calabria.* Turin: Einaudi.

Bevilacqua, P. 1993. *Breve storia dell'Italia meridionale dall'Ottocento a oggi.* Rome: Donzelli.

Bevilacqua, P., A. de Clementi, and E. Franzina 2001. *Storia dell'emigrazione italiana. Vol. 1, Partenze; vol. 2, Arrivi.* Rome: Donzelli.

Bianchi, B. 2001. "Lavoro ed emigrazione femminile (1880–1915)." In P. Bevilacqua, A. Clementi, and E. Franzina (eds.), *Storia dell'emigrazione italiana*, vol. 1, Partenze, 257–273. Rome: Donzelli.

Bidani, B., and M. Ravallion 1994. *How Robust is a Poverty Profile?*, World Bank Economic Review 8: 75–102.

Blanchard, O. 1997. *Macroeconomics.* Upper Saddle River, N.J. : Pearson Prentice Hall.

Bleakley, H., and F. Lange. 2009. "Chronic Disease Burden and the Interaction of Education, Fertility, and Growth." *Review of Economics and Statistics* 91, no. 1: 52–65.

Bleich, S., D. Cutler, C. Murray, and A. Adams. 2007. *Why Is the Developed World Obese?* NBER Working Paper, no. 12954.

Bodio, L. 1882. *Statistica della emigrazione italiana all'estero nel 1881, confrontata con quella degli anni precedenti e coll'emigrazione avvenuta da altri Stati.* Società Geografica Italiana, Roma: Società Geografica Italiana.

Boeri, T. 2000. *Uno stato asociale. Perché è fallito il welfare in Italia*, Rome: Laterza.

Boeri, T., M. De Philippis, E. Patacchini, and M. Pellizzari. 2014. *Immigration, housing discrimination and employment.* CReAM Discussion Paper Series 1414, London: University College.

Boeri, T., and R. Perotti. 2002. *Meno pensioni, più welfare.* Bologna: Il Mulino.

Bogin, B. 1999. *Patterns of Human Growth.* Cambridge: Cambridge University Press.

Bogin, B., P. Smith, A. B. Orden, M. I. Varela Silva, and J. Loucky 2002. "Rapid Change in Height and Body Porportions of Maya American Children." *American Journal of Human Biology* 14: 753–761.

Bonifazi, C., and F. Heins. 2000. "Long-term trends of internal migration in Italy." *International Journal of Population Geography* 2: 111–131.

Bonifazi, C., and F. Heins. 2011. *La mobilità interna nei 150 anni di storia unitaria*. In S. Avveduto (ed.), *Italia 150 anni: popolazione, welfare, scienza e società*. Rome: Gangemi. 51–55.

Bonnet, O., P. H. Bono, G. Chapelle, and É. Wasmer. 2014. *Does housing capital contribute to inequality? A comment on Thomas Piketty's Capital in the 21st Century*. Sciences Po Economics Discussion Paper 2014–07.

Bonoli, G. 2005. "The Politics of the New Social Policies: Providing Coverage against New Social Risks in Mature Welfare States." *Policy & Politics* 33, no. 3: 431–449.

Bordley, R. F., J. B. McDonald, and A. Mantrala. 1996. "Something New, Something Old: Parametric Models for the Size Distribution of Income." *Journal of Income Distribution* 6: 91–103.

Borgerhoff Mulder, M., et al. 2009. "Wealth Transmission and the Dynamics of Inequality in Small-Scale Societie." *Science* 326: 682–688.

Borjas, G. J. 1987. "Self-selection and the earnings of immigrants." *American Economic Review* 77: 531–553.

Borjas, G. J. 1988. Immigration and Self-selection. *NBER WP*, no. 2566, April.

Bosna, E. 1982. *L'obbligo scolastico in Italia da Casati ai giorni nostri*. Bari: Gemma.

Bottazzi, F., A. Niceforo, and G. Quagliariello. 1933. *Documenti per lo studio della alimentazione della popolazione italiana nell'ultimo cinquantennio*. Commissione per lo studio dei problemi dell'alimentazione, Napoli: Jovene.

Bourguignon, F., and C. Morrisson. 2002. "Inequality among World Citizens: 1820–1992." *American Economic Review* 92, no. 4: 727–744.

Bourguignon, F., C. Goh, and D. I. Kim. 2004. *Estimating Individual Vulnerability to Poverty with Pseudo-panel Data*. World Bank Policy Research Working Paper, no. 3375.

Boustan, L. P., M. E. Kahn, and P. W. Rhode. 2012. "Coping with Economic and Environmental Shocks: Institutions and Outcomes—Moving to Higher Ground: Migration Response to Natural Disasters in the Early Twentieth Century." *American Economic Review* 102, no. 3: 238–244.

Bowden, S. and A. Offer. 1994. "Household Appliances and the Use of Time: the United States and Britain since the 1920s." *Economic History Review* 47, no. 4: 725–748.

Bozzoli, C., A. Deaton, and C. Quintana-Domeque. 2009. "Adult Height and Childhood Disease." *Demography* 46, no. 4: 647–669.

Braghin, P. (ed.). 1978. *L'inchiesta sulla miseria*. Turin: Einaudi.

Brandolini, A. 1997. "Legge di Pareto, curva di Kuznets ed evoluzione «secolare» della disuguaglianza dei redditi." *Rivista di storia economica* 13, no. 2: 221–252.

Brandolini, A. 1999. "The Distribution of Personal Income in Post-War Italy: Source Description, Data Quality, and the Time Pattern of Income Inequality." *Giornale degli economisti e Annali di economia* 58, no. 2: 183–239.

Brandolini, A. 2000. "Appunti per una storia della distribuzione del reddito in Italia nel secondo dopoguerra." *Rivista di storia economica* 16: 213–232.

Brandolini, A. 2007. *On Applying Synthetic Indices of Multidimensional Well-being: Health and Income Inequalities in Selected EU Countries*. Themes of Discussion (Economic Working Papers) 668. Rome: Bank of Italy, Economic Research Department.

Brandolini, A. 2005. "La diseguaglianza di reddito in Italia nell'ultimo decennio." *Stato e mercato* 74: 207–229.

Brandolini, A., L. Cannari, G. D'Alessio, and I. Faiella. 2004. "Household Wealth Distribution in Italy in the 1990s." *Temi di Discussione*," 530. Rome: Bank of Italy.

Brandolini, A., L. Cannari, G. D'Alessio, and I. Faiella. 2004. *La distribuzione della ricchezza tra le famiglie italiane negli anni novanta*. "Temi di discussione," 530. Rome: Bank of Italy.

Brandolini, A., and T. M. Smeeding. 2008. "Inequality Patterns in Western Democracies: Cross-Country Differences and Changes over Time." In P. Beramendi and C. J. Anderson (eds.), *Democracy, Inequality, and Representation*. New York: Russell Sage Foundation. 25–61.

Brandolini, A., and R. Torrini. 2010. "Disuguaglianza dei redditi e divari territoriali: l'eccezionalità del caso italiano." *Rivista delle politiche sociali* 3: 37–58.

Brandolini, A., 2009. "L'evoluzione recente della distribuzione del reddito in Italia". In A. Brandolini, C. Saraceno and A. Schizzerotto (eds.), Dimensioni della disuguaglianza in Italia: povertà, salute, abitazione. Bologna: Il Mulino. 39–67

Brandolini, A., P. Cipollone, and P. Sestito. 2002. "Earning Dispersion, Low Pay and Household Poverty in Italy, 1977–1998." In D. Cohen, T. Piketty, and G. Saint-Paul (eds.), *The Economics of Rising Inequalities*. Oxford: Oxford University Press, 225–264.

Brandolini, A., and G. Vecchi. 2012. *The Well-Being of Italians: A Comparative Historical Approach*. Economic History Working Papers, 19, Bank of Italy.

Brandolini, A., and G. Vecchi. (2013). "Standards of Living." In G. Toniolo (ed.), *The Oxford Handbook of the Italian Economy since Unification*. Oxford: Oxford University Press, 227–248.

Brenner, Y. S., H. Kaelble, and M. Thomas (eds.). 1991. *Income Distribution in Historical Perspective*. Cambridge: Cambridge University Press; Paris: Maison des Sciences de l'Homme.

Bresciani-Turroni, C. 1937. *The Economics of Inflation: A Study of Currency Depreciation in Post-War Germany*. London: Allen & Unwin.

Bresciani-Turroni, C. 1939. "Annual Survey of Statistical Data: Pareto's Law and the Index of Inequality of Incomes." *Econometrica* 7: 107–133.

Bretoni Jovine, D. 1963. *L'alienazione dell'infanzia. Il lavoro minorile nella società moderna*. Rome: Editori Riuniti.

Bring, J. 1994. "How to Standardize Regression Coefficients." *American Statistician* 48, no. 3: 209–213.

Broadberry, S., C. Giordano, and F. Zollino. 2011. *A Sectoral Analysis of Italy's Development, 1861–2011*. "Quaderni di storia economica" (Economic History Working Papers) 20, Bank of Italy, Economic Research and International Relations Area.

Broadberry, S., and R. K. O'Rourke. 2010. *The Cambridge Economic History of Modern Europe*. Cambridge: Cambridge University Press.

Brosio, G., and C. Marchese. 1986. *Il potere di spendere. Economia e storia della spesa pubblica dall'unificazione a oggi*. Bologna: Il Mulino.

Brunetti, A., E. Felice, and G. Vecchi. 2011. *Reddito*. In G. Vecchi, *In ricchezza e in povertà*. Bologna: Il Mulino, 209–234.

Brunialti, A. 1870. "La funzione politica del potere giudiziario." *Archivio Giuridico* 3: 1–45.

Brugiavini, A., and G. Weber (eds.). 2014. *Longer-term Consequences of the Great Recession on the Lives of Europeans*. Oxford: Oxford University Press.

Bulmer, K., K. Bales, and K. Sklar. 1991. *The Social Survey in Historical Perspective, 1880–1940*. Cambridge: Cambridge University Press.

Burn, A. R. 1953. "Hic breve vivitur: A study of the expectation of life in the Roman Empire." *Past and Present*, 7: 635–678.

Cacciari, E., S. Milani, A. Balsamo, F. Dammacco, F. De Luca, F. Chiarelli, A. M. Pasquino, G. Tonini, and M. Vanelli. 2002. "Italian Cross-sectional Growth Charts for Height, Weight, and BMI (6–20 y)." *European Journal of Clinical Nutrition* 56: 171–180.

Cafiso, F. 2012. "Interventi a salvaguardia dei centri abitati: il caso della frana di San Fratello (ME)." *Bollettino dei Geologi di Sicilia* 20, no. 4: XXX.

Cagan, P. 1956. "The Monetary Dynamics of Hyperinflation." In M. Friedman, *Studies in the Quantity Theory of Money*. Chicago: University of Chicago Press. 25–117.

Camera dei Deputati. 1953. *Atti della Commissione parlamentare d'inchiesta sulla miseria e sui mezzi per combatterla*. Rome: Camera dei Deputati.

Cameron, R., and L. Neal. 2002. *A Concise Economic History of the World*. Oxford: Oxford University Press.

Campiglio, L. 1986. "Un'analisi comparata del sistema dei prezzi nei venti Comuni capoluogo di Regione." *Rivista internazionale di scienze sociali* 3, no. 94: 329–377.

Campiglio, L. 1996. *Il costo del vivere. Nord e Sud a confronto*. Bologna: Il Mulino.

Campiglio, L., and G. Rovati. 2009. *La povertà alimentare in Italia: prima indagine quantitativa e qualitativa*. Fondazione per la sussidiarietà, Milan: Guerini e Associati.

Cannari, L., and S. Chiri. 2003. "Le infrastrutture economiche dall'Unità." In P. Ciocca and G. Toniolo (eds.), *Storia economica d'Italia*, vol. 3.1. Rome-Bari: Laterza, 225–297.

Cannari L., and G. D'Alessio. 2002. "La distribuzione del reddito e della ricchezza nelle regioni italiane." *Rivista economica del Mezzogiorno* a. XVI, no. 4.

Cannari, L., and G. D'Alessio. 2006. *La ricchezza degli italiani*. Bologna: Il Mulino.

Cannari, L., and G. D'Alessio. 2003. *La distribuzione del reddito e della ricchezza nelle regioni italiane*. Rome: Bank of Italy.

Cannari, L., and G. D'Alessio. 2008. "Intergenerational Transfers in Italy." In Bank of Italy (ed.), *Household Wealth in Italy*. Rome: Bank of Italy.

Cannari, L., and G. Iuzzolino. 2009. *Le differenze nel livello dei prezzi al consumo tra Nord e Sud*. "Questioni di economia e finanza," 49. Rome: Bank of Italy.

Cannistraro, P. 1975. *La fabbrica del consenso. Fascismo e mass media*. Rome-Bari: Laterza.

Cannistrato, P. V., and G. Rosoli. 1979. "Fascist Emigration Policy in the 1920s: An Interpretative Framework." *International Migration Review* 13, no. 4: 673–692.

Cao Pinna, V. 1958. *Struttura ed elasticità dei consumi di un campione di famiglie italiane*. Rome: Doxa.

Capodiferro, A. 1965. "Abitazioni." *Annali di statistica* 7: 17.

Cappieri, M. 1971. "Le basi etniche della statura degli italiani." *Genus* 4: 267–324.

Caracciolo, A. 1958. *L'inchiesta agraria Jacini*. Torino: Einaudi.

Carattieri, M., P. Marchi, and M. Trionfini. 2009. *Ermanno Gorrieri (1920–2004). Un cattolico sociale nelle trasformazioni del Novecento*. Bologna: Il Mulino.

Caravaggio, E. 1911. "Beneficienza pubblica, di Stato o legale, e privata." In Accademia dei Lincei (ed.), *Cinquanta anni di storia italiana*, vol. 2. Milan: Hoepli.

Cardani, F., and F. Massara. 1868. *Sulle condizioni economico-morali del contadino comasco, milanese, pavese e lodigiano* "Atti della società italiana lombarda di economia politica del 1865, adunanza del 30 aprile."

Carmagnani, M., and G. Mantelli. 1975. "Fonti quantitative italiane relative all'emigrazione italiana verso l'America latina (1902–1914). Analisi Critica." *Annali Fondazione L. Einaudi Torino* 9: 286–287.

Carpi, L. 1887. *L'Italia all'estero*. Rome: Centenari.

Carson, C. S. 1975. "The History of the United States National Income and Product Accounts: The Development of an Analytical Tool". *Journal of Income and Wealth* 21: 153–181.

Caselli, G. 1991. "Health Transition and Cause-Specific Mortality." In R. Schofield, D. Reher, and A. Bideau (eds.), *The Decline of Mortality in Europe*. Oxford: Clarendon Press, 68–96.

Caselli, G., and R. M. Lipsi. 2002. *Evoluzione della geografia della mortalità in Italia, Tavole provinciali e probabilità di morte per causa. Anni 1971–73, 1981–83, 1991–93*, "Fonti e Strumenti," 4. Rome, University of Rome "La Sapienza," Department of Demographic Sciences.

Caselli, G., and R. M. Lipsi. 2006. "Survival Differences among the Oldest Old in Sardinia: Who, What, Where, and Why?" *Demographic Research* 14, no. 13: 267–294.

Castellano, C. 1965. *L'industria degli elettrodomestici in Italia*. Turin: Giappichelli.

Castles, F. G. 2006. *The Growth of the Post-war Public Expenditure State: Long-term Trajectories and Recent Trends*. TranState Working Papers, no. 35.

Cavelaars, A. E. J. M., A. E. Kunst, J. J. M. Geurts, R. Crialesi, L. Grötvedt, U. Helmert, E. Lahelma, O. Lundberg, A. Mielck, N. K. Rasmussen, E. Regidor, T. Spuhler, and J. P. Mackenbach. 2000. "Persistent Variations in Average Height between Countries and between Socio-economic Groups: An Overview of 10 European Countries." *Annals of Human Biology* 27, no. 4: 407–421.

CEI, Caritas. 2012. *Opere per il bene comune*. Bologna: Edizioni Dehoniane.

Cerase, F. P. 2001. "L'onda di ritorno: i rimpatri." In P. Bevilacqua, A. De Clementi, and E. e Franzina (eds.), *Storia dell'emigrazione italiana*. 113–125.

Cergas (Centro di Ricerche sulla gestione dell'assistenza sanitaria e sociale). 2009. *Rapporto OASI 2009*. Milan: Bocconi University.

Ceriani, L., and P. Verme. 2011. "The origins of the Gini index: Extracts from Variabilità e Mutabilità (1912) by Corrado Gini." *Journal of Economic Inequality* 10, no. 3: 421–443.

Chakravarty, S. R. 2003. "A Generalized Human Development Index." *Review of Development Economics*, 7, no. 1: 99–114.

Chakravarty, S. R., R. Kanbur, and D. Mukherjee. 2006. "Population Growth and Poverty Measurement." *Social Choice Welfare* 26: 471–483.

Chamla, M.-C. 1964. "L'Accroissement de la stature en France de 1880 à 1960; comparaison avec les pays d'Europe occidentale." *Bulletins et Mèmoires de la Sociètè d'anthropologie de Paris* XI, 6, no. 2: 201–278.

Chaudhuri, S. 2003. *Assessing Vulnerability to Poverty: Concepts, Empirical Methods and Illustrative Examples.* New York: Columbia University.

Checchi, D. 1997. "L'efficacia del sistema scolastico italiano in prospettiva storica." In N. Rossi (ed.), *L'istruzione in Italia: solo un pezzo di carta?* Bologna: Il Mulino, XXX–XXX.

Checchi, D. 2006. *The Economics of Education; Human Capital, Family Background and Inequality.* Cambridge: Cambridge University Press.

Chen S., Z. Luo, and X. Pan. 2013. "Natural Disaster in China: 1900–2011." *Natural Hazards* 69, no. 3: 1597–1605.

Cherubini, A. 1980. *Medicina e lotte sociali (1900–1920).* Rome: Il pensiero scientifico.

Chevry, G. 1970. "L'Institut international de statistique." *Economie et statistique* 13: 63–65.

Chianese, S., and G. Vecchi. 2011. "Bilanci di Famiglia." In G. Vecchi, *In ricchezza e in povertà.* Bologna: Il Mulino, XXX–XXX.

Choate, M. I. 2008. *Emigrant Nation: The Making of Italy Abroad.* Cambridge, MA: Harvard University Press.

Christiaensen, L. J., and K. Subbarao. 2005 "Towards an Understanding of Household Vulnerability in Rural Kenya." *Journal of African Economies* 14, no. 4: 520–558.

Ciampani, A. (ed.). 2002. *L'Amministrazione per gli Aiuti Internazionali. La ricostruzione dell'Italia tra dinamiche internazionali e attività assistenziali.* Milan: Franco Angeli.

Ciccarelli, C., and S. Fenoaltea. 2009. *La produzione industriale delle regioni d'Italia, 1861–1913: una ricostruzione quantitativa. 1. Le industrie non manifatturiere.* Rome: Bank of Italy.

Ciccarelli, C., and S. Fenoaltea. 2010. "Attraverso la lente d'ingrandimento: aspetti provinciali della crescita industriale nell'Italia postunitaria." *Quaderni di storia economica* 4, July, 5–67, Rome: Bank of Italy.

CIES (Commissione di indagine sull'esclusione sociale). 2015. http://www.commissionepoverta-cies.eu/Archivio/Archivio.htm

Cigno, A., and F. C. Rosati. 2005. *The Economics of Child Labour.* Oxford: Oxford University Press.

Cinel, D. 1991. *The National Integration of Italian Return Migration, 1870–1929.* Cambridge: Cambridge University Press.

Cinnirella, F. 2008. "Optimists or Pessimists? A Reconsideration of Nutritional Status in Britain, 1740–1865." *European Review of Economic History* 12: 325–354.

Ciocca, P. 2007. *Ricchi per sempre? Una storia economica d'Italia (1796–2005).* Turin: Bollati Boringhieri.

Cipolla, C. M. 1969. *Literacy and Developement in the West.* Baltimore: Penguin.

Citro, C. F., and R. T. Michael (eds.). 1995. *Measuring Poverty: A New Approach.* Washington, DC: National Academy Press.

CNEL (Consiglio nazionale dell'economia e del lavoro). 1993. *Rapporto sulla distribuzione e redistribuzione del reddito in Italia 1981–1991.* Ed. N. Rossi. Bologna: Il Mulino.

CNEL (Consiglio nazionale dell'economia e del lavoro). 1994. *II rapporto sulla distribuzione e redistribuzione del reddito in Italia 1992–1993.* Ed. N. Rossi. Bologna: Il Mulino.

CNEL (Consiglio nazionale dell'economia e del lavoro). 1996. *III rapporto sulla distribuzione e redistribuzione del reddito in Italia 1994–1995.* Ed. N. Rossi. Bologna: Il Mulino.

CNEL (Consiglio nazionale dell'economia e del lavoro). 1998. *IV rapporto sulla distribuzione e redistribuzione del reddito in Italia 1996–1997.* Ed. N. Rossi. Bologna: Il Mulino.

CNEL (Consiglio nazionale dell'economia e del lavoro). 2000. *V rapporto sulla distribuzione e redistribuzione del reddito in Italia ed in Europa 1998–1999.* Ed. V. Atella. Bologna: Il Mulino.

CNEL (Consiglio nazionale dell'economia e del lavoro). 2002. *VI rapporto sulla distribuzione e redistribuzione del reddito in Europa 2000–2001.* Ed. V. Atella. Bologna: Il Mulino.

Coccia, G., and A. Righi (eds.). 2009. *Il lavoro minorile: esperienze e problematiche di stima.* "Il lavoro che cambia" http://www.portalecnel.it/Portale/IndLavrapportiFinali.nsf/vwCapitoli?OpenView&Count=40.

Coccìa, M., and G. Della Torre. 2007. *La ricostruzione dei consumi pubblici nel campo dell'istruzione nell'Italia liberale: 1861–1913*. DEPFID Working Paper, 9/2007, University of Siena.

Cohen, J., and G. Federico. 2001. *Lo sviluppo economico italiano. 1820–1960*. Bologna: Il Mulino.

Cohen, M. 1982. "Changing Education Strategies among Immigrant Generations: New York Italians in Comparative Perspective." *Journal of Social History* 15, no. 3: 443–466.

Cohen, D., and M. Soto. 2007. "Growth and Human Capital: Good Data, Good Results." *Journal of Economic Growth* Springer, 12, no. 1: 51–76.

Coletti, F. 1911. *Dell'emigrazione italiana*. In AA. VV., *Cinquanta anni di storia italiana*, vol. III. Milan: Hoepli, 219.

Colli, A., and M. Vasta. 2010. *Forms of Enterprise in 20th Century Italy: Boundaries, Structures and Strategies*. Cheltenham: Edward Elgar.

Colucci, M. 2010. *La libertà solidale. Scritti 1942–45*. Rome: Donzelli.

Commissariato generale della emigrazione italiana. 1927. *Annuario statistico della emigrazione italiana dal 1876 al 1925 con notizie sull'emigrazione negli anni 1869–1875*. Rome: Edizione del commissariato dell'emigrazione.

Commissione di indagine sulla povertà. 1985. *La povertà in Italia. Rapporto conclusivo della Commissione di studio istituita presso la Presidenza del Consiglio dei ministri*. Rome: Presidenza del Consiglio dei ministri.

Commissione di indagine sulla povertà e l'emarginazione. 1996. *La povertà in Italia 1980–1994*. Rome: Presidenza del Consiglio dei ministri, Dipartimento per l'informazione e l'editoria.

Commissione di indagine sulla povertà e sull'emarginazione. 1997. *La spesa pubblica per l'assistenza in Italia*. Rome: Presidenza del Consiglio dei Ministri, Dipartimento per l'informazione e l'editoria.

Comune di Milano. 1928. *Annuario Statistico, Anni 1926–1930, IV–VIII*. Milan: Industrie Grafiche Italiane Stucchi.

Conte, L., G. Della Torre, and M. Vasta. 2007. *The Human Development Index in Historical Perspective: Italy from Political Unification to the Present Day*. "Quaderni," 491, Siena, Department of Economics, University of Siena.

Conte, L., M. Rossi, and G. Vecchi. 2011. "Vulnerabilità." In G. Vecchi, *In ricchezza e in povertà*. Bologna: Il Mulino.

Coppola, L., D. Di Laurea, and S. Gerosa. 2013. *The Immigrants Wage Gap in Italy*, June 25. Available at SSRN: http://ssrn.com/abstract=2514714.

Corner, P. 2002. *Fascismo e controllo sociale*, "Italia contemporanea," 228.

Corsini, C. A., and P. P. Viazzo (eds.). 1993. *The Decline of Infant Mortality in Europe, 1800–1950. Four National Case Studies*. Florence: Unicef-Istituto degli Innocenti.

Corti, P. 1984. "Malaria e società contadina nel Mezzogiorno." In F. Della Peruta (ed.), *Storia d'Italia, Annali 7, Malattia e medicina*. Turin: Einaudi, XXX–XXX.

Corti, P., and M. Sanfilippo (eds.). 2009. *Migrazioni*. "Storia d'Italia, Annali," 24, Turin: Giulio Einaudi Editore, 151–804.

Cosmacini, G. 1989. *Medicina e sanità in Italia nel ventesimo secolo. Dalla "spagnola" alla seconda guerra mondiale*. Rome-Bari: Laterza.

Cosmacini, G. 2005. *Storia della medicina e della sanità in Italia*. Rome-Bari: Laterza.

Costa, D. L., and R. H. Steckel. 1997. "Long-term Trends in Health, Welfare, and Economic Growth in the United States." In R. H. Steckel and R. Floud (eds.), *Health and Welfare during Industrialization*. Chicago: University of Chicago Press, 47–90.

Costanza, R., et al. 2014. "Time to leave GDP behind." *Nature*, January 16: 283–285.

Costanzo, A. 1940. "Risultati di una inchiesta sui bilanci di 744 famiglie operaie italiane." In Società italiana di Demografia e Statistica, *Atti della V riunione dedicata alla statistica del lavoro, Napoli, 18–20 dicembre 1939–XVIII*. Florence: Tipografia dell'Unione Arti Grafiche, 229–279.

Costanzo, A. 1942. "Modificazioni della struttura quantitativa e qualitativa dei bilanci alimentari in funzione delle variazioni della spesa per il vitto." *Rivista Internazionale di Scienze Sociali* 13, no. 4: 241–250.

Costanzo, A. 1943. "Relazioni tra redditi e fitti." In Società italiana di Demografia e Statistica, *Atti della VII riunione*. Rome: Tipografia dell'Unione Arti Grafiche, 475–502.

Costanzo, A. 1948. "La statura degli italiani ventenni nati dal 1854 al 1920." *Annali di statistica* VIII, no. 2: 59–123. Rome: Istat.

Cowell, F. A. 2011. *Measuring inequality*. 3rd edn. Oxford: Oxford University Press.

Cowell, F. A., and F. Mehta. 1982. "The Estimation and Interpolation of Inequality Measures." *Review of Economic Studies* 49, 273–290.

Cowell, F. A., and M.-P. Victoria-Feser. 1996. "Robustness Properties of Inequality Measures." *Econometrica* 64: 77–101.

Crafts, N. F. R. 1997a. "The Human Development Index and Changes in the Standards of Living: Some Historical Comparisons." *European Review of Economic History* 1, no. 3: 299–322.

Crafts, N. F. R. 1997b. "Some Dimensions of the 'Quality of Life' during the British Industrial Revolution." *Economic History Review* 4: 617–639.

Crafts, N. F. R. 2002. "The Human Development Index, 1870–1999: Some Revised Estimates." *European Review of Economic History* 6, no. 3: 395–405.

Crafts, N., and P. Fearon. 2010. "Lessons from the 1930s Great Depression." *Oxford Review of Economic Policy* 26, no. 3: 285–317.

Crafts, N., and G. Toniolo. 1996. *Economic Growth in Europe since 1945*. Cambridge: Cambridge University Press.

Crafts, N., and G. Toniolo. 2010. "Aggregate Growth, 1950–2005." In S. Broadberry and K. H. O'Rourke (eds.), *The Cambridge Economic History of Modern Europe*, vol. 2 Cambridge: Cambridge University Press, 296–332.

Crainz, G. 2005. *Storia del miracolo italiano: culture, identità, trasformazioni fra anni cinquanta e sessanta*. Rome: Donzelli.

Croce, B. 1928. *Storia d'Italia dal 1871 al 1915*. Bari: Laterza.

Cunningham, H. 2000. "The Decline of Child Labour: Labour Markets and Family Economics in Europe and North America since 1830." *Economic History Review* 53: 409–428.

Cunningham, H., and P. P. Viazzo. 1996. *Child Labor in Historical Perspective, 1800–1985: Case Studies from Europe, Japan and Colombia*. Florence: UNICEF.

Cuoco, V. 1991. *Statistica della Repubblica Italiana, Scritti inediti*. Ed. Vittorio Gatto. Rome: Archivio Guido Izzi.

D'Alessio, G. 2012. *Wealth and Inequality in Italy*. Bank of Italy Occasional Working Paper, 115. Rome: Bank of Italy.

D'Alessio, G., and R. Gambacorta. 2007. *L'accesso all'abitazione di residenza in Italia*. "Questioni di economia e finanza (Occasional papers)," 9, July 2007.

D'Amuri, F., and G. Peri. 2014. "Immigration, Jobs and Labor Market Institutions: Evidence from Europe". *Journal of European Economic Association*, 12, no. 2: 432–464.

D'Apice, C. 1975. "La povertà in Italia." *Economia e Lavoro* 9, nos. 2 and 4: XXX–XXX.

Dal Maso, L., R. De Angelis, and S. Guzzinati (eds.). 2010. *La prevalenza dei tumori in Italia, Rapporto AIRTum 2010*, "Epidemiolgia e prevenzione," September 2010, http://www.registri-tumori.it/cms/?q=Rapp2010.

Dalton, H. 1920. "The Measurement of the Inequality of Incomes." *Economic Journal* 30: 348–361.

Dang, H., and P. Lanjouw. 2014. *Welfare Dynamics Measurement: Two Definitions of a Vulnerability Line and Their Empirical Application*. Policy Research Working Paper Series 6944. Washington, DC: World Bank.

Daniele, V., and P. Malanima. 2007. "Il prodotto delle regioni e il divario Nord-Sud in Italia (1861–2004)." *Rivista di politica economica* 67, nos. 3–4: 267–315.

Daniele, V., and P. Malanima. 2011. *Il divario Nord-Sud in Italia. 1861–2011*. Rubbettino: Soveria Mannelli.

Danubio, M. E., E. Amicone, and R. Vargiu. 2005. "Height and BMI of Italian Immigrants to the USA, 1908–1970." *Economics and Human Biology* 3: 33–43.

Dasgupta, P., and W. Weale. 1992. "On Measuring the Quality of Life." *World Development* 20, no. 1: 119–131.

Datt, G., and M. Ravallion. 1992. "Growth and Redistribution Components of Changes in Poverty: A Pecomposition with Application to Brazil and India." *Journal of Development Economics* 38: 275–295.

Davies, D. 1795. *The Case of Labourers in Husbandry*. Bath: R. Cruttwell.

Davies, J. B., S. Sandstrom, A. Shorrocks, and E. N. Wolff. 2008. *The World Distribution of Household Wealth*. UNU-WIDER Working Paper, no. 2008/03.

De Bernardi, A. 1984. *Il mal della rosa: denutrizione e pellagra nelle campagne italiane fra '800e '900*. Milan: Franco Angeli.

De Bernardi, A. 1984. "Storia d'Italia, Pellagra, stato e scienza medica: la curabilità impossibile," in *Storia d'Italia*. Annali 7. Turin: Einaudi.

De Bonis, R., F. Farabullini, M. Rocchelli, and A. Salvio. 2011. *Il valore aggiunto del settore del credito dal 1861 al 2010*. Mimeo. Rome: Bank of Italy.

De Cecco, M. 2000. *L'economia di Lucignolo. Opportunità e vincoli dello sviluppo italiano*. Rome: Donzelli.

De Flora, S., A. Quaglia, C. Bennicelli, and M. Vercelli. 2005. "The Epidemiological Revolution of the 20th Century." *FASEB Journal* 19, no. 8: 892–897.

De Fort, E. 1995. *Scuola e analfabetismo nell'Italia del '900*. Bologna: Il Mulino.

De Fourcy, M. L. 1883. "L'Ingenieur Des Mines." *La Réforme sociale, Trosieme année, tome* 5: 29–44.

De Gérando, J.-M. 1867. "Della beneficenza pubblica, *trattati speciali*." *Biblioteca dell'Economista* II, no. 13: 1007–1033.

De Grauwe, P., and Y. Ji. 2013. "Are Germans Really Poorer than Spaniards, Italians and Greeks?" *Vox Europe*, 14 April: http://www.voxeu.org/article/are-germans-really-poorer-spaniards-italiano and greeks

De Herdt, R. 1996. "Child Labour in Belgium: 1800–1914." In H. Cunningham and P. P. Viazzo (eds.), *Child Labour in Historical Perspective, 1800–1985: Case Studies from Europe, Japan and Colombia*. Florence: UNICEF and Instituto degli Innocenti, 23–29.

De Luca, G. 1991. "La metafora sanitaria nella costruzione della città moderna in Italia." *Storia Urbana* 4: 43–62.

De Marco, R. 1939. "Risultati di una inchiesta alimentare nel comune di Scilla (Reggio Calabria). Nota I." *Quaderni della nutrizione* 6: 41–71.

De Mattia, R. 1959. *L'unificazione monetaria italiana*. Turin: Ilte.

De Mauro, T. 1963. *Storia linguistica dell'Italia unita*. Bari: Laterza.

De Mauro, T. 2010. *La cultura degli italiani*. Ed. F. Erbani. Rome: Laterza.

De Mauro, T. 2014. *Storia linguistica dell'Italia repubblicana*. Bari: Laterza.

De Meo, G. 1965. "Produttività e distribuzione del reddito in Italia nel periodo 1951–63." *Annali di statistica*, VIII, 15. Rome: Istituto Centrale di Statistica.

De Meo, G. 1967. "Redditi e produttività in Italia (1951–1966)." *Annali di statistica*, VIII, 20. Rome: Istituto Centrale di Statistica.

De Rosa, L. 1980. *Emigranti, capitali e banche*. Napoli: Banco di Napoli.

De Simoni, A., and R. M. Lipsi. 2005. "La mortalit per causa in Italia nell'ultimo trentennio. Tavole di mortalità 1971, 1976, 1981, 1986, 1991, 1996, 2000." *Fonti e Strumenti*, 6. Rome: University of Rome "La Sapienza," Department of Demographic Sciences.

De Vita, A. 1933. "La ricchezza privata dell'Italia al 1928 e la sua ripartizione regionale." *La vita economica italiana* 4: 48–64.

Deaton, A. S. 1975. "The Measurement of Income and Price Elasticities." *European Economic Review* 6, no. 3: 261–273.

Deaton, A. 1992. *Understanding Consumption*. Oxford: Oxford University Press.

Deaton, A. 1997. *The Analysis of Household Surveys: A Microeconometric Approach to Development Policy*. Washington, DC: World Bank.

Deaton, A. 2003. "Health, Inequality and Economic Development." *Journal of Economic Literature* 41: 113–158.

Deaton, A. 2007. "Height, Health and Development." *Proceedings of the National Academies of Science* 104, no. 33: 13232–13237.

Deaton, A. 2008. "Height, Health, and Inequality: The Distribution of Adult Heights in India." *American Economic Review: Papers and Proceedings* 98, no. 2: 468–474.

Deaton, A., and J. Muellbauer. 1980. *Economics and Consumer Behaviour*. Cambridge: Cambridge University Press.

Deaton, A., and S. Zaidi. 2002. *Guidelines for Constructing Consumption Aggregates for Welfare Analysis*. Living Standards Measurement Study Working Paper, 135. Washington, DC: World Bank.

Decancq, K., and M. Lugo. 2013. "Weights in Multidimensional Indices of Wellbeing: An Overview." *Econometric Reviews* 32, no. 1: 7–34.

Declich, C., and V. Polin 2005. "Povertà assoluta e costo della vita: un'analisi empirica sulle famiglie italiane." *Politica economica* 21, no. 2: 265–305.

Deeming, C. 2010. "The Historical Development of Family Budget Standards in Britain, from the 17th Century to the Present." *Social Policy & Administration* 44, no. 7: 765–788.

Dehejia, R., and A. Lleras-Mune. 2004. "Booms, Busts, and Babies' Health." *Quarterly Journal of Economics* 119, no. 3: 1091–1130.

Del Boca, D., and A. Venturini. 2003. *Italian migration*. IZA DP, no. 938.

Del Boca, D., and C. Wetzels. 2010. *Social Policies, Labour Markets and Motherhood: A Comparative Analysis of European Countries*. Cambridge: Cambridge University Press.

Del Panta, L. 1980. *Le epidemie nella storia demografica italiana (secoli XIV–XIX)*. Turin: Loescher.

Del Panta, L. 1997. "Infant and Child Mortality in Italy, Eighteenth to Twentieth Century: Long-Term Trends and Territorial Differences." In A. Bideau, B. Desjardins, and H. P. Brignoli (eds.), *Infant and Child Mortality in the Past*. Oxford: Clarendon Press, 7–21.

Del Vecchio, G. 1912. "Relazioni tra entrata e consumo." *Giornale degli economisti* 4, nos. 111–142; 220–251, 389 430.

Della Peruta, F. 1980. Sanità pubblica e legislazione sanitaria dall'Unità a Crispi. *Studi Storici* 21, no. 4: 713–759.

Della Peruta, F. 1985. *Società e classi popolari nell'Italia dell'800*. Milan: Franco Angeli.

Dercon, S. 2001. *Assessing Vulnerability to Poverty*. Center for the Study of African Economies, Department of Economies, Oxford University.

Dercon, S. 2005. "Risk, Poverty and Vulnerability in Africa." *Journal of African Economies* 14, no. 4: 483–488.

Dercon, S. 2007. *Insurance against Poverty*. Oxford: Oxford University Press.

Desai, M. 1991. "Human Development: Concept and Measurement." *European Economic Review* 35, nos. 2–3: 350–357.

Detti, T. 1994. *Salute, società e stato nell'Italia liberale*. Milan: Franco Angeli.

Devicienti, F., and V. Gualtieri. 2007. "Persistenza e transitorietà della povertà in Italia: soggettività, multidimensionalità e reddito a confront." In G. Rovati (ed.), *Povertà e lavoro. Giovani generazioni a rischio*. Rome: Carocci, 59–92.

Di Rollo, F. 1965. "Le retribuzioni dei lavoratori edili a Roma dal 1826 al 1880." *Archivio economico della unificazione italiana* I, 13, no. 4. Turin: Ilte.

Dickens, C. 1846. *Pictures from Italy*. London: Bradbury and Evans.

Diewert, W. E. 1993. "The Early History of Price Index Research." In W. E. Diewert and A. O. Nakamura (eds.), *Essays in Index Number Theory*. Amsterdam: Elsevier, 1: 33–71.

Diewert, W. E. 2009. "Durables and Owner-Occupied Housing in a Consumer Price Index." In W. E. Diewert, J. S. Greenlees, and C. R. Hulten (eds.), *Price Index Concepts and Measurements*. Chicago: University of Chicago Press, 445–500.

Disney, R. 1996. *Can We Afford to Grow Older?* Cambridge: MIT Press.

Dollar, D., and A. Kraay. 2002. "Growth Is Good for the Poor." *Journal of Economic Growth* 7, no. 3: 195–225.

Doria, M. 1989. *Ansaldo. L'impresa e lo stato*. Milan: F. Angeli.

Doxa. 1966. *Il volto sconosciuto dell'Italia*. Milan: Giuffrè.

Draghi, M. 2007. *Household Wealth in Central Bank Policy Analysis, Remarks by Mario Draghi, Governor of the Bank of Italy*. Rome, July 6.

Draghi, M. 2010. *Crescita, benessere e compiti dell'economia politica*. Lecture of the Governator of the Bank of Italy during the Conference in remembrance of Giorgio Fuà "Sviluppo economico e benessere," Ancona, November 5.

Drinkwater, S., P. Levine, and E. Lotti. 2003. *The Labour Market Effects of Remittances*. FLOWENLA Discussion Paper, no. 6. Hamburg Institute of International Economics.

Dronkers, J., and M. de Heus. 2010. *Negative Selectivity of Europe's Guest-worker Immigration?* MPRA Paper, no. 22213.

Dustmann, C., I. Fadlon, and Y. Weiss. 2011. "Return Migration, Human Capital Accumulation and the Brain Drain." *Journal of Development Economics* 95, no. 1: 58–67.

Dustmann, C., T. Trattini, and I. Preston. 2013. "The Effect of Immigration along the Distribution of Wages." *Review of Economic Studies* 80, no. 1: 145–173.

Du Tot, N. 1738. *Reflexions politiques sur les finances et le commerce*. The Hague: Vaillant frères et N. Prevost, 2 vols.

Easterlin, R. A. 1974. "Does Economic Growth Improve the Human Lot? Some Empirical Evidence." In P. A. David and M. W. Reder (eds.), *Nations and Households in Economic Growth: Essays in Honor of Moses Abramowitz*. New York: Academic Press, 89–125.

Easterlin, R. A. 1995. "Will Raising the Incomes of All Increase the Happiness of All?" *Journal of Economic Behavior & Organization* 27, no. 1: 35–47.

Eden, F. M. 1797. *The State of the Poor*. London, 3 vols.

Edmonds, E. V., and N. Pavcnik. 2005. "Child Labor in the Global Economy." *Journal of Economic Perspectives* 19, no. 1: 199–220.

Egidi, V. 2007. *Differenze di genere nella mortalità in Italia. Mortalità evitabile per genere e Usl*, Atlante ERA, http://www.atlantesanitario.it/index.php?option=com_content&view=articl e&id=65&Itemid=79.

Einaudi, L. 1936. "Il peccato originale e la teoria della classe eletta in Federico Le Play." *Rivista di storia economica* 2: 81–129.

Einaudi, L. 1940. "Schemi statistici e dubbi storici." *Rivista di storia economica* a. V: 125–129.

Einaudi, L. 1956. *Prediche inutili*. Turin: Einaudi.

EM-DAT: The OFDA/CRED International Disaster Database. n.d. www.emdat.be, Université Catholique de Louvain, Brussels (Belgium).

Engel, E. 1857. Die Productions- und Consumptionsverhaeltnisse des Koenigsreichs Sachsen, Zeitschrift des Statistischen Bureaus des Koniglich Sachsischen Ministeriums des Inneren, nos. 8 and 9.

Engels, F. 1845. *Die Lage der arbeitenden Klasse in England. Nach eigner Anschauung und authentischen Quellen*. Leipzig; trad. it. *La situazione della classe operaia in Inghilterra*, Roma: Editori Riuniti, 1992.

Engerman, S. L. 1997. "The Standard of Living Debate in International Perspective: Measure and Indicators." In R. H. Steckel and R. Floud (eds.), *Health and Welfare during Industrialization*. Chicago: University of Chicago Press/NBER, 17–45.

Erickson, C. L., and A. Ichino. 1995. "Wage Differentials in Italy: Market Forces, Institutions, and Inflation." In R. B. Freeman and L. F. Katz (eds.), *Differences and Changes in Wage Structures*. Chicago: University of Chicago Press, 265–305.

Errera, A. 1879. "Inchiesta sulle condizioni degli operai nelle fabbriche." *Archivio di statistica* 4: 113–185.

Esping-Andersen, G. 2002. *Why We Need a New Welfare State*. Oxford: Oxford University Press.

Esposto, A. G. 1997. "Estimating Regional per Capita Income: Italy, 1861–1914." *Journal of European Economic History* 26, no. 3: 585–604.

Esteves, R., and D. Khoudour-Castéras. 2009. "A fantastic rain of gold: European migrants' remittances and balance of payments adjustment during the gold standard period." *Journal of Economic History* 69, no. 4: 951–985.

Esteves, R., and D. Khoudour-Castéras. 2010. "Remittances, Capital Flows and Financial Development during the Mass Migration Period, 1870–1913." *European Review of Economic History* 15, no. 3 (December): 443–474.

Eurobarometer: http://ec.europa.eu/public_opinion/index_en.htm.

European Central Bank. 2013. *The Eurosystem Household Finance and Consumption Survey: Results from the First Wave*. Statistics Paper Series 2, April.

European Foundation for the Improvement of Living and Working Conditions. 2006. *First European Quality of Life Survey: Social Dimensions of Housing*. Luxembourg: Office for Official Publications of the European Communities.

Eurostat. 2010. http://epp.eurostat.ec.europa.eu/portal/page/portal/statistics/search_database.

Eurostat. 2013. European System of Accounts 2010 Manual. Available from: www.lb.lt/n22873/esa_2010-en_book.pdf.

Eurostat-OECD. 2006. *Methodological Manual on Purchasing Power Parities (PPPs)*. Paris: OECD.

Evans, S., and B. Jovanovic. 1989. "An Estimated Model of Entrepreneurial Choice under Liquidity Constraints." *Journal of Political Economy* 97, no. 4 (August): 808–827.

Eveleth, P. B., and J. M.Tanner. 1990. *Worldwide Variation in Human Growth*. 2nd edn. Cambridge: Cambridge University Press.

Evenepoel, P., B. Geypens, A. Luypaerts, M. Hiele, Y. Ghoos, and P. Rutgeerts. 1998. "Digestibility of Cooked and Raw Egg Protein in Humans as Assessed by Stable Isotope Techniques." *Journal of Nutrition* 128: 1716–1722.

Faina, E. (ed.) 1911. *Inchiesta parlamentare sulle condizioni dei contadini nelle province meridionali e nella Sicilia (1909–1911)*. Rome: Bertero.

Faini, R. 2003. *Is the Brain Drain an Unmitigated Blessing?* WIDER Discussion Paper 2003/64.

Faini, R., G. Galli, P. Gennari, and F. Rossi. 1997. "An Empirical Puzzle: Falling Migration and Growing Unemployment Differentials among Italian Regions." *European Economic Review* 41, nos. 3–5: 571–579.

Faini, R., and A. Venturini. 1994a. "Italian Emigration in the Pre-war Period." In Timothy J. Hatton and Jeffrey G. Williamson (eds.), *Migration and the International Labour Market 1850–1939*. London: Routledge, 72–90.

Faini, R., and A. Venturini. 1994b. *Migration and Growth: The Experience of Southern Europe*, Centro Studi Luca D'Agliano—Queen Elizabeth House, Development Studies Working Papers, no. 75, October.

Fallada, H. 1933. *Little Man, What Now?* "E adesso, pover'uomo?," Sellerio editore Palermo, 2008. New York: Simon & Schuster.

FAO (Food and Agriculture Organization). 2005. *Supply Utilization Accounts and Food Balance Sheets in the Context of a National Statistical System*. Rome.

FAO (Food and Agriculture Organization). 2008. *Fao Methodology for the Measurement of Food Deprivation. Updating the Minimum Dietary Energy Requirements*. Roma.

FAO (Food and Agriculture Organization). 2010. http://faostat.fao.org/site/368/default.aspx#ancor.

FAO/WHO/UNU. 2004. *Human Energy Requirements. Report of a Joint FAO/WHO/UNU Expert Consultation*. Rome.

Farrell-Vinay, G. 1977. *Povertà e politica nell'Ottocento: le Opere Pie nello Stato liberale*. Turin: Scriptorium.

Fauri, F. 2001. *L'Italia e l'integrazione economica europea, 1947–2000*. Bologna: Il Mulino.

Fauri, F. 2010. *Il piano Marshall e l'Italia*. Bologna: Il Mulino.

Favero, G. 2006. "I servizi statistici ufficiali in Italia dall'Unità alla Repubblica: strategie di organizzazione interna e pertinenza dell'informazione prodotta." *Note di Lavoro*, 2, Università Ca' Foscari di Venezia.

Favero, G. 2007. "Storia economica e storia delle scienze sociali: a proposito dell'edizione critica delle monografie di famiglie agrarie." *Storia e Società* XXX, no. 117: 581–592.

Federico, G. 1984. "Azienda contadina e autoconsumo fra antropologia ed econometria: considerazioni metodologiche." *Rivista di storia economica* 2: 222–268.

Federico, G. 1986 Mercantilizzazione e sviluppo economico italiano (1861–1940). *Rivista di storia economica* s.i., III, 2: 149–186.

Federico, G. 1991. "Household Budgets as a Source for the Study of Rural Economy (Italy, 1860–1940): Commercialization and Peasants' Behaviour." In T. Pierenkemper (ed.), *Zur Ökonomik des privaten Haushlts*. Dusseldorf: Campus, 182–197.

Federico, G. 1992. "Il valore aggiunto dell'agricoltura." In G. M. Rey (ed.), *I conti economici dell'Italia 2. Una stima del valore aggiunto per il 1911*. Rome-Bari: Laterza, 3–103.

Federico, G. 1996. "Italy, 1860–1940: A Little-Known Success Story." *Economic History Review* 49, no. 4: 764–786.

Federico, G. 2003a. "Heights, Calories and Welfare: A New Perspective on Italian Industrialization, 1854–1913." *Economics and Human Biology*, 1, no. 3: 289–308.

Federico, G. 2003b. "Le nuove stime della produzione agricola italiana, 1860–1910: primi risultati e implicazioni." *Rivista di storia economica* 19, no. 3: 359–381.

Federico, G. 2007a. "Ma l'agricoltura meridionale era davvero arretrata?" *Rivista di politica economica* 67, nos. 3–4: 317–340.

Federico, G. 2007b. "Market Integration and Market Efficiency: The Case of 19th Century Italy." *Explorations in Economic History* 44, no. 2: 293–316.

Federico, G., and G. Toniolo. 1991. "Italy." In R. Sylla and G. Toniolo (eds.), *Patterns of European Industrialization*. London: Routledge, 197–217.

Fehr, E., and K. M. Schmidt. 1999. "A Theory of Fairness, Competition and Cooperation." *The Quarterly Journal of Economics* 3: 817–868.

Feinstein, C. H. 1987. "Measurement of Economic Growth." In J. Eatwell, M. Milgate, and P. Newman (eds.), *The New Palgrave: A Dictionary of Economics Online*. Londra: Palgrave Macmillan.

Feinstein, C. H. 1988. "The Rise and Fall of the Williamson Curve." *Journal of Economic History* 48, no. 03: 699–729.

Feinstein, C. H., P. Temin, and G. Toniolo. 2004. *L'economia europea fra le due guerre*, Rome-Bari: Laterza (trading. *The World Economy between the World Wars*, Oxford: Oxford University Press, 2008).

Feldstein, M. 1998. *Income Inequality and Poverty*, NBER Working Paper Series, 6770, October.

Feldstein, M. 1999. "Reducing Poverty, not Inequality." *The Public Interest* 137: 33–41.

Felice, E. 2002. "Le politiche regionali in Italia e nel Regno Unito (1950–1989)." *Rivista economica del Mezzogiorno* 16, nos. 1–2: 175–235.

Felice, E. 2005a. "Il reddito delle regioni italiane nel 1938. e nel 1951. Una stima basata sul costo del lavoro." *Rivista di storia economica* 21, no. 1: 3–30.

Felice, E. 2005b. "Il valore aggiunto regionale. Una stima per il 1891 e per il 1911 e alcune elaborazioni di lungo periodo (1891–1971)." *Rivista di storia economica* 21, no. 3: 83–124.

Felice, E. 2007a. *Divari regionali e intervento pubblico. Per una rilettura dello sviluppo in Italia*. Bologna: Il Mulino.

Felice, E. 2007b. "I divari regionali in Italia sulla base degli indicatori sociali (1871–2001)." *Rivista di politica economica* 3–4: 359–405.

Felice, E. 2009a. *Estimating Regional Gdp in Italy (1871–2001): Sources, Methodology, and Results*, Universidad Carlos III de Madrid. Departamento de Historia Económica e Instituciones. Working Papers in Economic History 09-07, http://e-archivo.uc3m.es/handle/10016/5334.

Felice, E. 2009b. *Regional Value Added in Italy (1891–2001) and the Backbone of a Long Term Picture*, Working Papers in Economic History, Universidad Carlos III de Madrid.

Felice, E. 2010. "State Ownership and International Competitiveness: the Italian Finmeccanica from Alfa Romeo to Aerospace and Defence." *Enterprise and Society* 11, no. 3: 594–635.

Felice, E. 2011. "Regional Value Added in Italy (1891–2001) and the Foundation of a Long Term Picture." *The Economic History Review*, 64, in corso di stampa.

Felice, E. 2012. "Regional Convergence in Italy (1891–2001): Testing Human and Social Capital." *Cliometrica* 6, no. 3: 267–306.

Felice, E., and A. Carreras. 2012. "When Did Modernization Begin? Italy's Industrial Growth Reconsidered in Light of New Value-added Series, 1911–1951." *Explorations in Economic History* 49, no. 4: 443–460.

Felice, E., and M. Vasta. 2015. "Passive Modernization? Social Indicators and Human Development in Italy's Regions (1871–2009)." *European Review of Economic History* 19, no. 1: 44–66.

Felice, E., and G. Vecchi. 2015. "Italy's Growth and Decline, 1861–2011." *Journal of Interdisciplinary History* 45, no. 4: 507–548.

Felice, E. 2015. *Ascesa e Declino. Storia Economica d'Italia*. Bologna: Il Mulino.

Felice, E., and A. Lepore. 2016. "State Intervention and Economic Growth in Southern Italy: The Rise and Fall of the «Cassa per il Mezzogiorno» (1950–1986)." *Business History* (in press, available at: http://dx.doi.org/10.1080/00076791.2016.1174214)

Fenoaltea, S. 1988. "International Resource Flows and Construction Movements in the Atlantic Economy: the Kuznets Cycle in Italy, 1861–1913." *The Journal of Economic History* 48, no. 3: 605–638.

Fenoaltea, S. 1992. "Il valore aggiunto dell'industria nel 1911." In G.M. Rey (ed.), *I conti economici dell'Italia, 2. Una stima del valore aggiunto per il 1911*. Rome-Bari: Laterza, 105–190.

Fenoaltea, S. 1998. Lo sviluppo economico dell'Italia nel lungo periodo: riflessione su tre fallimenti." In P. Ciocca and G. Toniolo (ed.), *Storia economica d'Italia*, vol. 1. Rome-Bari: Laterza, 3–41.

Fenoaltea, S. 2002. "Production and Consumption in Post-Unification Italy: New Evidence, New Conjectures." *Rivista di storia economica* 5: 251–300.

Fenoaltea, S. 2003a. "Notes on the Rate of Industrial Growth in Italy, 1861–1913." *The Journal of Economic History* 63, no. 3: 695–735.

Fenoaltea, S. 2003b. "Peeking backward: Regional Aspects of Industrial Growth in Post-unification Italy." *The Journal of Economic History* 63, no. 4: 1059–1102.

Fenoaltea, S. 2005. "La crescita economica dell'Italia postunitaria: le nuove serie storiche." *Rivista di storia economica* 21, no. 2: 91–121.

Fenoaltea, S. 2006. *L'economia italiana dall'Unità alla Grande Guerra*, Rome-Bari: Laterza.

Fenoaltea, S. 2007. "I due fallimenti della storia economica: il periodo post-unitario." *Rivista Politica Economica* XCVII, no. 3–4: 341–358.

Fenoaltea, S. 2008. "A proposito del PIL." *Italianieuropei* 8, no. 1: 165–169.

Fenoaltea, S. 2010. "The Reconstruction of Historical National Accounts: The Case of Italy." *PSL Quarterly Review*, APSL 63, no. 252: 77–96.

Fenoaltea, S. 2011. "On the Structure of the Italian Economy, 1861–1913." *Rivista di storia economica, il Mulino* no. 1: 61–72.

Fenoaltea, S. 2014. *The Reinterpretation of Italian Economic History. From Unification to the Great War*. Cambridge: Cambridge University Press.

Fenoaltea, S., and C. Bardini. 2000. "Il valore aggiunto dell'industria." In G. M. Rey (ed.), *I conti economici dell'Italia*, 3.2. *Il valore aggiunto per agli anni 1891, 1938, 1951*, Rome-Bari: Laterza, 113–238.

Ferenczi, I., and W. Wilcox. 1929. *International Migrations*. New York: NBER.

Ferger, W. F. 1946. "Historical Note on the Purchasing Power Concept, and Index Number." *Journal of the American Statistical Association* 41, no. 233: 53–57.

Ferrario, M., G. Cesana, D. Vannuzzo, L. Pilotto, R. Sega, and S. Giampaoli. 2001. "Surveillance of Ischaemic Heart Disease: Results from the Italian MONICA Populations." *International Journal of Epidemiology* 30: S23–S29.

Ferrera, M. 1984. *Il welfare state in Italia. Sviluppo e crisi in prospettiva comparata*. Bologna: Il Mulino.

Ferrera, M. 1993. *Modelli di solidarietà. Politica e riforme sociali nelle democrazie*. Bologna: Il Mulino.

Ferrera, M. 1998. *Le trappole del Welfare*. Bologna: Il Mulino.

Ferrera, M. 2010. "The South European Countries." In F. Castles, S. Leibfried, J. Lewis, H. Obinger, and C. Pierson (eds.), *The Oxford Handbook of The Welfare State*. Oxford: Oxford University Press, 616–629.

Ferrie, J. P., and T. J. Hatton. 2013. *Two Centuries of International Migration*. IZA DP no. 7866, December.

Filosa, R., and I. Visco. 1980. "Costo del lavoro, indicizzazione e perequazione delle retribuzioni negli anni '70." In G. Nardozzi (ed.), *I difficili anni '70. I problemi della politica economica italiana 1973/1979*. Milan: Etas Libri, 107–139.

Finzi, R. 1975. "Il necessario e il superfluo. Note su storia dell'alimentazione e storicità dei bisogni." *Studi storici* 2: 424–438.

Finzi, R. 1982. *Quando e perché fu sconfitta la pellagra in Italia*, in M.L. Berti e A. Gigli Marchetti (ed.), *Salute e classi lavoratrici in Italia dall'Unità al fascismo*, Milano, Franco Angeli, 391–429.

Fiocca, G. 1957. "Monografia di una famiglia bracciantile con piccola proprietà e compartecipazione." *Rivista di Economia agraria*, marzo.

Fiocco, G. 2004. *L'Italia prima del miracolo economico: l'inchiesta parlamentare sulla miseria (1951–54)*. Manduria: Lacaita.

Fiori, A. 2005. *Poveri, Opere pie e assistenza. Dall'Unità al fascismo*. Rome: Studium.

Fisher, G. M. 2008. *Remarks on Mollie Orshansky's Life, Career, and Achievements*, http://www.ssa.gov/history/orshansky.html

Fleurbaey, M. 2009. "Beyond GDP: The Quest for a Measure of Social Welfare." *Journal of Economic Literature* 47, no. 4: 1029–1075.

Fleurbaey, M., K. Decancq, and E. Schokkaert. 2009. "What Good Is Happiness?" CORE.

Floud, R., and B. Harris. 1997. "Health, Height, and Welfare: Britain, 1700–1980." In R. H. Steckel and R. Floud (eds.), *Health and Welfare during Industrialization*. Chicago, IL: University of Chicago Press, 91–126.

Flora, P., and J. Alber. 1981. "Modernization, Democratization, and the Development of Welfare States in Western Europe." In Peter Flora and Arnold J. Heidenheimer (eds.), *The Development of Welfare States in Europe and America*. New Brunswick, NJ: Transaction Books.

Floud, R., K. Wachter, and A. Gregory. 1990. *Height, Health and History. Nutritional Status in the United Kingdom, 1750–1980*. Cambridge: Cambridge University Press.

Fogel, R. W. 1984. *Nutrition and the Decline in Mortality Since 1700: Some Preliminary Findings*. NBER Working Papers, no. 1402, Cambridge, MA, National Bureau of Economic Research, http://www.nber.org/papers/w1402

Fogel, R. W. 1964. *Railroads and American Economic Growth*. Baltimore: Johns Hopkins University Press.

Fogel, R. W. 1990. *The Conquest of High Mortality and Hunger in Europe and America: Timing and Mechanism*. NBER Working Paper Series on Historical Factors in Long-run Ggrowth, no. 16, Cambridge, MA, National Bureau of Economic Research.

Fogel, R. W. 1997. "New Findings on Secular Trends in Nutrition and Mortality: Some Implications for Population Theory." In M. R. Rosenzweig and O. Stark (eds.), *Handbook of Population and Family Economics*. Amsterdam: Elsevier, 433–481.

Fogel, R. W. 2000. *Simon S. Kuznets: April 30, 1901–July 9, 1985*. NBER Working Papers, 7787, National Bureau of Economic Research, Inc.

Fogel, R. W., S. Engerman, and J. Trussell. 1982. "Exploring the Uses of Data on Height: The Analysis of Long-term Trends in Nutrition, Labor Welfare, and Labor Productivity." *Social Science History* 6: 401–421.

Fornero, E., and O. Castellino. 2001. *La riforma del istema previdenziale italiano*. Bologna: Il Mulino.

Fornero, E., and P. Sestito (eds.). 2005. *Pension Systems: Beyond Mandatory Retirement*. Cheltenham: Edward Elgar Publishing.

Forti Messina, A. 1982. "I medici condotti all'indomani dell'Unità." In M. L. Berti and A. Gigli Marchetti (eds.), *Salute e classi lavoratrici in Italia dall'Unità al fascismo*. Milan: Franco Angeli, 663–698.

Fortunato, G. 1911. *l Mezzogiorno e lo Stato italiano. Discorsi politici, 1880–1910*. Bari: Laterza, 2. vols.

Foster, J. E. 1998. "Absolute versus Relative Poverty." *American Economic Review* 88, no. 2, Papers and Proceedings, 335–341.

Foster, J. E., J. Greer, and E. Thorbecke. 1984. "A Class of Decomposable Poverty Measures." *Econometrica* 52; 761–765.

Fracassi, R. 1961. *Dal censimento dell'Unità ai censimenti del centenario: un secolo di vita della statistica italiana, 1861–1961*. Rome: Abete.

Franco, D. 1993. *L'espansione della spesa pubblica in Italia*. Bologna: Il Mulino.

Francois, J., and H. Rojas-Romagosa. 2008. *The Construction and Interpretation of Combined Cross-section and Time Series Inequality Datasets*. IIDE Discussion Paper, 200708-05.

Frascani, P. 1986. *Ospedale e società in età liberale*. Bologna: Il Mulino.

Fisher, S., R. Sahay, and C. A. Vegh. 2002. "Modern Hyper—and High Inflations." *Journal of Economic Literature* 40, no. 3: 837–880, American Economic Association, September. Fratianni, M., and F. Spinelli. 2001. *Storia monetaria d'Italia. Lira e politica monetaria dall'Unità all'Unione Europea*. Mian: Etas.

Freedom House. 2013. Freedom in the World Country Ratings by Region 1972–2011, available at: https://freedomhouse.org/sites/default/files/FIW%202012%20Booklet%20-%20 FOR%Web_0.pdf

Freeman, C., and C. Perez. 1988. "Structural Crises of Adjustment, Business Cycles and Investment Behaviour." In G. Dosi, C. Freeman, R. Nelson, G. Silverberg, and L. Soete (eds.), *Technical Change and Economic Theory*. London: Printer, 38–66.

Fuà, G. (ed.). 1968. *Lo sviluppo economico in Italia*, III: *Studi di settore e documentazione di base*. Milan: Franco Angeli.

Fuller, M. 1979. "The Estimation of Gini Coefficients from Grouped Data." *Economic Letters* 3: 187–192.

Gaeta, L. 1996. "L'Italia e lo Stato sociale." In G. A. Ritter (ed.), *Storia dello Stato sociale*. Rome-Bari: Laterza, 227–276.

Gale, D. 1982. *Money in Equilibrium*. New York: Cambridge University Press.

Galimberti, F. and L. Paolazzi. 1998. *Il volo del calabrone. Breve storia dell'economia del Novecento*, Quaderni di Storia. Florence: Le Monnier.

Galor, O. 2005. "From Stagnation to Growth: Unified Growth Theory." In P. Aghion and S. Durlauf, *Handbook of Economic Growth*, vol. 1A. Amsterdam: North-Holland, XXX–XXX.

Galor, O. 2011. *Inequality, Human Capital Formation and the Process of Development*. Working Papers, 2011-7, Brown University, Department of Economics.

Galor, O. and O. Moav. 2006. "Das Human-Kapital: A Theory of the Demise of the Class Structure." *Review of Economic Studies* 73: 85–117.

Galor, O. and J. Zeira. 1993. "Income Distribution and Macroeconomics." *Review of Economic Studies* 60: 35–52.

García-Peñalosa, C. 2010. "Income Distribution, Economic Growth and European Integration." *Journal of Economic Inequality* 8: 277–292.

Gastil. 1986. *Freedom in the World*. New York: Freedom House.

Gavosto A., A. Venturini, and C. Villosio. 1999. "Do Immigrants Compete with Natives?" *Labour* 13, no. 3: 603–622.

Geary, F. and T. Stark. 2002. "Examining Ireland's Post-famine Economic Growth Performance." *Economic Journal* 112, no. 482: 919–935.

Genovesi, G. 1993. *Storia della scuola in Italia dal Settecento a oggi*. Rome-Bari: Laterza.

Geremek, B. 1986. *La pietà e la forca. Storia della miseria e della carità in Europa*. Rome-Bari: Laterza.

Genovesi, G. 2010. *Storia della scuola in Italia dal Settecento a oggi*. RomE-Bari: Laterza.

Gerschenkron, A. 1955. "Notes on the Rate of Industrial Growth in Italy, 1881–1913." *Journal of Economic History* 15, no. 4: 360–375.

Gerschenkron, A. 1959. "Rosario Romeo e l'accumulazione primitiva del capitale." *Rivista Storica Italiana* 71, no. 4: 557–586.

Gerschenkron, A. 1962. *Economic Backwardness in Historical Perspective*. Cambridge, MA: Cambridge University Press.

Gerschenkron, A. 1968. *Continuity in History and Other Essays*. Cambridge, MA: Cambridge University Press.

Gheza Fabbri, L. 2000. "Le società di mutuo soccorso italiane nel contesto europeo fra XIX e XX secolo." In V. Zamagni (ed.), *Povertà e innovazioni istituzionali in Italia. Dal Medioevo ad oggi*. Bologna: Il Mulino, 503–528.

Giampaoli, S., L. Palmieri, R. Capocaccia, L. Pilotto, and D. Vannuzz. 2001. "Estimating Population-Based Incidence and Prevalence of Major Coronary Events." *Internationa Journal of Epidemiology* 30: S5–S10.

Giannetti, M. 2001. "Complementarities and Migration Decisions: An Analysis of Human Capital Movements." *Labour* 15-1: 1–32.

Giannini, M. S. 1970. *Diritto Amministrativo*, I. Milano: Giuffrè

Giffoni, F. and M. Gomellini. 2015. *Brain Gain in the Age of Mass Migration* forthcoming in Economic History Working Paper 34, Bank of Italy.

Giglioli, G. C. 1891. *L'assistenza pubblica nella storia e nella legislazione*. Turin: Unione Tipografica Editoriale.

Giglioli, I. 1903 *Malessere agrario e alimentare in Italia*. Rome: Loescher.

Gini, C. 1912. *Variabilità e mutabilità*. Bologna: Tipografia di Paolo Cuppini.

Gini, C. 1914. "Sulla misura della concentrazione e della variabilità dei caratteri." *Atti del R. Istituto Veneto di SS.LL.AA.* 73: 1203–1248.

Gini, C. 1921. "Measurement of Inequality of Incomes." *Economic Journal* 31: 124–126.

Gini, C. 1950. "Contenuto e impiego delle valutazioni del reddito nazionale," "Studi sul reddito nazionale," *Annali di Statistica*, Serie VIII, vol. III, 3–70.

Gini, C. 1959. "*Ricchezza e reddito.*" Torino: UTET.

Gini, C. 1962. *L'ammontare e la composizione della ricchezza delle nazioni.*" Torino: UTET.

Ginsborg, P. 1989. *Storia d'Italia dal dopoguerra a oggi*. Torino: Einaudi.

Ginzburg, C. 1976. *Il formaggio e i vermi. Il cosmo di un mugnaio del Cinquecento*. Turin: Einaudi.

Giovannini Tappi, L. 1957. "Prezzi al minute." *Annali di statistica* VIII, no. 7: 716–733.

Giorgi, G. M. 1996. "Encounters with the Italian Statistical School. A Conversation with Carlo Benedetti." *Metron* 54: 3–23.

Giorgi, G. M. 2001. "Corrado Gini." In C. C. Heyde and E. Seneta (eds.), *Statisticians of the Centuries*. New York: Springer, 364–368.

Giovannini, C. 1996 *Risanare le città. L'utopia igienista di fine Ottocento*. Milan: Franco Angeli.

Giovannini, E. 2010. "Dal Pil al benessere: nuovi indicatori per misurare il progresso della società." In L. Paolazzi (ed.), *Libertà e benessere. L'Italia al futuro*. Rome: Centro Studi Confindustria.

Giuntti, F. 2004. *Welfare State. Storia, modelli e critica*. Rome: Carocci.

Giugliano, F. 2010. *Crisis? Which Crisis? New Estimates of Industrial Value Added in Italy during the Great Depression*, Banca d'Italia. Mineo.

Giunta Centrale di Statistica. 1868–1872. *Statistica del Regno d'Italia. Le Opere pie nel 1861*, Florence: Le Monier, 15 vols.

Giunta per la inchiesta agraria e sulle condizioni della classe agricola. 1881–1886. *Atti della giunta per la inchiesta agraria e sulle condizioni della classe agricola*. Rome: Forzani e C. tipografi del Senato.Giuntella, O. 2012. "Do Immigrants Squeeze Natives out of Bad Schedules? Evidence from Italy." *IZA Journal of Migration* 1: 7.

Giuntini, A. 1999a. "Gli ingegneri sanitari e l'utopia igienista." In A. Giuntini and M. Minesso (eds.), *Gli ingegneri in Italia tra '800.e '900*. Milan: Franco Angeli. 117–128.

Giuntini, A. 1999b. "Nascita, sviluppo e tracollo della rete infrastrutturale." In F. Amatori, D. Bigazzi, R. Giannetti, and L. Segreto (eds.), *Storia d'Italia. Annali 15. L'industria*. Turin: Einaudi, 551–616.

Giusti, F. 1965. "Bilancio demografico della popolazione italiana dal 1861 al 1961." *Annali di Statistica*, serie 8, no. 17. Rome: Istat.

Giusti, U. 1932. "Consumi e bilanci di una famiglia di impiegati dall'anteguerra ad oggi." *Economia* 10, no. 6: 551–568.

Giusti, U. 1952. "A che punto si trova la ricostruzione del bilancio di famiglia dei ceti medi meno fortunate?" *Rivista italiana di Economia Demografica e Statistica*, july–december, 159–167.

Glytsos, N. P. 2005. "The Contribution of Remittances to Growth: A Dynamic Approach and Empirical Analysis." *Journal of Economic Studies* 32, no. 6: 468–496.

Gnesutta, C. 2000. *Prospettive di sviluppo nazionale e rappresentazione della realtà economica negli "Annali di statistica" 1871–1996*, in Istat, *Statistica ufficiale e storia d'Italia*, Rome.

Go, S. and P. Lindert. 2010. "The Uneven Rise of American Public Schools to 1850." *Journal of Economic History* 70, no. 1: 1–26.

Goldin, C. 1994. "The Political Economy of Immigration Restriction in the United States, 1890 to 1921." In C. Goldin and G. Libecap (eds.), *The Regulated Economy: A Historical Approach to Political Economy*. Chicago: University of Chicago Press, 223–258.

Goldin, C., 2001. "The Human-Capital Century and American Leadership: Virtues of the Past." *Journal of Economic History* 61, no. 02: 263–292.

Goldin, C. and L. F. Katz. 2008. *The Race between Education and Technology*. Cambridge, MA: Harvard University Press.

Goldin, C., and Sokoloff, K. 1982. "Women, Children, and Industrialization in the Early Republic: Evidence from Manufacturing Censuses." *Journal of Economic History* 42: 741–774.

Goldsmith, R. W., and Zecchini, S. 1999. "The National Balance Sheet of Italy (1861–1973)." *Rivista di storia economica* 15, no. 1: 3–20.

Golini, A., 1976. "Le migrazioni interne." In *Storia d'Italia* Turin: Atlante, Einaudi.

Gollier, G., 2004. *The Economics of Risk and Time*. Cambridge: MIT Press.

Gordon, R. J. 2012. *Is U.S. Economic Growth Over? Faltering Innovation Confronts the Six Headwinds*. NBER Working Papers, 18315, National Bureau of Economic Research, Inc.

Gomellini, M., and C. Ó Gráda. 2013. "Migrations." In G. Toniolo (ed.), *The Oxford Handbook of The Italian Economy since Unification*. Oxford: New York: Oxford University Press.

Gormely, P. J. 1995. "The Human Development Index in 1994: Impact of Income on Country Rank." *Journal of Economic and Social Measurement* 21: 253–267.

Gorrieri, E. 2002. *Parti uguali fra disuguali*. Bologna: Il Mulino.

Gould, J. D. 1980. "European Inter-continental Emigration. The Role of 'Diffusion' and 'Feedback'." *Journal of European Economic History* 9: 267–315.

Hatton, T. J. 1995. "A Model of U.K. Emigration, 1870– 1913." *Review of Economics and Statistics* 77: 407–415.Gould, J. D. 2010. "The Cliometrics of International Migration: A Survey." *Journal of Economic Survey* 24: 941–969.

Grande, E., R. Inghelmann, S. Francisci, A. Verdecchia, A. Micheli, P. Baili, R. Capocaccia, and R. De Angelis. 2007. "Regional Estimates of All Cancer Malignancies in Italy." *Tumori* 93: 345–351.

Grasso, A. 2000. *Storia della televisione italiana*. Milan: Garzanti.

Grassi, D., and Pannuzi, N. 2005. "La misura della povertà: metodologie e aspetti critici." *Rivista non profit* 10: 4.

Gratton, B., and Moen, J. 2004. "Immigration, Culture and Child Labor in the United States, 1880–1920." *Journal of Interdisciplinary History* 34, no. 3: 355–391.

Graziani, A. 1981. "Regional Inequalities in Italy." In P. Bairoch and M. Lévy-Leboyer (eds.), *Disparities in Economic Development since the Industrial Revolution*, London: Macmillan, 319–330.

Greco, P. and S. Termini. 2007. *Contro il declino*. Turin: Codice Edizioni.

Greve, B. 2013. *The Routledge Handbook of the Welfare State*. London: Routledge.

Grew, R., P. J. Harrigan, J. B. Whitney, M.-B. Albaret, and J. Valensi. 1984. "La scolarisation en France, 1829–1906, Annales." *Économies, Sociétés, Civilisations* 39e année, N. 1: 116–157.

Grootaert, C., and R. Kanbur. 1995. "Child labour: An Economic Perspective." *International Labour Review* 134, no. 2: 187–203.

Gruber J. and D. Hungerman. 2007. "Faith-based Charity and Crowd out during the Great Depression." *Journal of Public Economics* 91, no. 5/ 6: 1043–1069.

Gualerni, G. 1995. *Storia dell'Italia industriale. Dall'Unità alla Seconda Repubblica*. Milan: Etas Libri.

Guerzoni, G. 1868. *La tratta dei fanciulli. Pagine del problema sociale in Italia*. Florence: Tipografia di Giovanni Polizzi.

Guidicini, P. (ed.). 1991. *Gli studi sulla povertà in Italia*. Milan: Franco Angeli.

Guidoboni E., G. Valensise. 2011. *Il peso economico e sociale dei disastri sismici in Italia negli ultimi 150 anni*. Bologna: Bononia University Press.

Guiso, L., P. Sapienza, and L. Zingales. 2006. "Does Culture Affect Economic Outcomes?" *Journal of Economic Perspectives* 20, no. 2: 23–48.

Günther I., and Harttgen K., 2009. "Estimating Households Vulnerability to Idiosyncratic and Covariate Shocks: A Novel Method Applied in Madagascar." *World Development* 37, no. 7: 1222–1234.

Halbwachs, M. 1913. *La classe ouvrière et les niveaux de vie*. Paris.

Hanushek, E. A., and L. Woessmann. 2008. "The Role of Cognitive Skills in Economic Development." *Journal of Economic Literature* 100 46, no. 3: 607–668.

Hanushek, R., G. Schwerdt, S. Wiederhold, and L. Woessmann. 2013. *Returns to Skill around the World: Evidence from PIACC*. NBER Working Paper, 19762.

Haq, M. 2003. "The Birth of the Human Development Index." In S. Fukuda-Parr and A. K. Shiva Kumar (eds.), *Readings in Human Development*. Oxford: Oxford University Press, 127–137.

Harris, B. 2004. "Public Health, Nutrition, and the Decline of Mortality: The McKeown Thesis Revisited." *Social History of Medicine* 17, no. 3: 379–407.

Hatton, T. J., and Bray, B. E. 2010. "Long Run Trends in the Heights of European Men, 19th-20th Centuries." *Economics and Human Biology*, Dec; 8, no. 3: 405–413.

Hatton, T. J., and J. G. Williamson. 1998a. *The Age of Mass Migration: Causes and Economic Impact.* New York: Oxford University Press.

Hatton, T. J., and J. G. Williamson. 1998b. "Segmented Markets, Multiple Destinations: Italian Experience," in *The Age of Mass Migration: Causes and Economic Impact.* New York: Oxford University Press, 95–122.

Hatton, T. J., and J. G. Williamson. 2005. *Global Migration and the World Economy: Two Centuries of Policy and Performance.* Cambridge, MA: MIT Press.

Hatton, T. J., and J. G. Williamson. 2008. "The Impact of Immigration: Comparing Two Global Eras." *World Development* 36, no. 3: 345–61.

Heitzmann, K., R. S. Canagarajah, and P. B. Siegel. 2002. *Guidelines for Assessing the Sources of Risk and Vulnerability.* World Bank Social Protection Discussion Papers, no. 218.

Heltosky, C. 2004. *Garlic & Oil. Food and Politics in Italy.* Oxford-New York: Berg.

Herlihy, D., and C. Klapisch-Zuber. 1978. *Le Toscans et leurs familles: un etude du catasto Florentine de 1427*, Paris: Presses de la Fondation Nationale des Sciences Politique; trad. it. *Toscani e le loro famiglie. Uno studio sul catasto fiorentino del 1427.* Bologna: Il Mulino, 1988.

Hermardinquer, J. J. 1970. "Pour une histoire de l'alimentation." *Cahiers des Annales*, 28, EPHE 5ème section, Paris.

Hicks, N., and P. Streeten. 1979. "Indicators of Development: The Search for a Basic Needs Yardstick," *World Development* 7: 567–580

Higgs, H. 1893. "Workmens Budgets." *Journal of the Royal Statistical Society* 56: 255–285.

Higgs, H. 1899. "Some Remarks on Consumption." *Economic Journal*, December, 505–519.

Hirschman, A. O. 1973. "The Changing Tolerance of Income Inequality in the Course of Economic Development." *Quarterly Journal of Economics* 87: 544–566.

HMD (Human Mortality Database). 2010. University of California, Berkeley and Max Planck Institute for Demographic Research, http://www.mortality.org/, release 2010, December.

Hobbs, S. 1999. *Child labor: A World History Companion.* Santa Barbara, CA: ABC-Clio.

Hobsbwam, E. J. 1994. *Age of Extremes—The Short Twentieth Century 1914–1991.* London: Abacus.

Hoddinott, J., and A. Quisumbing. 2003a. *Methods for Microeconometric Risk and Vulnerability Assessments.* World Bank Social Protection Discussion Papers, no. 324.

Hoddinott, J., and A. Quisumbin. 2003b. *Data Sources for Microeconometric Risk and Vulnerability Assessments*, International Food Policy Research Institute Washington, DC, June.

Hoffmann, W. 1965. *Das Wachstum der Deutschen Wirtschaft Seit der Mitte des 19. Jahrhunderts.* Berlin: Springer.

Holt, D., and T. M. F. Smith. 1979. "Post Stratification." *Journal of the Royal Statistical Society* 142: 33–46.

Hopkins, K. 1966. "On the Probable Age Structure of the Roman Population." *Population Studies* 20, no. 2: 245–264.

Horlings, E., and J.-P. Smits. 1998. "The Quality of Life in the Netherlands." In J. Komlos and J. Baten (eds.) *The Biological Standard of Living in Comparative Perspective.* Stuttgart: Franz Steiner Verlag, 321–343.

Horner, L. 1840. *On the Employment of Children in Factories.* Shannon (Ireland): Irish University Press.

Horrell, S., and J. Humphries. 1992. "Old Questions, New Data, and Alternative Perspectives: Families' Living Standards in the Industrial Revolution." *Journal of Economic History* 52, no. 4: 849–880.

Horrell, S., and J. Humphries. 1995. "The Exploitation of Little Children: Child Labor and the Family Economy in the Industrial Revolution." *Explorations in Economic History* XLVIII: 485–516.

Houthakker, H. S. 1957. "An International Comparison of Household Expenditure Patterns, Commemorating the Centenary of Engel's Law." *Econometrica* 25: 532–551.

Humphries, J. 1987. " 'The Most Free from Objection . . .' The Sexual Division of Labor and Women's Work in Nineteenth-Century England." *Journal of Economic History* 47: 929–950.

Humphries, J. 2003. "Child Labor: Lessons from the Historical Experience of Today's Industrial Economies." *World Bank Economic Review* 17, no. 2: 175–196.

Humphries, J. 2012. "Childhood and Child Labour in the British Industrial Revolution". *The Economic History Review* 66, no.2: 395–418.

Hungerman, D. 2005. "Are Church and State Substitutes? Evidence from the 1996 Welfare Reform." *Journal of Public Economics* 89, no. 11/12: 2245–2267.

Hurst, E. and A. Lusardi. 2004. "Liquidity Constraints, Household Wealth, and Entrepreneurship." *Journal of Political Economy* 112, no. 2: 319–347.

Iannitto M. T. 1990. *Guida agli archivi per la storia contemporanea regionale: Napoli.* Napoli: Guida Editori. 75.

Ilari, V. 1989. *Storia del servizio militare in Italia.* Vol. I: 1506–1870. Roma: Centro Militare di Studi Strategici/Rivista Militare.

International Labour Office. 1926. *Methods of Conducting Family Budget Enquiries.* Studies and Reports Series, no. 9, Geneva.

ILO (International Labour Organization). 1996. *Economically Active Population 1950–2010.* Geneve: Bureau of Statistics International Labour Office.

ILO (International Labour Organization). 2004. *Child Labour: A Textbook for University Students.* Geneve: International Labour Office.

ILO (International Labour Organization). 2013. *World Report on Child Labour.* Geneva: International Labour Office.

INEA (Istituto nazionale di economia agraria) 1931–1939 *Monografie di famiglie agricole.* Rome: Studi e Monografie, 14.

Institute of Medicine of the National Academies. 2005. *Dietary Reference Intakes for Energy, Carbohydrates, Fiber, Fat, Fatty Acids, Cholesterol, Protein and Amino Acids.* Washington, DC: National Academies Press.

Iorio, G. 2001.*La povertà. Analisi storico-sociologica dei processi di deprivazione.* Rome: Armando.

IPSOS Mori. 2013. Perceptions are not reality. The top 10 we get wrong, available at: https://www.ipsos-mori.com/researchpublications/researcharchive/3188/Perceptions-are-not-reality.aspx

ISCE. 1960. *Budgets Familiaux des Ouvriers de la C.E.C.A., 1956/1957.* Luxembourg: Office Statistique des Communautés Européennes.

ISCE. 1966. *Bilanci familiari – Budget-onderzoek 1963/64.* Luxembourg: Office Statistique des Communautés Européennes.

Istat (Istituto centrale di statistica). 1933. *Compendio statistico, VII, Assistenza e beneficenza.* Rome, 96–101.

Istat (Istituto centrale di statistica). 1936. *Statistica dell'istruzione elementare per gli anni scolastici dal 1927–28 al 1931–32.* Rome: Failli.

Istat (Istituto centrale di statistica). 1950. *Studi sul reddito nazionale.* Rome: tip. F. Failli.

Istat (Istituto centrale di statistica). 1957. "Indagine statistica sullo sviluppo del reddito nazionale dell'Italia dal 1861 al 1956." *Annali di statistica* s. VIII: 9.

Istat (Istituto centrale di statistica). 1958. *Sommario di statistiche storiche italiane 1861–1955.* Rome.

ISTAT (Istituto Centrale di Statistica). 1960. *Indagine statistica sui bilanci di famiglie non agricole negli anni 1953–1954.* Roma: ISTAT.

Istat (Istituto centrale di statistica). 1961. *Distribuzione territoriale della scuola d'obbligo.* Rome.

Istat (Istituto centrale di statistica). 1967. *I consumi alimentari in Italia nel periodo 1951–66. Note e Relazioni*, no. 32, Rome.

Istat (Istituto centrale di statistica). 1968a. "Indagine statistica sui bilanci delle famiglie italiane. Anni 1963–64." *Annali di statistica* 97, no. VIII: 21, Rome.

Istat (Istituto centrale di statistica). 1968b. *Sommario di statistiche storiche dell'Italia, 1861–1965.* Rome.

Istat (Istituto centrale di statistica). 1972. *Annuario di contabilità nazionale.* Rome: Istat.

Istat (Istituto centrale di statistica). 1973. *Annuario di contabilità nazionale.* Rome.

Istat (Istituto centrale di statistica). 1976. *Sommario di statistiche storiche italiane 1861–1975.* Rome.

Istat (Istituto centrale di statistica). 1986. *Sommario di statistiche storiche italiane, 1926–1985.* Rome.

Istat (Istituto centrale di statistica). 2002. *Bambini, lavori e lavoretti. Verso un sistema informativo sul lavoro minorile: primi risultati*, Giornata Internazionale sul Lavoro Minorile, 12 giugno 2002.

Istat (Istituto centrale di statistica). 2005. *Nuove evidenze nell'evoluzione della mortalità per tumori in Italia, 1970–1999. Indicatori statistici.* Rome: Istat.

Istat (Istituto centrale di statistica). 2008a. *Differenze nel livello dei prezzi tra i capoluoghi nelle regioni italiane per alcune tipologie di beni.* Rome.

Istat (Istituto centrale di statistica). 2008b. *Distribuzione del reddito e condizioni di vita in Italia. Anni 2005–2006*, Statistiche in breve.

Istat (Istituto centrale di statistica). 2009. http://www.istat.it/dati/dataset/20091111_00/

Istat (Istituto centrale di statistica). 2010a. *Differenze nel livello dei prezzi tra i capoluoghi nelle regioni italiane.* Rome.

Istat (Istituto centrale di statistica). 2010b. *Distribuzione del reddito e condizioni di vita in Italia. Anni 2008–2009*, Statistiche in breve, 29 December.

Istat (Istituto centrale di statistica). 2010c. http://www.istat.it/sanita/sociosan/

Istat (Istituto centrale di statistica). 2010d. http://www.istat.it/dati/dataset/20100813_01/

Istat (Istituto centrale di statistica). 2010e. *Conti economici nazionali per settore istituzionale. Tavole*, Roma: luglio, http://www.istat.it/salastampa/comunicati/non_calendario/20100722_00/tavole_diffusione_Ed10.zip

Istat (Istituto centrale di statistica). 2011. *L'Italia in 150 anni. Sommario di statistiche storiche 1861–2010*, Roma.

Istat (Istituto centrale di statistica). 2012. *Conti economici regionali*, http://www.istat.it/it/archivio/75111

Istat. 2014. *Annuario Statistico Italiano 2013*, Rome.

Istat—Iss (Istituto centrale di statistica—Istituto Superiore della Sanità) 1999. *La mortalità in Italia nel periodo, 1970–1992. Evoluzione e geografia.* Rome.

Istat, Unioncamere e Istituto G. Tagliacarne. 2010. *Le differenze nel livello dei prezzi al consumo tra capoluoghi delle regioni italiane, luglio*, http://www.istat.it/salastampa/comunicati/non_calendario/20100707_00/testointegrale20100707.pdf

Ivanov, A., and M. Peleah. 2010. *From Centrally Planned Development to Human Development.* Human Development Research Paper, 38.

Janssens, A. (ed.). 1998. "The Rise and Decline of the Male Breadwinner Family." *International Review of Social History Supplement* 5, 1–23.

Jappelli T., and F. Modigliani. 1987. "Fiscal Policy and Saving in Italy since 1860." In M. J. Boskin, J. S. Flemming, and S. Gorini (eds.), *Private Saving and Public Debt.* Oxford: Basil Blackwell, 126–170.

Jappelli T., and M. Padula. 2007. *Household Saving and Debt in Italy.* Working Paper CSEF, no. 183.

Jappelli, T., and M. Pagano. 1994. "Saving, Growth and Liquidity Constraints." *Quarterly Journal of Economics*, February, 106: 83–109.

Jappelli, T., and L. Pistaferri. 2006. "Intertemporal Choice and Consumption Mobility." *Journal of the European Economic Association* vol. 4, no. 1: 75–115.

Jarach, C. 1877. *Inchiesta parlamentare.* Rome: Italian Ministry of Education.

Jenkins, S. P. 2009. "Distributionally-sensitive Inequality Indices and the GB2 Income Distribution." *Review of Income and Wealth* 55, no. 2: 392–398.

Jenkins, S. P., A. Brandolini, J. Micklewright, and B. Nolan. 2011. *The Great Recession and the Distribution of Household Income*. Mimeo.

Jenkins, S. P., and N. C. O'Leary. 1996. "Household Income Plus Household Production: The Distribution of Extended Income in the U.K." *Review of Income and Wealth* 42: 401–419.

Johnson, D. S., J. M. Rogers, and L. Tan. 2001. "A Century of Family Budgets in the United States." *Monthly Labor Review* 119, no.9: 28–45.

Johnston, R., M. McKinney, and T. Stark. 1996. "Regional Price Level Variations and Real Household Incomes in the United Kingdom, 1979/80–1993." *Regional Studies* 30, no. 6: 565–578.

Jones, M. B. 1977. "Health Status Indexes: The Trade-off Between Quantity and Quality of Life." *Socio-Economic Planning Sciences* 11, no. 6: 301–305.

Jovanovic, B., and P. L. Rousseau. 2005. "General Purpose Technologies." In P. Aghion and S. Durlauf (eds.), *Handbook of Economic Growth*, vol. 1, cap. 18. Amsterdam: Elsevier, 1181–1224.

Judge, G. G., R. C. Hill, W. E. Griffiths, H. Lutkepohl, and T. Lee. 1988. *Introduction to the Theory and Practice of Econometrics*, II ed. New York: John Wiley & Sons.

Jureen, L. 1956. "Long-term Trends in Food Consumption: A multi-country Study." *Econometrica* 24: 1–21.

Kaati, G., L. O. Bygren, M. Pembrey, and M. Sjöström. 2007. "Transgenerational Response to Nutrition, Early Life Circumstances and Longevity." *European Journal of Human Genetics* 15, no. 7: 784–790.

Kakwani, N. 1976. "On the Estimation of Inequality Measures from Grouped Observations." *Review of Economic Studies* 48: 621–631.

Kakwani, N. 1993. "Performance in Living Standards. An International Comparison." *Journal of Development Economics* 41: 307–336.

Kakwani, N. 2003. *Issues in Setting Absolute Poverty Lines*. Poverty and Social Development Paper, 3, Asian Development Bank.

Kakwani, N., and E. M. Pernia. 2000. "What Is Pro-Poor Growth?" *Asian Development Review* 18, no. 1: 1–16.

Kanbur, S. M. R. 2000. "Income Distribution and Development." In A. B. Atkinson and F. Bourguignon (eds.), *Handbook of Income Distribution*, vol. 1. Amsterdam: North-Holland, 791–841.

Kaneda, H. 1968. "Long-term Changes in Food Consumption Patterns in Japan, 1878–1964." *Food Research Institute Studies in Agricultural Economics Trade and Development* 8: 1.

Kangas O. 2010. "Work Accident and Sickness Benefits." In F. Castles, S. Leibfried, J. Lewis, H. Obinger, and C. Pierson (eds.), *The Oxford Handbook of The Welfare State*. Oxford: Oxford University Press.

Katseli, L.T., R. E. B. Lucas, and T. Xenogiani. 2006. "Effects of migration on sending countries: what do we know?" OECD Development Centre Working Paper, no. 250.

Keeling, D. 1999. "The Transportation Revolution and Transatlantic Migration, 1850–1914." *Research in Economic History* 19: 39–74.

Kelley, C. A. 1991. "The Human Development Index: Handle with Care." *Population and Development Review* 17, no. 2: 315–324.

Kendall, M. G. 1969. "Studies in the History of Probability and Statistics, XXI. The Early History of Index Numbers." *Review of the International Statistical Institute* 37, no. 1: 1–12.

Kennedy, R. F. 1968. http://www.jfklibrary.org/Research/Research-Aids/Ready-Reference/RFK-Speeches/Remarks-of-Robert-F-Kennedy-at-the-University-of-Kansas-March-18-1968.aspx

Kersbergen, K., and P. Manow. 2010. *Religion, in The Oxford Handbook of The Welfare State*. Oxford: Oxford University Press.

Keuning, S. 1998. "A Powerful Link between Economic Theory and Practice: National Accounting." *Review of Income and Wealth* 3: 437–446.

Keynes, J. M. .1923. *A Tract on Monetary Reform*. London: Macmillan.

Keynes, J. M. 1936. *The General Theory of Employment, Interest and Money*. London: Macmillan.

King, B., and T. Okey. 1901. *Italy Today*. London: Nisbet.

Klepper, M., and R. Gunther. 1996. *The Wealthy 100: From Benjamin Franklin to Bill Gates. A Ranking of the Richest Americans, Past and Present*. New York: Citadel Press.

Knoll, K., M. Schularick, and T. M. Steger. 2014. *No Price Like Home: Global House Prices, 1870–2012*. CEPR Discussion Paper, no. 10166.

Komlos, J. 1987. *The Height and Weight of West Point Cadets: Dietary Changes in Antebellum America*, in "Journal of Economic History," 47, 897–927.

Komlos, J. 1998. "Shrinking in a Growing Economy? The Mistery of Physical Stature during the Industrial Revolution." *Journal of Economic History* 58, no. 3: 779–802.

Korpi W., and Palme J. 2008. The Social Citizenship Indicators Program (SCIP), Stockholm: Stockholm University, Swedish Institute for Social Research. Available at https://dspace.it.su.se/dspace/handle/10102/7

Klugman, J., F. Rodrìguez, and C. Choi. 2011. "The HDI 2010: New Controversies, Old Critiques." *Journal of Economic Inequality* 9, no. 2: 249–288.

Komlos, J., and B. Snowdon. 2005. "Measures of Progress and Other Tall Stories: From Income to Anthropometrics." *World Economics* 6, no. 2: 87–135.

Kotlikoff, L. J. 1989. *What Determines Saving*. Cambridge, MA: The MIT Press.

Kovacevic, M. 2010. *Review of HDI Critiques and Potential Improvements*. Human Development Research Paper, 33, UNDP-HDRO, New York.

Kravis, I. B., Z. Kenessey, A. Heston, and R. Summers. 1975. *A System of International Comparisons of Gross Product and Purchasing Power*. Baltimore: Johns Hopkins University Press.

Kravis, I. B., A. Heston, and R. Summers. 1978. *International Comparisons of Real Product and Purchasing Power*. Baltimore: Johns Hopkins University Press.

Krugman, P. R. 1991. "Increasing Returns and Economic Geography." *Journal of Political Economy* 99, no. 3: 483–499.

Krugman, P. 2012. *End This Depression Now!* New York: W.W. Norton & Company.

Kruskal, W. and F. Mosteller. 1980. "Representative Sampling, IV: The History of the Concept in Statistics, 1895–1939." *International Statistical Review* 47, no. 1: 13–24.

Kuhnle S., and A. Sander. 2010. "The Emergence of the Western Welfare State." In F. Castles, S. Leibfried, J. Lewis, H. Obinger, and C. Pierson (eds.), *The Oxford Handbook of The Welfare State*. Oxford: Oxford University Press.

Kuznets, S. 1934. *National Income 1929–1932*. New York: National Bureau of Economic Research.

Kuznets, S. 1953. *Shares of Upper Income Groups in Income and Savings*. New York: National Bureau of Economic Research.

Kuznets, S. 1955. "Economic Growth and Income Inequality." *American Economic Review* 45, no. 1: 1–28.

Kuznets, S. 1963 *Quantitative Aspects of the Economic Growth of Nations: VIII. Distribution of Income by Size*, in "Economic Development and Cultural Change," 11, 2, parte II, 1–80.

Kuznets, S. 1966. *Modern Economic Growth: Rate, Structure and Spread*. New Haven: Yale University Press.

La Gumina, S. 1973. *Wop!* San Francisco: Straight Arrow Books.

La Spina, A. 2003. *La politica per il Mezzogiorno*. Bologna: Il Mulino.

Land, K. C. 1983. "Social indicators." *Annual Review of Sociology* 9: 1–26.

Lasker, G. W., and C. G. N. Mascie-Taylor. 1989. "Effects of Social Differences and Social Mobility on Growth in Height, Weight and Body Mass Index in a British Cohort." *Annals of Human Biology* 16, no. 1: 1–8.

Latinobarometro: http://www.latinobarometro.org/lat.jsp

Layard, R. 2005. *Happiness: Lessons From a New Science*, London: Penguin; trad. it. *Felicità. La nuova scienza del benessere comune*. Milan: Rizzoli.

Le Play, F. 1855–1879. *Les Ouvriers Europeéns*, II ed. Tours: Alfred Mame et fils, 6 t.

Le Play, F. 1879, *La Méthode sociale*. Tours: Alfred Mame et fils.

Lepore, A. "Cassa per il Mezzogiorno e politiche per lo sviluppo," nel CD-ROM di

Lepore, A. 2011. "La valutazione dell'operato della Cassa per il Mezzogiorno e il suo ruolo strategico per lo sviluppo del Paese." *Rivista Giuridica del Mezzogiorno* 25, no. 12: 281–317.

Le Roy Ladurie, E., N. Bernageau, and Y. Pasquet. 1969. "Le Conscrit et l'ordinateur. Perspectives de recherches sur les archives militaires du XIX siecle francais." *Studi Storici* 10: 260–308.

Lemnitzer, K.-H. 1977. *Ernährungssituation and wirtschaftliche Entwicklung*. Saarbrücken: Verlag der SSIP-Schriften Breitenbach.

Lepre, S. 1986. "Opere pie anni Ottanta. L'inchiesta conoscitiva presieduta da Cesare Correnti." In M. Bigaran (ed.), *Istituzioni e borghesie locali nell'Italia liberale*. Milan: Franco Angeli, 146–175.

Lepre, S. 1988. *Le difficoltà dell'assistenza. Le Opere Pie in Italia fra '800 e '900*. Rome: Bulzoni.

Lequiller, F. and D. Blades. 2006. *Understanding National Accounts*, Paris: OECD.

Lewbel, A. 2008. "Engel Curves." In S. N. Durlauf and L. E. Blume (eds.), *The New Palgrave Dictionary of Economics*, 2nd ed. Basingstoke: Palgrave Macmillan.

Lewis, J. 2001. "The Decline of the Male Breadwinner Model: the Implications for Work and Care." *Social Politics* 8, no. 2: 152–169.

Ligon, E., and L. Schecther. 2003. "Measuring Vulnerability." *Economic Journal* 113, no. 486: 95–110.

Lindert, P. H. 1986. "Unequal English Wealth since 1670." *Journal of Political Economy* 94, no. 6: 1127–1162.

Lindert, P.H. 1994. *The Rise of Social Spending, 1880-1930*, in "Explorations in Economic History," 31, 1–37.

Lindert, P. H. 2000a. "Three Centuries of Inequality in Britain and America." In A. B. Atkinson and F. Bourguignon (eds.), *Handbook of Income Distribution*, vol. 1. Amsterdam: Elsevier, 167–216.

Lindert, P. H. 2000b. "When Did Inequality Rise in Britain and America?" *Journal of Income Distribution* 9: 11–25.

Lindert, P. H. 2004. *Growing Public. Social Spending and Economic Growth since the Eighteenth Century*, 2 vols., Cambridge: Cambridge University Press.

Lindert, P. H., and J. G. Williamson. 1980. *American Inequality: A Macroeconomic History*. New York: Academic Press.

Lindert, P. H., and J. G. Williamson. 1982. "Revising England's Social Tables, 1688-1812." *Explorations in Economic History* 19: 385–408.

Lindert, P. H., and J.G. Williamson. 1983. "Reinterpreting Britain's Social Tables, 1688-1913." *Explorations in Economic History* 20: 94–109.

Lindert, P. H., and J. G. Williamson. 1985. "Growth, Equality, and History." *Exploration in Economic History* 22, no. 4: 341–377.

Livi Bacci, M. 1993. *Popolazione ed alimentazione. Saggio sulla storia demografica europea*. Bologna: Il Mulino.

Livi Bacci, M. 2010. *In cammino. Breve storia delle migrazioni*. Bologna: Universale Paperbacks, Società editrice il Mulino.

Livi Bacci, M., E. Cialfa, and M. Masselli. 1997. *Studio di fattibilità per la definizione di un paniere minimo di beni e servizi*, relazione presentata al seminario su «Nuovi approcci per l'analisi della povertà e dell'esclusione sociale». Rome: 14 luglio.

Lo Cascio, E., and P. Malanima. 2005. "Cycles and Stability. Italian Population before the Demographic Transition." *Rivista di Storia Economica* 21, no. 3: 197–232.

Lo Monaco Aprile, A. 1931. *La politica assistenziale dell'Italia fascista*. Rome: Anonima Editoriale Romana.

Longfellow, H. W. (eds.). 1877. *Poems of Places: An Anthology in 31 Volumes*, vols. XI-XIII. Italy. Boston: Houghton Mifflin and Company.

Löning, E. 1892. "Assistenza pubblica." *Biblioteca dell'Economista* s. III, vol. 15, 561–848.

Lorry, A. 2000. "Les monographies des Ouvriers européens (1855 et 1877–1879) et des Ouvriers des deux mondes (1857–1930) Inventaire et classification." *Les études sociales* 131–132, 1° et 2° semestres.

Lowe, J. 1823. *The Present State of England in Regard to Agriculture, Trade and Finance*, II ed. London: Longman, Hurst, Rees, Orme and Brown.

Lucas, R. 2000. "Some Macroeconomics for the 21st Century." *Journal of Economic Perspectives* 14, no. 1: 159–168.

Luttmer, E. 2005. "Neighbors as Negatives: Relative Earnings and Well-Being." *Quarterly Journal of Economics* 120, no.3: 963–1002

Luzzatto Fegiz, P. 1949. *I redditi delle famiglie italiane nel 1948*. Milan: Doxa.

Luzzatto Fegiz, P. 1950. "La distribuzione del reddito nazionale." *Giornale degli economisti e Annali di economia* 9, no. 7–8: 341–354.

Luzzatto Fegiz, P. 1956. *Il volto sconosciuto dell'Italia: dieci anni di sondaggi Doxa*. Milan: Giuffrè.

Luzzi, S. 2004. *Salute e sanità nell'Italia repubblicana*. Rome: Donzelli.

Mac Donald, J. B. 1984. "Some Generalized Functions for the Size Distribution of Income." *Econometrica* 52, no. 3: 647–663.

Maccaferri S., F. Cariboni, F. Campolongo. 2012. "Natural Catastrophes: Risk relevance and Insurance Coverage in the EU." *Joint Research Center Scientific and Technical Reports*, Luxembourg.

Maccolini R. 1982. "Storia ed evoluzione della medicina pubblica in Italia." In M. La Rosa and P. Zurla (eds.), *Sistema informativo e Unità sanitaria locale*, 97–116. Milan: Franco Angeli.

Maddison, A. 1991. "A Revised Estimate of Italian Economic Growth, 1861–1989." *Banca Nazionale del Lavoro Quarterly Review* 177: 225–241.

Maddison, A. 2001. *The World Economy: A Millennial Perspective*. Paris: OECD.

Maddison, A. 2007. "Fluctuations in the Momentum of Growth within the Capitalist Epoch." *Cliometrica* 1, no. 2: 145–175.

Maddison, A. 2010. Historical Statistics of the World Economy: 1-2008 AD, http://www.ggdc.net/maddison/content.shtml

Magnani, I. 2004. Il Paretaio, Quaderni del Dipartimento di economia pubblica e territoriale (2004)-1: 69–100.

MAIC (Ministero dell'Agricoltura, Industria e Commercio). 1882a. *Bilanci comunali, anni 1880 e 1881*. Rome: Direzione generale della statistica.

MAIC (Ministero dell'Agricoltura, Industria e Commercio). 1882b. *Notizie intorno alle condizioni dell'agricoltura negli anni 1878–1879*. Rome: Stamperia Reale.

MAIC (Ministero dell'Agricoltura, Industria e Commercio). 1909a. *Materiale per lo studio delle condizioni dei lavoratori della terra nel Mezzogiorno*, Pubblicazioni dell'Ufficio del Lavoro, s. B, 24, parte 1, Capitanata e Puglie, Rome: Bertero.

MAIC (Ministero dell'Agricoltura, Industria e Commercio). 1909b. *Relazione sull'applicazione della legge 19/6/1902 n. 242 sul lavoro delle donne e dei fanciulli (1903–1907) presentata dal ministro Cocco-Ortu alla Camera dei deputati nella seduta del 10 luglio 1909*. Rome: Ufficio del lavoro.

MAIC (Ministero di Agricoltura Industria e Commercio). 1908. *Annuario statistico italiano, Direzione generale della statistica*, Rome: Tipografia Bertero.

MAIC (Ministero di Agricoltura Industria e Commercio). 1914. *Inchieste sui prezzi dei generi di consumo pagati dai convitti nazionali dal 1890 al 1913 e dall'amministrazione militare dal 1890 al 1913*, vol. 1. Rome: Officina poligrafica italiana.

Malanima, P. 2003. "Measuring the Italian Economy 1300–1861." *Rivista di storia economica* XIX: 265–295.

Malanima, P. 2006a. "Alle origini della crescita in Italia 1820–1913." *Rivista di storia economica* n.s., XXII: 306–330.

Malanima, P. 2006b. "Energy Crisis and Growth 1650–1850. The European Deviation in a Comparative Perspective." *Journal of Global History* I: 101–121.

Mallet, R. 1862. *Great Neapolitan Earthquake of 1857: The First Principles of Observational Seismology*. London: Royal Society.

Manacorda, M. 2004. "Can the Scala Mobile Explain the Fall and Rise of Earnings Inequality in Italy? A Semiparametric Analysis, 1977–1993." *Journal of Labour Economics* 22: 585–613.

Manfredi, L. 1893. "Sull'alimentazione delle classi povere del popolo in Napoli." *Annali dell'Istituto d'igiene sperimentale della Regia Università di Roma* III: 37–113 (new series).

Manfredini, M., and L. Pozzi. 2004. "Mortalità infantile e condizione socio-economica. Una riflessione sull'esperienza italiana fra '800 e '900." *Revista de Demografía Histórica* 22, no. 2: 127–156.

Mannheimer, R. 2009. "Quel no alle gabbie salariali divide giovani e anziani." *Corriere della Sera*, 28 September, 20.

Mantegazza, S., and G. Tassinari. 1992. *La coerenza delle valutazioni dei consumi privati nella contabilità nazionale e nell'indagine sui bilanci delle famiglie, CON PRI—La misura dei consumi privati*, Rapporto di ricerca n. 4, Dipartimento di Scienze Statistiche, Università di Bologna.

Maraffino, D. 2010. "Quel terribile autunno del 1918." *Medicina Pontina* 32, no. 2: 1–179.

Marescalchi, C. 1946. "Le condizioni di vita di una famiglia mezzadrile nella annata agraria 1944–1945." *Rivista di economia agraria*. September, 250–262.

Mariotto, A. B., K. R. Yabroff, Y.Shao, E. J.Feuer, and M. L. Brown. 2011. "Projections of the cost of cancer care in the United States: 2010–2020." *Journal of the National Cancer Institute* 103, no.2: 117–128.

Marshall, A. 1890. *Principles of Economics*; IX ed. London: Macmillan, 1961.

Martínez-Galarraga, J., J. R. Rosés, and D. A. Tirado. 2011. *The Long-Term Patterns of Regional Income Inequality in Spain (1860–2000)*. HIPOD Working Paper.

Martínez Carrión, J. M., and J. Puche-Gil. 2009. *La Estatura de los Españoles en el Espejo Francès. Una Historia Antropomètrica Comparada*, Asociación Española de Historia Económica, Documento de Trabajo, no. 0911.

Martino, E. 1878. *Commento alla legge 20 marzo 1865, n. 2248 (allegato C), e del relativo regolamento sulla sanità pubblica*. Milan: tipografia pirole.

Marucco, D. 2001. "Le statistiche dell'emigrazione italiana." In P. Bevilacqua, A. de Clementi and E. Franzina (eds.), *Storia dell'emigrazione italiana*, vol. 1. Partenze, 61–75, Rome.

Marx, K. 1867. *Das Kapital, Band I*; trad. it. *Il capitale*, vol. I. Rome: Editori Riuniti, 1973.

Marx, K., and F. Engels. 1848. *Manifest der kommunistischen Partei*, London; trad. it. *Manifesto del partito comunista*. Rome: Editori Riuniti, 1968.

Mas-Colell, A., M. D. Whinston, and J. R. Green. 1995. *Microeconomic Theory*. Oxford: Oxford University Press.

Masi, V. 1911. "Istruzione pubblica e privata." In R. Accademia dei Lincei (ed.), *Cinquant'anni di storia italiana*, vol. II. Milan: Hoepli, 2–78.

Massullo, G. 2001. "Economia delle rimesse." In P. Bevilacqua, A. de Clementi, and E. Franzina (eds.), *Storia dell'emigrazione italiana*, vol. 1. Partenze, 161–183, Rome: Donzelli.

Mattesini, F., and B. Quintieri. 1997. "Italy and the Great Depression: An Analysis of the Italian Economy, 1929–1936." *Explorations in Economic History* 34: 265–294.

Matteucci, C. 1867. *Raccolta di scritti varii intorno alla istruzione pubblica*. Prato: Tipografia Alberghetti.

Matthew, R. 1993. "Incorporating Fairness into Game Theory and Economics." *American Economic Review* 5: 1281–1302

Mattone A. V., and L. Berlinguer. 1998. "L'identità storica della Sardegna contemporanea." In L. Berlinguer and A. V. Mattone (eds.), *Storia d'Italia, Le regioni dall'unità ad oggi, La Sardegna*. Turin: Einaudi, XIX–XLVIII.

Mayr, K., and G. Peri. 2009. "Brain drain and brain return: theory and application to eastern-western Europe," *Contributions to Economic Analysis and Policy Berkeley Electronic Press* 9: 1.

McCloskey. 2014. "Measured, Unmeasured, Mismeasured, and Unjustified Pessimism: A Review Essay of Thomas Piketty's Capital in the Twenty-first Century." *Erasmus Journal for Philosophy and Economics* 7, 2: Autumn 2014.

McDonald, J. B. 1984. "Some Generalized Functions for the Size Distribution of Income." *Econometrica* 52: 647–663.

McKeown, T. 1976. *The Modern Rise of Population*. New York: Academic Press.

McMahon, W. W. 1988. *Geographical Cost of Living Differences: An Update*, MacArthur/Spencer Series, Report number 7, Illinois State University.

Megale, A., and A. Teselli. 2006. *Lavori minorili e percorsi a rischio di esclusione sociale*. Rome: Ediesse.

Memmo, G. 1894. "Sull'alimentazione in varie condizioni individuali e sociali." *Annali dell'Istituto d'igiene sperimentale della Regia Università di Roma* IV, no. 4: 270.

Meredith, D. D., and D. Oxley. 2013. "Food and Fodder: Feeding England, 1700–1900." *Past and Present* 222, no. 1: 163–214.

Merli, S. 1972. *Proletariato di fabbrica e capitalismo industriale. Il caso italiano 1880–1900*. Florence: La Nuova Italia.

Milanovic, B. 2005. *Worlds Apart. Measuring International and Global Inequality*. Princeton: Princeton University Press.

Milanovic, B. 2011. *The Have and the Have-Nots. A Brief and Idiosyncratic History of Global Inequality*. New York: Basic Books.

Milanovic, B., P. H. Lindert, and J. G. Williamson. 2010. "Pre-Industrial Inequality." *Economic Journal* 121: 255–272.

Milanovic, B. 2014. "The Return of 'Patrimonial Capitalism': A Review of Thomas Piketty's Capital in the Twenty-First Century." *Journal of Economic Literature* 52, no. 2: 519–534.

Millward, R., and J. Baten. 2010. "Population and Living Standards 1914–1945." In S. Broadberry and O'Rourke K. *The Cambridge Economic History of Modern Europe*. Cambridge: Cambridge University Press, 232–266.

Mineo, A., and G. Giammanco. 1968. *La mortalità in Italia dal 1899 al 1961. Evoluzione e cause della mortalità differenziale nei due sessi*. Palermo, Ingrana.

Minesso, M. 2007. (ed.) *Stato e infanzia nell'Italia contemporanea*. Bologna: Il Mulino.

Ministero degli Esteri. 1991. "Il fondo archivistico Commissariato Generale dell'Emigrazione (1901–1927)." In P. Santoni (ed.), *Inventario*. Rome: Istituto poligrafico e zecca dello Stato.

Ministero del Lavoro, della Salute e delle Politiche Sociali. 2007–08. *Relazione sullo Stato Sanitario del Paese*, http://www.salute.gov.it/imgs/C_17_pubblicazioni_1144_allegato.pdf.

Ministero della Pubblica istruzione. 1889–90. *Statistica per l'adempimento della Legge sull'istruzione obbligatoria del 15 Luglio 1877, n. 3961, e del relativo Regolamento in data 19 ottobre 1877, n. 4191*. Rome: Archivio Centrale dello Stato.

Ministero della Pubblica Istruzione. 1908. *L'istruzione primaria e popolare in Italia. Relazione presentata a S. E. il ministro della P.I. dal comm. dott. Camillo Corradini, direttore generale per l'Istruzione primaria e popolare*. Rome: Tipografia Operaia Romana Coop.

Mioni, F. 1986. (ed.) *Dopo il Rapporto Gorrieri sulla povertà in Italia: quali prospettive di politica sociale?* Bologna: 30 November 1985, atti dell'incontro, Bologna: Istituto De Gasperi.

Mira, G. 1940. *Vicende economiche di una famiglia italiana dal XIV al XVII secolo*. Milan: Vita e Pensiero.

Mises, L. V. 1949. *Human Action: A Treatise on Economics*. New Haven: Yale University Press.

Mitchell B. R. 2005. *Intenational Historical Statistics: Europe 1750–2005*. London: Palgrave Macmillan.

Modigliani, F., and R. H. Brumberg. 1954. "Utility Analysis and the Consumption Function: An Interpretation of Cross-section Data." In K. K. Kurihara (ed.), *Post-Keynesian Economics*. New Brunswick, NJ. Rutgers University Press, 388–436.

Moheling, C. 1999. "State Child Labor Laws and the Decline of Child Labor." *Explorations in Economic History* 36: 72–106.

Mokyr, J. 1990. *The Lever of Riches*. New York: Oxford University Press.

Molinari, A. 2001. "Porti, Trasporti, Compagnie." In P. Bevilacqua, A. de Clementi, and E. Franzina (eds.), *Storia dell'emigrazione italiana*. vol. 1. Partenze, 237–255.

Molinari, A. 2009. "Traversate." In P. Corti, and M. Sanfilippo (eds.), *Migrazioni, Storia d'Italia Annali 24*. Torino: Giulio Einaudi Editore.

Montgomery, J. E. 2000. "Ibn Fadlan and the Rusiyyah." *Journal of Arabic and Islamic Studies* 3: 1–25.

Monti P., and M. Pellizzari. 2010. "Implementing a Guaranteed Minimum Income in Italy: An empirical Analysis of Costs and Political Feasibility." *Giornale degli Economisti* 69, issue 1: 67/100.

Mookherjee, D., and A. Shorrocks. 1982. "A Decomposition Analysis of the Trend in UK Income Inequality." *Economic Journal* 92, no. 368: 886–902.

Moravia, A. 1957. *La ciociara*. Milan: Bompiani.

Morduch, J. 1994. "Poverty and Vulnerability." *American Economic Review*, Papers and Proceedings of the Hundred and Sixth Annual Meeting of the American Economic Association, 84, no. 2: 221–225.

Moretti, E. 1999. "Social Networks and Migrations: 1876–1913." *International Migration Review* 33, no. 3: 640–657.

Mori, G. 1981. "The Process of Industrialization in General and the Process of Industrialization in Italy: Some Suggestions, Problems and Questions." In P. Bairoch and M. Lévy-Leboyer (eds.), *Disparities in Economic Development since the Industrial Revolution*. London: Macmillan, 151–164.

Morris, D. M. 1979. *Measuring the Conditions of the World's Poor: The Physical Quality of Life*. New York: Pergamon.

Morrisson, C. 2000. "Historical Perspectives on Income Distribution." In A. B. Atkinson and F. Bourguignon (eds.), *Handbook of income distribution*. Amsterdam: Elsevier, 217–260.

Morrisson, C., and F. Murtin. 2009. "The Century of Education." *Journal of Human Capital* 3, no. 1: 1–42.

Mulhall, M. G. 1884. *Mulhall's Dictionary of Statistics*. London: New York: G. Routledge.

Murphy, K. M., A. Shleifer, and R. Vishny. 1989. "Income Distribution, Market Size, and Industrialization." *Quarterly Journal of Economics* 104: 537–564.

Murphy, K. M., A. Shleifer, and R. Vishny. 2008. *Growing Unequal? Income Distribution and Poverty in OECD Countries*. Paris: OECD Publishing.

Nitti, F. S. 1905. *La ricchezza dell'Italia, Casa Editrice Nazionale Roux e Viarengo*. Turin-Rome.

Myers, R. J. 1976. "An Instance of Reverse Heaping of Ages." *Demography* 13, no. 4: 577–580.

Nardinelli, C. 1990. *Child labor and the Industrial Revolution*. Bloomington: Indiana University Press, 155–266.

Nardo M., M. Saisana, A. Saltelli, S. Tarantola, A. Hoffman, and E. Giovannini. 2005. *Handbook on Constructing Composite Indicators: Methodology and User Guide OECD*, Statistics Working Paper, JT00188147.

Negri, N., and Saraceno, C. 1996. *Le politiche contro la povertà in Italia*. Bologna: Il Mulino.

Nelson, R. R., and E. D. Phelps. 1966. "Investment in Humans, Technological Diffusion, and Economic Growth." *American Economic Review* 56: 69–75.

Nenna, M. 2002. "Deviations from Purchasing Power Parity: Any Role for the Harrod-Balassa-Samuelson Hypothesis?" *Rivista di politica economica* 92, no. 4: 167–196.

Niceforo, A. 1901. *Italiani del Nord e italiani del Sud*. Turin Fratelli Bocca.

Niceforo, A. 1906. *Forza e ricchezza. Studi sulla vita fisica ed economica delle classi sociali*. Turin: Bocca.

Niceforo, A. 1933. "Dati statistici sull'alimentazione della popolazione italiana." In F. Bottazzi, A. Niceforo and G. Quagliarello (eds.), *Documenti per lo Studio dell'Alimentazione della Popolazione Italiana nell'Ultimo Cinquantennio*. Neaples: Tipografia Jovene, 77–267.

Niceforo, A. 1937. Per la storia numerica dell'alimentazione italiana." *Difesa sociale* 8–9: 747–763.

Nitti, F. S. 1892. "Poor Relief in Italy." *Economic Review* II, 1: 1892.

Novello, E. 2003. *La bonifica in Italia. Legislazione, credito e lotta alla malaria dall'Unità al fascismo*. Milan: Franco Angeli.

Noorbakhsh, F. 1998. "A Modified Human Development Index." *World Development* 25, 517–528.

Nordhaus, W. D., and J. Tobin. 1972. "Is Growth Obsolete?" In W. D. Nordhaus and J. Tobin, *Economic Research: Retrospect and Prospect. Economic Growth, Fiftieth Anniversary Colloquium V*. New York: National Bureau of Economic Research, 1–80.

Nuzzo, G. 2006. *Un secolo di statistiche sociali: persistenza o convergenza tra le regioni italiane?, Quaderni dell'Ufficio Ricerche Storiche*. Rome: Banca d'Italia.

Ó Gráda, C., and K. H. O'Rourke. 1997. "Migration as Disaster Relief: Lessons from the Great Irish Famine." *European Review of Economic History* 1, no. 1: 3–25. Cambridge University Press, April.

Obinger H., and U. Wagschal. 2010. "Social Expenditure and Revenues." In F. Castles, S. Leibfried, J. Lewis, H. Obinger, and C. Pierson (eds.), *The Oxford Handbook of The Welfare State*. Oxford: Oxford University Press.

Oddy, D. J. 1976. "A Nutritional Analysis of Historical Evidence: the Working- Class Diet, 1880-1914." In D. Oddy and D. Miller (eds.), *The Making of the British Diet*. London: Croom Helm.

Oddy, D. J. 1990. "Food, Drink and Nutrition." In F. M. L. Thompson (ed.), *The Cambridge Social History of Britain 1750–1950*, vol. 2. New York: Cambridge University Press.

OECD. 1985. *Social Expenditure 1960–1990*. OECD Publishing: Paris.

OECD. 1999. *Social Expenditure Database 1980–1996* (CD-Rom).

OECD. 2008a. *Growing Unequal? Income Distribution and Poverty in OECD Countries*. OECD Publishing: Paris.

OECD. 2008b. http://www.oecd.org.

OECD. 2010. *PISA 2009. Results: What Students Know and Can Do*, vol. 1. Paris.

OECD. 2012. *Divided We Stand: Why Inequality Keeps Rising.* Paris: OECD Publishing.

OECD. 2013a. *OECD Skills Outlook 2013: First Results from the Survey of Adult Skills.* Paris: OECD Publishing.

OECD. 2013b. *International Migration Outlook 2013.* Paris: OECD Publishing.

OECD. 2013c *Education at a Glance* 2013: OECD Indicators. Paris: OECD Publishing.

OECD. 2014a. *Education at a Glance* 2014: OECD Indicators. Paris: OECD Publishing.

OECD. 2014b. *Education at a Glance 2014: Country Note, Italy.* Paris: OECD Publishing.

Offer, A. 2005. *The Challenge of Affluence. Self-Control and Well-Being in the United States and Britain since 1950.* Oxford: Oxford University Press.

Ogburn, W. F. 1912. "Progress and Uniformity in Child-Labor Legislation: A Study in Statistical Measurement." *Studies in History, Economics and Public Law* 48, no. 2. Columbia University.

Ohlsson, H., J. Roine, and D. Waldenström. 2014. *Inherited Wealth over the Path of Development: Sweden, 1810–2010.* Working Paper, available at: www.uueconomics.se/danielw/Research_files/Inherited_wealth_in_Sweden.pdf.

Onida, V. 2007. *La costituzione.* Bologna: Il Mulino.

Orshansky, M. 1963. "Children of the Poor." *Social Security Bulletin* 26, no. 7: 3–13.

Orshansky, M. 1965. "Counting the Poor: Another Look at the Poverty Profile." *Social Security Bulletin* 28: 3–29.

Orshansky, M. 1969. "How Poverty Is Measured." *Monthly Labor Review* 92: 37–41.

Osberg, L., and A. Sharpe. 2005. "How Should We Measure the 'Economic' Aspects of Well–being?" *Review of Income and Wealth* 51: 311–336.

Ostenc, M. 1981. *La scuola italiana durante il fascismo.* Rome-Bari: Laterza.

Pagani, A. 1960. *La linea della povertà.* Milan: Anea.

Pagliani, L. 1876. "Sopra alcuni fattori dello sviluppo umano." *Archivio per l'Antropologia e l'Etnologia* 6, no. 2: 129–183.

Pagliani, L. 1879. "Lo sviluppo umano per età, sesso, condizione sociale ed etnica, studiato nel peso, statura, circonferenza toracica, capacità vitale e forza muscolare." *Giornale della Società italiana di Igiene* 1: 1, 357–376, 453–491, 589–610.

Pagliani, L. 1878. "La demografia italiana all'esposizione universale di Parigi nel 1878. II, Studi antropometrici sullo sviluppo dell'organismo umano." *Annali di statistica* s. 2, vol. II: 228–236.

Pantaleoni, M. 1884. *Dell'ammontare probabile della ricchezza in Italia.* Rome: Tip. A. Befani.

Pantaleoni, M. 1890. "Dell'ammontare probabile della ricchezza in Italia dal 1872 al 1889." *Giornale degli economisti* II, sec. II: 139–176.

Pantaleoni, M. 1925. "*Il secolo Ventesimo secondo un individualista*, Conferenza tenuta a Venezia alla Fenice il 6 aprile 1900." In M. Pantaleoni, *Erotemi di economia* vol. I. Bari: Laterza, 259–281.

Paolazzi, L. 2011. (ed.) *Libertà e benessere in Italia. 150 anni di storia unitaria e i traguardi del futuro.* Rome-Bari: Laterza.

Paoloni, G. 2013. "I 'bianchi': la tecnologia in cucina, in Istituto della Enciclopedia Italiana (2013)." *Enciclopedia Italiana: Appendice VIII: Il contributo italiano alla storia del pensiero.* Tecnica.

Pareto, V. 1897. *Cours d'Economie politique professé à l'Université de Lausanne,* t. II, Lausanne, F. Rouge Editeur, 1897; trad. it.: *Corso di economia politica.* Turin: Utet, 1971.

Pareto, V. 1984. *Lettere a Maffeo Pantaleoni 1890–1923,* vol.XXVIII of *Oeuvres complètes.* Ed. G. De Rosa. Genève: Droz.

Parola, L. 1849. *Della tubercolosi in genere e della tisi polmonare in specie.* Torino: Tipografia di G. Favale.

Pascall, G. 2008. "Gender and New Labour: after the Male Breadwinner Model." *Social Policy Review-Harlow* 20: 315. Policy Press, Bristol.

Pascoli, G. 1914. *Pensieri e discorsi, 1895–1906.* Bologna: Zanichelli.

Pasolini, M. 1892. "Monografie di alcuni operai braccianti nel Comune di Ravenna." *Giornale degli economisti,* 5, n.s.: 311–343 e 411–427.

Pella, G. 1961. *Discorso del Presidente del Comitato Italia "61, in Comitato nazionale per la celebrazione del primo centenario dell" unita d'Italia (1961).* Turin: Celebrazione del primo centenario dell'unita d'Italia, May–October.

Pen, J. 1971. *Income Distribution*. London: Allen Lane.

Perotti, R. 1993. "Political Equilibrium, Income Distribution, and Growth." *Review of Economic Studies* 60, 755–776.

Persky, J. 1998. "Price Indexes and General Exchange Values." *Journal of Economic Perspectives* 12, no. 1: 197–205.

Persson, K. G. 2010. *An Economic History of Europe: Knowledge, Institutions and Growth, 600 to the Present*. Cambridge: Cambridge University Press.

Persson, T., and G. Tabellini. 1994. "Is Inequality Harmful for Growth?" *American Economic Review* 84: 600–621.

Petitti di Roreto, C. I. 1841. "Del lavoro de' fanciulli nelle manifatture. Dissertazione." *Memorie della Regia Accademia delle Scienze di Torino* M2, III2: 209–306.

Petri R. 2002. *Storia economica d'Italia. Dalla grande guerra al miracolo economico (1918–1963)*. Bologna: Il Mulino.

Pettersson, P., T. Ekstrand, and N. Edgardh. 2004. "Welfare, Church and Gender in Sweden." In Ninna Edgardh Beckman (ed.), *Welfare, Church and Gender in Eight European Countries, Working Paper 1 from the Project Welfare and Religion in a European Perspective*. Uppsala: SLU Repro.

Petty, W. 1899. *The Economic Writings of Sir William Petty, together with The Observations upon Bills of Mortality, more probably by Captain John Graunt*. Ed. Charles Henry Hull 1. Cambridge: Cambridge University Press, 1899. Online at <http://oll.libertyfund.org/titles/1677>.

Piazza, A., N. Cappello, E. Olivetti, and S. Rendine. 1988. "A Genetic History of Italy." *Annals of Human Genetics* 52: 203–213.

Piccialuti Caprioli, M. 1980. "Il patrimonio del povero. L'inchiesta sulle opere pie del 1861." *Quaderni storici* n. 45, a. XV, 3: 918–941.

Picozzi, L. 2012. "La ricostruzione del conto delle risorse e degli impieghi per l'anno 1970." In G. M. Rey, L. Picozzi, P. Piselli, and S. Clementi (eds.), *Una revisione dei conti nazionali dell'Italia (1951–1970)*. Banca d'Italia, Quaderni di Storia Economica, 27.

Pigou. 1920. *The Economics of Welfare*. London: McMiller.

Piketty, T. 1997. "The Dynamics of the Wealth Distribution and the Interest Rate with Credit Rationing." *Review of Economic Studies* 2: 173–189.

Piketty, T. 2003. "Income Inequality in France, 1901–1998." *Journal of Political Economy* 5: 1004–1042.

Piketty, T. 2014. *Capital in the Twenty-first Century*. Cambridge: MA: Belknap of Harvard UP.

Piketty, T., and E. Saez. 2006. "The Evolution of Top Incomes: A Historical and International Perspective." *American Economic Review* 2: 200–205.

Piketty, T., and G. Zucman. 2013. "Capital Is Back: Wealth-Income Ratios in Rich Countries 1700–2010." *Quaterly Journal of Economics* 29, no.3: 1155–1210.

Pineau, J. C. 1993. "La stature en France depuis un siècle: évolution générale et régionale." *Bulletins et Mémoires de la Société d'Anthropologie de Paris* 5, no. 1: 257–268.

Pinnelli, A., and P. Mancini. 1991. "Differences de mortalite par sexe de la naissance a la puberte en Italie: un siecle d'evolution." *Population* 46, no. 6: 1651–1676.

Pinnelli, A., and P. Mancini. 1999. "Mortality Peaks in Italy in the Late 19th and Early 20th Centuries: Trends by Age and Sex." *European Journal of Population* 14: 333–365.

Pliskin, J. S., D. S. Shepard, and M. C. Weinstein. 1980. "Utility Functions for Life Years and Health Status." *Oper Res* 28: 206–224.

Pogliano, C. 1984. "L'utopia igienista (1870–1920)." In F. Della Peruta (ed.), *Storia d'Italia, Annali*, vol. VII, *Malattia e medicina*. Turin Einaudi, 589–631.

Pope, C. 2009. "Measuring the Distribution of Material Well-being: U.S. Trends." *Journal of Monetary Economics* 56: 66–78.

Poston, D. L., and R. G. Rogers. 1985. "Toward a Reformulation of the Neonatal Mortality Rate." *Biodemography and Social Biology* 32, nos. 1–2: 1–12.

Pozzi, L. 1990. *La mortalità per cause nelle province italiane dal 1890 al 1950: differenziazioni geografiche e fattori esplicativi*. Tesi di dottorato in Demografia, III ciclo, Università degli Studi di Firenze, Padova, Rome, 1989–1990.

Prados de la Escosura, L. 2010. "Improving Human Development: A Long-run View." *Journal of Economic Surveys* 24, no. 5: 841–894.

Prados de la Escosura, L. 2013a. "Human Development in Africa: A Long-run Perspective." *Explorations in Economic History* 50, no. 2 (April): 179–204.

Prados de la Escosura, L. 2013b. "World Human Development: 1870–2007." Working Papers, 0034, European Historical Economics Society (EHES).

Prados de la Escosura, L. 2014. "World Human Development: 1870–2007." *Review of Income and Wealth*. doi: 10.1111/roiw.12104.

Preti, A., and C. Venturoli. 2000. "Fascismo e Stato sociale." In V. Zamagni (ed.), *Povertà e innovazioni istituzionali in Italia. Dal Medioevo ad oggi*. Bologna: Il Mulino, 729–749.

Preti, D. 1982. "Per una storia sociale dell'Italia fascista: la tutela della salute nell'organizzazione dello stato corporativo (1922–1940)." In M. L. Betri and A. Gigli Marchetti (eds.), *Salute e classi lavoratrici in italia dall'unità al fascismo*. Milan: Franco Angeli, 797–834.

Preti, D. 1984. "La questione ospedaliera nell'età fascista (1922–1940): un aspetto della 'modernizzazione corporativa.'" In F. Della Peruta (ed.), *Storia d'Italia. Annali, VII, Malattia e medicina*. Turin Einaudi, 335–387.

Pritchett, L. 2013. *The Rebirth of Education: Schooling Ain't Learning*. Washington, DC: Center for Global Development.

Pugliese, E., and S. Sabatino. 2006. *Emigrazione e immigrazione*. Napoli: Guida.

Puissant, J. 1976. "Un lent et difficile processus de démocratisation." In H. Hasquin (ed.), *La Wallonie, le Pays et les Hommes. Histoire-Economies-Sociétés, II: de 1830 a nos jours*. Brussels: La Renaissance du Livre.

Putnam, R. D. 1993. *Making Democracy Work. Civic Traditions in Modern Italy*. Princeton, NJ: Princeton University Press.

Quaglia, A., M. Vercelli, R. Lillini, E. Mugno, J. W. Coebergh, M. Quinn, C. Martinez-Garcia, R. Capocaccia, and A. Micheli. 2005. "Socio-Economic Factors and Health Care System Characteristics Related to Cancer Survival in the Elderly. A Population-Based Analysis in 16 European Countries (ELDCARE project)." *Critical Reviews in Oncology Hematology* 54, no. 2: 117–128.

Quirino. 1962. "Le valutazioni della ricchezza italiana dal 1908 ai nostri giorni." In C. Gini, *L'ammontare e la composizione della ricchezza delle nazioni*. Turin: UTET.

Ragioneria Generale dello Stato. 1914. *Il bilancio del regno d'Italia negli esercizi finanziari dal 1862 al 1912–13*. Rome: Tipografia dell'Unione.

Ragioneria Generale dello Stato. 1931. *Il bilancio dello stato dal 1913–14 al 1929–30 e la finanza fascista a tutto l'anno VIII*. Rome: Istituto Poligrafico dello Stato.

Ragioneria Generale dello Stato. 1957. *Note informative sul Bilancio dello Stato per gli esercizi finanziari dal 1945–46 al 1955–56*. Rome: Istituto Poligrafico dello Stato.

Ragioneria Generale dello Stato. 1961. *Note informative sul Bilancio dello Stato nella ricorrenza del Centenario dell'Unità d'Italia*. Rome: Istituto Poligrafico dello Stato.

Ragioneria Generale dello Stato. 1969. *Il bilancio dello stato italiano dal 1862 al 1967*. Rome: Istituto Poligrafico dello Stato.

Ranci, C. 1999. *Oltre il welfare state. Terzo settore, nuove solidarietà e trasformazioni del welfare*. Bologna: Il Mulino, 155.

Raseri, E. 1879. "Materiali per l'etnologia italiana raccolti per cura della Società Italiana di Antropologia ed Etnologia." *Annali di statistica* s. II, no. 8: 91–96.

Raseri, E. 1882. "Le condotte mediche in Italia." *Rivista della beneficenza pubblica e delle Istituzioni di previdenza* 10, no. 9: 821–828.

Ravallion, M. 1988. "Expected Poverty under Risk-Induced Welfare Variability." *Economic Journal* 98, no. 393: 1171–1182.

Ravallion, M. 1994. *Poverty Comparisons*. Fundamentals of Pure and Applied Economics, vol. 56. Chur: Harwood Academic Publishers.

Ravallion, M. 1996. "Issues in Measuring and Modelling Poverty." *Economic Journal* 106, no. 438: 1328–1343.

Ravallion, M. 1997. "Good and Bad Growth: The Human Development Reports." *World Development* 25, no. 5: 631–638.

Ravallion, M. 1998. *Poverty Lines in Theory and Practice*. LSMS Working Paper, 133. Washington, DC: World Bank.

Ravallion, M. 2004. *Pro-Poor Growth: A Primer, The World Bank*. Policy Research Working Paper, no. 3242.

Ravallion, M. 2012a. "Troubling Tradeoffs in the Human Development Index." *Journal of Development Economics* 99L: 201–209.

Ravallion, M. 2012b. "Mashup Indices of Development." *The World Bank Research Observer*, vol. 27, no. 1, pp. 1–32.

Ravallion, M., and S. Chen. 2003. "Measuring Pro-poor Growth." *Economics Letters* 78: 93–99.

Ravallion, M., S. Chen, and P. Sangraula. 2008. *Dollar a Day Revisited*. Policy Research Working Paper, 4620, World Bank.

Ravallion, M., G. Datt, and D. van de Walle. 1991. "Quantifying Absolute Poverty in the Developing World." *Review of Income and Wealth* 37: 345–361.

Reinhart, C. M., and K. S. Rogoff. 2010. "Growth in a Time of Debt." *American Economic Review* 100, no. 2: 573–78.

Reingold, D. A., M. Pirog, and D. Brady. 2007. "Empirical Evidence on Faith-Based Organizations in an Era of Welfare Reform." *Social Service Review* 81, no.2: 245–283.

Reinhart, C. M., and K. S. Rogoff. 2011. *This Time Is Different: Eight Centuries of Financial Folly*. Princeton: Princeton University Press.

Remarque, E. M. 1957. *The Black Obelisque: A Novel of War's Aftermath*. New York: Random House Trade Paperbacks Edition, 2013.

Repaci, F. A. 1937. "Il bilancio dello stato italiano dalla unificazione ad oggi (1862–1934/35)." *Rivista di storia economica,* giugno, 138–168.

Repaci, F. A. 1962. *La finanza pubblica italiana nel secolo 1861–1960*. Bologna: Zanichelli.

Revelli, M. 2010. *Poveri noi*. Turin: Einaudi.

Rhum, C. J. 2007. *Current and Future Prevalence of Obesity and Severe Obesity in the United States*. Forum for Health Economics and Policy (Obesity) 10(2), Article 6, 1–22.

Rhum, C. J. 2010. *Understanding Overeating and Obesity*. NBER Working Paper, 16149, July 2010.

Ricchioni, V. 1929. *Lavoro agricolo e trasformazioni fondiarie in terra di Bari*. Bari: Laterza.

Ricchioni, V. 1930. "Studi sulla piccola proprietà coltivatrice. L'azienda e la famiglia di un piccolo proprietario autonomo." *Archivio Scientifico dell'istituto Superiore di Scienze Economiche e Commerciali di Bari* 4: 75–143.

Ricci, R. 1997. *Povertà abitativa in Italia, 1989–1993*. Presidenza del Consiglio dei ministri, Dipartimento per l'informazione e l'editoria.

Ricuperati, G. 1968. "Il problema della scuola da Salvemini a Gramsci." *Rivista Storica Italiana a* LXXX, IVL: 964–1001.

Ricuperati, G. 1973. "La scuola nell'Italia unita." In *Storia d'Italia*, V/2, *I documenti*. Turin: Einaudi, 1695–1736.

Riley, J. C. 2001. *Rising Life Expectancy: A Global History*. Cambridge: Cambridge University Press.

Rinauro, S. 2002. *Storia del sondaggio d'opinione in Italia, 1936–1994: dal lungo rifiuto alla Repubblica dei sondaggi*. Venezia: Istituto veneto di scienze, lettere ed arti.

Ritter, A. 1996. *Storia dello stato sociale*. Bari: Laterza.

Rizzi, D., and N. Rossi. 1990. "Benessere, disuguaglianza e povertà nell'Italia del 'secondo miracolo economico' (1973–1987)." *Politica economica* 6, no. 1: 77–96.

Rizzo, T. L. 1988. *La legislazione sociale della nuova Italia 1876–1900*. Naples: Edizioni Scientifiche Italiane.

Roberti, P. 1971 "Le variazioni nella distribuzione personale del reddito in Italia: 1948–1966." *Rassegna economica* 4: 801–828.

Robeyns, I. 2005. "The Capability Approach: A Theoretical Survey." *Journal of Human Development* 6, no. 1: 93–114.

Rodgers, G., and G. Standing (eds.). 1981. *Child Work, Poverty, and Underdevelopment*. Geneva: International Labour Office.

Rodotà, S. 1995. *Tecnologie e Diritti*. Bologna: Il Mulino.

Rodotà, S. 2011. *Diritti e Libertà nella storia d'Italia: Conquiste e conflitti 1861–2011*. Rome: Donzelli.

Roemer, J. E. 2009. "Equality: Its Justification, Nature, Domain." In W. Slaverda, B. Nolan, and T. M. Smeeding, (eds.), *The Oxford Handbook of Economic Inequality*. Oxford: Oxford University Press, 23–39.

Romanelli, R. 1995. *Storia dello stato italiano*. Rome: Donzelli.

Romero, F. 2001. "L'emigrazione operaia in Europa (1948–1973)." In P. Bevilacqua, A. De Clementi, and E. Franzina (eds.), *Storia dell'emigrazione italiana*, vol. 1. Partenze, 397–413.

Rondini, L. L. 2003. *Storia della statistica pubblica in Italia*. Milan: Franco Angeli.

Roncaglia, A. 2006. *The Wealth of Ideas*. Cambridge: Cambridge University Press.

Rosenstein-Rodan, N. P. 1943. "Problems of Industrialisation of Eastern and South-Eastern Europe." *Economic Journal* 53, nos. 210/211: 202–211.

Rosoli, G. (ed.). 1978. *Un secolo di emigrazione italiana: 1876–1976*. Rome: Centro Studi Emigrazione.

Rosoli, G., and A. M. Ostuni. 1978. "Saggio di bibliografia statistica dell'emigrazione italiana." In G. Rosoli (ed.), *Un secolo di emigrazione italiana: 1876–1976*. Rome: Centro Studi Emigrazione.

Rossi, E. 1946. *Abolire la miseria*. Milan: La Fiaccola.

Rossi, L. 1982. "Appunti per una storia della malaria nell'agro romano nella seconda metà dell'Ottocento." In M. L. Betri and A. Gigli Marchetti (eds.), *Salute e classi lavoratrici in Italia dall'Unità al fascismo*. Milan: Franco Angeli, 227–253.

Rossi, M. 2009. "Examining the Interaction between Saving and Contributions to Personal Pension Plans: Evidence from the BHPS." *Oxford Bulletin of Economics and Statistics* 71, no. 2: 253–271.

Rossi, N. (ed.). 1993. *La crescita ineguale*. Bologna: Il Mulino.

Rossi, N. (ed.). 1994. *La transizione equa*. Bologna: Il Mulino.

Rossi, N. (ed.). 1995. *Competizione e giustizia sociale*. Bologna: Il Mulino.

Rossi, N. 1997. *Meno ai padri più ai figli. Stato sociale e modernizzazione dell'Italia*. Bologna: Il Mulino.

Rossi, N. (ed.). 1998. *Il lavoro e la sovranità sociale*. Bologna: Il Mulino.

Rossi, N., and G. Toniolo. 1994. "Un secolo di sviluppo economico." In P. Ciocca (ed.), *Il progresso economico dell'Italia. Permanenze, discontinuità, limiti*. Bologna: Il Mulino, 15–46.

Rossi, N., and G. Toniolo. 1996. "Italy." In N. Crafts and G. Toniolo (eds.), *Economic Growth in Europe since 1945*. Cambridge: Cambridge University Press, 427–454.

Rossi, N., and V. Visco. 1995. "National Savings and Social Security in Italy." *Ricerche economiche* 49: 329–356.

Rossi, N., G. Toniolo, and G. Vecchi. 2001. "Is the Kutznets Curve Still Alive? Evidence from Italy's Household Budgets, 1881–1961." *Journal of Economic History* 61, no. 4: 904–925.

Rossi, S. 2007. *La politica economica italiana. 1968–2007*. Bari: Laterza.

Rostow, W. W. 1960. *The Stages of Economic Growth*. Cambridge, MA: Cambridge University Press; trad. it. *Gli stadi dello sviluppo economico*, Turin: Einaudi, 1962.

Rovida, A., R. Camassi, P. Gasperini, and M. Stucchi (eds.). 2011. *CPTI11, the 2011 version of the Parametric Catalogue of Italian Earthquakes*. Milano. Bologna: http://emidius.mi.ingv. it/CPTI.

Rowbottom, J. 2010. *Democracy Distorted: Wealth, Influence and Democratic Politics*. Cambridge: Cambridge University Press.

Rowland, D. T. 2003. *Demographic methods and concepts*. Oxford: Oxford University Press.

Rowntree, B. S. 1901. *Poverty: A Study of Town Life*. London: Longmans Green.

Ruggles, P. 1990. *Drawing the Line: Alternative Poverty Measures and Their Implications for Public Policy*. Washington, DC: Urban Institute Press.

Runciman, W. G. 1966. *Relative Deprivation and Social Justice*. Berkeley: University of California Press.

Sacchi, S. 2007. "L'esperienza del reddito minimo di inserimento." In A. Brandolini and C. Saraceno (eds.), *Povertà e benessere. Una geografia delle disuguaglianze in Italia*. Bologna: Il Mulino, 423–448.

Sagar A. D., and A. Najam. 1998. "The Human Development Index: A Critical Review." *Ecological Economics* 25: 249–264.

Saint-Paul, G., and T. Verdier. 1992. "Historical Accidents and the Persistence of Distributional Conflict." *Journal of the Japanese and International Economies* 6: 406–422.

Saint-Paul, G., and T. Verdier. 1993. "Education, Democracy and Growth." *Journal of Development Economics* 42: 399–407.

Saito, O. 1996. *Children's work, industrialism and the family economy in Japan, 1872–1926.* in Cunningham and Viazzo 1996.

Sakula, A. 1982. "Robert Koch: Centenary of the Discovery of the Tubercle Bacillus, 1882." *Thorax* 37: 246–251.

Sala-i-Martin, X. 1996. "The Classical Approach to Convergence Analysis." *Economic Journal* 106, 437: 1019–1036.

Sala-i-Martin, X. 2002. *The World Distribution of Income.* NBER Working Paper, no. 8905, May.

Salsano, F. 2010. "La sistemazione degli sfrattati dall'area dei Fori Imperiali e la nascita delle borgate nella Roma fascista." *Città e storia* VII, no. 2: 207–234.

Samuelson, P. A. 1964. "Theoretical Notes on Trades Problems." *Review of Economics and Statistics* 46(2), no. 27: 145–154.

Samuelson, Paul A. 1983. *Foundations of Economic Analysis,* enlarged edn. Cambridge, MA: Harvard University Press.

Samuelson, P. A. 1994. "Facets of Balassa-Samuelson Thirty Years Later." *Review of International Economics* 2, no. 3:, 201–26. Wiley Blackwell, October.

Sanfilippo, M. 1990. "La storiografia sui fenomeni migratori a lungo raggio nell'Italia dell'età contemporanea." *Bollettino di demografia storica* 12: 55–66.

Saposnik, R. 1981. "Rank Dominance in Income Distribution." *Public Choice* 36: 147–151.

Saraceno, C. 1985. "Problemi teorici e metodologici nella definizione della povertà." In *La povertà in Italia,* Rapporto conclusivo della Commissione di studio istituita presso la Presidenza del Consiglio dei ministri, 120–151.

Saraceno, C. 1997. "Growth, Regional Imbalance, and Child Well-Being: Italy over the Last Four Decades." In G. A. Cornia and S. Dazinger (eds.), *Child Poverty and Deprivation in the Industrialized Countries, 1945–1995.* Oxford: Clarendon Press.

Sarpellon, G. 1977. "La riscoperta della povertà." *Promozione Sociale* 6: 5–14.

Sarpellon, G. 1978. "Come si dice povertà oggi?" *Schema* 2: 92–96.

Sarpellon, G. (ed.). 1982. *La povertà in Italia.* Milan: Franco Angeli.

Sarpellon, G. 1983 *Rapporto sulla povertà in Italia. La sintesi della grande indagine Cee.* Milan: Franco Angeli.

Sarpellon, G. 1993. "Dalla povertà nascosta alle nuove povertà e oltre." In P. Guidicini and G. Pieretti (eds.), *La residualità come valore. Povertà urbane e dignità umana.* Milano: Franco Angeli, 300–308.

Sarpellon G. (ed.). 2002. *Chiesa e solidarietà sociale. Terza indagine sui servizi socio-assistenziali collegati con la Chiesa cattolica in Italia.* Turin: Elledici.

Saunders, P. 1998. *Using budget standards to assess the well-being of families. SPRC Discussion Paper No. 93,* Social Policy Research Centre, University of New South Wales, Sydney.

Save the Children Italia Onlus and Associazione B. Trentin. 2013. "Game Over, Indagine sul lavoro minorile in Italia, Risultati preliminari."

Sawyer, M. C. 1976. *Income Distribution in OECD Countries.* Paris: OECD.

Scheitle, C. 2010. *Beyond the Congregation: The World of Christian Nonprofits.* Oxford: Oxford University Press.

Schizzerotto, A. 2002. *Vite ineguali.* Bologna: Il Mulino.

Schofield, R., D. Reher, and A. Bideau. (ed.). 1991. *The Decline of Mortality in Europe.* Oxford: Clarendon Press.

Schulze, M. 2007. *Regional Income Dispersion and Market Potential in the Late Nineteenth Century Habsburg Empire,* LSE Working Paper, 106/07.

Schumpeter, J. A. 1954. *History of Economic Analysis,* London: Allen and Unwin; trad it. *Storia dell'analisi economica.* Turin: Bollati Boringhier, 1990.

Scruggs, L. 2007. "Welfare State Decommodification in Time and Space." In N. Siegal and J. Clasen (eds.), *Welfare Reform in Advanced Societies: The Dependent Variable Problem in Comparative Welfare State Analysis*. Cheltenham: Edward Elgar.

Sen, A. K. 1976a. "*Poverty: An Ordinal Approach to Measurement.*" *Econometrica* 44: 219–231.

Sen, A. K. 1976b. "Real National Income." *Review of Economic Studies* 43: 19–39.

Sen, A. 1979 *Equality of What? Tanner Lecture on Human Values in: Tanner Lectures*. Stanford University.

Sen, A. K. 1985. *Commodities and Capabilities*. Amsterdam: North Holland.

Sen, A. K. 1992. *Inequality Reexamined*. Oxford: Oxford University Press; trad. it. *La diseguaglianza: un riesame critico*. Bologna: Il Mulino, 1992.

Sen, A. K. 1998. "Mortality as an indicator of economic success and failure." *The Economic Journal* 108 (January): 1–25.

Sen, A. 2003. "Sraffa, Wittgenstein, and Gramsci." *Journal of Economic Literature* 41, no. 4: 1240–1255.

Sen, A. K. 2005. "Human Rights and Capabilities." *Journal of Human Development* 6, no. 2: 151–166.

Seng, Y. P. 1951. "Historical Survey of the Development of Sampling Theories and Practice." *Journal of the Royal Statistical Society*. Series A, 114, 2: 214–231.

Senofonte [IV secolo a.c.]. 1991. *L'economico*. Milan: Rizzoli.

Sensini, G. 1904. *Le variazioni dello stato economico d'Italia nell'ultimo trentennio del secolo XIX*. Rome: Loescher.

Sepe, S. 1999. *Le amministrazioni della sicurezza sociale nell'Italia unita. 1861–1998*. Milan: Giuffrè.

Serpieri, A. 1929. *Guida e ricerche di economia agraria*. Rome: Treves.

Serraino, D., E. Bidoli, P. Piselli, C. Angeletti, S. Bruzzone, V. Puro, E. Girardi, and G. Ippolito. (eds.). 2004. *Atlante di mortalità. 30 anni di malattie infettive in Italia*, Istituto Nazionale per le malattie infettive Lazzaro Spallanzani, IRCCS, Dipartimento di Epidemiologia, Rome.

Shammas, C. 1984. "The Eighteenth-Century English Diet and Economic Change" *Explorations in Economic History* 21, no. 10: 254–269.

Shay, T. 1994. "The Level of Living in Japan, 1885–1938," In Id. (ed.), *Stature, Living Standards, and Economic Development*. Chicago: University of Chicago Press, 173–201.

Shields, J. 1962. *Monozygotyc Twins Brought Up Apart and Brought Up Together*. London: Oxford University Press.

Shorrocks, A. F. 1980. "The Class of Additively Decomposable Inequality Measures." *Econometrica* 48: 613–625.

Shorrocks, A. 1983. "Ranking Income Distributions." *Economica*, 50: 3–17.

Shorrocks, A. 2005. *Inequality values and unequal shares*. Mimeo.

Shorrocks, A., and G. Wan. 2008. *Ungrouping Income Distributions: Synthesising Samples for Inequality and Poverty Analysis*, Working Papers, RP2008/16, World Institute for Development Economic Research (UNU-WIDER).

Silei, G. 2000. "Dalle assicurazioni sociali alla Social Security. Politiche sociali in Europa e negli Stati Uniti fra le due guerre (1919–1939)." In V. Zamagni (ed.), *Povertà e innovazioni istituzionali in Italia. Dal Medioevo ad oggi*. Bologna: Il Mulino, 751–773.

Silei, G. 2003. *Lo Stato sociale in Italia. Storia e documenti*, I, *Dall'Unità al fascismo (1861–1943)*, Manduria-Bari-Rome: Lacaita.

Silei, G. 2004. *Lo Stato sociale in Italia. Storia e documenti*, II, *Dalla caduta del fascsmo ad oggi (1943–2004)*. Manduria-Bari-Rome: Lacaita.

Silventoinen, K. 2003. "Determinants of Variation in Adult Body Height." *Journal of Biosocial Science* 35: 263–285.

Simpson, J. 1989. "La producción agraria y el consumo español en el siglo XIX." *Revista de Historia Económica* 7: 355–388.

Singh-Manoux, A., Gourmelen, J., Ferrie, J., Silventoinen, K., Guèguen, A., Stringhini, S., Nabi, H., Kivimaki, M. 2010. "Trends in the Association Between Height and Socioeconomic Indicators in France, 1970–2003." *Economics and Human Biology*, in corso di stampa.

Slesnick, D. T. 2001. *Consumption and Social Welfare: Living Standards and Their Distribution in the United States*. Cambridge University Press.

Slottje, D. J. 1990. "Using Grouped Data for Constructing Inequality Indices. Parametric vs. Non-parametric Methods." *Economic Letters* 32: 193–197.

Smeeding, T. M. 2004. "Twenty Years of Research on Income Inequality, Poverty, and Redistribution in the Developed World: Introduction and Overview." in Socio-Economic Review, 2, 149–163.

Smith, W., W. Wayte, and G. E. Marindin. 1890. *A Dictionary of Greek and Roman Antiquities*. London: Harper & brothers.

Società Italiana di Nutrizione Umana. 1986–87. *Livelli di Assunzione Giornalieri di Energia e Nutrienti per la Popolazione Italiana (LARN)*, Revisione 1986–87, Istituto Nazionale della Nutrizione e Ministero dell'Agricoltura e Foreste, Rome.

Solow, R. M. 1956. "A Contribution to the Theory of Economic Growth." *Quarterly Journal of Economics* 70, no. 1: 65–94.

Soltow, L. 1968. "Long–Run Changes in British Income Inequality." *Economic History Review* 21, no. 1: 17–29.

Société d'économie sociale. 1857–1862. *Les Ouvriers des deux mondes*. SES: Paris.

Société d'économie sociale. 1885–1913. *Les Ouvriers des deux mondes*. SES: Paris.

Soltow, L. 1992. "Inequalities in the Standard of Living in the United States,1798–1875." In R. E. Gallman and J. J. Wallis (eds.), *American Economic Growth and Standards of Living before the Civil War*. Chicago: University of Chicago Press, 121–172.

Somogyi, S. 1959. "Cento anni di bilanci familiari in Italia (1857–1956)." *Annali della Fondazione Giangiacomo Feltrinelli* II: 121–263.

Somogyi, S. 1973. *L'alimentazione dell'Italia unita*, in *Storia d'Italia*, vol. 5, *I Documenti*. Turin: Einaudi, 839–887.

Son, H. H. 2004. "A Note on Pro-Poor Growth." *Economics Letters* 82, no. 3: 307–314.

Son, H. H. 2007. *Pro-Poor Growth: Concepts and Measures*, ERD Techincal Note Series, 22, Asian Development Bank.

Sorcinelli, P. 1995. *Gli italiani e il cibo. Appetiti, digiuni e rinunce dalla realtà contadina alla società del benessere*. Bologna: Clueb.

Soresina, M. 1987. *La tutela della salute nell'Italia unita (1860–1980)*, in *Storia della società italiana*, vol. XVII, *La struttura e le classi nell'Italia unita* . Milan: Teti.

Soresina, M. 2001.*Conoscere per amministrare: Luigi Bodio. Statistica, economia e pubblica amminis-trazione*. Milan: Franco Angeli.

Sori, E. 1979. *L'emigrazione italiana dall'Unità alla seconda guerra mondiale*. Bologna: Il Mulino.

Sori, E. 1996. "Movimenti migratori. Il caso italiano." In *Enciclopedia delle Scienze Sociali*, vol. V. Rome: Istituto dell'Enciclopedia Italiana.

Spanos, A. 1986. *Statistical Foundations of Econometric Modelling*. Cambridge: Cambridge University Press.

Srinivasan T. N. 1994. "Human Development: A New Paradigm or Reinvention of the Wheel?" *American Economic Review, Papers and Proceedings*, 84, no. 2: 238–243.

SSA (Social security Administration, US Department of Health and Human Services). 2012, 2013. *Social Security Programs Throughout the World*. Washington, DC: USGPO, Social Security Administration. Available at http://www.ssa.gov/policy/docs/progdesc/ssptw/

Staehle, H. 1934. "Annual Survey of Statistical Information: Family Budgets." *Econometrica* 2, no: 4: 349–362.

Staehle, H. 1935. "Family Budgets." *Econometrica* 3, no. 1: 106–118.

Stapleford, T. A. 2009. *The Cost of Living in America. A Political History of Economic Statistics, 1880–2000*. New York: Cambridge University Press.

Stark, T. 1997. *The Distribution of Income in Eight Countries Background Paper to Report 5*, Royal Commission on the Distribution of Income and Wealth. London: HMSO.

Statistique générale de la France. 1911–1933; 1937; 1945; 1948–1950; 1953. *Bulletin de la Statistique générale de la France*. Paris: Presses Universitaires de France.

Steckel, R. H. 1995. "Stature and the Standard of Living." *Journal of Economic Literature* 33: 1903–1940.

Steckel, R.H. 2004 *New Light on the "Dark Ages". The Remarkably Tall Stature of Northern European Men during the Medieval Era*, in "Social Science History," 28, 2, 211–229.

Steckel, R. H. 2008. "Biological Measures of the Standard of Living." *Journal of Economic Perspectives* 22, no. 1: 129–152.

Steckel, R. H. 2009. "Heights and Human Welfare: Recent Developments and New Directions." *Explorations in Economic History* 46: 1–23.

Stella, G. A. 2002. *L'orda. Quando gli albanesi eravamo noi.* Milan: Rizzoli.

Stella, G. A. 2009. Mercati e rimesse: il ruolo dell'emigrazione nell'economia italiana. In P. Corti and M. Sanfilippo (eds.), *Migrazioni*, Storia d'Italia Annali 24. Turin: Giulio Einaudi Editore.

Stark, O., C. Helmenstein, and A. Prskawetz 1997. "A Brain Gain with a Brain Drain." *Economic Letters* 55: 227–234.

Stephan, F. 1948. "History of the Uses of Modern Sampling Procedures." *Journal of the American Statistical Association* 43, no. 241: 12–39.

Stigler, G. 1954. "The Early History of Empirical Studies of Consumer Behavior." *Journal of Political Economy* LXII: 95–113.

Stone, R. 1986. "Nobel Memorial Lecture 1984: The Accounts of Society." *Journal of Applied Econometrics* 1, no. 1: 5–28.

Streeten, P. 1994. "Human Development: Means and Ends." *American Economic Review, Papers and Proceedings* 84, no. 2: 232–237.

Strömberg, D. 2007. "Natural Disasters, Economic Development, and Humanitarian Aid." *Journal of Economic Perspective* 21, no.3: 199–222.

Subramanian, S. 2002. "An elementary interpretation of the Gini inequality index." *Theory and Decision* 52, no. 4: 375–379.

Supple, B. 1994. *The Economic History of Britain since 1700.* Cambridge, MA: Cambridge University Press.

Svedberg, P. 2000. *Poverty and Undernutrition: Theory, Measurement, and Policy.* Oxford: Clarendon Press.

Svimez (Associazione per lo sviluppo dell'industria nel Mezzogiorno). 1961. *Un secolo di statistiche storiche italiane: Nord e Sud, 1861–1961.* Rome: Stabilimento tipografico F. Failli.

Svimez (Associazione per lo sviluppo dell'industria nel Mezzogiorno). 1993. *I conti del Mezzogiorno e del Centro-Nord nel ventennio 1970–1989.* Bologna: Il Mulino.

Sydenstricker, E., and King, M. 1931. "The Incidence of Influenza among Persons of Different Economic Status During the Epidemic of 1918." *Public Health Reports* 46, no. 4: 154–170.

Sylos Labini, P. 1974. *Saggio sulle classi sociali.* Bari: Laterza

Talamo, G. 1960. *La scuola. Dalla legge Casati alla inchiesta del 1864.* Milan: Giuffrè.

Tanner, J. M. 1981. *A History of the Study of Human Growth.* Cambridge: Cambridge University Press.

Tanner, J. M. 1989. *Foetus into Man. Physical Growth from Conception to Maturity.* Ware: Castlemead Publications.

Tanzi V., and Schuknecht L. 2000. *Public Spending in the 20th Century. A Global Perspective.* Cambridge: Cambridge University Press.

Tatarelli Murer, A. 1978. "Sulla distribuzione del benessere economico. Un'analisi basata sui consumi." *Rivista di politica economica* 6: 795–833.

Taubenberger, J. K., and Morens, D. 2006. "1918 Influenza: the Mother of All Pandemics." *Emerging Infectious Diseases* 12, no. 1: 15–22.

Taubenberger, J. K. 2005. "The Virulence of the 1918 Pandemic Influenza Virus: Unraveling the Enigma." In Peters, C.J. e Calisher, C.H. (eds.), *Infectious Diseases from Nature: Mechanisms of Viral Emergence and Persistence.* Vienna: Springer, 101–115.

Taylor, C. L., and D. A. Jodice. 1983. *World Handbook of Political and Social Indicators*, Vol. 1. New Haven, CT: Yale University Press.

Taylor, A. M., and J. G. Williamson. 1997. "Convergence in the Age of Mass Migration." *European Review of Economic History* 1: 27–63.

Taylor-Gooby, Peter F. 2004. *New Risks, New Welfare: The Transformation of the European Welfare State.* Oxford: Oxford University Press.

Temin, P. 2002. "Price Behavior in Ancient Babylon." *Explorations in Economic History* 39, no. 1: 46–60.

Tenti, B. 1940. *Le spese familiari per alloggio, acqua, gas ed energia elettrica in relazione al reddito.* Citta di Castello, Tip. Unione arti grafiche.

Tentori, T. (ed.). 1966. *Ricerche sociali in Italia (1945–1965).* Rome: Aai.

Terrenato, L., and Ulizzi, L. 1983. "Genotype and Environment Relationship: An Analysis of the Stature Distribution Curves during the Last Century in Italy." *Annals of Human Biology* 10: 335–346.

Teselli A., and G. Paone. (eds.). 2000. *Lavoro e lavori minorili in Italia. L'inchiesta Cgil.* Rome: Ediesse.

Thoday, J. M. 1965. "Geneticism and Environmentalism." In J. E. Meade and A. S. Parkes (eds.), *Biological Aspects of Social Problems.* London: Oliver and Boyd.

Tizzano, A. 1965. "Sviluppo della popolazione italiana dal 1861 al 1961. Mortalità generale." *Annali di statistica* 94, s. VIII, 17: 441–465.

Tognotti, E. 1996. *Per una storia della malaria in Italia: il caso della Sardegna.* Milan: Franco Angeli.

Tognotti E. 2000. *Il mostro asiatico. Storia del colera in Italia.* Rome-Bari: Laterza.

Tognotti, E. 2002. *La Spagnola in Italia: storia dell'influenza che fece temere la fine del mondo (1918–19).* Milan: Franco Angeli.

Tognotti, E. 2008. "E il Ddt cambiò *per sempre l'isola.*" *La Nuova Sardegna*, 2 December, 36.

Tomasi, T. 1978. *L'educazione infantile tra Chiesa e Stato.* Florence: Vallecchi.

Toniolo, G. 1980. *L'economia dell'Italia fascista.* Rome-Bari: Laterza.

Toniolo, G. 1981. "Aspetti macroeconomici del problema della povertà in Italia, 1860–1963." *Ricerche di storia sociale e religiosa*, 19–20: 7–55.

Toniolo, G. 1988. *Storia economica dell'Italia liberale (1850–1918).* Bologna: Il Mulino.

Toniolo, G. 1998. "Europe's Golden Age, 1950–1973: Speculations from a Long-run Perspective." *Economic History Review* 51, no. 2: 252–267.

Toniolo, G. 2003. "La storia economica dell'Italia liberale: una rivoluzione in atto." *Rivista di storia economica* 3: 247–264.

Toniolo, G. 2004. "L'Italia verso il declino economico? Ipotesi e congetture in una prospettiva secolare." *Rivista Italiana degli Economisti* 9: 29–46.

Toniolo, G. 2007. "Stefano Fenoaltea, L'economia italiana dall'Unità alla Grande Guerra (Rome and Bari: Laterza, 2006)." *Journal of Modern Italian Studies* 12, no. 1: 130–132.

Toniolo, G. 2013. *The Oxford Handbook of the Italian Economy Since Unification.* Oxford: Oxford University Press.

Toniolo, G., and Vecchi, G. 2007. "Italian children at work, 1881–1961." *Giornale degli economisti e Annali di economia* 66, no. 3: 410–427.

Toniolo, G., and Vecchi, G. 2010. "Nel secolo breve il lungo balzo del benessere degli italiani." In L. Paolazzi (ed.), *Libertà e benessere: l'Italia al futuro*, Centro studi Confindustria. Rome: SIPI, 15–59 (nuova ed. Roma-Bari: Laterza, 2011).

Toniolo, G., and V. Visco. (ed.). 2004. *Il declino economico dell'Italia. Cause e rimedi.* Milan: B. Mondadori.

Toniolo, G., L. Conte, and G. Vecchi. 2003. "Monetary Union, Institutions and Financial Market Integration: Italy, 1862–1905." *Explorations in Economic History* 40, no. 4: 443–461.

Torelli, L. 1882. *Carta della malaria in Italia.* Florence: Stabilimento di Giuseppe Pellas.

Torrance, G. W. 1976. "Health Status Index Models: A Unified Mathematical View." *Management Science* 22: 99–1001.

Torvik, R. 1993. "Talent, Growth and Income Distribution." *Scandinavian Journal of Economics* 95: 581–596.

Toutain, J.-C. 1971. "La consommation alimentaire en France de 1789 à 1964." *Économies et Sociétés* 5: 1909–2049.

Townsend, P. 1962. *The Meaning of Poverty*, in "British Journal of Sociology," XIII, 3,

Townsend, P. 1979. *Poverty in the United Kingdom.* London: Penguin.

Tremonti, G. 2008. *La paura e la speranza.* Milan: Mondandori.

Treves, A. 1976. *Le migrazioni interne nell'Italia fascista.* . Turin: Piccola Biblioteca Einaudi.

Trigilia, C. 1992.*Sviluppo senza autonomia. Effetti perversi delle politiche nel Mezzogiorno.* Bologna: Il Mulino.

Trivellato, U. 1998. "Il monitoraggio della povertà e della sua dinamica: questioni di misura e evidenze empriche." *Statistica* 58, no. 4: 549–575.

Trombetta, S. 1994. "Le strategie dell'abbandono: luoghi, esposti, espositori nei fascicoli proces-suali del tribunale criminale comasco (1815–1860)." *Il Risorgimento* 1: 87–138.

Tukey, J. W. 1977. *Exploratory Data Analysis.* Reading, MA: Addison-Wesley.

Tuttle, C. 1998. "A Revival of the Pessimist View." *Research in Economic History* 18: 53–82.

UNESCO 2011, Institute of Statistics database: http://stats.uis.unesco.org/unesco/TableViewer/document.aspx?ReportId=143&IF_Language=eng

United Nations Development Programme (UNDP). 1990. *Human Development Report 1990.* New York: Oxford University Press.

United Nations Development Programme (UNDP). 1991. *Human Development Report 1991.* New York: Oxford University Press.

United Nations Development Programme (UNDP). 1992. *Human Development Report 1992.* New York: Oxford University Press.

United Nations Development Programme (UNDP). 1994. *Human Development Report 1994.* New York: Oxford University Press.

United Nations Development Programme (UNDP). 2013a. *Human Development Report 2013.* New York: Oxford University Press.

United Nations Development Programme (UNDP). 2013b. *Human Development Report 2013: Technical Notes.* New York: Oxford University Press.

Ura, K., S. Alkire, T. Zangmo, and K. Wangdi. 2012. An extensive analysis of GNH index, Centre for Bhutan Studies. Thimphu, Bhutan.

USDA (United States Department of Agriculture). 2007. *Nutrient Content of the U.S. Food Supply,* 1909–2004.

U.S. Congress. 1911. *Report of the Dillingham Immigration Commission,* 41 vols. Washington, DC: US Governmennt Printing Office.

Usher, D. 1973. "An Imputation to the Measure of Economic Growth for Changes in Life Expectancy." In M. Moss (ed.), *The Measurement of Economic and Social Performance, Studies in Income and Wealth,* vol. 38. New York: National Bureau of Economic Research, 193–226.

Vaccai, M. 1914. "Eccessi del lavoro delle donne e dei fanciulli nelle campagne," *Bollettino della Società degli agricoltori italiani,* maggio.

Vaccaro, G. 1999. "Problemi di comparabilità spaziale delle statistiche dei prezzi al consumo." *Studi e note di economia* 1: 33–49.

Vanoli, A. 2005. *A History of National Accounting.* Amsterdam: IOS Press.

Vardaro, L. 1943. "Rilievi sulle condizioni dei poveri dell'Irpinia." *Rivista Internazionale di Scienze Sociali* 14, nos. 3, 2: 85–95.

Vardaro, L. 1946. "Guadagni, consumi e tenor di vita in un comune dell'Irpinia." *Rivista Internazionale di Scienze Sociali* 17, no. 2: 112–131.

Vecchi, G. 1994. "I bilanci familiari in Italia:1860–1960." *Rivista di storia economica* 11: 9–95.

Vecchi, G. 1999. *La distribuzione personale della spesa in Italia: 1860–1960,* Univ. di Rome "Tor Vergata," PhD. dissertation.

Vecchi, G. 2003. "Il benessere dell'Italia liberale (1861–1913)." In P. Ciocca and G. Toniolo (eds.), *Storia economica d'Italia.* Rome-Bari: Laterza, 71–98.

Vecchi, G. 2010. "Cooperazione e benessere: un'analisi territoriale di lungo periodo." In *Cooperare per cambiare,* Reggio Emilia: Legacoop.

Vecchi, G. 2011. *In ricchezza e in povertà. Il benessere degli italiani dall'Unità a oggi.* Bologna: Il Mulino.

Vecchi, G. and M. Coppola. 2003. "Nutrizione e povertà in Italia, 1861–1911." *Rivista di storia economica* 19, no. 3: 383–401.

Vecchi, G. and M. Coppola. 2006. "Nutrition and Growth in Italy, 1861–1911. What Macroeconomic Data Hide." *Explorations in Economic History* 43: 438–464.

Veenhoven, R. 2014. *Happiness in Nations World Database of Happiness.* The Netherlands: Erasmus University Rotterdam. Assessed on January 17th, 2014 at: http://worlddatabaseofhappiness.eur.nl/hap_nat/nat_fp.php?mode=1

Ventura, A. 2009. "La composizione dei panieri per gli indici dei prezzi in Italia (1927–1978)." *Storia e Futuro*, 20, June.

Venturini, A. 2004. *Postwar Migration in Southern Europe, 1950-2000: An Economic Analysis.* Cambridge: Cambridge University Press.

Vercelli, M., R. Lillini, R. Capocaccia. *et al.* 2006. "Cancer survival in the elderly: effects of socio-economic factors and health care system features (ELDCARE project)." *European Journal of Cancer* 42, no. 2: 234–242.

Verdecchia, A., M. Caldora, L. Frova, R. Crialesi, and F. Berrino (eds.). 2005. *Nuove evidenze nell'evoluzione della mortalità per tumore in Italia, Anno 1970–1999*, Istat, Indicatori statistici, 5.

Verdecchia, A., R. De Angelis, S. Francisci, and E. Grande. 2007. "Methodology for Estimation of Cancer Incidence, Survival and Prevalence in Italian Regions." *Tumori* 93, no. 4: 337–344.

Verga, G. 1881. *I Malavoglia.* Milano: Mondadori, 2010.

Vidari, E. 1886. *I fallimenti*, Milan: Hoepli.

Vigorelli, E. 1948. *L'offensiva contro la miseria. Idee e esperienze per un piano di sicurezza sociale.* Milan: Mondadori.

Villari, P. 1872. "La scuola e la quistione sociale in Italia."*Nuova Antologia* 21: 477–512.

Villari, P. 1885. *Lettere meridionali ed altri scritti sulla questione sociale in Italia*, II ed. riveduta e accresciuta.Turin: Bocca.

Vinci, F. 1940. *I bilanci di famiglia nella prassi e nella teoria economica.* Bologna: Zanichelli.

Visco, I. 2008. *Crescita, capitale umano, istruzione*, intervento all'inaugurazione dell'anno accademico 2007/08 dell'Università degli studi di Genova.

Vitali, O. 1968. *La popolazione attiva in agricoltura attraverso i censimenti italiani.* Rome: Istituto di Demografia dell'Università di Roma.

Vitali, O. 1969. "La stima del valore aggiunto a prezzi costanti per rami di attività." In: Fuà, Giorgio (Ed.), *Lo sviluppo economico in Italia: Studi di settore e documentazione di base, 3*. Milan: Franco Angeli, 463–477.

Vitali, O. 1970. *Aspetti dello sviluppo economico italiano alla luce della ricostruzione della popolazione attiva.* Rome: Istituto di Demografia dell'Università di Roma.

Von Tunzelmann, G. N. 1978. *Steam Power and British Industrialization to 1860.* Oxford: Oxford University Press.

Wagstaff, A., and E. van Doorslaer. 2000. "Equity in Health Care Finance and Delivery." In A. J. Culyer and J. P. Newhouse (eds.), *Handbook of Health Economics.* Amsterdam: Elsevier, ch. 34: 1803–1862.

Walsh, C. 2010. *Monetary Theory and Policy.* Cambridge, MA: MIT Press.

Watts, H. W. 1968. "An Economic Definition of Poverty." In D. P. Moynihan (ed.), *On Understanding Poverty.* New York: Basic Books.

Wheatcroft, S. G. 1999. "The Great Leap Upwards: Anthropometric Data and Indicators of Crises and Secular Change in Soviet Welfare Levels, 1880–1960." *Slavic Review* 58: 27–60.

WHO (World Health Organization). 1946. *Constitution,* http://www.who.int/governance/eb/who_constitution_en.pdf

WHO (World Health Organization). 2010. http://www.who.int/gho/en/index.html, December.

Wilensky H. 1975. *The Welfare State and Equality: Structural and Ideological Roots of Public Expenditures.* Berkeley: University of California Press.

Wilkinson, R. 1996. *Unhealthy Societies: The Affliction of Inequality.* London: Routledge.

Wilkinson, R., and K. Pickett. 2006. "Income inequality and population health: A review and explanation of the evidence." *Social Science and Medicine* 62: 1768–1784.

Wilkinson, R., and K. Pickett. 2009. *The Spirit Level: Why More Equal Societies Almost Always Do Better.* London: Allen Lane; trad. it. *La misura dell'anima. Perché le diseguaglianze rendono le società più infelici.* Milan: Feltrinelli, 2009.

Williamson, J. G. 1965. "Regional Inequality and the Process of National Development: A Description of the Patterns." *Economic Development and Cultural Change* 13: 3–84.

Williams, F. M., and C. C. Zimmerman. 1935. *Studies of Family Living in the United States and Other Countries: An Analysis of Material and Method*. United States Department of Agriculture, Miscellaneous Publications, no. 323.

Williamson, J. G. 1985. *Did British Capitalism Breed Inequality?* Winchester: Allen & Unwin.

Williamson, J. G. 1995. "The Evolution of Global Labor Markets since 1830: Background Evidence and Hypotheses." *Explorations in Economic History* 32, no. 2: 141–196.

Williamson, J. G. 2004. "The Inaugural Noel Butlin Lecture: World Factor Migrations and Demographic Transitions." *Australian Economic History Review* 44, no. 2: 118–141.

Williamson, J. G. 2006. "Inequality and Schooling Responses to Globalization Forces: Lessons from History." New York: *National Bureau of Economic Research*, no. w12553.

Williamson, J. G., and P. H. Lindert. 1980. *American Inequality: A Macroeconomic History*. New York: Academic Press.

Winkworth, G., and P. Camilleri. 2004. "Keeping the faith: the impact of Human services restructuring on catholic social welfare services." *Australian Journal of Social Issues* 39, no. 3: 315.

Wolff, E. N. 1998. "Recent Trends in the Size Distribution of Household Wealth." *Journal of Economic Perspectives* 12, no. 3 (Summer): 131–150.

Woolf, S. 1988. *Porca miseria. Poveri e assistenza nell'età moderna*. Rome-Bari: Laterza.

World Bank. 2014. *World Development Indicators*. Washington, DC: World Bank.

WVS: http://www.worldvaluessurvey.org/

Zamagni, V. 1978 *Industrializzazione e squilibri regionali in Italia. Bilancio dell'età giolittiana*. Bologna: Il Mulino.

Zamagni, V. 1980. "The Rich and the Richest in a Late Industrializer: the Case of Italy 1800–1945." In W. D. Rubinstein (ed.), *Wealth and the Wealthy in the Modern World*. London: Croom Helm.

Zamagni, V. 1981. *Lo Stato italiano e l'economia: storia dell'intervento pubblico dall'unificazione ai giorni nostri*. Florence: Le Monnier.

Zamagni, V. 1990. *Dalla periferia al centro. La seconda rinascita economica dell'Italia (1861–1990)*. Bologna: Il Mulino.

Zamagni, V. 1991. "Industrial Wages and Workers' Protest in Italy during the 'Biennio Rosso' (1919–1920)." *Journal of European Economic History* 20: 137–153.

Zamagni, V. 1992. "Il valore aggiunto del settore terziario italiano nel 1911." In G. M. Rey (ed.), *I conti economici dell'Italia, 2. Una stima del valore aggiunto per il 1911*. Rome-Bari: Laterza, 191–239.

Zamagni, V. 1993a. *Dalla periferia al centro. La seconda rinascita economica dell'Italia (1861–1990)*. Bologna: Il Mulino.

Zamagni, V. 1993b. *L'offerta di istruzione in Italia 1861–1987: un fattore guida dello sviluppo o un ostacolo?* Università degli Studi di Cassino, Working Paper, no. 4, July.

Zamagni, V. 1995. "Redditi e consumi privati in Italia ed Europa nel XX secolo." In G. Aliberti (ed.), *L'economia domestica, sec. XIX–XX*. Pisa-Roma: Istituti editoriali e poligrafici internazionali.

Zamagni, V. (ed.). 1997. *Come perdere la guerra e vincere la pace: l'economia italiana tra guerra e dopoguerra, 1938–1947*. Bologna: Il Mulino.

Zamagni, V. 1998. "L'evoluzione dei consumi fra tradizione e innovazione." In *Storia d'Italia, Annali, XIII, L'alimentazione*. Turin: Einaudi.

Zamagni, V. (ed.) 2000. *Povertà e innovazioni istituzionali in Itali. Dal Medioevo ad oggi*. Bologna: Il Mulino.

Zamagni, V. 2002. "La grande guerra come elemento di rottura della crescita equilibrata dell'economia italiana." In F. Garcia Sanz (ed.), *España e Italia en la Europa contemporánea: desde finales del siglo XIX a las dictaduras*. Madrid: Csic, 323–334.

Zamagni, V. 2003. *Dalla periferia al centro. La seconda rinascita economica dell'Italia*. Bologna: Il Mulino.

Zamagni, V. 2011. "Ricchi e poveri: pensare all'economia del benessere," In *Cristiani d'Italia*, Treccani.

Zamagni, V., and P. Battilani. 2000. "Stima del valore aggiunto dei servizi." In G. M. Rey (ed.), *I conti economici dell'Italia*, 3.2. *Il valore aggiunto per agli anni 1891, 1938, 1951*. Rome-Bari: Laterza, 239–371.

Zhang, Y. e Wan, G. 2009. "How Precisely Can We Estimate Vulnerability to Poverty?" *Oxford Development Studies* 37, no. 3: 277–287.

Zheng, B. 1997. "Aggregate Poverty Measures." *Journal of Economic Surveys* 11, no. 2: 123–162.

Zola, E. 1877. *L'Assommoir*. Paris: G. Charpentier Éditeur.

Zola, E. 1880. *L'inondation* ("L'inondazione"). Milan: Società editoriale Milanese, 1909.

Zucman, G. 2014. "Taxing across Borders: Tracking Personal Wealth and Corporate Profits." *Journal of Economic Perspectives* 28, no. 4: 121–148.

Analytical Index

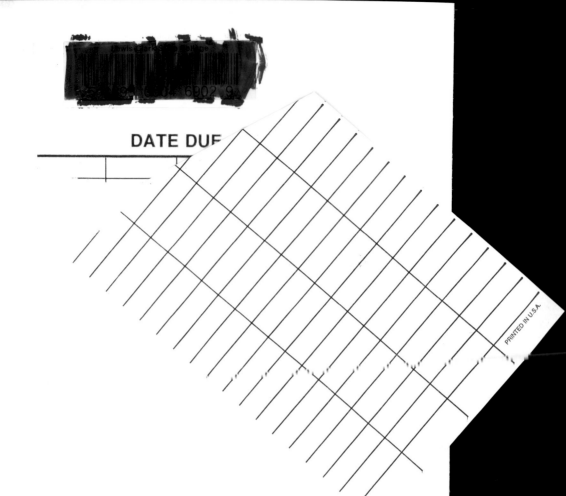

PRINTED IN U.S.A.